South-Western

ECONOMICS

Wraparound Teacher's Edition — Volume 1

J. Holton Wilson
Professor
Central Michigan University

J.R. Clark
Probasco Chair
University of Tennessee/Chattanooga

Editor-in-Chief

Development

Technology and Media

Production

Design

Photos

Marketing and Promotion

Manufacturing

Editorial Support

SOUTH-WESTERN EDUCATIONAL PUBLISHING
Cincinnati, Ohio

ISBN: 0-538-65605-0

1 2 3 4 5 6 7 8 9 D2 04 03 02 01 00 99 98 97 96

Printed in the United States of America

I(T)P

International Thomson Publishing

South-Western Educational Publishing is a division of International Thomson Publishing Inc. The ITP trademark is used under license.

South-Western

ECONOMICS

Wraparound Teacher's Edition — Volume 1

Comprehensive instruction in an

Designed to meet the curriculum standards set by the National Council on Economic Education, South-Western *ECONOMICS* is an easy-to-use system containing the most up-to-date courseware on the economics topics that teachers tell us they want, with print and media components built into one complete instructional package. Select the materials that work with your teaching priorities and schedule and your school's technology to enhance and personalize your students' knowledge and application of economics.

FOR LEARNERS

Learn by Doing, Do by Learning

It's easy to make *ECONOMICS* relevant to daily life! The clear, lively student text engages your students in reading about and solving problems in contemporary economics and is supported by software and print supplements to ensure that your students' learning keeps pace with our everchanging world. But, don't stop there! Motivate your students to build a solid foundation for lifelong application of key concepts as they get ready to enter the "real" world as productive citizens.

Capture Your Students' Untapped Interest in Economics! Allow them to:

- personally apply economics life skills, designed expressly for young adults and their growing roles in society,
- learn career information,
- "rub elbows" with the key names in economics today,
- converse intelligently about primary source documents that reflect the latest issues in economics,
- immerse themselves in the timely special features that highlight relevant topics of interest,
- support the mathematics behind the key economic measurement concepts, and
- interact with technology designed expressly for *ECONOMICS*—Internet applications; CNBC video segments; Interactive *ECONOMICS*, a chapter-by-chapter computer tutorial; template software; and Arctic Express, a computer simulation.

Easy-to-Manage System

FOR INSTRUCTORS

Those Who Can, Do. Those Who Care, Teach.

As many variations as there are on the saying above, educators are special people and South-Western ECONOMICS provides you with the highest quality instructional support to enhance student learning and make your classes more enjoyable. Pick and choose from these resources: a highly visual and appealing textbook; template, simulation, and tutorial software; reproducible masters and independent workbooks; overhead transparencies; colorful posters; formal and informal assessment; and reteaching, enrichment, special needs, and portfolio activities—a comprehensive system to support your planning, teaching, and assessment goals.

Features of the Student Text

Learning Objectives emphasize for students the key concepts for every chapter. Plus, *Checkpoints*, Section Quizzes, *Chapter Assessment*, and *Reteach* and *Enrich* worksheets and activities correlate to the objectives for on-target skill assessment and reinforcement.

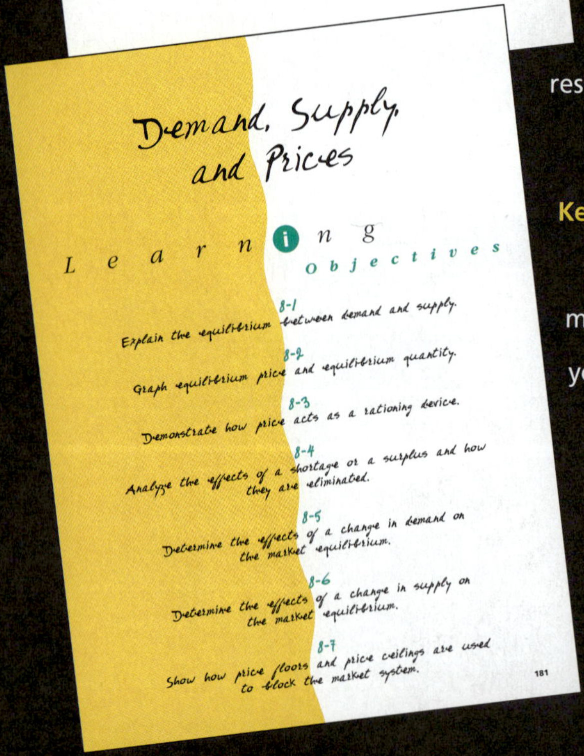

From the first minutes of every lesson, the section **Focus** engages students in active learning by posing a contemporary, real-life issue to be resolved through the application of the lesson content.

Key terms are introduced at the point of use through succinct marginal definitions that keep your students focused and on target throughout the lesson.

Lively, captioned **instructional graphics** support students visually as they explore and apply the economic content of every lesson.

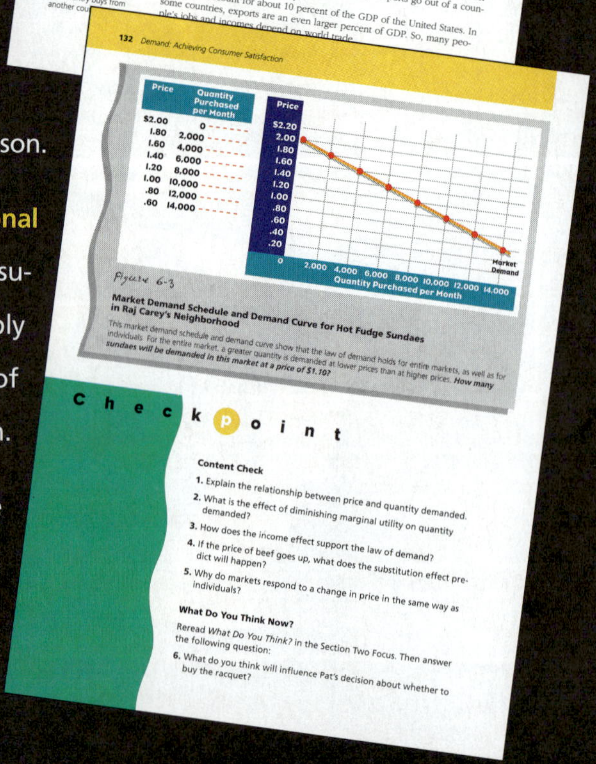

Section **Checkpoint** features are informal opportunities for students to assess their understanding and challenge students to apply what they're learning.

Comprehensive **Chapter Review** provides your students with a review of the key concepts and additional opportunities to assess their mastery of new vocabulary and content before you offer formal evaluation. *Thinking Critically About Economics, Economic Enrichment, Math and Economics,* and *Writing About Economics* features allow students to apply in real-life situations what they have learned .

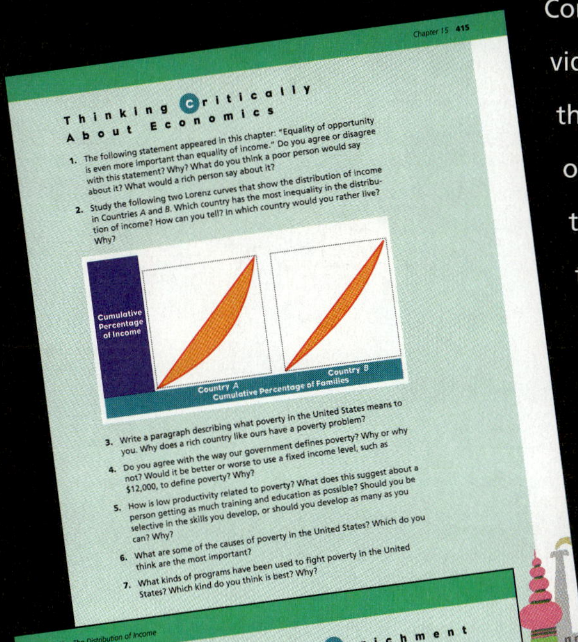

Chapter 15 415

Thinking Critically About Economics

1. The following statement appeared in this chapter: "Equality of opportunity is even more important than equality of income." Do you agree or disagree with this statement? Why? What do you think a poor person would say about it? What would a rich person say about it?
2. Study the following two Lorenz curves that show the distribution of income in Countries *A* and *B*. Which country has the most inequality in the distribution of income? How can you tell? In which country would you rather live? Why?

3. Write a paragraph describing what poverty in the United States means to you. Why does a rich country like ours have a poverty problem?
4. Do you agree with the way our government defines poverty? Why or why not? Would it be better or worse to use a fixed income level, such as $12,000, to define poverty? Why?
5. How is low productivity related to poverty? What does this suggest about a person getting as much training and education as possible? Should you be selective in the skills you develop, or should you develop as many as you can? Why?
6. What are some of the causes of poverty in the United States? Which do you think are the most important?
7. What kinds of programs have been used to fight poverty in the United States? Which kind do you think is best? Why?

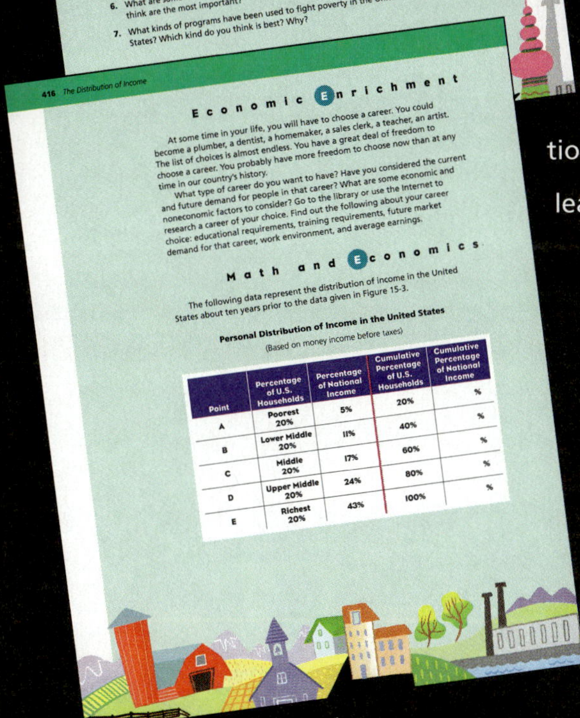

416 The Distribution of Income

Economic Enrichment

At some time in your life, you will have to choose a career. You could become a plumber, a dentist, a homemaker, a sales clerk, a teacher, an artist. The list of choices is almost endless. You have a great deal of freedom to choose a career. You probably have more freedom to choose now than at any time in our country's history.

What type of career do you want to have? Have you considered the current and future demand for people in that career? What are some economic and noneconomic factors to consider? Go to the library or use the Internet to research a career of your choice. Find out the following about your career choice: educational requirements, training requirements, future market demand for that career, work environment, and average earnings.

Math and Economics

The following data represent the distribution of income in the United States about ten years prior to the data given in Figure 15-3.

Personal Distribution of Income in the United States
(Based on money income before taxes)

Point	Percentage of U.S. Households	Percentage of National Income	Cumulative Percentage of U.S. Households	Cumulative Percentage of National Income
A	Poorest 20%	5%	20%	%
B	Lower Middle 20%	11%	40%	%
C	Middle 20%	17%	60%	%
D	Upper Middle 20%	24%	80%	%
E	Richest 20%	43%	100%	%

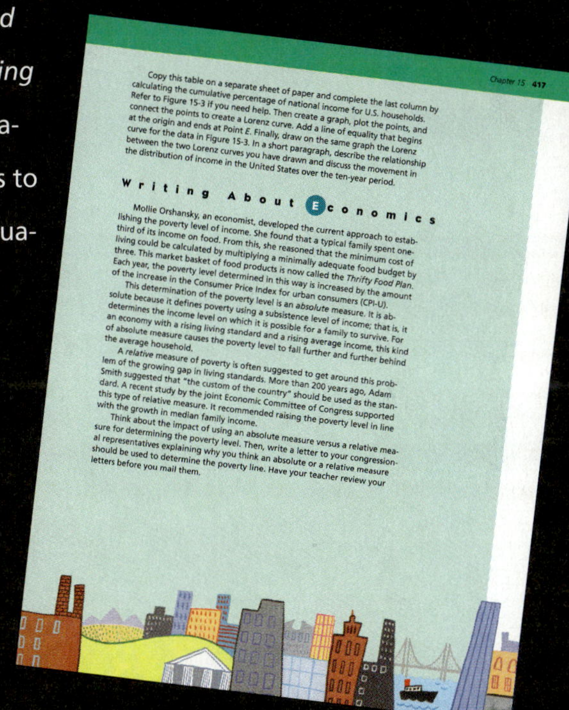

Chapter 15 417

Copy this table on a separate sheet of paper and complete the last column by calculating the cumulative percentage of national income for U.S. households. Refer to Figure 15-3 if you need help. Then create a graph, plot the points, and connect the points to create a Lorenz curve. Add a line of equality that begins at the origin and ends at Point *E*. Finally, draw on the same graph the Lorenz curve for the data in Figure 15-3. In a short paragraph, describe the relationship between the two Lorenz curves you have drawn and discuss the movement in the distribution of income in the United States over the ten-year period.

Writing About Economics

Mollie Orshansky, an economist, developed the current approach to establishing the poverty level of income. She found that a typical family spent one-third of its income on food. From this, she reasoned that the minimum cost of living could be calculated by multiplying a minimally adequate food budget by three. This market basket of food products is now called the *Thrifty Food Plan*. Each year, the poverty level determined in this way is increased by the amount of the increase in the Consumer Price Index for urban consumers (CPI-U).

This determination of the poverty level is an *absolute* measure. It is absolute because it defines poverty using a subsistence level of income; that is, it determines the income level on which it is possible for a family to survive. For an economy with a rising living standard and a rising average income, this kind of absolute measure causes the poverty level to fall further and further behind the average household.

A *relative* measure of poverty is often suggested to get around this problem of the growing gap in living standards. More than 200 years ago, Adam Smith suggested that "the custom of the country" should be used as the standard. A recent study by the joint Economic Committee of Congress supported this type of relative measure. It recommended raising the poverty level in line with the growth in median family income.

Think about the impact of using an absolute measure versus a relative measure for determining the poverty level. Then, write a letter to your congressional representatives explaining why you think an absolute or a relative measure should be used to determine the poverty line. Have your teacher review your letters before you mail them.

Special Features Enhance Instruction

Economic Dilemma

provides opportunities in every chapter for students to interact with the ethical, environmental, political, and social issues that relate to economics and, ultimately, to them.

Internet Connection

activities actively engage your students (and you!) on the Internet, starting with useful information for logging on and then progressing to hands-on application as you and they manipulate the fastest growing technology of the decade. Plus, a **Teachers' Connection to the Internet** manual provides you with additional Internet support you'll want to share with your classes.

Global Economy

provides insight into the economies of other nations and how they work. Thought-provoking and informative in nature, these features provide a natural opportunity for comparison and contrast and for extending the core concepts in the lesson.

Economic Spotlight

centers on a culturally diverse group of "movers and shakers" that play a key role in our economy. Students learn who these individuals are and why they are so important.

in Every Chapter

Econ & You

provides students with regular opportunities to apply economics concepts to their own lives, creating a foundation for lifelong learning based on a solid knowledge of the economics behind the issues.

In every part, special features add additional dimensions to your students' study of economics. You'll find your students **Analyzing Primary Source Documents,** applying **Economic Measurement Concepts,** and examining the **Social Goals of the U.S. Economy.**

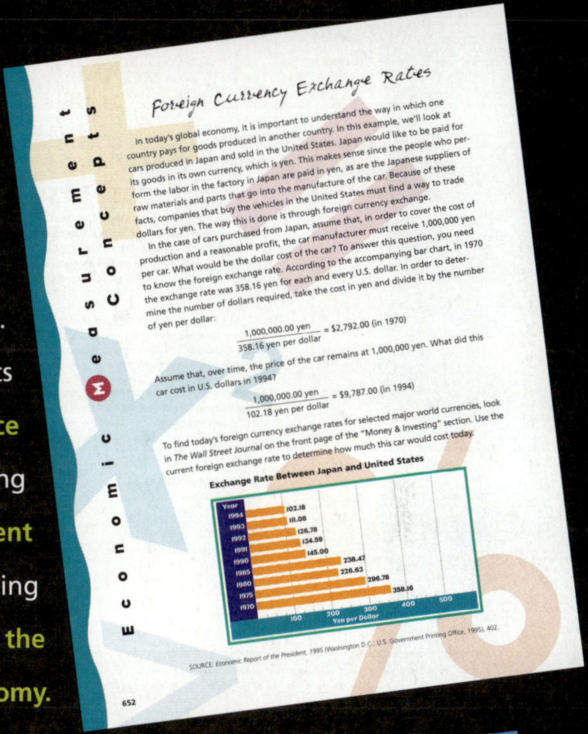
Economic Measurement Concepts

Foreign Currency Exchange Rates

In today's global economy, it is important to understand the way in which one country pays for goods produced in another country. In this example, we'll look at cars produced in Japan and sold in the United States. Japan would like to be paid for its goods in its own currency, which is yen. This makes sense since the people who perform the labor in the factory in Japan are paid in yen, as are the Japanese suppliers of raw materials and parts that go into the manufacture of the car. Because of these facts, companies that buy the vehicles in the United States must find a way to trade dollars for yen. The way this is done is through foreign currency exchange.

In the case of cars purchased from Japan, assume that, in order to cover the cost of production and a reasonable profit, the car manufacturer must receive 1,000,000 yen per car. What would be the dollar cost of the car? To answer this question, you need to know the foreign exchange rate. According to the accompanying bar chart, in 1970 the exchange rate was 358.16 yen for each and every U.S. dollar. In order to determine the number of dollars required, take the cost in yen and divide it by the number of yen per dollar:

$$\frac{1{,}000{,}000.00 \text{ yen}}{358.16 \text{ yen per dollar}} = \$2{,}792.00 \text{ (in 1970)}$$

Assume that, over time, the price of the car remains at 1,000,000 yen. What did this car cost in U.S. dollars in 1994?

$$\frac{1{,}000{,}000.00 \text{ yen}}{102.18 \text{ yen per dollar}} = \$9{,}787.00 \text{ (in 1994)}$$

To find today's foreign currency exchange rates for selected major world currencies, look in *The Wall Street Journal* on the front page of the "Money & Investing" section. Use the current foreign exchange rate to determine how much this car would cost today.

Exchange Rate Between Japan and United States

Year	Yen per Dollar
1994	102.18
1993	111.08
1992	126.78
1991	134.59
1990	145.00
1985	238.47
1980	226.63
1975	296.78
1970	358.16

SOURCE: *Economic Report of the President,* 1995 (Washington D.C.: U.S. Government Printing Office, 1995), 402.

652

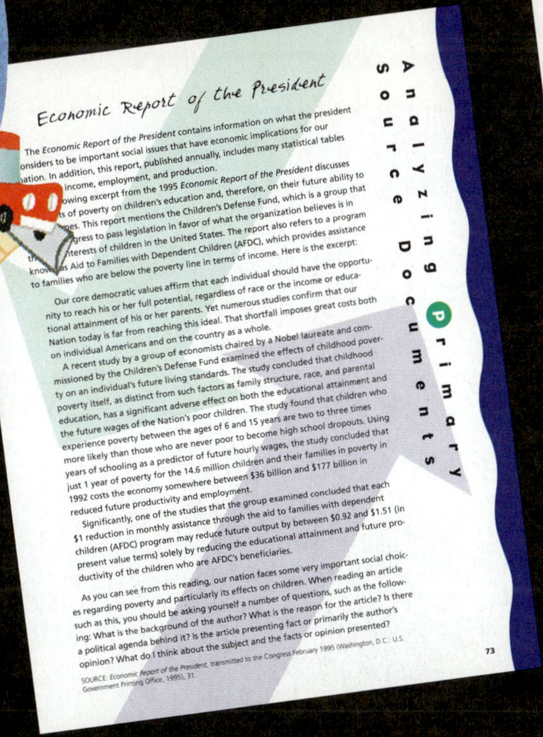
Analyzing Primary Source Documents

Economic Report of the President

The *Economic Report of the President* contains information on what the president onsiders to be important social issues that have economic implications for our ation. In addition, this report, published annually, includes many statistical tables income, employment, and production.

owing excerpt from the 1995 *Economic Report of the President* discusses ts of poverty on children's education and, therefore, on their future ability to es. This report mentions the Children's Defense Fund, which is a group that gress to pass legislation in favor of what the organization believes is in terests of children in the United States. The report also refers to a program th know as Aid to Families with Dependent Children (AFDC), which provides assistance to families who are below the poverty line in terms of income. Here is the excerpt:

Our core democratic values affirm that each individual should have the opportunity to reach his or her full potential, regardless of race or the income or educational attainment of his or her parents. Yet numerous studies confirm that our Nation today is far from reaching this ideal. That shortfall imposes great costs both on individual Americans and on the country as a whole.

A recent study by a group of economists chaired by a Nobel laureate and commissioned by the Children's Defense Fund examined the effects of childhood poverty on an individual's future living standards. The study concluded that childhood poverty itself, as distinct from such factors as family structure, race, and parental education, has a significant adverse effect on both the educational attainment and the future wages of the Nation's poor children. The study found that children who experience poverty between the ages of 6 and 15 years are two to three times more likely than those who are never poor to become high school dropouts. Using years of schooling as a predictor of future hourly wages, the study concluded that just 1 year of poverty for the 14.6 million children and their families in poverty in 1992 costs the economy somewhere between $36 billion and $177 billion in reduced future productivity and employment.

Significantly, one of the studies that the group examined concluded that each $1 reduction in monthly assistance through the aid to families with dependent children (AFDC) program may reduce future output by between $0.92 and $1.51 (in present value terms) solely by reducing the educational attainment and future productivity of the children who are AFDC's beneficiaries.

As you can see from this reading, our nation faces some very important social choices regarding poverty and particularly its effects on children. When reading an article such as this, you should be asking yourself a number of questions, such as the following: What is the background of the author? What is the reason for the article? Is there a political agenda behind it? Is the article presenting fact or primarily the author's opinion? What do I think about the subject and the facts or opinion presented?

SOURCE: *Economic Report of the President,* transmitted to the Congress February 1995 (Washington, D.C.: U.S. Government Printing Office, 1995), 31.

73

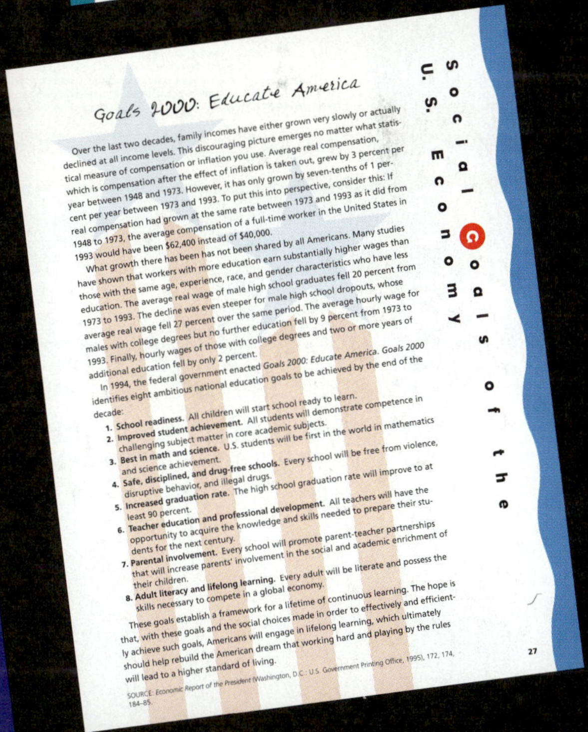
Social Goals of the U.S. Economy

Goals 2000: Educate America

Over the last two decades, family incomes have either grown very slowly or actually declined at all income levels. This discouraging picture emerges no matter what statistical measure of compensation or inflation you use. Average real compensation, which is compensation after the effect of inflation is taken out, grew by 3 percent per year between 1948 and 1973. However, it has only grown by seven-tenths of 1 percent per year between 1973 and 1993. To put this into perspective, consider this: If real compensation had grown at the same rate between 1973 and 1993 as it did from 1948 to 1973, the average compensation of a full-time worker in the United States in 1993 would have been $62,400 instead of $40,000.

What growth there has been has not been shared by all Americans. Many studies have shown that workers with more education earn substantially higher wages than those with the same age, experience, race, and gender characteristics who have less education. The average real wage of male high school graduates fell 20 percent from 1973 to 1993. The decline was even steeper for male high school dropouts, whose average real wage fell 27 percent over the same period. The average hourly wage for males with college degrees but no further education fell by 9 percent from 1973 to 1993. Finally, hourly wages of those with college degrees and two or more years of additional education fell by only 2 percent.

In 1994, the federal government enacted *Goals 2000: Educate America*. *Goals 2000* identifies eight ambitious national education goals to be achieved by the end of the decade:

1. **School readiness.** All children will start school ready to learn.
2. **Improved student achievement.** All students will demonstrate competence in challenging subject matter in core academic subjects.
3. **Best in math and science.** U.S. students will be first in the world in mathematics and science achievement.
4. **Safe, disciplined, and drug-free schools.** Every school will be free from violence, disruptive behavior, and illegal drugs.
5. **Increased graduation rate.** The high school graduation rate will improve to at least 90 percent.
6. **Teacher education and professional development.** All teachers will have the opportunity to acquire the knowledge and skills needed to prepare their students for the next century.
7. **Parental involvement.** Every school will promote parent-teacher partnerships that will increase parents' involvement in the social and academic enrichment of their children.
8. **Adult literacy and lifelong learning.** Every adult will be literate and possess the skills necessary to compete in a global economy.

These goals establish a framework for a lifetime of continuous learning. The hope is that, with these goals and the social choices made in order to effectively and efficiently achieve such goals, Americans will engage in lifelong learning, which ultimately should help rebuild the American dream that working hard and playing by the rules will lead to a higher standard of living.

SOURCE: *Economic Report of the President* (Washington, D.C.: U.S. Government Printing Office, 1995), 172, 174, 184–85.

27

At-A-Glance Organizers Help You

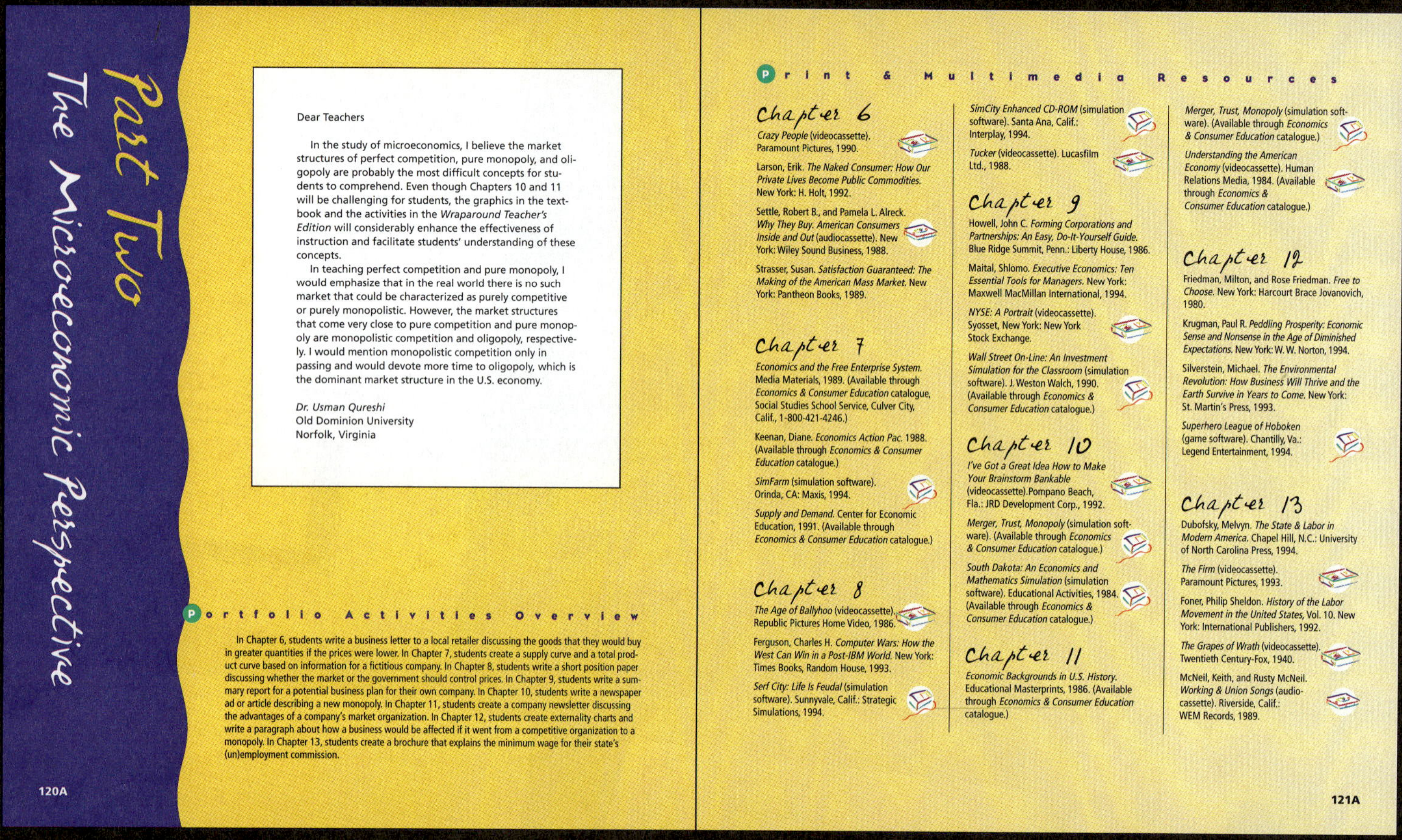

Part Two
The Microeconomic Perspective

Dear Teachers

In the study of microeconomics, I believe the market structures of perfect competition, pure monopoly, and oligopoly are probably the most difficult concepts for students to comprehend. Even though Chapters 10 and 11 will be challenging for students, the graphics in the textbook and the activities in the *Wraparound Teacher's Edition* will considerably enhance the effectiveness of instruction and facilitate students' understanding of these concepts.

In teaching perfect competition and pure monopoly, I would emphasize that in the real world there is no such market that could be characterized as purely competitive or purely monopolistic. However, the market structures that come very close to pure competition and pure monopoly are monopolistic competition and oligopoly, respectively. I would mention monopolistic competition only in passing and would devote more time to oligopoly, which is the dominant market structure in the U.S. economy.

Dr. Usman Qureshi
Old Dominion University
Norfolk, Virginia

Portfolio Activities Overview

In Chapter 6, students write a business letter to a local retailer discussing the goods that they would buy in greater quantities if the prices were lower. In Chapter 7, students create a supply curve and a total product curve based on information for a fictitious company. In Chapter 8, students write a short position paper discussing whether the market or the government should control prices. In Chapter 9, students write a summary report for a potential business plan for their own company. In Chapter 10, students write a newspaper ad or article describing a new monopoly. In Chapter 11, students create a company newsletter discussing the advantages of a company's market organization. In Chapter 12, students create externality charts and write a paragraph about how a business would be affected if it went from a competitive organization to a monopoly. In Chapter 13, students create a brochure that explains the minimum wage for their state's (un)employment commission.

120A

Print & Multimedia Resources

Chapter 6

Crazy People (videocassette). Paramount Pictures, 1990.

Larson, Erik. *The Naked Consumer: How Our Private Lives Become Public Commodities.* New York: H. Holt, 1992.

Settle, Robert B., and Pamela L. Alreck. *Why They Buy. American Consumers Inside and Out* (audiocassette). New York: Wiley Sound Business, 1988.

Strasser, Susan. *Satisfaction Guaranteed: The Making of the American Mass Market.* New York: Pantheon Books, 1989.

Chapter 7

Economics and the Free Enterprise System. Media Materials, 1989. (Available through *Economics & Consumer Education* catalogue, Social Studies School Service, Culver City, Calif., 1-800-421-4246.)

Keenan, Diane. *Economics Action Pac.* 1988. (Available through *Economics & Consumer Education* catalogue.)

SimFarm (simulation software). Orinda, CA: Maxis, 1994.

Supply and Demand. Center for Economic Education, 1991. (Available through *Economics & Consumer Education* catalogue.)

Chapter 8

The Age of Ballyhoo (videocassette). Republic Pictures Home Video, 1986.

Ferguson, Charles H. *Computer Wars: How the West Can Win in a Post-IBM World.* New York: Times Books, Random House, 1993.

Serf City: Life Is Feudal (simulation software). Sunnyvale, Calif.: Strategic Simulations, 1994.

SimCity Enhanced CD-ROM (simulation software). Santa Ana, Calif.: Interplay, 1994.

Tucker (videocassette). Lucasfilm Ltd., 1988.

Chapter 9

Howell, John C. *Forming Corporations and Partnerships: An Easy, Do-It-Yourself Guide.* Blue Ridge Summit, Penn.: Liberty House, 1986.

Maital, Shlomo. *Executive Economics: Ten Essential Tools for Managers.* New York: Maxwell MacMillan International, 1994.

NYSE: A Portrait (videocassette). Syosset, New York: New York Stock Exchange.

Wall Street On-Line: An Investment Simulation for the Classroom (simulation software). J. Weston Walch, 1990. (Available through *Economics & Consumer Education* catalogue.)

Chapter 10

I've Got a Great Idea How to Make Your Brainstorm Bankable (videocassette).Pompano Beach, Fla.: JRD Development Corp., 1992.

Merger, Trust, Monopoly (simulation software). (Available through *Economics & Consumer Education* catalogue.)

South Dakota: An Economics and Mathematics Simulation (simulation software). Educational Activities, 1984. (Available through *Economics & Consumer Education* catalogue.)

Chapter 11

Economic Backgrounds in U.S. History. Educational Masterprints, 1986. (Available through *Economics & Consumer Education* catalogue.)

Merger, Trust, Monopoly (simulation software). (Available through *Economics & Consumer Education* catalogue.)

Understanding the American Economy (videocassette). Human Relations Media, 1984. (Available through *Economics & Consumer Education* catalogue.)

Chapter 12

Friedman, Milton, and Rose Friedman. *Free to Choose.* New York: Harcourt Brace Jovanovich, 1980.

Krugman, Paul R. *Peddling Prosperity: Economic Sense and Nonsense in the Age of Diminished Expectations.* New York: W. W. Norton, 1994.

Silverstein, Michael. *The Environmental Revolution: How Business Will Thrive and the Earth Survive in Years to Come.* New York: St. Martin's Press, 1993.

Superhero League of Hoboken (game software). Chantilly, Va.: Legend Entertainment, 1994.

Chapter 13

Dubofsky, Melvyn. *The State & Labor in Modern America.* Chapel Hill, N.C.: University of North Carolina Press, 1994.

The Firm (videocassette). Paramount Pictures, 1993.

Foner, Philip Sheldon. *History of the Labor Movement in the United States,* Vol. 10. New York: International Publishers, 1992.

The Grapes of Wrath (videocassette). Twentieth Century-Fox, 1940.

McNeil, Keith, and Rusty McNeil. *Working & Union Songs* (audiocassette). Riverside, Calif.: WEM Records, 1989.

121A

Start each of the four ECONOMICS parts with a four-page planner designed to help you organize the unit of study and get a head start on preparing for upcoming classes.

Have you ever wondered how other teachers respond to a textbook you are using? Gain another perspective of ECONOMICS from our **personalized letters of reference** and learn how other teachers anticipate integrating ECONOMICS into their classes. Perhaps you'll find a new approach or gain a teaching tip you'll want to add to your own repertoire.

Portfolio activity summaries for each chapter make it easy for you

Gather Resources for Every Unit

to preview or adapt suggestions for portfolio assessment to meet the distinct needs of your classes.

A comprehensive, chapter-by-chapter **bibliography** of current print and multimedia resources provides a wealth of extension and reference information for you and your students and makes it easier to explore key topics and concepts in greater depth.

A brief **overview** of the contents of each chapter in the part allows you to rapidly transition from the focus of one part to the next and prepares you for the economics content to be addressed in the weeks to come.

Chapter Interleaf Sections Facilitate Planning.

Chapter Themes preview the content in each chapter.

Special Features—12 in each chapter—add informative, lively learning opportunities to the student text and teacher edition and empower your economics learners to experience real-world perspectives.

Activities for Special Learners—Auditory, Visual, Kinesthetic, Cooperative Learning, and Special Needs opportunities provide suggestions for integrating a variety of learning modalities and formats to help all your learners perform at their peak.

Chapter 6

Demand: Achieving Consumer Satisfaction

Chapter Theme

Chapter 6 explores demand, the relationship between quantity demanded and price, and the reasons for the relationship. Changes in demand and factors that affect the demand for goods and services also are explored. In Section Four, the relationship between price, unit sales, and revenue is analyzed.

Section	Special Features
Demand Schedules and Demand Curves	Economic Spotlight
The Law of Demand	Perspectives: Thinking Like a Consumer Economics & Your Community Internet Connection
Determinants of Demand	Eye on Market News Economic Talk Global Economy Economic Dilemma
Price Elasticity of Demand	Multicultural Highlights Econ & You Media Link

Video Activity

Chapter 6, British Retail

Search Chapter 6, Play to 7

Ask students to discuss what kinds of cultural differences or other considerations U.S. retailers need to be aware of to succeed in other countries (limited product exposure, different social customs, or unfamiliar terminology). Have students suggest kinds of changes that corporations might make to achieve consumer satisfaction in particular countries.

122A

Video Activities maximize hands-on opportunities for students to analyze the video clips they view in class and respond to thought-provoking questions.

Conducting, and Assessing Your Daily Lessons

	Print Resources	Media Resources	Assessment
	Effective Teaching Model Lesson Plans *Skills & Concepts* worksheet *Problem Solving* worksheet *Casebook* *Economic Measurement Workbook* *Content Review Workbook* *Spanish Resources*	VHS CD-ROM Videodisc *Arctic Express* *Interactive ECONOMICS* Template software	*Your Economic Portfolio* Chapter *Assessment* Chapter *MicroExam*

Special Learners	Print Resources	Media Resources	Assessment
		Overhead and *Transparencies 6-1 and 6-2* Computer	*Checkpoint* Section 1 Quiz
Attention Deficit Disorder	*Teacher's Connection to the Internet*	Overhead and *Transparency 6-3* Computer Camcorder VCR	*Checkpoint* Section 2 Quiz
Visual Activity Kinesthetic Activity Auditory Activity	*Enrich* worksheet	Overhead and *Transparency 6-4* Computer	*Checkpoint* Section 3 Quiz
Cooperative Learning Activity	*Life Skills* worksheet *Reteach* worksheet	Overhead and *Transparencies 6-5 and 6-6* Computer Audio	*Checkpoint* Section 4 Quiz

Careers Activity

The job of advertising is to create or increase consumer demand. Advertising art directors use visuals to accomplish this. They create, or direct the creation of, art that captures the consumer's interest and promotes a product or service.

Besides having artistic ability, advertising art directors must understand marketing, layout, typography, design methods, and basic printing processes. A knowledge of video production also may be helpful. Art directors should maintain a portfolio of their best work to show to potential employers. Earnings generally range from $15,000 to $30,000 per year but can reach as high as $100,000.

Tell students to imagine that they are art directors who have been asked to create an ad campaign for a well-established line of clothing. Because of recent increases in cloth prices, the clothes have become very expensive and sales have dropped. Have students create full-page ads to win back old customers and to entice new ones to buy the product.

123A

Print, Media, and **Assessment** resources are built into your teaching plan for every chapter. Consisting of a variety of modalities from print, to video, to disk- and CD-ROM-based learning, these resources give you and your students maximum flexibility to best meet your classroom's needs and schedules.

Section-by-section annotations of **print, media,** and **assessment** opportunities are sequenced in the order in which they are offered in the program. Use this handy resource to gather the materials and equipment you'll want to have on hand to conduct the suggested teaching activities.

Careers Activities profile 24 employment opportunities that require a working background in economics. Entry-level requirements, salary histories, job descriptions, and a hands-on activity are provided in every chapter.

Features of the Two-Volume Wraparound

A fully developed, multistep teaching plan provides a blueprint to focus, teach, apply, assess, reteach, enrich, and bring closure to each instructional lesson.

Two **Focus** activities bridge students' prior knowledge to the new concepts presented in the lesson. Engage students actively in economics—before the bell rings.

Following a multistep lesson plan, **Teach** activities synthesize key content and provide you with a variety of teaching suggestions to emphasize the main points of each lesson.

Guided Practice and Independent Practice activities allow your students to **Apply** the concepts developed in the lesson. Choose those activities that best meet your class needs and interests.

Suggested solutions to the end-of-section *Checkpoint* questions allow you to **Assess** student comprehension before continuing to the next lesson.

Do you want to reinforce a learning objective before a particular student continues to the next lesson?

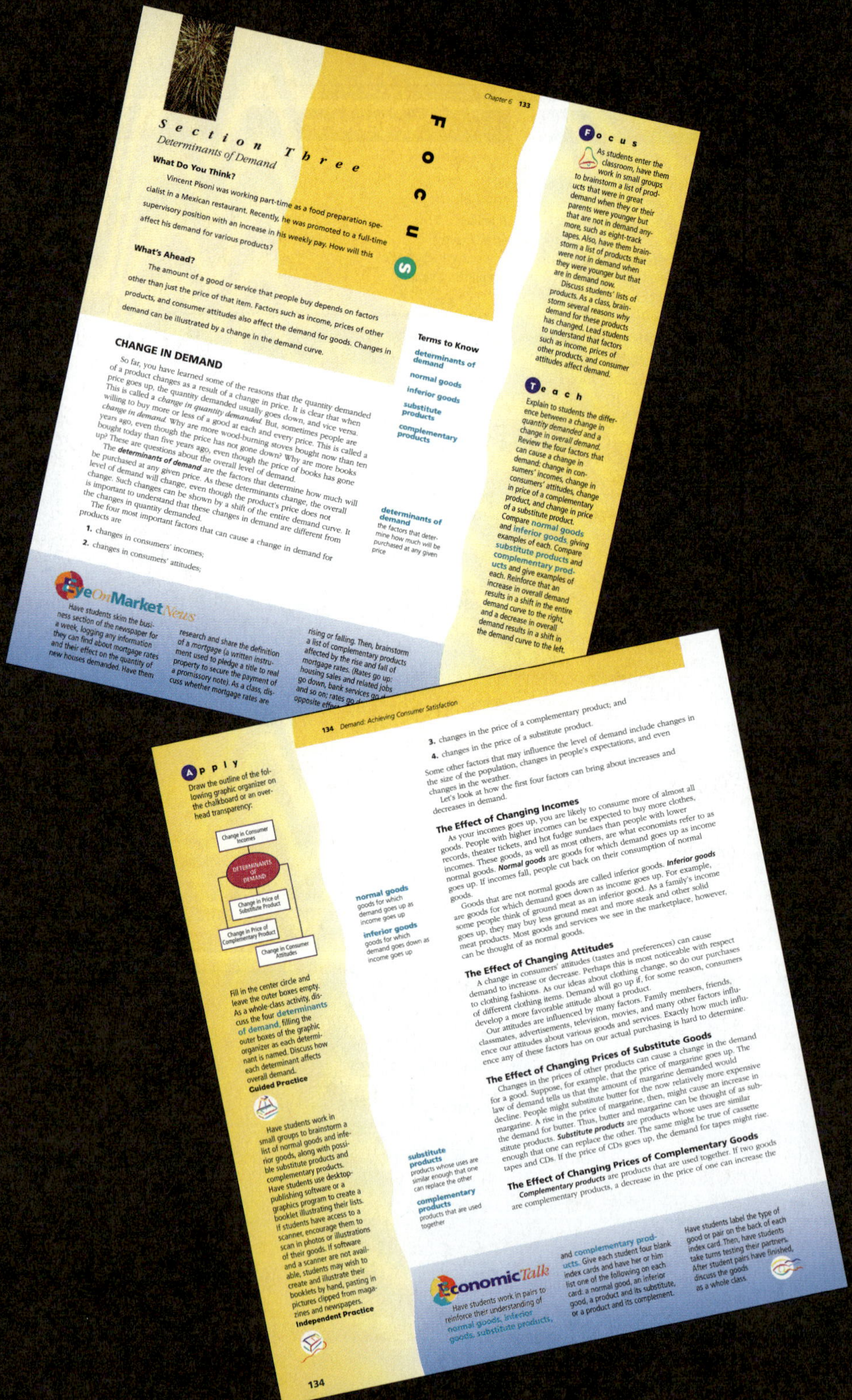

Teacher's Edition

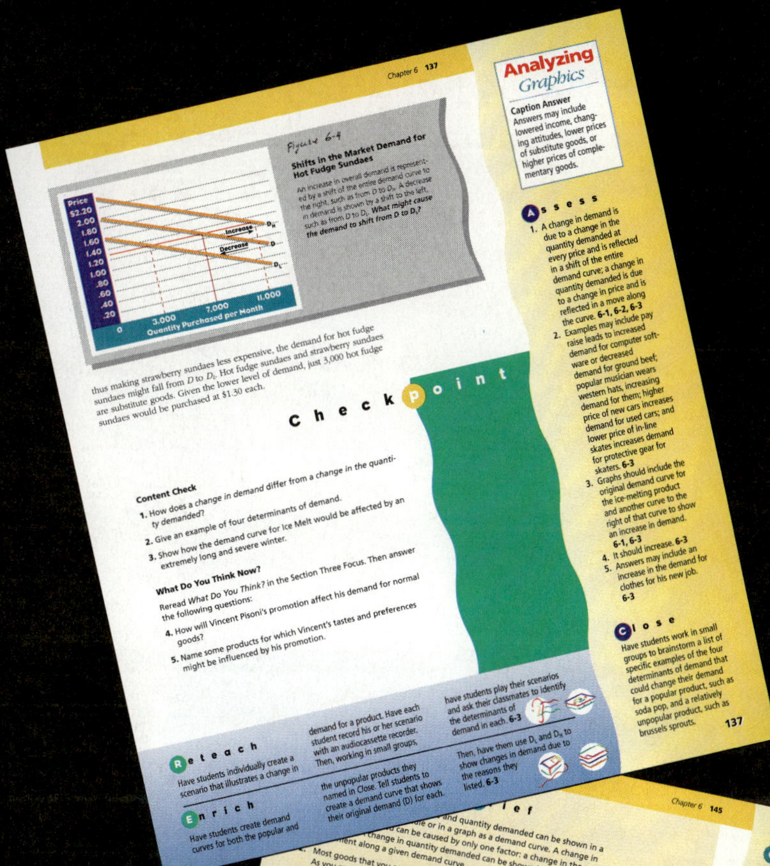

Figure 6-4

Shifts in the Market Demand for Hot Fudge Sundaes

An increase in overall demand is represented by a shift of the entire demand curve to the right, such as from D to D_I. A decrease in demand is shown by a shift to the left, such as from D to D_D. **What might cause the demand to shift from D to D_I?**

thus making strawberry sundaes less expensive, the demand for hot fudge sundaes might fall from D to D_D. Hot fudge sundaes and strawberry sundaes are substitute goods. Given the lower level of demand, just 3,000 hot fudge sundaes would be purchased at $1.50 each.

Checkpoint

Content Check

1. How does a change in demand differ from a change in the quantity demanded?
2. Give an example of four determinants of demand.
3. Show how the demand curve for Ice Melt would be affected by an extremely long and severe winter.

What Do You Think Now?

Reread *What Do You Think?* in the Section Three Focus. Then answer the following questions:

4. How will Vincent Pisoni's promotion affect his demand for normal goods?
5. Name some products for which Vincent's tastes and preferences might be influenced by his promotion.

Analyzing Graphics

Caption Answer Answers may include lowered income, changing attitudes, lower prices of substitute goods, or higher prices of complementary goods.

Assess

1. A change in demand is due to a change in the quantity demanded at every price and is reflected in a shift of the entire demand curve; a change in quantity demanded is due to a change in price and is reflected in a move along the curve. **6-1, 6-2, 6-3**
2. Examples may include pay raise leads to increased demand for computer software or decreased demand for ground beef; popular musician wears western hats, increasing demand for them; higher price of new cars increases demand for used cars; and lower price of in-line skates increases demand for protective gear for skaters. **6-3**
3. Graphs should include the original demand curve for the ice-melting product and another curve to the right of that curve to show an increase in demand. **6-1, 6-3**
4. It should increase. **6-3**
5. Answers may include an increase in the demand for clothes for his new job. **6-3**

Close

Have students work in small groups to brainstorm a list of specific examples of the four determinants of demand that could change their demand for a popular product, such as soda pop, and a relatively unpopular product, such as brussels sprouts.

Reteach

Have students individually create a scenario that illustrates a change in demand for a product. Have each student record his or her scenario with an audiocassette recorder. Then, working in small groups, have students play their scenarios and ask their classmates to identify the determinants of demand in each. **6-3**

Enrich

Have students create demand curves for both the popular and the unpopular products they named in Close. Tell students to create a demand curve that shows their original demand (D) for each. Then, have them use D_I and D_D to show changes in demand due to the reasons they listed. **6-3**

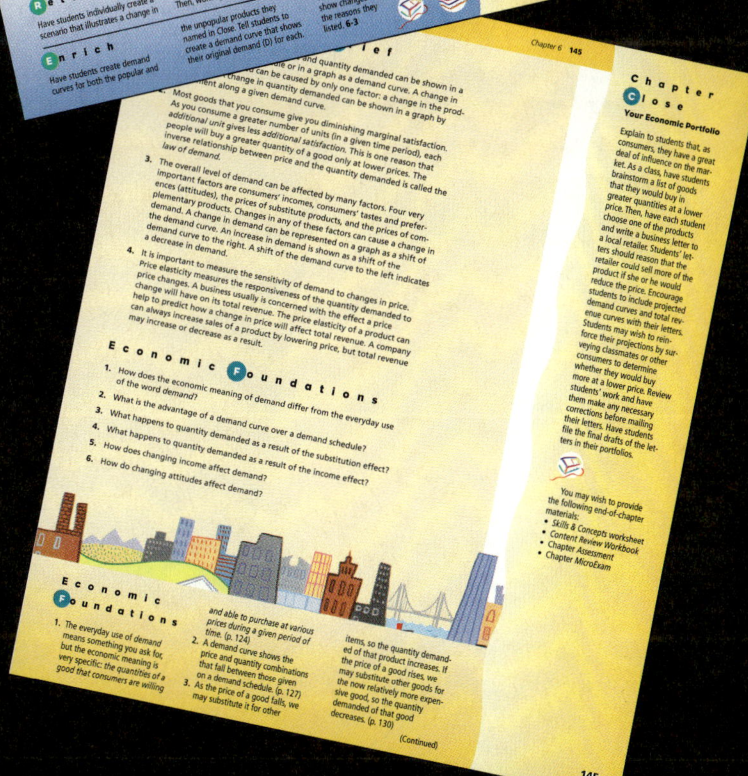

...and quantity demanded can be shown in a ... or in a graph as a demand curve. A change in ... can be caused by only one factor: a change in the prod... change in quantity demanded can be shown in a graph by ...ment along a given demand curve.

2. Most goods that you consume give you diminishing marginal satisfaction. As you consume a greater number of units (in a given time period), each additional unit gives less additional satisfaction. This is one reason that people will buy a greater quantity of a good only at lower prices. The inverse relationship between price and the quantity demanded is called the *law of demand*.
3. The overall level of demand can be affected by many factors. Four very important factors are consumers' incomes, consumers' tastes and preferences (attitudes), the prices of substitute products, and the prices of complementary products. Changes in any of these factors can cause a change in demand. A change in demand can be represented on a graph as a shift of the demand curve. An increase in demand is shown as a shift of the demand curve to the right. A shift of the demand curve to the left indicates a decrease in demand.
4. It is important to measure the sensitivity of demand to changes in price. Price elasticity measures the responsiveness of the quantity demanded to price changes. A business usually is concerned with the effect a price change will have on its total revenue. The price elasticity of a product can help to predict how a change in price will affect total revenue. A company can always increase sales of a product by lowering price, but total revenue may increase or decrease as a result.

Economic Foundations

1. How does the economic meaning of demand differ from the everyday use of the word *demand*?
2. What is the advantage of a demand curve over a demand schedule?
3. What happens to quantity demanded as a result of the substitution effect?
4. What happens to quantity demanded as a result of the income effect?
5. How does changing income affect demand?
6. How do changing attitudes affect demand?

Chapter Close

Your Economic Portfolio

Explain to students that, as consumers, they have a great deal of influence on the market. As a class, have students brainstorm a list of goods that they would buy in greater quantities at a lower price. Then, have each student choose one of the products and write a business letter to a local retailer. Students' letters should reason that the retailer could sell more of the product if she or he would reduce the price. Encourage students to include projected demand curves and total revenue curves with their letters. Students may wish to reinforce their projections by surveying classmates or other consumers to determine whether they would buy more at a lower price. Review students' work and have them make any necessary corrections before mailing their letters. Have students file the final drafts of the letters in their portfolios.

You may wish to provide the following end-of-chapter materials:

- *Skills & Concepts* worksheet
- *Content Review Workbook*
- *Chapter Assessment*
- *Chapter MicroExam*

Economic Foundations

1. The everyday use of demand means something you ask for, but the economic meaning is very specific: the quantities of a good that consumers are willing and able to purchase at various prices during a given period of time. (p. 124)
2. A demand curve shows the price and quantity combinations that fall between those given on a demand schedule. (p. 127)
3. As the price of a good falls, we may substitute it for other items, so the quantity demanded of that product increases. If the price of a good rises, we may substitute other goods for the now relatively more expensive good, so the quantity demanded of that good decreases. (p. 130)

(Continued)

Do you need to challenge and extend the core content? Reteach and Enrich activities let you accomplish both objectives—in each instructional lesson. The worksheet icon identifies the Reteach and Enrich activities that are further supported by worksheets in the Teacher's Resource Box.

Close activities allow you to wrap up each lesson before continuing to the next.

Visually distinct media icons identify activities that integrate technology into your economics curriculum and alert you to gather the necessary materials before class begins.

Your Economic Portfolio is an informal assessment opportunity built into every chapter. Enhance higher-order thinking skills as students follow a progression of writing assignments that build in scope as your students acquire economic knowledge. The portfolio activity allows you to discuss students' work with them and document their efforts throughout the course.

Integrated Activities Bring ECONOMICS

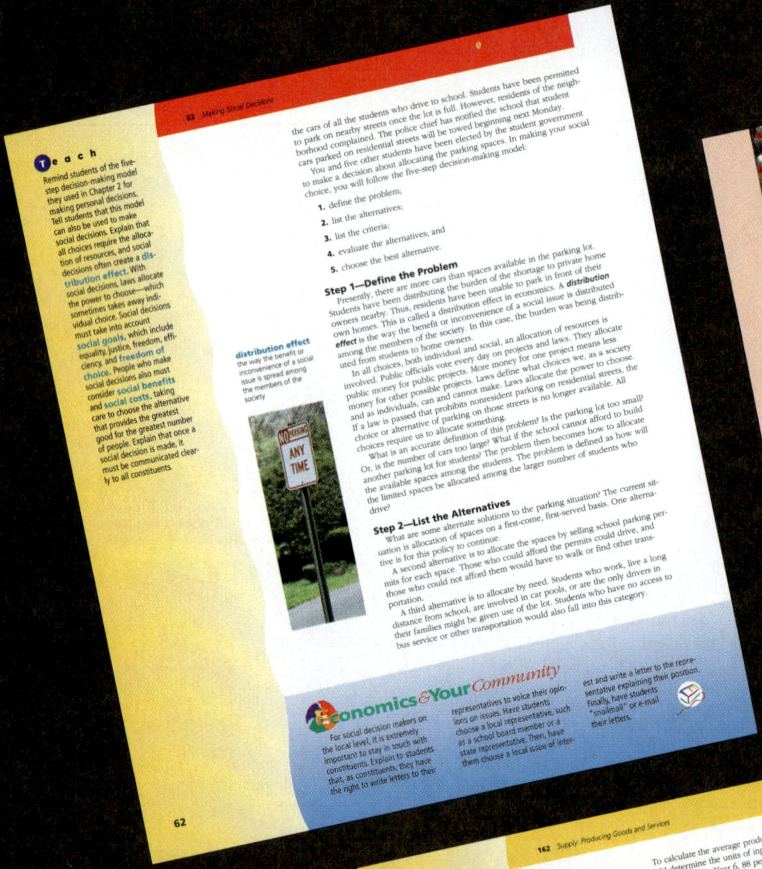

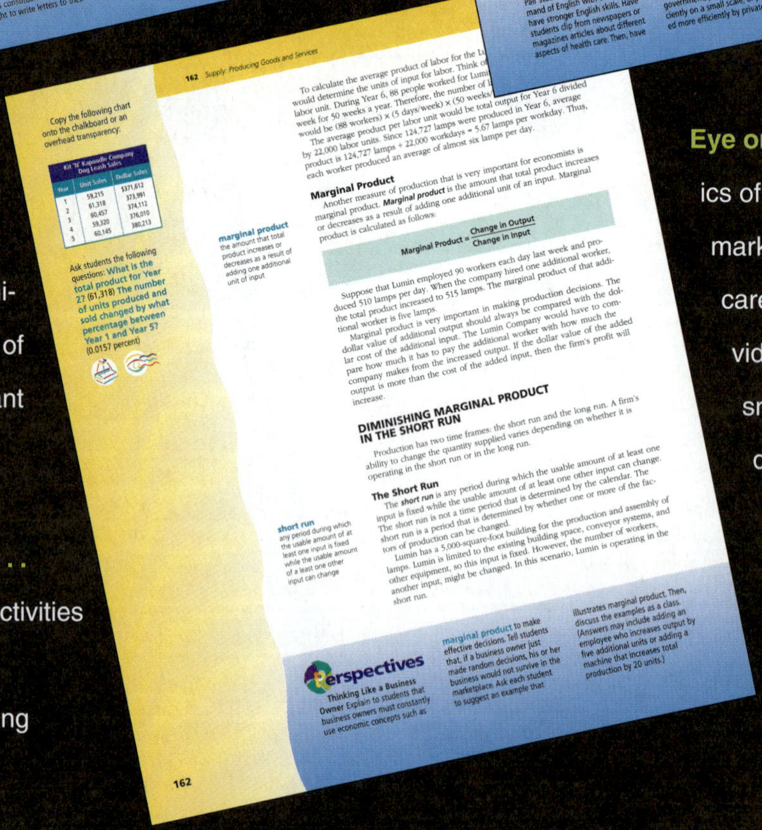

Economics & Your Community Students use current events and local economics issues in your community to apply their understanding of economics to personally relevant scenarios.

Perspectives: Thinking Like . . . Open-ended, critical-thinking activities challenge students to consider alternate points of view regarding related economics issues.

Eye on Market News Recurring topics of interest such as the stock market and the impact of health care on our nation's economy provide a focal point for individual, small-group, and class-based discussions and projects.

to Life

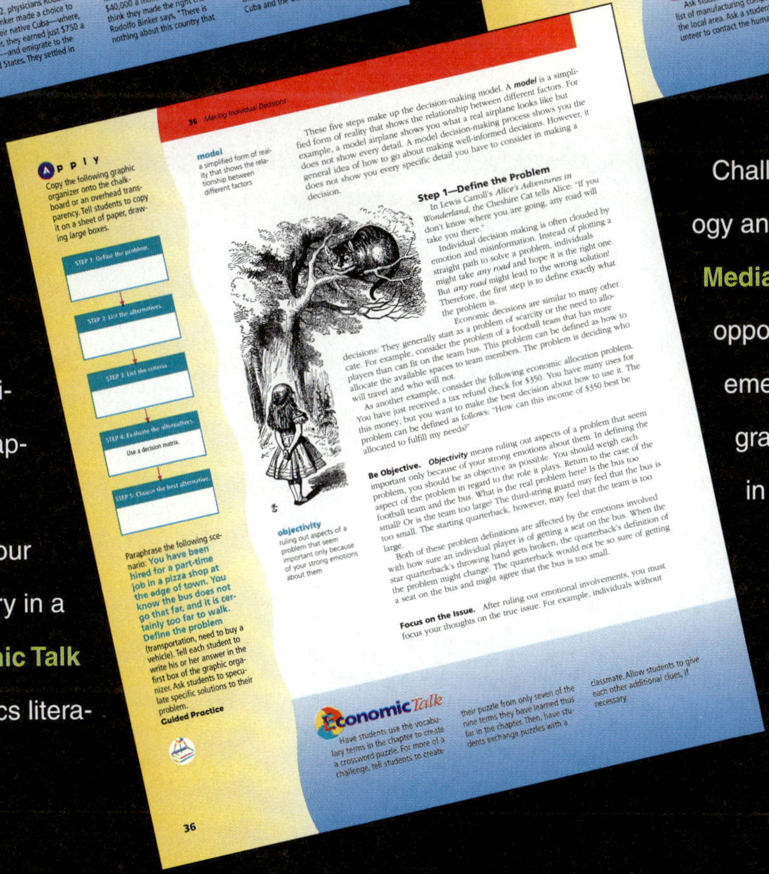

Background information highlighting cultural or ethnic contributions related to the chapter content are offered in **Multicultural Highlights** activities, which appear in every chapter of *ECONOMICS*.

Would you like to develop your students' economics vocabulary in a fun, less-formal way? **Economic Talk** is your answer! Build economics literacy as you teach.

Challenge students to use technology and multimedia resources in **Media Link**, which offers hands-on opportunities for students to use emerging technologies and integrated software to solve problems in economics.

Technology and Print Components Complete

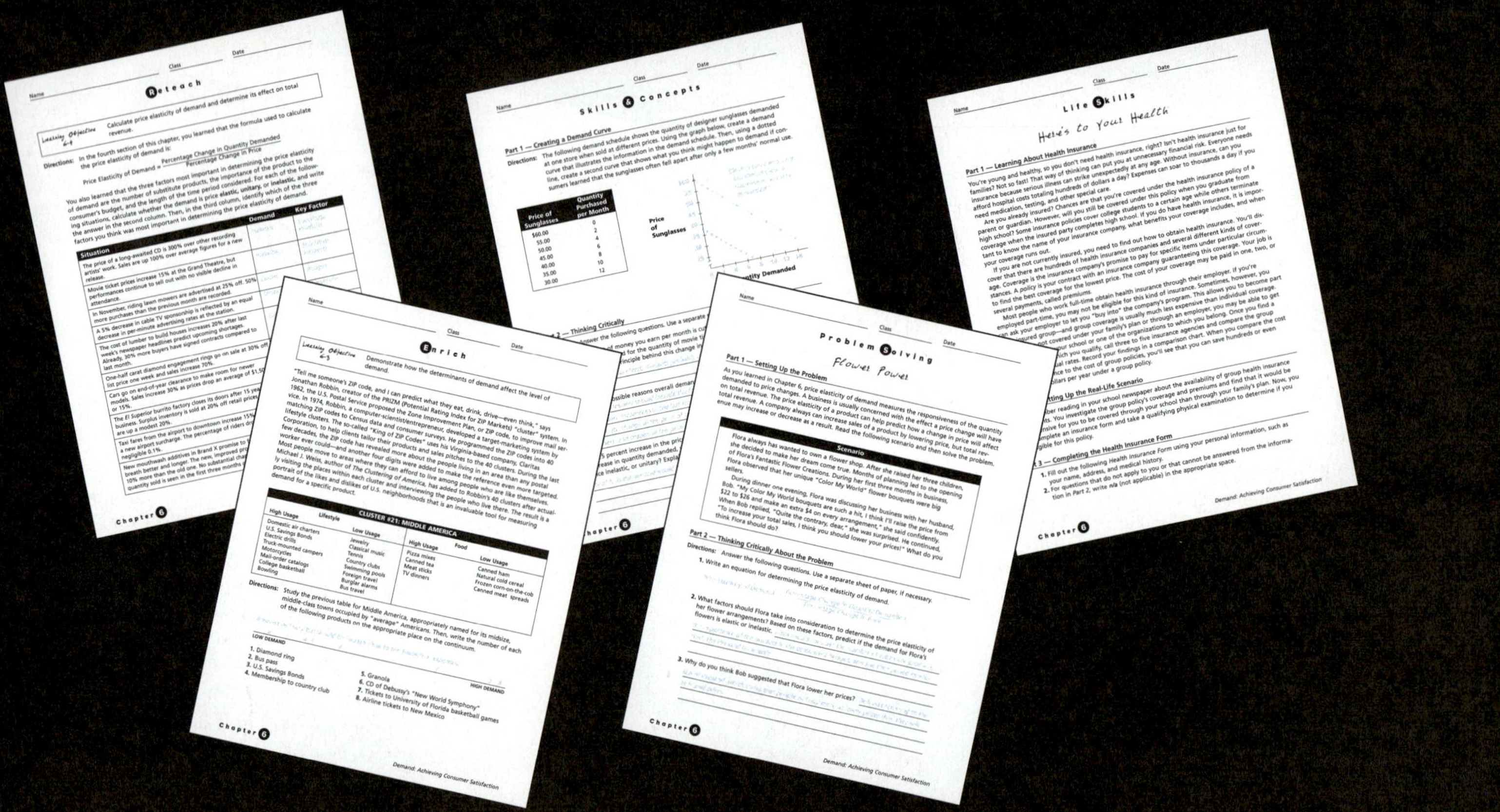

The **Teacher's Resource Box** contains a wealth of support materials. Teacher overprints of the section and chapter tests, *Casebook*, *Economic Measurement Workbook*, and *Content Review Workbook* are provided. The demo software, multistep lesson plans, transparency masters, and five blackline master ancillaries (*Reteach*, *Enrich*, *Skills & Concepts*, *Problem Solving*, and *Life Skills*) focus and enhance the learning experiences provided in every chapter. *Teacher's Connection to the Internet* contains the support you need to bring your classroom online. Use the Teacher's Resource Binder to store and organize your ECONOMICS resources and the Professional Organizer to prepare for class. Display the multicultural poster and let your students celebrate our heritage. In addition, *Spanish Resources,* which contains chapter learning objectives, summaries, and a comprehensive English-Spanish program glossary, is available free by request.

Dynamic, four-color **Teaching Transparencies** allow you to demonstrate concepts as you teach them. **Casebook** offers a selection of 24 contemporary profiles in economics. These scenarios allow students to explore the relationship between the chapter content and its real-world application.

The **Economic Measurement Workbook** provides substantial opportunities for students to develop and practice the core mathematics and measurement concepts

Your instructional Package

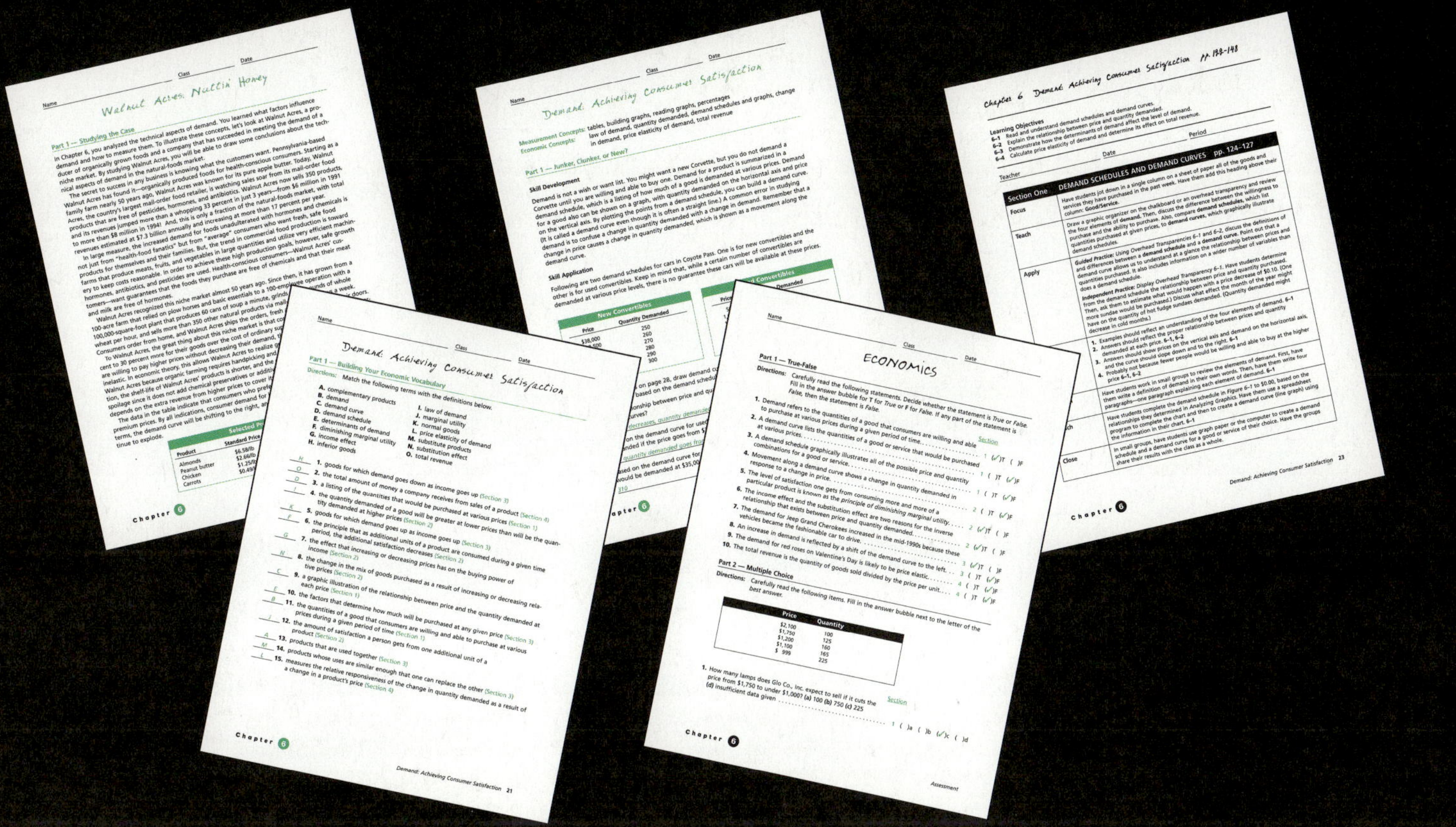

identified by the National Council on Economic Education.

Wrap up each chapter with the **Content Review Workbook**, which provides vocabulary and content review opportunities in standardized test formats so students can pre-assess their own economic competency.

Assessment Booklets and **Micro-Exam software** provide true/false and multiple/choice tests, in both print and electronic formats.

Interactive ECONOMICS lets students explore the main economic concepts in each chapter at their own pace. The hands-on, interactive nature of this program is ideal for reteaching. Interactive ECONOMICS is available for Windows and Macintosh, on both disk and CD-ROM.

Arctic Express allows students to compete with one another as they make economic decisions while running an ice-cream shop. Arctic Express is available for Windows and Macintosh, on both disk and CD-ROM.

CNBC Video Segments bring real-world events and their economic implications into the classroom. CNBC segments are available on videodisc, videotape, and CD-ROM.

The Stock Market: A Computer Simulation exposes students to the stock market experience through a fun, exciting simulation. This computer simulation is available for Windows and Macintosh.

Template Software provides the opportunity for students to use spreadsheet software to solve economic measurement problems. Template software is available for Windows and Macintosh spreadsheet software.

PREFACE

ECONOMICS IS ALL AROUND YOU

Economics plays a vital role in society. Trade and exchange reach every aspect of your life through the choices you make in the marketplace and eventually the voting booth. Relationships between nations are likely to revolve as much around economic matters as around everyday political affairs of state.

The role that economics plays in the life of every individual actually is nothing new or different. People always have made choices, and choices always have been the essence of economics. It is true, however, that in the past several decades we have become increasingly aware that much of our decision making is highly economic in nature. You can expect that through the end of the twentieth century and into the new millennium, people throughout the world will be faced with more and more decisions that have important economic components.

One of the primary goals of South-Western *ECONOMICS* is to explain to you the role that economics plays in improving the quality of your decision-making process. We have brought together a variety of learning tools to help you not only learn about economics but also appreciate the importance of economics in your personal life as well as in the functioning of our domestic and global economies.

COVERAGE OF *ECONOMICS*

This edition of the text has involved a very major revision; however, it continues to follow the guidelines suggested by the National Council on Economic Education's *Master Curriculum Guide*. This textbook covers every aspect of high school economics.

Part One, Making Economic Decisions, examines the choice process from individual and social viewpoints. A five-step decision process is presented that enables you to make informed and relevant choices in the marketplace, the voting booth, and your own life. You learn to identify the opportunity costs of any choice and to evaluate these costs against the expected benefits. Different economic systems are explained and you learn how these systems answer such economic questions as "What should be produced?," "How should things be produced?," and "For whom should the goods be produced?"

Once the role of choice in economics is firmly established, **Part Two, The Microeconomic Perspective,** explains the choices made by individual

consumers and producers in the marketplace. **Part Two** shows how these individual choices affect supply and demand. It describes the organization of individual business firms and markets, ways to improve the market system, the labor market, and how individual incomes are determined.

Part Three, The Macroeconomic Perspective, explains the choices made by the whole economy. Topics explored include gross domestic product (GDP); unemployment; inflation; the money supply and the banking system; and monetary, tax, and fiscal policies.

Part Four, The World Economy, explores economic topics related to the world economy. These include international trade and the problems of less-developed countries. Again, the role of choice is examined in relation to these topics.

LEARNING WITH ECONOMICS

The world you live in requires people who are well-educated, creative, and determined. Economics is a big part of that world. The following sections identify some of the key features of South-Western ECONOMICS and how you can use this book to get the most out of the time you spend learning about economics.

Preview with the Chapter Opener

The first two pages of each chapter include a unique illustration by Robert de Michiell and clearly defined **Learning Objectives.** Take a moment to view the illustration and see if you can link it to the chapter content. Then read the **Learning Objectives** to preview the economic concepts that you will be learning about in the chapter.

Investigate by Sections

Chapters are divided into several sections, each of which covers an economic concept in its entirety. Within the **Focus** at the start of each section be sure to read the feature entitled ***What Do You Think?*** These are short scenarios that end with a question for you to think about as you read the section. The **Checkpoint** at the end of the section then asks you to reconsider the scenario in light of what you have just learned. When you are asked, ***What Do You Think Now?,*** you might be surprised!

Explore with the Special Features

Every chapter contains the following five features that let you have fun while you explore a diversity of experiences related to the topic of the chapter.

Global Economy. This feature examines the global aspects of economic concepts covered in the chapter. You might learn about current events, important historic events, or activities that have global economic results. Take a look at Chapter 4, where the question "Can We Afford to Save the Environment?" is examined in economic terms.

Economic Spotlight. Individuals who have made important contributions to economics and/or are interesting because of their personal economic activities are highlighted in this feature. Chapter 14 takes a look at why L. L. Bean started a company that has grown into one of the most successful mail-order companies in the United States. (Hint: It has to do with wet feet.)

Internet Connection. This feature provides general information about how the Internet works, as well as economic uses of the Internet. Actual Internet addresses are provided so that you can find sites that have information to supplement what you have read about in the chapter and sites that are just plain fun. Don't miss Chapter 6, where you visit South-Western's ECONOMICS Web page and are given the addresses of many fun sites.

Economic Dilemma. In making economic decisions, you, as an individual or as a member of society, are frequently faced with dilemmas. This feature draws attention to specific situations in which economic dilemmas exist. One dilemma facing you is whether to work or attend college after high school. Chapter 2 gives you some information on the economic trade-offs involved in that critical decision.

Econ & You. This feature relates the concepts in each chapter directly to you. Do you know what type of employee the business is looking for when you apply for a job? Find out in Chapter 7, as you read "Why Should I Hire You?"

As you have read, this book is divided into four parts: **Making Economic Decisions, The Microeconomic Perspective, The Macroeconomic Perspective,** and **The World Economy.** Three special features are included in each of the four parts. **Analyzing Primary Source Documents** presents the original text of an important document for you to read and analyze. **Economic Measurement Concepts** presents examples of how mathematical relationships and measurement tools are used in economic analysis. Finally, **Social Goals of the U.S. Economy** examines how we incorporate the goals of freedom, security, equity, and full employment into our national economic decisions.

Improve Your Vocabulary with Key Terms

Key economic terms are highlighted in bold type and defined in the margins. These are terms to know, because you'll be using them throughout this

course and throughout your life. A complete **Glossary** of all these economic terms is provided at the end of the text, giving you easy access to definitions of any terms you do not understand.

Analyze the Illustrations and Photos

Graphs, tables, photographs, and maps provide graphic representation of the concepts presented. Take some time to look at these, as economic information is often made clearer with graphic images.

Review with the End-of-Chapter Activities

The activities at the end of each chapter are there for your review and assessment. Read **Concepts in Brief** and then review any section of the chapter that remains unclear. The activities provide opportunities for you to demonstrate understanding of and to apply the economic concepts you've studied.

Supplement with the Appendices

Several appendices are available at the end of your book for your use in exploring economic material. Use these appendices to gain an understanding of geography, consumer issues, career options, measurement concepts, and economic data.

Search with the Index

A detailed **Index** is provided at the end of the text. The in-depth nature of this **Index** will be a valuable aid to you when you are trying to find particular concepts in the text.

THE REST OF THE PACKAGE

There are many resources available to support this text and enhance your economic education. On the computer, you may have the opportunity to compete with other students in ***Arctic Express,*** test your knowledge with ***Interactive*** ECONOMICS, hone your math skills with template problems, and even view some video clips from CNBC. These video clips, at least one for every chapter, are also available on VHS and videodisc.

Several workbooks are also available. You can develop your critical-thinking skills when you analyze cases about real companies in the ***Casebook.*** If you would like to improve your math skills, use the ***Economic Measurement Workbook.*** Need to review the chapter content? Try the ***Content Review Workbook.***

ECONOMICS IN YOUR LIFE

Economics is both challenging and interesting. South-Western ECONOMICS will help you understand decision making, economics, and the role of both in business and government. By using this book and the accompanying supplementary materials, you can develop the knowledge and skills needed to become a better citizen, consumer, and worker. This package of learning materials makes learning economics interesting and even fun. Gone are the days of economics as a dismal science. Enjoy your study of economics!

CONTRIBUTORS

The fourth edition of ECONOMICS would not be the powerful learning package it is without the feedback received from teachers and students who have used the first three editions. These comments and suggestions are greatly appreciated and encouraged. This edition also has benefited from the observations of high school teachers who had not used the earlier editions, but who generously participated in focus groups and written surveys designed to elicit insight into what works and what doesn't work in helping students learn about economics.

Program Reviewers and Consultants

The following individuals have been instrumental in the development of South-Western ECONOMICS.

Eleanor Allen
Foothill High School
Sacramento, California

John Burton
Palm Harbor University High School
Palm Harbor, Florida

Danny L. Cole
Dunedin High School
Dunedin, Florida

Norman B. Cregger
Central Michigan University
Mt. Pleasant, Michigan

Dr. Harlan Day
Purdue University
West Lafayette, Indiana

Dennis Dowling
Lakota High School
West Chester, Ohio

Steven A. Greenlaw
Mary Washington College
Fredericksburg, Virginia

Helen I. Humbert
Kent-Meridian High School
Kent, Washington

Thomas A. Kessinger
Wyoming High School
Wyoming, Ohio

Dr. Usman A. Qureshi
Old Dominion University
Norfolk, Virginia

Holly Sagues
Winter Park High School
Winter Park, Florida

Linda Smith
Clearwater High School
Clearwater, Florida

Jeffrey H. Trout
Mynderse Academy
Seneca Falls, New York

Dr. Mark S. Walbert
Illinois State University
Normal, Illinois

Tom Welch
Jessamine County High School
Nicholasville, Kentucky

Dr. Terry Wilson
Mt. Carmel High School
San Diego, California

THE AUTHORS

Dr. Holt Wilson is a professor at Central Michigan University. Building on his undergraduate degrees in economics and chemistry, Dr. Wilson took major course work and exams in both economics and marketing in his doctoral program. In his nearly 30 years of teaching, Dr. Wilson has taught college and university economics courses in Ohio, Oklahoma, Montana, and Michigan. He was named to Outstanding Educators in America and in 1995 received Central Michigan University's College of Business Administration Dean's Teaching Award.

In addition to his academic credentials, Dr. Wilson has worked in quality control at H. J. Heinz Company and as a partner in a market research firm. He also has consulted with firms in the banking, manufacturing, and chemical industries. Dr. Wilson is a member of the American Economic Association and the National Association of Business Economists. Dr. Wilson has published numerous textbooks and articles on economics and continues his research in the areas of managerial economics, economic forecasting, and economic statistics.

Dr. J. R. Clark holds the Probasco Chair at the University of Tennessee at Chattanooga. In his more than two decades in teaching, Dr. Clark has also been a professor at Fairleigh Dickinson University and the University of Tennessee at Martin. He received the University of Tennessee Outstanding Research Award in 1991 and the Association of Private Enterprise Education Distinguished Scholar Award in 1992.

In addition to his academic credentials, Dr. Clark has consulted in both the public and private sectors, including Fortune 500 companies, government agencies, and universities. He is a member of the American Economic Association and the Secretary/Treasurer of the Association of Private Enterprise Education. Dr. Clark is the author of textbooks and articles in the areas of public choice and economics.

CONTENTS

Special Features

SOCIAL GOALS OF THE U.S. ECONOMY

ECONOMIC MEASUREMENT CONCEPTS

ANALYZING PRIMARY SOURCE DOCUMENTS

ECONOMIC SPOTLIGHT

ECONOMIC DILEMMA

GLOBAL ECONOMY

Internet Connection

xviii

ECON & YOU

Part One
Making Economic Decisions

Dear Teachers

As one teacher to another, you probably would agree with me that teachers and economics share the same basic problem—scarcity. To make the most of our limited resources, we know that we need to effectively allocate our time in the classroom and make intelligent choices. For my classes, I would combine the first five chapters and teach them as an introduction to economics, allowing additional time to teach the more difficult concepts in subsequent chapters. I would quickly move through Chapter 1, stressing to students that economic scarcity causes us to become effective decision makers. I would combine Chapters 2 and 3 by comparing individual decision making to social decision making. I also would teach Chapters 4 and 5 together, comparing private sector decisions to public sector decisions.

As you delve into this first part, I think you'll discover a number of relevant and creative activities that encompass a wide range of cognitive skills. Activities are offered for students with different learning styles and abilities, with an appropriate balance between individual, small-group, and whole-class instruction. I place particular emphasis on small-group activities because they develop problem-solving skills in a cooperative-learning environment.

As I reviewed the student and teacher materials, I found them to be much better than those I currently use—I think you will, too.

Dennis Dowling
Lakota High School
West Chester, Ohio

Portfolio Activities Overview

In Chapter 1, students write a summary describing a purchasing decision that they have made to show how economics affects their lives. In Chapter 2, students create a decision matrix and write a paragraph summarizing the process and results of purchasing a house to recognize the importance of making smart economic decisions. In Chapter 3, students write journal entries describing personal decisions and evaluate the effectiveness of their decisions. In Chapter 4, students keep a daily log of their purchases for a week and write a summary analyzing common purchasing patterns. In Chapter 5, students write a business letter to a government representative, detailing a concern or problem in their community.

Chapter 1

Anderson, Quentin. *Making Americans: An Essay on Individualism and Money.* New York: Harcourt Brace Jovanovich, 1992.

Covey, Stephen R., A. Roger Merrill, and Rebecca R. Merrill. *The 7 Habits of Highly Effective People.* New York: Simon and Schuster, 1989.

Henderson, David R., ed. *The Fortune Encyclopedia of Economics.* New York: Warner Books, 1993.

Landsburg, Steven E. *The Armchair Economist: Economics and Everyday Life.* New York: Maxwell Macmillan International, 1993.

Pass, Christopher, et al. *The HarperCollins Dictionary of Economics.* New York: HarperCollins, 1991.

SimFarm (simulation software). Orinda, Calif.: Maxis, 1994.

Chapter 2

Finegan, Patrick G. *Master Your Budget: Taming the Beast.* Washington, D.C.: Palindrome Press, 1992.

Keenan, Diane, and Roger Cannon. *Slamdunk: Teaching Economics Through the Sports, Music and Film Industries.* 1990. (Available through *Economics & Consumer Education* catalogue, Social Studies School Service, Culver City, Calif., 1-800-421-4246.)

Krugman, Paul R. *Peddling Prosperity: Economic Sense and Nonsense in the Age of Diminished Expectations.* New York: W. W. Norton, 1994.

Lawrence, Judy. *The Budget Kit: The Common Cent$ Money Management Workbook.* Chicago: Dearborn Financial Publishing, 1992.

Chapter 3

Caesar (simulation software). Cambridge, Mass.: Impressions Software, Inc., 1993.

Eggert, Jim. *What Is Economics?* Kaufmann. 1993. (Available through *Economics & Consumer Education* catalogue, Social Studies School Service, Culver City, Calif., 1-800-421-4246.)

Marx, Karl. *The Communist Manifesto.* New York: Appleton Century-Crofts, 1955.

Serf City: Life Is Feudal (simulation software). Sunnyvale, Calif.: Strategic Simulations, 1994.

SimCity Enhanced CD-ROM (simulation software). Santa Ana, Calif.: Interplay, 1994.

SimCity 2000 (simulation software). Orinda, Calif.: Maxis, 1994.

Chapter 4

Carr, Glenna D., et al. *The Economic Costs of Crime.* Center of Economic Education, University of Florida, 1990. (Available through *Economics & Consumer Education* catalogue, Social Studies School Service, Culver City, Calif., 1-800-421-4246.)

Cohen, Laurie P. "Dirty Dozen?: Tampering with Injuries Appeals to Defendants Facing Steep Sentences" in *The Wall Street Journal* (January 10, 1995).

The Crystal Ball: Your Financial Future (simulation software). Learning Seed, 1985. (Available through *Economics & Consumer Education* catalogue, Social Studies School Service, Culver City, Calif., 1-800-421-4246.)

Ekins, Paul, et al. *The GAIA Atlas of Green Economics.* Doubleday, 1992. (Available through *Economics & Consumer Education* catalogue, Social Studies School Service, Culver City, Calif., 1-800-421-4246.)

Forrest Gump (videocassette). Paramount Pictures, 1994.

Chapter 5

Forkner, Jerry, and Gail Schatz. *Consumer Education Learning Activities.* Social Science Education Consortium, 1989. (Available through *Economics & Consumer Education* catalogue, Social Studies School Service, Culver City, Calif., 1-800-421-4246.)

SimCity Enhanced CD-ROM (simulation software). Santa Ana, Calif.: Interplay, 1994.

SimCity 2000 (simulation software). Orinda, Calif.: Maxis, 1994.

SimHealth (simulation software). Orinda, Calif.: Maxis Business Simulations, 1994.

Stein, Herbert, and Murray Foss. *An Illustrated Guide to the American Economy.* AEI, 1992. (Available through *Economics & Consumer Education* catalogue, Social Studies School Service, Culver City, Calif., 1-800-421-4246.)

Part One
Making Economic Decisions

PART ONE

Making Economic Decisions

Chapter 1

Understanding economics helps us to allocate our resources and weigh the alternatives to make more informed decisions.

Chapter 2

A five-step decision-making model can help us arrive at more effective individual choices—ones that maximize the utility of the choice and minimize associated opportunity costs.

Chapter 3

Although in market economies such as the United States most economic decisions are based on individual choice, some decisions are based on social choice, making it important to elect candidates who share our views.

Chapter 4

Individual choice and competition in the private sector encourage producers and consumers to be efficient, and profit motivates entrepreneurs to take risks. The market system, however, is not without its pitfalls.

Chapter 5

The public sector performs some tasks more efficiently than does the private sector and also performs tasks that the private sector is unwilling or unable to perform. However, the public sector is not without its problems.

Chapter 1 The Economic Way of Thinking

Chapter Theme

Individuals and societies both must answer the basic economic questions of what, how, and for whom to produce although they use different combinations of individual and social choices to arrive at the answer and to allocate resources. An understanding of economics helps you understand the basic problems and the trade-offs between alternatives.

Section	Special Features
Economics and Choice	Perspectives: Thinking Like an Economic Citizen Economic Spotlight
Opportunity Costs and Benefits	Economics & Your Community Economic Dilemma Media Link
Basic Economic Questions	Multicultural Highlights Global Economy Eye on Market News Internet Connection
Economic Systems	Economic Talk Econ & You

Video Activity

Chapter 1, Property Rights

Search Chapter 1, Play to 2

Divide the class into two groups to debate whether wildlife protection should take priority over individual property rights.

	Print Resources	Media Resources	Assessment
	Effective Teaching Model Lesson Plans *Skills & Concepts* worksheet *Problem Solving* worksheet *Casebook* *Economic Measurement Workbook* *Content Review Workbook* *Spanish Resources*	VHS CD-ROM Videodisc *Arctic Express* *Interactive* ECONOMICS Template software	*Your Economic Portfolio* Chapter *Assessment* Chapter *MicroExam*

Special Learners	Print Resources	Media Resources	Assessment
Auditory Activity Kinesthetic Activity	*Enrich* worksheet	Overhead Camcorder VCR	*Checkpoint* Section 1 Quiz
	Life Skills worksheet	Computer Overhead and *Transparencies 1-1* and *1-2*	*Checkpoint* Section 2 Quiz
Visual Activity	*Teacher's Connection to the Internet*	Computer Overhead	*Checkpoint* Section 3 Quiz
At Risk Cooperative Learning Activity	*Reteach* worksheet	Computer Overhead	*Checkpoint* Section 4 Quiz

Careers Activity

You don't have to be a Wall Street broker to be affected by economics. Even rural horse ranchers make many economic decisions every day as they buy hay, feed, and medicines; match breeding stock; monitor offspring; and hire personnel.

An aspiring horse rancher must work on farms and ranches for several years to learn about horses. She or he also must research and study various bloodlines to learn how to pick horses for breeding. A rancher's earnings may vary from $20,000 to more than $1 million per year, depending upon the fees earned for breeding certain horses.

Tell students to imagine that they own a horse ranch. Have them write an essay that answers these three basic economic questions for the ranch: **What will I produce? How will I produce it? For whom will I produce?**

CHAPTER 1

Teaching Materials

Program Resources

- Student text
- *Effective Teaching Model Lesson Plans*
- *Overhead Transparencies 1-1 and 1-2*
- *Life Skills* worksheet
- *Problem Solving* worksheet
- *Reteach* worksheet
- *Enrich* worksheet
- *Skills & Concepts* worksheet
- *Casebook*
- *Economic Measurement Workbook*
- *Content Review Workbook*
- *Spanish Resources*
- Video package
- *Teacher's Connection to the Internet*
- *Arctic Express*
- *Interactive ECONOMICS*
- Template software

Assessment

- Section Quizzes
- Chapter *Assessment*
- Chapter *MicroExam*

Overview

Section One
Economics and Choice

Section Two
Opportunity Costs and Benefits

Section Three
Basic Economic Questions

Section Four
Economic Systems

Teacher to Teacher

To reinforce the concept of different economic systems, create a continuum that shows the varying levels of government involvement in each system. On the chalkboard or an overhead transparency, draw a horizontal line. Label the left end of the line **Command (Total Gov't Involvement).** Label the middle section **Mixed (Limited Gov't Involvement)** and label the right end of the line **Market/Traditional (No Gov't Involvement).** Then, work with students to plot different nations along the continuum according to the type of economic system each possesses.

Dennis Dowling
Lakota High School
West Chester, OH

2

The Economic Way of Thinking

Learning Objectives

1-1 Present reasons why it is important for everyone to understand economics.

1-2 Explain why economics is called the science of choices.

1-3 Identify the opportunity cost and the opportunity benefit of an economic choice.

1-4 Relate individual and social choices to microeconomics and macroeconomics.

1-5 Distinguish between the three basic economic questions that must be answered in all societies.

1-6 Analyze market, command, and mixed economic systems by how they answer the three basic economic questions.

1-7 Demonstrate how economic theory is used in economic decision making.

3

Vocabulary

scarcity, p. 6
unlimited wants and needs, p. 6
limited resources, p. 7
allocation, p. 7
economics, p. 7
opportunity cost, p. 8
opportunity benefit, p. 11
microeconomics, p. 13
macroeconomics, p. 13
economic system, p. 18
theory, p. 19
budget constraint, p. 20

Outside Resources

- Blank overhead transparencies
- Camcorder and VCR
- Covey, Stephen R., A. Roger Merrill, and Rebecca R. Merrill. *The 7 Habits of Highly Effective People.* New York: Simon and Schuster, 1989.
- Toy Monopoly® money ($100 bills)
- Local newspapers
- Computer
- Integrated software (spreadsheets, charting)
- Business section of local newspaper
- Index cards

Focus

Write the following on the chalkboard: **Relax all summer.** As students enter the classroom, ask them to list on the chalkboard what they would be giving up or missing if they spent their entire summer relaxing.

Relate students' ideas to Anthony's dilemma posed in *Focus.* Explain that choosing to swim and play basketball all summer is an economic choice. By studying economics, students will learn to make informed choices as consumers, workers, and citizens.

Teach

Write the term **economics** on the chalkboard. Brainstorm with students all the words they think of when they think of economics. Explain that, although the words may define **economics,** the study of economics is much more than any of these words alone. Discuss the meaning of the term **scarcity.** Explain that there are two sides to scarcity: **unlimited wants and needs** and **limited resources.** Emphasize that the problem of scarcity results in **allocation,** which is the process of choosing which needs will be satisfied and how much of the resources will be used to satisfy them. Discuss *tradeoffs,* or choices among alternatives. Finally, define **economics** as the social science that deals with how society allocates its scarce resources.

FOCUS

Section One
Economics and Choice

What Do You Think?

Anthony and his mother were watching a news report about the lack of jobs for teens in their area. Anthony was a little discouraged by the report, since he was looking for a summer job. On the other hand, he wouldn't mind a whole summer full of swimming and playing basketball. He was relieved he wouldn't have to make a choice between working and relaxing. "After all, if there aren't any jobs available," he figured, "I'm not really losing out on anything." Anthony's mom said to think again.

Terms to Know

- scarcity
- unlimited wants and needs
- limited resources
- allocation
- economics

What's Ahead?

Economics is important because it affects your life every day. An understanding of economics will help you make more informed decisions and be a more effective citizen. Economics deals with the basic problem of scarcity and how you make tradeoffs between alternatives.

ECONOMICS IS IMPORTANT

Why should you study economics? What will you gain from learning about it? Almost everyone hears something every week about economics. It is difficult to pick up a newspaper, watch television, or have contact with the world outside your home without encountering some economic information. In order to understand the economic information you hear every day, you will need to become familiar with the economic way of thinking.

Economics Affects Your Everyday Life

Economic concerns are the topics of many newspaper headlines: "Teen Unemployment Rate Remains High," "U.S. Auto Makers See Brighter Times Ahead," "College Tuition to Rise," "Concern About Inflation Remains High." You can see that these are topics that affect aspects of your everyday life—cars, school, jobs, and so on. Economics not only identifies economic problems, it provides you with a logical, effective decision-making process. This process helps you make the most of your resources and satisfy many of your wants and needs every day.

Economics Helps You Make More Informed Decisions

As a worker and a consumer, you will have to make many economic decisions. You will have to decide how to spend your income. The cost of all the goods and services you will want to buy will most likely be greater than your income. So, you will have to choose among them carefully. You also will have to choose a career for yourself, and this choice will surely affect your lifetime income, personal happiness, and success. You will make decisions about working, learning, earning, and spending. You can make all these decisions more effectively with a basic understanding of economics.

Economics Makes You a More Effective Citizen

As a citizen in this country, you have the opportunity to vote. You can help decide the future course the economy will take. Do you want to pay higher taxes for more new roads and schools? Or, do you want to pay lower taxes and accept poorer roads and schools? The candidates will have to make these economic choices, and you must decide which candidates to vote for. As you cast your vote, you should understand what these choices will mean to you.

You might even want to become a political candidate yourself. However, before you could take a position on an issue, you would need to understand how it affects the economy. Perhaps you would favor a tax cut that would reduce unemployment. But what if the tax cut also increased inflation? Would you favor free trade with other countries, or would you expect people to buy only U.S.-made products?

The study of economics helps people and societies make better choices. An understanding of economics is vital to your success in the workplace, the marketplace, and the voting booth.

A SCIENCE OF CHOICES

When you think of the term *economics,* many impressions come to mind. Perhaps you associate the term with money, the stock market, inflation, taxes, and unemployment. But, economics is much more. It is a scientific body of knowledge that can analyze, explain, and in many cases predict people's economic behavior. This behavior is centered around the basic economic problem.

Apply

To help students relate economics to their everyday lives, make a chart on the chalkboard or an overhead transparency with the following three column headings (or have students create their own headings): **Consumer, Worker,** and **Citizen.** Brainstorm the kinds of economic choices students make as consumers, workers, and citizens. List students' responses in the appropriate columns.

Guided Practice

To serve in their constituents' best interests, elected officials should have a good understanding of economics and use this knowledge to vote in an informed manner. Assist students in contacting your local city hall or mayor's office to obtain a list of the current elected officials. As a class, select one area of local government, such as your school board, and have the class chart the names of their representatives, recent issues voted upon, and how the officials voted. Determine whether the elected officials acted in the best interests of your students. Draft a class letter to each official supporting or opposing the vote and stating students' concerns.

Perspectives

Thinking Like an Economic Citizen Have students brainstorm how they can utilize economics to make better informed personal decisions. Pair small groups of four or five students and ask them to sit facing each other. On a sheet of paper, have each group independently list five economic issues of importance (job search, salary, purchases, and so on). Ask one group to read its issues aloud, one at a time. The other group is to suggest how a knowledge of economics can lead to more effective decisions.

Explain to students that economic decision making helps them satisfy their wants and needs by making the most of their available resources. Copy the following graphic organizer onto the chalkboard or an overhead transparency:

SCARCITY
Unlimited Wants/Needs
Limited Resources

Have students copy the chart onto a sheet of paper. Individually, have them list their unlimited wants and needs and then list the limited resources used to fulfill these wants and needs. **Independent Practice**

The Basic Economic Problem: Scarcity

scarcity
the condition that occurs because people's wants and needs are unlimited, while the resources needed to produce goods and services to meet these wants and needs are limited

unlimited wants and needs
the human characteristic of never having all wants and needs satisfied

The basic economic problem is scarcity. ***Scarcity*** is the condition that occurs because people's wants and needs are unlimited, while the resources needed to produce goods and services to meet these wants and needs are limited.

There are two sides to the scarcity problem. One of the basic human characteristics is that people are never fully satisfied. Psychologists say that as soon as the basic needs for food, clothing, and shelter are met, the mind creates new needs, such as physical security. When this need is fulfilled, the mind finds even more new needs. This need creation and fulfillment process has no end. Every time a need is satisfied, a new need is created. No matter if you are rich, poor, or in between, you probably can think of many things you need right now. ***Unlimited wants and needs*** is the human characteristic of never having all wants and needs satisfied.

Economic Spotlight

CAN YOU TELL A NEED FROM A WANT?

Does Oscar de la Renta's luxurious clothing fulfill a need or a want? Oscar de la Renta dresses some of the most prominent women in the United States for their main events. He is the first American to head a Paris *couture house,* a clothing studio that hand makes clothing to fit each individual customer.

De la Renta is a shrewd, industrious fashion designer who works very hard but does it with grace. According to De la Renta, "I could work harder and have a bigger business, but there is so much more to life." He presents a high-class image in the fashion world—a far cry from his humble beginnings. An orphan, born in Santo Domingo in the Dominican Republic, he is the sixth child in a large family. At 17 years old, this son of an insurance salesman headed to Madrid, Spain, to study art. There he developed an interest in fashion design.

His big break came when he was commissioned to design a debutante gown for the daughter of U.S. politician Henry Cabot Lodge. The gown ended up on the cover of *Life* magazine, giving De la Renta his entry into the world of fashion design. After working for Balenciaga and Elizabeth Arden, he opened his own salon in 1965. He now has more than 45 licensees and three perfumes and sells more than $500 million of products each year.

While De la Renta and his wife Annette Reed may be a wealthy, socially ambitious couple, they still find the time to serve on the boards of many nonprofit organizations. They also have founded and funded an orphanage for 350 children, the only institution of its kind in Santo Domingo. By donating time and money to worthy causes, De la Renta fulfills many people's unmet needs, but does his custom-designed clothing fulfill a need or a want?

Economic Spotlight

After students have read the *Economic Spotlight* feature, lead them to understand that Oscar de la Renta's designs fulfill a want, rather than a need. As a class, brainstorm a list of circumstances that might cause consumers not to want his products as much in the future. (Designs become outdated, consumers have less money to spend on fashion, and so on.) Ask students how they think a downturn such as this might affect the needs that currently are met by De la Renta's company and the programs it supports. (Company probably would downsize and lay off workers; not as much funding available for the orphanage; and so on.)

Fulfilling most needs requires goods and services of one kind or another. To produce goods and services, resources or the raw materials of production are needed. For example, building houses to fulfill the human need for shelter requires wood, glass, concrete, steel, copper, and the services of builders. However, there is only so much lumber, glass, concrete, steel, and labor available. There is a limit to resources. ***Limited resources*** means that there are never enough resources to fulfill all wants and needs. Limited resources available to satisfy unlimited wants and needs creates *scarcity,* the basic economic problem.

limited resources
the condition of there not being enough resources to fulfill all wants and needs

allocation
the process of choosing which needs will be satisfied and how much of our resources we will use to satisfy them

economics
the social science that deals with how society allocates its scarce resources among its unlimited wants and needs

Definition of Economics

The problem of scarcity results in allocation. ***Allocation*** is the process of choosing which needs will be satisfied and how much of our resources we will use to satisfy them. You must choose which needs to neglect and just how much to neglect them. This allocation process requires making *trade-offs* or choosing among alternatives. When you allocate, you choose among alternatives or make trade-offs in deciding how to use your resources.

Economics, then, is the science of making effective choices or decisions by examining the alternatives. As a social science, economics studies how people interact in their society in an economic way. Broadly defined, ***economics*** is the social science that deals with how society allocates its scarce resources among its unlimited wants and needs.

Checkpoint

Content Check

1. What is the economic way of thinking?
2. Identify the basic economic problem and explain why it occurs in our society.
3. How does allocation apply to the basic economic problem?

What Do You Think Now?

Reread *What Do You Think?* in the Section One Focus. Then answer the following questions:

4. How would a basic understanding of economics help Anthony make a good decision about how to spend his time this summer?
5. What is scarce for Anthony?

Assess

1. A logical, effective decision-making process that helps make the most of unlimited wants and needs and limited resources **1-1**
2. Scarcity; because there are unlimited wants and needs and limited resources **1-1, 1-2**
3. It is what results because of scarcity, and it is a way of choosing which wants and needs to satisfy with how much of the resources. **1-1, 1-2**
4. Answers should reflect an understanding of unlimited wants and needs and limited resources and how this creates scarcity. **1-1**
5. Answers may include jobs, money, and time. **1-2**

Close

Have groups of students visit specific locales where economic transactions take place, such as shopping centers or malls. Provide each group with a camcorder and have students interview each other about the purchases they would like to make, based on a realistic income. Have students view the footage in class and discuss these examples of economic decision making.

Reteach

Pair students who need additional support to review the graphic organizer they completed in the *Apply* activity. Ask each student to look at the other's graphic organizer and, with your guidance, summarize orally the partner's unlimited needs and wants, explaining how limited resources affect economic choices. **1-2**

Enrich

Bring to class toy Monopoly® money and, before class, count out three fewer $100 bills than there are students. When class begins, have a volunteer distribute the bills to students. When some students realize they are not receiving a $100 bill, begin a class discussion of the problem of scarcity. **1-2**

Focus

After students have read *Focus,* have them copy the following chart onto a sheet of paper and list in the appropriate columns what was given up and what was gained by Maria and Teresa.

What Maria Gave Up	What Maria Gained
What Teresa Gave Up	**What Teresa Gained**

Discuss what each student listed under each heading. On the chalkboard or an overhead transparency, draw a balance or scale. Discuss with students that benefits should always outweigh opportunity costs in a well-thought-out economic decision.

FOCUS

Section Two
Opportunity Costs and Benefits

What Do You Think?

Teresa and Maria work at The Sports Machine, a sporting goods store near their school. Teresa spends most of what she earns on clothes and jewelry. The rest she uses for going out on the weekends. When she asks Maria why she never goes out on the weekends, Maria tells her that she's saving for a used car so she can drive to school and work. Teresa says she'll just keep riding the bus.

Terms to Know

opportunity cost

opportunity benefit

What's Ahead?

Costs and benefits guide the choice process of individuals and countries. They determine what, how, and for whom goods are produced. Every time you make a choice, you give up the value of any alternatives. If you determine the value of what you are giving up, you can make better decisions.

COSTS AND BENEFITS

You have learned that economics is the science of making choices. However, in order to make effective choices, you must understand the costs and the benefits of any given choice. When you make a purchase decision, you weigh the price you must pay against the satisfaction or use you believe you will get from the purchase. There is more to cost, however, than just the dollar price. Economists consider the *opportunity costs* and *opportunity benefits* of each choice.

Opportunity Cost

opportunity cost the value of any alternative that you must give up when you make a choice

Opportunity cost is the value of any alternative that you must give up when you make a choice. In short, the opportunity cost is the value of the opportunity lost. If you choose to study for a test rather than ski, the opportunity cost is the skiing time you must give up to study.

Let's develop another example of opportunity cost and use some of the tools that an economist would use to make a decision. Assume for the moment that you have a weekly income of $30 and that you spend that

Economics & Your Community

Write **bond referendum** on the chalkboard. Ask students if they know what a referendum (when citizens vote directly on an issue) is. Explain that with a bond referendum, citizens are voting to allocate public moneys to support a specific issue, such as education. Bring to class a stack of local newspapers. Have students individually or in small groups scan the newspapers for any mention of articles on bond referendums or other community-based economic issues such as changes in zoning ordinances. Have students share these articles with the rest of the class. Discuss the opportunity costs and benefits of each story.

income on only two different goods: movies and paperback books. To keep the numbers very simple, assume that a movie ticket and snack cost $10 and that books sell for $5 each. Figure 1-1 shows how many of each item you can buy with your income.

As Figure 1-1 shows, you could spend all of your income on three movies or on six books. However, you may wish to have some of both goods. If so, you will spend some of your income on movies and some of your income on books. Of course, how much you spend on movies will determine how much income you have left to spend on books.

Assume you have only two choices. That will make it easier to see the opportunity costs. One choice is to buy four books and use the remaining income to go to one movie. This will be called Combination *A*.

4 books @ $5 = $20	
1 movie @ $10 = $10	Combination *A*
TOTAL = $30	

Another choice is to buy two books and use the remaining income to go to two movies. This will be called Combination *B*.

2 books @ $5 = $10	
2 movies @ $10 = $20	Combination *B*
TOTAL = $30	

Teach

Explain to students that what Maria and Teresa gave up is the cost of their decisions. Cost is more than just the actual dollar price of doing something; it is the value of the opportunity lost, which is called **opportunity cost.** Write **Opportunity Costs** on the *Focus* chart above what Maria and Teresa gave up. Tell students that what Maria and Teresa gained was more than just money. What you get from making an economic choice is called **opportunity benefit.** Write **Opportunity Benefits** on the chart above what Maria and Teresa gained. Review the definitions of both concepts with students.

Economic Dilemma

NO ONE CAN BE SUPERWOMAN!

Since the early 1960s, women have entered the work force in large numbers. While for families there are many advantages to this situation, including increased income, economics reminds us that there must be an opportunity cost as well.

Some women have attempted to be mother, homemaker, and breadwinner all at the same time, believing they can "have it all." To believe this is to deny that scarcity exists, which is clearly not true. While both women and men have taken on new roles in the 80s and 90s, scarcity will always be with us. Time spent on the job cannot at the same time be spent caring for children, nurturing families, homemaking, and participating in leisure or recreational activities.

It is highly probable that much of the increased stress reported by working women and men today is due to inability or unwillingness to recognize the opportunity costs of a working career. The most basic economic dilemma will always be a part of life because, at least in the sense of opportunity costs, no one can "have it all."

Economic Dilemma

Divide the class into two groups: students who would define "having it all" as having enough and those who interpret the phrase literally. Focus the discussion on the different opportunity costs and opportunity benefits of having it all, depending upon the way the phrase is defined. Have one student from each group volunteer to record examples of costs and benefits on the chalkboard under the appropriate column headings: **Opportunity Costs** and **Opportunity Benefits.** At the end of the discussion, count the number of examples in each column and declare the group with the most examples the "winner."

Apply

Copy the heads for columns two to five of *Figure 1–1* onto the chalkboard. Give column one the heads **CDs You Can Buy** and **Videos You Can Rent.** Tell students to assume that their weekly income is $40 and that videos rent for $2 each and CDs sell for $10 each. Have students create a chart to show what their money could buy. Discuss how the chart shows **opportunity costs** and **opportunity benefits.**
Guided Practice

Analyzing *Graphics*

Caption Answer
Three books cost $15. This leaves $15, or enough for only one movie.

By using the information in the chart from the *Guided Practice* activity, have students write about how they would choose to spend their $40 income. Ask them to explain the reasons for their decisions.
Independent Practice

Analyzing *Graphics*

Caption Answer
The two endpoints of the line represent the realistic combinations of no movies and six books and three movies and no books.

To help students who are having difficulty understanding line graphs, enlist the help of students who have mastered the concept. Display *Overhead Transparency 1-2*
(Continued)

Figure 1-1

Use of Income to Attend Movies and Buy Books

With a fixed income of $30, more movies means fewer books. ***If you buy three books, how many movies can you go see?***

Movies You Can Attend	Price	Total Cost	Your Total Income	Income Left Over
1	$10	$10	$30	$20
2	$10	$20	$30	$10
3	$10	$30	$30	$ 0
Books You Can Buy	**Price**	**Total Cost**	**Your Total Income**	**Income Left Over**
1	$5	$ 5	$30	$25
2	$5	$10	$30	$20
3	$5	$15	$30	$15
4	$5	$20	$30	$10
5	$5	$25	$30	$ 5
6	$5	$30	$30	$ 0

Either choice is possible since you have $30 to allocate. How, then, will you decide which alternative to choose? Will you choose *A* or *B?* The best way to make that choice is to look at the opportunity cost of each alternative. Suppose you are presently considering Combination *A* with four books and one movie. What, then, will you have to give up to move to Combination *B,* which allows you two books and two movies? As the graph in Figure 1-2 shows, to get the additional movie in Combination *B,* you will have to give up two of the four books you would have had in Combination *A.* Therefore, the opportunity cost of one movie is two books.

You should make your decision based on how much you like movies compared with how much you like books. You need to decide if you like one movie enough to give up two books. On the other hand, you also can con-

Figure 1-2

The Opportunity Benefit and Opportunity Cost of Two Alternatives

As you move from Combination *A* to Combination *B,* you gain one movie (opportunity benefit) and give up two books (opportunity cost). ***Identify two other combinations of books and movies and explain where they are represented on this graph.***

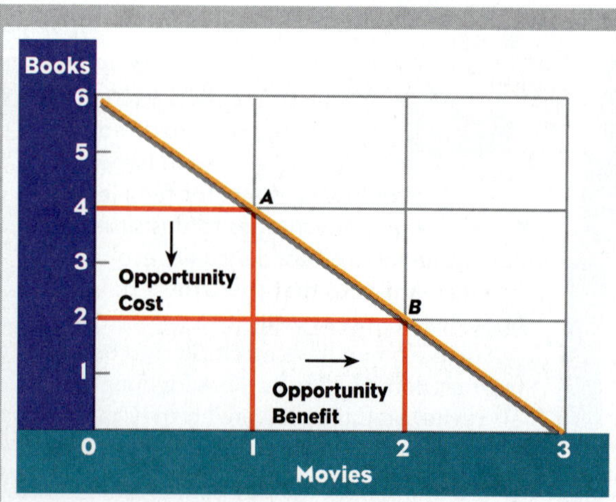

Media*Link*

Using a spreadsheet program with charting capabilities, have small groups of students create a double line graph from the data in *Figure 1-1.* Have them label one column **Total Cost** and the other column with two economic alternatives of their choice, such as **Movies I Can Attend/Books I Can Buy.** Remind students to carefully input the information in the spreadsheet, making sure they key in the appropriate data and the appropriate column headings to serve as labels on the graph.

sider whether you like two books enough to give up one movie. What is the opportunity cost of two additional books? It is one movie.

You can now add the concept of opportunity cost to the definition of economics. Economics includes the study of how we make effective choices or decisions by examining the alternatives and considering the opportunity cost of each alternative.

Opportunity Benefit

Another way of making choices is to look at the opportunity benefits of the alternatives. The ***opportunity benefit*** is what is gained by making a particular choice. If, in the previous case, the opportunity cost of moving from Combination *A* to Combination *B* is two books, then the opportunity benefit is one movie. In the case of choosing to study rather than to ski, the opportunity benefit is receiving a better grade on your test.

Every economic choice has an opportunity benefit and an opportunity cost. When you make an informed choice, you compare the opportunity benefit (what you gain) with the opportunity cost (what you lose). This simple concept will serve as a good guide as you further your knowledge of economics. It will also be useful as you make more complicated individual and social decisions.

opportunity benefit
what is gained by making a particular choice

Checkpoint

Content Check

1. What is opportunity cost?
2. What is opportunity benefit?
3. How are opportunity costs and opportunity benefits applied to everyday life?

What Do You Think Now?

Reread *What Do You Think?* in the Section Two Focus. Then answer the following questions:

4. Do you think Maria and Teresa considered the opportunity costs of their choices before they reached decisions?
5. Why do you think Teresa and Maria made different decisions?
6. What would you have decided? Why?

Reteach

Pair students who understand opportunity costs and opportunity benefits with those who do not. Assign a scenario, such as going to the movies or doing homework, to each pair, and have them make a chart listing the opportunity costs and benefits. **1-3**

Enrich

Have students brainstorm ways to increase their opportunity benefits while decreasing their opportunity costs when purchasing particular items (with grocery coupons, rebates on videos, and so on). Then, have students create a pamphlet on how to save money. You may wish to compare students' pamphlets to government brochures on saving money. For a free catalog, write to Consumer Information Center, Pueblo, CO 81009. **1-3**

(Continued)

and circle various points on the graph. Have students identify the combination of books and movies represented by each point and explain how they got their answers. You may wish to have students use spreadsheet software or draw programs to create line graphs comparing two items of their choice.

Assess

1. The value of any alternative given up to make a choice **1-3**
2. What is gained by making a choice **1-3**
3. They are a part of every informed economic choice. **1-3**
4. Answers should reflect an understanding of the definition of opportunity costs. **1-3**
5. Answers may include that they identified different opportunity costs and benefits. **1-3**
6. Answers should include students' descriptions of their opportunity costs and benefits. **1-3**

Close

Tell students to imagine that their teacher has donated one class period next week for students to "spend" as they wish. Have students discuss, debate, and vote on how to spend the class period. Have students explain why they voted as they did and the **opportunity costs** and **opportunity benefits** of their decision.

Focus

Before students enter the classroom, place the following labels on the walls (one on each wall):

- **Same Pay for All**
- **Equal Pay for Equal Work**
- **Better Pay for Harder Workers**
- **Better Pay for Well-Known Workers**

As students enter the classroom, explain that each sign represents one way they might prefer to be paid as workers. Ask students to stand next to the sign of the payment method of their choice.

Have students remain in their groups and, after they have read *Focus,* list the reasons they chose to be paid in that manner. Then, discuss as a class the costs and benefits of each method of payment.

Section Three

Basic Economic Questions

FOCUS

What Do You Think?

In the People's Republic of China, the state owns almost all factories and businesses. Farming is done mostly on huge communal farms. Each job pays the same wage to everyone holding that specific job, regardless of how hard they work. Some people work harder and do more work than others in the same job. Which type of worker do you think you would be and why? In the United States, some professional ballplayers get paid much more than others. Some construction workers get paid more than others for the same job. Why do you think this is true?

Terms to Know

microeconomics

macroeconomics

What's Ahead?

Every society must answer the basic economic questions of what, how, and for whom to produce. These decisions are reached through some combination of individual and social choice. When answering the basic economic questions, societies must balance the needs of individuals with the needs of society as a whole.

INDIVIDUAL AND SOCIAL CHOICES

There are at least two kinds of choices made in a society: individual choices and social choices. First, individuals make choices every day as they try to satisfy their needs with limited resources. Second, society must make social choices to try to satisfy the needs of society as a whole. Some social choices determine how much of society's income is spent on national defense, roads, schools, or cultural affairs for citizens. Individual and social choices play large roles in the functioning of the economy. Economics is divided into two separate branches that deal with these two basic types of choices: microeconomics and macroeconomics.

Multicultural *Highlights*

In 1982, physicians Rodolfo and Josefa Binker made a choice to leave their native Cuba—where, together, they earned just $750 a month—and emigrate to the United States. They settled in Miami, Florida, and now their medical practice brings in about $40,000 a month! The Binkers think they made the right choice. Rodolfo Binker says, "There is nothing about this country that Josefa and I don't love." Discuss with students the opportunity costs and opportunity benefits of the Binkers' individual choices and the differences in pay between Cuba and the United States.

Individual Choices and Microeconomics

Microeconomics is the branch of economics that examines the choices of individuals concerning one product, one firm, or one industry. It is concerned primarily with individual decision making. The unit of analysis is one person, one product, one firm, or one industry. An example of a microeconomic choice would be how individual beef farmers respond to higher beef prices in the market. Each farmer must decide whether to supply more, less, or the same amount of beef to the market at the new price. Individual consumers of beef must decide whether they wish to buy more, less, or the same amount of beef at the new, higher price. Each individual, both on the buying and selling sides, will make an individual choice.

microeconomics
the branch of economics that examines the choices of individuals concerning one product, one firm, or one industry

Social Choices and Macroeconomics

Macroeconomics is the branch of economics that examines the behavior of the whole economy at once. Thus, the unit of analysis is the whole economy.

macroeconomics
the branch of economics that examines the behavior of the whole economy at once

Global Economy

SCARCITY WINS THE ARMS RACE

Scarcity, the most basic economic concept, plays many surprising roles in the global economy. For example, in the 1980s under the Reagan administration it was clear that the Soviet Union and the United States were involved in an arms race. Each of the two countries would respond to every new costly weapons system developed by the other country with much larger, frequently more complex, and always more costly weapons systems of its own.

At the same time, the Soviet economy, because of basic economic scarcity, was producing fewer and fewer consumer goods to satisfy the everyday needs of the people. Its resources were going into military production. The command economy of the Soviet Union was much less efficient at producing goods and services in general than were the market economies of other countries. Soviet citizens began to complain bitterly about the lack of consumer goods as their lifestyles declined more each day.

Meanwhile, the Reagan administration announced its Star Wars Defense System or Strategic Defense Initiative. This was the most complex and costly defense system ever conceived. Simultaneously, several other new costly weapons systems were reaching completion in the United States.

These announcements, it is believed, stimulated many huge new costly weapons programs in the Soviet Union that diverted so many resources away from consumer goods into military production that the decline in living standards became unacceptable to the Soviet people. They began to overthrow their communist government and its command economy.

Scarcity is everywhere all the time. It will play an increasingly important role in the global economy of the twenty-first century.

Teach

Discuss the significance of individual versus social choices. Explain to students that **microeconomics** focuses on individual choices—analyzing one person, product, firm, or industry—and **macroeconomics** focuses on social choices—analyzing the whole economy. Some governments concentrate more on social choices or on individual choices, but all use a combination of the two to answer the three basic economic questions. Focus students' attention on these three questions presented in the textbook on p. 14.

Apply

Write **micro-** and **macro-** on the chalkboard or an overhead transparency. Ask students the following question: **What, do you think, do these prefixes mean?** (Micro—little, minute; macro—large, big) Relate student answers to the definitions of **microeconomics** and **macroeconomics,** pointing out that **microeconomics** studies smaller pieces of the economy and **macroeconomics** studies larger pieces, such as the economy itself.

Guided Practice

Global Economy

In many command economies, such as in the former USSR, there are shortages of basic consumer goods, such as food, clothing, and shelter. Often, citizens in these countries wait in long lines to purchase basic necessities. Ask students to describe the last time they waited in a long line to purchase something. Then, ask for a show of hands of people who would wait in a long line to purchase a basic necessity such as food. Ask students if they think scarce resources always mean long lines. Explain that scarcity depends on how the economic system allocates resources.

Macroeconomics asks, How much total output is the economy producing? Are the resources of the economy fully employed? How high is the rate of inflation in the economy?

An example of a macroeconomic choice is how the government of a country deals with inflation. The government could cut back its spending, make credit more difficult for consumers to get, and raise taxes to encourage consumers to cut spending. This is a social decision made by government to deal with the macroeconomic issue of inflation.

THREE BASIC ECONOMIC QUESTIONS

Some countries make many more *social* decisions than others because of how their systems of government are designed. Other countries conduct most of their economic affairs through *individual* decision making. Regardless of the relative amounts of social and individual decision making in an economy, all societies use some combination of social and individual decisions to answer three basic economic questions:

1. *What* will be produced with the limited resources?
2. *How* will the goods and services be produced?
3. *For whom* will the goods and services be produced?

What to Produce?

All societies try to produce certain basic goods such as food, clothing, and shelter. The real questions are, How much food? How much clothing? How much shelter? Remember, if more food is produced, there will be an opportunity cost of this additional food. The society must give up some shelter or clothing or something else that is being produced.

The questions get more difficult if the society considers other essentials such as national defense, roads, and schools. If education takes top priority, then perhaps the roads used to get to the schools will not be repaired as often. The society must decide exactly what mix of goods and services to produce. In the United States, this decision is made mostly by the interaction of individual buyers and sellers.

How to Produce?

There are many different ways to produce most goods and services. For instance, a highway can be built with large bulldozers and earth movers. A highway of equal quality can be built with thousands of individual workers using wheelbarrows, picks, and shovels. In the United States, highways are usually constructed with heavy machinery. This does not mean that the use of many laborers and smaller tools is less effective. Decisions about how to produce take into account the resources that are available. A country with a large population and very few machines may decide that the best road building method is *labor intensive;* that is, using many laborers and few machines. In such a country, the opportunity cost of machines is higher than the opportunity cost of labor.

Copy the outline of the following graphic organizer onto the chalkboard or an overhead transparency with the word **Question** listed in each of the circles:

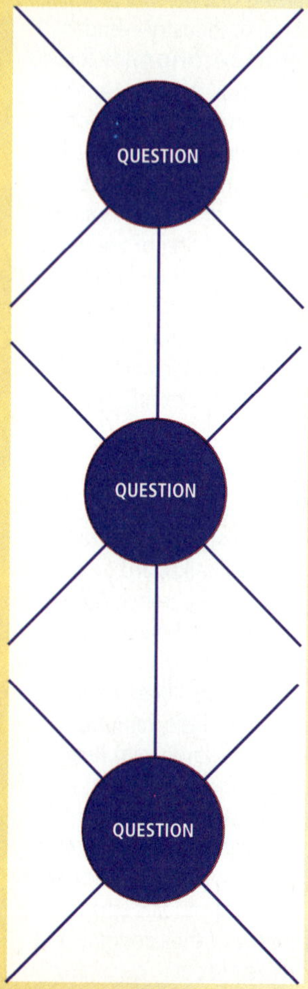

In groups of four or five, have students complete the graphic organizer by first filling in the three basic economic questions (what will be produced?; how will it be produced?; and for whom will it be produced?) and then listing more specific questions (what type of pastries will I produce?; will I make the pastries by hand or by machine?; and will I market my pastries to individuals or restaurants?). Have each group present its completed organizer to the class.

Independent Practice

Divide the class into teams of four or five students to debate providing essential goods or services, such as providing free public schooling for all students. Have half of each team represent either the individual or the social decision-making school of thought and half take the opposing viewpoint. For each good or service, have students debate the issues of what to produce, how to produce, and for whom to produce. Conclude the activity by having the whole class summarize the strengths and weaknesses of each argument. You may wish to extend the activity by having students debate other issues, such as a national defense and a public road system.

A historical example of this concept occurred in the coal industry. Several decades ago, coal mining in the United States was a relatively low-paying profession with many dangers. About 1 million miners worked with picks, shovels, and drills to remove coal from the ground. These coal miners eventually formed unions and demanded higher wages. Thus, it became much cheaper, in many cases, for coal companies to develop and use huge machines, a *capital-intensive* approach, than to hire laborers to mine coal. Today, the coal output of the United States is much greater than it was in the 1940s; yet only half a million workers are employed in mining. Why is coal produced with a capital-intensive process now, when the process used to be labor intensive? Because the opportunity cost of labor (workers) relative to capital (machines) went up.

For Whom to Produce?

Once goods and services are produced, all economies must decide who will use them. Will every citizen get the same quality and amount of goods and services or will there be differences? In the United States, who gets what is decided by consumers and the price system in the market. How individuals choose to spend their income varies according to their personal preferences as well as their income levels. If you can pay the price for a Rolls Royce, you may have one. You also have the option of buying a Ford Taurus or any number of other cars. In the U.S. economy, the question of for whom to produce is primarily an individual choice.

EyeOnMarketNews

Ask students if they have ever heard the adage, "Buy low, sell high." Explain that, although this makes good common sense, many investors actually buy high and sell low. Monitor the up and down fluctuations of the stock market for one week by checking in the business section of the local newspaper or by checking daily stock market news and listings on the Internet. Ask students why they think investors would sell when the market was going down. Why would investors feel like buying when the market was going up? Explain that, although economics is a science, it is affected by people's behavior and feelings.

In the United States, the three basic economic questions are answered primarily by individual choice. Some other societies make many more social decisions. Have students name ten or more countries at random as a scribe lists each country on the chalkboard in a vertical column titled **Country.** Add a second column named **Predominant Type of Decision Making.** Have students discuss whether the countries they chose conduct most of their economic affairs through social or individual decision making and chart their responses. Correct any misconceptions before wrapping up this section.

Internet Connection

ECONOMICS ON THE INTERNET

The Internet links more than four million computers in schools, government agencies, and businesses around the world and it's growing everyday. Mainframes, minicomputers, and PCs are connected to small networks connected to even larger networks, making up what we call the Internet.

The economic resources of the Internet include online encyclopedias, studies by economists, economic reports of government agencies, and a wide range of economic statistics. The Clinton administration has adopted a policy of making all government documents, including the text of all bills before Congress, accessible electronically.

The tools of the Internet range from the simple to the powerful. These tools include electronic mail, newsgroups and list serves, file transfer protocol, telnet, gopher, and World Wide Web browsers. There are electronic methods for searching for information, very similar to online catalogs in your local libraries. An additional feature is the ability to communicate easily with anyone connected to the Internet, including the authors of many economic reports and studies. You can use the computer to ask an author a question about his or her work.

You will learn how to use the specific tools of the Internet by completing the applications in each chapter. Here are the first of these applications.

Internet Application: The first step to using the Internet is learning how to connect to a computer on the Internet using a "log-in" procedure. Find out how to log-in to and log-out from the Internet using a user i.d. and password and try it out before the next lesson. If you gain access through a modem, find out the baud rate or speed of the modem. Some high school PCs are automatically connected to an Internet computer via a local area network. If the PCs at your school are like this, you may skip this application.

Economics Application: If the Internet is such a useful tool for education, you might think all schools would have access to it, but many don't. This might be explained by applying the economic principles in Chapter 1. What are the opportunity costs and benefits of having access to the Internet? Use these concepts to explain why some schools do not yet have access.

Internet Connection

Be sure to read *Teacher's Connection to the Internet,* a manual that is included in your ECONOMICS Teacher's Resource Box.

Teacher's Connection to the Internet supplements the *Internet Connection* activities in the textbook, lists Internet reference texts, and will help you make the Internet a successful resource in your classroom. Throughout this program, e-mail and Internet addresses are provided.

Should you have difficulty accessing any of these, search the World Wide Web at **http://www.thomson.com/swpco/internet/hb29da1.html**. If the information you seek is not listed there, contact this publisher at **econ_connect@swpco.com**.

Other societies allocate goods and services by other means. Some societies provide housing for all workers which, by and large, is identical in design, space, location, and even color. Individuals can't make many choices in this situation. They may choose any housing they desire but only from the location, design, or color that is provided. Here, the social decision to provide identical housing for the whole society takes away much of the individual choice.

Checkpoint

Content Check

1. What are microeconomic choices and macroeconomic choices? Give an example of each.
2. How do social and individual decision making answer each of the three basic economic questions?
3. Why would a company in the United States change from labor-intensive processes to capital-intensive processes?

What Do You Think Now?

Reread *What Do You Think?* in the Section Three Focus. Then answer the following questions:

4. How are decisions about the basic economic questions made in the People's Republic of China?
5. Why do some construction workers in the United States get paid more than others for the same job?
6. Would you want to live and work in the People's Republic of China? Why or why not?

Assess

1. Microeconomic: individual choices—car purchase, which brand of sneaker to purchase. Macroeconomic: social, whole-economy choices—increase taxes, tighten credit. **1-4**
2. What will be produced with the limited resources? How will the goods and services be produced? For whom will the goods and services be produced? Answers should include an understanding of each question and the difference between social and individual choices. **1-5**
3. Because the opportunity cost of labor relative to capital has gone up **1-4, 1-5**
4. As social choices **1-4**
5. Answers may include differences in skills, type of project being worked on, area of the country, and so on. **1-5**
6. Answers should address the fact that workers are paid the same for the same job no matter how hard they work. **1-4, 1-5**

Close

Have students suggest different kinds of workers, such as military pilots and doctors. Ask them to discuss how these workers in different countries would respond to the three basic economic questions raised in this section.

Reteach

Have students work independently to create and complete a table as you prompt their responses to the three basic economic questions. Ask students to title the first column **Question** and identify the three questions. Title the second column **Example** and, in it, provide examples of each question. **1-5**

Enrich

Explain to students that, basically, there are three different kinds of assets: physical, financial, and human. Have students form three groups. Assign one kind of asset to each group. Have students brainstorm examples of their assets and record their answers on a group list. Discuss with students which type of asset they think is the most important to them and why. **1-4**

Focus

Write the following on the chalkboard: **Describe in one word the U.S. economic system.** As students enter the classroom, hand out index cards. Have each student write his or her word on an index card.

Divide the class into groups of three or four. Have students brainstorm more words to describe the U.S. economy. Have them write each word on a separate card. Allow two to three minutes. Then, as a whole-class activity, discuss all words and post them on a bulletin board labeled **What Is the U.S. Economy?**

Teach

Discuss the four basic types of **economic systems:** traditional, market, command, and mixed. Remind students that all economic systems answer the three basic questions: what, how, and for whom; they just differ in the way they answer these questions.

Explain that a **theory** is like a map; it is a simplified description of reality to be used as a guide for a specific purpose. Relate the theoretical tool **budget constraint** to opportunity cost.

Section Four

Economic Systems

What Do You Think?

In command economies, government planners decide what is produced and available for sale. In these countries, goods such as handguns, alcohol, and tobacco products are not readily available in state stores. In the United States, consumers primarily decide what is produced by choosing what products to buy and not to buy. In the United States, there seem to be plenty of handguns, alcohol, and tobacco products. Why is this so?

Terms to Know

economic system
theory
budget constraint

What's Ahead?

Scarcity and choice exist in all economies. However, societies use different combinations of individual and social choices to allocate resources. That is why traditional, market, command, and mixed economies all answer the three basic economic questions in different ways. Economic theory will help you understand economic systems and the choices they make.

ECONOMIC SYSTEMS ANSWER ECONOMIC QUESTIONS

economic system the combination of social and individual decision making a society uses to answer the three economic questions

You have learned that all economies must answer three basic economic questions: what to produce, how to produce, and for whom to produce. The way a society answers these questions determines the kind of economic system it will have. Every society uses a different combination of individual and social choices to answer the economic questions. A society's ***economic system*** is the combination of social and individual decision making it uses to answer the three economic questions.

There are four basic types of economic systems: traditional economies, market economies, command economies, and mixed economies. These economic systems differ in how the basic economic questions of what, how, and for whom to produce are answered. In traditional economies, the three economic questions are decided mainly by social customs. In market economies,

Economic*Talk*

Pair students that have a good grasp of the vocabulary in this chapter with students who are having difficulty understanding some of the concepts. Hand out index cards to each pair and have them write the vocabulary words on the cards. Then, have the student who is having difficulty hold up a card for the other student to define and illustrate with an example. Encourage the student who is having difficulty to ask questions of the other student after each definition and example are given. Then, change roles.

At Risk

the economic questions are decided mostly by individuals in the marketplace. In command economies, they are decided by government. In mixed economies, they are decided by a combination of market decision making and government order. Many different combinations of these four kinds of economic systems are operating around the world today, with different degrees of success.

Market Economies and Economic Questions

In market economies, the question of what to produce is decided by individual consumers and producers in the marketplace. Consumers, in effect, cast dollar "votes" by spending money in the marketplace. Thus, producers of the products consumers want most are rewarded with profits. Consumers do not buy goods and services that they do not want. Those goods and services do not get as many dollar votes. This tells producers that there are other goods of better quality or lower price that consumers want more. Producers then must respond quickly to consumer desires or lose money and perhaps go out of business.

In market economies, individual producers decide what resources they need and in what amounts. Producers try to use less of the most costly resources and more of the cheapest resources. Individual producers closely monitor their own production processes in an effort to produce the same quality of goods at the least cost. Because producers' profits are the difference between the cost of producing a product and the price consumers will pay for it in the market, each producer has a strong reason to economize, use resources wisely, and buy the right amounts of each resource.

Market economies decide for whom to produce using the price system as well. Usually anyone who can pay the market price of the good gets the good. However, the government makes some decisions about for whom to produce; for example, alcohol and tobacco products cannot be sold legally to those below the legal age. In addition, some goods are only sold to specific legal buyers; for example, some weapons are sold legally only to governments.

Scarcity and Choice Exist in All Economies

Just as individuals make choices because of scarcity, so must economic systems. There simply are not enough of the productive resources to make all of everything everyone wants. For every choice made, there are opportunity costs.

THE IMPORTANCE OF ECONOMIC THEORY

All economic systems are guided in their economic decision making by the use of economic theory. A ***theory*** (also called a *model*) is a simplified description of reality. Theory is not always perfect, however. Sometimes economic decisions do not produce the results that theory might have predicted. Why, then, is it important to understand economic theory?

theory
a simplified description of reality

Economic Theory Simplifies Reality

Earlier, you read about the concept of opportunity cost as applied to buying books or going to the movies. This case used a theoretical tool that

Apply

Copy the following Venn diagram onto the chalkboard or an overhead transparency:

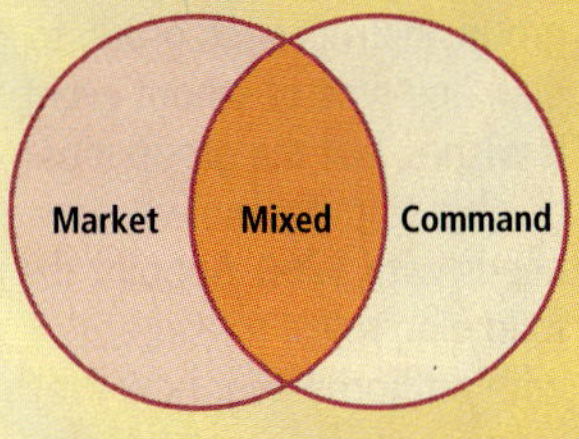

Ask students who answers the basic economic questions in a market economy (individuals), in a command economy (the government), and in a mixed economy (a mixture of individuals and the government). Write students' answers in the appropriate circles and then shade in the overlapping areas on the Venn diagram.
Guided Practice

Have each student make a chart with the four types of economic systems listed across the top of the paper and the three basic economic questions listed down the side. Have each student complete the chart.
Independent Practice

To emphasize the concepts **budget constraint** and **scarcity,** divide the class into groups of three or four. Hand out $200 in toy Monopoly® money to each group. Instruct each group to plan any type of school event it wishes, but the group must be able to purchase what it needs with $200. Appoint the following roles: treasurer, with authority over how the money is spent; social director, with ultimate authority over which types of events/activities are sponsored; marketing director, responsible for advertising and promoting the event; and recorder, who records all decisions. (If only three students are in a group, have one student also serve as the recorder.) Allow eight to ten minutes for students to make their decisions and report their findings to the class.
Cooperative Learning

Individually, have students write an essay explaining how **budget constraints** and **scarcity** affected their choices in the previous activity.

budget constraint the mix of goods that can be purchased with a limited amount of income

economists call a budget constraint. A ***budget constraint*** is the mix of goods that can be purchased, given a limited amount of income. The budget constraint in the earlier example was that you had $30 to spend on two goods: books and movies.

In reality, an individual can and usually does choose among many goods. Why, then, do we use simplified theoretical tools such as budget constraints? Can they tell us anything about the real economic world? The answer is a definite yes! Remember, theory is merely a simplified description of reality.

To describe reality in detail would be an endless task. If you tried to consider every thought an individual has in making choices about all goods and services, there would be no end to the process. The description would be so complicated that you could not draw any meaningful conclusions from it.

Theory, on the other hand, is like a road map. A road map is a guide to be used for a specific purpose. It does not show every street or even every small town. Trees, rocks, mountains, and fields are not generally part of the road map because they do not affect the decisions of a driver. A road map is helpful to a driver because it simplifies reality.

A hiker, on the other hand, would benefit more from a relief map showing mountains, fields, streams, and landmarks. This kind of map simplifies reality for the purposes of a hiker. Streets are not much help to the hiker and are, therefore, unnecessary information. A theory must include only the useful data. In simplifying reality, it is important to develop the right theory for the problem to be solved.

Economic theory is very much like the map example. To study how individuals make decisions (microeconomic theory), we may need a different theory from the one we use to study how whole societies make decisions

Econ & You

A PERMANENT PAIR

Economics is about scarcity, choice, and opportunity cost, and it touches your life every day in many ways. If you study for your math test for two hours, you cannot at the same time study for your English test. There is a scarcity of time. You must allocate the available time among your competing needs, including study time, leisure, sleeping, eating, and exercising. In the same way, you also must choose how to allocate your limited income among your unlimited wants and needs.

Choosing a career also involves trade-offs. If you decide to be an economist, you cannot at the same time work as an airline pilot. If and when you choose to marry, you will bear the opportunity cost of not being able to spend time with and enjoy other potential spouses.

You will always be subject to scarcity of some type, and the choices you make will all have an opportunity cost. Econ and you are a permanent pair.

Econ & You

A basic, underlying principle of the U.S. economy, government, and society is freedom of choice. Discuss with students the idea that every action is a choice. If economics is a graduation requirement, it may be difficult to get students to realize that taking the course still is their choice; but, if they choose not to take it, they won't graduate. Students interested in the perspective that everything is a choice should read "Part Two: Habit One" from *The 7 Habits of Highly Effective People*, by Stephen R. Covey.

(macroeconomic theory). The theory we use to understand problems such as inflation and unemployment differs from the theory we use to understand gasoline prices. Before we simplify our description of reality, we must know what we are trying to describe.

With the budget constraint for books and movies, we were trying to simplify the process that individuals use in making informed choices between two alternatives. We *assumed* that there were only two choices. This assumption told us under what conditions our theory was valid. We could have used much more complicated theories and not needed this assumption. However, the concept of opportunity cost might not have been as clear.

Economic Theory Is Relevant

As you go through life, you will make economic decisions as a consumer, as a worker, and as a citizen. An understanding of economic theory will be relevant to your everyday life. It will help you to make the most informed decisions possible on every economic issue you will face.

Look for the relevance in every economic theory you learn in this book. Ask yourself how and under what conditions each concept applies. As you do this, you will train your mind in the economic way of thinking.

Checkpoint

Content Check

1. Compare the four basic types of economic systems.
2. How do market economies answer the three basic economic questions?
3. Why is it important to understand economic theory?
4. Why are different economic theories needed to make microeconomic and macroeconomic decisions?

What Do You Think Now?

Reread *What Do You Think?* in the Section Four Focus. Then answer the following questions:

5. How does scarcity affect decisions made in command economies regarding consumer products, such as handguns, alcohol, or tobacco?
6. Do command economies and market economies often make different decisions about allocating limited resources? Why or why not?

Reteach

On the chalkboard, write the following: **tax increases, climbing interest rates,** and **new fast-food restaurant in town.** Have students who need reinforcement on how economic theory applies to their lives explain how the items on the list affect them. Reinforce that economic theory helps them make informed decisions about how to respond to economic factors such as these. **1-7**

Enrich

In small groups, have students scan business-section newspaper articles on economic issues. Ask each group to determine whether the articles are examples of microeconomic or macroeconomic choices. Then, have students list how each macroeconomic choice affects society and how each microeconomic choice affects individuals. **1-7**

Assess

1. Traditional, market, command, and mixed **1-6**
2. Through the choices and actions of individual consumers and producers **1-6**
3. To make informed decisions **1-7**
4. Because different choices are being made—individual vs. whole-society **1-7**
5. Government planners decide to make them scarce. **1-6**
6. Answers may be yes or no but should include an understanding of how each economic system allocates resources. **1-6**

Close

Divide the class into two groups. Have the first group support the position that economic theory is useful because it helps us make informed economic decisions, such as how much to spend on clothes, food, and entertainment. Ask the second group to defend the position that our economic decisions would be just as sound even if we never considered economic theory. Conduct a debate, making sure that students back up their viewpoints with real-life examples and then summarize the main ideas expressed by both sides.

Chapter Close

Your Economic Portfolio

Ask students to think about how economics—from theory to microeconomics to macroeconomics—affects their everyday lives.

Have students summarize a real-life economic scenario they have experienced. Then, ask them to explain what roles scarcity, needs, and wants played in their purchasing decision. Individually, review students' work, correct any misconceptions, and have them make needed alterations. Then, file the final draft of their essay in their portfolio.

You may wish to provide the following end-of-chapter materials:

- *Skills & Concepts* worksheet
- *Content Review Workbook*
- Chapter *Assessment*
- Chapter *MicroExam*

Concepts in Brief

1. An understanding of economics is important to your everyday life. Economics helps you make more informed decisions as a consumer, worker, and citizen.
2. Economics is a social science concerned with the basic economic problem of scarcity. Scarcity arises because limited resources are available to satisfy unlimited wants and needs. Because of scarcity, choices must be made to allocate limited resources among unlimited wants and needs.
3. With every decision, there is an opportunity cost and an opportunity benefit. The opportunity cost is the value of the alternative that is not chosen. The opportunity benefit is what is gained by choosing an alternative.
4. Economics is divided into two major types of theory. Microeconomics is concerned with the individual producing or consuming units and generally involves individual decisions. Macroeconomics is concerned with the economy as a whole and generally examines social economic decisions.
5. All economies must answer the three basic economic questions of what to produce, how to produce, and for whom to produce.
6. Countries and their economic systems use a variety of approaches to answer the basic economic questions. Command economies are ruled by social decisions, while market economies operate mostly by individual decisions.
7. Economic theory is a broad description that simplifies reality. Economic theory is not precise in all situations. It is, however, extremely useful and relevant when correctly applied.

Economic Foundations

1. What is the basic economic problem?
2. Why does scarcity occur in a society?
3. What is the solution to the basic economic problem?
4. What is the opportunity cost of asking for a day off from work to attend your cousin's wedding? What is the opportunity benefit?
5. Name the two kinds of choices that societies must make and give an example of each.
6. What are the three basic economic questions?

7. In the United States today, why is coal produced by a capital-intensive process instead of a labor-intensive process?
8. How are the basic economic questions answered in a command economy? How are they answered in a market economy?

Your Economic Vocabulary

Build your economic vocabulary by matching the following terms with their definitions.

1. the social science that deals with how society allocates its scarce resources among its unlimited wants and needs
2. the branch of economics that examines the behavior of the whole economy at once
3. the value of any alternative that you must give up when you make a choice
4. a simplified description of reality
5. the human characteristic of never having all wants and needs satisfied
6. the mix of goods that can be purchased with a limited amount of income
7. the branch of economics that examines the choices of individuals concerning one product, one firm, or one industry
8. the process of choosing which needs will be satisfied and how much of our resources we will use to satisfy them
9. the condition of there not being enough resources to fulfill all wants and needs
10. what is gained by making a particular choice
11. the combination of social and individual decision making a society uses to answer the three economic questions
12. the condition that occurs because people's wants and needs are unlimited, while the resources needed to produce goods and services to meet these wants and needs are limited

allocation
budget constraint
economics
economic system
limited resources
macroeconomics
microeconomics
opportunity benefit
opportunity cost
scarcity
theory
unlimited wants and needs

Economic Foundations

1. The basic economic problem is scarcity. (p. 6)
2. Scarcity occurs because only limited resources are available to satisfy unlimited wants and needs. (p. 6)
3. The solution to the basic economic problem of scarcity is allocation—we must choose which needs to neglect and just how much to neglect them. (p. 7)
4. Answers may include that the opportunity cost would be getting behind at work; an opportunity benefit might be enjoying the experience of the wedding. (pp. 8-11)
5. Answers may include that the two kinds of choices societies must make are individual choices, such as whether to buy a stereo, and social choices, such as how much tax money to spend on roads. (p. 12)
6. (1) What will be produced with the limited resources? (2) How will the goods and services be produced? (3) For whom will the goods and services be produced? (pp. 14-15)
7. Coal production in the United States today is capital intensive instead of labor intensive because the opportunity cost of labor relative to capital is now higher. (p. 15)
8. In a command economy, the basic economic questions are answered by the government; in a market economy, they are answered by individuals in the marketplace. (p. 19)

Your Economic Vocabulary

1. **economics**
2. **macroeconomics**
3. **opportunity cost**
4. **theory**
5. **unlimited wants and needs**
6. **budget constraint**
7. **microeconomics**
8. **allocation**
9. **limited resources**
10. **opportunity benefit**
11. **economic system**
12. **scarcity**

Thinking Critically About Economics

1. If you had to choose between going swimming or raking your neighbor's lawn for $10, which two economic concepts would enter into your decision? What would you decide and why? If the opportunity to swim were lost, but the offer from the neighbor remained, would your decision change?
2. If you had an income of $1 million a year, would you escape the basic economic problem of scarcity? If so, how? If not, why not?
3. If you were a highly skilled brain surgeon and your brother or sister were a school teacher, which of you would have the larger opportunity cost if drafted into the army? Why? Can opportunity cost be measured only in terms of money?
4. Would you rather live in a country that makes most of its decisions socially or one in which individuals make most of the decisions? In which of these countries would there be more freedom of choice?
5. Candidates for political office often speak of what their administration will give voters if they are elected. Candidate *A* promises more roads, new schools, more public parks, and new fire trucks. From what you have learned in this chapter about scarcity, choices, and cost, what are the obvious questions for you to ask Candidate *A*?
6. Can you develop a simple theory about how much water people drink in the summer relative to how much they drink in the winter? Will your theory always be correct for all people? If not, is your theory worthless in describing human behavior? Is your theory more effective than trying to observe how much water each person drinks in each season? Why or why not?

Economic Enrichment

Read the first section of your local newspaper each day for one week and cut out all the articles that relate directly to economics. You will be surprised at how many there are. Make a collage on poster board with the articles you find. Attach a brief report that contains the following:

1. a list of some of the most frequently discussed economic topics;
2. a summary of an article that you would not have thought was related to economics before you read this chapter; and
3. a paragraph giving your opinion on whether or not the economic way of thinking can be applied to almost any issue.

Thinking Critically About Economics

1. The opportunity cost and benefit of the choice would be the most important considerations. Answers may include that you would choose to rake the lawn if and only if you valued the $10 (the opportunity benefit) more than the chance to go swimming (the opportunity cost). If the opportunity to swim were lost, the opportunity cost of raking the lawn would obviously decrease and you might be more inclined to choose raking.
2. Regardless of your income, scarcity always will exist because you always will have to make choices. You must choose how to spend your time, what to eat, and so on, and since you cannot do all things at the same time, choice is inevitable. With every choice there is an opportunity cost, so you cannot avoid scarcity.
3. Answers may include that, on a monetary basis, the surgeon would have the higher opportunity cost because the lost earnings of the surgeon would be higher than the lost earnings of the teacher; however, others may answer that there is no way to know because all opportunity costs are not monetary.
4. Students will choose between social (government) choice and individual choice according to their personal preferences. Either choice is correct, but more freedom of choice exists in an economy ruled by individual choice.

(Continued)

Thinking Critically About Economics (Continued)

5. Answers may include the following: What will be the opportunity costs of your promises, and who will bear these costs? How will the new goods and services be paid for? Will you increase taxes or cut some other goods and services from the government's budget? Students should understand that whatever is provided must, by definition, have an opportunity cost.
6. Answers may include that, in general, people drink more water in the summer because temperatures are higher. The theory will not always be correct for all people, but it is an excellent and valuable behavioral rule. It tells much more about people in general than does attempted observation of each person's drinking habits because it would be impossible to observe all people all the time.

Math and Economics

Assume you have a budget constraint of $90 to spend on new shorts and shirts for the summer. To keep things simple, in this situation shorts cost $10 and shirts cost $15. On a separate sheet of paper, complete the following table to show how many shorts you could buy if you spent all of your money on shorts and how many shirts you could buy if you spent all of your money on shirts.

Shorts You Can Buy	Price	Total Cost	Your Total Income	Income Left Over
1	$10	$10	$90	$80
2	$10	$	$90	$
3	$10	$	$90	$
4	$10	$	$90	$
5	$10	$	$90	$
6	$10	$	$90	$
7	$10	$	$90	$
8	$10	$	$90	$
9	$10	$	$90	$

Shirts You Can Buy	Price	Total Cost	Your Total Income	Income Left Over
1	$15	$15	$90	$75
2	$15	$	$90	$
3	$15	$	$90	$
4	$15	$	$90	$
5	$15	$	$90	$
6	$15	$	$90	$

Before you go shopping, you think you would like to buy three pairs of shorts and four shirts. This is your first choice, Choice *1*. However, when you get to the store, you see six pairs of shorts you really like, leaving only enough money for two shirts. This is Choice *2*. Work through the following tasks to help you decide between Choice *1* and Choice *2*.

1. Sketch a graph that illustrates the many ways you can spend your $90 on shorts and shirts. (See Figure 1-2 for an example of this type of graph.)
2. Use your graph to help calculate the opportunity cost of changing your mind at the store and moving from Choice *1* to Choice *2*.
3. Use your graph to help calculate the opportunity benefit of changing your mind at the store and moving from Choice *1* to Choice *2*.
4. What choice would you make?

Math and Economics

Shorts You Can Buy	Total Cost	Income Left Over
1	$10	$80
2	$20	$70
3	$30	$60
4	$40	$50
5	$50	$40
6	$60	$30
7	$70	$20
8	$80	$10
9	$90	$ 0

Shirts You Can Buy	Total Cost	Income Left Over
1	$15	$75
2	$30	$60
3	$45	$45
4	$60	$30
5	$75	$15
6	$90	$ 0

1.

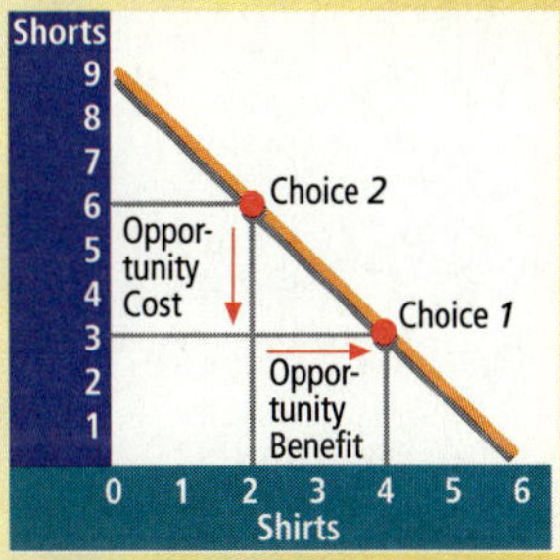

2. The opportunity cost of Choice *2* is the two other shirts that you will no longer be able to afford.
3. The opportunity benefit of Choice *2* is the three extra pairs of shorts that you will own.
4. Answers will vary but should reflect each student's assessment of the opportunity costs and benefits associated with either choice.

Economic Enrichment

Students' reports will vary but should contain information relating to the articles they chose for their collages. Reports should point out the most frequently discussed economic topics in their articles and should name an article that they wouldn't have related to economics prior to reading Chapter 1. Each report also should include a paragraph stating the student's personal opinion about applying the economic way of thinking to everyday life.

Writing About Economics

Students should record prices for regular unleaded gasoline at ten different gas stations in their city and note why they think prices vary as they do. Students' memos will vary but should reflect an understanding of the specific opportunity costs to consumers if the new gas station is built in an inconvenient location or if Shelby Oil's gas prices are higher than its competitors' prices. Students should explain to Victor Pumba that customers will be likely to purchase gas at the station that offers them the most opportunity benefits and fewest opportunity costs.

Writing About Economics

You are a market analyst for Shelby Oil. Shelby is considering your town as a location for a new gas station. Your job is to analyze your town with regard to current gas station locations and write a memo to the marketing manager, Victor Pumba, summarizing your results.

First, observe and record the prices in your town for regular unleaded gasoline at ten different locations. Are all of the prices the same? Why or why not? Are the prices at locations that are near each other fairly similar?

In your memo to Victor Pumba, present in a table the prices at different locations. Then discuss what role location and transportation costs might play in setting gasoline prices. Include information about the impact of opportunity costs on purchasers' decisions about where to buy gasoline.

Goals 2000: Educate America

Over the last two decades, family incomes have either grown very slowly or actually declined at all income levels. This discouraging picture emerges no matter what statistical measure of compensation or inflation you use. Average real compensation, which is compensation after the effect of inflation is taken out, grew by 3 percent per year between 1948 and 1973. However, it has only grown by seven-tenths of 1 percent per year between 1973 and 1993. To put this into perspective, consider this: If real compensation had grown at the same rate between 1973 and 1993 as it did from 1948 to 1973, the average compensation of a full-time worker in the United States in 1993 would have been $62,400 instead of $40,000.

What growth there has been has not been shared by all Americans. Many studies have shown that workers with more education earn substantially higher wages than those with the same age, experience, race, and gender characteristics who have less education. The average real wage of male high school graduates fell 20 percent from 1973 to 1993. The decline was even steeper for male high school dropouts, whose average real wage fell 27 percent over the same period. The average hourly wage for males with college degrees but no further education fell by 9 percent from 1973 to 1993. Finally, hourly wages of those with college degrees and two or more years of additional education fell by only 2 percent.

In 1994, the federal government enacted *Goals 2000: Educate America. Goals 2000* identifies eight ambitious national education goals to be achieved by the end of the decade:

1. **School readiness.** All children will start school ready to learn.
2. **Improved student achievement.** All students will demonstrate competence in challenging subject matter in core academic subjects.
3. **Best in math and science.** U.S. students will be first in the world in mathematics and science achievement.
4. **Safe, disciplined, and drug-free schools.** Every school will be free from violence, disruptive behavior, and illegal drugs.
5. **Increased graduation rate.** The high school graduation rate will improve to at least 90 percent.
6. **Teacher education and professional development.** All teachers will have the opportunity to acquire the knowledge and skills needed to prepare their students for the next century.
7. **Parental involvement.** Every school will promote parent-teacher partnerships that will increase parents' involvement in the social and academic enrichment of their children.
8. **Adult literacy and lifelong learning.** Every adult will be literate and possess the skills necessary to compete in a global economy.

These goals establish a framework for a lifetime of continuous learning. The hope is that, with these goals and the social choices made in order to effectively and efficiently achieve such goals, Americans will engage in lifelong learning, which ultimately should help rebuild the American dream that working hard and playing by the rules will lead to a higher standard of living.

SOURCE: *Economic Report of the President* (Washington, D.C.: U.S. Government Printing Office, 1995), 172, 174, 184–85.

After students have read the feature article on this page, facilitate a discussion on the opportunity costs and benefits to individual members of society of obtaining and receiving (from society as a whole) higher education. First, have students draw a one-sentence conclusion from the second paragraph of the reading. (Answers may include that the average real wage earned between 1973 and 1993 fell for all males, but it fell more for those who had less education.) On the chalkboard or an overhead transparency, copy the eight national education goals identified by the government in 1994. (Leave sufficient writing space between goals to add more text later on in this activity.) As a class, have students review each of the goals. Ask what implied, or unstated, problems the goals are designed to address. (Answers may include that education in the United States must be more focused and more strongly supported by teachers, parents, and the learners themselves to be beneficial and that the value of education must have greater priority—both socially and economically—to enable workers to prosper.) Note for the class that the education goals listed unfortunately do not contain prescriptions for *how* they will be accomplished. Have students brainstorm three ways each of the eight goals can be reached. Act, or have a class member act, as scribe and transfer students' suggestions into the spaces you left earlier in your list of eight goals. Guide students to see the economic costs and benefits—to society and to individual members of society—of supporting national education goals.

Chapter 2
Making Individual Decisions

Chapter Theme

Individuals must consider the costs and benefits of each choice before making a decision. A five-step decision-making model can help you arrive at more effective individual choices—ones that maximize the utility of the choice and minimize associated opportunity costs.

Section	Special Features
Individual Choice	Economics & Your Community Economic Spotlight Perspectives: Thinking Like a Producer Global Economy
The Decision-Making Model	Economic Talk Economic Dilemma Eye on Market News Media Link
Maximizing Utility	Multicultural Highlights Internet Connection Econ & You

Video Activity

Chapter 2, Better Light Bulb

Search Chapter 2, Play to 3

Ask students to vote by a show of hands whether they would buy the Solium light bulb featured in the video clip. Then, lead a class debate on both sides of the issue. On the chalkboard or an overhead transparency, record the different arguments students make in defense of their positions. After the debate, as a class, discuss the merit of each argument.

	Print Resources	Media Resources	Assessment
	Effective Teaching Model Lesson Plans *Skills & Concepts* worksheet *Problem Solving* worksheet *Casebook* *Economic Measurement Workbook* *Content Review Workbook* *Spanish Resources*	VHS CD-ROM Videodisc *Arctic Express* *Interactive* ECONOMICS Template software	*Your Economic Portfolio* Chapter *Assessment* Chapter *MicroExam*

Special Learners	Print Resources	Media Resources	Assessment
Kinesthetic Activity At Risk Auditory Activity		Overhead Computer	*Checkpoint* Section 1 Quiz
Visual Activity	*Life Skills* worksheet	Computer Overhead and *Transparency 2-1*	*Checkpoint* Section 2 Quiz
Cooperative Learning Activity	*Teacher's Connection to the Internet* *Reteach* worksheet *Enrich* worksheet	Computer Overhead	*Checkpoint* Section 3 Quiz

Careers Activity

The individual decisions that people make about how to spend their money can have a great effect on the need for travel agents. Travel agents arrange leisure and business trips for individuals and groups. For international travel, agents also inform clients of fees, required papers, customs regulations, and currency exchange rates.

Many travel agencies require a liberal arts degree and fluency in a foreign language. A good agent also will have visited many of the places to which he or she sends clients. Travel agents may earn a salary of less than $20,000. Most of their income is from commissions paid by hotels, airlines, and resorts.

Tell students to imagine that they are travel agents specializing in Florida vacations. Have them work in small groups to develop a travel brochure. Tell students to address the vacation pros and cons listed in *Figure 2-1* of their textbook and to include pictures and information about Florida's vacation features.

Teaching Materials

Program Resources

- Student text
- *Effective Teaching Model Lesson Plans*
- *Overhead Transparency 2-1*
- *Life Skills* worksheet
- *Problem Solving* worksheet
- *Reteach* worksheet
- *Enrich* worksheet
- *Skills & Concepts* worksheet
- *Casebook*
- *Economic Measurement Workbook*
- *Content Review Workbook*
- *Spanish Resources*
- Video package
- *Teacher's Connection to the Internet*
- *Arctic Express*
- *Interactive ECONOMICS*
- Template software

Assessment

- Section Quizzes
- Chapter *Assessment*
- Chapter *MicroExam*

Overview

Section One
Individual Choice

Section Two
The Decision-Making Model

Section Three
Maximizing Utility

28

Teacher to Teacher

Have students brainstorm a list of problems facing them at school (such as unsatisfactory cafeteria food and parking problems). On the chalkboard, use one of the problems to demonstrate how to use the decision-making process. Divide students into groups of five or six and have each group apply the five-step process to decide how to solve one of the other problems on the list. As a class, have each group compare its results with the other groups.

Dennis Dowling
Lakota High School
West Chester, OH

Making Individual Decisions

Learning Objectives

2-1

Explain how economic incentives guide individual decisions in a market economy.

2-2

Discuss how individual self-interest results in decisions that are in the best interest of society.

2-3

Describe how the decision-making model provides a logical approach to problem solving.

2-4

Apply the five-step decision-making model.

Outside Resources

- Blank overhead transparencies
- Outside speakers: Local producers
- Want ads
- Sales circulars from newspapers
- Computer
- Integrated software (spreadsheets)
- Catalogs
- Butcher paper

Vocabulary

individual choice, p. 30
market economy, p. 30
economic incentive, p. 31
psychic income, p. 31
economic profit, p. 32
invisible hand, p. 33
model, p. 36
objectivity, p. 36
alternative, p. 37
criteria, p. 38
decision matrix, p. 39
utility, p. 41
util, p. 41

Focus

Before class begins, write the following questions on the chalkboard: **Are you selfish? Are you self-interested?** Ask students to answer the questions on a sheet of paper.

Ask student volunteers to explain the difference between being *selfish* and *self-interested.* Have students debate whether a person can have one characteristic and not the other.

Teach

On the chalkboard or an overhead transparency, draw the following graphic organizer to show the characteristics of a **market economy**.

Explain to students the meanings of the terms and how each plays a part in the U.S. economy.

FOCUS

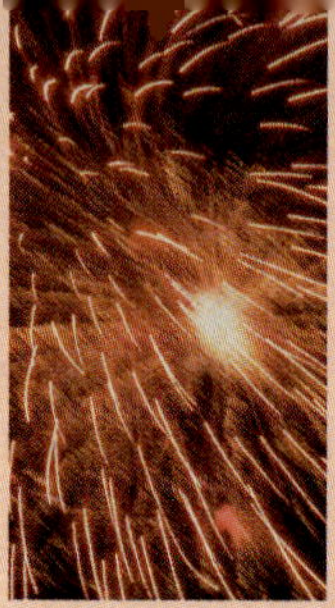

Section One
Individual Choice

What Do You Think?

Adam Smith, a Scottish economist, believed that the interests of the whole society were best served by each individual pursuing his or her own self-interest and that everyone should take care of themselves. Karl Marx believed that people were greedy and selfish, that the state should control this greed by owning almost all forms of property, and that everyone should get only what they needed. What do you think? Is self-interest bad? How can self-interest lead to a strong economy?

Terms to Know

- **individual choice**
- **market economy**
- **economic incentive**
- **psychic income**
- **economic profit**
- **invisible hand**

What's Ahead?

The economic questions of what, how, and for whom to produce are answered by individual choice in a market economy. Individual choice is guided by self-interest and the goal of gaining economic incentives. Individuals must consider the costs and benefits of each choice before making a decision. When individuals directly benefit from their decisions, the whole society benefits. Adam Smith described this effect as the *invisible hand.*

INDIVIDUAL DECISIONS AND THE MARKET ECONOMY

Economics is a science of choices because of scarcity. The economic questions of what, how, and for whom to produce must be answered in every society. Some economies rely mainly on individual choice to answer these economic questions. ***Individual choice*** means decisions are made by people acting separately from one another. To make intelligent choices, individuals must carefully consider the costs and benefits of each choice.

individual choice decisions made by people acting separately

market economy an economy in which the economic questions are decided mostly by individuals in the marketplace

Economic Incentives

An economy in which the economic questions are decided mostly by individuals in the marketplace is called a ***market economy.*** *Capitalist economy* is another name for a market economy. The U.S. economy is an example of a market, or capitalist, economy.

Economics & Your Community

Ask students to listen to the news on the radio or television and to read the newspaper to find examples of economic incentives that include **psychic income** (such as working fewer hours, becoming famous, and working with famous people). Using these examples, have students debate how economic incentives and individual choices help or hinder a market economy.

People's actions in a market economy result from their motives or incentives for personal gain. ***Economic incentive*** is the increase in personal satisfaction that may result from some economic activity. This increase in satisfaction may be the result of having more money income; for example, fixing an old bike and selling it for $30. However, money is not the only economic incentive.

Psychic income is the nonmonetary reward we get from taking some action. For example, you may feel a sense of pride from knowing that a child now has a safe bike to ride. You are happier because of that pride and so have some personal gain. The economic incentive of psychic income is very important in determining how economic questions are answered in a market economy.

economic incentive
the increase in personal satisfaction that may result from some economic activity

psychic income
the nonmonetary reward we get from taking some action

Economic Questions

In a market economy, *what to produce* is decided by consumers voting in the marketplace with their dollars. If many individual consumers decide to

Economic Spotlight

WHERE ARE YOU GOING?

Would you like to become the first . . . ? Barbara Brandon, the first nationally syndicated African-American female cartoonist, is stunned that even in the 1990s she still could "become the first black something."

Following in the footsteps of her cartoonist father who created the strip "Luther," about the life of an inner-city child, Brandon knew early on that she wanted to be a cartoonist. As a child, she helped her father by coloring in silhouettes and drawing borders for his strips. Her comic strip was picked up by Universal Press Syndicate in 1991 and now runs in more than 400 newspapers across the country.

Her weekly comic strip "Where I'm Coming From" illustrates difficult life choices that young adults face about relationships, parenthood, and human rights. Brandon takes these difficult choices and, in a lighthearted way, shows the decision-making process that her characters use. Only her characters' heads and arms appear in her strip because she does not want to focus on physical appearances. Brandon wants her readers to learn to look hard at people's faces and gaze into their eyes, so they'll think more about what the person is saying rather than what the person looks like.

Her strip features a range of female characters—from socially conscious to self-absorbed to man obsessed—who shatter many common stereotypes about women. Her main character, Lekesia, is an active, sassy, street-smart African-American woman who battles oppression of all kinds.

Brandon believes that her strip will help people understand themselves better. The artist says she would like, years from now, for "people to read these strips and see what they were going through." So, would you like to become the first . . . ? The choice is up to you.

Economic Spotlight

Collect several of Barbara Brandon's comic strips that deal with economic choices and bring them to class for students to read. Ask students to think of a difficult economic choice they have faced or are facing. Have them illustrate a five-frame comic strip using one frame for each of the five steps in the decision-making process. Encourage students to use the graphic tools or programs available on computer. You may wish to post students' strips on a bulletin board entitled *Where We're Coming From.*

A pply

On the chalkboard or an overhead transparency, create a chart with the headings **Economic Incentive** and **Psychic Income.** Ask students what the economic incentives and psychic incomes, if any, are for the following jobs: senator (answers may include *EI:* high salary, expense-paid trips, chauffeurs; *PI*: prestige, power, making a difference) and hospital volunteer (answers may include *EI*: none; *PI*: pride, joy, fulfillment). Write students' responses on the chart. Discuss with students how economic incentives and psychic income can help them evaluate their career choices. **Guided Practice**

In small groups, have students discuss why they think certain products, such as Cabbage Patch Dolls and Mighty Morphin Power Rangers, are very popular for a while and then eventually decrease in popularity. (Answers may include market saturation, consumable vs. nonconsumable product, and decreased advertising.) **Independent Practice**

Tell students to imagine that they want to start their own part-time business, such as a lawn-care service or a car-washing service, but they need to borrow money from their parents or guardians to get started. Have students write persuasive letters to their parents or guardians explaining how their business will make a profit. Make sure students include the answers to the following questions: **What information will I need to know to ensure that I will make a profit? What can I do to maximize my income? Will I buy or rent the equipment that I need? Will I hire workers? If so, how much will I pay them? Who will be the consumers of my service or product?** Bring to class want ads, sales circulars from newspapers, and catalogs for students to research the prices of new and used equipment for their business.

buy a good or service, the product succeeds in the market. When a product succeeds, its producers earn money and so they have an incentive to provide more of those products consumers want.

However, if many consumers individually choose not to buy a product, the product fails in the market. The producer then faces loss and individually chooses not to produce the item and the product disappears from the market. This process of individual choice by consumers and producers in a marketplace thus determines what will be produced.

How to produce is also decided by individual choice in a market economy. Assume that you are an individual producer in a highly competitive industry such as wheat production. The market price for wheat might be $3.50 a bushel. How will you produce the wheat so that you can make a profit? There are many ways to grow wheat. For instance, you can employ hundreds of farm workers who use hand tools or you can employ fewer workers and more machinery (tractors). How will you choose between these two methods? You will choose the one that produces the greatest amount of wheat at the lowest cost.

It might take 100 hours of plowing with a tractor to cultivate the crop. The tractor might cost $75 an hour to rent and operate. Your cost of plowing with the tractor would then be $7,500. You could do the same amount of plowing in 100 hours with 100 workers each of whom earns $3.25 an hour. Then your plowing cost would be $32,500 (100 hours × 100 workers × $3.25 an hour = $32,500). You would probably choose the method that costs less—using the tractor.

Hundreds of other production decisions will be made the same way. You, as an individual producer, will choose as effectively as you can with the best information you can find. Your incentive will be personal gain. You will want to maximize your income from the production of your product.

For whom to produce also is answered in a market economy by individual choice. Anyone who has enough money can buy any product. Producers will make their products for the people who will be able to buy them.

BENEFITS OF INDIVIDUAL CHOICE

It is important to understand the issues of individual choice and personal gain in order to understand market economies. During the past 50 years, U.S. capitalism has produced a standard of living that is unparalleled. One reason for this high standard of living is that individuals in a market economy directly benefit from their decisions, so their decisions are guided by self-interest. Self-interest is a strong incentive. In other economies, individuals do not necessarily benefit from their own decisions.

Self-Interest

economic profit the difference between the money you obtain from selling a product and the cost of producing the product

In a market economy, if you do not seek out the correct information—and therefore choose poorly—your costs will rise and your profits will decline. ***Economic profit*** is the difference between the money you obtain from selling a product and the cost of producing the product. For example, in the production of wheat, you might have chosen to use laborers instead of a tractor.

Perspectives

Thinking Like a Producer
Invite one or more local producers to visit your class. Ask the speaker(s) to discuss ways a producer can succeed in a market economy. As a whole group, before the speaker arrives, have students brainstorm questions to ask the producer, such as **"How do producers determine what consumers will buy?"** and **"How do producers determine how to produce a product to gain the most profit?"**

Your profits would have been $25,000 more if you had chosen the tractor. You will pay a price in a market economy for choosing poorly.

The power of self-interest cannot be overstated. It is the driving force behind market economies. Self-interest is not merely an advantage to individuals. It is what makes individual choice influence the marketplace. Many economists believe that self-motivated individual choice does the greatest good for society as a whole.

invisible hand
the incentive that guides individuals to choose in the best interest of society by pursuing their own self-interests

The Invisible Hand

When the producer and the consumer meet in the marketplace, they pursue their own self-interests. The producer wants to maximize profits and the consumer wants to minimize costs. The bargain that is struck must benefit both producer and consumer, or they would have no reason to trade or exchange. The incentive that guides individuals to choose in the best interest of society by pursuing their own self-interests is called the ***invisible hand.*** This role of self-interest is best explained in Adam Smith's description of the invisible hand more than 200 years ago:

> An individual neither intends to promote the public interest, nor knows he is promoting it. . . . He intends only his own gain, and he is led by an invisible hand to promote an end which was no part of his intention. . . . It

Global Economy

INDIVIDUALS ARE INTERDEPENDENT

The growing emphasis on global economics comes from the fact that the world's economies are becoming much more interdependent than in the past. World trade is a very important part of the economics of almost all countries now, and the information age is speeding up communication, transportation, specialization, trade, and exchange.

Many decisions made by individuals every day are a part of this global economy. For example, the gasoline for your trip to school, the automobile itself, the TV carrying the morning news, the clothing you are wearing, and the computer game you may play this afternoon all might have been produced in other countries. Your individual decision to use them has direct effects on the foreign producers of those goods and on the livelihood of the employees who work for them.

U.S. investors can now buy and sell shares of stock in foreign companies by phone daily. The same is true of citizens in other countries. They can and do buy U.S. products and invest in U.S. companies, and their individual choices affect the U.S. economy every day.

The world is moving toward a global economy, and the individual choices you make are a part of it. In the future, there will be increased demand for professionals in international business.

Divide the class into two groups: producers and consumers. Pair each producer with a consumer. Using role-playing techniques and the information from the previous activity, have the producers persuade the consumers to buy their services or products. Encourage the consumers to be self-interested and to ask probing questions. Then, have students switch roles.

At Risk

Ask students to reread Adam Smith's description of the **invisible hand** in their textbook. Have students trace an outline of one of their hands on a sheet of paper. Then, tell students to rewrite the quote in their own words in any format, such as a song or a poem. Have students write their work inside the outline of their hand.

Have students create a chart comparing and contrasting **market economy** and **social economy**. Be sure to have students include the advantages and disadvantages of each to both the economy and individual workers.

Global Economy

As a class, ask students to think about and name many of the products that they have used, worn, and eaten during the past week. **Where were these products produced or grown?** Using the chalkboard or an overhead transparency, create a chart to show how many different countries produce the products that students frequently use. Have students discuss how individual decisions positively and negatively affect foreign and U.S. producers.

is not from the benevolence of the butcher, the brewer, or the baker that we expect our dinner, but from their regard to their self-interest. We address ourselves not to their humanity, but to their self-love and never talk to them of our necessities, but of their advantages.[1]

Individual Incentives and Social Choice

Social choice can reduce the incentive of direct self-interest and therefore, at times, discourage individual productive efforts. Consider the case of wheat production again. This time, however, assume that the government decides workers must work eight hours each day and everyone must be paid equally. What if you, a worker on this farm, work very hard, put in extra hours, and spend your off hours thinking of ways to improve output? As a result of your efforts, the farm increases output by 1,000 bushels. You, however, continue to receive the same pay and rewards as your coworkers who do not try to produce as much. You would have little or no economic incentive to produce more than your coworkers.

The government's decision that the whole society should benefit from the farm equally fails to reward the value of any individual decisions you might make. It is highly likely that you will choose in your own self-interest not to work extra hard to improve. You will still enjoy the same benefits as your coworkers. From the standpoint of productivity, social decisions are generally not as effective as individual decisions.

Checkpoint

Content Check

1. In a market economy, how do individual choices affect the economic questions of what to produce and how to produce?
2. How does individual self-interest influence the marketplace?
3. How are individuals affected by social choices?

What Do You Think Now?

Reread *What Do You Think?* in the Section One Focus. Then answer the following questions:

4. Do you think Adam Smith's belief that self-interest benefits all of society makes sense in today's economy? Why or why not?
5. Can a government that owns almost all of the economic resources in a country provide economic incentives to workers? If so, how? If not, why not?

[1]Adam Smith, *An Inquiry into the Nature and Causes of the Wealth of Nations*, Edwin Cannan, ed. (Chicago: University of Chicago Press, 1976), 18.

Assess

1. What to produce: individual consumers decide to buy specific goods and services. How to produce: individual producers decide to use methods that produce the most profit. **2-1**
2. It motivates both consumers and producers to maximize their benefits, which benefits society. **2-1, 2-2**
3. Individual productive efforts are sometimes discouraged. **2-1**
4. Answers may include that self-interest promotes productivity, which benefits the economy. **2-1, 2-2**
5. Answers may include that workers usually have no incentive to excel in this situation. **2-1**

Close

Divide the class into two teams. Have the teams debate the views of Adam Smith and Karl Marx concerning self-interest.

Reteach

Have students create a chart with the headings **Selfish** and **Self-Interested**. Ask students to fill in both columns with examples of selfish and self-interested behaviors. Have students compare their own examples with those of a classmate and, together, discuss how each example does or does not benefit society. **2-1, 2-2**

Enrich

As a class, discuss people's spending habits and how a market economy might be jeopardized if all of us either spent all our income or saved all except what was spent for necessities. **2-1, 2-2**

FOCUS

Section Two
The Decision-Making Model

What Do You Think?

Sometimes in the heat of an argument you say things that you later wish you had not. Sometimes when you have to make choices in a hurry, you wish you had chosen differently. Sometimes after you make a decision, you discover that there were other choices that you did not consider. Everyone has to make choices every day and yet some people seem to make better choices than others most of the time. All of these problems revolve around the choice process. What can economics teach you about how to make better choices?

What's Ahead?

Making good decisions increases your satisfaction and the satisfaction of others. Individual decisions are improved with a five-step decision-making model. A clear definition of the problem, well-thought-out alternatives, appropriate criteria, and a careful evaluation process will result in better decisions.

Terms to Know

model
objectivity
alternative
criteria
decision matrix

INDIVIDUAL DECISION-MAKING MODEL

As both consumers and producers of goods and services, your individual or personal decisions affect your own satisfaction as well as the satisfaction of others. Making a correct decision the first time around is always better than trying to correct a poor decision once it has been made. A logical, well-reasoned approach to individual or personal problem solving involves five steps:

1. define the problem;
2. list the alternatives from which you must choose;
3. list the criteria by which you must evaluate the alternatives;
4. evaluate the alternatives based on the criteria you have chosen; and
5. choose the alternative that best meets the criteria you have chosen.

Focus

Before class begins, write the following on the chalkboard: **What process do you use to make a decision?** As students enter the classroom, ask them to jot down their answer on a sheet of paper.

Ask students to share their answers to the previous question. (Answers may include making a list, asking the opinions of friends and family, and doing research.) Have a class discussion of the advantages and disadvantages of each of the processes students listed.

Teach

Explain to students that it is important to make good decisions and that, usually, the best ones are those that are well thought out. Tell students that there is a five-step process that they can use to help them make good decisions throughout their life. Explain to students each of the five steps in the process.

Apply

Copy the following graphic organizer onto the chalkboard or an overhead transparency. Tell students to copy it on a sheet of paper, drawing *large* boxes.

STEP 1: Define the problem.

STEP 2: List the alternatives.

STEP 3: List the criteria.

STEP 4: Evaluate the alternatives.
Use a decision matrix.

STEP 5: Choose the best alternative.

Paraphrase the following scenario: **You have been hired for a part-time job in a pizza shop at the edge of town. You know the bus does not go that far, and it is certainly too far to walk. Define the problem** (transportation, need to buy a vehicle). Tell each student to write his or her answer in the first box of the graphic organizer. Ask students to speculate specific solutions to their problem.

Guided Practice

model
a simplified form of reality that shows the relationship between different factors

These five steps make up the decision-making model. A ***model*** is a simplified form of reality that shows the relationship between different factors. For example, a model airplane shows you what a real airplane looks like but does not show every detail. A model decision-making process shows you the general idea of how to go about making well-informed decisions. However, it does not show you every specific detail you have to consider in making a decision.

Step 1—Define the Problem

In Lewis Carroll's *Alice's Adventures in Wonderland,* the Cheshire Cat tells Alice: "If you don't know where you are going, any road will take you there."

Individual decision making is often clouded by emotion and misinformation. Instead of plotting a straight path to solve a problem, individuals might take *any road* and hope it is the right one. But *any road* might lead to the wrong solution! Therefore, the first step is to define exactly what the problem is.

Economic decisions are similar to many other decisions: They generally start as a problem of scarcity or the need to allocate. For example, consider the problem of a football team that has more players than can fit on the team bus. This problem can be defined as how to allocate the available spaces to team members. The problem is deciding who will travel and who will not.

As another example, consider the following economic allocation problem. You have just received a tax refund check for $350. You have many uses for this money, but you want to make the best decision about how to use it. The problem can be defined as follows: "How can this income of $350 best be allocated to fulfill my needs?"

objectivity
ruling out aspects of a problem that seem important only because of your strong emotions about them

Be Objective. ***Objectivity*** means ruling out aspects of a problem that seem important only because of your strong emotions about them. In defining the problem, you should be as objective as possible. You should weigh each aspect of the problem in regard to the role it plays. Return to the case of the football team and the bus. What is the real problem here? Is the bus too small? Or is the team too large? The third-string guard may feel that the bus is too small. The starting quarterback, however, may feel that the team is too large.

Both of these problem definitions are affected by the emotions involved with how sure an individual player is of getting a seat on the bus. When the star quarterback's throwing hand gets broken, the quarterback's definition of the problem might change. The quarterback would not be so sure of getting a seat on the bus and might agree that the bus is too small.

Focus on the Issue. After ruling out emotional involvements, you must focus your thoughts on the true issue. For example, individuals without

EconomicTalk

Have students use the vocabulary terms in the chapter to create a crossword puzzle. For more of a challenge, tell students to create their puzzle from only seven of the nine terms they have learned thus far in the chapter. Then, have students exchange puzzles with a classmate. Allow students to give each other additional clues, if necessary.

emotional involvement in the problem of the football team's bus will view the issue differently. The school principal may feel that the team is too large. The coach, however, may argue that the team needs to carry as many players as possible in order to train young talent. The problem should be defined objectively and clearly. Buses are limited in size, and most teams usually have more players than seats. The problem definition then becomes how to allocate the limited seats among the players.

Step 2—List the Alternatives

An ***alternative*** is a possible course of action. Once the problem has been defined, the next step in the personal decision-making model is to list the alternatives.

alternative
a possible course of action

Let's take another look at the tax refund problem: "How can this income of $350 best be allocated to fulfill my needs?" To solve the problem, you should make a list of the alternate uses for this income. Remember that your alternate solutions are limited by the amount of the tax refund: $350.

Limit Your Alternatives. There are many ways to use $350. You could consider every item in the world before making your choice. However, that would take more time and effort than you are willing to spend. So, you must list a reasonably small number of alternatives from which to choose.

Expand the previous activity by reminding students that they need to remain focused on the primary objective, which is obtaining a reliable car—not necessarily the "coolest" car—to get to work and back. Have students brainstorm a list of all the vehicles they would be interested in buying for this purpose. Remind students to be realistic and to limit their alternatives to only those cars they think they can afford. From that list, have students choose four used cars that they think fall within their budget. Tell students that they need to decide which of the four alternatives will be the best buy and write their choices in Step 2 of the graphic organizer they drew in the previous *Guided Practice* activity.

Economic Dilemma

WORK OR COLLEGE?

One of the first major dilemmas faced by high school students is the choice between taking a job as soon as they graduate or going on to college. College is very expensive; you have to pay for tuition, books, and fees. Attending college for four years or more usually means giving up earnings from a full-time job during that period as well. In other words, the opportunity cost of college can frequently be greater than the financial cost.

With that in mind, it is even more important to consider this decision using the five-step choice process. The alternatives might be immediate full-time college and no work, part-time college with full-time work, or some combination of these. Weighing the opportunity costs and benefits of each alternative will clearly lead to better decisions.

Expect this type of dilemma to come up many times in your life, such as when you graduate from college. There will be decisions about graduate school, marriage, and family. All of these decisions are dealt with best by using the five-step decision process. Better process yields better decisions.

Economic Dilemma

Ask students to consider their personal options for the next five years. Do they think they will continue on to college? Go to work after high school graduation? Get married? Have children? What careers or jobs will they pursue? Using *Figure 2-1* as a model, have students create and complete a decision-making matrix. After they have completed the matrix, have students write a poem, essay, or short story describing where they see themselves in five years.

Have students brainstorm a list of the criteria that could be used when shopping for a used car. Ask students if they think durability, acceptability to authority figures, related expenses, and trade-in value are important. Then, in Step 3 of their graphic organizers, have students list the criteria that are important to them.

Independent Practice

Have students think of a personal dilemma that would benefit from the application of the decision-making model and ask volunteers to share their issue. Copy the graphic organizer from p. 36 onto the chalkboard. Ask the volunteers to identify what they have considered for steps 1 through 5. Classmates are to offer other alternatives and assist in the process of arriving at a good solution to the problem.

Be Realistic. While you might want a new car, the $350 you have to spend makes this an unrealistic alternative. On the other hand, you might be able to buy a used car for $350, but it probably would not be dependable. Step 2 requires you to list realistic alternatives.

Let's assume that you consider the following four items to be your most important choices:

1. a new CD player;
2. a one-week vacation to Florida during spring break;
3. a new electronic keyboard; and
4. a new 18-speed bike.

Step 3—List the Criteria Used to Evaluate Your Alternatives

Now that you have defined the problem and listed your alternatives, you need some way to evaluate the alternatives. The characteristics that you will use to judge a group of alternatives are called ***criteria.***

criteria
the characteristics of a group of alternatives that will be judged to make a choice

Ask yourself the following questions: "Given these alternatives, on what criteria should I base my choice?" Should I consider cost, usefulness, product life, or some other aspect of the product? The answers will vary from person to person, but you should select your criteria objectively and realistically.

Let's assume that the important criteria in this case include the following:

1. *Durability*—how long the goods or services will last;
2. *Acceptability to authority figures*—how parents, police, school authorities, and others will accept your choice (another way of looking at this criterion is to think about how a given choice will affect your relationship with others);
3. *Related expenses*—The costs of other items that will be needed to enjoy each alternative, such as compact discs, keyboard lessons, or a bike helmet; and
4. *Salvage or trade-in value*—The value, if any, of the alternative when you are finished with it.

Having chosen your criteria, you may also want to rank them in order of importance. For example, you might feel that product durability is more important to you than acceptability to parents because you will be moving into a college dorm soon. However, if you are living at home and working your way through college, other expenses might be the most important criterion.

Step 4—Evaluate the Alternatives

You have now defined the problem, listed the alternatives, and selected some criteria. The next step involves evaluating each alternative using the criteria. To do this, set up a table of alternatives and criteria, such as the one in Figure 2-1. This is sometimes called a decision matrix. A ***decision matrix*** is a table comparing possible decisions.

decision matrix
a table comparing possible decisions

EyeOnMarketNews

Remind students that good decision making is not only an important skill for individuals to master but that a lack of this skill also continues to be identified as one of the problems of today's government. In small groups, have students choose one problem, such as unemployment, homelessness, or crime, that plagues the economy today. Then, tell students to use the five steps of the decision-making model to create a decision matrix to solve the problem that they chose.

	Alternatives			
	CD Player	**Florida Vacation**	**Electronic Keyboard**	**18-Speed Bike**

Criteria: Durability and Product Life	Ten years or more — 4 points	One week; memories good or bad, one lifetime — 2 points	Two years — 2 points	Eight years — 3 points
Criteria: Acceptability to Authority Figures	Somewhat acceptable — 3 points	Not acceptable — 1 point	Acceptable with volume control — 3 points	Very acceptable — 4 points
Criteria: Related Expenses	Moderate and flexible; new CDs — 2 points	Some, but flexible; entertainment, shopping, etc. — 3 points	High; lessons, music, electricity — 1 point	Low; bike helmet — 4 points
Criteria: Salvage or Trade-in Value	Moderate — 3 points	None — 1 point	Low — 2 points	Moderate — 3 points
Final Score and Rank of Alternative	12 points 2nd choice	7 points 4th choice	8 points 3rd choice	14 points 1st choice

Figure 2-1

A Decision Matrix

The four alternatives are listed at the top of the last four columns. The four criteria for evaluating the alternatives are listed in the first column. Note the final score and rank for each alternative. ***Would these ranks vary depending on who assigns the scores?***

Each alternative listed in this decision matrix is given a score for each criterion. A score of four points is given for very desirable alternatives and one point is given for very undesirable alternatives. After the points for each alternative are totaled, final scores are figured. The higher the number of total points, the more desirable the alternative.

This example uses hypothetical scores for each alternative. Your individual evaluation may be different. Every individual places a different and unique value on each good or service in the world. You may listen to music twice as much as you would practice on your keyboard. One of your friends may feel just the opposite. Both of you are entitled to your preference, and both of you are right.

Step 5—Choose the Best Alternative

From the decision matrix in Figure 2-1, you can see that the best alternative is the 18-speed bike. It has the highest total score. Remember, however, that your own final choice depends on the criteria you choose and on your own preferences. If you live only for today, then product durability

Have students use the information in the first three steps of the graphic organizers they completed on p. 36 to set up a decision matrix similar to *Figure 2-1.* Next, have students fill in their charts, describing how the criteria match up with the four cars. Then, have students rank the criteria from 1 point (very undesirable) to 4 points (very desirable). Have them add the points to get the scores of their four alternatives. (Instruct students to keep their matrices in a safe place because they will be used again in Section Three.)

Analyzing *Graphics*

Caption Answer

The scores that depend on personal differences, such as the acceptability of a Florida vacation to parents, will vary. The scores that do not depend on personal differences, such as related expenses for a CD player, will not vary much.

Media*Link*

Using a spreadsheet program, have students create their own decision matrices. Tell students to use the decision matrix in their textbook (*Figure 2-1*) as a model but to choose four new alternatives. Ask students to program formulas to calculate the scores of their alternatives. Have students discuss their results. (Instruct students to keep their matrices in a safe place because they will be used again in Section Three.)

may not be important to you and your choice might be the vacation. If you get lots of enjoyment from your music, the electronic keyboard may be a better choice for you. There is an important issue here. If you make your personal decisions in the logical, organized, and effective way described, the satisfaction you get probably will be greater than a choice made another way. This will be true no matter what individual preferences enter into your evaluation and no matter what choice you make.

Checkpoint

Content Check

1. What are the five steps in the decision-making model?
2. Why should you define problems in an objective and focused manner?
3. How are alternatives chosen, criteria selected, and alternatives evaluated?

What Do You Think Now?

Reread *What Do You Think?* in the Section Two Focus. Then answer the following questions:

4. Can the decision-making model help you avoid saying things you later regret? Explain.
5. Can the economic concepts you have learned about help you make better choices? Explain.
6. If you combine what you know about economics with what you know about the decision-making model, will you make better choices? Explain.

Assess

1. Define the problem, list the alternatives, list the criteria, evaluate the alternatives, and choose the best alternative. **2-3**
2. To rule out emotional issues **2-3**
3. Alternatives should be reasonable in number and scope. Criteria should be the decision maker's most important considerations. Alternatives should be ranked. **2-4**
4. Answers may include that it can help you think through a decision rather than speak in haste. **2-3**
5. Answers should reflect an understanding of the concepts of scarcity and trade-off and their connection to decision making. **2-3, 2-4**
6. Answers should reflect an understanding of the value of using the decision-making model when making economic choices. **2-3**

Close

Have students discuss the last step in the decision-making process: choosing the best alternative. Tell students to add their choice to Step 5 in their graphic organizers. Ask students how close their speculation, which they made in the first *Apply* activity, was to their highest scoring alternative. Have the class discuss how the five-step decision-making process and the decision matrix are or are not helpful.

Reteach

Display *Overhead Transparency 2-1* to students who are having difficulty understanding the five-step decision-making process. Encourage peer-tutoring by asking students who grasp the concept to explain how the matrix was completed. **2-3, 2-4**

Enrich

Ask students to write an essay explaining why they think some people are not good decision makers. Ask why some people are quicker and more confident decision makers. **Is it a learned skill? How might our decision-making skills change from age 18 to age 50? How is a decision matrix useful? 2-3**

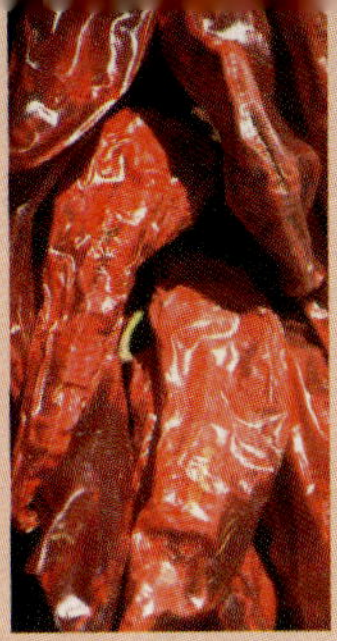

FOCUS

Section Three
Maximizing Utility

What Do You Think?

Nikki was having a hard time making a decision about Friday night. She had been invited to a party *and* offered a chance to usher at a performance of "Phantom of the Opera." She wouldn't get paid to usher, but she would see the show for free. She wanted to go to the party too, however, because a friend who had moved away last year was going to be there. It was already Wednesday and Nikki couldn't decide. What should Nikki do?

What's Ahead?

The five-step process helps you maximize the utility of your choice and minimize the opportunity cost. Although the decision-making process seems lengthy at first, you will find it can work quickly and easily with practice. You can use it every day to make better choices.

Terms to Know

utility

util

THE DECISION-MAKING PROCESS IN REAL LIFE

It is important to remember that every time you make a choice, there is an opportunity cost. That is, you give up some alternative that you could have chosen. By using the five-step decision-making model to make choices, you can make comparisons between your opportunity costs.

Individual Choice and Opportunity Cost

Economists use the term *utility* to describe the strength of your preference. ***Utility*** is the satisfaction one receives from the consumption, use, or ownership of a good or service. The unit of measurement for utility is the ***util.*** For example, listening to music may have twice as many utils as playing the keyboard.

Wise choices are those that maximize the utility of the choice. A related concept economists use is psychic income. As you learned earlier in this chapter, *psychic income* is the nonmonetary satisfaction received from taking

utility
the satisfaction one receives from the consumption, use, or ownership of a good or service

util
the unit of measurement for utility

Focus

As students enter the classroom, ask them to jot down the important and unimportant decisions that they have made in the past week.

Write students' responses in a list on the chalkboard or an overhead transparency. Ask students which decisions were hard to make. Elicit the reasons some decisions are more difficult to make than others. (Answers may include opportunity costs and whether a decision was life-altering.)

Teach

Tell students that every decision has an opportunity cost. Explain the definitions of **utility** and **util.** Ask students to think about this question: **If the decision-making matrix ranks a product highly based on practical criteria, but you will not receive any utility from it, will you choose that product?**

Multicultural *Highlights*

Evelyn Lauder, a vice president of the cosmetics company Estée Lauder, colors the world beautiful. In 1990, Lauder, a European American, became a member of the Board of Overseers at Memorial Sloan-Kettering Cancer Center in New York City, where she spearheads fund-raising drives for breast cancer research. Lauder has given her time and decorating talents to create a warm, nurturing atmosphere for patients. Have students make a chart showing what they choose to do with their free time. Discuss how they make these decisions.

Apply

On the chalkboard or an overhead transparency, create a two-column chart with the headings **Individual Choice** and **Opportunity Cost.** Use the information from the *Focus* activity to fill in the first column. Then, ask students what the opportunity cost was for making each decision. For example, if a student chose to bring his or her lunch to school, then the opportunity cost may have been school-cafeteria pizza. Add that information to the second column of the chart. Discuss with students if the choices were worth the opportunity costs.

Guided Practice

Have students refer to one of the decision matrices that they created in Section Two. Ask students to determine what utility they would receive from the use or ownership of the good they listed in the matrix. Tell them to rank the utility by using utils to compare and contrast the goods.

Independent Practice

Internet Connection

E-MAIL OR SNAILMAIL?

Exploration on the Internet often begins with electronic mail, e-mail. E-mail allows you to send written messages to anyone who has an account on any computer on the Internet or on a commercial network, such as CompuServe, Prodigy, and America Online. You can use e-mail to communicate with your teacher or with other students in your school or in schools around the world.

E-mail is a lot faster than "snail-mail," as the regular postal service is now known to e-mail users. E-mail can arrive from across town or across the globe within minutes. By contrast, snailmail usually takes days to deliver.

E-mail also can be used to obtain Internet resources. However, since there are more sophisticated, easy-to-use tools for that purpose, e-mail is principally used for communication.

E-mail programs have a number of common features. They allow you to create messages using a word processor. You can send e-mail messages to other people and save or print e-mail messages you receive. To take advantage of e-mail communication offerings, you need to know how to address outgoing messages.

Each computer on the Internet, or "Internet host," has a unique name, such as s850.mwc.edu or www.ibm.com or whitehouse.gov. The last block of letters explains the type of organization operating the computer: *edu* represents an educational institution, *com* represents a commercial business, and *gov* represents a government agency. For computers located outside of the United States, the last block of letters is the country code. For example, the *ca* in schoolnet.carleton.ca stands for *Canada.* The next block of letters (reading right to left) identifies the organization: Mary Washington College, or IBM corporation, or the White House. If there are additional blocks of letters, they identify the specific computer at the organization. What is the "host" name of the computer through which your class can access the Internet?

In the last lesson, we described *user-i.d.,* a person's "name" on the Internet. To send e-mail to someone, simply address it to their user i.d. @internet.host.name. For example, suppose a user whose i.d. is "Econ_Connect" can access the Internet through a computer called "swpco.com". Then Econ_Connect@swpco.com is the complete Internet address. (This is pronounced "Econ Connect at swpco dot com.")

Internet Application: Your teacher will assign one or more of the questions at the end of Chapter 2. Do the assignment and turn it in using e-mail instead of paper.

Internet Connection

Like mail sent through the regular postal service, e-mail doesn't always go through without a hitch. The most common problem occurs when e-mail is addressed incorrectly. Make sure you write the address in this format: *user-i.d.@internet.host.name.* Leave no spaces between the different components of the address. If there is a problem with delivery, e-mail will return to the sender. A later lesson will discuss how to find correct e-mail addresses. In many cases, the easiest solution is to ask the addressee.

some action. (Psychic income is also called *psychic utility*.) For example, volunteer work at a hospital may not pay anything, but those who do it receive psychic income, or the personal satisfaction or utility from doing such work.

In Figure 2-1, the 18-speed bike was the clear-cut first choice. Owning the bike might also hold some psychic utility. Perhaps it would give you status, peer acceptance, or the attention and admiration of your friends. Psychic utility is another criterion you may want to use to evaluate your alternatives.

If you choose the bike, your opportunity costs are the alternatives you have given up—the vacation, keyboard, and CD player. By using the decision-making model, you have chosen the alternative that will give the most satisfaction and have the lowest possible opportunity costs.

It is possible that prices of bikes may rise. You might find that you cannot buy an 18-speed bike for $350, so you may have to make a second choice. From the decision matrix, note that the CD player follows as a close second choice. Therefore, you may not suffer greatly if you settle for the CD player. Also, note that the vacation and the keyboard, while ranked lower than the bike or CD player, were almost equal choices. They scored only one point apart. If both the bike and the CD player became unavailable, you might have to carefully consider whether to select the vacation or the keyboard. At that point, you might even want to add more criteria to help you decide.

Econ & You

CAREERS IN YOUR ECONOMIC FUTURE

Many personal decisions will affect your own economic future. One of these is your career selection. Clearly, the level of education you obtain will influence your earning power. On average, college graduates earn twice as much each year as people who do not complete high school and about 1.7 times as much as those who stop going to school after graduating from high school.

In considering a career, some of the questions you need to think about include the following:

1. What do you do well?
2. What do you enjoy doing?
3. How much education is required?
4. How will economic trends affect your choices?
5. What careers will most likely have the greatest growth potential for you over your working life?

Your school counselors can probably help you identify answers to the first three questions in this list. Library research and your study of economics will help you with the last two. As you think about different jobs, be sure to include the idea of opportunity costs in your thinking. The decision-making process discussed in this chapter will help you with your career choices.

Divide the class into groups of five or six students. Assign each student responsibility for one of the following five steps in the decision-making process: defining the problem, listing the alternatives, listing the criteria, evaluating the alternatives, and choosing the best alternative. If applicable, assign the sixth student the task of creating the decision matrix. Allow students 20 to 30 minutes to fulfill their responsibilities and to complete a decision matrix. Then, as a class, have the groups compare their matrices.
Cooperative Learning

Econ & You

After students have read *Econ & You* in their textbook, have them answer the five questions on a separate sheet of paper. (You may wish to give students time to conduct research or to consult with family members for the answers.) Then, have students determine three to five careers or jobs that they think they are well-suited for based on the answers to the five questions. Tell students to write about why they chose the careers that they did.

Making Decisions Every Day

The decision-making process described here may seem very complicated. It seems like a lot of work just to make a choice. However, think about the allocation decisions you make every day. Over and over again, you make decisions concerning how to allocate your limited free time among a variety of activities, such as study, work, and leisure. You also decide how to spend your income and your energy. To make good choices, you must first define each individual problem.

In reality, the first few times you try the process, it may take some time. After a few times, however, you will get accustomed to using the five-step process, and things will move more quickly. In the first few attempts, it might be wise to write out a decision matrix like the one in Figure 2-1. After a few times, this should not be necessary. Just think through the process:

1. define the problem;
2. list the alternatives;
3. list the criteria;
4. evaluate the alternatives; and
5. choose the best alternative.

Remember, the utility received from a particular good, service, or action varies from person to person. The important point here is not how you *feel* about each choice. Instead it is important that you develop an organized, logical approach to making choices.

Assess

1. It helps minimize costs and maximize utility. **2-3**
2. Answers should reflect an understanding of decision-making steps and opportunity costs. **2-1, 2-2, 2-3**
3. Decision matrices should include two alternatives: criteria (such as time, cost, and comfort) and scores. A first choice should be identified clearly. **2-3**
4. Answers may include an understanding of the problem, appropriate criteria, and a clear choice. **2-3, 2-4**

Close

Tell students to imagine that the local PTO has donated $500 to your class to spend however it wants. On a large sheet of butcher paper, have the class work together to create a decision matrix to determine how to spend the money.

Checkpoint

Content Check

1. How can the five-step decision-making model result in greater satisfaction from personal decisions?
2. Give an example of individual choice and opportunity cost as they apply to you.
3. Construct and complete a decision matrix like the one in Figure 2-1 to rank the alternatives of driving to a city 500 miles away and flying to the same city. Select appropriate criteria.

What Do You Think Now?

Reread *What Do You Think?* in the Section Three Focus. Then answer the following questions:

4. How would you use the five-step decision-making process to choose between the party and ushering? What criteria would you use to evaluate the alternatives? What would be your choice?

Reteach

Have students interview someone who is in the process of making a decision. Have students find answers to the following questions: **What decision is being made? What are the alternatives? What are the criteria? How do the alternatives compare? What is the maximum utility of that choice?** Have students help the interviewee evaluate the alternatives. Then, have each student list the information in a graphic organizer. **2-3, 2-4**

Enrich

Ask students to interpret the following statement: **By *not* making a decision, you really *are* deciding not to decide.** Have students write their responses to this statement. **2-3**

Concepts in Brief

1. Economies must make choices because of scarcity. In a market economy, the economic questions of what, how, and for whom to produce are decided mostly in the marketplace by individual producers and consumers.
2. Self-interest guides individual choices in a market economy. Adam Smith, a Scottish economist, said that self-interest and individual choice would produce the greatest benefit for the individual and the whole economy.
3. Individual choice plays a major role in a market economy. Therefore, it is important to use a well-reasoned decision-making process. To make effective individual choices, five steps can be followed:
    1. define the problem;
    2. list the alternatives;
    3. list the criteria;
    4. evaluate the alternatives; and
    5. choose the best alternative.
4. Every decision results in an opportunity cost. Using the decision-making model in real life allows individuals to minimize opportunity costs. The more the decision-making model is used, the easier it is to make good decisions.

Economic Foundations

1. How are the economic questions of what to produce and how to produce decided in a market economy such as the United States?
2. What is the guiding force behind individual decisions in a market economy?
3. Why are individual decisions important in a market economy?
4. List the five steps in the decision-making model.
5. What two actions should be taken to clearly define a problem?
6. How should alternatives be chosen?
7. How should criteria be selected?
8. How should the criteria be used to evaluate the alternatives?
9. How can you get the most satisfaction from any personal decision you make?

Chapter Close

Your Economic Portfolio

As a class, discuss the importance of making sound, effective economic decisions. Then, ask students to consider three types of homes they would like to live in five years from now. On a sheet of paper, have each student list the economic incentive and psychic income of his or her choices, ranking each according to its utility. Then, have students draw a decision matrix, filling in their information for the five decision-making steps. Below the matrix, in one paragraph, have students explain which type of home they chose and how they made their decision. Review students' work and have them make any necessary corrections before filing the final draft in their portfolio.

You may wish to provide the following end-of-chapter materials:

- *Skills & Concepts* worksheet
- *Content Review Workbook*
- Chapter *Assessment*
- Chapter *MicroExam*

Economic Foundations

1. These questions are decided in a market economy mostly by individuals in the marketplace. (p. 31)
2. Self-interest (p. 32)
3. Because many economists believe that individuals choosing in their own self-interest do the greatest good for the society as a whole (pp. 32-33)
4. (1) Define the problem. (2) List the alternatives from which you must choose. (3) List the criteria by which you must evaluate the alternatives. (4) Evaluate the alternatives based on the criteria you have chosen. (5) Choose the alternative that best meets the criteria you have chosen. (p. 35)
5. To clearly define a problem, you should (1) objectively weigh each aspect of the problem in

(Continued)

Economic Foundations
(Continued)

regard to the role it plays and (2) focus your thought on the true issue. (pp. 36-37)

6. By listing a reasonably small number of realistic alternatives (p. 37)
7. Objectively and realistically (p. 38)
8. Create a decision matrix to rank the desirability of the alternatives. (p. 39)
9. By making it in a logical, organized, and effective way; the five-step decision model helps in this process. (p. 40)

Your Economic Vocabulary

1. **economic incentive**
2. **economic profit**
3. **alternative**
4. **utility**
5. **invisible hand**
6. **individual choice**
7. **util**
8. **psychic income**
9. **objectivity**
10. **criteria**
11. **decision matrix**
12. **market economy**
13. **model**

Thinking Critically About Economics

1. Answers will vary but should include the idea that self-interest is the guiding beneficial force in a market economy.
2. Answers will vary but students should understand that, if the government makes these decisions, there is less individual freedom of choice; it is preferable for individuals, acting through the market system, to decide what goods and services are to be produced.

(Continued)

Your Economic Vocabulary

Build your economic vocabulary by matching the following terms with their definitions.

alternative
criteria
decision matrix
economic incentive
economic profit
individual choice
invisible hand
market economy
model
objectivity
psychic income
util
utility

1. the increase in personal satisfaction that may result from some economic activity
2. the difference between the money you obtain from selling a product and the cost of producing the product
3. a possible course of action
4. the satisfaction one receives from the consumption, use, or ownership of a good or service
5. the incentive that guides individuals to choose in the best interest of society by pursuing their own self-interests
6. decisions made by people acting separately
7. the unit of measurement for utility
8. the nonmonetary reward we get from taking some action
9. ruling out aspects of a problem that seem important only because of your strong emotions about them
10. the characteristics of a group of alternatives that will be judged to make a choice
11. a table comparing possible decisions
12. an economy in which the economic questions are decided mostly by individuals in the marketplace
13. a simplified form of reality that shows the relationship between different factors

Thinking Critically About Economics

1. "Self-interest is selfish, greedy, and not in the best interest of our market economy." Do you agree or disagree with this statement? Why?
2. "In a modern society, the government should decide what to produce and how so that enough goods and services are produced to meet everyone's needs." Do you agree or disagree? Why?

3. Assume that you have just ended a dating relationship and now have six more hours of free time per week. You can allocate this time among studying, working, dating others, or spending time with your family. Use the five-step decision-making process to decide how you will spend your time. Select your own criteria and set up a decision matrix.

4. Which do you prefer: an economy based primarily on individual choice or one based on social choice? Why?

Economic Enrichment

In 1995, newspapers and television news broadcasts carried many stories of the continuing struggle between the People's Republic of China and the United States to settle the dispute over copyrights and patents on U.S. goods. The issue had a lot to do with how goods and services are produced in both countries and the incentive those countries provide to producers.

Review articles about this conflict from appropriate editions of *The Wall Street Journal* and other periodicals. Make a brief presentation to your class that answers the following questions: Why was the United States so interested in protecting copyrights and patents? What role do copyrights and patents play in providing incentive to producers?

Math and Economics

Many young people go to camp in the summer. The camp a person chooses depends on many criteria, some of which include the main focus of the camp, the length of the camp, the cost, whether it is a day camp or overnight camp, and the extra activities available at the camp.

Your grandparents have given you $750 to attend a computer camp this summer. Any money you do not spend on camp you get to put in your savings account. You are saving to buy a used car. You have the choice between three summer computer camps: one that teaches you how to produce multimedia reports (audio, video, print), one that teaches you how to navigate the Internet, and one that teaches you to use authoring software to create CD-ROM games. Information about each of these camps is summarized in the decision matrix on page 48.

1. Copy the decision matrix on a separate piece of paper. Based on your own evaluation of the criteria, assign a score to each of the alternatives in the decision matrix. The scores can range from 1 to 5, with 1 being undesirable and 5 being very desirable. Write the scores in the boxes in the bottom right corner of each box.

Thinking Critically About Economics (Continued)

3. Decision matrices will vary but should identify the specific criteria that students have chosen and the one alternative that they feel best meets these criteria.
4. Answers will vary depending upon students' personal evaluations of social and individual choices. Either answer is correct, but should be supported by an explanation of the costs and benefits of each choice.

Economic Enrichment

Answers will vary but should be supported by research and may include that the sale of U.S.-made products helps the United States maintain its status as a world trade leader. If copyrights and patents were no longer valid, anyone could produce the goods and the resulting competition would hurt U.S. producers. When a copyrighted or patented product succeeds, its producers earn money and have an incentive to produce more, which strengthens the U.S. economy.

Math and Economics

1. Individual scores for each criterion should reflect students' personal preferences.
2. Students' circled choices will vary but should reflect the highest overall score of the three alternatives.
3. Rankings will vary, but each student's first choice should be the alternative with the highest overall score, the second choice should be the alternative with the next-highest score, and the third choice should be the lowest scoring alternative.

Writing About Economics

Information in the posters will vary, but each poster should include a chart listing several different milk prices from different types of retailers; the highest and lowest milk prices should be clearly identified; and the price differences should be explained as they relate to each store's location and the specific opportunity costs and benefits consumers realize by purchasing their milk there.

Criteria	Alternatives: Multimedia Reports	Navigating the Internet	Authoring CD-ROM Games
Cost	$650	$600	$750
Day Camp or Overnight	Overnight	Overnight	Day
Length of Camp	7 Days	7 Days	5 Days
Extra Activities Available	Swimming, boating, tennis, horseback riding	Swimming, tennis, hiking trails	None
Total Score			
Ranking of Alternatives			

2. Add the scores for each camp and complete the Total Score row in the decision matrix. Circle your first choice, the camp with the highest total score.

3. Rank the alternatives, with 1 being your first choice, in the Ranking of Alternatives row in the decision matrix.

Writing About Economics

Observe and record the prices for a half gallon of 2 percent milk at ten different locations in your town. Be sure to include grocery stores, gasoline and convenience stores, milk retailers, and discount grocery outlets.

Summarize your findings in a table that includes the price, location, and type of store. Identify the highest and lowest price. Then prepare a poster that includes your table and a written explanation of the price differences. Consider the following when preparing your explanation: the role of location in setting milk prices and the impact of opportunity costs on purchasers' decisions about where to buy milk.

The Personal Consumption Pie

A useful thing to know about the economy is how people spend their money. Do they spend it on durable goods, such as cars and household furniture? Do they spend it on nondurable goods, such as clothing and gasoline? Or, do they spend it on services, such as housing and medical care? The proportion spent in each of these areas has an impact on what type of jobs are created and what level of wages are earned by people performing those jobs.

The accompanying table shows data on personal consumption expenditures for the United States broken down into three categories: durable goods, nondurable goods, and services.

Total Personal Consumption Expenditures for Durable Goods, Nondurable Goods, and Services (1990–1994)

Year	Total Personal Consumption Expenditures (in billions)	Durable Goods (in billions)	Nondurable Goods (in billions)	Services (in billions)
1990	$3,265.90	$433.20	$1,057.50	$1,775.20
1991	3,265.40	427.70	1,040.40	1,797.30
1992	3,403.40	468.80	1,074.20	1,860.40
1993	3,506.20	510.80	1,088.00	1,907.40
1994	3,625.20	552.40	1,121.10	1,951.70

Although tables are very useful, it is a bit difficult to really see from the table what relationship there might be between the numbers. Another way to look at this information is in a pie chart. The accompanying pie chart presents the same data on total personal consumption expenditures for 1994 as does the table but in a different format. The pie chart shows visually how total personal consumption, on average, is divided among the categories of durable goods, nondurable goods, and services. It is clear from the pie chart that services accounted for the greatest percentage of total personal consumption. Look for pie charts as you read the newspaper or magazines—they can make numbers and their relationships easier to understand.

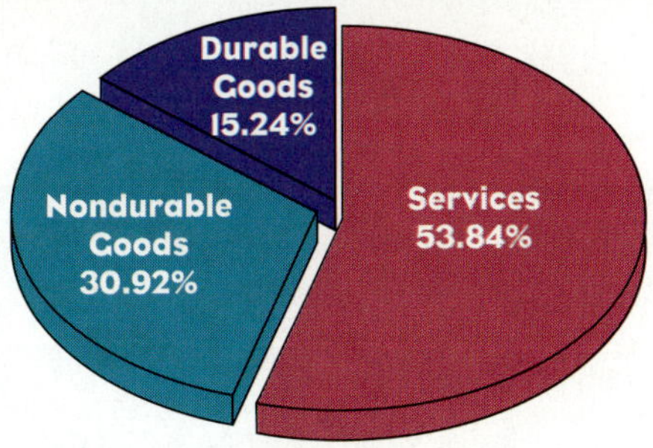

Remind students that, in a market economy, the economic questions of what to produce, how to produce, and for whom to produce are answered by individual consumers who decide independently how to spend their dollars. Have students look at the data on this page on personal consumption expenditures for the United States and draw conclusions about why services ranked first, nondurable goods were second, and durable goods placed third. (Answers may include that services such as housing and medical care are really nondiscretionary expenditures that take a regular, big bite out of the average American's paycheck. Nondurable goods have a built-in obsolescence that require frequent repurchasing, and durable goods, although often big-ticket items, are not purchased as frequently so the cost doesn't add up as much over time.) Have students imagine that they are recent high school graduates who have been offered a salary of $22,000 per year at their first job. Using conservative figures reflective of the costs in your area of the country, have students create personal consumption expenditures pie charts that divide their salary into the three categories. Ask students to identify the individual items that (will) make up the subtotals for their "pies."

Throughout this program, students will have frequent opportunities to use technology to enhance their study of economics. These opportunities are indicated by the symbol in your *Teacher's Edition*. As appropriate for and available to your students in and outside of class, encourage students' use of the computer throughout this course to prepare reports, complete projects, make calculations, and graphically illustrate data.

(Continued at left)

(Continued)

Have students use spreadsheet software with charting capabilities to subtotal and total the information in the chart on this page. Then, have students create a pie chart to show the percentages of expenditures for durable goods, nondurable goods, and services for each year.

Chapter 3 Making Social Decisions

Chapter Theme

In social economies, governments decide what, how, and for whom to produce. In market economies such as the United States, most economic decisions are based on individual choice. Some important decisions, however, are based on social choice; therefore, it is important to elect to office those decision makers who reflect your views on the issues.

Section	Special Features
Social Choice	Multicultural Highlights Global Economy Economic Spotlight
Market Economies Use Social Choice	Eye on Market News Economic Dilemma Internet Connection
Effective Social Decisions	Economic Talk Economics & Your Community Media Link Perspectives: Thinking Like an Elected School Board Member Econ & You

Video Activity

Chapter 3, Workfare

Search Chapter 3, Play to 4

Have students discuss the short-range and long-range effects of the "workfare" program on the individuals involved and on society in general. Then, divide the class in half and have each group develop an alternative plan to workfare and the current welfare system. Have the two groups present their ideas to the class, analyzing the social costs and benefits of each plan.

	Print Resources	Media Resources	Assessment
	Effective Teaching Model Lesson Plans *Skills & Concepts* worksheet *Problem Solving* worksheet *Casebook* *Economic Measurement Workbook* *Content Review Workbook* *Spanish Resources*	VHS CD-ROM Videodisc *Arctic Express* *Interactive* ECONOMICS Template software	*Your Economic Portfolio* Chapter *Assessment* Chapter *MicroExam*

Special Learners	Print Resources	Media Resources	Assessment
		Computer Overhead	*Checkpoint* Section 1 Quiz
Limited English Proficiency Auditory Activity	*Teacher's Connection to the Internet* *Reteach* worksheet *Enrich* worksheet	Overhead Computer Video Audio	*Checkpoint* Section 2 Quiz
Visual Activity Cooperative Learning Activity Kinesthetic Activity	*Life Skills* worksheet	Overhead and *Transparency 3-1* Computer	*Checkpoint* Section 3 Quiz

Careers Activity

One essential job provided by our tax dollars is that of firefighter. Firefighters help protect our lives and property from the hazards of fire. They contain and extinguish fires, rescue people trapped or injured by fire or smoke, inspect buildings for unsafe conditions, and educate the public about fire safety.

Beginning firefighters must be 21 to 31 years old and in excellent physical condition. Most candidates are required to have a high school diploma, and all must complete several weeks of intensive training and testing, including a rigid physical performance test. Many firefighters work as volunteers; however, a full-time, career firefighter can earn from $20,000 to $35,000.

Since fire departments are funded with tax dollars, politicians often warn that fire protection will suffer if taxes are not raised. Have students list the disadvantages of having too few firefighters to serve a community. Then, for each problem, have them describe a possible solution that does not involve spending more tax dollars.

CHAPTER 3

Teaching Materials

Program Resources

- Student text
- *Effective Teaching Model Lesson Plans*
- *Overhead Transparency 3-1*
- *Life Skills* worksheet
- *Problem Solving* worksheet
- *Reteach* worksheet
- *Enrich* worksheet
- *Skills & Concepts* worksheet
- *Casebook*
- *Economic Measurement Workbook*
- *Content Review Workbook*
- *Spanish Resources*
- Video package
- *Teacher's Connection to the Internet*
- *Arctic Express*
- *Interactive ECONOMICS*
- *Template software*

Assessment

- Section Quizzes
- Chapter *Assessment*
- Chapter *MicroExam*

Overview

Section One
Social Choice

Section Two
Market Economies Use Social Choice

Section Three
Effective Social Decisions

Teacher to Teacher

To help students better understand socialist philosophy, distribute copies of short passages from *The Communist Manifesto* by Karl Marx to small groups of students. Have one student in each group read aloud a passage. Ask students to analyze how Marx advocates socialism through his writing. Then, as a whole class, have students share their analyses with the other groups.

Dennis Dowling
Lakota High School
West Chester, OH

Making Social Decisions

Learning Objectives

3-1
Explain how the three basic economic questions are answered in a social economy.

3-2
Discuss the role of personal incentives under social choice.

3-3
Describe the conditions under which social choice is preferable to individual choice.

3-4
Apply the five-step decision-making model to social decisions.

Outside Resources

- Marx, Karl, *The Communist Manifesto* (New York: Appleton Century-Crofts, 1955).
- Blank overhead transparencies
- Newspaper or magazine articles about health care
- Copies of the Bill of Rights
- Camcorder and VCR or cassette recorder
- Butcher paper
- Art supplies or old magazines
- Computer
- Integrated software (word processing, desktop publishing)
- Poster board

Vocabulary

social economy, p. 52
social choice, p. 55
equity, p. 55
public goods, p. 57
economies of scale, p. 57
public goods rationale, p. 58
free rider, p. 60
distribution effect, p. 62
social goals, p. 63
social costs, p. 63
freedom of choice, p. 63
social benefits, p. 63

Focus

Before students enter the classroom, write the following on scraps of paper: **high school students, police officers, city council, senior citizens, parents,** and **downtown business owners.** Fold the scraps of paper and place them in a bag. As students enter the classroom, form six groups. Tell students to imagine that the city is going to play music in the downtown shopping district. Have each group choose one of the scraps of paper from the bag and then decide what type of music that identified group would prefer. Allow a few minutes for group discussion.

Have each group of students state whose interests it represents and then describe what type of music it selected. After all groups have reported their selections, ask the following questions: **Do you think you faithfully represented the tastes of the group you selected? Can you really know what a certain group of people will like and not like? Do you think you can truly represent someone else's interests?** Explain to students that this type of decision making is much like that performed by a central planning committee that makes decisions for the entire country in a **social economy.**

FOCUS

Section One
Social Choice

What Do You Think?

In social economies, what, how, and for whom goods are produced is decided by a central planning committee. Who makes up that committee bears directly on the decisions made. If the committee were made up of high school students, would there be more classical music concerts offered to the public or more rock and rap concerts? If the committee were made up of senior citizens, how would the mix of goods and services produced differ? Why? Do you think it is possible for a small group of people to accurately reflect the diverse preferences of an entire population? Who would you like to choose what goods are available for you: your grandmother or your classmates? Would it make any difference?

Terms to Know

social economy
social choice
equity

What's Ahead?

In social economies, governments make the decisions about what, how, and for whom to produce. Social economies use the social choice process to satisfy most wants and needs with public goods. Karl Marx had a strong influence on the development of socialist ideas.

ECONOMIC QUESTIONS IN SOCIAL ECONOMIES

Some economies in the world operate through mostly *social* decision making. An economy in which the major economic questions of what, how, and for whom to produce are determined by a government representing the interests of the entire society is called a ***social economy.*** A social economy is sometimes called a *command economy.*

social economy an economy in which the major economic questions are determined by a government representing the interests of the entire society

What to Produce?

The question of what to produce with a nation's given stock of resources presents an interesting problem of economic choice. While market economies operate mostly through individual choice, social economies use committees of experts who pool their knowledge.

Multicultural *Highlights*

Self-proclaimed "Ex-hippies" Ben Cohen and Jerry Greenfield, of Ben & Jerry's Homemade Inc., held a "Find-a-CEO" (chief executive officer) contest for their company. All entrants had to write an essay stating why they wanted to be the company's CEO. Their pick, Robert Holland Jr., never officially entered the contest but submitted a poem, "Time, Values and Ice Cream," after he was selected. Holland, possibly the most visible African-American CEO in the United States, vowed to uphold the company's funky yet socially responsible image. Have students write a description of whom they would have entered in the contest and why.

These central planning committees work out elaborate plans about what the economy will produce. Decisions about what goods and services will be produced are based on what the central planning committee thinks will benefit the whole society. Individuals do not directly make these decisions. Rather, the goods and services are produced by order of the planning committee and appear in the marketplace when completed. The varieties and choices of goods and services in the market are limited to what the central planning committee decides will benefit the whole society. The goods and services produced do not have to pass the difficult test of individual market choice. If they did, many might not survive.

This lack of individual choice in a social economy greatly affects the consumer and the producer. When only one kind of product is made to fill a given need, the consumer still must make a choice; however, the choice is very limited. The consumer can either buy the available product or completely do without it. Producers do not have profit incentives, but it is extremely difficult for their products to fail in the marketplace since there are few competing goods.

Teach

Explain to students that in a **social economy,** or command economy, the government makes decisions about what, how, and for whom to produce. What to produce is based on social choice, not individual choice. How to produce is determined by government decree and is usually regulated by a quota. For whom to produce is based on **equity,** or making sure that all members of society get their fair share. Discuss Karl Marx's role as the "Father of Communism" and his reasons for believing that the State can better control the factors of production than can business owners.

Global Economy

Social Decisions vs Free Trade

International trade is the life blood of the global economy. Two people decide to engage in trade for the simple reason that each has what the other wants at a price they are both willing to pay. Both parties are better off because of the exchange, or they would not continue to trade. However, social decisions sometimes interfere with the individual decisions of free trade. For example, governments place tariffs (taxes) on international trade to protect domestic industries or to raise revenue for their own benefit. Governments also set quotas (limits) on how much of a certain good can be traded across borders.

These social decisions may be made with good intentions, but they always reduce the amount of trade that takes place. Since trade benefits both trading partners, both trading parties are worse off when tariffs and quotas are imposed. The social decision may well be in the best interest of the whole country, but they are not in the best interest of the individual trading parties.

In times of war or as a result of specific foreign policy, trade with a given country or in specific goods may be prohibited entirely. In 1992, the United Nations prohibited Iraq from selling oil on the world market as a punishment for the Gulf War. This social decision may have been in the best interest of preserving world peace in the future, but it injured not only Iraq but all its trading partners in the process. In the global economy, as in the U.S. economy, when sweeping social decisions are made, the economic impact is felt by individuals.

Global Economy

Brainstorm with students products they use that are imported (foreign cars, computers, TVs, VCRs, and so on). Ask students if they remember paying the tariff on the imported products they bought. Then, ask if they remember paying the sales tax. Explain the difference between a direct tax (such as sales tax) and an indirect tax (such as a tariff). Explain that students did pay a tariff, but it was indirect, or hidden, by being built into the price. Have students write an explanation of which type of tax they prefer and why.

Apply

On the chalkboard or an overhead transparency, make a chart with four columns. Leave the first column blank and enter the following headings above the next three columns: **What to Produce, How to Produce,** and **For Whom to Produce.** Brainstorm with the class how a social economy answers these three economic questions. Write students' responses in the appropriate columns of the chart. Have students copy the completed chart into their notebooks.

Guided Practice

	What to Produce	How to Produce	For Whom to Produce

Economic Spotlight

CAN A FOR-PROFIT COMPANY HAVE A HEART?

What do Princess Di and Oprah Winfrey have in common? They both wear RYKÄ shoes, made specifically for women. Thanks to Sheri Poe, women can now find shoes that really fit their feet. Poe, founder, president, and CEO of RYKÄ, came up with the idea for her product when she couldn't find an athletic shoe that fit her properly. At the time, most women's athletic shoes were only scaled-down versions of men's shoes, so the entrepreneur decided to create a shoe made *for women, by women*.

When Poe tried to find financing to start her athletic shoe company, bankers laughed at her idea. Her small company would be up against the heavy-hitting footwear giants Nike and Reebok, among others. Finally, Poe was given a chance by the Denver-based investment firm R. B. Marich; the "B" in R. B. stood for *Betty,* an aerobics enthusiast who convinced the male members in the firm that there was, indeed, a market for women's athletic shoes. With $25,000 in bank loans and $50,000 from her family, Poe at the age of 34 started RYKÄ in her kitchen in 1987.

Since then, the company has grown into a publicly held, multimillion dollar corporation with distributorships in more than 15 countries. But, even with this phenomenal growth, RYKÄ is a model of a profitable yet socially responsible corporation. Five years after she started RYKÄ, Poe examined her past and found herself reconsidering her silence about being raped when a college student. She wanted to help other women avoid the pain that she experienced as a rape survivor. She decided to give her company a soul and a conscience. In 1992, Poe founded the RYKÄ ROSE (Restore One's Self-Esteem) Foundation, a charitable, nonprofit foundation separate from her shoe company.

RYKÄ ROSE funds programs that battle violence against women. Since RYKÄ was not yet profitable in 1992, Poe pledged $250,000 of her own money to start the foundation, and her principal retail partner, Lady Footlocker, donated additional funding. Now, every time a consumer purchases a pair of RYKÄ shoes at an average retail price of $40 to $75, RYKÄ donates 7 percent of the profits to the RYKÄ ROSE Foundation. According to Poe, "I believe in an ethical *and* a financial bottom line."

Economic Spotlight

After students have read *Economic Spotlight,* ask them to brainstorm a list of companies that are socially responsible (Body Shop, Patagonia, Mrs. Fields Cookies, and so on). Discuss what social values each company upholds (Body Shop: environment, self-sufficiency; Patagonia: environment; Mrs. Fields: sharing with the less fortunate). Discuss how social responsibility might affect a company's profitability (expensive, but might actually help business because of attractiveness to consumers).

The main idea in social economies is that the government, rather than individuals, decides what to produce. This decision-making structure implies that individuals may not be capable of choosing for themselves as well as their government can. ***Social choice,*** then, is decision making by government in the interest of society.

social choice
decision making by government in the interest of society

How to Produce?

The question of how to produce is decided in social economies primarily by government decree. Central planning authorities decide which producers will produce what goods and services. Quantities of resources are allocated to those producers only. Usually, output quotas are set, but producers do not risk market failure since there are few competing goods. Of course, if resources are used wastefully, there is concern. But, with government support, producers cannot incur losses and are not in danger of going out of business.

In a social economy, there is little difference in reward to the producer who is very efficient and to the producer who is only moderately efficient. Profits are not a major goal and self-interest is not a socially acceptable incentive. Therefore, there is no profit incentive. Producers decide how resources are to be used by what is allocated to them, not by what individuals will choose to buy in the marketplace. Producers do not have an extremely accurate resource price system to guide their choices.

For Whom to Produce?

The question of how goods are distributed in a social economy is made primarily in an effort to provide equity. ***Equity*** means dealing fairly and equally with all concerned. All members of the society are supposed to be given a fair share of the fruits of the entire economy's labor. Equity, however, is a difficult objective. What you think is fair or equitable probably is different from what your neighbor thinks is equitable. There are probably as many different opinions about what is equitable in any society as there are citizens.

equity
dealing fairly and equally with all concerned

Social economies try to provide equitable goods and services. This, however, means that individuals do not have the right to choose among many significantly different goods and services. If everyone gets an equitable house, for instance, there certainly cannot be any significant differences among houses. You can choose any house you want, but they all may be alike.

Social Decision Making and Karl Marx

Throughout history, many economists and philosophers have strongly advocated socialism and social decision making. Karl Marx is probably the best known. He certainly had the most influence on the development of socialist ideals.

Marx was born in 1818 and attended the Universities of Bonn and Berlin. He received a doctoral degree from the University of Jena in 1841 and wrote widely about his views on social decision making. Marx believed that the State (entire society) should own the factors of production and make decisions about the production and distribution of wealth. He openly advocated violent revolution by the working class (proletariat) to overthrow the capitalist ruling class (bourgeoisie).

Marx saw communism as a natural evolution of capitalism. He felt that capitalism and individual decision making would lead to the development

Explain to students that the answers to the three economic questions in the chart are the *benefits* of a social economy. Have students write **Benefits** in column one beside the answers they wrote earlier. Then, have them draw a line beneath all the answers and write **Costs** in column one below that line. Have students complete their chart by filling in the costs (lack of individual choice, limited kinds of products, no profit incentives, quotas, little reward for efficient production, and so on).
Independent Practice

Benefits	What to Produce	How to Produce	For Whom to Produce
Costs			

of a few very wealthy and all-controlling people who would produce nothing. They would live on the labors of the working class. The evolution of a nonproductive bourgeoisie would lead to violent revolution. Then the power and ownership of the society would revert to the common people.

Marx envisioned a classless society of equals. In this society, all people would contribute to the society according to their ability and take from the society according to their needs. He wrote that once the bourgeoisie was overthrown, all power would be in the hands of the State. The State would then gradually distribute power to the people, and the population would make cooperative decisions in the best interest of society.

Marx's most famous writings were *The Communist Manifesto,* written with Friedrich Engels in 1848, and *Das Kapital,* part of which was published in 1867. These books laid much of the groundwork for socialist philosophy.

Checkpoint

Content Check

1. How does a social economy decide what, how, and for whom to produce?
2. What was Karl Marx's vision of how economies would evolve over time?

What Do You Think Now?

Reread *What Do You Think?* in the Section One Focus. Then answer the following questions:

3. What changes would you propose if you were on the central planning committee that makes decisions for your school about how classes are "produced"?
4. What changes would you propose if you were on the central planning committee that made decisions for your city or town about what, how, and for whom community services are produced?

Assess

1. Central planning committees and government decree determine what, how, and for whom to produce. The decisions are made based on what will benefit the whole society. **3-1, 3-2**
2. A working-class revolution would overthrow capitalism, leading to socialism and, eventually, communism. **3-1**
3. Answers should reflect an understanding of limited resources (teachers, classrooms, time schedules, course requirements) and unlimited needs and wants. **3-1, 3-2**
4. Answers should reflect an understanding of the problems of having a limited resource (money) and unlimited needs and wants from citizens. **3-1, 3-2**

Close

Divide the class into three groups. Assign each group one of the three economic questions. Then, assign one social choice, such as schooling, the military, or housing, to each group. Have each group describe to the class how its social choice would be answered in a social economy.

Reteach

Have students write a brief description of how a social economy answers the three basic economic questions. Have them write one paragraph for each of the three questions. **3-1**

Enrich

Discuss the incentives and disincentives for producers in a social economy. Then, have students write one paragraph about the incentives, one paragraph about the disincentives, and one paragraph explaining whether they would like to own a business in a social economy. **3-2**

FOCUS

Section Two

Market Economies Use Social Choice

What Do You Think?

Ask your classmates if they watch public television. Now ask if they send donations to public television stations. The number of watchers will probably be larger than the number of contributors. How many people use public parks for ball games and other recreation in other towns? What causes people to choose to use free services without helping to support them? How do we, as a society, deal with this issue?

What's Ahead?

Market economies make some important decisions based on social choice. Public goods that the government provides in a market economy are cheaper due to economies of scale and the public goods rationale. Your views about these social choices are represented by your votes.

Terms to Know

public goods

economies of scale

public goods rationale

free rider

SOCIAL CHOICE IN MARKET ECONOMIES

In market economies such as the United States, most economic decisions are based on individual choice in the marketplace. It is important to note, however, that a number of important decisions are also based on social choice.

The Government Provides Public Goods

As a society, we choose to provide public goods. ***Public goods*** are goods and services available to the whole society. Roads, schools, national defense, and police and fire protection are examples of public goods.

public goods
goods and services available to the whole society

Economies of Scale. There are several important reasons that governments provide public goods. One reason, however, is clearly more valid than the rest. Governments provide public goods because sometimes it is cheaper due to economies of scale. ***Economies of scale*** is the concept that some economic activities become more efficient when done on a large scale. Many people can enjoy a large public park at a lower cost per person than if individuals tried to provide their own parks, for example.

economies of scale
the concept that some economic activities become more efficient when done on a large scale

EyeOnMarketNews

Pair students with a limited command of English with others who have stronger English skills. Have students clip from newspapers or magazines articles about different aspects of health care. Then, have them classify each article: provided more efficiently on a large scale; provided more efficiently by the government; provided more efficiently on a small scale; or provided more efficiently by private businesses. Post articles in their appropriate categories on a bulletin board entitled **To Your Health: A Public or Private Good?**

Limited English Proficiency

Focus

Write the following question on the chalkboard and have students jot down on a sheet of paper as many answers as they can: **What government-provided goods and services do you use every day but don't pay for as you use them?** (Roads, schooling, parks, and so on)

As a whole-class activity, discuss students' answers. Write their answers on the chalkboard or an overhead transparency. Explain to students that the examples they listed are **public goods** and services. In our market economy, we have made a social choice to provide these goods and services to everyone in our society.

Teach

Explain to students that, even in market economies, where most economic decisions are based on individual choice, a whole society may choose to provide **public goods** such as roads, schools, and police protection. Governments in a market economy provide public goods for two main reasons: **economies of scale** and the **public goods rationale.** Explain that, in order to minimize **free riders,** a market economy must back social choice with the power of laws made by government officials elected by individual citizens to be their representatives.

Apply

Draw the following graphic organizer on the chalkboard or on an overhead transparency.

Brainstorm with students examples of the public goods provided by the government under each rationale. (Some goods could fall into both categories.) Write their examples on the spokes.
Guided Practice

public goods rationale
the argument that some public goods can be produced more efficiently by the government

Public Goods Rationale. Even Adam Smith agreed that government could provide some public goods more efficiently than could individuals. In economics, this is called the public goods rationale (reason) for social choice. The ***public goods rationale*** is the argument that some public goods can be produced more efficiently by the government. Consider a public road. Everyone who uses the road benefits from it. Each individual pays for only a very small part of the total cost of the road. If each of us had to buy or build a road to wherever we wanted to go, no one could afford to travel by road. By joining together, we can realize an economy of scale by spreading the cost of creating the road over everyone in the society.

The public goods rationale can be applied to police protection or any other public good. For instance, suppose you need a police officer to guard your home from burglars. You could hire a guard to walk around outside your house all day. This would be expensive, however. The mere presence of

Economic Dilemma

WELFARE REFORM

Welfare reform has been a major political issue since the 1980s. Critics contend that huge amounts of federal money are being spent on welfare programs and that the programs themselves take away incentives for people to work and earn their own livelihood. In most welfare programs, recipients are not allowed to work and receive welfare payments at the same time. The government's social choice, in an effort to help welfare recipients, overrode the individual choices recipients might have made to work on their own if they had the opportunity.

Welfare reformers propose that welfare payments be reduced and that recipients without small children be required to work at public service jobs in exchange for their benefits. It is argued that these reforms would create stronger incentives for recipients to find full-time work in the private sector and get off of welfare programs. The dilemma is that some welfare recipients have few job skills, making them unqualified for the required work.

There are many economic dilemmas involving conflict between social choices and individual choices. Most social choices prohibit some individual actions in the belief that society is being protected from the potential of individual harm. For example, while speed limits make driving safer for everyone, they deny the possible thrill of high-speed driving to those who might enjoy it. Smoking is prohibited in many public places in an effort to protect society from secondhand smoke. However, such laws deny the pleasure of smoking to individuals who might enjoy it enough to knowingly endanger their health by doing so. When society makes value judgments for individuals, such as in the case of welfare reform, economic dilemmas are likely to be present.

Economic Dilemma

Discuss with students the economic dilemma of social choices that inhibit individual choices but are enacted to protect individuals from harm. Brainstorm examples, such as seat-belt laws and gun-control laws. Relate the discussion to different interpretations of the freedoms in the Bill of Rights. (You may wish to bring to class copies of the Bill of Rights.) Divide the class into two groups with one group defending personal freedoms over social protection and the other group defending the freedoms of society as a whole.

the officer would probably frighten burglars away from your home and your neighbor's home. The officer might even be protecting the whole block at your expense. Unfortunately, you would be paying the bill individually. How could this situation be improved? You and your neighbor could split the bill. You might offer the police officer's services to everyone in the neighborhood if they would share the cost. One officer could patrol 50 homes and each home owner could pay 1/50 of the expense. All would share in the benefit, and the cost to each individual would be much less. Services such as these are provided more efficiently by a group or society than by an individual.

Internet Connection

PUTTING GOVERNMENT ONLINE

The government is a major contributor to the information superhighway. By making it easier for the government to give information to and receive information from citizens, the Internet may actually enhance social decision making. Many U.S. government agencies—the Commerce Department, the Extension Service of the Agriculture Department, NASA, the National Archives, the U.S. Geological Survey—are making their reports and a variety of statistical information available online.

All U.S. government documents will be published electronically. The current U.S. budget and the latest U.S. census already are obtainable online. The Declaration of Independence, the U.S. Constitution, bills in Congress, committee reports, and the Congressional Record also are available. Even the White House has an Internet site. You can obtain copies of the President's speeches and other press releases.

Let's look at how e-mail has the potential to make government more accessible and responsive to the people. More and more government officials are reachable via e-mail. President@whitehouse.gov and vice.president@whitehouse.gov are e-mail addresses for the president and vice president.

Many senators and members of Congress have e-mail addresses. While many people are reluctant to call or write a letter to a government official, they are willing to communicate via e-mail, because it is so easy to use.

Internet/Economics Application: Effective representative government requires that you inform your elected officials of your views on important issues. Who represents your district in the U.S. House of Representatives? Send e-mail to congress@hr.house.gov with no message to get a list of representatives and their e-mail addresses. If your representative has an e-mail address, send a message letting him or her know what you think is the nation's most pressing economic problem right now. If your representative has no e-mail address, send your message to the President.

Divide the class into six groups. Write each of the following on a slip of paper and distribute one slip to each group: **taxes, national defense, schools, money system, roads,** and **police and fire protection.** Have the groups decide which rationale, economies of scale or the public goods rationale, allows the government to provide each public good. Then, have each group decide whether they think the government should continue to provide each public good. If not, have group members describe who could better provide the public good and how. If so, have them explain how the government could better provide the public good. Also, have students describe how they would minimize free riders. Have students record their recommendations on videotape or audio tape. As a class, play all the groups' tapes and compare the recommendations.

Independent Practice

Internet Connection

You may wish to point out to students that sending a blank e-mail message to **congress@hr.house.gov** will elicit the current list of congressional e-mail addresses. There is no publicly available list of Senate e-mail addresses. E-mail sent to **president@whitehouse.gov** is read by a member of the White House staff, who will return a generic acknowledgment. Sending e-mail to a member of Congress is more likely to result in a real response—but that depends on the member.

The Free Rider Problem

Suppose a society was going to build an army to protect itself. If funding for the army were left to individual choice, there would be a problem. Even if most individuals banded together to pay for the army, some persons would not agree to pay. A person who benefits from a public good without sharing its cost is called a ***free rider.***

free rider
a person who benefits from a public good without sharing its cost

It would be impossible to protect those who did pay without also protecting the free riders. In order to eliminate free riders, it is necessary to back social choice with the power of law. Eliminating free riders is also efficient in spreading the cost of the public good over the whole society.

Social Choice in Representative Government

Now that you know why social decisions are made in market economies, let's look at how your individual view is reflected in the government's social choices. Representative government implies that individual citizens, through their votes, elect government officials. These officials are expected to make social choices for the voters they represent, their constituents. Therefore, you should vote for the candidates who most closely represent your views. If your elected officials choose differently from how you would have, you have the right to vote for other candidates.

Unfortunately, representative government, just like social choice, reduces the number of alternatives you have to choose from. A candidate must vote for or against an issue. You must choose with your vote among two or three candidates. There is little chance that any candidate would vote just as you would on every social choice.

Checkpoint

Content Check

1. Why do governments in market economies provide public goods?
2. What is the public goods rationale?
3. What is the free rider problem and how can it be minimized?

What Do You Think Now?

Reread *What Do You Think?* in the Section Two Focus. Then answer the following questions:

4. Are those who watch public television without financially supporting it free riders? How do public television stations deal with this issue?
5. Describe a situation in your school where there is a problem with free riders. How can this situation be minimized?
6. Is it possible that people who are free riders in one situation provide more than their share of support in another situation? Give an example.

Assess

1. Because of economies of scale and the public goods rationale **3-3**
2. Some goods are produced more efficiently by the government. **3-3**
3. Some benefit without sharing cost; with the power of law **3-3**
4. Yes. Answers should reflect an understanding of how public television stations raise funds, such as through mail campaigns, televised auctions, and telethons. **3-3**
5. Answers may include not helping to keep a clean campus and not working on committees. Answers should reflect methods of making sure all students share responsibilities. **3-3**
6. Answers should include that, yes, it is possible because some people may contribute substantially to causes that they are enthusiastic about. **3-3**

Close

On the chalkboard or an overhead transparency, have students create a chart listing the costs and benefits of public goods that are justified by economies of scale and the public goods rationale.

Reteach

Pair students who understand economies of scale and the public goods rationale with those who do not. Have students imagine that they are elected officials who must vote on whether to spend more money to hire more local police officers. Have each pair write a speech relating its position to economies of scale and the public goods rationale. Have the student who understands the concepts present the speech to the other student. Then, have the other student present the speech to the class. **3-3**

Enrich

Have students write a position paper debating the following basic principle of economics: "There is no such thing as a free lunch." **3-3**

Section Three
Effective Social Decisions

What Do You Think?

Winton Creek has new legislation that calls for waste materials to be sorted into recyclables, yard waste, and trash. City residents can recycle as much material as they want at no charge. Each home is allowed only one can of trash per week and each additional can costs $1 for pickup. Yard waste must be placed in a clearly marked container and pickup costs $0.75. Payment for yard waste and extra trash pickup is made by purchasing stickers and attaching them to containers. Some people are complaining that the system is not fair: They do all the work of sorting and recycling and the city gets all the money. Do you think the system is fair?

What's Ahead?

Social decisions impact many people and should be made very carefully. Decision makers can improve the quality of the choices they make by using the five-step decision-making model. You can use the decision-making process to clarify your position on social issues and communicate the reasons for your social choices.

Terms to Know

distribution effect
social goals
social costs
freedom of choice
social benefits

Focus

Write the following scenario on the chalkboard or an overhead transparency for students to answer on paper as they enter class: **Your city's garbage dump is filling up quickly with local residents' trash. Much of the waste is recyclable, but most people don't take time to sort their garbage. How would you solve this problem?**

Brainstorm ways in which this problem can be resolved. Discuss the costs and benefits of each decision. Ask students to describe the decision-making process they used to solve this problem.

MAKING EFFECTIVE SOCIAL CHOICES

Representative government concentrates the power to make social decisions in the hands of a very few people. The choices made by a few public officials affect the lives of everyone in a society and so should be made very carefully. It is important to clarify the benefits and the costs of each choice.

Let's look at an example of a social decision at school. Assume that enrollment at your school has increased during the last five years. The parking lot is not big enough to hold

EconomicTalk

Using the vocabulary words from all three sections of this chapter, have students describe in writing how social decisions are made in a social economy and in a market economy. Have students emphasize the vocabulary words used in their explanations by underlining them or by making them appear in boldface type.

Teach

Remind students of the five-step decision-making model they used in Chapter 2 for making personal decisions. Tell students that this model can also be used to make social decisions. Explain that all choices require the allocation of resources, and social decisions often create a **distribution effect.** With social decisions, laws allocate the power to choose—which sometimes takes away individual choice. Social decisions must take into account **social goals,** which include equality, justice, freedom, efficiency, and **freedom of choice.** People who make social decisions also must consider **social benefits** and **social costs,** taking care to choose the alternative that provides the greatest good for the greatest number of people. Explain that once a social decision is made, it must be communicated clearly to all constituents.

the cars of all the students who drive to school. Students have been permitted to park on nearby streets once the lot is full. However, residents of the neighborhood complained. The police chief has notified the school that student cars parked on residential streets will be towed beginning next Monday.

You and five other students have been elected by the student government to make a decision about allocating the parking spaces. In making your social choice, you will follow the five-step decision-making model:

1. define the problem;
2. list the alternatives;
3. list the criteria;
4. evaluate the alternatives; and
5. choose the best alternative.

Step 1—Define the Problem

Presently, there are more cars than spaces available in the parking lot. Students have been distributing the burden of the shortage to private home owners nearby. Thus, residents have been unable to park in front of their own homes. This is called a distribution effect in economics. A ***distribution effect*** is the way the benefit or inconvenience of a social issue is distributed among the members of the society. In this case, the burden was being distributed from students to home owners.

distribution effect
the way the benefit or inconvenience of a social issue is spread among the members of the society

In all choices, both individual and social, an allocation of resources is involved. Public officials vote every day on projects and laws. They allocate public money for public projects. More money for one project means less money for other possible projects. Laws define what choices we, as a society and as individuals, can and cannot make. Laws allocate the power to choose. If a law is passed that prohibits nonresident parking on residential streets, the choice or alternative of parking on those streets is no longer available. All choices require us to allocate something.

What is an accurate definition of this problem? Is the parking lot too small? Or, is the number of cars too large? What if the school cannot afford to build another parking lot for students? The problem then becomes how to allocate the available spaces among the students. The problem is defined as how will the limited spaces be allocated among the larger number of students who drive?

Step 2—List the Alternatives

What are some alternate solutions to the parking situation? The current situation is allocation of spaces on a first-come, first-served basis. One alternative is for this policy to continue.

A second alternative is to allocate the spaces by selling school parking permits for each space. Those who could afford the permits could drive, and those who could not afford them would have to walk or find other transportation.

A third alternative is to allocate by need. Students who work, live a long distance from school, are involved in car pools, or are the only drivers in their families might be given use of the lot. Students who have no access to bus service or other transportation would also fall into this category.

Economics & Your Community

For social decision makers on the local level, it is extremely important to stay in touch with constituents. Explain to students that, as constituents, they have the right to write letters to their representatives to voice their opinions on issues. Have students choose a local representative, such as a school board member or a state representative. Then, have them choose a local issue of interest and write a letter to the representative explaining their position. Finally, have students "snailmail" or e-mail their letters.

A fourth alternative is to allocate parking spaces by seniority. Seniors would have first choice and then juniors and then sophomores. This would, no doubt, be popular among seniors, but sophomores might think it is unfair.

You and the other student representatives decide to consider the following alternatives:

1. first come, first served;
2. selling permits;
3. need; and
4. seniority.

Step 3—List the Criteria

There are advantages and disadvantages to each alternative. In order to evaluate the alternatives, you must select some criteria. In social decision making, the criteria are social goals. ***Social goals*** are the goals of an entire society.

What social goals should be considered for the parking lot problem? Some of the social goals societies strive for include justice, equality, efficiency, and freedom of choice.

Clearly, your choice should be fair or just. It should not give one group of students advantage over another without a very good reason. Consider, too, that if a decision is easy to understand, more students probably will feel that it is fair.

Equity might also be a part of your considerations. You might think that everyone should have an equal chance to use the parking lot. Remember, however, that equity is a difficult goal, as you will see later.

The costs of the decision, including its enforcement, should also be a criterion. The more efficient the choice is to administer, the lower the social costs. ***Social costs*** are the costs to a society of a social choice. If the decision is easy to understand, more students will probably feel that it is fair.

Freedom of choice also might be an important goal. ***Freedom of choice*** is the individual power to choose and receive both the costs and the benefits of a choice. Your rule might want to offer students an individual choice rather than simply dictate a course of required action.

Social benefits could be another criterion. ***Social benefits*** are the benefits received by a society from a social choice. You might want to guide your choice by trying to produce benefits for the largest part of society. Here, a plan that shares the benefits of the choice among many people or groups would be preferable to one that benefits a few individuals or groups. You are trying to do the most good for the most people.

Step 4—Evaluate the Alternatives

Having defined your problem, determined your alternatives, and established your criteria (social goals), you now must evaluate each alternative. Through evaluation, you will get a clear idea of the advantages and disadvantages of each possible choice.

Figure 3-1 on page 64 is a decision matrix like the one in Chapter 2. In Figure 3-1, the four criteria (social goals) are listed in the first column. The four alternatives are in the first row. Each alternative, beginning with first-come, first-served, is given a score on each criterion. A score of four points is

social goals
the goals of an entire society

social costs
the costs to a society of a social choice

freedom of choice
the individual power to choose and receive both the costs and the benefits of a choice

social benefits
the benefits received by a society from a social choice

Apply

As a whole-class activity, discuss with students the scenario posed in their textbook on pp. 61-62 concerning the student parking problem. Divide the class into five groups. Assign each group one of the five steps in the decision-making model. Starting with the group that was assigned the first step, have each group explain to the whole class what it does at its assigned step to help make a decision about the parking problem. Have the class critique each group's understanding of the specific problem, its understanding of the step that it was assigned, and its presentation of the step to the rest of the class.
Guided Practice

Divide the class into groups of four or five. Hand out butcher paper to each group. Then, have each group create a flowchart of the five-step decision-making process. Encourage students to illustrate each step of their decision-making models with original artwork or pictures cut out of magazines. You may wish to bind the flowcharts into a class book or display them on a bulletin board.
Independent Practice

Analyzing *Graphics*

Caption Answer
Social goals chosen may include economic efficiency, improving educational opportunities, eliminating discrimination, and preserving the environment.

Ask students to rank the social goals on the left side of *Figure 3-1* in order of importance from the most valued goal to the least. Have them record their rankings on paper. Then, ask students to reevaluate the rank order of the items in the decision matrix based on their own rankings of the social goals.

Explain to students that social decisions in the United States are based on majority rule, with protected minority rights. Divide the class into groups of five or six. Explain that each group is to make five new rules for the classroom. Assign the following roles: president, senator, representative, constituent, judge, and recorder. (The judge may also serve as recorder if there are only five students.) Have all students suggest rules, with the whole group voting until five rules are approved. Each rule must pass by three votes in groups of five and by four votes in groups of six. Assign the following powers: president has veto power on all rules; senator and representative must agree on their votes before voting in the group; constituent votes alone on every rule; judge can declare rules unfair; and recorder documents everyone's votes and all decisions. After 10 to 15 minutes, have each group present to the class the rules it approved, discussing the ups and downs of its approval process.
Cooperative Learning

given for very desirable alternatives and one point for very undesirable alternatives. The higher the number of total points, the more desirable the alternative.

Notice that the parking permit alternative in Figure 3-1 scores high on social costs and fairly high on freedom of choice. However, compared to the other alternatives, it is third in social benefit and third in equity. The good aspects of this alternative are that the people who get the benefit of parking spaces are the ones who pay the fees and it allows some individual freedom of choice. In this way, the policy would function a lot like the marketplace. This alternative is weak in equity because those who cannot pay the fee have no opportunity to use the lot. The social benefits also are received only by those who pay the fee. Given its strong and weak points, this alternative ranks second among the four alternatives.

Criteria	Alternatives: First Come First Served	Parking Permits	Need	Seniority
Equity	Everyone has an equal chance — 4 points	Limited to those who can afford the fee — 2 points	Different treatment for individuals with different needs — 3 points	Limited to seniors and some juniors — 1 point
Social Cost	No costs—no more room when spaces are full — 4 points	Very low; pays for itself through fees — 4 points	Difficult to measure and classify individual needs — 1 point	Low cost; students easily identified — 3 points
Social Benefit	Benefits only those who get there first — 2 points	Limited; only those who can pay can benefit — 2 points	Limited to those who need it most — 4 points	Benefits only older students — 2 points
Freedom of Choice	Individuals can choose how early they want to arrive — 4 points	Some choice allowed; individuals can choose to pay to drive — 3 points	Not much choice; individuals can only change their needs such as by moving farther from school — 2 points	No choice — 1 point
Final Score and Rank of Alternative	14 points 1st choice	11 points 2nd choice	10 points 3rd choice	7 points 4th choice

Figure 3-1

A Decision Matrix for the Parking Lot Case

In this decision matrix, the criteria are the social goals. ***What social goals would you choose for the criteria?***

MediaLink

Using *Figure 3-1* as a guide, have students use word-processing or desktop-publishing software to create blank decision matrices. Explain that these diagrams can be used as a template, or guide, for making future decisions. After students have created their templates, assign a topic or use the scenario in *Math and Economics* and have students enter their information. Have students print out their blank templates and their completed decision matrices. Then, allow time for students to show them and explain them to their classmates.

The first-come, first-served alternative is the best social choice of the four. This alternative is strong on individual freedom and equity since everyone has an equal chance to try for the available spaces. Students can choose how early they are willing to leave home each day. However, only those who can regularly get to school early can receive the benefits of this choice. Enforcement costs are zero, since when the available spaces are taken no one else can occupy them.

The real shortcoming of the first-come, first-served rule falls under another criterion that we did not consider. What happens if you try for a space and the lot is full? Are the unlucky individuals supposed to take their cars home or do something else with them? Under such a situation, it is likely that some people would park on the streets again and eventually be towed away. This is an example of how difficult it is to include every possible consideration in the social decision-making process. This is probably why some social decisions do not work out as planned.

Allocating parking spaces by need gets high points for equity and social benefit. At first glance, it may seem very fair to let the people who have the greatest need for parking use the spaces. This does the greatest good for as many people as there are parking spaces available. However, need is very difficult to determine. If you are handicapped, you have an obvious need to park near the building. On the other hand, what if you live a half mile closer to school than another student does. Do you have less need than the other student for transportation? This is a matter of judgment. The individual case of every student would have to be considered separately which would require large amounts of time and effort. Individual circumstances would change with time and the judgment process would have to continue for as long as the parking rules were in force. Considering all the criteria, this alternative ranked third.

Assigning space by seniority ranks poorly on almost all social goals. Such a rule would provide no individual choice. All seniors can drive, but few juniors or sophomores have the privilege. The social benefit goes to upper class students only. Since all students do not stay in school until they are seniors, not everyone has an equal chance to park in the school lot. This alternative turns out to be the worst choice, based on the social goals that were established.

Step 5—Choose the Best Alternative

After evaluating the alternatives based on the social goals, the first-come, first-served rule is the best choice. Don't forget, however, that the outcome is based on the alternatives you have considered and the value the society places on each of the social goals. If there were a social goal of trying to provide convenience for student drivers, the outcome might have been different. If the certainty of getting a parking space were very important to students, this might have been a criterion and another alternative might have been chosen. As the values of a society change, its social choices reflect those changes.

Explain to students that, for social decisions to truly reflect what the majority wants, public officials need to know what their constituents want. A popular way to find this out is through public-opinion polls, which question a sample population about social decisions. Ask if anyone in the class has ever completed an opinion questionnaire. If so, have those students describe the types of questions they were asked, whether they answered the questions honestly, and whether they thought their answers to the questions reflected what they really believed. Use the textbook scenario of school parking spaces to develop a questionnaire to find out students' opinions on which alternative they think is best. You may wish to bring in samples of questionnaires or use the market survey questionnaire on the Chapter 11 *Life Skills* worksheet as an example.

Perspectives

Thinking Like an Elected School Board Member Tell students to imagine that they will run as candidates in the local school board election. Explain that, to determine the major issues at stake, each person is to poll at least ten students and four adults to find out their opinions. Then, have students use the results of their polls to identify the three issues they believe are the most important. Remind students to use the five-step decision-making model to help them decide. Then, have them create campaign posters or write campaign speeches that reflect their stands on these issues.

Divide the class into groups of four to five students. Assign students the task of creating their own problem-solving model. Have students develop an acronym for their decision-making steps. Explain to students that, in an acronym, the first letter of each word is used to form another word. For example, an acronym for the Great Lakes is HOMES: Huron, Ontario, Michigan, Erie, and Superior. After students have determined their steps and decided on their acronyms, have them create posters by cutting out the letters of their acronyms in brightly colored paper and then listing the steps beside the appropriate letters. When all the posters are complete, have students vote on the one with the best steps and the one with the best acronym (not necessarily the same poster).

The quality of any social choice depends on defining the problem accurately and weighing carefully the costs and benefits of each alternative. Following a logical and well-organized method of decision making will improve your ability to understand and participate in the social decision-making process.

SOCIAL DECISIONS IN REAL LIFE

Remember how the individual decision-making process, described in Chapter 2, seemed very complex at first? After several tries, however, you probably learned to use the process quickly and efficiently. The social decision-making process also may seem complex. If you repeat the process with several different issues, however, you will quickly come to understand its value. The five-step decision-making model will not give you a specific

Econ & You

STANDING BEHIND YOUR DECISIONS

As a social decision maker, once you have decided which alternative is in the best interest of the people, your work is just beginning. You have only worked out the costs and benefits in an understandable form. Your next and most important task is to clearly communicate the costs and benefits of each possible alternative to your constituents. Constituents are the individual citizens or voters in a democracy who are represented by a particular public official.

You must be able to explain your stand on the issue and support it with facts. You have to convince the people that your decision was based on how each possible alternative measured up to the social goals that were considered. You must be sure that the social goals reflect values that most of the constituents have in common. This process should also protect you from criticism regarding acting in your own self-interest.

Once you have communicated the costs and benefits of each alternative to those affected, you must measure the responses. You might try to get a general impression of how people feel about your choice and if your decision was best for the majority. Whether you like it or not, your social choice will override the individual choices of the individuals who disagree with the majority. Your action, by necessity, will take away the power of their individual choice.

With this in mind, your challenge is to convince as many people as possible that your choice is the best for the society. You must exercise your power of social choice with the greatest of care. You must be mindful that when you choose for others, they may not agree with your choice. Thus, in the long run, they may choose some other social decision maker who more closely represents their views.

Econ & You

Explain to students that it is important for a social decision maker to be a good communicator, which includes being a good listener. Divide the class into groups of five or six. Have one student in each group explain to another student directions to follow when traveling from his or her house to the school. Then, have the second student explain the same directions to the next student and so on until the directions are repeated back to the first student. Have each group critique how well each student listened and then determine where the directions changed.

answer to any problem. But, it will help you organize your thinking and more effectively develop your own solutions to problems involving social choices. The selection of social goals and the value your society places on each goal is up to you to determine.

The five-step decision-making model is, in some respects, more important in making social decisions than it is in making individual decisions. When you choose only for yourself, you usually do not have to justify or explain your choice to others. Your criteria reflect your own values. With social choices, however, you not only will have to make careful decisions, you also will have to clearly communicate to members of the society how and why you make these decisions.

The five-step decision-making process clarifies your decisions and makes it much easier to communicate the *why* and *how* of your decision to society. It also gives you the opportunity to see if your ranking of the criteria (goals) agrees with that of the society. You may have overlooked a major consideration. Through discussions with voters, you might change the outcome of your decision. Finally, if you can communicate the five-step decision-making process to the society, each individual may be able to make more effective decisions in the future. All these outcomes will be to the benefit of the society and to the individuals who belong to it.

Checkpoint

Content Check

1. How can social decisions be improved with the five-step decision-making model?
2. Give examples of social goals, social costs, and social benefits.
3. Why is the five-step decision-making process sometimes more important in making social decisions than in making individual decisions?

What Do You Think Now?

Reread *What Do You Think?* in the Section Three Focus. Then answer the following questions:

4. What criteria would you use to evaluate the waste collection problem in Winton Creek?
5. What other alternatives can you suggest to Winton Creek residents for waste collection?

Assess

1. The problem, alternatives, and criteria are more clearly defined. **3-4**
2. Examples will vary but should reflect an understanding of goals of an entire society, societal costs of a social choice, and societal benefits of a social choice. **3-4**
3. Many more people are affected by the decision. **3-4**
4. Answers should reflect an understanding of social goals as criteria. **3-4**
5. Alternatives should be realistic and might include a strict can-by-can payment; no charge, no separation into recyclables, yard waste, and trash; and central recycling locations with no curbside pickup. **3-4**

Close

Copy the outline of the following graphic organizer on the chalkboard.

Add the following type: **New Prison, Social Costs,** and **Social Benefits.** Tell students to imagine that the government is building a prison in your community. Ask students to fill in the graphic organizer with the costs and benefits to your community.

Reteach

Have students take out the decision-making templates they created in the *Media Link* activity and complete them for the school parking scenario from their textbook. Have students list their own social goals and alternatives and rank the alternatives from 1 (most negative impact) to 5 (most positive). **3-4**

Enrich

Have students reread *Economic Dilemma: Welfare Reform* and then complete a decision matrix using welfare reform as a social choice. Use *Figure 3-1* as a guide and have students use the same scoring as in *Reteach.* **3-4**

Chapter Close

Your Economic Portfolio

Ask students to keep a journal of the decisions they make each day. Tell them to describe each problem, the steps they took to solve it, and the outcome of their decision. Have students reread their journals at the end of each week and evaluate how effective their decisions were.

Explain to students that, after they make decisions, they should evaluate how well their choices worked so they can learn from their successes and mistakes. As a class, have students share the decision-making tips they learned through their experiences. Individually, review students' work, correct any misconceptions, and have them make any needed alterations. Then, file the final draft of their essays in their portfolios.

You may wish to provide the following end-of-chapter materials:

- *Skills & Concepts* worksheet
- *Content Review Workbook*
- Chapter *Assessment*
- Chapter *MicroExam*

Concepts in Brief

1. Social economies answer the three basic economic questions of what, how, and for whom to produce mostly by government decree. Central planning committees decide which resources will be used to produce the goods and services selected for production. This process limits the amount of individual choice given to the citizens of social economies.

2. Personal incentives are not as strong in a social economy as they are in a market society. Even in market economies, however, there are many situations in which social choice is more efficient and more equitable than private choice. Decisions about public goods such as roads, schools, and national defense are examples of situations in which public choice may be superior to individual choice.

3. In cases where public choice is preferable to individual choice, the power of law is frequently necessary to deal with the free rider problem. The free rider problem refers to providing a public good to those who do not share in the cost of the good. Laws taxing everyone in a society (regardless of their preference) in order to provide for national defense is an example of such a situation. It is difficult or impossible to defend the society and yet not defend some of its citizens. With this in mind, everyone is taxed by law, whether they wish to be defended or not.

4. A society can make more efficient social choices by applying the five-step decision-making model to its choice process:
    1. define the problem;
    2. list the alternatives;
    3. list the criteria or social goals;
    4. evaluate the alternatives in regard to the criteria; and
    5. choose the best alternative that meets the criteria (social choice).

5. A logical, organized, and effective decision-making process may be even more important in making social decisions than in making individual decisions. Social decision makers must clearly communicate the costs and benefits of each alternative to the society and explain the reasons for their choices. The five-step decision-making model clearly presents these costs and benefits.

Economic Foundations

1. How are the major economic questions of what, how, and for whom to produce answered in a social economy?
2. What personal incentives exist for the producer of goods or services under social choice?
3. Under what conditions is social choice preferable to individual choice?
4. What are the public goods rationale and the free rider problem?
5. How can the five-step decision-making model be applied to social choice?
6. Why is an effective decision-making process often more important in social choices than in individual choices?

Your Economic Vocabulary

Build your economic vocabulary by matching the following terms with their definitions.

1. dealing fairly and equally with all concerned
2. the costs to a society of a social choice
3. the way the benefit or inconvenience of a social issue is spread among the members of the society
4. the individual power to choose and receive both the costs and the benefits of a choice
5. the benefits received by a society from a social choice
6. the goals of an entire society
7. an economy in which the major economic questions are determined by a government representing the interests of the entire society
8. decision making by government in the interest of society
9. a person who benefits from a public good without sharing its cost
10. goods and services available to the whole society
11. the argument that some public goods can be produced more efficiently by the government
12. the concept that some economic activities become more efficient when done on a large scale

distribution effect
economies of scale
equity
freedom of choice
free rider
public goods
public goods rationale
social benefits
social choice
social costs
social economy
social goals

Economic Foundations

1. In a social economy, these questions are answered primarily by the government representing the best interests of the entire society. (p. 52)
2. In a system based on social choice, there are very few, if any, personal incentives. (p. 55)
3. Answers will vary but should be based on the idea that social choice is preferable to individual choice when it is more efficient than individual choice. (pp. 57-59)
4. The public goods rationale is the argument that some public goods can be produced more efficiently by the government than by individuals. The free rider problem is the fact that some people (free riders) will benefit from public goods without sharing in their cost. (pp. 58-60)
5. The five-step decision-making model is applied to social choice in the same way that it is applied to individual choice, but the criteria are social goals rather than individual goals. (p. 67)
6. It is often more important because it helps clarify decisions, makes communication of the reasons for decisions easier, and ensures that logic is applied to decisions that could affect large numbers of people. (p. 67)

Your Economic Vocabulary

1. **equity**
2. **social costs**
3. **distribution effect**
4. **freedom of choice**
5. **social benefits**
6. **social goals**
7. **social economy**
8. **social choice**
9. **free rider**
10. **public goods**
11. **public goods rationale**
12. **economies of scale**

Thinking Critically About Economics

1. If you were a producer or worker in a social economy, what personal incentives would motivate you to strive for excellence or efficiency? If you were in the same position in a system of primarily individual decision making, would your incentives be any different? If so, how? If not, why not? Which kind of system do you prefer? Why

2. What do you feel is the strongest argument in favor of social decision making? In what types of situations do you feel social decision making would be better or more efficient than individual decision making?

3. Karl Marx's dream of a socialist economy was a state in which individuals would contribute to society to the fullest of their abilities and take from society only what they needed. Do you believe this to be a workable reality? If so, why? If not, why not?

4. If social decision makers make choices that do not agree with your preferences, what is your recourse under representative government? Can a representative government make social decisions that completely reflect your individual preferences? If so, how? If not, why not? What would you suggest as an alternate form of government?

5. As president of the student council, you and your fellow council members must decide how the council's social events budget will be spent this year. There are sufficient funds for only one event. Alternatives include a junior/senior prom, an all-school picnic, or a recognition banquet for this year's volleyball team. Your criteria or goals might be equity, social benefit, and any other two you feel are important. Use the five-step decision-making process to develop your position on this issue. Once you have decided, clearly communicate your decision and supporting reasons to the class. Do other students agree or disagree and why?

Economic Enrichment

Assume that your school is suffering both from a shortage of parking places in the school parking lot and poor conditions in the girls' locker room. Assume that there definitely are not enough resources to do both projects. Examine this problem using the five-step decision-making process and present your decision to the class. After your arguments and those of other students are presented, the class will vote on which project should be undertaken.

Thinking Critically About Economics

1. Answers may include that, in a social economy, the reward for an average amount and quality of work would be the same as for superior work, so it would be in one's best interest not to work very hard—personal incentives are diminished. In a system based on individual decision making, rewards are based on the quality and quantity of one's work, so the personal incentive to strive for excellence is increased. Students' preferences will vary but should be supported with sound reasoning.
2. Social decision making is superior to individual decision making in cases where public goods can be provided more efficiently than private goods. Answers will vary but might include road building, maintaining a national defense, or providing police and fire protection.
3. Answers should be supported by arguments for efficiency or personal incentive. Some students may answer that Marx's dream is not a workable reality because it is impossible to identify what individuals need as opposed to what they want, and it is impossible to determine whether people are contributing to the full extent of their ability.
4. You may vote for someone else in the next election. Representative government must represent all people with their individual preferences, so all of one individual's preferences will not be reflected in every social decision. Suggestions will vary, but

(Continued)

Thinking Critically About Economics (Continued)

students should understand that representing everyone's individual choices all the time results in anarchy.

5. Students' positions on how to spend the funds will vary but should be supported by reasons identified through the five-step decision-making process.

Math and Economics

Your town recently received a donation of land that is located within a growing residential area. There is some disagreement within the town over what is the best use of this land. You are on the town council and have been asked to chair a committee that will make a recommendation about how the land can be used to best meet the needs of the townspeople.

At a series of town meetings, suggestions for alternate uses of the land are received. The final list of alternatives includes selling the land to the state as a site for a new prison; building a multipurpose recreation complex with athletic fields, swimming pool, and gymnasium; or selling the land to the state university for the purpose of building a college branch. Your committee has agreed that the social goals to be used for evaluation should be reducing unemployment, maintaining a clean environment, encouraging economic growth, and striving for economic equity. The following decision matrix summarizes the alternatives and the criteria.

Criteria	Alternatives		
	State Prison	Recreation Complex	College Branch
Full Employment			
Clean Environment			
Economic Growth			
Economic Equity			
Total Score			
Ranking of Alternatives			

Economic Enrichment

Arguments will vary depending upon each student's individual preferences and what he or she perceives as the alternative that will produce the greatest social benefit and the least social cost. Students should complete the five-step decision-making process to support their choices.

Math and Economics

1. Scores will vary according to students' personal evaluations of how well each alternative meets each criterion.
2. Individual scores should be supported by logical written explanations.
3. Scores for each alternative should be added correctly, and the total should be written in the Total Score row of each column. The highest score should be circled.
4. Alternatives should be ranked in descending order, with 1 denoting the highest score, 2 the next-highest score, and 3 the lowest score.
5. Criteria will vary according to each individual's opinions about the most important goals for the use of the land. Students should perform the five-step decision-making process a second time using their new criteria and then compare the results with those from the first decision matrix.

Writing About Economics

Students' collages of social issues may vary, but each article should be accompanied by a list of logical alternative solutions. Students should identify their preferred alternatives and should be able to support their preferences with sound reasoning derived from the five-step decision-making process.

1. Assign a score to each alternative that evaluates how that alternative would affect the criteria. The scores can range from 1 to 5, with 1 representing a very negative impact on the criteria and 5 representing a very positive impact on the criteria. On a separate sheet of paper, copy the decision matrix on page 71 and write the scores in the boxes in the bottom right corner of each box.
2. Within each box, write a brief explanation for your score.
3. Add the scores for each alternative use of the land and complete the Total Score row in the decision matrix. Circle your first choice, which should be the land use with the highest total score.
4. Rank the alternatives, with 1 being your first choice, in the Ranking of Alternatives row in the decision matrix.
5. If you had a chance to choose the criteria, would they be the same as those in the decision matrix? Are there other criteria you think are more important for this decision? If so, what are they? How would different criteria affect your final decision?

Writing About Economics

Collect five to seven newspaper articles about pressing social issues in your city or town. Perhaps the town is raising property taxes or building new roads or schools. Maybe more police are needed or the city is losing an industry that has employed many people for a long time. Prepare a large collage of the articles. Under each article, include a list of alternative solutions and identify the solution you support.

Economic Report of the President

Analyzing Primary Source Documents

The *Economic Report of the President* contains information on what the president considers to be important social issues that have economic implications for our nation. In addition, this report, published annually, includes many statistical tables relating to income, employment, and production.

The following excerpt from the 1995 *Economic Report of the President* discusses the effects of poverty on children's education and, therefore, on their future ability to earn incomes. This report mentions the Children's Defense Fund, which is a group that lobbies Congress to pass legislation in favor of what the organization believes is in the best interests of children in the United States. The report also refers to a program known as Aid to Families with Dependent Children (AFDC), which provides assistance to families who are below the poverty line in terms of income. Here is the excerpt:

> Our core democratic values affirm that each individual should have the opportunity to reach his or her full potential, regardless of race or the income or educational attainment of his or her parents. Yet numerous studies confirm that our Nation today is far from reaching this ideal. That shortfall imposes great costs both on individual Americans and on the country as a whole.
>
> A recent study by a group of economists chaired by a Nobel laureate and commissioned by the Children's Defense Fund examined the effects of childhood poverty on an individual's future living standards. The study concluded that childhood poverty itself, as distinct from such factors as family structure, race, and parental education, has a significant adverse effect on both the educational attainment and the future wages of the Nation's poor children. The study found that children who experience poverty between the ages of 6 and 15 years are two to three times more likely than those who are never poor to become high school dropouts. Using years of schooling as a predictor of future hourly wages, the study concluded that just 1 year of poverty for the 14.6 million children and their families in poverty in 1992 costs the economy somewhere between \$36 billion and \$177 billion in reduced future productivity and employment.
>
> Significantly, one of the studies that the group examined concluded that each \$1 reduction in monthly assistance through the aid to families with dependent children (AFDC) program may reduce future output by between \$0.92 and \$1.51 (in present value terms) solely by reducing the educational attainment and future productivity of the children who are AFDC's beneficiaries.

As you can see from this reading, our nation faces some very important social choices regarding poverty and particularly its effects on children. When reading an article such as this, you should be asking yourself a number of questions, such as the following: What is the background of the author? What is the reason for the article? Is there a political agenda behind it? Is the article presenting fact or primarily the author's opinion? What do I think about the subject and the facts or opinion presented?

SOURCE: *Economic Report of the President,* transmitted to the Congress February 1995 (Washington, D.C.: U.S. Government Printing Office, 1995), 31.

Make individual photocopies of the excerpt from the 1995 *Economic Report of the President* and distribute them to each student. As a class, brainstorm the definition of *primary source* and write the agreed-upon meaning on the chalkboard or an overhead transparency. (Answers may include a supply of information such as a document or artifact that has been unaltered by others and is, essentially, in its original state.) Point out, however, that primary sources can be impartial (for example, artifacts) or they can reflect the biases of their creator or author (such as this written text). Have students use a highlighter, pen, or pencil to call out the portions of this document that indicate that the author has a particular point to make and that the words used were chosen to make the point. (Accept all logical responses.) Point out to students that, at the end of every chapter, they will have the opportunity to complete a portfolio activity in which they, too, will practice different styles of writing, including the persuasive writing modeled in this document.

Have students work in small groups of four or five to create and use decision matrices to support or refute the value of the Aid to Families with Dependent Children (AFDC) program. Review the matrices as a class, exploring similarities as well as differences.

Chapter 4
Private Sector Decisions

Chapter Theme

The private sector is that part of the economy owned by and operated for the benefit of private individuals. Competition in the private sector encourages producers *and* consumers to be efficient. The market system, however, does not solve all economic problems, three of which are explored in this chapter.

Section	Special Features
The Private Sector	Economics & Your Community Multicultural Highlights Internet Connection Eye on Market News
Private Sector Markets	Media Link Economic Spotlight Perspectives: Thinking Like an Entrepreneur Economic Dilemma
Private Sector Problems	Global Economy Econ & You Economic Talk

Video Activity

Chapter 4, Clothing Prices

Search Chapter 4, Play to 5

Have students debate the best way to win back consumers (from the outlets, from reduced demand, and so on). Give three to five ways this could be accomplished and have a group of students present each plan to the class. Then, have the class vote for a winner.

	Print Resources	Media Resources	Assessment
	Effective Teaching Model Lesson Plans *Skills & Concepts* worksheet *Problem Solving* worksheet *Casebook* *Economic Measurement Workbook* *Content Review Workbook* *Spanish Resources*	VHS CD-ROM Videodisc *Arctic Express* *Interactive* ECONOMICS Template software	*Your Economic Portfolio* Chapter *Assessment* Chapter *MicroExam*
Special Learners	**Print Resources**	**Media Resources**	**Assessment**
Limited English Proficiency Auditory Activity Kinesthetic Activity Cooperative Learning Activity	*Life Skills* worksheet *Reteach* worksheet *Teacher's Connection to the Internet*	Overhead Computer Camcorder VCR	*Checkpoint* Section 1 Quiz
Visual Activity	*Enrich* worksheet	Computer Overhead	*Checkpoint* Section 2 Quiz
		Overhead and *Transparency 4-1* Computer Camcorder Video Audio	*Checkpoint* Section 3 Quiz

Careers Activity

A retail store buyer must read market trends accurately to effectively anticipate and respond to consumer demands. A buyer must obtain the best available, lowest priced merchandise for quick resale.

Although a college degree is not required, it is preferred. Courses in economics, marketing, fashion, buying, and business administration are helpful, and experience in retailing is also advantageous. A buyer for an average store may earn between $17,000 and $35,000, depending upon sales volume. Additionally, buyers often receive cash bonuses and employee discounts.

Have students imagine that they are buyers for a small kitchen supply store competing with a large department store for customers. On the chalkboard, create a three-column chart with these headings: Tactic, Cost, Result. Have students fill in the chart with five ways to get consumers to choose their store over the competition, the cost of each tactic, and the specific results they hope to achieve.

CHAPTER 4

Teaching Materials

Program Resources

- Student text
- *Effective Teaching Model Lesson Plans*
- *Overhead Transparency 4-1*
- *Life Skills* worksheet
- *Problem Solving* worksheet
- *Reteach* worksheet
- *Enrich* worksheet
- *Skills & Concepts* worksheet
- *Casebook*
- *Economic Measurement Workbook*
- *Content Review Workbook*
- *Spanish Resources*
- Video package
- *Teacher's Connection to the Internet*
- *Arctic Express*
- *Interactive ECONOMICS*
- Template software

Assessment

- Section Quizzes
- Chapter *Assessment*
- Chapter *MicroExam*

Overview

Section One
The Private Sector

Section Two
Private Sector Markets

Section Three
Private Sector Problems

Teacher to Teacher

To help students understand the U.S. economy draw this graphic without the endpoints on the arrows.

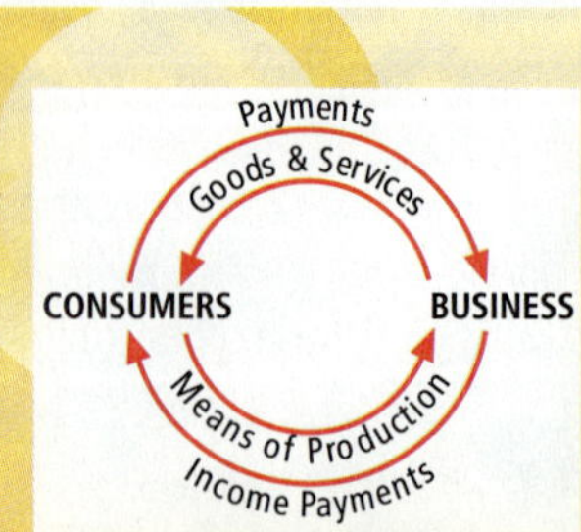

Ask students to copy the graphic onto a sheet of paper and add the arrow endpoints to show the circular flow of the U.S. economy. Then, have students explain why they placed the arrows in the direction that they did.

Dennis Dowling
Lakota High School
West Chester, OH

Private Sector Decisions

Learning Objectives

4-1

Explain how economic decisions are affected by private ownership and private choice.

4-2

Describe how competition and individual choice improve the efficiency of exchanges.

4-3

Discuss how markets benefit consumers.

4-4

Identify the role of profits and risk for producers in private sector markets.

4-5

Present three major pitfalls associated with the market system in the private sector.

Outside Resources

- Blank transparencies
- Copies of utility bills from competitive companies
- Outside speakers: Executives from local businesses
- Advertisements for local businesses
- China markers, colored pens, and highlighters
- Camcorder and VCR
- Four-color circulars from Sunday newspapers for competitive products such as computers, jewelry, or seasonal merchandise
- Catalogs and sale circulars
- *Yellow Pages* from telephone book
- Computer
- Integrated software (databases)
- Variety of cereal boxes
- Laurie P. Cohen, "Dirty Dozen?: Tampering with Juries' Appeals to Defendants Facing Steep Sentences," in *The Wall Street Journal* (January 10, 1995): 1.
- Advertisements for a variety of competitive products
- Business magazines
- Poster board
- Business sections of local or national newspapers
- Cassette recorder

Vocabulary

private sector, p. 76
private goods, p. 76
public sector, p. 77
exchange, p. 77
efficiency, p. 77
competition, p. 79
market, p. 81
entrepreneurs, p. 83
private enterprise, p. 84
externalities, p. 90

Focus

Write **Private sector** and **Public sector** on the chalkboard or an overhead transparency. Then, write the following to the left of the two terms: **health club, electric company, golf course, car, highway, local library, state college, cable TV company,** and **health insurance provider.** Ask students to use check marks to categorize each good, service, or institution as public or private, according to what they know about it. (Some items fit under both categories.) Have students record their thoughts on a sheet of paper.

As a class, have students infer the meaning of **private sector** and **public sector** from the context of the chart. Discuss students' lists, correcting misconceptions as necessary. Point out that this chapter focuses on the decisions businesses and consumers make in the private sector of our economy.

Limited English Proficiency

FOCUS

Section One

The Private Sector

What Do You Think?

Hernandez's fruit orchard is located near a major highway. Despite the signs that clearly identify the orchard as private property, motorists occasionally stop by the side of the road to pick pieces of fruit. Lately, this has become more of a problem. Hernandez's has asked police to increase their patrols and arrest the offenders, even those taking just one or two pieces of fruit. Do you think Hernandez's is overreacting?

Terms to Know

- private sector
- private goods
- public sector
- exchange
- efficiency
- competition

What's Ahead?

The private sector is made up of individuals making private choices for their personal benefit. Exchanges in the private sector contribute to the efficiency of the economy. Individual choice and competition in the private sector improve efficiency.

WHAT IS THE PRIVATE SECTOR?

private sector the part of an economy that is owned by individuals and operated for their personal benefit

The ***private sector*** is the part of an economy that is owned by individuals and operated for their personal benefit. It is made up of private citizens. You are a member of the private sector.

Private Ownership—Private Benefit

private goods goods that are privately owned and used to benefit only their owners

In the private sector, individuals own goods for their private gain. If you own a house, you have the right to reside in it. It is not public property and you can exclude the public from using it. You may even sell your house at a profit. As the owner, you, not the public, benefit from the sale. ***Private goods*** are goods that are privately owned and used to benefit only their owners.

Members of the private sector produce private goods and services mostly for the benefit of private owners. For example, General Motors is a private firm that produces automobiles which it then sells to earn profits. These profits are private benefits paid to owners of the company. If you buy a GM car, you own it privately and can use it to your benefit. You control the rights to

Economics & Your Community

Have students do some comparison shopping in the private sector of your community. Tell students to choose at least four shops in your local area and compare prices of three particular items (snack foods, CDs, jeans, or any other products) sold by all the stores. After students have gathered their information, have them organize it in a chart or spreadsheet to compare the prices. As a class, discuss students' findings.

your private property just as General Motors controls the rights to the private property it owns.

Private institutions also are designed to produce private benefits. If individuals form a private country club, the members bear the cost and enjoy the benefits. The private club, the private auto, and the private company are all private properties that benefit their owners. In general, they are not meant to benefit everyone in society.

There is a public sector in our economy as well. The ***public sector*** is the part of an economy that is owned by the whole society and operated for its benefit. All public goods are found in this sector. All members of the economy own and share the public goods, and no one can exclude anyone from their use. As a citizen, you are part owner of such public goods as roads and schools. You share your classroom with your classmates. You share the use of highways with other drivers. Neither you nor others can exclude anyone from lawful use of the roads and schools.

public sector
the part of an economy that is owned by the whole society and operated for its benefit

Private Choice—Private Benefit

The private sector is controlled by individual or private choice. You individually choose which house or car to buy. Companies, which are owned by one individual or a group of individuals, decide what to produce and how to produce it. Private institutions decide not only who will receive their benefits but also how. Individuals decide how to allocate their time among study, leisure, and work activities so that they receive the maximum benefit.

All these individual choices will be guided by one important principle of economics: Individuals will choose the alternative that produces the maximum private benefit or the minimum private cost to them. This principle is important because it guides the whole private sector. The private sector today produces the majority of all the income in our economy. Therefore, it is reasonable to say that the U.S. economy is primarily an economy of private ownership.

PRIVATE SECTOR EXCHANGES

Economic activity involves exchanges. An ***exchange*** is the giving of one thing in return for some other thing. In economic terms, a voluntary exchange occurs only when both parties benefit from the exchange. In the United States, most property is privately owned. Therefore, most of the economic activity involves the exchange of private property between private individuals, businesses, and institutions. Because private sector decisions involve exchanges, they generally are made in some kind of market situation. Two parties exchange something of value, and both parties are better off because of the exchange.

exchange
giving one thing in return for some other thing

Efficiency and Individual Choice

Individuals make private choices to maximize their benefits or minimize costs. This makes the private sector very efficient. ***Efficiency*** is using a given

efficiency
achieving the maximum benefit from a given amount and combination of resources

Teach

Review students' understanding of the terms **private sector** and **public sector** as introduced in *Focus*. Ensure that students grasp that, in the private sector of our economy, goods, services, and organizations are owned and operated by individuals or private groups for their personal benefit; the public sector, on the other hand, is a collective ownership and operation of goods and services to benefit all citizens.

Write the words **benefit** and **cost** on the chalkboard. Summarize for students the guiding principle of private sector exchanges: **Individuals determine what to produce and how to produce it by calculating either the maximum private benefit or the minimum private cost of the exchange.** Provide examples to help students grasp the concept, such as setting the sales price of a car or buying a wanted but unneeded item because it is on sale at the "right" price.

Define **efficiency** as the use of a fixed amount and combination of resources to reap the maximum benefit. Point out that competition forces producers to produce goods or provide services more efficiently and at a lower cost. Provide students with examples to clarify the relationship between competition and individual, private choices in the marketplace.

Multicultural Highlights

Frank Carney had only tasted pizza once before he and his brother opened the first Pizza Hut in Wichita, Kansas, in 1958. Although successful, the Irish-American brothers claim they "had more guts than brains." To start the business, they took out a $600 loan on their mother's life insurance policy. They named the restaurant "Pizza Hut" because it allowed them to use the sign of the restaurant they bought.

Have small groups of students brainstorm ways restaurants can be efficient in order to minimize their costs or maximize their benefits. (Answers may include serving water or bread only upon request, using dishes instead of paper plates, and charging extra for incidentals.)

Apply

On the chalkboard or overhead transparency, draw a circle with the words **Private Sector** written in the center. Ask students to provide you with descriptive words that characterize the private sector (profits, exchange, efficiency, competition, and so on). As a student responds, draw a spoke radiating from the center circle and write the student's answer on it.

Guided Practice

Invite local businesspeople to speak to your class about the costs and benefits of private business ownership. Ask guests to focus their discussion on their target market, how ownership or rights to the property are controlled or transferred, and how they make business decisions to maximize benefits and minimize costs. Ask guests to bring examples of tools, forms, and so on that help them with these aspects of their business.

Provide students with newspaper ads for local, private sector businesses. Have students independently circle three ads of interest with a china marker, red pen, or highlighter. Ask a volunteer to define **exchange** (the giving of one thing in return for something else). Then, have students read their most appealing ads aloud to the class. As a group, have students identify what is exchanged and the role efficiency plays in determining the value of the exchange.

Internet Connection

THE PRIVATE SECTOR OF CYBERSPACE

The Internet was developed as a government project by the Defense Department. When the Internet became established, a number of commercial computer networks sprang up to offer similar online services. The largest of these are CompuServe, Prodigy, and America Online.

All three provide the same fundamental services: e-mail, news reports, stock market information, weather forecasts, online encyclopedias, and bulletin boards for special interest group discussions. CompuServe is the oldest and has the most information to offer, but the majority of its resources are text based. Prodigy is more family oriented and uses more graphics. America Online (AOL) is the newest and offers the most extensive Internet access.

Initially, the commercial services were more user friendly than the Internet. However, while they were easier to use, they were less powerful and offered fewer services. Now that the federal government is phasing out financial support for the Internet, the commercial networks and the Internet are converging. Commercial networks are offering more of the Internet services, and with applications such as the World Wide Web, the Internet is getting much easier to use.

To send e-mail from the Internet to a commercial network, you must know the commercial e-mail address. Suppose you have a friend whose e-mail address on Prodigy is "friend." From the Internet, her address should read "friend@prodigy.com." If she subscribed to AOL, her address would be "friend@aol.com." CompuServe is a little more complicated. CompuServe addresses have the form "number,number," or "12345,123," for example. When sending e-mail from the Internet, the address should read "12345.123@compuserve.com". Notice that the comma is replaced with a period.

Internet Application: Since most commercial vendors allow a free trial period, talk with your teacher about setting up a class account. Discuss strengths and weaknesses of the different vendors. Use the account to send an e-mail message to your teacher.

Economics Application: In Chapters 3 and 4, you learned about public and private sector decision making. Use what you have learned to explain the following: Why was the first large-scale network (i.e. the Internet) created by the government and not some private firm? Why then did CompuServe, Prodigy, and America Online get created?

Internet Connection

Economics Application: The "public goods" nature of the Internet created an imbalance between private costs and benefits. The costs to a private firm seemed very large, and the benefits appeared uncertain and moderate at best. (See the discussion of *public goods* in chapters 3 and 5.) Once government showed a demand for such a service and the technology improved, it became clear that computer networks offered a profit-making opportunity for business. Therefore, private networks were created.

amount and combination of resources to get the maximum amount of benefit. You might say that efficiency is the primary concern of the private sector.

Suppose you are going to make sandwiches. You have a one-pound jar of peanut butter and 24 slices of bread. Each sandwich should have 1⅓ ounces of peanut butter. If you are efficient, you can make 12 sandwiches. If you are not efficient, you may not get 12 sandwiches. If you drop slices of bread on the floor and spoil them, your output (sandwiches) will be less than 12. Spreading more than 1⅓ ounces of peanut butter on the sandwiches will result in an output of less than 12 sandwiches.

Efficiency is not a negative word! In the private sector, firms must try to be efficient to stay in business. When a firm tries to produce at the lowest cost, it is not trying to cheat customers. For example, you buy a pair of jeans because you are willing to pay the price in exchange for the benefit you receive from having the jeans. If the company that makes your favorite jeans reduces the quality of its jeans, you would notice. You would then reevaluate whether the price you must pay is worth the benefit you receive. You might decide to buy another brand of jeans. If another company provides better jeans at the same price, that company is more efficient.

Competition Improves Efficiency

The existence of many individual jeans producers and many individual consumers of jeans contributes to the efficiency of that industry. Levi's, Lee, Wrangler, and all other jeans companies must compete with each other for the consumer's buying decision.

Competition is the rivalry between two or more parties to gain benefits from a third party. Competition forces producers to aim for efficiency. A local tailor shop may not be able to produce jeans that you feel are equal to the major brands at a competitive price. This leaves only two possibilities for that local tailor shop if it wants to compete with such firms as Levi's at the same price. The shop must improve its ability to produce an equal or better pair of jeans at an equal price *or* go out of the jeans business. Competition not only encourages producers to be more efficient; it also forces weaker, less efficient companies out of the industry.

competition
the rivalry between two or more parties to gain benefits from a third party

Competition among producers in the marketplace works to the consumer's advantage. However, there is also competition among consumers. If everyone in the United States wanted a pair of Levi's jeans right away, it is doubtful that Levi's could produce rapidly enough the amount consumers wanted. Prices would rise and only those willing and able to pay the higher price would get the Levi's jeans. Some consumers would be priced out of the market. If the Levi's jeans cost $45, fewer consumers would buy them. Only consumers willing and able to pay $45 would get those particular jeans. The competition among consumers for the available jeans might mean that you must purchase some other brand of jeans instead.

Competition on the consumer side exists all the time, just like competition among producers. Suppose you wanted to buy tickets for a particular concert. However, once you reached the ticket counter you found that there were no tickets left. Because there was a limited number of tickets, not everyone who

Divide the class into groups of three or four students to create a commercial for one competitive product, such as jeans or sneakers. Allow students in each group to select from the following roles: cameraperson and/or producer to time and record a 30-second commercial and on-air talent (one or two students) to hawk (sell) the product. All students in the group should collaborate on outlining the commercial, creating the props, and writing the script. Allow students one classroom period to complete this portion of the assignment. Then, identify a location away from the classroom where students can record their work independently. As a class, view the commercials, pausing after each one to identify the **exchange, individual purchasing decisions, efficiency,** and the role **competition** plays in the success of the product or service in the marketplace. **Cooperative Learning**

Divide the class into small groups of three or four students. Distribute to each group Sunday newspaper circulars advertising highly competitive products, such as computers, jewelry, or seasonal merchandise. Have groups look at several vendors' ads for one type of merchandise, comparing prices and other specific attributes. Have students determine which vendor they would buy from and which economic factors impacted their selection. **Independent Practice**

EyeOnMarket*News*

Ask students to think about the economic characteristic that household utilities, such as gas, electricity, and water, have in common. (There is no private choice since none of these has any competition.) As a contrast, have students bring in bills or advertisements from competitive long-distance phone companies (MCI, Sprint, AT&T, and so on) and compare the rates. As a whole-class activity, have students discuss the pros and cons of having competition among utility companies.

wanted one received one. Some people settled for less than exactly what they wanted. For example, you might have decided to buy tickets for some other concert.

This competition process causes you to choose so that you get the maximum benefit for a given sacrifice or opportunity cost. It makes you a more efficient consumer. If the sold-out concert had been more important to you, you might have bought your tickets earlier. However, you decided that the benefit was not worth the cost to you of getting there earlier. Therefore, you were forced out of the market for this concert, just as inefficient producers are forced out of their markets. Competition improves the efficiency of both producers and consumers.

Checkpoint

Content Check

1. What is the guiding principle behind private sector decisions?

2. How does individual choice affect efficiency?

3. How does competition affect efficiency?

What Do You Think Now?

Reread *What Do You Think?* in the Section One Focus. Then answer the following questions:

4. Do you think Hernandez's is acting reasonably? If so, why? If not, what actions should be taken?

Assess

1. Producing the maximum private benefit or minimum private cost **4-1**
2. Choices are made to maximize private benefits or minimize private costs, leading to greater efficiency. **4-2**
3. It forces consumers and producers to become more efficient or leave the marketplace. **4-2**
4. Answers should reflect students' understanding of private benefits, free riders, private property, efficiency, and private choice. Answers may include building a high fence, hiring a private guard, and ignoring the problem. **4-1, 4-2**

Close

Write the names of a variety of local businesses on slips of paper. Fold and put them in a bag or other container. Have pairs of students select one paper per pair. Then, have one student read the name of the business to his or her partner. Student pairs should then discuss the private ownership of the business: what exchanges take place, the efficiency, the competition in the marketplace, and so on.

Reteach

With permission, have students visit two car dealerships that offer the same make and model of automobile. Have students "shop" to determine the role of competition in the efficiency of the exchange. Have students summarize their findings in a paragraph. **4-1, 4-2**

Enrich

Instruct students to explain on paper the quote from p. 77 of their textbook: ". . . it is reasonable to say that the U.S. economy is primarily an economy of private ownership." **4-1**

FOCUS

Section Two

Private Sector Markets

What Do You Think?

Severe flooding destroyed much of the lettuce crop in California. The cost of lettuce all across the United States went up as a result of the shortage. Some restaurants and grocers raised the price of salads, sandwiches, and heads of lettuce to reflect the increased cost. Miller's Market, a large supermarket, decided to keep the price of lettuce down by earning a smaller profit. Miller's thought the lettuce shortage was a short-term problem and that keeping the price down would build customer loyalty. Do you think Miller's decision to keep the price down will build customer loyalty?

What's Ahead?

Private sector markets provide price information and a variety of product choices to consumers through competition. The profit motive increases the efficiency of producers and encourages entrepreneurs to take risks. Private markets help you maximize your well-being.

Terms to Know

market

entrepreneurs

private enterprise

PRIVATE SECTOR MARKETS AND CONSUMERS

Exchanges in the private sector usually take place in a market setting. The term ***market*** refers to the exchange activities between buyers and sellers of goods and services. Goods and services of value are exchanged in the market and buyers and sellers benefit from the exchange. Markets provide information through advertising, public relations, promotions, and demonstrations, enabling buyers and sellers to make more efficient private choices.

market
exchange activities between buyers and sellers of goods and services

Markets Give You Price Information

Markets give you important information with which to make your exchange decisions. First of all, markets establish and provide price information. You make your buying decisions based on the price of the item and its benefit to you. A market quickly establishes prices through competition. It takes only a minute to find out the market price of a pair of jeans.

Focus

As students enter the classroom, ask them to list on the chalkboard one or more breakfast cereals that their families eat, if any.

Begin a discussion with students about what they perceive as the benefits of various product choices (lasts a long time, looks appealing, is made of fine materials, is a good economic value, provides good nutrition, tastes good, and so on). Then, ask students to name several cereal manufacturers (Kellogg, General Mills, Post, and so on). Ask students if they think choosing some cereals over others allows them to enjoy greater benefits. Discuss the ways students think these breakfast-food producers compete with each other.

MediaLink

Ask students to think of a product or service that they are considering buying. Then, have them look in the *Yellow Pages* to find information on the companies that supply what they are looking for. Tell students to create a database of the available information on that product or service. Be sure students include the following fields in their database: store name, address, phone number, brand, and cost.

Teach

On an overhead transparency or the chalkboard, draw the following graphic organizer, including only the three headings.

Producers/Entrepreneurs
- Make Profits
- Satisfy Needs
- Take Risks

↓

Private-Sector Market
- Exchanges Goods and Services
- Provides Price Information
- Offers Product Choices

↓

Consumers
- Make Choices
- Fulfill Wants and Needs
- Maximize Satisfaction

Explain to students the relationship among producers, the market, and consumers. Elicit from students characteristics of each entity and add the information to the graphic organizer.

Economic Spotlight

ROAD RUNNER ON THE INFORMATION HIGHWAY

Time Warner Inc. is one of the largest diversified media, entertainment, and publishing companies in the world. Its operations range from publishing to music to movies to cable TV—even to Bugs Bunny and Road Runner cartoons—with a market capitalization of more than $15 billion. The company is an industry leader; in fact, its film entertainment subsidiary, Warner Brothers Studios, was ranked number one at the box office for three consecutive years.

Time Warner is also a major player on the information superhighway, traveling in the fast lane with Richard Parsons, one of the country's most prominent African-American executives, in the driver's seat. As president of Time Warner Inc., Parsons has launched his fourth career after successful careers as a government policy maker, lawyer, and chairman of Dime Bancorp. Parsons is no stranger to the wonders of technology. He attributes much of his success at Dime Bancorp—which he rescued from a three-year struggle with loan problems to make it the fourth-largest savings bank in the country—to technology, which he used to keep his employees informed. He believed that the more informed employees were about the company's numbers, the more effective they would be at their jobs—and his strategy worked!

Brooklyn born, the second of five children, and the son of an electronics technician, Parsons skipped two school grades, graduating from high school at age 16. He ventured on to a fun-filled but academically disastrous experience at the University of Hawaii, leaving school just six credits shy of a degree. Overcoming this "failure" in his life, he was allowed to enroll at Albany Law School in New York without an undergraduate degree. Three years later, he finished first in his class. Parsons attributes his drive for success to his father, who always encouraged him to think for himself.

According to people who know him, Parsons is effective because he is able not only to see the big picture, but also to "grasp the fine point of the details." As Time Warner speeds down the information highway, Parsons sees many challenges ahead. So many, he believes, that "This is the first time I've ever landed somewhere where I think I could be there the rest of my life."

Economic Spotlight

Richard Parsons serves as proof that a person can work his or her way up from Bedford-Stuyvesant, a poor neighborhood in Brooklyn, to become one of the most prominent executives in the United States. Point out to students that Parsons learned from his "mistakes" in undergraduate school and better applied himself in law school. Explain that there really are no mistakes or failures if you learn from your experiences. Have students describe on paper a personal "failure," how they felt about it, and what they learned from it.

A quick call to several stores will give you this information. If one seller's price is much higher, you may buy somewhere else. If the market price for a pair of jeans is more than you are willing to pay, you might check the market price of other types of pants.

Markets Provide Many Choices

The second important function of markets is that they usually provide many choices. Not only can you get price information, you can also find substitutes to fill your need quickly. If competitive markets did not exist, there might not be a large variety of goods and services from which to choose. There also might not be a range of prices from which to choose.

Suppose you needed a means of transportation to get to school. A quick look in the phone book would turn up references to buses, taxis, trains, automobile dealers, bicycle stores, and other alternatives. Even if you decided to consider just one of these alternatives to fill your transportation needs, the market is still very large. For instance, assume you decided to buy a bicycle. The market for bicycles would offer you everything from a simple one-speed model to racing bikes, with new models entering the market constantly.

Markets usually provide you with many choices to satisfy your needs. You make those choices based on what has the greatest private benefit for you relative to the market price you must pay. The market rewards consumers with the benefits of new and better products to fulfill their wants and needs. Consumers who choose carefully and allocate their incomes efficiently through the market increase their satisfaction. Consumers who choose poorly do not receive the same satisfaction per dollar spent.

PRIVATE SECTOR MARKETS AND PRODUCERS

So far, you have learned mostly about the consumer's view of the private sector. Consumers use market information to make choices that maximize their satisfaction. Now consider the situation from the producer's point of view.

Profit Drives Producers

The success of producers depends on their ability to satisfy the wants and needs of consumers more efficiently than others do. Therefore, producers must find out what consumers want or need. Once the consumer's needs are identified, producers must decide what resources to use and in what quantities to make a product that satisfies these needs. Resource prices guide producers just as final goods prices guide consumers' choices. For example, what if the price of metal buttons rises? Levi's might then change to plastic buttons or some other substitute. Then Levi's could earn the same profit without raising its prices. Profits benefit producers. Therefore, producers in the market try to maximize profits.

Entrepreneurs Take Risks

One major difference between consumer choices and producer decisions is that producers take greater risks in making their decisions. Individuals who organize a company to produce a product for a profit are called ***entrepreneurs.*** Entrepreneurs bring together the inputs of production (raw materials,

entrepreneurs
individuals who take the risk of producing a product for a profit

Apply

Display, one at a time, advertisements from catalogs, sale circulars, and newspapers. Have students brainstorm common characteristics of the ads and list them on the chalkboard (price information, product descriptions, and so on). As a class, discuss how students could change the ads to encourage more buyers and then ask them to make the changes.

Guided Practice

If possible, load onto a computer an electronic *Yellow Pages* program, such as *PowerFinder* or *Select Phone* (available on CD-ROM from a variety of software distributors). Discuss with students how this type of resource can assist producers and consumers in making exchanges in the marketplace.

Display or distribute a variety of cereal boxes to students and have each student create an advertisement for one of the cereals. Remind students to use the advertising elements that they listed in the *Guided Practice* activity at the beginning of *Apply* in this section. Encourage students to use a desktop-publishing program or a graphics program to make their ads realistic.

Independent Practice

Perspectives

Thinking Like an Entrepreneur
Tell students that, for many people, the American dream is to create something new or to become one's own boss—in other words, to become an entrepreneur. Have students brainstorm a list of entrepreneurs, such as Donna Karan, Steven Spielberg, and George Lucas. Discuss with students common characteristics of successful entrepreneurs. (Answers may include perseverance, desire for independence, and willingness to take risks.)

Have students imagine that they are entrepreneurs. In small groups, have students create a service or product (possibly even an invention). Tell students to draw a rough sketch of their marketable item and then write a description of it, including a selling price, who the consumers will be, and a list of potential business risks. Allow time for students to present their ideas to the class.

Allow students to read independently the *Economic Dilemma* feature on this page. Then, as a class, discuss the question posed in the last paragraph of the feature. For a primary-source application of an economist's view of crime, you may wish to locate an article entitled "Dirty Dozen?: Tampering with Juries' Appeals to Defendants Facing Steep Sentences," by Laurie P. Cohen (from *The Wall Street Journal*, January 10, 1995, p. 1). Distribute copies of the article to students. In small groups, have students discuss the pros and cons of the article's viewpoint.

workers, and machines) to produce a product to satisfy consumer wants and needs. While consumers can see the products that they can buy to satisfy their needs, entrepreneurs cannot see their products until they are produced. Therefore, entrepreneurs must take the risk that their finished products can satisfy a need, be attractive to consumers, and sell at a price that covers the cost of production. Entrepreneurs take the risk that the product will produce profits.

private enterprise a system in which individuals take the risk of producing goods or services to make a profit

Sometimes our economy is referred to as a private enterprise economy. ***Private enterprise*** is a system in which individuals take the risk of producing goods or services to make a profit. In private enterprise, an entrepreneur is willing to take risks or try something that has not been done before. If entrepreneurs did not risk producing new products, you would not have the variety of choices you have today. If reasonable profits were not possible, entrepreneurs would not risk producing new and better products. The market rewards successful entrepreneurs with profits.

On the other hand, the market punishes entrepreneurs who produce products that consumers do not want. In the early 1980s, Adam Osborne identi-

Economic Dilemma

DOES CRIME PAY?

Crime is a social problem that you hear about all the time in the news media. Economists believe that criminals weigh the costs against the benefits when making a decision about committing a particular crime. Remember that this is only a discussion about the economic part of the decision process. Moral and ethical concerns also have a large impact on a person's decision.

Suppose that Sam, who earns $10,400 a year, notices several color television sets on the loading dock at work. These TVs sell for about $800 each. If Sam were to steal a TV, he would gain a piece of property worth $800. However, his decision to steal would not be without its costs. Sam has read that the police apprehend one out of every ten thieves (10 percent). Furthermore, only 10 percent of those apprehended are actually convicted and sentenced to three years in jail. If only 10 percent of the thieves get caught, and only 10 percent of those are convicted and jailed, then Sam's chance of going to jail for stealing is only one in 100 (1 percent).

Sam figures that three years in jail would cost him $31,200, in lost salary ($10,400 × 3). However, if he has only a 1 percent chance of going to jail, the real "cost" is 1 percent of $31,200 or $312. Since the TV is worth $800, from a purely economic standpoint it would be rational for Sam to risk stealing the TV.

Realizing that crime is a costly problem to society, what does economics suggest as a solution? There are many options available to society. To reduce crime, society can (1) raise the opportunity cost of committing the crime, (2) increase the probability of apprehension, (3) increase the probability of conviction, and/or (4) increase the penalties for criminal acts.

Economic Dilemma

Divide the class into four groups. Assign each group one of the four suggested solutions to crime listed in the *Economic Dilemma* in their textbook. Allow students time to brainstorm a persuasive argument that their assigned solution is the best. Then, choose one member from each group to become part of a panel discussion about crime. Give each panel member 60 seconds to tell the benefits of his or her solution. Then, encourage the remaining students to ask the panel members probing questions.

fied the need for a small portable computer. At first his idea was very successful in the marketplace. His company, Osborne Computer, became one of the best-known names in technology. However, the company failed to keep up with current market trends. New products introduced by Apple, IBM, and others were favored by consumers. The Osborne computers failed in the eyes of consumers and Osborne Computer eventually filed for bankruptcy.

In summary, the private sector functions primarily through markets. Markets give power to both producer and consumer through competition. The market encourages producers to take risks and to produce new and better products. Markets help producers and consumers make more efficient decisions that maximize their own well-being.

Checkpoint

Content Check

1. What benefits do consumers receive as a result of competition in private sector markets?
2. What is the role of profit in private sector markets?
3. What is the role of entrepreneurs in private sector markets?

What Do You Think Now?

Reread *What Do You Think?* in the Section Two Focus. Then answer the following questions:

4. What other options did Miller's have in response to an increase in the cost of lettuce?
5. What risks is Miller's taking?

Assess

1. Lower prices and many product choices **4-2, 4-3**
2. Profit increases efficiency. Inefficient firms will go out of business. Producers must provide products consumers want and can pay for. **4-2, 4-4**
3. They provide consumers with many choices by taking risks and organizing productive resources. **4-4**
4. Answers may include increasing the price of lettuce, increasing the price of other goods and keeping the price of lettuce unchanged, or some combination of price changes to lettuce and other goods. **4-4**
5. Miller's is risking profit and taking a chance that keeping the lettuce price down will not build significant customer loyalty. **4-3, 4-4**

Close

Divide the class into groups of three or four students. Assign students in each group the following roles: producer, the market, and consumer (a fourth student may role-play a different type of producer). Have students discuss how the private sector works from the perspective of these three roles.

Reteach

Have students make a chart with the headings **Producer, Market,** and **Consumer** and then independently fill in some examples, such as Elizabeth Arden (producer), department store (market), and women (consumer). Have students leave at least one hole in each row of their chart and then exchange and complete each other's charts. **4-2, 4-3, 4-4**

Enrich

Distribute business magazines to students and have them skim for articles on entrepreneurs. Have each student glean information on why the featured people are entrepreneurs and then write ten profiles, creating a "Success Stories" booklet. **4-4**

Focus

Write the following question on the chalkboard for students to discuss informally before class begins: **How do producers and consumers deliberately reduce competition in the marketplace?**

Make an overhead transparency showing a collage of advertisements for same-model cars, computers, or other highly marketable products. Elicit from students that producers force competitors out of the marketplace by price-fixing or deeply discounting items, and consumers force competitors out by boycotting products or specific businesses. Tie this discussion to the following *Teach* activity, which allows you to provide students with an overview of the major problems of the market system in the private sector.

FOCUS

Section Three

Private Sector Problems

What Do You Think?

The rumbling sounds of road construction equipment break the morning silence in Oak Grove. Everyone in this rural community is tired of the noise, dust, and traffic congestion caused by the three-year project to build a new interstate highway nearby. At a town meeting last week, a government representative reassured the townspeople that the highway was worth the inconvenience because it would benefit the community when completed. Some of the farmers agreed because they believe the highway will open new markets for them. Other residents weren't convinced. They feel like they're paying the price for everyone who will eventually use the highway. How would you feel?

Term to Know

externalities

What's Ahead?

Market systems are associated with three major pitfalls. First, producers and consumers can reduce competition within the private sector. Second, public goods are used to support the efficiency of the private sector market. Third, private sector decisions can create costs that spill over to the public sector.

MARKET PITFALLS

The market system and private enterprise have produced one of the highest standards of living in the twentieth century. The efficiency of the private sector can take much of the credit for the large assortment of goods and services you enjoy today. You should be aware, however, that this market system in the private sector does have three major pitfalls: the possibility of reduced competition, the use of public goods for private benefit, and the production of costs that affect individuals outside the market.

Reduced Competition

Competition among buyers and sellers makes private sector markets efficient. However, sometimes competition is not as strong as it could be. Competition can be reduced by both producers and consumers, thus making markets less efficient.

How Producers Reduce Competition. Competition makes producers try to produce at the lowest possible cost the goods that consumers want. Competition among buyers allows producers to offer their goods to many buyers and sell to the highest bidders. Sometimes, however, producers try to swing the forces of the market in their favor. All the producers of milk might get together and agree to set a uniform price higher than the existing market price. If no producer will sell below the agreed-upon price, consumers must

Global Economy

CAN WE AFFORD TO SAVE THE ENVIRONMENT?

The environment is something we all share. Environmental problems, such as depletion of the rain forest and major oil spills, deserve our attention because they have the potential to endanger the future of our lives and our planet. But what can be done and at what cost? Efforts to solve these problems will all have opportunity costs.

Since we do not have unlimited resources, we cannot simultaneously solve all environmental concerns. We must once again allocate our resources among unlimited needs. If a government requires a corporation to install millions of dollar's worth of pollution control equipment, we cannot at the same time use those resources to have cleaner water. The question is not how clean an environment we want, but how clean an environment we are willing and able to pay for.

How many goods and services, how many jobs, and how much income are we willing to give up to get how much more of a clean environment? Individuals must eventually make these choices based upon the costs and benefits of each alternative. This is even more true on a global scale. For example, some less-developed and developing countries who want very much to industrialize and grow are burning off portions of the rain forest. In other words, scarcity in these developing and less-developed countries has lead them to prefer a less clean environment in pursuit of economic development. Some scientists believe this will affect the global climate and have negative effects on agriculture and the quality of life in many other countries, such as the United States. The externality of polluting the environment is producing a global economic issue.

Teach

On the chalkboard or an overhead transparency, create a graphic organizer to help explain the problems of a market system. Draw a circle and write **Market System Pitfalls** in the center. Then, draw three spokes radiating from the center. Write one pitfall on each spoke: **Reduced producer and consumer competition, Public goods used for private benefit,** and **Spillover effect of costs and benefits.** Discuss each issue in relation to the market system and private enterprise.

Apply

Tell students to imagine that gasoline prices have gone up by $0.25 in the past two months and most likely will continue to rise. Ask students if they think that consumers should refuse to buy gas. If so, how will this affect producers? Consumers? What are the alternatives? Then, ask students to imagine that the price of silk skyrocketed. How would the effect be similar to or different from that of rising gasoline prices? (More people need gasoline to fuel their vehicles to get to work and school. People can more easily buy clothing made out of other fibers.) **Guided Practice**

Global Economy

Divide the class into two groups. Tell students to imagine that Costa Rica is considering opening part of its rain forest to development. Have one group represent the fictitious corporation BigBiz Inc., which claims that it will train and employ thousands of Costa Ricans in its manufacturing plant. Have the other group represent an environmentalists' coalition, arguing that BigBiz will do nothing but hire cheap labor and ruin the environment. Have students make posters and write letters to convince American consumers and the Costa Rican government of their particular positions.

Give students this scenario: **A national discount chain advertises the top ten CDs or tapes for $5.99 each—but it's for this Sunday only and only for the first 500 consumers. There's no limit on quantity. How is this seller reducing competition?** Allow students sufficient time to think before they respond. Then, discuss the benefits and repercussions of this strategy to the seller, other sellers, and consumers.

Divide the class into small groups of three or four students. Supply each group with pages from the business section of several local or national newspapers. If necessary, photocopy the pages so each group has access to multiple pages. Tell students to look for articles, headlines, or advertisements that directly or indirectly reflect a decrease in competition. Have students circle these examples and then identify whether producers or consumers are responsible. Discuss their findings. **Independent Practice**

pay the higher price. The choices available to consumers are reduced. If they want milk, they must pay the price. The producers gain at a cost to the consumer.

These same producers can use their extra profits to build larger and more efficient plants, and thus further reduce their costs. They now are able to produce milk at lower costs because of these large plants. Newer and smaller milk producers cannot afford such large plants. They cannot produce milk at as low a cost as the large companies can, and, therefore, they cannot enter or succeed in the market. Competition is reduced.

How Consumers Reduce Competition. Consumers sometimes agree not to buy a particular item from a particular producer. Assume that a dairy is charging the fair market price for milk. However, consumers band together and refuse to buy from that dairy until it lowers its price. Consumers then benefit at the cost of the dairy.

Econ & You

PUBLIC EDUCATION FOR PRIVATE BENEFIT

When students gain a good education, they themselves get the primary benefit. An educated individual has more job skills, is more valuable to an employer, and usually earns more income. Education also adds to the individual's knowledge of many other matters, such as nutrition, health care, and financial security. On average, educated people are healthier, live longer, have more stable marriages, earn higher incomes, and commit fewer crimes than others. It would seem, therefore, that education really does provide significant benefits to the individuals that receive it.

If education produces significant private benefits, why would our government spend billions of tax dollars each year to provide education free of charge to students as a public good? The answer is that education also produces positive externalities for society as a whole. Educated people earn higher incomes so they end up paying higher taxes to support the public sector. Healthier people spread fewer diseases throughout the population. Educated people commit fewer crimes, which decreases the cost of crime on the law abiding population. Stronger and more stable marriages reduce the number of families on welfare.

In reality, education has both private and public benefits, and this is one reason why both society and individuals are willing to spend so much money, time, and effort on good education. As the economy of the future becomes more and more complex, the benefits of an education, both public and private, are sure to increase.

Econ & You

In small groups, have students create a public-service announcement (PSA) promoting both the private and public benefits of education. Encourage students to be creative and informative. Tell them that they also may wish to use humor or drama to capture the audience's attention. Have students use camcorders and cassette recorders to record their PSAs. Then, as a class, watch and/or listen to all the groups' presentations.

The action of milk producers or the consumers working together to reduce competition destroys the efficiency of the market. It enriches one party in an exchange at the cost of another. Eventually, it leads to inefficient production on the part of producers and inefficient buying decisions on the part of consumers.

Public Sector Reaction to Reduced Competition. The private sector has a definite interest in keeping markets competitive. Both producers and consumers stand to benefit from competitive markets. Unfortunately, neither group is really in a position to force competitive behavior from the other. So far, the only partial solution to the problem has been public laws against noncompetitive behavior. This moves the solution to the problem from the private sector to the public sector. You will learn in the next chapter how the public sector deals with this problem.

Public Goods for Private Benefit

Many aspects of the private sector depend on public goods to operate efficiently. For example, roads, which are public goods, increase the efficiency of shipping goods to markets. Early in our country's history, there were few paved roads. There were just dirt paths and trails for people to use. Farmers drove their pigs, cattle, or sheep to market on foot through these crude trails and paths. The animals lost a great deal of weight on the long journey. This caused farmers to earn smaller profits on their products. Consumers received smaller animals in poorer physical condition in return for the price paid. In this situation, producing a public good, such as a road, was in the interest of both producers and consumers.

Once roads were built, the exchange of private goods between producers and consumers was more efficient. Because the trip to market was not as long, animals didn't lose as much weight, and the farmers got a better price for them. Also, consumers received a better quality animal. In addition, producers, consumers, and the public were able to use the roads for many other purposes besides bringing animals to market. You can see that in this case private sector exchange is made more efficient through public goods.

Public goods, however, do cause problems for the private sector. Public goods cannot easily be provided by the private sector. Private benefits usually are less than private costs. For example, if only farmers pay to have a road built, the cost to each farmer is very large. Their individual use cannot justify such a cost. Also, it is very difficult to keep the public from using a private road. Guards or expensive fences only increase the cost of the road. There is no easy way to exclude those who did not pay to have the road built. If it is difficult to exclude nonpayers, some farmers might even refuse to pay but use the road anyway.

Private goods yield benefits only to their owners. They are goods that exclude the public from their use. Goods such as roads or schools surely contribute to the efficiency of the private sector, but they also benefit the whole economy. Public goods cannot be provided as effectively by the private sector, since individuals cannot keep all the benefits for themselves. The problem is that, to some extent, the public sector supports the efficiency of the private sector.

Using the following outline as a model, have students create a two-column chart with the headings **Public Good** and **Private Benefit.** Have students fill in at least three public goods and their corresponding private benefits. (Some examples of correct answers are shown in the following outline.)

Public Good	Private Benefit
• Police Dept.	• Protects Merchandise, Citizenry
• Fire Dept.	• Protects Property
• Public Bus System	• Transports Employees to Work

Remind students that private sector decisions can create costs and benefits that spill over into the public sector. Then, have students work in pairs to create two scenarios: one showing a negative externality and one a positive externality. Have them use their scenarios to create two cause-and-effect graphic organizers. On the chalkboard or an overhead transparency, display the following graphic organizer as an example.

Initiating Event
- Need for New School Across the Street from your Apartment Building

Event 2
- Lose View of Flower Garden
- Gain View of Concrete Wall

Final Outcome
- Reduces Personal Satisfaction

Analyzing *Graphics*

Caption Answer
Pollution from the automobile and, possibly, depletion of natural resources

Using the same student pairs from the previous activity, have students role-play one of their scenarios. Ask the remaining students to determine whether the scenario is of a positive or negative externality.

Costs and Benefits Flow Outside the Market

When producers provide goods and services to the market, sometimes they pass on some costs and benefits to citizens outside the private sector market. Costs or benefits passed on outside of the market system are called ***externalities.*** Another term for externalities is *spillover effect.*

externalities
costs or benefits passed on outside of the market system

Negative Externalities. A new apartment building may be built across from your home on a lot now occupied by a flower garden. When the building is finished, your view will be a concrete wall instead of the flower garden. Your satisfaction or well-being will be reduced by the construction of the building. In effect, a cost will be passed on to you. This is not a cost in dollar terms but a reduction of your satisfaction.

The garbage produced at a local restaurant is another example of costs outside a market. It costs money to clean up and carry away the garbage. The restaurant would save money by cutting back to two garbage pickups a month. As a result, the restaurant could offer lower food prices or enjoy larger profits. However, the garbage would accumulate and pass a cost on to residents of the neighborhood in terms of smell and unsightly appearance. Again, this is not a dollar cost but a reduction of satisfaction. It is an externality, a cost passed on to others outside of the market system.

Figure 4-1

The impact of a negative externality is sometimes hard to measure. ***What negative externalities are illustrated in this editorial cartoon?***

Scott Willis ©1989 San Jose Mercury News

One solution to the restaurant's garbage situation is to have the garbage collected more often, passing the additional cost on to consumers through higher food prices. Getting rid of the garbage is then a true part of the cost of the food. Those who benefit from eating in the restaurant pay the full cost of the benefit. If, on the other hand, garbage collection is reduced to keep food prices low, consumers are not paying the full cost of the food. Local residents are paying part of the cost by enduring the smell and mess.

Positive Externalities. Externalities also can be positive. They can pass on benefits as a by-product of some action. If your neighbor buys a very large

Economic*Talk*

To reinforce the concept of the vocabulary term **externalities,** have each student draw a political cartoon. Using *Overhead Transparency 4-1* or *Figure 4-1* as a model, students should create cartoons that illustrate negative or positive externalities. Encourage students to use a graphics program or electronic clip art to create their cartoons.

dog, it may frighten burglars away from your house, too. You receive a benefit for which you did not have to pay.

In the business world, a positive externality might occur when one company hires guards to patrol its offices and grounds. Other businesses in the area receive some benefit, because the patrol might keep some criminals away from the whole area. Fewer burglaries benefit all companies in the area, not just the company that hired the guards. Whether externalities are positive or negative, they are not reflected in market prices. Therefore, they are a true problem for the market system.

Checkpoint

Content Check

1. How do producers and consumers reduce competition in a market?

2. How do public goods support private sector markets? Give an example in your school.

3. How do externalities spill over to the public sector? Give an example in your community.

What Do You Think Now?

Reread *What Do You Think?* in the Section Three Focus. Then answer the following questions:

4. Who benefits from a new interstate highway?

5. What are some positive and negative externalities of the road construction near Oak Grove?

6. What actions can people who are opposed to the new highway take? What actions could they have taken before construction began?

Assess

1. Producers agree to set prices at a level that is higher than the market price. Consumers agree not to buy from a particular producer. **4-5**
2. They increase the efficiency of private sector activities without direct cost to users. Good schools and an educated workforce encourage businesses to locate in the community. **4-5**
3. Pollution, added security, and other by-products created when private sector goods and services are produced sometimes affect the public sector. **4-5**
4. Travelers, consumers, businesses, producers, and other highway users. **4-5**
5. Positive externalities: increased business for local firms and more efficient transportation. Negative externalities: traffic noise and increased pollution. **4-5**
6. Answers may include moving, requesting a sound barrier along the highway, and not using the highway. Before construction, people could have lobbied the decision makers, organized broad public opposition, and physically blocked construction work. **4-5**

Close

Divide the class into three groups. Assign each group one of the three major pitfalls in a market system. Have students discuss each pitfall from the perspectives of a producer and a consumer.

Reteach

Have students create a three-column chart identifying the three major pitfalls in a market system. Have students fill in the chart with at least one example for each pitfall. **4-5**

Enrich

In small groups, have students brainstorm a list of ideas of what our society can do to avoid the three major pitfalls of a market system. Ask for one student volunteer from each group and form a panel. Have the panel members share their groups' ideas with the class. **4-5**

Chapter Close

Your Economic Portfolio

Have students keep a daily log for a week's time on the items they purchase from the private sector. Ask students to answer the following questions for each purchase: **What was your purchase or individual choice? What was the price? Where was the exchange? What information did the market provide? Did your choice maximize your benefits? Did it minimize your costs? Why was your decision efficient or inefficient? Why did you not choose any of the competitive products?** Ask students to analyze any common patterns in their purchasing decisions and to write a summary of their analysis in their log. Review students' work and have them make any necessary corrections before filing the final drafts in their portfolios.

You may wish to provide the following end-of-chapter materials:

- *Skills & Concepts* worksheet
- *Content Review Workbook*
- Chapter *Assessment*
- Chapter *MicroExam*

Concepts in Brief

1. The private sector is that part of the economy owned by and operated for the benefit of private individuals. It includes private business, institutions, and individual citizens. The owners of private property can exclude the public from the use and benefits of their property. The private sector engages in individual choice for private benefit.
2. Efficiency is achieved when individuals make decisions that maximize benefits and minimize costs. Competition in the private sector strongly encourages producers and consumers to be efficient. Each producer attempts to provide at the lowest cost to them goods of a specific quality to the market. This makes producers choose carefully and improves their efficiency. Competition among buyers for the available goods causes buyers to choose carefully as well.
3. Exchanges take place because both parties benefit from the exchange. Markets enable exchange to take place more efficiently by providing price information and a variety of substitutes for consumers.
4. In market situations, producers must take risks in trying to produce goods that they think consumers will buy. Profits are the incentives that encourage producers to take risks and to provide goods and services to consumers.
5. The market system does not solve all economic problems. There are some pitfalls. For one, the competition that encourages efficiency in markets does not always exist. Either buyers or sellers may band together to swing the market in their favor. In some cases, price fixing by producers can force up market prices. In other cases, consumer actions can force market prices down. A second problem is that the private sector depends, in part, on public goods. Some productive parts of our society, therefore, cannot be provided by the private sector. Finally, producing goods and services often results in by-products, such as air or water pollution, that are passed on to consumers outside of the marketplace.

Economic Foundations

1. List some of the differences between the private sector and the public sector.
2. What guides individual choices in the private sector?
3. What is the effect of competition on producers?
4. What is the effect of competition on consumers?

5. How do markets increase the efficiency of individual decisions?
6. How do profits and entrepreneurs benefit consumers?
7. What are three major pitfalls associated with the private sector market system?
8. How can producers reduce competition?
9. How can consumers reduce competition?
10. Why does the private sector avoid producing public goods?
11. Who pays the cost of negative externalities?

Your Economic Vocabulary

Build your economic vocabulary by matching the following terms with their definitions.

1. individuals who take the risk of producing a product for a profit
2. the rivalry between two or more parties to gain benefits from a third party
3. giving one thing in return for some other thing
4. a system in which individuals take the risk of producing goods or services to make a profit
5. achieving the maximum benefit from a given amount and combination of resources
6. goods that are privately owned and used to benefit only their owners
7. exchange activities between buyers and sellers of goods and services
8. costs or benefits passed on outside of the market system
9. the part of an economy that is owned by individuals and operated for their personal benefit
10. the part of an economy that is owned by the whole society and operated for its benefit

competition
efficiency
entrepreneurs
exchange
externalities
market
private enterprise
private goods
private sector
public sector

Your Economic Vocabulary

1. **entrepreneurs**
2. **competition**
3. **exchange**
4. **private enterprise**
5. **efficiency**
6. **private goods**
7. **market**
8. **externalities**
9. **private sector**
10. **public sector**

Economic Foundations

1. Answers may include that the private sector is owned by private individuals while the public sector is owned by the whole society, and that private goods are used to benefit only their owners while public goods are used to benefit the whole society. (pp. 76-77)
2. The principle that individuals will choose the alternative that produces the maximum private benefit or minimum private cost (p. 77)
3. Competition forces producers to aim for efficiency. (p. 79)
4. Competition makes consumers more efficient. (p. 80)
5. Markets provide many choices to satisfy individual needs, forcing consumers to make choices based on what has the greatest private benefit relative to the market price. (p. 83)
6. Profits encourage entrepreneurs to provide consumers with a wide variety of products as well as new and better products. (pp. 83-84)
7. (1) Sometimes, competition is reduced. (2) The public sector supports the efficiency of the private sector to some extent. (3) Some production costs beyond the prices of goods can be passed on to the citizens. (p. 86)
8. By joining together to set prices above the market price (pp. 87-88)
9. By joining together and refusing to buy products at the market price (pp. 88-89)
10. Because private benefits would be less than private costs (p. 89)
11. Others outside of the market system (p. 90)

Thinking Critically About Economics

1. Is it fair that our economy permits private property? Should individuals have the sole benefit of their property? If so, why? If not, why not?
2. What role do markets play in conducting exchanges between private parties?
3. What should be done about markets where producers or consumers band together to swing the market in their favor?
4. Are negative externalities fair to the consumer? Would you feel the same way if the externalities were positive?
5. Should all of our economy be privately owned? If so, why? If not, why not? Can the private sector meet all the needs of the citizens of our society?
6. What are the industries that might be difficult for new entrepreneurs to enter?

Economic Enrichment

Look through some large metropolitan newspapers, such as the *The New York Times* or *Washington Post,* to identify two articles that address negative externalities. Use an online search on your computer or go to the library to find the actual newspapers. Write a one-page report that explains the negative externality and presents two or more proposed solutions. Indicate in the report who you believe will end up paying the price for the externality under each proposed solution. Attach a copy of each article to your report.

Thinking Critically About Economics

1. Answers will vary, but students should understand that it not only is fair but essential to permit private property because it produces private benefit, which creates an incentive system that causes a market economy to work.
2. Markets bring together buyers and sellers and provide price information and substitutes from which the buyer and seller may choose, making exchange more efficient.
3. Answers may include that laws can be created to prohibit this behavior and keep markets functioning efficiently.
4. Answers may include that externalities—either positive or negative—are passed on to third parties without their consent so, in this sense, they are not fair; however, few third parties complain when they are affected by positive externalities.
5. No. If all of the economy were privately owned, there would be no public goods such as roads or a national defense. These goods would have to be provided by the private sector, which could not provide them as efficiently as the public sector. By itself, the private sector cannot meet all the needs of society.
6. Answers will vary but might include such industries as automobile manufacturing or electric-power generation because of the tremendous capital investment needed to get started and the need for government permission to enter into the market.

Economic Enrichment

Students' reports will vary. One or more negative externalities should be identified for each article and two or more possible solutions should be suggested for each externality. Solutions should be supported by logical reasoning and should take into consideration any new externalities that they may create. Students also should indicate who will bear the cost of eliminating each externality.

Math and Economics

Conduct a market survey to see how market prices affect consumers' willingness to buy. Ask 15 people how many 1-pound bags of Hershey Kisses they would be willing and able to buy at $0.75 per bag. Record the results. Ask the same group of people how many bags they would be willing and able to buy at $1.50 per bag. Record this price and quantity. Now raise the price to $2.00 per bag and record the responses. Finally, raise the price to $4.00 per bag and record the price and quantity. Prepare a table that summarizes the price and quantity combinations from highest price to lowest price.

1. What happens to quantity demanded as price goes up?
2. What happens to quantity demanded as price goes down?
3. What kind of mathematical relationship is there between price and quantity demanded?

Writing About Economics

Markets reward successful professional athletes and entertainers with very large salaries. Teachers, who shape the minds of students around the world, are usually paid much less. Research the average salary for high school teachers, college professors, NBA basketball players, professional soccer players in the United States, and professional actors.

What does this salary information tell you about wages paid to educators, athletes, and entertainers? Write an article for your school newspaper that explains why teachers earn less than professional athletes and entertainers. Be sure to discuss how wages are determined for teachers as well as for athletes and entertainers.

Math and Economics

Students' survey responses will vary but should be recorded in a table that lists price and quantity combinations from highest price to lowest price. Students also should provide the following answers:

1. Quantity demanded decreases.
2. Quantity demanded increases.
3. There is an inverse relationship between price and quantity demanded; as price decreases, quantity demanded increases, and vice versa.

Writing About Economics

Students' articles should be supported by research and may suggest that teachers earn less than professional athletes and entertainers because most teachers work in the public sector while athletes and entertainers work in the private sector where there is more available funding. Students should point out that teachers' wages are determined by the state and the school district based on such factors as available funding, education level, seniority, and merit. Wages for professional athletes and entertainers are determined by such factors as quality of performance, mass appeal, and personal business savvy.

Chapter 5 Public Sector Decisions

Chapter Theme

The public sector is that part of the economy owned by and operated for the benefit of the whole society. We give our government great economic power to carry out five major functions that either can be performed more efficiently by the public sector or that the private sector is unwilling or unable to perform. Public sector problems do exist, however, and actions by citizens can help resolve these issues.

Section	Special Features
The Public Sector	Eye on Market News Economic Spotlight Economic Dilemma
Public Sector Contributions	Economics & Your Community Multicultural Highlights Internet Connection Media Link Perspectives: Thinking Like a Politician
Public Sector Problems	Global Economy Econ & You Economic Talk

Video Activity

Chapter 5, Affirmative Action

Search Chapter 5, Play to 6

Divide the class into two groups to debate whether affirmative action is a fair and worthwhile government policy in today's society.

	Print Resources	Media Resources	Assessment
	Effective Teaching Model Lesson Plans *Skills & Concepts* worksheet *Problem Solving* worksheet *Casebook* *Economic Measurement Workbook* *Content Review Workbook* *Spanish Resources*	VHS CD-ROM Videodisc *Arctic Express* *Interactive* ECONOMICS Template software	*Your Economic Portfolio* Chapter *Assessment* Chapter *MicroExam*

Special Learners	Print Resources	Media Resources	Assessment
Visual Activity Attention Deficit Disorder		Overhead and *Transparency 5-1* Computer	*Checkpoint* Section 1 Quiz
Auditory Activity Kinesthetic Activity	*Teacher's Connection to the Internet* *Life Skills* worksheet	Overhead Computer Camcorder VCR	*Checkpoint* Section 2 Quiz
Cooperative Learning Activity	*Reteach* worksheet *Enrich* worksheet	Overhead Camcorder VCR Computer Audio	*Checkpoint* Section 3 Quiz

Careers Activity

One well-known public sector service in the United States is the postal service. The postal service employs mail carriers, who are responsible for collecting and delivering mail in a safe and timely manner. They also carry out special delivery instructions, collect postage and C.O.D. moneys, and obtain signatures for registered mail.

While there are no specific education requirements for mail carriers, a high school education will prove helpful on the job and will aid candidates in passing the required civil service exam. A good memory, strong people skills, and physical strength are also helpful. A mail carrier earns from $23,000 to $30,000 per year.

From time to time, the U.S. government has considered turning over the nation's postal service to private enterprise. Tell students to imagine that the year is 2060 and the postal service is no longer run by the government. Instead, it is privately owned and operated. Have them write a letter to their great-grandchildren describing how the postal service has changed since the mid-1990s.

CHAPTER 5

Teaching Materials

Program Resources

- Student text
- *Effective Teaching Model Lesson Plans*
- *Overhead Transparency 5-1*
- *Life Skills* worksheet
- *Problem Solving* worksheet
- *Reteach* worksheet
- *Enrich* worksheet
- *Skills & Concepts* worksheet
- *Casebook*
- *Economic Measurement Workbook*
- *Content Review Workbook*
- *Spanish Resources*
- Video package
- *Teacher's Connection to the Internet*
- *Arctic Express*
- *Interactive* ECONOMICS
- Template software

Assessment

- Section Quizzes
- Chapter *Assessment*
- Chapter *MicroExam*

Overview

Section One
The Public Sector

Section Two
Public Sector Contributions

Section Three
Public Sector Problems

Teacher to Teacher

To help students understand the role of the government in the economy and how that role has changed over the last four decades, draw the pie charts on page 97 on the chalkboard and then ask students to describe how federal spending has changed and why. (Shifted toward social spending and away from national defense; threat of war has decreased)

Harlan Day
Purdue University
W. Lafayette, IN

Public Sector Decisions

Learning Objectives

5-1

Explain the roles of public institutions and government in the economy.

5-2

Distinguish between the five major functions of the public sector.

5-3

Present three problems with the public sector.

Vocabulary

public sector, p. 98
public institutions, p. 99
property rights, p. 105
contract, p. 106
special interest group, p. 115
lobbying, p. 115

Outside Resources

- Blank overhead transparencies
- Index cards
- Copies of the U.S. Constitution
- Camcorder and VCR
- Paper bags, empty soda cans, and food wrappers
- Newspapers
- Outside speaker: Parks and Recreation Department representative
- Cassette recorder

Teacher to Teacher

(Continued from p. 96)

Distribution of the Federal Budget: 1960 and 1994

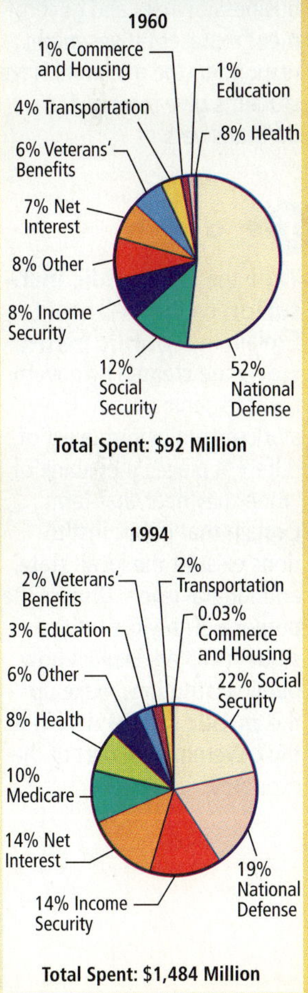

FOCUS

Section One

The Public Sector

What Do You Think?

Jamison and her dad were surfing the Internet one night, doing research for Jamison's history project on resistance movements in World War II. Some of the photos and other visual images they came across were fairly gruesome. Jamison's dad was surprised that just anybody, no matter how young, could access these photos of mutilation and torture. Jamison told him there are people who want the government to regulate what can be carried on the Internet. Jamison's dad said that might not be the best solution—legislation would just get bogged down in regulatory agency rulings and court decisions. Are regulations going to solve this problem?

Terms to Know

public sector

public institutions

What's Ahead?

The public sector is that part of the economy that is owned by and operated for the benefit of the whole society. Government and public institutions at all levels have been given great power to carry out the functions of the public sector. Economists differ in their views about whether the government should play an active or limited role in our economy.

WHAT IS THE PUBLIC SECTOR?

public sector the part of an economy that is owned by and operated for the benefit of the whole society

The ***public sector*** is the part of an economy that is owned by and operated for the benefit of the whole society. The public sector consists of government at all levels in our economy—federal, state, and local—and public institutions. Individual citizens acting together as a society create the public sector (government) to carry out certain functions. As citizens, we give this vast economic power to government. Therefore, it is important to understand the economic role of government.

Focus

Write the following on the chalkboard: **Should the government be involved by controlling or regulating?** Beneath this question, make a two-column chart with the headings **Food** and **Automobiles.** As they enter the classroom, ask each student to write either **yes, sometimes,** or **no** under each heading.

Tally the responses in both columns. Ask students if they answered as consumers, business owners, or government representatives. Have students discuss their points of view. Then, ask students how business owners and government representatives might respond to the question. Have students give reasons for their answers.

Teach

Write the term **public institution** on the chalkboard. Explain that **public institutions** are created by government to serve society. Have students brainstorm a list of different places they think of when they hear that term. Explain that public institutions exist at the local, state, and federal levels. Discuss the purpose of the institutions students listed. Explain how public institutions make up the **public sector,** which is the governmental part of the economy.

Government's Role in the Public Sector

No single force in our economy is more powerful than government. Government makes the laws of the land, thereby establishing rules that all producers and consumers must obey. Our government sets broad limits on what can and cannot be produced and how it can be produced. For example, our government permits and encourages the production of milk. It also sets safety standards and regulations on how milk must be produced. Government also allows the mining of coal. However, it closely regulates the safety and health conditions under which coal is mined. Government creates and enforces the laws by which organizations, such as the miners' unions and the coal companies, must settle their differences.

Government also prohibits the unlicensed production of some goods and services, such as nuclear power, radio and television broadcasts, and military weapons. The government's decisions to regulate or prohibit the production of such items are made by our whole society through our votes. It is government, however, that enforces these decisions.

Public Institutions

Public institutions are publicly owned organizations established by government to serve the wants and needs of a whole society. Our courts, state universities, and Federal Reserve Bank System are examples of public institutions. Government establishes public institutions to help our society function efficiently.

public institutions publicly owned organizations established by government to serve the wants and needs of a whole society

The public sector makes up a large part of our entire economy. By one measure, about 43 percent of U.S. gross domestic product is government expenditures (see Figure 5-1 on page 100).[1]

[1] *Statistical Abstract of the United States: 1994,* 114th ed. (Washington, D.C.: U.S. Bureau of the Census, 1994), 298, 448.

Apply

On the chalkboard or an overhead transparency, ask students to name the services they use that are in the public sector (school bus, public library, and so on). Ask students the following questions: **If these services were not available, how would you get to school? How could you research a written report?** Brainstorm alternatives, including costs and benefits.

Guided Practice

Point out to students that the federal government has established organizations such as the Federal Communications Commission (FCC) to regulate the public airwaves. For example, the FCC prohibits some forms of nudity and profanity from being broadcast on TV or radio. Some people believe that the laws are not strict enough. Others believe that the government is too involved. Divide the class into two groups and have them debate whether it is the government's responsibility or our responsibility to control what we see and hear.

EyeOnMarketNews

Explain to students that health care costs have increased at a much faster pace than inflation in recent years. Ask students if they think the government should be involved in health care reform. You may wish to have students research the topic briefly before discussing the positives and negatives of controlling health care prices. Explain that changing societal rules might be good in some respects and bad in others. Have students discuss and then list the pros and cons of having a national health care program.

Analyzing *Graphics*

Caption Answer
Answers should reflect an understanding of the trade-offs between the benefits of government spending, such as jobs and services, and the costs, such as taxes.

Display *Overhead Transparency 5-1.* Ask students the following question: **In your opinion, what percentage of the U.S. economy should be in the public sector?** Explain that certain services are carried out by the government and others by the private sector. Have students discuss whether they think the government should claim a larger or smaller portion than is shown on the transparency and why. (Responses may include larger so more people are served or smaller so taxes can be reduced.) For a comparison of past and current government spending, ask students if they think government spending has increased since the 1920s. Since the 1960s? Tell students to back up their speculation with data from an online resource or the library.

To reinforce the importance of government institutions, have students make a three-column chart with the following headings: **Institution, Purpose,** and **Nonexistent.** In small groups, have students brainstorm at least five public institutions and their purposes. After the first two columns are complete, have the groups exchange charts and fill in what might happen if each of the institutions did not exist. **Independent Practice**

Figure 5-1

Government Expenditure as a Percentage of Gross Domestic Product

The federal government is by far the single largest segment of our economy. It accounts for almost one-fourth of the U.S. gross domestic product. ***Do you think there is too much government spending?***

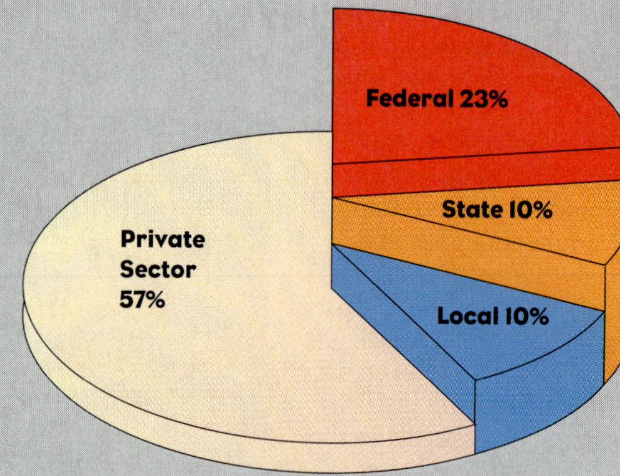

While providing an environment in which the private sector can function, the public sector also provides

1. courts to define rights and settle disputes;
2. monetary institutions, such as the Federal Reserve System, to control our system of money; and
3. regulatory agencies to promote competition among producers.

LEADERS IN ECONOMIC THOUGHT

Economic leaders do not always agree on the appropriate role that government and public institutions should play in our economy. Let's see what two leaders in economic thought believe about government involvement in our economy.

Milton Friedman

Milton Friedman is a strong supporter of *laissez-faire.* The concept of laissez-faire means that government involvement in economic matters should be highly limited. Friedman's main argument is that while trying to do good, government actions usually end up doing just the opposite. Most government efforts to protect consumers by regulating business create higher prices or services and goods of lesser quality. Many of the regulatory agencies are not very efficient in promoting competition in markets. They frequently end up representing the interests of the very businesses they regulate. Friedman has contended for more than three decades that minimal government ownership and control in the economy is in everyone's best interest.

Friedman won the Nobel Prize in Economics in 1976 for his work on monetary theory. He is professor emeritus at the University of Chicago and a fellow at Stanford University's Hoover Institute. Milton and his wife, Rose Friedman, have written three books together and are perhaps best known for their television series, "*Free to Choose.*"

Economic Spotlight

PUBLIC SERVANT, PRIVATE CONCERNS

One of 11 children of a Dutch-Irish mother and a Cherokee Indian father, Wilma Mankiller spent most of her childhood away from the Cherokee Indian Reservation of her birth. However, she later came back to her roots to help the Cherokees restore their self-sufficiency. As the first female principal chief of the Native-American Cherokee tribe, Mankiller wants to be remembered "as the person who helped us restore faith in ourselves."

As a child, her family fled the reservation for California after a severe drought ruined any chances of eking out a living from the poor Oklahoma soil. After becoming a social worker actively involved in Native-American rights, Wilma Mankiller moved back to the reservation. There she found most of the Cherokees living at the poverty level. On the reservation, she worked hard to revive the Cherokee nation's cultural pride and to restore the people to economic self-sufficiency. She won the respect of male leaders in the tribe by obtaining a grant that enabled rural Cherokees to build their own 26-mile waterline. In 1985, she filled the vacated position of principal chief of the Cherokee Nation. She was subsequently elected to that position in 1987 and 1991, retiring after completion of her 1991 term.

As chief, Mankiller worked 14-hour days to bring national attention to the plight of the Native-American people and to show Cherokees how they can overcome adversity to live productively. Applying the skills that she learned as a social worker, Mankiller's focus as chief was on two issues: self-help as a source of self-esteem and solving economic problems without looking for a handout from the government.

According to Mankiller, "My goal has always been for Indians to solve their own economic problems. Although we have been affected by a lot of historical factors, nobody is going to pull us out but ourselves." She certainly is off to a good start. In 1975, nearly all Cherokee income came from the federal government. But today, more than 50 percent of the tribe's income comes from a Cherokee-owned electronics plant and other private enterprises.

Economic Spotlight

After students have read the *Economic Spotlight* feature, tell them that the government does not tax commerce that occurs on reservations, yet it provides social services and aid to the Native Americans who live there. Divide the class into two groups and have students debate whether this policy is fair or unfair. (Responses may include that it is fair because the U.S. government has taken away almost all Native American lands or unfair because individuals on reservations reap benefits that they do not help fund.) Conclude by having students weigh the societal costs and benefits of this policy.

Explain that the government is involved in some issues and not in others. Tell students that, with laissez-faire, government involvement is *limited* but not *eliminated*. To help students who are demonstrating symptoms of Attention Deficit Disorder (ADD) such as difficulty in concentrating, low frustration tolerance, and inappropriately high levels of activity, encourage peer tutoring. This will help to filter out distractions in the classroom, focus attention one-on-one, and simplify the task at hand. Have one student who understands the need for some government involvement describe to the target student what it would be like if there were no regulation of military weapons, no laws regarding minimum wages, or no restaurant health inspections. Then, have the second student repeat the description and tell a story involving that scenario.

Attention Deficit Disorder

On the chalkboard or an overhead transparency, create a two-circle Venn diagram. Write **Public Sector** above one of the circles and **Private Sector** above the other. Ask students to brainstorm a list of businesses and organizations and then determine to which sector each entity belongs. Write each in the appropriate circle. If a business could be in both sectors, as with a golf course or university, write it in the space where the two circles overlap.

Copy the following graphic organizer onto the chalkboard or an overhead transparency.

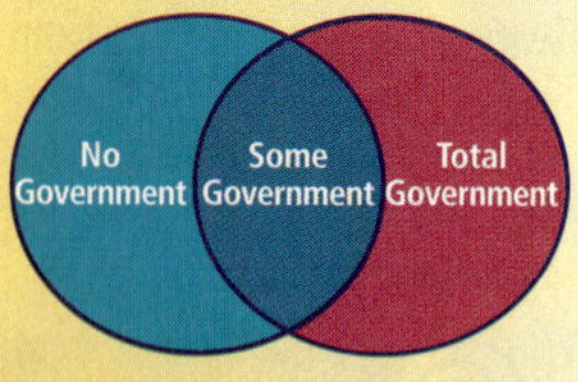

Ask students to copy the graphic organizer onto a sheet of paper and then fill in the circles with types of services that involve *no, some,* or *total* government involvement.

Divide the class into two groups. Tell one group that it represents Milton Friedman's viewpoint of laissez-faire. Tell the other group that it supports John Kenneth Galbraith's viewpoint of strong government. Have students debate why their viewpoint is the better choice.

Ask the class to vote for or against laissez-faire teacher involvement in the classroom. Have students write a persuasive essay defending their point of view about how this would affect the educational environment and students' grades.

John Kenneth Galbraith

John Kenneth Galbraith urges an affirmative role for government. He argues that because of their size, corporations have too much influence in modern society. This influence is so strong that it sometimes overpowers the classical market forces of supply and demand. Through advertising, corporations tend to *create* wants and needs for consumers. Thus, more private goods are produced, sometimes to the detriment of needed public goods. Galbraith has gained attention and respect in the field of economics.

Economic Dilemma

THE ECONOMICS OF POLITICS AND THE POLITICS OF ECONOMICS

If economists know what policies are good for the economy, why don't those policies always get used? Unfortunately, the system of representative government we have in the United States sometimes links good economics with bad politics and good politics with bad economics. There are at least three major reasons why this is true. The national debt gives us an example of how these three reasons create conflict between good economics and good politics.

First, some voters are rationally ignorant. This means that people make a rational decision to be poorly informed about the national debt. They feel that their individual votes make little difference (little benefit) and it is time consuming to gather information on which to base their votes (high cost). So they rationally decide not to inform themselves about an issue such as the national debt.

Second, special interest groups benefit a great deal from influencing decisions surrounding the national debt. Therefore, they spend a lot of money to influence the government to vote to their advantage, which is often to the disadvantage of the rest of society. Since the cost of the resulting policies is spread over the general public, no one person has too high a cost and there is usually little opposition to special interest groups.

Third, politicians are rationally shortsighted. They are more likely to vote for government spending than against it because it often benefits their voters—in the short run. Rational politicians would rather be in office explaining an increased national debt than defeated and explaining why they did not support spending programs for their state.

When these three effects combine in the political arena, the economic policy that gets voted in is frequently far from what is best for the whole economy. That's when good politics leads to bad economics.

Economic Dilemma

Divide the class into three groups: voters, a special interest group, and politicians. Remind voters that they are only a very small percentage of the total population. Then, tell the class that condominium builders want to build on land that is currently protected by the government. Ask the special interest group to come up with a strategy to convince politicians to allow the land to be used for condominiums. Have voters, who are against the construction, and special interest group members (lobbyists) debate their viewpoints. Finally, have the politicians vote on the issue.

John Kenneth Galbraith has been a professor of economics at Harvard University and president of the American Economic Association. He has served as ambassador to India and provided economic advice to several presidents. His books, *The Affluent Society, The New Industrial State,* and *Economics and the Public Purpose,* have been widely read and have contributed to economic thinking for more than two decades.

Checkpoint

Content Check

1. What makes up the public sector?

2. What are public institutions? Give two examples.

3. How do Milton Friedman's views about the role of government in our economy differ from John Kenneth Galbraith's views?

What Do You Think Now?

Reread *What Do You Think?* in the Section One Focus. Then answer the following questions:

4. Do you think the federal government should play a role in regulating content on the Internet? Why or why not?

5. What other actions, besides government regulation, can be taken to control content and access to the Internet?

6. Do you think any actions need to be taken to oversee information exchanges on the Internet?

Assess

1. Public institutions and the government **5-1**
2. Publicly owned organizations established by government to serve the wants and needs of a whole society (FCC, Federal Reserve, and state universities) **5-1**
3. Friedman believes in a limited role for government, whereas Galbraith believes in a strong, affirmative role for government. **5-1**
4. Students' opinions should be based on an understanding of public institutions and should identify the consequences of their decisions. **5-1**
5. Answers might include parental control, software that can monitor/limit access, or industry standards and self-regulation. **5-1**
6. Student answers should be supported by reasoned arguments and/or examples of similar situations. **5-1**

Close

Ask students to list several services that are provided by institutions in the public sector such as sanitation and public education. Have students discuss which services would be more efficient or inefficient if they were the responsibility of the private sector.

Reteach

Write the headings **Less Government** and **More Government** on the chalkboard or an overhead transparency. Ask students which heading could be renamed **Laissez-Faire.** Then, tell them to list some services that have substantial government involvement and some services that have less. **5-1**

Enrich

Tell students that the total budget for Parks Town is $500,000. They must divide the funds among the city's library, police department, fire department, and schools. Have students create a pie chart to show how they would allocate the funds and then explain their disbursement. **5-1**

Focus

Write the following on the chalkboard: **Why do sports teams promote competition among players and teams?** (To create drive, incentive, and an attitude of trying one's hardest to be the best) As students enter the classroom, hand out index cards and have students write their responses on them.

Collect all the index cards and read them to the class. Lead students to see a parallel between competition in sports and competition in business.

Teach

Identify the five major functions of the public sector: **promote competition, define and enforce property rights, provide public goods, reduce negative externalities,** and **redistribute income.**

Explain the function of **promoting competition** by describing what would happen if there were only one place where you could see movies. (That theater would not have to worry about having competitive prices.)

To help students understand **property rights,** point out how they serve as an authority to peacefully resolve disagreements over issues such as excessive noise.

Explain **public goods** from the perspective that it is cheaper to have one fire department protect an area rather than to have everyone try to do it individually.

To explain **negative externalities,** give an example such as a neighbor's smelly trash compost.

Discuss **redistributing income** from the perspective of equity. Explain that creating greater equity over time creates more stability in a society.

FOCUS

Section Two

Public Sector Contributions

What Do You Think?

The copper smelting company located outside of Madison produces smoke, fly ash, and other chemicals that drift down and settle on neighboring homes and farms. Recently, a lawsuit was filed by the residents of Madison against the smelter. The suit asks the company to pay for damage to the homes, public buildings, and farms in Madison. The company says its factory did not produce all the damaging pollutants and that if anyone has to pay, it should be everyone that produces smoke in the valley. The company specifically refers to the Army facility down the valley that still burns coal in its power plant. What do you think the solution is?

Terms to Know

property rights

contract

What's Ahead?

The public sector performs some tasks more efficiently than the private sector. The public sector also performs some tasks that the private sector is unwilling or unable to perform. Five major tasks of the public sector are to promote competition, define and enforce property rights, provide public goods, reduce negative externalities, and redistribute income.

FIVE MAJOR FUNCTIONS OF THE PUBLIC SECTOR

The public sector often does what the private sector either cannot do or is not willing to do. Let's take a closer look at the five major functions of the public sector. These are tasks that the public sector performs more effectively than the private sector.

Promoting Competition in the Private Sector

The efficiency of the private sector is improved by competition. Producers compete for the consumers' dollar votes by producing the most wanted goods at the lowest possible prices at which they can make a profit. If one

Economics & Your *Community*

Have students read newspapers and watch the local television news to see which companies are making news because they are affecting the local community in some way. Ask students to bring in the newspaper clippings or share with the class what they heard on the television news. Tell students to think about how these companies' competitors might be reacting to the news. Ask students what they think might happen if these businesses had no competition in the community. (Wouldn't worry about externalities) company grows so strong in the market that it pushes out all other producers, there will be no competition. The remaining giant company will be the only producer. Then it may not work as hard to produce the goods consumers want most at the lowest possible prices. Once a single producer grows so powerful that it controls an entire market, other producers will not be able to grow strong enough to compete.

Many times in this country's history, several companies joined together to set higher prices or to refuse to compete with each other in certain geographical areas. By joining together, they eliminated competition. The cooperating producers were able to control market forces in their favor. They reduced the supply of goods or services, therefore driving up prices and often profits.

The only force in our economy powerful enough to change this situation is government. In our history, government often has intervened in such cases by passing laws prohibiting companies from working together to dominate a market. The *Clayton Antitrust Act* (1914) is one of many such laws against unfair competition. The government also has established the *Federal Trade Commission* (1914) which promotes competition in industry and prevents unfair competition. The Federal Trade Commission polices the nation's businesses to keep our markets competitive.

Most economists agree that there is a need for government to do this kind of work. However, they do not agree on how it should be done. Government regulation is not always able to do everything that we would like it to do. We can pass laws forbidding producers from cooperating in setting prices. It is difficult, however, to detect this kind of behavior. It is also very expensive to pass and enforce laws against unfair competition. To pass and enforce these laws requires the efforts of many people such as legislators, investigators, judges, and office workers. Your tax dollars pay the salaries of all these people. Therefore, a small price increase may be less costly to you as a consumer than the cost of prosecuting businesses that are cooperating unlawfully.

Defining and Enforcing Property Rights

In our economy, the whole productive process depends on the concept of private property. All productive resources, such as land, labor, capital, and management skills, are owned by people. When you own property, you have certain rights. The government defines and enforces these rights.

property rights
the rules that government has established to define who owns what property and how owners may use their property

What Are Property Rights? ***Property rights*** are the rules that government has established to define who owns what property and how owners may use their property. As a worker, you own your own labor and sell that labor to an employer. The employer uses the labor you have sold to produce some good or service. The producer also buys raw materials, such as steel, iron, electric power, lumber, plastic, and glass, to use in producing the good or service. The producers own these goods and services until they sell them.

In most cases, once the goods or services are sold, they become the private property of the buyers. The buyers or owners have the private right to benefit from the ownership and use of these goods or services. They can enjoy

Apply

To help explain property rights, hold a mock trial. Choose two students to role-play feuding neighbors. Explain that one of the neighbors plays music loudly and the other complains that it prevents him or her from sleeping. Choose another student to act as a judge, presiding over the proceedings. Have the other students act as the jury. After hearing both neighbors' arguments, have the judge and jury decide who is right and then set down rules to resolve the situation. Ask probing questions to ensure understanding of property rights.
Guided Practice

Ask students to read Amendment XIV, Section 1, of the U.S. Constitution and write an essay discussing the limitations of ownership when it conflicts with the rights of others.
Independent Practice

Have the class brainstorm examples of how a property owner might unreasonably or unlawfully use property in a way that might injure someone else. Then, have students determine whether each example endangers public safety or health and, if so, what the government involvement should be.

Multicultural Highlights

U.S. Army General Colin Powell, an African American and former Chairman of the Joint Chiefs of Staff, has been a key player in U.S. public service. Powell was responsible for the country's entire defense budget and helped lead the United States successfully through the Gulf War against Iraq. Discuss with students the importance of how these types of federal-level decisions affect our economy. Have students discuss the impact on the economy when the country's national defense budget is decreased or increased.

the goods or services, or they have the right to sell them to others. The right to benefit from the use or sale of the items is a private right for the direct benefit of the owner. This system of private property rights strongly influences us to work hard to produce goods and services. We have this incentive because we can benefit directly from our hard work.

How Are Property Rights Protected? How is this system of private property rights enforced? Who is powerful enough to enforce these laws? The answer is *government*. Government defines what rights individuals and producers have. Government establishes and enforces the laws that give us the use and benefit of our private property. Without this system of rights and enforcement, our system of production would not be as efficient as it is.

contract
a legally binding agreement between two or more competent persons

When you sell your labor to an employer, you and your employer enter into a contract. A ***contract*** is a legally binding agreement between two or more competent persons. Suppose you decide to sell your labor to an employer and that employer cheats you or breaks the contract. The employer would be breaking the law, and you would have the power of the law behind you. You could force your employer to live up to the contract under the law.

The law also protects the employer's rights. Suppose your employer paid you in advance for a week's work, and then you only worked two days. The power of the law would be on the employer's side. The employer could force repayment from you through the legal system.

The law establishes a system of property rights and enforces contracts between individuals and businesses. In short, the law defines the rights of all parties and protects those parties equally.

If there were no laws to enforce contracts, individuals and businesses probably would break their agreements more often. Then all businesses would become less efficient because they could not be sure that agreements would be fulfilled. Employers could not depend on employees to fulfill their promise to work. Production would go up and down depending on how many workers decided to work on any given day. A producer could not promise buyers any specific delivery date. Also, workers would not be able to count on an employer to pay the agreed-upon wages. If producers could not deliver goods to buyers, they might not have enough revenues to pay the workers. Therefore, a system of contracts in which all parties must fulfill their legal obligations is extremely important to our economic system.

The legal system defines what you can and cannot do with your property. If you own a piece of residential land, you may legally occupy that land yourself or sell it. You own the private property rights to that land. The law also defines what you and your neighbors cannot do with your land. For example, you may not build a slaughterhouse on your land in a residential neighborhood. You cannot do anything that would injure your neighbors' property rights. And, your neighbors cannot do anything that would injure your property rights. If you decide to build a house on property that you own, there are many legal restrictions. For example, you must follow electrical safety codes. You cannot build a firetrap that might burn down and

Divide the class into groups of four or five students. Have the groups discuss the ethics of breaking an employment contract.(Answers may include poor ethics on the part of the employee if it unjustly leaves the employer in a bind or poor ethics on the part of the employer if it unjustly leaves an employee without a salary.) Then, have each group choose a spokesperson to sit on a panel at the front of the classroom. Ask each panel member to speak for 60 seconds on his or her group's viewpoint. Encourage the remainder of the class to ask probing questions of the panel.

Have each student write a business letter to a real or fictitious company that has not fulfilled a contract with him or her. (Examples might include a yearbook or class ring order.) Have students use appropriate business-letter style to state the terms of their contract, the obligation that was not fulfilled, and the course of action they would like to take to fulfill or end the contractual obligation. Post students' letters on a bulletin board and allow students time to read their classmates' work. Discuss selected letters and the options that were chosen to fulfill or end the contracts. Ask students how governmental laws might affect the disputes.

Internet Connection

BURROWING FOR INFORMATION WITH GOPHER

The best thing about the Internet is the tremendous amount of information it offers. Gopher allows you to search for and retrieve information.

If you connect to the Internet through a text-based computer (DOS or UNIX), you can access gopher by typing *gopher*. To move around the menu that appears, use the up and down arrow keys or type in the number of an item you wish to examine. Move to a subsequent screen by pressing the space bar. To return to an earlier screen, type *b* for back.

To select a menu item, put the cursor on the item and press *Enter*. Either a new menu will appear or a document will appear. To retrieve a document, type *m* to e-mail yourself a copy or *s* to save a copy in your home directory on the computer that allows you Internet access. To return to a previous menu, type *u* for up. To exit gopher, type *q* for quit.

While you can reach any gopher site on the Internet by moving through the menus from your local gopher, if you know the Internet address of a remote gopher site, it is quicker to access that site directly. To connect directly to a remote gopher, type *gopher remote-gopher-name*.

Economics/Internet Application: One measure of the importance of government is its share of total spending in the economy. Using gopher, connect to the Economics Bulletin Board, **una.hh.lib.umich.edu**. Make the following selections: EBB, National Income and Product Accounts, Latest National Income and Product Account (NIPA) Detail, Latest BEA Annual NIPA (A) Tables. From Table 101, compute the federal government's share of total spending by dividing Government Purchases by Gross Domestic Product. E-mail your answer to your teacher. If you cannot access una.hh.lib.umich.edu, it might be that the address has changed. Connect to gopher.thomson.com. Choose "South-Western Education, Resources, Internet Activities," and then choose "Economics." Print the page that appears and use the address listed for Chapter 5.

Divide the class into groups of four or five students. Choose one student to be a judge, presiding over the following debate: The mayor of a medium-sized town has recommended that the city build one additional fire station. Explain that, no matter where the fire station is located, everyone will pay for it because it will help the entire community. Remind students that a fire could damage any community's resources. Then, assign one of the following resources to each group: city schools, hospital, business district, residential area, and a historic museum. Have the groups of students act as citizen committees, arguing that the new fire station should be located in their neighborhood. After five to seven minutes, stop the debate. As a class, discuss the strengths and weaknesses of the groups' arguments.

Have each student recreate the following chart, listing what benefit the public receives from each of the listed public goods. Have students add three more public goods and their benefits to the chart.

Public Good	Benefit
Yellowstone National Park	
Public Library	
Lincoln Memorial	

Internet Connection

Before assigning this application, connect to the University of Michigan Gopher to confirm that the Internet address given here is still valid. If there is any problem accessing the Gopher, check for a new address in the **thomson.com** Gopher site, discussed in Chapter 1 of *Teacher's Connection to the Internet. Teacher's Connection* explains ways of accessing Gopher if you have a World Wide Web browser and gives complete steps for solving the application.

Have students re-create the following three-column chart. Have them list who in a neighborhood would be affected by each negative externality and how. (Answers may include motorists, car dings; neighborhood, noise pollution; and community, air pollution.)

NEGATIVE EXTERNALITIES

Cause	Who's Affected	How
Gravel Trucks		
Airport		
Steel Factory		

spread fire to your neighbors' homes. In general, laws are designed to protect the property rights of all owners. You can do whatever you want with your property as long as it does not threaten or hurt the property rights of others.

The legal system is for your benefit. It protects your rights. Government, by defining these rights, sets up a system in society that helps all of us to live and work together more efficiently. By defining what is fair or equitable, government contributes to the efficiency of an economy. It settles disputes between individuals and forces everyone to fulfill their legal agreements.

Providing Public Goods

As you learned in Chapter 3, many goods and services are produced more efficiently in the public sector. Roads, schools, national defense, and police and fire protection are some of these goods and services. Obviously, it is more efficient for a country to maintain one army than for citizens to try to defend themselves individually. Roads are too expensive to build to be used efficiently by just one individual. The public goods rationale explains why these goods are most efficiently produced by government.

Government also often undertakes activities that the private sector will not. For example, several private railway companies once provided rail service, but they failed financially. They could not generate enough profit to stay in business. The private sector thus stopped providing rail service to some parts of the country. The U.S. government took over much of the railway system in the 1980s and partially paid for its operation through a corporation called Amtrak. Many people in the government tried to eliminate this subsidy in the 1990s, with varying results. Believing that train service is important to our economy, the public sector still spends tax dollars to keep trains running.

Some economists say this is a wasteful and inefficient use of tax dollars. This may be a fair criticism. However, keeping the trains running does provide train service in places where it is vital to our nation's interest. It also provides competition for the trucking industry and other kinds of businesses that transport freight and people. Every government action clearly has both benefits and costs. If train service is important and the private sector cannot provide that service profitably, the public sector must step in.

Dealing with Negative Externalities

Many kinds of costs and benefits are passed on to individuals who are not involved in the market. In Chapter 4, you learned that when these spillover effects are *costs*, they are called *negative externalities*. Negative externalities affect people who are "external" to (or outside of) the market that produces the costs.

Measuring Negative Externalities. When discussing externalities, the term *cost* does not necessarily mean a dollar cost. Instead, cost can be a reduction in individual satisfaction or well-being. For example, assume your neighbors are playing their radio at high volume while you are trying to sleep. Your neighbors are passing on a negative externality to you. They are reducing your satisfaction or well-being by passing on a cost to you outside the market system. There is no dollar price involved, just a reduction in your well-being. A business world equivalent of this is the pollution of a stream by a chemical plant. Air pollution by a coal-burning electric power plant is another example. These activities reduce the quality of life of people downstream or

MediaLink

Have students prepare two to three questions to use in a survey about the role of government in the economy. (For example, "Is it the government's responsibility to provide all citizens with health care?", "How much control should the government have over radio broadcasting?", and "Where does government responsibility for financial aid to families end and individual responsibility begin?") Then, using a camcorder, have students survey others at school. View the recorded surveys as a class and, after each one, pause to discuss people's different opinions about the role of government.

downwind. Clean air and clean water clearly contribute to our health and well-being. Pollution of the environment reduces our satisfaction and quality of life.

Controlling Negative Externalities. Government is often called on to deal with negative externalities in the private sector. If a local chemical plant is polluting the river, you might complain directly to the plant. Many of your neighbors might do the same. However, most plants will not stop polluting if measures needed to stop the pollution are expensive. You and your neighbors will probably need the power of the law behind you. So far, only the public sector has been powerful enough to force companies to spend a large amount of money to stop pollution. It is not that most companies want to pollute. They are simply trying to produce the goods and services consumers desire at the lowest possible price. If a business must spend millions of dollars on pollution control, its costs of production must rise. You and your neighbors, with the help of government, may be successful in forcing a company to clean up its pollution. However, you may end up paying higher prices for goods made by that company.

Pollution and other kinds of externalities are often hard to detect. It is also difficult to find a sole cause of an externality and apply the blame to the proper party. A chemical plant may be the main cause of pollution. On the other hand, every plant that uses the river probably contributes to the pollution in some way. The city sewer system, run by government itself, might be dumping sewage. The large research and monitoring effort needed to control externalities can be provided most efficiently by government.

In controlling externalities, the government defines and enforces property rights. The public sector can deal with this issue more effectively than the private sector. The public sector can protect you by passing laws that prohibit companies or individuals from injuring you by polluting air and water or by making your property less attractive. The public sector also can force companies to buy pollution control equipment. It can even force persons or companies to pay for damages due to externalities they caused. All this effort,

Tell students that one way the government regulates negative externalities is through court orders called *injunctions.* An injunction forbids an individual or company from continuing an action. The action must be halted immediately and can only be resumed if the injunction is removed. As a class, discuss how easy or difficult it should be for a citizen to obtain an injunction. Then, divide the class into three groups. One group should role-play a community that is upset about dangerous potholes in the streets created by trucks traveling to and from a local plant. The other group should role-play the company's management team, arguing that, if the trucks can't use those streets, the company will go out of business, and many people in the community will lose their jobs. Have the third group decide whether to issue an injunction against the company based on the two groups' arguments. Bring closure to the activity by having students summarize why and how injunctions regulate negative externalities.

At random, divide the class into three socioeconomic groups. Have the first group consist of two students representing the upper class; the second group, four students representing the middle class; and the third group, the remaining students, representing the lower class. Make sure that inclusion in any particular group is purely random. Remind students that, if the government didn't help redistribute income, the wealthy might become wealthier and the poor might become poorer. Have group members sit together. Ask each group to discuss its wealth status, to debate the pros and cons of wealth redistribution, and to determine the group's position on the topic. Then, bring the class together and have a spokesperson for each group summarize the group's debate. Discuss conclusions as a class.

however, will be paid for by the individual in one way or another. The costs to pass and enforce the laws will be paid for through tax dollars. The costs to clean up the pollution or install better equipment will be paid for through higher market prices.

The real choice as to how much externality will be tolerated and at what cost is up to the consumer. The consumer's voice in these matters is heard in two places. First, the consumer's voice reaches producers in the marketplace. What consumers buy and do not buy tells producers how they feel about the goods and services offered at various prices. Second, the consumer's voice reaches government in the voting booth. How individuals vote determines the reactions of the public sector to externalities.

Redistributing Income

In our economy there are some individuals who are unable to earn enough income to survive. Often, this is not their fault. There are members of our society who are handicapped or simply unable to work at a productive job. The public sector taxes the income of those who work and redistributes part of that income to those who cannot earn.

This is more than just an attempt to be compassionate. In our system of private enterprise, the ability to earn income increases with wealth. The more private property you own, the more income you have and the more chances you have of being able to produce. This situation tends to make the rich get richer. By redistributing income, our government attempts to provide equity. It tries to make the opportunity to earn income more equitable, which is a social goal in our society.

This redistribution effort does not give everyone an equal income. However, it does keep all the income in our economy from going only to a few individuals. Income redistribution programs that provide public assistance to low-income households help make more opportunities available. This attempts to break the cycle of poverty.

The United States still has its share of poverty. The distribution of income in this country, however, is more equitable than in many capitalistic countries of the world. Extremely uneven distribution of income in a country is often the cause of revolutions. Much of the political upheaval in Latin America has been due, in part, to an uneven distribution of income. In some Latin American countries, a very small part of the population controls most of the country's income.

We realize, then, that income redistribution may be an equitable and desirable act. To redistribute income on any large scale takes the power of law. Americans give large sums to charity every year, but this is a very small amount compared to the income redistributed by government. Each year, our

Perspectives

Thinking Like a Politician

In many countries, there is an uneven distribution of wealth. Even in the United States, the wealthiest 1 percent of the population owns a large share of the country's total wealth. In many countries, citizens have forced the government to make changes. U.S. politicians do not want political upheaval, so they are concerned about achieving equity. However, they also know that the wealthy have a great deal of power. Ask students what strategies some politicians might use while in office in order to satisfy enough voters in every socioeconomic group to become reelected.

government redistributes hundreds of billions of dollars to needy people. It is highly unlikely that any individuals or businesses willingly would turn over large parts of their incomes to be redistributed if it were not required by law. You might feel that everyone should do her or his share and that if everyone else chipped in, you would too. However, if everyone did not give their share, you might refuse to bear the redistribution burden alone. Redistribution without the power of law is not likely to be effective. Therefore, the public sector can redistribute income more efficiently than the private sector. The public sector's primary concern is to serve the wants and needs of our society in an equitable manner.

Checkpoint

Content Check

1. What tasks does the public sector perform because it is more efficient than the private sector?
2. What tasks does the public sector perform because the private sector is not able to perform them?
3. Why are property rights important in a market economy?

What Do You Think Now?

Reread *What Do You Think?* in the Section Two Focus. Then answer the following questions:

4. Do you think it is possible to identify everyone responsible for polluting the air? Explain.
5. What functions are the citizens of Madison asking the government to perform?

Assess

1. Providing public goods and redistributing income **5-2**
2. Promoting competition, controlling negative externalities, enforcing property rights **5-2**
3. They provide an economic incentive for owners, who can benefit from ownership and use of the property. **5-2**
4. No, very difficult to assign private responsibility for polluting a public good such as clean air **5-2**
5. Defining and enforcing property rights; controlling negative externalities **5-2**

Close

Divide the class into five groups, one for each of the five functions of the public sector. Ask each group to determine what would happen if its function were eliminated from government's role. Then, as a class, discuss how society would be different if the public sector were not responsible for these functions.

Reteach

Distribute newspapers to the class and have each student cut out an article that is an example of one of the five major functions of the public sector. Have each student exchange his or her article with another student and then identify the function represented. **5-2**

Enrich

Have students discuss negative externalities from the perspective of property values. For example, would living next to a football stadium be good or bad? Have students create a list of other negative externalities that might affect property value and determine which ones could be eliminated through government involvement. **5-2**

Focus

Before students arrive, "litter" the classroom with crumpled paper bags, clean but empty soda cans, newspapers, and food wrappers. As students enter class, ask them to observe the classroom and to jot down how the room looks different today.

Ask students to note how the surroundings make them feel. Discuss that leaving trash in a public place is littering, which is one example of a public abuse. Elicit from students reasons they think people litter and engage in other forms of destruction of public property.

Teach

On the chalkboard or an overhead transparency, create a graphic organizer. In the center circle, write **Public Sector Problems.** Draw three lines radiating from the center with the following three labels: **Special Interest Groups, Abuse of Public Goods,** and **Problems of Size.** As students view the graphic organizer, describe the problems associated with the public sector.

Explain that **special interest groups** have a concern for an issue and lobby to get laws passed in their favor. Tell students that **lobbying** affects all of us when the groups are successful and new laws are passed. Explain that milk prices may go up or cars might become more costly due to new tests or safety standards required by law.

Explain that citizens tend to abuse public goods because they think of public property as having less value to them than private property.

Finally, explain that problems of size occur when an organization is too large to control and its production cannot be monitored, which leads to inefficiency.

Section Three

Public Sector Problems

What Do You Think?

Trevor was at the main library looking for books on his favorite subject, the Civil War. As he searched the stacks, he found many books out of place. Two of the Civil War atlases were missing the pages he really wanted to see. One of the very old books about Andersonville had been damaged badly by water and the spine was broken in half. Someone had written notes throughout the margins of a biography of Robert E. Lee. Trevor couldn't understand why some people were so careless with library books. It seemed as if they didn't care that someone else was going to use them later. Do you think that this is a common problem?

Terms to Know

special interest group

lobbying

What's Ahead?

The public sector has some problems carrying out its economic functions. Problems in the public sector include the abuse of public goods, the influence of special interest groups, and a tendency to grow too large. Your actions can help to solve these problems.

PROBLEMS WITH THE PUBLIC SECTOR

You have learned about the five major areas where the public sector plays a major role in a market economy. These five areas seem to function best in the public sector. You should also be aware of some of the major problems that can occur in the public sector.

Abuse of Public Goods

Public goods, such as schools, roads, public housing, parks, and recreational facilities, are goods the whole community or society owns. These goods are provided through public ownership. This is an application of the concept of economies of scale (that some economic activities become more efficient when done on a large scale). People can enjoy a large public park at a lower cost per person than if individuals tried to provide their own parks.

Public Ownership and Individual Responsibility. Public ownership does not always encourage the pride and conscience of individual ownership. Often, individuals do not take care of publicly owned goods as well as they do their own property. For example, graffiti frequently appears on public goods, such as school buildings, but rarely on privately owned property. Individuals who deface or destroy public property usually do not ruin their individually owned property. Other examples of this disregard for public property are litter on highways and destruction of play equipment in parks. These activities detract from the satisfaction we get from the use of public goods. To repair, clean up, and maintain public property is costly. This cost is passed on to all members of society, even though only a few citizens cause the problem.

Global Economy

RIGHTS AROUND THE WORLD

In the mid-1980s, technology that was protected by copyrights and patents in the United States was frequently pirated and sold in other countries. Copyrights and patents are legal property rights granted to those who invest their time, energy, and money to produce new inventions and innovations. The protection of copyrights and patents gives people the right to profit from their invention or innovation for a specified period of time. This provides a strong incentive for entrepreneurs to risk their time, energy, and money to bring new goods and services to market.

The research and development costs of creating new software are very high. Without the protection guaranteed by copyrights and patents, many entrepreneurs would not develop these new products. In a case that drew international attention, it was found that individuals and whole organizations in China frequently copied U.S. computer software and sold it in their country without paying royalties to the copyright holder. When governments allow software to be copied and sold in their countries without paying the proper royalties, they steal from U.S. producers. Since the global market for software is so large, this theft deprives the original producers of royalties, to which they are legally entitled.

In 1995, the Clinton administration notified China that if they did not help protect and enforce U.S. patent and copyright laws, the United States would institute trade restrictions against China. China then agreed to make additional efforts to enforce U.S. copyright and patent laws in China. Just how permanent these efforts will be is not clear. However, the threat of trade restrictions, while potentially injuring individual trading partners, may help all future producers who need the protection of copyrights and patents. Property rights will be a major issue as the world moves toward a single global economy in the future.

Apply

To help students relate public sector problems to their everyday lives, make a chart on the chalkboard or an overhead transparency with the following three column headings: **Public Institution, Purpose,** and **Problem.** Ask students to brainstorm a list of institutions in their community and their purposes. Then, have them list a problem associated with each. Write students' responses in the appropriate columns of the chart.
Guided Practice

Tell students to imagine that they work for the Parks and Recreation Department for their county. Ask them how they would deal with people who abuse their county's public parks. Would they treat a classmate who spray paints graffiti differently from a classmate who litters? Would they relate the penalty to the cost of cleaning up the site? Have students write an essay on this topic. Then, invite a member of your Parks and Recreation Department to speak to your class about abuses such as vandalism, graffiti, and litter on public property. Ask the speaker to be prepared to discuss fines and other solutions the department has come up with to deter abuse.
Independent Practice

Global Economy

In the past, the typical consumer would buy many of his or her goods and services locally. All parties involved in these transactions were under the same authority: U.S. law. In recent times, however, we have moved from a local economy to a global economy. Ask students to think of ways that our government can protect the property rights of U.S. citizens conducting business internationally. (Answers may include United Nations involvement, cooperative sanctions, and special coding.)

Emphasize to students how costly it is to the public to hire crews to clean up litter, erase graffiti, and repair or replace destroyed property. Encourage students to start their own street, neighborhood, or community "clean-up task force." Have students ask their family, friends, and neighbors if they will volunteer a certain amount of time each month to help clean up a particular area in their neighborhood. Have students create a class database of volunteers, making sure they include volunteers' names, addresses, phone numbers, supplies they can donate, and time of availability.

Have students create public-service announcements to stop a public abuse such as graffiti, litter, or vandalism that is occurring in their school. Tell students to create posters with slogans (for example, "Keep our school cool: Keep graffiti off the walls and trash out of the halls") or record radio or TV spots using cassette recorders or camcorders. Encourage all students' creative ideas.

Once started, the problem of public property abuse grows. People throw even more garbage on a badly littered highway in the mistaken belief that "everyone does it." Some people who would never throw a soda can in their own front yard think nothing of throwing one out their car window. Many people do not see these acts as the costly activities that they really are. This simply increases the costs all citizens will pay for public goods in the future.

Working Toward a Solution. Abusive private behavior toward public goods has been a problem for many years in our country. Some societies, however, have been able to improve this kind of behavior. The Montreal subway system in Canada is a public good in which many citizens take great pride of ownership. There is almost no graffiti there. The public parks of

Econ & You

EVERYONE'S SPECIAL

Almost all Americans have become part of some type of special interest group. In 1956, there were 4,900 national trade associations in the United States. By 1989, there were 23,000. In 1960, there were 365 paid lobbyists registered with the U.S. Senate, but today there are 40,111.

Lobbyists are highly skilled (and paid) professionals whose function is to promote the well-being of their special interest groups. They represent every kind of interest imaginable in Washington, including every known industry. The Tobacco Lobby openly spends millions of dollars each year in efforts to prevent legislation that would ban smoking. The Automobile Lobby opposes federal legislation that would require higher gasoline mileage and safety standards for cars. If your parents are members of a retirement plan at work, they are represented by lobbyists who work for the securities industry. Your grandparents may be members of the American Association of Retired Persons (AARP). Teachers are represented by the National Federation of Teachers and the National Education Association. The American Bar Association lobbies for lawyers and the American Medical Association lobbies for doctors. The American Lung Association, The American Cancer Society, and many other nonprofit organizations use lobbyists to represent their interests.

It is easy to see why it is difficult to get legislation passed with so many varied interests. It is entirely possible that in the future you may become a member of two special interest groups with completely opposing views on a given law. If, for example, you were a New York teacher who enjoyed hunting, your teachers union would openly advocate more gun control while the National Rifle Association would openly oppose such legislation.

Special interests are something we seem to want to have less of except when it comes to our own individual special interests. The problem of the power of special interest groups is obviously very complex and probably will continue to be a problem for a long time.

Econ & You

Ask the class to think of a special interest it would like to see occur in its school or city. For example, would students like to have more athletic groups or social hangouts available in the area for teenagers? Have the class form and name its own special interest group. Then, have students write letters or send videotaped or audiotaped messages lobbying their cause to their local or state government. Share responses when received.

Japan are a showplace of public pride. Citizens who foolishly litter or foul the area are quickly reminded by other citizens of their civic responsibility. These examples of changing private behavior show some hope for improving the problem of private abuse of public goods.

Special Interest Groups

Laws are made through our system of representative government in Washington, D.C., that determine how the many functions of the public sector will be carried out. The federal government has tremendous power when it defines and enforces property rights and redistributes income. There will always be people who try to use the system to their own advantage. A ***special interest group*** is an organization of people who are bound together by a common concern. Special interest groups are very active in lobbying. ***Lobbying*** is the act of communicating with government representatives to influence their votes on a specific issue.

special interest group
an organization of people who are bound together by a common concern

lobbying
the act of communicating with government representatives to influence their votes on a specific issue

How Does Lobbying Work? Over the years, many special interest groups have developed to lobby for laws that will benefit them. The National Rifle Association lobbies against gun control. The Sierra Club lobbies in Congress against the use of wilderness lands for public parks and recreation. The National Dairy Association lobbies for higher subsidized, or legally set, minimum prices on dairy products. All these organizations devote large amounts of money and time to make sure that government representatives hear their points of view. If a particular member of Congress votes against laws the organization favors, the organization tries to influence its members against reelecting that representative. These organizations are believed to influence tens of thousands of votes for each candidate.

Individuals do not have the time and resources to lobby for their own interests. It would be difficult for you to write thousands of letters to Congress or to go to Washington to make your views known. So, like all other individual voters, you participate in the process of representative government by electing individuals who represent your views. Perhaps you support with membership dues organizations that will lobby for you.

Lobbying Affects All of Us. Special interest groups are very powerful politically. They strongly influence the passing of laws that will benefit the special interest groups at the cost of all citizens. If the National Dairy Association succeeds in getting laws passed that raise the minimum price of milk, everyone pays higher milk prices. The producer of dairy products receives the benefits of such laws. The cost is passed on to every member of the economy who buys milk. The outcome is the same anytime a law benefiting only one particular group in society is passed. The whole society pays for a benefit that is enjoyed by only a small group. This is not necessarily bad. You and others in society may be willing to pay a small price individually to pass on a large benefit to a special interest group. You should be aware, however, that special interest groups number in the thousands. When you pay your taxes or buy the goods and services these groups represent, you are supporting their cause whether you like it or not.

Economic *Talk*

Ask the class to take at least three vocabulary terms from the chapter and use them in a song, rap, poem, or other form of presentation. (For example: "Some people with a cause like to lobby/They're called special interest groups/ Swaying politicians is their hobby/ For their cause, they'll jump through hoops.") Videotape students as they perform. Then, review the presentations as a class having each student write down all the vocabulary terms used. Review students' lists and add any terms missed in the presentations.

Explain to the class that lobbyists are involved in many issues. For example, some lobbyists are in favor of a flat tax as part of the U.S. tax system, while other lobbyists are in favor of keeping the current tax structure, which allows deductions for home ownership. Ask students what concerns they have regarding specific issues in their school and what they would like to see changed. Ask students how lobbying might help them accomplish their objectives.

Divide the class into groups of three or four students. Have two students in each group role-play members of special interest groups for opposite causes. (For example, one could be for gun control and one against it.) Ask both students to formulate lobbying strategies. Tell the third student to role-play a politician that the lobbyists are trying to influence. Have the special interest group members present their cases to the politician, who should respond favorably or unfavorably to the arguments. If there is a fourth student, have him or her write down the different strategies used. Allow 15 minutes for the activity. Then, bring the whole class together to discuss the strategies used by each side in their presentations.
Cooperative Learning

As a class, lead students to brainstorm as many special interest groups as possible. In the library or through an online information service, have volunteers research an address and the name of one contact person for each group on the list. Then, have students create a class database of this information. You may wish to have students call or write for specific information about each cause and update the database periodically.

Have students think of reasons it could be detrimental for some organizations to get too large. Ask the class to brainstorm a list of ways technology (such as computers, faxes, modems, and cellular phones) has given organizations the ability to be smaller and more efficient (decreased chance of errors; one computer does the work of many, so not as many salaries to pay; and so on).

Unfortunately, when political power is concentrated in any organization or group, individual interests of all citizens are sometimes not well represented. There will always be individuals and groups who try to use the public sector to their advantage. There will always be situations where smaller groups and individuals benefit at a cost passed on to everyone in the society. This is very much the nature of the social decision-making process you learned about in Chapter 3.

Problems of Size

Some goods and services are produced in the public sector because of economies of scale. On the other hand, some productive activities can be done more efficiently on a smaller scale. In the private sector, many companies realize this. Therefore, they break their companies down into several smaller subsidiaries or smaller companies. This structure helps to maintain control of a giant company's efforts. However, even with this structure, it is difficult to control any very large organization.

In the past, the public sector has had problems with size. For example, the Department of Agriculture employed 128,595 people in 1981. There were only about 2,434,000 farms in the United States in that year, which means there was nearly one federal employee for every 19 farms. By 1992, the Department of Agriculture served 2,197,000 farms with 128,324 employees, so there was nearly one federal employee for every 18 farms. Many people believe the Department of Agriculture does not need that many employees.

Streamlining government is more difficult than it seems. In the years ahead, we may see a more streamlined and more efficient government. Even though there will always be problems in the public sector, new and innovative solutions are a primary goal of economists.

Assess

1. Abusers lack the pride that comes with individual ownership. **5-3**
2. Through lobbying, which may affect lawmakers' votes **5-3**
3. When organizations get too large, they become inefficient. The government often suffers from the inefficiencies associated with size. **5-3**
4. Answers may include closer security, public involvement in monitoring public areas, heavier penalties, peer pressure, and limited access. **5-3**
5. Answers will range from verbal confrontation to no action. **5-3**

Checkpoint

Content Check

1. Why are public goods misused by individuals who treat their private property with respect?
2. How does a special interest group influence the law making process?
3. What is the effect of size on the efficiency of the public sector?

What Do You Think Now?

Reread *What Do You Think?* in the Section Three Focus. Then answer the following questions:

4. How can our society minimize the type of abuse of public goods Trevor observed?
5. How would you deal with a situation in which you saw one of your friends destroying public property?

Close

Explain to the class that problems with the public sector cannot be solved easily. Ask the class to develop a plan that would help prevent future problems in public schools. Ask students where they would get the money to implement these plans and what types of difficulties they might encounter.

Reteach

Have students skim through newspapers to find several examples of public sector problems. Have them state in their own words on an index card the general problem of each article. Tell each student to exchange his or her article and card with another student and match each summary card to an article. **5-3**

Enrich

Ask students to think of appropriate penalties for students who litter, vandalize, paint graffiti, and steal supplies or equipment. Have students find out the school's actual penalties for these abuses and then compare them to the penalties they listed. **5-3**

Concepts in Brief

1. The public sector includes all levels of government and its institutions that assist the functioning of the entire economy. The primary concern of the public sector is to provide equity in our system which, in turn, improves efficiency. The public sector undertakes activities that the private sector cannot do or is not willing to do.
2. Some of the functions of the public sector, such as controlling negative externalities, promoting competition, and enforcing property rights, come about because they require the power of law. Other activities of the public sector, such as providing public goods and redistributing income, are undertaken because generally they are not profitable for private industry. The government serves as a referee to encourage competition among firms. The government also sets up the legal system to define and enforce the property rights of individuals and the public. The public sector provides public goods, such as roads and police protection, that improve the efficiency of the private sector. The public sector deals with negative externalities that pass costs on to those outside of the market. Finally, the public sector redistributes income to improve equity within the economy.
3. The public sector encounters problems in performing economic activities. First, public goods are frequently abused by a small number of individuals at the expense of the whole society. Second, special interest groups try to manipulate the process of government to gain benefits for themselves at the cost of all members of the society. Third, the public sector has grown so large that portions of its efforts are not very efficient.

Economic Foundations

1. What are five major functions of the public sector?
2. How does the public sector promote competition?
3. How does the public sector enforce property rights?
4. What can the public sector do about negative externalities?
5. Give one major reason why the public sector redistributes income.
6. Why does abuse of public goods affect all members of a society?
7. How can a special interest group affect those individuals who do not support the cause of the special interest group?
8. How can the size of government affect its ability to carry out economic activities?

Chapter Close

Your Economic Portfolio

Tell students to think of a concern or problem in their community that is the responsibility of the public sector, such as potholes in the roads or outdated reference materials in the libraries. Ask students to each write a letter to the mayor, governor, or other appropriate government representative that states what the problem is, how it affects the public, and what some possible solutions are. Tell students to look in the government section of the phone book to find the phone number of the representative's office. Then, have them call to obtain the name and address of the state official they need to contact. Remind students to use a proper business-letter format, which includes the return address, date line, inside address, formal salutation, and complimentary closing. Review each letter with its author. Have the student make any necessary changes, proofread the final letter, and mail it. Be sure to make a copy of each student's letter to put in his or her portfolio.

You may wish to provide the following end-of-chapter materials:

- *Skills & Concepts* worksheet
- *Content Review Workbook*
- Chapter *Assessment*
- Chapter *MicroExam*

Economic Foundations

1. (1) Promoting competition in the private sector, (2) defining and enforcing property rights, (3) providing public goods, (4) attempting to deal with externalities, and (5) redistributing income (pp. 104-111)
2. By passing laws such as antitrust laws (pp. 104-105)
3. By establishing and enforcing laws that give us the use and benefit of our private property (pp. 105-106)
4. The public sector can pass and enforce laws that prohibit companies or individuals from injuring others. (pp. 108-110)
5. To provide equity (pp. 110-111)
6. Because the costs of such abuse are paid for by all members of a society (p. 113)

(Continued)

Your Economic Vocabulary

Build your economic vocabulary by matching the following terms with their definitions.

contract
lobbying
property rights
public institutions
public sector
special interest group

1. the rules that government has established to define who owns what property and how owners may use their property
2. an organization of people who are bound together by a common concern
3. a legally binding agreement between two or more competent persons
4. publicly owned organizations established by government to serve the wants and needs of a whole society
5. the act of communicating with government representatives to influence their votes on a specific issue
6. the part of an economy that is owned by and operated for the benefit of the whole society

Thinking Critically About Economics

1. Do you think that equity or efficiency is a more important goal for our economy? Why? Do you feel that both are necessary? If so, why? If not, why not?
2. What do you feel is the single most important function of the public sector? Why is this function more important to you than the other major functions provided by the public sector?
3. Are property rights necessary for an advanced industrial society to function efficiently? If so, are private property rights necessary? What do you think is the difference between property rights in general and private property rights? Are there property rights involved with a public good like a park? If so, are they public or private property rights?
4. Are externalities sometimes efficient but not equitable? If so, give an example of an efficient, but inequitable, externality. If not, explain why not.
5. Suggest a solution to each of the three problems of the public sector.
6. Do you feel that the public sector should keep businesses from cooperating to set prices or from competing with each other? If so, explain.

Economic Foundations (Continued)

7. When a special interest group succeeds in getting government support for its programs, all members of society pay the costs—even those individuals who do not support the special interest group's cause. (p. 115)
8. When a government grows too large, its efforts are not very efficient. (p. 116)

Your Economic Vocabulary

1. **property rights**
2. **special interest group**
3. **contract**
4. **public institutions**
5. **lobbying**
6. **public sector**

Thinking Critically About Economics

1. Both equity and efficiency contribute vitally to our economy, and equity tends to improve efficiency.
2. Answers will vary but may include defining and enforcing property rights because property rights determine who can do what and how in our economy.
3. Yes. Private property rights are necessary in order to define who may do what with each type of property. Public property rights provide equity while private property rights provide private benefits for individuals. Yes, the rights to a public park are public because everyone owns the park and has equal rights to its benefits.

(Continued)

Thinking Critically About Economics (Continued)

4. Externalities are efficient but not equitable when the cost passed on to third parties is less than the benefit received by the rest of society. Examples may include forcing one homeowner to move if his or her house stands in the path of a new highway that will benefit an entire city.
5. Answers may include reducing the size of some bureaucracies, passing and enforcing more stringent laws dealing with the abuse of public property, and passing laws to reduce the power of special interest groups.
6. Students should understand that it is an important function because competition makes most markets more efficient.

Economic Enrichment

Identify three special interest groups that affect how your school operates. Create a poster that illustrates the beliefs and issues important to each special interest group, the activities the special interest groups undertake to communicate their views, and how the interests of each group might compete with one another.

Math and Economics

Use library resources, commercial online services, or the Internet to find the number of business enterprises in the United States and the number of employees in the U.S. Department of Commerce. Calculate the number of business enterprises for every commerce department employee. How does this number compare with the number of farms in the United States for each employee of the Department of Agriculture?

Writing About Economics

Research a current economic issue that you are interested in, such as government waste, increasing or decreasing taxes, welfare reform, cost of recycling, or education reform. Be sure to examine the facts surrounding the issue and investigate the views of the special interest groups involved. Then write a letter to your senator, representative, or appropriate local political representative that presents your views on the issue and what you think the solution should be. Use the five-step decision-making model to arrive at your proposed solution.

Economic Enrichment

Students' posters will vary according to the specific groups chosen. Examples of special interest groups are the American Civil Liberties Union (ACLU), Students Against Drunk Driving (SADD), specific citizen committees, and other locally or nationally organized groups.

Math and Economics

Students should divide the current number of U.S. business enterprises by the number of employees in the Department of Commerce. Then, they should compare that figure to the number of U.S. farms per Department of Agriculture employees as stated in their textbook on p. 116 (19 farms per federal employee).

Writing About Economics

Students should complete the five-step decision-making process to arrive at possible solutions to the economic issues they choose. They should describe their individual issues and solutions in letters to political representatives, making sure to use proper business-letter style and to proofread and correct any errors in grammar and spelling.

Part Two
The Microeconomic Perspective

Dear Teachers

In the study of microeconomics, I believe the market structures of perfect competition, pure monopoly, and oligopoly are probably the most difficult concepts for students to comprehend. Even though Chapters 10 and 11 will be challenging for students, the graphics in the textbook and the activities in the *Wraparound Teacher's Edition* will considerably enhance the effectiveness of instruction and facilitate students' understanding of these concepts.

In teaching perfect competition and pure monopoly, I would emphasize that in the real world there is no such market that could be characterized as purely competitive or purely monopolistic. However, the market structures that come very close to pure competition and pure monopoly are monopolistic competition and oligopoly, respectively. I would mention monopolistic competition only in passing and would devote more time to oligopoly, which is the dominant market structure in the U.S. economy.

Dr. Usman Qureshi
Old Dominion University
Norfolk, Virginia

Portfolio Activities Overview

In Chapter 6, students write a business letter to a local retailer discussing the goods that they would buy in greater quantities if the prices were lower. In Chapter 7, students create a supply curve and a total product curve based on information for a fictitious company. In Chapter 8, students write a short position paper discussing whether the market or the government should control prices. In Chapter 9, students write a summary report for a potential business plan for their own company. In Chapter 10, students write a newspaper ad or article describing a new monopoly. In Chapter 11, students create a company newsletter discussing the advantages of a company's market organization. In Chapter 12, students create externality charts and write a paragraph about how a business would be affected if it went from a competitive organization to a monopoly. In Chapter 13, students create a brochure that explains the minimum wage for their state's (un)employment commission.

Chapter 6

Crazy People (videocassette). Paramount Pictures, 1990.

Larson, Erik. *The Naked Consumer: How Our Private Lives Become Public Commodities.* New York: H. Holt, 1992.

Settle, Robert B., and Pamela L. Alreck. *Why They Buy. American Consumers Inside and Out* (audiocassette). New York: Wiley Sound Business, 1988.

Strasser, Susan. *Satisfaction Guaranteed: The Making of the American Mass Market.* New York: Pantheon Books, 1989.

Chapter 7

Economics and the Free Enterprise System. Media Materials, 1989. (Available through *Economics & Consumer Education* catalogue, Social Studies School Service, Culver City, Calif., 1-800-421-4246.)

Keenan, Diane. *Economics Action Pac.* 1988. (Available through *Economics & Consumer Education* catalogue.)

SimFarm (simulation software). Orinda, CA: Maxis, 1994.

Supply and Demand. Center for Economic Education, 1991. (Available through *Economics & Consumer Education* catalogue.)

Chapter 8

The Age of Ballyhoo (videocassette). Republic Pictures Home Video, 1986.

Ferguson, Charles H. *Computer Wars: How the West Can Win in a Post-IBM World.* New York: Times Books, Random House, 1993.

Serf City: Life Is Feudal (simulation software). Sunnyvale, Calif.: Strategic Simulations, 1994.

SimCity Enhanced CD-ROM (simulation software). Santa Ana, Calif.: Interplay, 1994.

Tucker (videocassette). Lucasfilm Ltd., 1988.

Chapter 9

Howell, John C. *Forming Corporations and Partnerships: An Easy, Do-It-Yourself Guide.* Blue Ridge Summit, Penn.: Liberty House, 1986.

Maital, Shlomo. *Executive Economics: Ten Essential Tools for Managers.* New York: Maxwell MacMillan International, 1994.

NYSE: A Portrait (videocassette). Syosset, New York: New York Stock Exchange.

Wall Street On-Line: An Investment Simulation for the Classroom (simulation software). J. Weston Walch, 1990. (Available through *Economics & Consumer Education* catalogue.)

Chapter 10

I've Got a Great Idea How to Make Your Brainstorm Bankable (videocassette).Pompano Beach, Fla.: JRD Development Corp., 1992.

Merger, Trust, Monopoly (simulation software). (Available through *Economics & Consumer Education* catalogue.)

South Dakota: An Economics and Mathematics Simulation (simulation software). Educational Activities, 1984. (Available through *Economics & Consumer Education* catalogue.)

Chapter 11

Economic Backgrounds in U.S. History. Educational Masterprints, 1986. (Available through *Economics & Consumer Education* catalogue.)

Merger, Trust, Monopoly (simulation software). (Available through *Economics & Consumer Education* catalogue.)

Understanding the American Economy (videocassette). Human Relations Media, 1984. (Available through *Economics & Consumer Education* catalogue.)

Chapter 12

Friedman, Milton, and Rose Friedman. *Free to Choose.* New York: Harcourt Brace Jovanovich, 1980.

Krugman, Paul R. *Peddling Prosperity: Economic Sense and Nonsense in the Age of Diminished Expectations.* New York: W. W. Norton, 1994.

Silverstein, Michael. *The Environmental Revolution: How Business Will Thrive and the Earth Survive in Years to Come.* New York: St. Martin's Press, 1993.

Superhero League of Hoboken (game software). Chantilly, Va.: Legend Entertainment, 1994.

Chapter 13

Dubofsky, Melvyn. *The State & Labor in Modern America.* Chapel Hill, N.C.: University of North Carolina Press, 1994.

The Firm (videocassette). Paramount Pictures, 1993.

Foner, Philip Sheldon. *History of the Labor Movement in the United States,* Vol. 10. New York: International Publishers, 1992.

The Grapes of Wrath (videocassette). Twentieth Century-Fox, 1940.

McNeil, Keith, and Rusty McNeil. *Working & Union Songs* (audiocassette). Riverside, Calif.: WEM Records, 1989.

Part Two

The Microeconomic Perspective

PART TWO

The Microeconomic Perspective

Chapter 6

Consumers' buying decisions determine demand, the quantities of a good that consumers are willing and able to purchase at various prices during a given period of time.

Chapter 7

Changes in price result in a change in the quantity supplied; changes in production costs or technology can lead to a change in supply.

Chapter 8

The goal of a market economy is equilibrium; that is, for the quantity of goods supplied to be equal to the quantity demanded.

Chapter 9

Each company—big or small—falls into one of three business organizations: proprietorship, partnership, or corporation.

Chapter 10

Knowing how businesses in perfect competition and a monopoly are organized helps us understand the economic issues that face these market organizations.

Chapter 11

Examining the characteristics of monopolistic competition and oligopoly helps us see why these market organizations prevail in the U.S. market economy.

Chapter 12

Sometimes in a competitive free market economy, people's actions result in externalities.

Chapter 13

The interaction between the supply of labor and the demand for labor determines the amount of labor that is hired and the wage rate that is paid.

Chapter 6

Demand: Achieving Consumer Satisfaction

Chapter Theme

Chapter 6 explores demand, the relationship between quantity demanded and price, and the reasons for the relationship. Changes in demand and factors that affect the demand for goods and services also are explored. In Section Four, the relationship between price, unit sales, and revenue is analyzed.

Section	Special Features
Demand Schedules and Demand Curves	Economic Spotlight
The Law of Demand	Perspectives: Thinking Like a Consumer Economics & Your Community Internet Connection
Determinants of Demand	Eye on Market News Economic Talk Global Economy Economic Dilemma
Price Elasticity of Demand	Multicultural Highlights Econ & You Media Link

Video Activity

Chapter 6, British Retail

Search Chapter 6, Play to 7

Ask students to discuss what kinds of cultural differences or other considerations U.S. retailers need to be aware of to succeed in other countries (limited product exposure, different social customs, or unfamiliar terminology). Have students suggest kinds of changes that corporations might make to achieve consumer satisfaction in particular countries.

	Print Resources	Media Resources	Assessment
	Effective Teaching Model Lesson Plans *Skills & Concepts* worksheet *Problem Solving* worksheet *Casebook* *Economic Measurement Workbook* *Content Review Workbook* *Spanish Resources*	VHS CD-ROM Videodisc *Arctic Express* *Interactive* ECONOMICS Template software	*Your Economic Portfolio* Chapter *Assessment* Chapter *MicroExam*

Special Learners	Print Resources	Media Resources	Assessment
		Overhead and *Transparencies 6-1 and 6-2* Computer	*Checkpoint* Section 1 Quiz
Attention Deficit Disorder	*Teacher's Connection to the Internet*	Overhead and *Transparency 6-3* Computer Camcorder VCR	*Checkpoint* Section 2 Quiz
Visual Activity Kinesthetic Activity Auditory Activity	*Enrich* worksheet	Overhead and *Transparency 6-4* Computer	*Checkpoint* Section 3 Quiz
Cooperative Learning Activity	*Life Skills* worksheet *Reteach* worksheet	Overhead and *Transparencies 6-5 and 6-6* Computer Audio	*Checkpoint* Section 4 Quiz

Careers Activity

The job of advertising is to create or increase consumer demand. Advertising art directors use visuals to accomplish this. They create, or direct the creation of, art that captures the consumer's interest and promotes a product or service.

Besides having artistic ability, advertising art directors must understand marketing, layout, typography, design methods, and basic printing processes. A knowledge of video production also may be helpful. Art directors should maintain a portfolio of their best work to show to potential employers. Earnings generally range from $15,000 to $30,000 per year but can reach as high as $100,000.

Tell students to imagine that they are art directors who have been asked to create an ad campaign for a well-established line of clothing. Because of recent increases in cloth prices, the clothes have become very expensive and sales have dropped. Have students create full-page ads to win back old customers and to entice new ones to buy the product.

CHAPTER 6

Teaching Materials

Program Resources

- Student text
- *Effective Teaching Model Lesson Plans*
- *Overhead Transparencies 6-1 to 6-6*
- *Life Skills worksheet*
- *Problem Solving worksheet*
- *Reteach worksheet*
- *Enrich worksheet*
- *Skills & Concepts worksheet*
- *Casebook*
- *Economic Measurement Workbook*
- *Content Review Workbook*
- *Spanish Resources*
- Video package
- *Teacher's Connection to the Internet*
- *Arctic Express*
- *Interactive* ECONOMICS
- Template software

Assessment

- Section Quizzes
- Chapter *Assessment*
- Chapter *MicroExam*

Chapter 6

Overview

Section One
Demand Schedules and Demand Curves

Section Two
The Law of Demand

Section Three
Determinants of Demand

Section Four
Price Elasticity of Demand

Teacher to Teacher

To help students understand how quantity demanded is related to price, allow them to set a market price for doughnuts. Bring to class one doughnut. Show students a list of prices and ask them how many doughnuts they would buy at each price. Have the class work together to create a demand curve from the data and decide at which price the most doughnuts would be sold. Tell students that you will allow them to purchase doughnuts at that price tomorrow if they bring money to class. The next day, sell the doughnuts to students. Determine whether students purchased as many doughnuts as they said they would. Then, introduce the concept of diminishing marginal utility.

Harlan Day
Purdue University
W. Lafayette, IN

Demand: Achieving Consumer Satisfaction

Learning Objectives

6-1
Read and understand demand schedules and demand curves.

6-2
Explain the relationship between price and quantity demanded.

6-3
Demonstrate how the determinants of demand affect the level of demand.

6-4
Calculate price elasticity of demand and determine its effect on total revenue.

Outside Resources

- Doughnuts
- Blank overhead transparencies
- Graph paper
- Pictures of hamburgers
- Camcorder and VCR
- Construction paper
- Computer
- Integrated software (desktop publishing or graphics, spreadsheets)
- Image scanner
- Magazines and newspapers
- Outside speaker: Head of hospital ethics committee
- Index cards
- Newspaper business sections showing mortgage rates
- Audiocassette recorder and tapes
- "Elastic" items, such as rubber bands or lycra

Vocabulary

demand, p. 124
demand schedule, p. 125
demand curve, p. 127
law of demand, p. 128
marginal utility, p. 129
diminishing marginal utility, p. 129
income effect, p. 129
substitution effect, p. 130
determinants of demand, p. 133
normal goods, p. 134
inferior goods, p. 134
substitute products, p. 134
complementary products, p. 134
price elasticity of demand, p. 138
total revenue, p. 143

Focus

Have students jot down in a single column on a sheet of paper all of the goods and services they have purchased in the past week. Have them add this heading above their column: **Good/Service.**

After students have completed their lists, have them add two more columns to create a chart. Label one column **Reasons for Buying** and the other **Reasons Met.** In these columns, have students list their reasons for purchasing and whether those reasons were satisfied. Have students share their lists of purchases and their reasons for buying. Discuss Larry Sanchez's pricing dilemma in *Focus*. Point out that, if there is little or no demand for his computer table, he will have little success selling it at any price.

Teach

Remind students that *microeconomics* studies how individuals behave and make decisions. To make sure students understand the definition of **demand,** draw the following graphic organizer on the chalkboard or an overhead transparency and review the four elements of **demand: ability to purchase, willingness to purchase, time period, and price.**

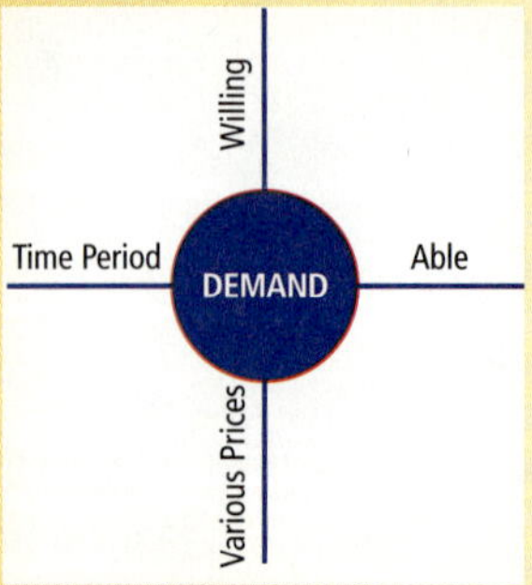

Section One
Demand Schedules and Demand Curves

What Do You Think?

Larry Sanchez makes computer tables out of solid maple. Larry has been selling about five tables a month at a price of $340 each. He has decided to increase his price to $380 so he can make more money. What should Larry consider before he raises his price?

What's Ahead?

Microeconomics is the study of how individual economic units (like a person or a business) behave and make decisions. Individuals buy goods and services to increase satisfaction. These buying decisions are an important factor in determining demand. Demand schedules and demand curves summarize the relationship between the quantity demanded and price.

Terms to Know
- demand
- demand schedule
- demand curve

DEMAND

In this chapter, you begin your study of the branch of economics called *microeconomics.* Microeconomics involves looking at *small* parts of the total economy. It includes the choices we all make as individual consumers. Should we spend our limited amount of money on clothes or on recreation? Or should we spend some money on each? Exactly how we choose to allocate our money is an important factor in determining the demand for various goods and services in the economy.

Economic Meaning of Demand

demand
the quantities of a good that consumers are willing and able to purchase at various prices during a given period of time

Demand refers to the quantities of a good that consumers are willing and able to purchase at various prices during a given period of time. Let's take a closer look at the important elements of this definition.

First, you must be *able* to make a purchase; that is, you must have enough money to make the purchase. There are many items you may want to purchase. For example, you might want to buy a ski lodge in the Colorado Rockies and a private jet to get you there. But, if you do not have the money to purchase these luxuries, you do not have an effective demand for them.

Second, you must be *willing* to make the purchase. There are products that you can afford, but you may not be willing to spend your income on them.

Examples might include a pet snake or prune-flavored yogurt. If you are not willing to purchase these items, you do not have an effective demand for them.

Third, when we discuss demand, we are referring to purchases made during a *given period of time*. For example, you might have a weekly demand for candy bars. If you are willing and able each week to buy four candy bars at a price of $0.50 each, your demand is four candy bars a week.

Fourth, demand represents the *quantities* consumers would purchase at *various prices*. If the price of candy bars drops to $0.25 each, you might increase the number you buy each week from four candy bars to six. If the price rises to $0.90, you might only buy two candy bars a week.

Demand Schedules

It is often convenient to look at demand in the form of a listing of the quantities that would be purchased at various prices. A listing of the quantities that would be purchased at various prices is called a ***demand schedule***. Figure 6-1 shows a demand schedule for the number of hot fudge sundaes Raj Carey would buy per month at different prices. You see that at $2 a sundae, Raj would not be willing to buy any. However, if the price were lower, Raj would have a demand. For example, at a price of $1.80 a sundae, she would buy two sundaes each month. At a price of $1.20, her quantity demanded would increase to eight sundaes a month.

demand schedule
a listing of the quantities that would be purchased at various prices

Demand Curves

A demand schedule shows only a small number of the possible price and quantity combinations. For example, Figure 6-1 shows only eight such combinations. From that table, you can see how many sundaes Raj would buy at certain prices, such as $1.40 or $1.20. But, what if the price of a hot fudge sundae was $1.30? How many sundaes would Raj buy? You cannot answer this question directly from the demand schedule.

Price	Quantity Purchased per Month
$2.00	0
1.80	2
1.60	4
1.40	6
1.20	8
1.00	10
.80	12
.60	14

Figure 6-1

Raj Carey's Demand Schedule for Hot Fudge Sundaes

This table summarizes an individual's demand for hot fudge sundaes at different prices. ***If price fell to $0.40, how many sundaes would Raj want to purchase?***

Discuss the difference between the willingness to purchase and the ability to purchase. Also, compare **demand schedules,** which list quantities purchased at given prices, to **demand curves,** which graphically illustrate demand schedules.

Apply

Using *Overhead Transparencies 6-1* and *6-2*, discuss the definitions of and differences between a **demand schedule** and a **demand curve.** (A **demand schedule** lists in table format the quantities that would be purchased at various prices; a **demand curve** graphically illustrates the quantities of a product that would be bought at each price within a range of prices.) Point out that a demand curve allows us to understand at a glance the relationship between prices and quantities purchased. It also includes information on a wider number of variables than does a demand schedule.

Guided Practice

Analyzing Graphics

Caption Answer
Probably 16 sundaes

Display *Overhead Transparency 6-1* (*Figure 6-1* on p. 125). Have students determine from the demand schedule the relationship between price and quantity purchased. (With each price decrease of $0.20, two more hot fudge sundaes would be purchased.) On the transparency, insert price decreases at $0.10 intervals from $2.00 to $0.60. Ask students to estimate what would happen with a price decrease of $0.10 and mark suggested responses in the **Quantity Purchased Per Month** column. (One more sundae would be purchased.) Discuss what effect the month of the year might have on the quantity of hot fudge sundaes demanded. (Quantity demanded might decrease in cold months at all prices.) Ask students whether this demand schedule accurately shows the demand in specific months of the year. (No)

Using graph paper or the computer, have each student create a demand schedule for a product he or she buys often. Then, have students use their demand schedule to plot a demand curve. Point out that the horizontal axis on the demand curve graph shows *quantity* and the vertical axis shows *price*.

Independent Practice

Economic Spotlight

WHO IS THE #1 ENTREPRENEUR IN AMERICA?

H. Wayne Huizenga knows how to grow a business. Take Blockbuster Entertainment, for example. Huizenga grew the company to more than 4,000 percent of its original value before selling it to the media giant Viacom. A pure entrepreneur at heart, Huizenga gained his business savvy early on in the Illinois Dutch Reform community where he was born and raised. There he learned a strong work ethic and was taught by his father that nobody ever got rich by working for someone else.

As a young man, Huizenga followed in the footsteps of his Dutch immigrant grandfather, entering the garbage-hauling business quietly and then dominating the industry only a few years later. He began by managing a garbage company for a friend of his father. Later, he went out on his own, eventually merging with his grandfather's company to form Waste Management, a global giant generating profits of more than $200 million per year. However, once the company was thriving on its own, Huizenga resigned from the board of Waste Management "to pursue other interests."

In 1987, a friend told Huizenga about a little firm called Blockbuster Video. Blockbuster Entertainment had been founded by Dallas businessman David Cook, who opened the first Blockbuster superstore in October 1985. Cook's display, tracking, and security innovations had eliminated many of the problems associated with the video rental business. But, his company needed money. In short, Cook was looking to expand and Huizenga was looking to invest. Two months after Huizenga invested in Blockbuster, Cook resigned, allowing Huizenga to grow Blockbuster his way—"building by buying" and not by franchising. Huizenga rapidly bought up other video chains that dominated local and regional areas and converted them to Blockbusters. At one point, a new Blockbuster store was opening every 17 hours.

In 1994, Huizenga backed the merger of Blockbuster and Viacom and resigned six months later. Although Huizenga may have stepped out of the video game, the owner of the Florida Marlins and the Miami Dolphins is still playing in the big leagues as the number-one entrepreneur in America.

Economic Spotlight

After students have read the *Economic Spotlight* feature, ask them to think about the types of economic decisions the leader of a large corporation might have to make. Working in groups of four or five, have students draw up a business plan detailing changing demands in the video movie rental and sales market and how Blockbuster Video might meet them and remain a competitive force in the marketplace. You may wish to have students use a business plan computer template such as *BizPlan Builder*® from Jian to complete this activity.

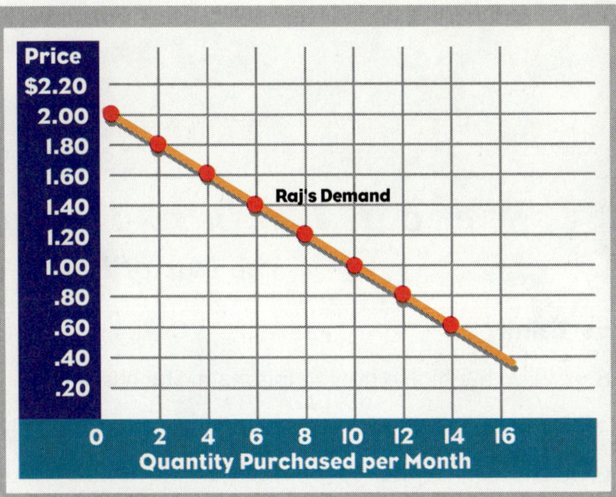

Figure 6-2

Raj Carey's Demand Curve for Hot Fudge Sundaes

This demand curve is based on Raj Carey's demand schedule for hot fudge sundaes. ***How many hot fudge sundaes will Raj purchase at $1.70?***

You can construct a demand curve to help you find the quantity that Raj would demand at any price. A ***demand curve*** is a graphic illustration of the relationship between *price* and the *quantity demanded* at each price. Figure 6-2 is a demand curve that represents Raj Carey's demand for hot fudge sundaes. Prices are measured along the vertical axis. The horizontal axis measures the quantities demanded. Each of the eight price-quantity combinations in Raj's demand schedule (Figure 6-1) is represented as a point in Figure 6-2.

Connecting all the points shows Raj's demand curve for hot fudge sundaes at each possible price. Using this demand curve allows you to determine how many sundaes Raj would buy at prices that are not shown in Figure 6-1. It is reasonable to expect that at a price of $1.30, Raj would buy seven sundaes each month. You can tell this from the demand curve in Figure 6-2 but not from the demand schedule in Figure 6-1.

demand curve
a graphic illustration of the relationship between *price* and the *quantity demanded* at each price

Checkpoint

Content Check

1. Give an example of the economic concept of demand.
2. Make a demand schedule for your favorite dessert for one month.
3. Draw a demand curve for your favorite dessert for one month.

What Do You Think Now?

Reread *What Do You Think?* in the Section One Focus. Then answer the following questions:

4. Can Larry Sanchez expect to sell as many tables per month at $380 as he had been selling at $340? Why or why not?

Reteach

Have students work in small groups to review the elements of demand. First, have them write a definition of **demand** in their own words. Then, have them write four paragraphs—one paragraph explaining each element of demand. **6-1**

Enrich

Have students complete the demand schedule in *Figure 6-1* to $0.00, based on the relationships they determined in *Analyzing Graphics.* Have them use a spreadsheet program to complete the chart and then to create a demand curve (line graph) using the information in their chart. **6-1**

Analyzing Graphics

Caption Answer
Probably three sundaes

Have students study *Figure 6-2* to find the change in quantity demanded when there is a price decrease of $0.10. Did they estimate correctly in the previous activity?

Assess

1. Examples should reflect an understanding of the four elements of demand. **6-1**
2. Answers should reflect the proper relationship between prices and quantity demanded at each price. **6-1, 6-2**
3. Answers should show prices on the vertical axis and demand on the horizontal axis, and the curve should slope down and to the right. **6-1**
4. Probably not because fewer people would be willing and able to buy at the higher price **6-1, 6-2**

Close

In small groups, have students use graph paper or the computer to create a demand schedule and a demand curve for a good or service of their choice. Have the groups share their results with the class as a whole.

Focus

Write the following on the chalkboard for students to discuss in pairs before the start of class: **Think of something that you have purchased more than once in one day. Describe how you felt as you purchased the first item. Did you feel different as you paid for the second identical item? The third? The tenth? Why do you think your feelings changed?**

Discuss this scenario as a class. Lead students to discover that, usually, the more times they purchase an item in a set period of time, the less satisfaction they receive from the purchase. Tell the class that this is known as **diminishing marginal utility**.

Teach

Explain to students the law of demand, which shows an inverse relationship between price and quantity demanded. (Be sure students understand that *inverse* means *opposite*.) Point out that the law of demand focuses on what happens to the quantity *demanded* when the price goes up or down—not what happens when the actual quantity *available* changes. This relationship between price and quantity demanded holds true with individual consumers and in the marketplace as a whole. Point out to students the three reasons for the law of demand stated in their textbook. Then, relate them to the inverse relationship between price and quantity demanded.

FOCUS

Section Two

The Law of Demand

What Do You Think?

Pat Keats plays on her high school tennis team. She has one Wilson Pro Staff 3.5 racquet and a Prince Extender racquet. A friend called Pat last night to tell her about a great sale on the newest Head tennis racquet at the MX Sports Center in the mall. Pat is trying to decide whether to buy this new racquet. Do you think Pat will buy the racquet?

Terms to Know

- law of demand
- marginal utility
- diminishing marginal utility
- income effect
- substitution effect

What's Ahead?

People tend to buy more of a good or service at a lower price than at a higher price. This is true for individual consumers and the market as a whole. In this section, you will learn three reasons for this relationship between price and quantity demanded.

THE LAW OF DEMAND

For most goods, consumers are willing to purchase more units at a lower price than at a higher price. The relationship between price and quantity demanded holds true as long as other factors, such as income, do not change. You saw this illustrated with Raj's demand for hot fudge sundaes. As the price went down, Raj purchased more and more sundaes.

This pattern is true with most products and services. The inverse relationship between price and the quantity consumers will buy is called the law of demand. The ***law of demand*** states that the quantity demanded of a good will be greater at lower prices than will be the quantity demanded at higher prices (as long as other influences are constant). This movement along the demand curve shows a change in the *quantity demanded* in response to a change in price. Let's look at some reasons the law of demand is true.

law of demand the quantity demanded of a good will be greater at lower prices than will be the quantity demanded at higher prices

Diminishing Marginal Utility

You have already learned that consumers make purchases to increase satisfaction. The amount of satisfaction a person gets from *one* additional unit of a product is called ***marginal utility***. For example, the additional satisfaction Raj gets when she eats the second sundae is the marginal utility of that sundae.

As a person consumes more and more units of a particular product, the satisfaction gained from each *additional* unit starts to lessen. For example, that first hot fudge sundae Raj eats probably tastes wonderful and brings her a lot of satisfaction. By the time she eats 14 hot fudge sundaes, however, one additional sundae does not bring as much satisfaction as the first one did. ***Diminishing marginal utility*** is the principle that as additional units of a product are consumed during a given time period, the additional satisfaction decreases. A person's *total* satisfaction may continue to increase but at a slower rate.

marginal utility
the amount of satisfaction a person gets from *one* additional unit of a product

diminishing marginal utility
the principle that as additional units of a product are consumed during a given time period, the additional satisfaction decreases

Stop to think about the products that you consume. The principle of diminishing marginal utility applies to most of them. Shoes, sweaters, CDs, and posters all follow this principle. Buying additional units of each good during a given time period provides less and less additional satisfaction.

The Income Effect

A second reason for the inverse relationship between price and quantity demanded is the income effect. The effect that increasing or decreasing prices has on the buying power of income is called the ***income effect.*** As the price of a product changes, your buying power changes as well.

If prices go up, your buying power goes down and your income appears to be less. Suppose, for example, that Taylor has a part-time job that pays $30 a week. Taylor collects CDs of her favorite recording artists and usually buys two CDs each week. If the store where she shops has a sale reducing the

income effect
the effect that increasing or decreasing prices has on the buying power of income

Apply

Copy the following flowchart on the chalkboard or an overhead transparency:

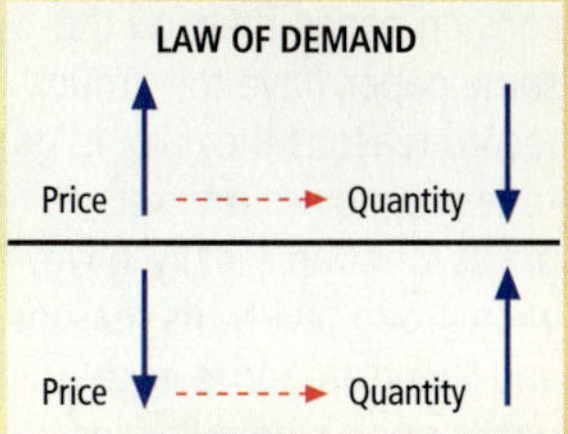

Ask for volunteers to explain the flowchart. Explain that the **law of demand** states that as the price goes up, the quantity demanded goes down, and as price goes down, the quantity demanded goes up. Reinforce that this is an inverse relationship. Have students create their own flowcharts describing the law of demand. Ask for volunteers to copy their flowcharts onto the chalkboard.
Guided Practice

Perspectives

Thinking Like a Consumer
Divide the class into groups of three or four students and provide each group with a picture of a hamburger. Tell each student to imagine that he or she has only $10 (total) to spend on hamburgers during several auctions. Students may buy as many burgers as they can afford. Then, have students take turns auctioning off burgers to their group. Record the auctions with a camcorder and review the video with the class. Discuss how students' satisfaction (or marginal utility) diminished after their initial purchases.

price of each CD by $2, Taylor can buy three CDs rather than two. This change in her buying habits results from the fact that her $30 income now goes further. This supports the law of demand: As price goes down, quantity demanded goes up.

The income effect works in the other direction, too. As the price of an item goes up, your income doesn't go as far. You cannot buy as much with a given amount of money since prices are higher. Your buying power and quantity demanded go down as a result of an increase in price.

The Substitution Effect

A third reason for the inverse relationship between price and quantity demanded is the substitution effect. Let's return to our example of the lowered price of CDs. As the price of CDs goes down, CDs become cheaper *relative* to other goods, such as concerts or cassette tapes. Taylor is likely to change her buying habits and purchase more CDs and attend fewer concerts. This is called the substitution effect of a price change. The ***substitution effect*** is the change in the mix of goods purchased as a result of increasing or decreasing relative prices.

substitution effect
the change in the mix of goods purchased as a result of increasing or decreasing relative prices

The substitution effect works in two directions. If the price of a good falls, you may substitute it for other items. But, if the price of a good rises, you may substitute other items for the now relatively more expensive good. This substitution effect is seen relatively often. As the prices of oil and natural gas go up, people substitute wood-burning stoves and solar collectors for heating their homes. When the price of coffee goes up, people substitute with tea and chicory. When the price of beef falls, consumers substitute beef for chicken and pork.

MARKETS AND THE LAW OF DEMAND

You have seen that Raj's demand for hot fudge sundaes follows the law of demand. Raj would eat more sundaes at lower prices than at higher prices. Other consumers in Raj's community also have a demand for hot fudge sundaes. It is reasonable to expect that their individual demand schedules would also follow the law of demand. That is, we would expect them to purchase a greater number of hot fudge sundaes at lower prices than at higher prices.

Let's say that there are 1,000 people in Raj's neighborhood who like hot fudge sundaes. For simplicity, we also will say that each consumer has a demand schedule exactly like Raj's. If the price is $1.40 a sundae, those 1,000 consumers would *each* be willing and able to buy six sundaes a month. In *total,* they would have a demand for 6,000 sundaes at a price of $1.40 a sundae. If the price went down to $1.20 a sundae, the quantity demanded would increase to 8,000. If the price increased to $1.60 a sundae, only 4,000 sundaes would be demanded. When you list the quantities bought at each price for all 1,000 people, you have a market demand schedule. By plotting the market

In small groups, have students brainstorm reasons they would go to more movies if ticket prices went down. Have a member of each group record these reasons on paper. Then, on the same paper, have the groups record reasons they would go to fewer movies if ticket prices went up. Finally, have each group review its reasons and then categorize each under one of the following headings on a chart: **Marginal Utility** (includes **diminishing marginal utility**), **Income Effect**, and **Substitution Effect**. While students are categorizing their reasons, have a student volunteer make a similar chart on the chalkboard or an overhead transparency. Have volunteers from each group record their groups' reasons in the appropriate categories on the class chart.

Independent Practice

Economics & Your Community

With permission, have the class visit a local retailer to determine which of its products is demanded in the highest quantity. In class, have students analyze the current demand for this product based on what students consider to be the product's marginal utility, the income effect on the product, and the substitution effect. Have each student write four paragraphs: one describing the business and its top-selling product and the other three describing the three reasons why the quantity demanded of the product might change.

Attention Deficit Disorder

demand schedule on a graph and connecting the points, you have a market demand curve. These are shown in Figure 6-3 on page 132.

Both the market demand schedule and the market demand curve show that the quantity purchased goes up from 2,000 to 12,000 units as price falls from $1.80 to $0.80. As the price falls, a greater quantity is demanded. As the price goes up, a smaller quantity is demanded. A change in quantity demanded is caused by a change in the price of the product for any given demand curve. This is true of an individual consumer's demand, as well as for the market demand.

Internet Connection

SURFING THE NET WITH WORLD WIDE WEB BROWSERS

While the Internet has a huge amount of information and services available, until recently it was not very user-friendly. This changed with World Wide Web. The Web is an easy way of accessing virtually all Internet resources and services.

The Web is a set of resources called *home pages* or *web pages,* located on hundreds of computers around the Internet. Web pages are screens with text and images, with some words and images highlighted. Highlighted items are links to other screens. A web page is like a document with footnotes. A footnote in the middle of a document might give a reference for further information; a link on a web page allows you to jump to a copy of that document. The new document has links to even more documents.

To access World Wide Web, use a program called a *web browser.* There are a variety of browsers available. The major distinction is between those that display text and images (Netscape or Mosaic) and those that only display text (Lynx). This chapter will focus on Netscape. If you have access to Lynx, see your teacher for additional information.

Netscape is a web browser for a Windows environment. If you are familiar with Windows or Macintosh systems, using Netscape will be easy because Netscape uses the same commands. Click on the Netscape icon or select Netscape from a pull-down menu. After a few moments, a home page should appear.

Internet Application: If you have access to WWW, find out what browser you use. Key in **http://www.thomson.com/swpco/internet/hb29da1.html** to check out Thomson Publishing's Economics Internet activities. The Internet Application address is shown as two lines; however, it should be keyed in as one line. Describe some of what you learn in an e-mail message to your teacher.

Economics Application: Once students find out about the Internet, a large number want to use it. Use the law of demand to explain why quantity demanded is so great.

Emphasize to students that the law of demand applies to both individual consumers and the marketplace as a whole. To emphasize this, have students compare *Figures 6-1* and *6-2* (p. 125 and p. 127), which show individual demand for hot fudge sundaes, to *Figure 6-3* (p.132), which shows market demand. Ask students if they see any patterns between individual demand and market demand. (Answers may include that, for individual demand, every price change of $0.20 brings about a change by two in quantity and, for market demand, every price change of $0.20 brings about a 2,000 change in quantity. For both, as price goes up, quantity goes down, and as price goes down, quantity goes up. Larger quantities are demanded in the market than individually.)

Internet Connection

Economics Application: Since Internet access through your school is usually free to students, the money price is zero. (The time price due to waiting may be higher.) A low price implies a large demand.

Be sure to keep the address **http://www.thomson.com/swpco/internet/hb29da1.html** available for future chapters. Additional activities, interesting sites, and address changes are given on this page. If you find that you can't access a particular address and it isn't indicated on the thomson site, please send an email to **econ_connect@swpco.com** and let us know about the change so that we can update the page.

Price	Quantity Purchased per Month
$2.00	0
1.80	2,000
1.60	4,000
1.40	6,000
1.20	8,000
1.00	10,000
.80	12,000
.60	14,000

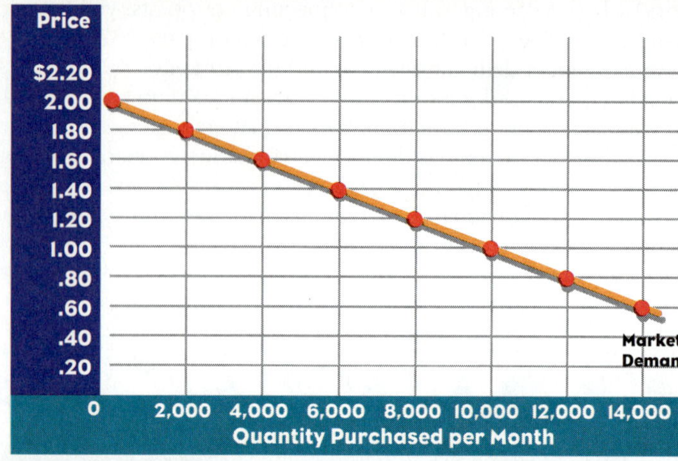

Figure 6-3

Market Demand Schedule and Demand Curve for Hot Fudge Sundaes in Raj Carey's Neighborhood

This market demand schedule and demand curve show that the law of demand holds for entire markets, as well as for individuals. For the entire market, a greater quantity is demanded at lower prices than at higher prices. ***How many sundaes will be demanded in this market at a price of $1.10?***

Checkpoint

Content Check

1. Explain the relationship between price and quantity demanded.
2. What is the effect of diminishing marginal utility on quantity demanded?
3. How does the income effect support the law of demand?
4. If the price of beef goes up, what does the substitution effect predict will happen?
5. Why do markets respond to a change in price in the same way as individuals?

What Do You Think Now?

Reread *What Do You Think?* in the Section Two Focus. Then answer the following question:

6. What do you think will influence Pat's decision about whether to buy the racquet?

Analyzing Graphics

Caption Answer
9,000 sundaes

Assess

1. As price increases, quantity demanded decreases and vice versa. **6-2**
2. As marginal utility diminishes, you are less willing to pay a higher price, so quantity demanded decreases. **6-2**
3. As price increases, the buying power and quantity demanded decrease and vice versa. **6-2**
4. The demanded quantity of beef will decrease and the demand for substitute products, such as chicken, will increase. **6-2**
5. Markets are the sum of the decisions of individuals. **6-2**
6. Answers should reflect an understanding that, since Pat already has a spare, the marginal utility of another racquet is decreased. Therefore, price will be the most important factor. **6-2**

Close

Have students write a scenario that describes how the law of demand works. Encourage students to use real-life examples and to include information about the marginal utility of the product(s), the income effect, and the substitution effect. Review students' work, correcting any misconceptions before proceeding to the next section.

Reteach

Pair students who understand demand schedules and demand curves with those who are demonstrating difficulty. Have each pair complete the demand schedule and demand curve in *Figure 6-3* to show every price change of $0.10. **6-1, 6-2**

Enrich

Have students work in pairs. Have one student create an individual's demand schedule for a product and the other create a demand curve from that information. Then, have students make an additional demand schedule and demand curve for a market of 5,000 consumers with the same purchasing habits as that individual. **6-1, 6-2**

Section Three

Determinants of Demand

What Do You Think?

Vincent Pisoni was working part-time as a food preparation specialist in a Mexican restaurant. Recently, he was promoted to a full-time supervisory position with an increase in his weekly pay. How will this affect his demand for various products?

What's Ahead?

The amount of a good or service that people buy depends on factors other than just the price of that item. Factors such as income, prices of other products, and consumer attitudes also affect the demand for goods. Changes in demand can be illustrated by a change in the demand curve.

Terms to Know

determinants of demand

normal goods

inferior goods

substitute products

complementary products

CHANGE IN DEMAND

So far, you have learned some of the reasons that the quantity demanded of a product changes as a result of a change in price. It is clear that when price goes up, the quantity demanded usually goes down, and vice versa. This is called a *change in quantity demanded.* But, sometimes people are willing to buy more or less of a good at each and every price. This is called a *change in demand.* Why are more wood-burning stoves bought now than ten years ago, even though the price has not gone down? Why are more books bought today than five years ago, even though the price of books has gone up? These are questions about the overall level of demand.

The ***determinants of demand*** are the factors that determine how much will be purchased at any given price. As these determinants change, the overall level of demand will change, even though the product's price does not change. Such changes can be shown by a shift of the entire demand curve. It is important to understand that these changes in demand are different from the changes in quantity demanded.

determinants of demand the factors that determine how much will be purchased at any given price

The four most important factors that can cause a change in demand for products are

1. changes in consumers' incomes;
2. changes in consumers' attitudes;

Focus

As students enter the classroom, have them work in small groups to brainstorm a list of products that were in great demand when they or their parents were younger but that are not in demand anymore, such as eight-track tapes. Also, have them brainstorm a list of products that were not in demand when they were younger but that are in demand now.

Discuss students' lists of products. As a class, brainstorm several reasons why demand for these products has changed. Lead students to understand that factors such as income, prices of other products, and consumer attitudes affect demand.

Teach

Explain to students the difference between a change in *quantity demanded* and a change in *overall demand.* Review the four factors that can cause a change in demand: change in consumers' incomes, change in consumers' attitudes, change in price of a complementary product, and change in price of a substitute product. Compare **normal goods** and **inferior goods,** giving examples of each. Compare **substitute products** and **complementary products** and give examples of each. Reinforce that an increase in overall demand results in a shift in the entire demand curve to the right, and a decrease in overall demand results in a shift in the demand curve to the left.

EyeOnMarketNews

Have students skim the business section of the newspaper for a week, logging any information they can find about mortgage rates and their effect on the quantity of new houses demanded. Have them research and share the definition of a *mortgage* (a written instrument used to pledge a title to real property to secure the payment of a promissory note). As a class, discuss whether mortgage rates are rising or falling. Then, brainstorm a list of complementary products affected by the rise and fall of mortgage rates. (Rates go up: housing sales and related jobs go down, bank services go down, and so on; rates go down: the opposite effect occurs.)

Apply

Draw the outline of the following graphic organizer on the chalkboard or an overhead transparency:

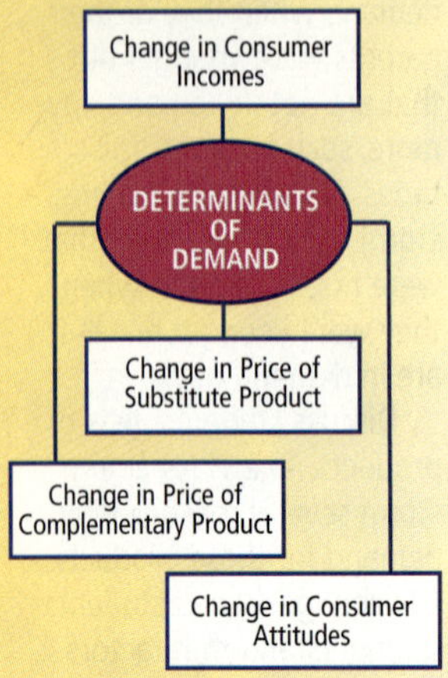

Fill in the center circle and leave the outer boxes empty. As a whole-class activity, discuss the four **determinants of demand,** filling the outer boxes of the graphic organizer as each determinant is named. Discuss how each determinant affects overall demand.

Guided Practice

Have students work in small groups to brainstorm a list of normal goods and inferior goods, along with possible substitute products and complementary products. Have students use desktop-publishing software or a graphics program to create a booklet illustrating their lists. If students have access to a scanner, encourage them to scan in photos or illustrations of their goods. If software and a scanner are not available, students may wish to create and illustrate their booklets by hand, pasting in pictures clipped from magazines and newspapers.

Independent Practice

3. changes in the price of a complementary product; and

4. changes in the price of a substitute product.

Some other factors that may influence the level of demand include changes in the size of the population, changes in people's expectations, and even changes in the weather.

Let's look at how the first four factors can bring about increases and decreases in demand.

The Effect of Changing Incomes

As your incomes goes up, you are likely to consume more of almost all goods. People with higher incomes can be expected to buy more clothes, records, theater tickets, and hot fudge sundaes than people with lower incomes. These goods, as well as most others, are what economists refer to as normal goods. ***Normal goods*** are goods for which demand goes up as income goes up. If incomes fall, people cut back on their consumption of normal goods.

Goods that are not normal goods are called inferior goods. ***Inferior goods*** are goods for which demand goes down as income goes up. For example, some people think of ground meat as an inferior good. As a family's income goes up, they may buy less ground meat and more steak and other solid meat products. Most goods and services we see in the marketplace, however, can be thought of as normal goods.

normal goods
goods for which demand goes up as income goes up

inferior goods
goods for which demand goes down as income goes up

The Effect of Changing Attitudes

A change in consumers' attitudes (tastes and preferences) can cause demand to increase or decrease. Perhaps this is most noticeable with respect to clothing fashions. As our ideas about clothing change, so do our purchases of different clothing items. Demand will go up if, for some reason, consumers develop a more favorable attitude about a product.

Our attitudes are influenced by many factors. Family members, friends, classmates, advertisements, television, movies, and many other factors influence our attitudes about various goods and services. Exactly how much influence any of these factors has on our actual purchasing is hard to determine.

The Effect of Changing Prices of Substitute Goods

Changes in the prices of other products can cause a change in the demand for a good. Suppose, for example, that the price of margarine goes up. The law of demand tells us that the amount of margarine demanded would decline. People might substitute butter for the now relatively more expensive margarine. A rise in the price of margarine, then, might cause an increase in the demand for butter. Thus, butter and margarine can be thought of as substitute products. ***Substitute products*** are products whose uses are similar enough that one can replace the other. The same might be true of cassette tapes and CDs. If the price of CDs goes up, the demand for tapes might rise.

substitute products
products whose uses are similar enough that one can replace the other

complementary products
products that are used together

The Effect of Changing Prices of Complementary Goods

Complementary products are products that are used together. If two goods are complementary products, a decrease in the price of one can increase the

EconomicTalk

Have students work in pairs to reinforce their understanding of **normal goods, inferior goods, substitute products,** and **complementary products.** Give each student four blank index cards and have her or him list one of the following on each card: a normal good, an inferior good, a product and its substitute, or a product and its complement. Have students label the type of good or pair on the back of each index card. Then, have students take turns testing their partners. After student pairs have finished, discuss the goods as a whole class.

demand for the other. For example, suppose that the price of snow skis goes down. More people could afford to buy skis. Thus, the demand for ski clothing and ski facilities would go up.

If the price of a product goes up, the demand for the complementary product would go down. Consider the effect of gasoline prices on the demand for automobile tires. As the price of gas goes up, people may reduce the number of miles they drive. This will result in less overall tire wear; therefore, tire demand will go down.

Global Economy

GROWING COFFEE IN THAILAND

Nestlé is a Swiss company you may know best for its chocolate candy products. This is a company that is very familiar with global markets. But, trying to sell a hot coffee beverage in a tropical country where tea is a favorite drink posed a real challenge. It took about ten years to establish coffee as a breakfast drink in Thailand, where Nestlé focused its attention mainly on the cities.

To do this Nestlé had to abandon its usual western advertising themes that centered on coffee taste and aroma as well as on its use as a stimulant. In Thailand, Nestlé found it more effective to focus on coffee as a relaxing beverage used to reduce the stresses caused by hectic traffic and the other pressures of life in Thailand's large cities.

Nestlé also borrowed a concept that had been developed by Nestlé Greece: promotion of a cold coffee beverage called the *Nescafe Shake.* As a result of these strategies, Nestlé captured 80 percent of the growing coffee market in Thailand, with sales increasing from $25 million to $100 million in a seven-year period.

How did Nestlé influence consumer choices in a country where coffee was not a popular beverage at one time? How does the concept of substitute goods relate to this discussion?

Have each student create a diagram showing how the four determinants of demand affect demand. Tell students to use up arrows to illustrate increases and down arrows to illustrate decreases. Ask a student volunteer to draw the following diagram on the chalkboard for students to view as one possible way to illustrate this concept.

DETERMINANTS OF DEMAND

Changing Incomes

NORMAL GOODS
Income ↑ ----► Demand ↑

INFERIOR GOODS
Income ↑ ----► Demand ↓

Changing Attitudes

Attitude ↑ ----► Demand ↑

Changing Prices of Substitute Products

Price of Substitute Product ↑ ----► Demand for Original Product ↑

Changing Prices of Complementary Products

Price of Complementary Product ↑ ----► Demand for Original Product ↓

Global Economy

Have groups of four or five students use the graphic organizer from the *Apply* activity on p. 134 as a guide to brainstorming the determinants of demand that affect international demand for automobiles, shrimp, or some other predetermined product. Have each group cut shapes out of construction paper to create a unique graphic organizer that illustrates these determinants. (Determinants may include the country's economy, consumer characteristics, culture and customs, level of technological development, and so on.) You may wish to display the groups' organizers on a bulletin board during the study of this chapter.

Have students study *Figure 6-4* on p. 137. Point out to students what **D**, **D_H**, and **D_L** stand for: **D** stands for the original demand; **D_H** stands for higher demand; and **D_L** stands for lower demand. As a class, discuss the difference between a change in overall demand and a change in quantity demanded. Point out that, when a different quantity is demanded, movement is *along* the demand curve. But, with an overall change in demand, the *entire curve* shifts right or left. Ask students to explain the placement of a higher demand curve (**D_H**) in relationship to the original demand curve (appears to the right of the original curve) and placement of a lower demand curve (**D_L**) in relationship to the original demand curve (appears to the left of the original curve).

Graphing Increases in Demand

An increase in demand causes the entire demand curve to shift to the right. This is shown as a move from the demand curve *D* to the demand curve D_H in Figure 6-4. Demand curve *D* is the market demand curve for hot fudge sundaes first shown in Figure 6-3. As shown in Figure 6-4, at a price of $1.30, the initial level of demand for hot fudge sundaes is 7,000. If the incomes of consumers in this market area went up, the demand for hot fudge sundaes might rise from *D* to D_H. If demand increases to D_H, consumers would purchase 11,000 units at a price of $1.30 rather than the 7,000 units along the demand curve *D*.

Graphing Decreases in Demand

A decrease in demand can be illustrated by a shift of the whole demand curve to the left. In Figure 6-4, this is represented by a move from the original demand *D* to a lower demand D_L. If the price of strawberries decreased,

Economic Dilemma

WE DEMAND HEALTH CARE!

As the age distribution in the United States shifts toward a more elderly population, what are the consequences in terms of consumer demand? The demand for certain types of products and services will certainly increase. Examples abound but would include nursing home space, home health care, elderly day care, wheelchairs, various medications, and other health-related products and services. Some people suggest that as a society we spend too much on often futile medical treatment for people who have short life expectancies. Others point out that the potential savings by reducing such treatments is only about 3 percent of total health care expenditures.

There are ethical considerations that impinge on our decisions about who gets health care and how it is paid for. Should a 60-year-old woman who does not have a large savings account or medical insurance be prohibited from having a life-saving heart transplant? Should health care for the elderly be allowed to so deplete a family's savings that the entire family must take a substantial cut in their standard of living?

What are some other products or services, beyond health care, for which you think demand will increase due to the aging of the population? What choices in terms of costs and benefits must we, as a society, make to answer the questions raised in this discussion?

Economic Dilemma

Because of the many ethical issues in health care, there has been a growth of *ethics committees* in hospitals. Have students contact a local hospital to find out if it has an ethics committee and who heads the committee. Have students find out the decision-making model the committee uses to address ethical issues. Compare that model to the five-step decision-making model students learned. If possible, have the head of the committee visit the class and relate some of the tough decisions that the committee has made.

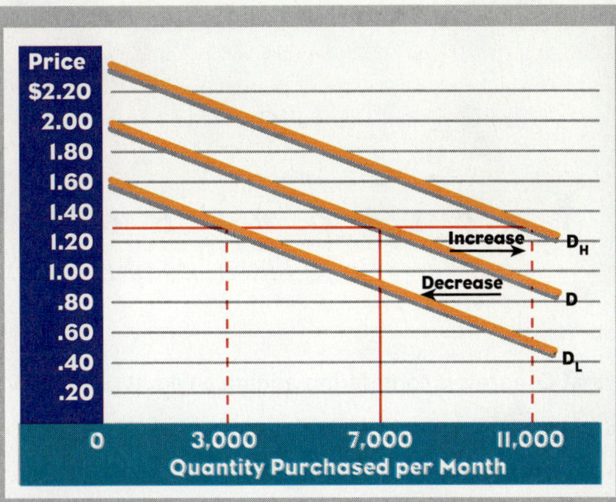

Figure 6-4

Shifts in the Market Demand for Hot Fudge Sundaes

An increase in overall demand is represented by a shift of the entire demand curve to the right, such as from *D* to D_H. A decrease in demand is shown by a shift to the left, such as from *D* to D_L. ***What might cause the demand to shift from D to D_L?***

thus making strawberry sundaes less expensive, the demand for hot fudge sundaes might fall from *D* to D_L. Hot fudge sundaes and strawberry sundaes are substitute goods. Given the lower level of demand, just 3,000 hot fudge sundaes would be purchased at $1.30 each.

Checkpoint

Content Check

1. How does a *change in demand* differ from a *change in the quantity demanded*?
2. Give an example of four determinants of demand.
3. Show how the demand curve for Ice Melt would be affected by an extremely long and severe winter.

What Do You Think Now?

Reread *What Do You Think?* in the Section Three Focus. Then answer the following questions:

4. How will Vincent Pisoni's promotion affect his demand for normal goods?
5. Name some products for which Vincent's tastes and preferences might be influenced by his promotion.

Reteach

Have students individually create a scenario that illustrates a change in demand for a product. Have each student record his or her scenario with an audiocassette recorder. Then, working in small groups, have students play their scenarios and ask their classmates to identify the determinants of demand in each. **6-3**

Enrich

Have students create demand curves for both the popular and the unpopular products they named in *Close*. Tell students to create a demand curve that shows their original demand (D) for each. Then, have them use D_L and D_H to show changes in demand due to the reasons they listed. **6-3**

Analyzing *Graphics*

Caption Answer
Answers may include lowered income, changing attitudes, lower prices of substitute goods, or higher prices of complementary goods.

Assess

1. A change in demand is due to a change in the quantity demanded at *every* price and is reflected in a shift of the entire demand curve; a change in quantity demanded is due to a change in price and is reflected in a move along the curve. **6-1, 6-2, 6-3**
2. Examples may include pay raise leads to increased demand for computer software or decreased demand for ground beef; popular musician wears western hats, increasing demand for them; higher price of new cars increases demand for used cars; and lower price of in-line skates increases demand for protective gear for skaters. **6-3**
3. Graphs should include the original demand curve for the ice-melting product and another curve to the right of that curve to show an increase in demand. **6-1, 6-3**
4. It should increase. **6-3**
5. Answers may include an increase in the demand for clothes for his new job. **6-3**

Close

Have students work in small groups to brainstorm a list of specific examples of the four determinants of demand that could change their demand for a popular product, such as soda pop, and a relatively unpopular product, such as brussels sprouts.

Focus

As students enter the classroom, have them jot down on the chalkboard all the words they associate with the word *elastic.* Erase any duplicate entries.

Brainstorm with the whole class different items that seem "elastic" (rubber band, lycra clothing, an inner tube, and so on). Discuss the common characteristics of the items (flexible, springy, return to original shape after being stretched, easily adapted to fit specific shapes, and so on). If possible, bring to class and display several items that have the characteristic of elasticity.

Teach

Explain that **price elasticity of demand** has the same characteristics as anything else elastic: As price moves, so does quantity demanded. Point out that the converse is true about *inelasticity*: As price moves, the quantity demanded does not move substantially. Explain that **price elasticity of demand** is calculated by dividing the percentage of change in quantity demanded by the percentage of change in price. Values greater than 1 indicate products that are price *elastic,* values of less than 1 indicate products that are price *inelastic*, and values of exactly 1 indicate *unitary* price elasticity.

FOCUS

Section Four

Price Elasticity of Demand

What Do You Think?

Suppose that Congress is considering adding an additional $0.10 per gallon tax on gasoline. Your senators are supporting this tax because they say reduced consumption of gasoline will improve air quality and reduce our oil imports. Do you agree with your senators?

What's Ahead?

It is important for business people and government officials to be able to measure the effect a price change will have on the quantity demanded. In this section, you will learn about the relationship between price, unit sales, and the revenue a firm receives.

Terms to Know

price elasticity of demand

total revenue

PRICE ELASTICITY OF DEMAND

It is often useful to be able to measure the sensitivity of the quantity demanded to a change in the product's price. Price elasticity is the measure that is used for this purpose. The ***price elasticity of demand*** measures the relative responsiveness of the change in quantity demanded as a result of a change in the product's price. It can be calculated as the ratio of the percentage change in quantity demanded to the percentage change in price. The formula for price elasticity of demand is as follows:

price elasticity of demand measures the relative responsiveness of the change in quantity demanded as a result of a change in the product's price

$$\text{Price Elasticity of Demand} = \frac{\text{Percentage Change in Quantity Demanded}}{\text{Percentage Change in Price}}$$

Elastic Demand with Respect to Price

The term *elastic* implies responsiveness. If something is elastic, it is responsive. Thus, when economists say that a product is price elastic, they mean that the quantity demanded is quite responsive to a change in price. If the calculated value of a price elasticity is greater than 1, we classify demand as being *price elastic*.

Multicultural *Highlights*

If possible, bring to class several ethnic publications, such as *Esteem* (for teenage African Americans), *Yolk* (for Asian Americans), or *Hispanic* (for Hispanic Americans). Explain that the ethnic publications market is growing rapidly, with an estimated 200 ethnic magazines published in English in the United States today. As a class, discuss what might cause a reader to buy an ethnic magazine (ethnic-oriented content, reasonable price, and so on). Ask students to discuss whether they think the demand for ethnic magazines is price elastic or price inelastic. (Probably price elastic—loyal readers may be willing to pay slightly more but may not support a significant price increase.) Have students support their positions with concepts from the textbook.

CD players may be a good example of a product for which demand is elastic. Since there are many substitutes (radios, tape players, and other forms of entertainment), the consumer demand for CD players may be quite elastic. The number of substitute products available is one important determinant of price elasticity. The more substitutes that are available, the more price elastic is demand. Another important influence is the size of the purchase in relation to the buyer's total income. Demand for an expensive item is more likely to be price elastic than demand for an inexpensive item.

Suppose that a 5 percent decrease in the price of CDs stimulated a 10 percent increase in the quantity demanded. Economists would say this demand was quite elastic with respect to price. The price elasticity of demand would be 2:

$$\text{Price Elasticity of Demand} = \frac{\text{10\% Change in Quantity Demanded}}{\text{5\% Change in Price}}$$

$$= 10\% \div 5\%$$
$$= 2$$

Think of some other products that you consider to be price elastic. That is, try to think of products for which you would expect the quantity demanded to be very responsive to a price change.

Inelastic Demand with Respect to Price

When the quantity demanded is not very sensitive to a change in price, we say that demand is *price inelastic*. Table salt is a good example of a product that has an inelastic demand. There are few good substitutes and spending on salt is a small part of total household spending. Thus, people are not very sensitive to the price of salt.

When a product has an inelastic demand, the percentage change in quantity is less than the percentage change in price. This results in a calculated

Review the three determinants of **price elasticity of demand**: the number of substitute products, the importance of the product in the consumer's budget, and the time period considered. Expand students' focus of the **price elasticity of demand** from consumer to producer by relating this concept to **total revenue.**

Apply

Remind students that, in the *Analyzing Graphics* activity for *Figure 6-1,* they speculated that the demand schedule for hot fudge sundaes is different during different months of the year. Price changes may have a different effect on the quantity demanded, depending upon what month it is. Explain that this illustrates **price elasticity of demand,** which measures the responsiveness of a change in the quantity demanded resulting from a change in price. Ask students whether they think hot fudge sundaes illustrate *elastic* or *inelastic* demand (elastic) and have them explain their reasons. List students' reasons under the following headings on the chalkboard or an overhead transparency: **Number of Substitute Products** (many), **Importance of Product in Consumer's Budget** (not very important), and **Time Period Considered** (as the time period is extended, consumers may adjust to spending more).

Guided Practice

Ask student volunteers to copy the following problems on the chalkboard or an overhead transparency for students to use to calculate price elasticity of demand:

1. $\frac{\text{20\% change in quantity demanded}}{\text{5\% change in price}}$
2. $\frac{\text{1\% change in quantity demanded}}{\text{10\% change in price}}$
3. $\frac{\text{12\% change in quantity demanded}}{\text{2\% change in price}}$
4. $\frac{\text{10\% change in quantity demanded}}{\text{10\% change in price}}$

Have students copy each ratio onto a sheet of paper and calculate the price elasticity of demand. After they are finished, have them label each answer as elastic, inelastic, or unitary. (**1.** 4, elastic; **2.** 0.1, inelastic; **3.** 6, elastic; **4.** 1, unitary)

Independent Practice

value of price elasticity that is less than 1. For example, suppose that a 4 percent increase in price for salt caused the quantity demanded to fall by just 1 percent. The numeric value of the price elasticity would be calculated as follows:

$$\text{Price Elasticity of Demand} = \frac{\text{1\% Change in Quantity Demanded}}{\text{4\% Change in Price}}$$

$$= 1\% \div 4\%$$
$$= 0.25$$

A price elasticity of 0.25 signifies that the quantity demanded is not very responsive to a price change. Gasoline is another product for which demand is price inelastic. The price elasticity for gasoline is close to 0.1.

Unitary Price Elasticity

It is possible that the percentage change in quantity demanded would exactly equal the percentage change in price. In such a case, the calculated value of the price elasticity would equal 1. For example, suppose that a 3 percent decrease in price caused a 3 percent increase in the quantity demanded. The price elasticity of demand would be calculated as follows:

$$\text{Price Elasticity of Demand} = \frac{\text{3\% Change in Quantity Demanded}}{\text{3\% Change in Price}}$$

$$= 3\% \div 3\%$$
$$= 1$$

This is a case of unitary price elasticity because the calculated value is equal to 1 (or unity).

WHAT DETERMINES THE PRICE ELASTICITY OF DEMAND?

It is possible to make some predictions about the price elasticity for a product. The following three factors are generally considered important in determining the price elasticity of demand:

1. number of substitute products;
2. importance of the product in the consumer's budget; and
3. time period considered.

Number of Substitute Products

The most important factor in determining the elasticity of a product with respect to the price is the number of substitute products available. The more substitutes available, the more price elastic we can expect demand to be. If there are few substitute products available, we would expect demand to be inelastic.

Consider some specific examples to illustrate this point. As noted earlier, the demand for gasoline in the United States has been estimated to have a price elasticity of about 0.10. Thus, we would classify gas as price inelastic. How does this fit with our explanation of the number of substitute products available? Given the current state of technology, there are virtually no substitutes for gasoline. Gasohol and even electric-powered cars may one day provide important substitutes. Until then, the only real substitute is to use other forms of transportation that use no gas or that conserve on gas. Bicycles use no gas. Riding on buses, in car pools, or in more efficient cars also conserves gas. Americans have shown that they are not willing to reduce gas consumption by very much as the price increases.

There are products that are much more sensitive to price changes. It has been found, for example, that the demand for haddock (an Atlantic fish) is quite price elastic. The price elasticity for haddock has been estimated to be 2.2. There are many substitutes for haddock, such as codfish and other fish. Even meats such as beef, lamb, pork, chicken, and turkey are substitutes for haddock.

Importance of the Product in the Consumer's Budget

A second factor that often influences the price elasticity of demand is the importance of the product in the consumer's budget. If expenditures on a product are a small fraction of a consumer's budget, demand will tend to be price inelastic. If the product represents a large fraction of consumer spending, demand will tend to be more elastic. For example, it is reasonable to expect table salt to have a very inelastic demand. Few consumers purchase enough salt to even remember if it is $0.20 per pound or $0.60 per pound. At either price, a pound of table salt would be a small fraction of a consumer's budget. On the other hand, products that represent major purchases would be expected to have a more elastic demand. Examples include appliances such as refrigerators, ranges, or microwave ovens.

Have students work in small groups to set up a computerized spreadsheet to calculate price elasticity of demand. You may wish to have students use the percentages given in the *Apply* activity on p. 138 as examples in their spreadsheets.

After students have read the section entitled *What Determines the Price Elasticity of Demand?* (pp. 140–142), have them create a graphic organizer to illustrate the determinants of price elasticity of demand. Tell students their graphic organizer should be similar to the one they completed earlier to illustrate the four determinants of demand (the *Guided Practice* in the third section). One possible answer follows.

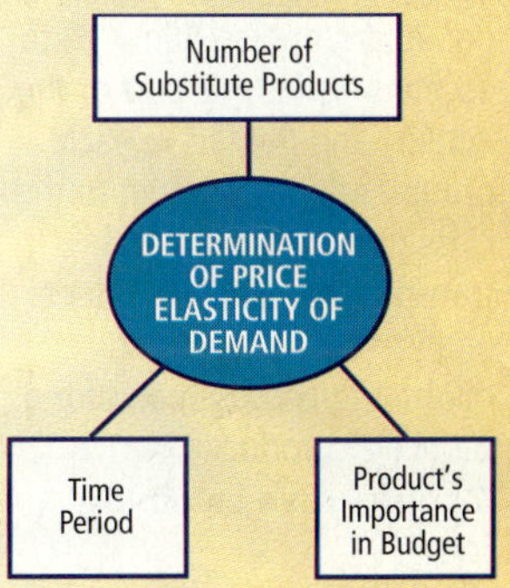

Divide the class into groups of three or four students. Hand out three blank overhead transparencies to each group. Have each group brainstorm a product with elastic demand that would fill a market need. Explain to students that their job is to "sell" others in their company (the class) on the feasibility of their product. In order to do this, they must work together to creatively present their ideas. Have one student create a demand schedule for market demand for the product, another create a demand curve based on that schedule, and a third determine the total revenue based on the demand schedule. If there is a fourth member of the group, he or she should create a slogan or logo for the product. Then, on the computer or by hand, have students create overhead transparencies, being sure to include their slogan and graphics. Allow 10 to 15 minutes for this part of the activity and then have each group "sell" its product to the class using the overhead transparencies. Help students analyze how advertising might influence demand for a particular product.
Cooperative Learning

Time Period Considered

Finally, price elasticity may depend on the length of the time period being considered. The shorter the time period, the more inelastic demand will be. As the time period considered increases, estimates of demand will usually be more elastic. Consumers will have more time to adjust to price changes and perhaps to find substitute products. If your home is heated with fuel oil and its price doubles, you may not be able to do much about it this winter. You can keep the house cooler, but you cannot do much more. Over a longer period of time, you may be able to convert to other energy sources, such as natural gas, wood, or solar heating.

TOTAL REVENUE AND DEMAND

So far, we have looked at demand from a consumer's point of view. Let's now shift our attention to the seller. Sellers of products have a strong interest

Econ & You

INELASTIC CIGARETTES

There is a great deal of debate about the health effects of smoking on those who smoke and on those who are subjected to secondhand smoke. Various policies have been enforced, by both the private and public sectors, to eliminate smoking in many places where smoking was once common. Excise taxes have been placed on cigarettes to raise revenues for the public sector, to reduce consumption, or both, depending on which argument one happens to believe.

Some economic concepts can help you decide which argument makes the most sense. The price elasticity of demand for cigarettes has been estimated to be about 0.4, which means the demand is quite price inelastic. Thus, policy makers are well aware that raising price (via a tax) will have only a slight effect on consumption. However, as a result of the tax, there will be a considerable increase in tax revenues. In Canada, for example, cigarette taxes were increased by 152 percent over a ten-year period spanning parts of the 1980s and 1990s. As a result, cigarette tax revenues increased by nearly 400 percent, while consumption dropped by only 38 percent.

What do you see as some of the costs and benefits of placing a higher tax on cigarettes? Are there both private and public costs and benefits? Why is a knowledge of price elasticity useful to those who must deal with this issue?

Econ & You

Divide the class into groups of four or five students. Have students consider the issue of raising taxes on cigarettes. Tell them to work together to list the private opportunity costs and opportunity benefits on one sheet of paper and the public ones on another. Discuss both lists with the class and ask whether students think the private opportunity costs are truly private, considering the public effects of secondary smoke and the increased costs of health care.

in understanding the demand for products. In particular, the sellers of a product are interested in the amount of money they can obtain from various levels of sales.

Measuring Total Revenue

The total amount of money a company receives from sales of a product is called ***total revenue.*** The formula for calculating total revenue is as follows:

Total Revenue = (Price) × (Quantity Sold)

total revenue
the total amount of money a company receives from sales of a product

Let's go back to the hot fudge sundae example. Suzanne's shop gets one-fifth (20 percent) of the market demand presented in Figure 6-3. The total revenue for hot fudge sundaes is the price multiplied by the quantity sold at that price. At a price of $1.40 per sundae, Suzanne's total revenue, $1,680, would be equal to the price, $1.40, times the quantity sold, 1,200. The demand schedule for Suzanne's Sundae Shop is shown in Figure 6-5. The total revenue at each price is presented in the third column.

Price ×	Quantity Sold per Month =	Total Revenue
$2.00	0	$ 0
1.80	400	720
1.60	800	1,280
1.40	1,200	1,680
1.20	1,600	1,920
1.00	2,000	2,000
.80	2,400	1,920
.60	2,800	1,680

Figure 6-5

Demand and Total Revenue for Hot Fudge Sundaes at Suzanne's

As Suzanne lowers her price for hot fudge sundaes, the quantity that she can sell increases. ***What happens to total revenue as Suzanne lowers the price of sundaes?***

Relationship Between Price and Total Revenue

You already know that the quantity sold is determined in part by the product's price. Figure 6-5 shows some interesting relationships. You see that, at first, price cuts stimulate enough new sales that total revenue goes up. But, note that this is not always the case. Down to a price of $1, total revenue rises as price falls and quantity goes up. However, if price is reduced below $1, the additional sales do not compensate for the lower price per unit. This results in lower total revenue.

When considering what price to charge it is important for a business to think about the price elasticity of demand. You know that according to the law of demand, lowering price will always increase unit sales. But, lowering price may cause total revenue to either increase or decrease depending on the price elasticity of demand. This important relationship is summarized in Figure 6-6.

Analyzing *Graphics*

Caption Answer
Total revenue goes up as the price moves from $2 to $1, and then it goes down at prices below $1. The product then becomes price inelastic.

Have students use the computer or graph paper to create a demand curve and a total revenue curve. Point out that a demand curve shows demand from a consumer's point of view while a total revenue curve tracks demand from a business's point of view. Tell students that, to create a total revenue curve, they should first create a line graph, plotting price on the vertical axis and total revenue on the horizontal axis. Point out how the graph makes it easy to see the exact point at which total revenue stops increasing and starts decreasing.

Media*Link*

Have students work in small groups to calculate the total revenue for hot fudge sundaes according to *Figure 6-2* on p. 127. Have students use *Figure 6-5* in their textbook or photocopies of *Overhead Transparency 6-5* as a guide. Tell students to use spreadsheet software, keying in the price in one column and the quantity in another. Have them create a third column for total revenue and then write a formula to calculate total revenue. Have students find the price at which total revenue stops going up and starts coming down ($1). Lead students to understand that this is the point at which the sundaes show unitary price elasticity. Below this point, they become price inelastic.

Analyzing Graphics

Caption Answer
More total revenue

Display *Overhead Transparency 6-6.* Ask students whether they would rather produce a product with consistently elastic demand or consistently inelastic demand. Brainstorm a class list of products with a highly elastic demand (such as fast-food tacos) and products with an inelastic demand (such as motor oil).

Assess

1. Relative responsiveness of the change in quantity demanded as a result of a change in price **6-4**
2. Examples should reflect an understanding of these determinants: number of substitute products, importance to consumer's budget, and time period. **6-4**
3. $1.60, $6,400; $1.20, $9,600; $0.80, $9,600 **6-4**
4. Total revenue would increase. **6-4**
5. Demand for gas will decrease only slightly because gas has a price elasticity of only about 0.1. Pollution and imports will not be affected much. **6-4**
6. Yes, since the public will not cut its consumption by much, the government will collect a great deal of additional revenue. **6-4**

Close

Have students create a table on the computer or in their notebooks that outlines all of the formulas used in this chapter. Review the formulas as a class.

Figure 6-6

The Relationship Between Price, Elasticity, and Total Revenue

This figure summarizes how price, price elasticity, and total revenue are related. ***If the demand for movie tickets is price elastic, would a theater get more or less total revenue if it lowered the price of tickets?***

Elastic Demand	Inelastic Demand
Decreasing price increases total revenue.	**Decreasing price decreases total revenue.**
Increasing price decreases total revenue.	**Increasing price increases total revenue.**

You can see from the relationships in Figure 6-6 that you should consider price elasticity carefully when thinking about changing price. If you have an objective of increasing total revenue, you need to decide if a price decrease or a price increase would have that effect.

Checkpoint

Content Check

1. What does price elasticity of demand measure?
2. Name three factors that affect the price elasticity of demand and give an example of each.
3. Using the following table, calculate total revenue at each price:

Price	Quantity Demanded per Month
$1.60	4,000
1.20	8,000
.80	12,000

4. If a product has a price elasticity of 1.3, what would happen to total revenue if the price decreased?

What Do You Think Now?

Reread *What Do You Think?* in the Section Four Focus. Then answer the following questions:

5. Explain whether you agree or disagree with your senators' analysis. Will people cut back on their consumption of gas, reducing pollution and oil imports?
6. Will this tax provide much additional revenue to the government?

Reteach

Pair students who understand how to calculate price elasticity with those who do not. Have the student who understands the concept write five problems for calculating price elasticity and then give them to the other student to solve. Then, together, have each pair identify whether their answers indicate elastic, inelastic, or unitary demand. **6-4**

Enrich

Have students work in small groups to create a demand schedule and a demand curve for two products—one with a price elasticity of 5 (very elastic) and one with a price elasticity of 0.2 (very inelastic). Ask students to compare how the two curves look (elastic: modestly sloping line; inelastic: very steep slope, almost vertical). **6-4**

Concepts in Brief

1. The relationship between price and quantity demanded can be shown in a table as a demand schedule or in a graph as a demand curve. A change in quantity demanded can be caused by only one factor: a change in the product's price. A change in quantity demanded can be shown in a graph by movement along a given demand curve.
2. Most goods that you consume give you diminishing marginal satisfaction. As you consume a greater number of units (in a given time period), each *additional unit* gives less *additional satisfaction.* This is one reason that people will buy a greater quantity of a good only at lower prices. The inverse relationship between price and the quantity demanded is called the *law of demand.*
3. The overall level of demand can be affected by many factors. Four very important factors are consumers' incomes, consumers' tastes and preferences (attitudes), the prices of substitute products, and the prices of complementary products. Changes in any of these factors can cause a change in demand. A change in demand can be represented on a graph as a shift of the demand curve. An increase in demand is shown as a shift of the demand curve to the right. A shift of the demand curve to the left indicates a decrease in demand.
4. It is important to measure the sensitivity of demand to changes in price. Price elasticity measures the responsiveness of the quantity demanded to price changes. A business usually is concerned with the effect a price change will have on its total revenue. The price elasticity of a product can help to predict how a change in price will affect total revenue. A company can always increase sales of a product by lowering price, but total revenue may increase or decrease as a result.

Economic Foundations

1. How does the economic meaning of demand differ from the everyday use of the word *demand*?
2. What is the advantage of a demand curve over a demand schedule?
3. What happens to quantity demanded as a result of the substitution effect?
4. What happens to quantity demanded as a result of the income effect?
5. How does changing income affect demand?
6. How do changing attitudes affect demand?

Chapter Close

Your Economic Portfolio

Explain to students that, as consumers, they have a great deal of influence on the market. As a class, have students brainstorm a list of goods that they would buy in greater quantities at a lower price. Then, have each student choose one of the products and write a business letter to a local retailer. Students' letters should reason that the retailer could sell more of the product if she or he would reduce the price. Encourage students to include projected demand curves and total revenue curves with their letters. Students may wish to reinforce their projections by surveying classmates or other consumers to determine whether they would buy more at a lower price. Review students' work and have them make any necessary corrections before mailing their letters. Have students file the final drafts of the letters in their portfolios.

You may wish to provide the following end-of-chapter materials:

- *Skills & Concepts* worksheet
- *Content Review Workbook*
- Chapter *Assessment*
- Chapter *MicroExam*

Economic Foundations

1. The everyday use of *demand* means something you ask for, but the economic meaning is very specific: *the quantities of a good that consumers are willing and able to purchase at various prices during a given period of time.* (p. 124)
2. A demand curve shows the price and quantity combinations that fall between those given on a demand schedule. (p. 127)
3. As the price of a good falls, we may substitute it for other items, so the quantity demanded of that product increases. If the price of a good rises, we may substitute other goods for the now relatively more expensive good, so the quantity demanded of that good decreases. (p. 130)

(Continued)

7. How do the changing prices of other goods affect demand?
8. Explain the differences between the three kinds of price elasticity of demand.
9. What three major factors influence the price elasticity of demand?

Your Economic Vocabulary

Build your economic vocabulary by matching the following terms with their definitions.

- **complementary products**
- **demand**
- **demand curve**
- **demand schedule**
- **determinants of demand**
- **diminishing marginal utility**
- **income effect**
- **inferior goods**
- **law of demand**
- **marginal utility**
- **normal goods**
- **price elasticity of demand**
- **substitute products**
- **substitution effect**
- **total revenue**

1. the effect that increasing or decreasing prices has on the buying power of income
2. a listing of the quantities that would be purchased at various prices
3. products whose uses are similar enough that one can replace the other
4. the total amount of money a company receives from sales of a product
5. a graphic illustration of the relationship between *price* and the *quantity demanded* at each price
6. products that are used together
7. the change in the mix of goods purchased as a result of increasing or decreasing relative prices
8. goods for which demand goes down as income goes up
9. measures the relative responsiveness of the change in quantity demanded as a result of a change in the product's price
10. the quantity demanded of a good will be greater at lower prices than will be the quantity demanded at higher prices
11. the quantities of a good that consumers are willing and able to purchase at various prices during a given period of time
12. the amount of satisfaction a person gets from *one* additional unit of a product
13. goods for which demand goes up as income goes up
14. the principle that as additional units of a product are consumed during a given time period, the additional satisfaction decreases
15. the factors that determine how much will be purchased at any given price

Economic Foundations
(Continued)

4. As the price of anything we buy goes down, our income appears greater because we feel that we can afford to buy more; therefore, the quantity we demand rises. Conversely, as the prices of products go up, our incomes appear smaller and so the quantity we demand decreases. (pp. 129–130)
5. We tend to consume more normal goods and less inferior goods as our incomes go up. (p. 134)
6. As our tastes and preferences toward a good become more positive, we tend to consume more of that good. Conversely, a negative change in attitude can cause us to consume less of that good. (p. 134)
7. As the price of a good increases, people buy substitute products instead. If the price of substitute goods decreases, people also tend to buy the substitute goods. For complementary products, if the price of the complementary product decreases, demand for the other can increase. (p. 134–135)
8. Price elastic demand means that price elasticity is greater than 1 and demand is very responsive to changes in price. Price inelastic demand means that price elasticity is less than 1 and demand is not very responsive to changes in price. Unitary price elasticity of demand means that price elasticity is equal to 1 and the percentage of change in quantity is the same as the percentage of change in price. (p. 138–140)
9. The number of substitute products, the importance of the product in the consumer's budget, and the time period considered (p. 140)

Your Economic Vocabulary

1. **income effect**
2. **demand schedule**
3. **substitute products**
4. **total revenue**
5. **demand curve**
6. **complementary products**
7. **substitution effect**
8. **inferior goods**
9. **price elasticity of demand**
10. **law of demand**
11. **demand**
12. **marginal utility**
13. **normal goods**
14. **diminishing marginal utility**
15. **determinants of demand**

Thinking Critically About Economics

1. Why are people willing to pay a price for the right to consume any product or service? Why would you be willing to pay for a cassette tape?
2. Explain how the principle of diminishing marginal utility would influence your consumption of hot fudge sundaes. Give several other examples of goods you buy that have diminishing marginal utility.
3. Explain the difference between a demand schedule and a demand curve. Construct an example of each.
4. What factors have influenced the demand for bicycles in the last few years? Focus your attention on income, attitudes, and the prices of other products. Explain how changes in these factors would either increase or decrease the demand for bicycles.
5. If the price of housing (rent or house payments) goes up, there may be an income effect on your family. What does this mean? What is the relationship between prices and income?
6. Since the early 1970s, much public attention has been focused on the demand for gasoline. Economists have found that the demand for gas is inelastic with respect to price. What does this mean? Why would the demand for gasoline be price inelastic?
7. A simple demand schedule for a company follows:

Price	Quantity
$6	0
$5	1
$4	2
$3	3
$2	4
$1	5

   Find the dollar value of total revenue at each of the six prices. At what price will total revenue be the greatest? How many units will sell at that price?
8. Choose two products and explain why you think their demand is price elastic or price inelastic. Be sure to consider the three factors that determine price elasticity in preparing your answer.
9. Explain the difference between a change in quantity demanded and a change in demand. Draw a graph to show this difference.

Thinking Critically About Economics

1. Because people get satisfaction, or utility, from the consumption of a product or service; answers may include that the student is willing to pay a price for the benefit of listening to a tape.
2. The first sundae would give a lot of satisfaction, but subsequent sundaes would be decreasingly satisfying, so students would be less likely to want an additional sundae as the number consumed during a given time period increased; answers may include bicycles, soft drinks, and TVs.
3. A demand schedule is a list of the quantities that would be

(Continued)

Thinking Critically About Economics (Continued)

purchased at various prices. A demand curve is a graphic way of presenting the same information, but it has the advantage of showing the price and quantity combinations that fall between those on a demand schedule.

Demand Schedule

(Prices/quantities may vary.)

Price	Quantity
$10	20
$8	40
$6	60
$4	80

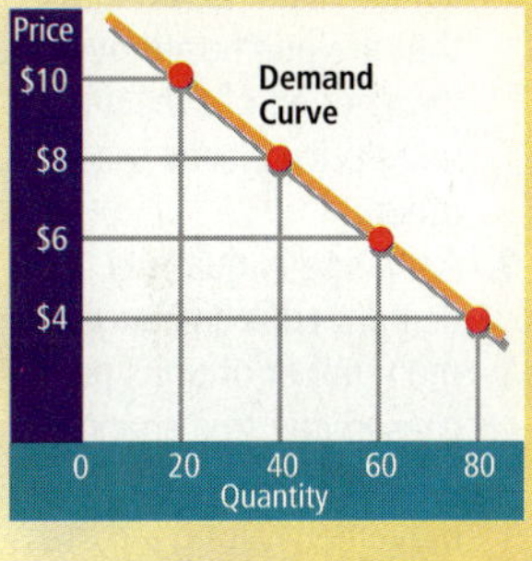

4. Answers may include that, today, there are more favorable attitudes about energy conservation and increased exercise, and high gasoline prices may contribute to a rise in the quantity of bicycles demanded.
5. The income effect shows that, as the price of housing goes up, people have less income available to spend on other goods if the dollar amount of their incomes stays the same. In general, rising prices result in lower real incomes (purchasing power), and falling prices result in higher real incomes.
6. The quantity of gasoline demanded does not respond very much to price changes. We depend heavily on gasoline for transportation, which is critical to maintaining our lifestyles, and there are few substitutes for gas.

(Continued)

Thinking Critically About Economics (Continued)

7. Students' completed demand schedules should show the following figures in the Total Revenue column: \$0, \$5, \$8, \$9, \$8, \$5. Total revenue is greatest at a price of \$3; three units will be demanded at that price.
8. Answers will vary but should include a consideration of the three factors that determine elasticity and should explain that products (1) with many substitutes, (2) that are important to the consumer's budget, and (3) that are purchased over a long period of time will be more price elastic than others.
9. A change in quantity demanded is a change in the number of units purchased due to a change in price and is indicated by movement along a curve. A change in demand is a shift of the entire demand curve showing a new set of price and quantity combinations.

   Students' graphs should be similar to the following:

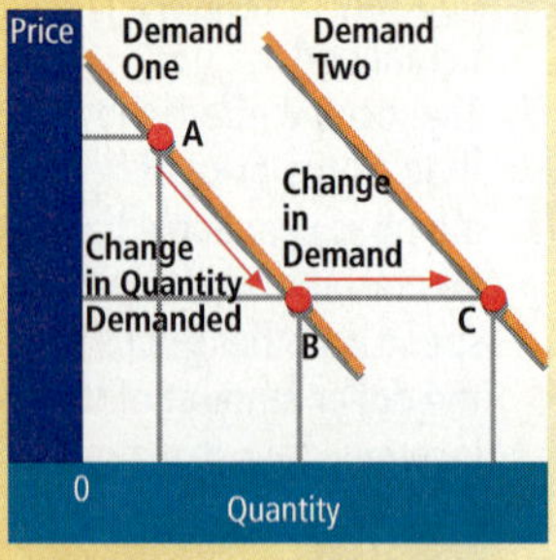

Economic Enrichment

Students' learning exercises will vary but should include the following four determinants of demand: (1) changes in consumers' incomes, (2) changes in consumers' attitudes, (3) changes in the price of a complementary product, and (4) changes in the price of a substitute product.

Economic Enrichment

LearnComp is a new company that is making pocket-sized computers that weigh just 5 ounces and are specifically designed to aid learning. These little computers run on solar power or on a single AAA battery if enough light is not available to power the system. Each of the computers has a slot where the user can slide in "LearnCards." Each LearnCard has an active learning exercise for a specific subject area. For example, there are LearnCards for basic algebra, geography, grammar, and biology.

You have been asked to develop the contents for the "Demand" unit on an economics LearnCard. There is limited space available so you cannot include everything you have learned about demand. Identify four concepts that you think would be the most important to include. Write a short learning exercise that could be used to illustrate each of the concepts you select.

Math and Economics

You have seen that consumers' demand is affected by their level of income. Current income can, however, be supplemented by the use of credit (borrowing). Often, the availability of credit makes it easy for people to spend more than they really can afford. You need to be careful about how much you borrow. How much credit can you afford? As a rule of thumb, the amount of credit payments you make each month should be less than 20 percent of your take-home pay. Thus, if you have take-home pay of \$1,500, you should not have more than \$300 a month in credit payments (\$1,500 × 0.2 = \$300). This amount does not include housing.

A family has an after-tax (take-home) income of \$3,600 per month after paying for their housing. Currently, the family's monthly payment on their Sear's charge is \$122. They also have a VISA payment of \$110 per month. Last week, they decided to replace the family car with a new minivan. Assuming that they have no other credit payments, how large a monthly car payment can they afford?

Writing About Economics

Look at advertisements in a local newspaper and a national magazine. From each publication, pick two advertisements for products or services a typical household might buy. Write a short report explaining the kind of information in each ad and discussing how that information may affect the demand for that product or service. In your report, cover the following: What differences in the kind of information did you find? What substitute and complementary goods also may be affected by each of the ads? How might the demand for these goods be affected by advertising?

Math and Economics

The family should not have monthly credit payments totaling more than \$720 (\$3,600 x 0.2); the family is already making monthly payments totaling \$232 (\$122 + \$110), so the monthly car payment should not exceed \$488 (\$720 – \$232).

Writing About Economics

Students' reports will vary but should include analyses of all four advertisements. Students should compare and contrast the content of the ads, list substitute and complementary goods for each product, and hypothesize about how the ads might increase or decrease demand for the products that they advertise. Students should cite one or more of the four determinants of demand when hypothesizing about changes in demand for these products.

Seasonality at the GAP

Sales in many types of retail establishments are seasonal. This means that sales during some parts of the year are consistently higher or lower than they are during other parts of the year. In the case of the GAP, we find that fourth-quarter sales are considerably stronger than sales the rest of the year.

Managers need to look at how much of the increased (or decreased) sales in any quarter is due to actual sales trends and how much of it is due to seasonality. When you think of the clothing industry, think of any reasons that might cause sales to be greater in some parts of the year than others. Some reasons to consider are people's decision to buy clothes at the beginning of the school year, clothing purchases in November and December for Christmas gifts, and the fact that sweaters, jackets, and heavier fall and winter clothing cost more than do shorts and T-shirts.

If you look closely at the accompanying line graph of the GAP's quarterly sales, you will see that the trend over time is toward increasing sales but with noticeable upward spikes (increases in sales) in the fourth quarter of the year followed by a steep decline in sales for the first quarter. Managers must be aware of this factor, which is called *seasonality,* and make allowances for it in decision making. As you read the newspaper or magazines and come across other line graphs, look for indications of seasonality.

Seasonality of GAP Sales

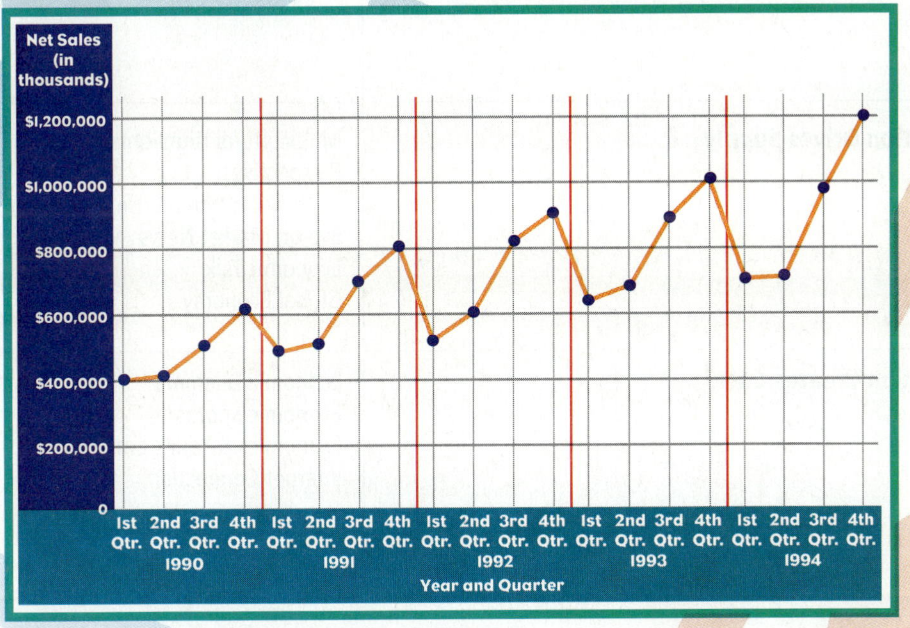

SOURCE: GAP, Inc., Annual Reports 1990–1994.

Economic Concepts

Measurement

149

After students have read the feature article on this page, discuss the buying habits of consumers by comparing each of the four quarters in 1990 to those in 1991, 1992, 1993, and 1994. (In all five years, the first quarter was the lowest selling one, the second quarter was higher than the first, the third quarter was higher than the second, and the fourth quarter was the highest selling quarter.) Then, distribute to students or have students research the national sales figures from last year, which can be found in the *GAP Annual Reports.* On butcher paper, have students create a large line graph of last year's four quarters. Then, divide the class into four groups and assign each of the groups one of the quarters of the year. Ask students to decorate their quarters of the line graph with collages of magazine and newspaper clippings, original drawings, and computer graphics to represent possible reasons their quarter had higher or lower sales compared to the other three quarters of the year. (Answers will vary but may include that the first quarter is affected by Valentine's Day and debt from Christmas bills; the second quarter includes spring/summer wardrobe shopping, Easter, summer clothing purchases, graduations, and weddings; the third quarter involves shopping for fall wardrobe, back-to-school clothes, and supplies; and the fourth quarter includes winter wardrobe purchases, Halloween, Thanksgiving, and Christmas.) Display the completed mural on a classroom wall. Then, have one member from each group explain to the class the significance of the groups's section of the collage. Then, precipitate a discussion on the roles that supply and demand play in the sales trends during the year.

Chapter 7
Supply: Producing Goods and Services

Chapter Theme

The process of producing a good or service results in costs of production. Changes in production costs or productivity can lead to a change in quantity supplied at every cost. The quantity of a good or service that is produced is related to the price at which the product can be sold.

Section	Special Features
Supply	Media Link Econ & You
Production Drives Supply	Multicultural Highlights Perspectives: Thinking Like a Business Owner Eye on Market News Economic Talk Global Economy
Production Creates Costs	Economic Dilemma Economic Spotlight Economics & Your Community Internet Connection

Video Activity

Chapter 7, Coffee Prices

Search Chapter 7, Play to 8

Ask students if they think the crop freeze featured in the video clip resulted in a change in supply or a change in quantity supplied (a change in supply). Have students support their answers. Then, ask students how they think they would be affected if a sudden decrease in production caused the price of soda or bottled water to soar. Ask students how much they would pay for the item and what product they might likely substitute if their preferred item became too expensive.

	Print Resources	Media Resources	Assessment
	Effective Teaching Model Lesson Plans *Skills & Concepts* worksheet *Problem Solving* worksheet *Casebook* *Economic Measurement Workbook* *Content Review Workbook* *Spanish Resources*	VHS CD-ROM Videodisc *Arctic Express* *Interactive* ECONOMICS Template software	*Your Economic Portfolio* Chapter *Assessment* Chapter *MicroExam*

Special Learners	Print Resources	Media Resources	Assessment
	Reteach worksheet	Overhead and *Transparencies 7-1 to 7-5* Computer Camcorder VCR Audio	*Checkpoint* Section 1 Quiz
Visual Activity Auditory Activity At Risk Activity	*Enrich* worksheet *Life Skills* worksheet	Overhead and *Transparencies 7-6 to 7-8* Audio	*Checkpoint* Section 2 Quiz
Cooperative Learning Activity Kinesthetic Activity	*Teacher's Connection to the Internet*	Overhead and *Transparencies 7-9 to 7-11* Computer	*Checkpoint* Section 3 Quiz

Careers Activity

With today's computer technology explosion, it's no wonder that many people are using their computers to produce goods and services for profit. Desktop publishers use their computer skills and creativity to provide original writing, typesetting, graphics, design work, and publications that meet the specific needs of businesses and individuals.

Desktop publishing requires an extensive background in writing, layout, and design and experience using various publishing software products. Strong sales skills are essential since income is based solely on the number of projects and clients a desktop publisher develops.

Tell students to imagine that they own desktop-publishing companies. They work alone out of their homes, each using one computer, about a dozen clip-art programs, and a fast, high-quality printer. They can serve about 15 full-time clients. Have each student write a business plan designed to bring in more profits in the long run.

CHAPTER 7

Teaching Materials

Program Resources

- Student text
- *Effective Teaching Model Lesson Plans*
- *Overhead Transparencies 7-1 to 7-11*
- *Life Skills* worksheet
- *Problem Solving* worksheet
- *Reteach* worksheet
- *Enrich* worksheet
- *Skills & Concepts* worksheet
- *Casebook*
- *Economic Measurement Workbook*
- *Content Review Workbook*
- *Spanish Resources*
- Video package
- *Teacher's Connection to the Internet*
- *Arctic Express*
- *Interactive ECONOMICS*
- Template software

Assessment

- Section Quizzes
- Chapter *Assessment*
- Chapter *MicroExam*

Overview

Section One
Supply

Section Two
Production Drives Supply

Section Three
Production Creates Costs

150

Teacher to Teacher

Hold a class auction of an item, such as a notebook, that students use and need everyday. Ask a student volunteer to record information about price and quantity demanded as the auction is going on. After the auction, work together with students to make a bar graph of the various prices and quantities demanded for the auctioned item. Ask students how much of the auctioned item each would be willing to supply at each price. Work together to make another bar graph of the prices and quantities supplied. Then, with students' input, create a line graph showing the relationships between price and the quantities supplied and demanded.

John Burton
Palm Harbor University High School
Palm Harbor, FL

Supply: Producing Goods and Services

Learning Objectives

7-1
Explain the relationship between price and quantity supplied.

7-2
Distinguish between a change in quantity supplied and a change in supply.

7-3
Discuss how and why people produce goods and services.

7-4
Recognize the impact of diminishing marginal product on production costs and the supply curve.

7-5
Understand the relationship between scale of production and production costs.

Outside Resources

- Blank overhead transparencies
- Camcorder and VCR or audiocassette recorder
- Graph paper
- Outside speaker: Business manager of your city or school district or from a local factory
- Outside speaker: Small-business owner or Small Business Administration representative
- Newspapers

Vocabulary

supply, p. 152
supply schedule, p. 152
supply curve, p. 153
law of supply, p. 156
change in the quantity supplied, p. 156
price elasticity of supply, p. 156
change in supply, p. 157
factor of production, p. 160
land, p. 160
labor, p. 160
capital, p. 160
entrepreneurship, p. 160
total product, p. 161
average product, p. 161
marginal product, p. 162
short run, p. 162
diminishing marginal product, p. 163
long run, p. 165
scale of production, p. 165
returns to scale, p. 166
explicit costs, p. 168
opportunity costs, p. 168

Focus

Have students jot down in a single column on a sheet of paper all of the goods and services that they can remember seeing advertised on TV during the past week. Have them add the heading **Available Goods and Services.**

After students have completed their list, have them add one more column. Tell students to label it **Reasons for Producing.** In this column, have students list the reasons they think these goods and services are produced. As a class, have students discuss situations in which a company might decide to produce more or less of a good. Point out that the quantity produced may be adjusted depending on the cost of production and price in the market.

Teach

Explain to students that firms are willing to supply a greater quantity of a product if they will receive a higher price. That is, **supply** is the quantities a firm is willing to produce at different prices. Display *Overhead Transparency 7-1.* Explain that a **supply schedule** is merely the information that appears on the horizontal and vertical axes of a supply curve.

FOCUS

Section One

Supply

What Do You Think?

In one year, wheat farmers in the United States produced 54 million tons of wheat at a price of $3.00 per bushel. When the price went up to $3.24 per bushel, wheat farmers produced 67 million tons of wheat. Was there an increase in the supply of wheat?

What's Ahead?

Businesses are successful when they supply the goods or services that people demand at a fair price. As the price increases, the quantity of goods supplied increases too. If there is a change in productivity or production costs, the quantity supplied at every price might change.

Terms to Know

- supply
- supply schedule
- supply curve
- law of supply
- change in the quantity supplied
- price elasticity of supply
- change in supply

supply
the quantities of a product or service that a firm is willing and able to make available for sale at different prices

supply schedule
a table that shows the quantities of a good or service that would be supplied by a firm at different prices

SUPPLY FOR THE INDIVIDUAL FIRM

In our economy, people produce goods and services to gain certain benefits. These benefits include money income and psychic income. One goal of firms is to make money for the owners of the business. So, firms will only produce goods and services that sell at prices that cover the cost of making those goods available. ***Supply*** is the quantities of a product or service that a firm is willing and able to make available for sale at different prices.

Supply Schedules

A list of the various prices of a product and the quantities made available for sale at those prices can be summarized in a table. A ***supply schedule*** is a table that shows the quantities of a good or service that would be supplied by a firm at different prices. A supply schedule for Ramano's Sandwich Shop, located in Sycamore Bend, is shown in Figure 7-1.

At a price of $2 per sandwich, Ramano's is willing to make 120 sandwiches each day. But, at higher prices, Ramano's is willing to make a greater quantity. For example, if the price went up to $4, Ramano's would supply 160 sandwiches each day. At a price of $7, Ramano's would be willing to make 220 sandwiches per day.

Price	Quantity Supplied per Day
$2.00	120
$3.00	140
$4.00	160
$5.00	180
$6.00	200
$7.00	220

Figure 7-1

Supply Schedule for Ramano's Sandwich Shop

This supply schedule summarizes the number of sandwiches Ramano's will supply at six different prices. ***Is Ramano's willing to supply more or fewer sandwiches as the price goes up?***

Supply Curves

The supply schedule for Ramano's also can be illustrated as a graph. A ***supply curve*** is a graphic representation of the quantities that would be supplied at each price. A supply curve shows the quantity supplied at every price, not just the prices in a supply schedule. A supply curve depicts price and the quantity supplied in a way that makes the relationship between them easy to see. Ramano's supply curve is shown in Figure 7-2.

supply curve
a graphic representation of the quantities that would be supplied at each price

You can read any price/quantity supplied combination from this supply curve. For example, the quantity of sandwiches supplied at a price of $2 is identified by the dashed lines. To find a price/quantity supplied combination that is not in the table in Figure 7-1, do the following:

1. Find the price on the vertical axis.
2. Go from that point straight across to the supply curve.
3. Go straight down from the supply curve to the horizontal axis to find the quantity supplied.

Using Figure 7-2, find out how many sandwiches Ramano's would supply if the price were $5.50 each.

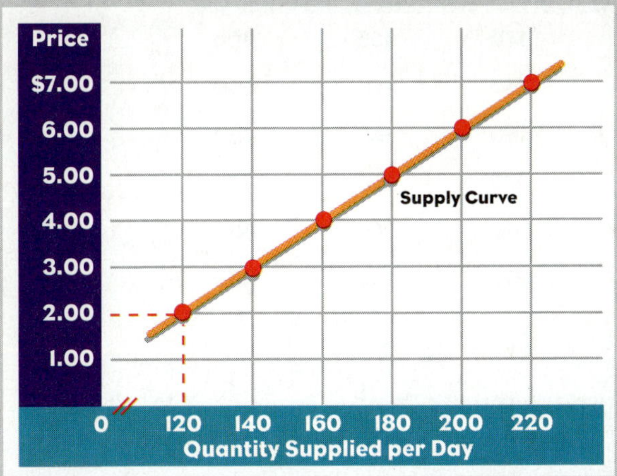

Figure 7-2

Supply Curve for Ramano's Sandwich Shop

This supply curve, based on the information in Figure 7-1, illustrates how quantity supplied increases with price. ***How many sandwiches do you think Ramano's will be willing to make each day at a price of $4.50?***

To clarify students' understanding of supply curves, display *Overhead Transparency 7-2.* Tell students that a **supply curve** is a graphical depiction of a **supply schedule.** Ask students to think about producing a good from a firm's perspective. Ask students if it would make sense for a firm to produce more of a product if the price it would receive were to increase. Explain that the **law of supply** states that a firm will supply a greater quantity if it can get a higher price. A firm will supply a lower quantity at a lower price. Explain that a change in production level along a supply curve is called a **change in the quantity supplied.**

Explain that the **price elasticity of supply** is a responsiveness indicator that shows how a change in price affects the quantity supplied. Explain that, with some products, the quantity supplied will be very responsive to a price change while, with other products, it will not. Finally, explain that the **supply curve** can shift because of reasons such as technology. That is, technology can make it cheaper to produce a good. This can alter market forces, which might make the whole supply curve shift.

Apply

Analyzing Graphics

Caption Answers

7-1 More sandwiches as the price goes up

7-2 170 sandwiches at a price of $4.50

Make a supply schedule on the chalkboard or an overhead transparency. Label the first column of the table **Price** and the second column **Quantity Supplied.** Ask students to imagine that they own a local bike shop and they currently sell 5,000 bicycles per year at $300 per bike. Ask students to estimate how many bikes they would supply if they could receive $350 per bike. With students' help, fill in the schedule with higher and lower prices to help them determine their answer. Ask students what quantity of bikes they would supply for each price they list.

Guided Practice

MARKET SUPPLY

Market supply is the total quantity of a product or service that all firms in a market will make available for sale at various prices. To get the market supply, you add up all the quantities that each firm in the market would supply at each price.

The Market Supply Schedule

In Sycamore Bend, the market served by Ramano's Sandwich Shop, there are four other restaurants that serve sandwiches: The Food Emporium, The Village Deli, Singh's Subs, and Damon's Diner. The supply schedules for these four firms are given in Figure 7-3, along with Ramano's supply schedule. The last column of Figure 7-3 is the market supply schedule for sandwiches in Sycamore Bend, which is the sum of columns two through six.

Price	Ramano's Sandwich Shop +	The Food Emporium +	The Village Deli +	Singh's Subs +	Damon's Diner =	Total Market Supply
$2.00	120	90	115	140	135	600
$3.00	140	100	120	150	140	650
$4.00	160	110	125	160	145	700
$5.00	180	120	130	170	150	750
$6.00	200	130	135	180	155	800
$7.00	220	140	140	190	160	850

Figure 7-3

Market Supply Schedule for Sandwiches in Sycamore Bend

This market supply schedule summarizes the individual supply schedules for five sandwich shops in Sycamore Bend. ***What is the relationship between price and the quantity supplied by the market?***

Analyzing *Graphics*

Caption Answer
Quantity supplied increases as price increases, and it decreases as price decreases.

Media*Link*

Ask students to brainstorm a list of manufacturing companies in the local area. Ask a student volunteer to contact the human resources department at one of the companies to set up an interview with one of its manufacturing department executives. Tell the student to ask permission to videotape or audio tape the interview. As a class, have students prepare interview questions ahead of time that relate to how supply is determined. After the interview, have students share and discuss the tape as a class.

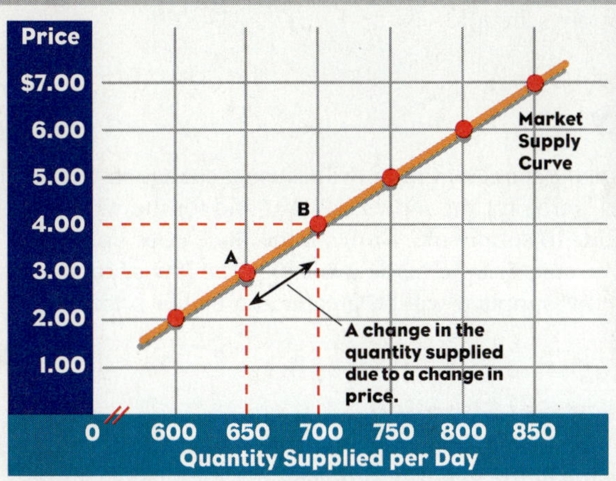

Figure 7-4

Market Supply Curve for Sandwiches in Sycamore Bend

The market supply curve for sandwiches is the sum of the supply curves for all firms in the market. ***How many sandwiches do you think would be supplied by this market if the price were $3.50?***

The Market Supply Curve

The market supply curve is a graph of the information contained in the market supply schedule. The market supply curve for sandwiches is illustrated in Figure 7-4. You can use the market supply curve to identify the quantity

Econ & You

WHY SHOULD I HIRE YOU?

Businesses find it increasingly important to maintain a highly productive work force. As a result, they expect more and more from the people they hire to help in the production of their products or services. It is very likely that you will be asked questions such as "What have you done?" and "What do you know?" at some point in your job search.

Education and training are critical to being a productive participant in today's fast-moving economy. The skills you have today won't be sufficient tomorrow. Continual learning is an important element of success. In the last two decades, the real wages of high school dropouts have dropped nearly 24 percent. For those workers with only high school educations, the decline has been more than 12 percent.

Business Week reported what a variety of workers suggested as important personal skills. Here are some examples:

- ability to communicate;
- positive attitude;
- ability to listen;
- willingness to work overtime; and
- self-confidence.

These personal skills, along with a good education, may be your keys to success.

Analyzing Graphics

Caption Answer
675 sandwiches at a price of $3.50

Divide the class into groups of four or five students. On the chalkboard or an overhead transparency, write the terms **Price** and **Quantity Supplied.** Tell students that each group is willing to supply 100 candy bars for a price of $10. Ask each group to determine how many units it will provide at a price of $5, $8, $12, and $15. Ask each group to develop its own supply curve and supply schedule, using spreadsheet software with graphing capability, if possible. Have each group share its results with the class. Then, as a class, develop a market supply schedule for all the groups and create a graph of the market supply curve.

Econ & You

Have students make a list of their personal and professional skills and any accomplishments that they think might help them get a job. Divide the class into student pairs and tell each pair to choose a specific job opportunity. Then, have one student in each pair role-play a potential employer and the other student role-play a potential employee as the class members watch. As a whole class, have students vote (by secret ballot) on how many of them would have considered hiring their job candidates. Discuss the reasons students voted as they did and how requirements might differ for job candidates in different areas of employment, such as professional and blue collar.

Ask students to imagine that they work for a fast-food restaurant. Due to a sudden change in the marketplace, consumers now will pay only $1 per jumbo hamburger—$1 less than the restaurant is accustomed to charging. So, the restaurant must lower its price. The problem is that it often costs the restaurant $1 or more to produce each hamburger. Explain that the law of supply can be applied when producing goods. Have students explain in writing how they think this price change will ultimately affect supply at that restaurant. Encourage students to apply the principles of the law of supply to their explanations.

Distribute graph paper and ask students to plot a change in the quantity supplied and the corresponding price change for products and numbers of their choosing. (You may wish to refer students to *Figure 7-4* for an example.) After their supply curves are complete, have each student trade graphs with a partner. Ask students to determine the price elasticity of supply for their partners' supply curves.
Independent Practice

of sandwiches that would be supplied by the market at a price that is not represented in the supply schedule.

LAW OF SUPPLY

law of supply
states that the quantity of goods supplied will be greater at a higher price than it will at a lower price

You have learned that a change in price will cause a change in the number of units supplied. This is true for the individual firm and for the whole market as well. Firms are willing to supply more units if the price goes up. If the price goes down, fewer units will be made available. The ***law of supply*** states that the quantity of goods supplied will be greater at a higher price than it will at a lower price.

Change in the Quantity Supplied

change in the quantity supplied
change in the number of units made available for sale due to a *price change*

This change in the number of units made available for sale due to a *price change* is called a ***change in the quantity supplied***. For the market supply curve in Figure 7-4, movement from Point *A* to Point *B* is an example of a change in quantity supplied. When price goes from $3 to $4, the quantity supplied goes up from 650 to 700 sandwiches per day. If the price fell again from $4 to $3, firms in the marketplace would cut production from a total of 700 to 650 per day.

A change in the quantity supplied is always shown as a change *along* a given supply curve. The change in quantity supplied in response to a price rise will be upward along the supply curve. For a fall in price, the change in quantity supplied will be downward along the supply curve. This is illustrated by the double-headed arrow between Points *A* and *B* in Figure 7-4.

Price Elasticity of Supply

price elasticity of supply
measures the responsiveness of the quantity supplied to changes in the product's price

The ***price elasticity of supply*** measures the responsiveness of the quantity supplied to changes in the product's price. This concept is very similar to the price elasticity of demand. The price elasticity of supply is calculated as the ratio of the percentage change in the quantity supplied to the percentage change in the product's price. The formula for price elasticity of supply follows:

$$\text{Price Elasticity of Supply} = \frac{\text{Percentage Change in Quantity Supplied}}{\text{Percentage Change in Price}}$$

When the quantity supplied is very responsive to price changes, supply is elastic and the price elasticity of supply is greater than 1. If a certain percentage change in price brings about a relatively small percentage change in the quantity supplied, supply is considered inelastic and the price elasticity of supply is less than 1. Supply is said to be unitarily price elastic if the calculated price elasticity of supply equals 1. Unitary price elasticity indicates that the percentage change in quantity supplied exactly equals the percentage change in price.

CHANGE IN SUPPLY

A ***change in supply*** means a change in the number of units supplied at every price. An increase in supply means *more* units will be supplied at *each* price. A decrease in supply means *fewer* units will be supplied at *each* price.

change in supply
a change in the number of units supplied at every price

Ask students to develop a scenario that could cause a change in the supply curve for a particular product. On graph paper, have students plot two curves—one before the change and one after. Then, have them write a paragraph explaining why the supply curve shifted. Ask student volunteers to share their scenarios and illustrate their supply curves on the chalkboard or overhead transparency.

Shifts in the Supply Curve

A change in supply means a shift of the whole supply curve. Changes in the supply of sandwiches in Sycamore Bend are illustrated in Figure 7-5.

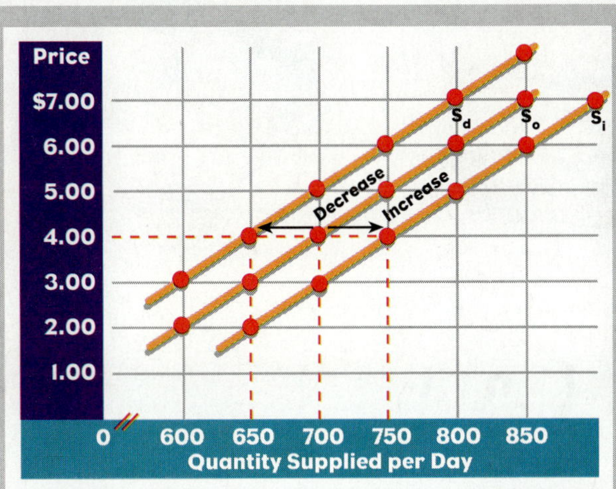

Figure 7-5

Shifts in the Sandwich Market Supply Curve

Shifts of the supply curve to the right or left represent changes in the supply at every price. ***If the market supply of sandwiches changed to 800 at a price of $4, would that be an increase in supply or a decrease in supply?***

Analyzing Graphics

Caption Answer
An increase in supply

An increase in the market supply of sandwiches is shown by supply curve S_i, which is to the right of the original supply curve S_o. For example, at a price of $4, originally there were 700 units supplied. Curve S_i reflects that at the same $4 price, 750 units were supplied. More is supplied at each price along S_i than along S_o.

A decrease in supply is shown by curve S_d, which is to the left of the original supply curve. For example, at a price of $4, the original supply was 700 units. After the decrease in supply, only 650 units were supplied at that same price. Less would be supplied at each price along S_d than along S_o.

What Causes a Change in Supply?

Changes in supply can be caused by a number of factors. The two most common causes are technological change and a change in the cost of inputs. Technological changes generally increase productivity. This in turn lowers the cost of production. If the cost of production is lower, firms can sell more output at any given level of price. For example, a technological change that increases productivity and lowers cost may allow firms to sell 650 units at a price of $2 rather than 600.

A change in the cost of inputs often causes costs to rise. Higher labor costs, a rise in the cost of raw materials used in production, and higher energy costs all cause the cost of production to increase. If production costs go up, firms may either charge a higher price for the same level of output or cut production back at the present price. That is, there would be a decrease in supply. If input costs fall, the reverse would be true and supply would increase.

Checkpoint

Content Check

1. Draw a graph of the relationship between price and quantity supplied for sport utility vehicles.
2. How would magazine publishers probably respond to an increase in the price of paper? Draw an illustration to support your answer.
3. What does the price elasticity of supply measure?
4. Explain the difference between a change in quantity supplied and a change in supply.

What Do You Think Now?

Reread *What Do You Think?* in the Section One Focus. Then answer the following questions:

5. Was there an increase in the *supply* of wheat or in the *quantity supplied* of wheat between the two years? Explain.
6. Describe what may cause a change in supply and a change in quantity supplied. Could both have happened in this case? Explain.

Assess

1. Graphs should show price on the vertical axis and quantity supplied on the horizontal axis; the line should show a positive relationship between price and quantity supplied. **7-1**
2. They would probably charge a higher price or decrease production at the existing price; either action results in the supply curve moving to the left. **7-1**
3. Relative responsiveness of a change in quantity supplied due to a change in price **7-1**
4. Change in quantity supplied is caused only by a change in price with movement along the supply curve; change in supply is a change in supply at each and every price and results in a shift of the entire supply curve. **7-2**
5. An increase in *quantity supplied* because it was caused by a price increase **7-2**
6. Yes; some of the 13 million tons could be due to a higher price (change in quantity supplied) and some due to lower production costs (change in supply). **7-2**

Close

In small groups, have students use graph paper or the computer to create a supply schedule and its corresponding supply curve for a good or service of their choice. Have the groups explain their scenarios and then share their results with the whole class.

Reteach

Ask students to think of a business and various situations that might cause either a shift in the supply curve or a change in the quantity supplied. Have students present their scenarios to the class. After evaluating each scenario, have the class decide if the quantity supplied increased or decreased or if the supply curve shifted to the left or right. **7-2**

Enrich

Ask students to consider price elasticity of supply and then brainstorm how a company's marketing strategy might change if its inelastic product suddenly became elastic or vice versa. **7-1**

FOCUS

Section Two

Production Drives Supply

What Do You Think?

Gerry Lamdon owns the Shaggy Dog grooming business. Over the past five years, Gerry has employed between one and five groomers, depending on the season. The following table summarizes the number of groomers at Shaggy Dog and the total number of dogs they groomed per month.

Number of Groomers	Number of Dogs Groomed per Month
1	140
2	270
3	370
4	420
5	410

Gerry currently has four groomers. They have been complaining that they can't get all the dogs groomed on time. Do you think Gerry should hire another groomer?

What's Ahead?

To understand economics, you must understand concepts related to production. In this section, you will learn about why people get involved in production and how production is measured.

Terms to Know

- **factor of production**
- **land**
- **labor**
- **capital**
- **entrepreneurship**
- **total product**
- **average product**
- **marginal product**
- **short run**
- **diminishing marginal product**
- **long run**
- **scale of production**
- **returns to scale**

PRODUCING GOODS AND SERVICES

Production is the act of providing the supply of goods and services to the market. Production is what makes it possible to meet consumer demand. It is often said that the desire to make money fuels the great engine of a productive economy. But, you know that earning money involves opportunity costs.

Focus

Write the following question on the chalkboard or an overhead transparency: **What is needed to produce a good or service?** Ask students to answer the question in list form.

On the chalkboard or an overhead transparency, jot down students' responses to the previous *Focus* question in a single column. Help students see how their responses fall under one of these categories: **land, labor, capital,** or **entrepreneurship** by labeling each response **L, LAB, C,** or **E.**

Teach

Explain the definition of each factor of production. You may wish to use examples from a movie theater, such as the popcorn machine, which is an example of **capital.** Explain that **capital** is previously produced goods that help produce other goods, such as popcorn.

Explain the terms **total product, marginal product,** and **average product.** Explain that **total product** is all units produced by a set of inputs for a given period. Explain that **marginal product** is how total product changes (increasing, decreasing, or staying the same) with the addition of one unit of a variable input. Explain that marginal product can be very useful in determining whether it is cost effective to hire a new employee. Finally, introduce to students the concept of average product. Point out that **average product** is the number of units of output produced per unit of input. Therefore, average product is a useful tool for determining the overall productivity of employees.

Apply

Copy the following graphic organizer onto the chalkboard or an overhead transparency:

Factors of Production	Examples
Land	
Labor	
Capital	
Entrepreneurship	

Ask students to provide an example of each of the four factors of production listed in the chart. Discuss students' responses and add them to the chart.

Guided Practice

Most of us would rather play tennis, dance, hike, or enjoy some activity other than work. To make up for those opportunity costs, we must get some benefits from working. We work because of the compensation, particularly money, that we receive for our efforts. We then use this money to buy the goods and services we need and enjoy.

The Four Factors of Production

factor of production anything used to produce a good or service

land a broad measure representing all the basic natural resources that contribute to production

labor the human factor of production

capital previously produced goods used to produce other goods

entrepreneurship the managerial ability and risk taking that contribute so much to a productive economy

A ***factor of production*** is anything used to produce a good or service. There are four broad categories of factors of production or productive resources: land, labor, capital, and entrepreneurship. ***Land*** is a broad measure representing all the basic natural resources that contribute to production. A Midwestern farm, a coal field in Wyoming, a Florida orange orchard, and natural gas in Oklahoma are all examples of the factor of production called *land*.

Labor represents the human factor of production. Each of us is free to follow our own best interests in using our productive abilities. Truck drivers, nurses, dockworkers, baseball players, teachers, and authors are all part of the factor of production called *labor*. The jobs and skills are very different, but they all fall into this broad category of labor.

Capital includes previously produced goods used to produce other goods. For example, a sewing machine used in making jeans is a form of capital. Office buildings, schools, factories, automobiles, tractors, and computers are all forms of capital equipment. Look around and you will note other kinds of capital equipment.

Entrepreneurship includes the managerial ability and risk taking that contribute so much to a productive economy. Few people can organize, direct, and control other people and resources efficiently and productively. Only an able person who is willing to accept risks will be a successful entrepreneur. We all benefit from the work of such people.

Ownership and Control of Factors of Production

In a free enterprise economy, most factors of production are owned or controlled by individuals. In such an economy, you can use your labor and the other factors you control to produce goods and services in exchange for monetary and nonmonetary rewards. If you own a large truck, you can use it to haul any goods you wish. You probably will choose to haul those items for which you can receive the most money. However, even in a free enterprise economy, there may be legal limits on how you use your productive resources.

Production takes place as owners of the factors of production allocate their land, labor, capital, and entrepreneurship in a manner that maximizes their expected returns. Thus, the profit motive is of great importance in guiding the production of goods and services in the economy.

MEASURING PRODUCTION

Businesses measure how much is produced or supplied during different time periods. For example, a company may keep track of how much is pro-

Multicultural Highlights

Bo Jackson, an African-American athlete, not only has won the Heisman Trophy, but also the admiration of countless fans. Jackson is unusual because he is highly skilled in two different sports. He played football for the Los Angeles Raiders until 1991 and major league baseball for the Kansas City Royals until 1995. Ask students which factor of production Jackson represented. (Labor) Then, have them list examples of one or more factors of production that they could offer in the production of a good or service.

duced on a yearly, monthly, weekly, or even hourly basis. Without accurate measures of production, it is impossible to manage a business well.

Counting Units Versus Counting Dollars

Output can be measured in units or dollars. Using units makes it easier to compare sales from one time period to another. To see why this is so, consider the example of the Lumin Company. Lumin produces table lamps. Figure 7-6 shows Lumin Company's sales of table lamps for six years.

Year	Unit Sales	Dollar Sales
1	121,292	$6,082,662.00
2	128,570	6,360,358.00
3	124,998	6,492,834.00
4	121,747	6,576,924.00
5	126,253	6,956,750.00
6	124,727	7,078,885.00

Figure 7-6

Lumin Company Lamp Sales (Years 1–6)

A company can measure production in units and dollars. ***How would you describe this company's sales history during these six years?***

A sales pattern such as this is fairly common and can be misleading. If you look at the dollar amount of sales, the company seems to be doing quite well. As measured in dollars, sales have increased every year. But what has really happened? The number of units produced and sold has increased in some years and decreased in other years. Part of the year-to-year increase in dollar sales must have been due to price changes, not changes in actual units produced. Measuring production only in dollars would have given the misleading impression that the company has been selling more and more every year. Thus, it is better to measure output in units than in dollars.

Total Product

The production and sales listed in units for the Lumin Company represent a measure of output called *total product*. ***Total product*** is all the units of a product produced in a given period of time. For the Lumin Company, 124,727 lamps represent the total product for Year 6.

total product
all the units of a product produced in a given period of time

Average Product

Average product is an important measure of output. ***Average product*** is the number of units of output produced per unit of input.

average product
the number of units of output produced per unit of input

$$\text{Average Product} = \frac{\text{Units of Output}}{\text{Units of Input}}$$

Divide the class into small groups of four or five students each. Tell group members to imagine they have just started a new business, such as a restaurant or bicycle store. Ask each group to list what it needs in order to start its business. Have students create a four-column chart in which to categorize each listed item as one of the four factors of production. **Independent Practice**

Analyzing *Graphics*

Caption Answer
Dollar sales have increased steadily, but unit sales have fluctuated.

Display *Overhead Transparency 7-6*. Have students use the data to develop a line graph that visually compares the unit and dollar sales. Tell students to plot unit sales and dollar sales on the vertical axis and years on the horizontal axis.

Copy the following chart onto the chalkboard or an overhead transparency:

Kit 'N' Kapoodle Company Dog Leash Sales		
Year	Unit Sales	Dollar Sales
1	59,215	$371,612
2	61,318	373,991
3	60,457	374,112
4	59,320	376,010
5	60,145	380,213

Ask students the following questions: **What is the total product for Year 2?** (61,318) **The number of units produced and sold changed by what percentage between Year 1 and Year 5?** (0.0157 percent)

To calculate the average product of labor for the Lumin Company, first you would determine the units of input for labor. Think of one workday as one labor unit. During Year 6, 88 people worked for Lumin for five days each week for 50 weeks a year. Therefore, the number of labor units used in Year 6 would be (88 workers) × (5 days/week) × (50 weeks/year) = 22,000 workdays.

The average product per labor unit would be total output for Year 6 divided by 22,000 labor units. Since 124,727 lamps were produced in Year 6, average product is 124,727 lamps ÷ 22,000 workdays = 5.67 lamps per workday. Thus, each worker produced an average of almost six lamps per day.

Marginal Product

marginal product the amount that total product increases or decreases as a result of adding one additional unit of input

Another measure of production that is very important for economists is marginal product. ***Marginal product*** is the amount that total product increases or decreases as a result of adding one additional unit of an input. Marginal product is calculated as follows:

$$\text{Marginal Product} = \frac{\text{Change in Output}}{\text{Change in Input}}$$

Suppose that Lumin employed 90 workers each day last week and produced 510 lamps per day. When the company hired one additional worker, the total product increased to 515 lamps. The marginal product of that additional worker is five lamps.

Marginal product is very important in making production decisions. The dollar value of additional output should always be compared with the dollar cost of the additional input. The Lumin Company would have to compare how much it has to pay the additional worker with how much the company makes from the increased output. If the dollar value of the added output is more than the cost of the added input, then the firm's profit will increase.

DIMINISHING MARGINAL PRODUCT IN THE SHORT RUN

Production has two time frames: the short run and the long run. A firm's ability to change the quantity supplied varies depending on whether it is operating in the short run or in the long run.

The Short Run

short run any period during which the usable amount of at least one input is fixed while the usable amount of a least one other input can change

The ***short run*** is any period during which the usable amount of at least one input is fixed while the usable amount of at least one other input can change. The short run is not a time period that is determined by the calendar. The short run is a period that is determined by whether one or more of the factors of production can be changed.

Lumin has a 5,000-square-foot building for the production and assembly of lamps. Lumin is limited to the existing building space, conveyor systems, and other equipment, so this input is fixed. However, the number of workers, another input, might be changed. In this scenario, Lumin is operating in the short run.

Perspectives

Thinking Like a Business Owner Explain to students that business owners must constantly use economic concepts such as **marginal product** to make effective decisions. Tell students that, if a business owner just made random decisions, his or her business would not survive in the marketplace. Ask each student to suggest an example that illustrates marginal product. Then, discuss the examples as a class. (Answers may include adding an employee who increases output by five additional units or adding a machine that increases total production by 20 units.)

If sales are good, Lumin might hire more assemblers to increase production. But, adding more workers will not continue to increase output for long. Eventually, Lumin will need extra space and more equipment. As all factors of production begin to change, Lumin will move out of the short run.

Diminishing Marginal Product

Marginal product is a short-run measure because there is some base of fixed factors of production and one variable factor of production. Calculating the marginal product of labor, for example, assumes that the other factors are not changing.

Diminishing marginal product is the principle that as more of one input is added to a fixed amount of other inputs, the marginal product decreases. This does not mean that total output necessarily declines as more of the input is used. It means that output increases less and less rapidly as additional units of the input are used.

diminishing marginal product
the principle that as more of one input is added to a fixed amount of other inputs, the marginal product decreases

Suppose that Lumin has decided to open a small retail store named Lights Unlimited. If the store hires no labor (clerks, cashiers), no sales can be made. If only one person is hired, not many customers can be served. But, as more people are hired, more customers can be served and more sales can result.

Will each extra employee increase Lights Unlimited's sales by an equal amount? Even if you assume that each worker is equally skilled, the answer is *no.* As more and more workers are added, the amount they add to total output (sales) decreases. Indeed, Lights Unlimited could hire so many workers that sales per worker would decrease. If there were 60 employees in the store, there would be no room for customers. Sales would fall to zero, just as if the store had hired no workers. Figure 7-7 summarizes the marginal product of labor for Lights Unlimited.

Figure 7-7

Number of Employees	Total Product	Marginal Product (Change in Output / Change in Input)
0	0	*
10	100	100 ÷ 10 = 10
20	160	60 ÷ 10 = 6
30	180	20 ÷ 10 = 2
40	160	-20 ÷ 10 = -2
50	100	-60 ÷ 10 = -6

* A value cannot be determined at this point.

Marginal Product of Labor for Lights Unlimited

In the short run, adding additional workers causes total product to increase for a while, but by a decreasing amount. Eventually, even total product begins to decrease. ***Why doesn't total product always increase as more workers are hired?***

Invite the business manager from your city or school district or from a local factory to speak to your class. Explain to the guest speaker that your class is discussing the concepts of **long run** and **short run** as well as **marginal product.** If possible, provide the business manager with information from the textbook to explain students' understanding of these economic concepts. Then, ask him or her to explain how he or she takes these concepts into consideration in a professional decision-making process.

Analyzing Graphics

Caption Answer
If other factors remain unchanged, adding more workers will eventually result in overcrowding and inefficient operations.

EyeOnMarketNews

Divide the class into groups of four or five students. Have each group develop a list of famous people, such as athletes or entrepreneurs, who are making the news. Have students in each group determine what labor skills these individuals use in their profession as well as the type of capital they need. As a class, discuss the types of labor and capital these people have used in order to succeed.

To help students who are having difficulty understanding the concepts of short run, diminishing marginal product, and long run, encourage peer tutoring. Have each student who understands the concept describe to another student what is measured in the short run (changes in marginal product) and in the long run (returns to scale). Also, have him or her develop an example of diminishing marginal product. After the first student explains each concept, have the student who needs support suggest a scenario that involves that concept.

At Risk

Notice in Figure 7-7 that marginal product can be negative. This happens when total output declines as additional units of the input are used. This could happen if too many workers were hired. The concept of diminishing marginal product is very important. It is not possible to go on adding any one factor of production without getting less and less *additional* output. This is true in the short run in nearly all situations, from farming to retailing to education to steel production.

Figure 7-8 is a graph of the information in the table in Figure 7-7. Notice that total output increases rapidly at first when labor units are increased. Then as more labor units are added, output increases less rapidly and finally declines.

Analyzing *Graphics*

Caption Answer
No, the 45th person would not add to the total product.

Figure 7-8

Graph of Diminishing Marginal Product for Lights Unlimited

Total product increases rapidly at first when labor usage is increased. Output increases less rapidly when the number of employees goes from 10 to 20 and from 20 to 30. After hiring 30 people, output actually declines. ***If you knew the information in this figure, would you hire the 45th unit of labor?***

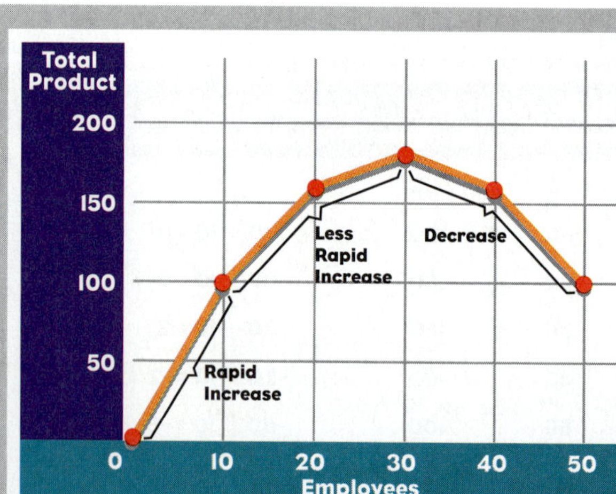

EconomicTalk

Divide the class into groups of three or four students. To reinforce the vocabulary terms in the first and second sections, have each group develop a business scenario. Explain that the business has decided to expand its facilities and the number of units it produces. Ask students to use in their narratives at least ten terms from the first two sections of this chapter. Encourage students to be creative by adding humor and drama to their scenarios. Have each group present its story aloud to the class.

CHANGING PRODUCTION IN THE LONG RUN

Remember that in the short run, only one of the factors of production can change. The rest are fixed or constant. What happens if a producer can change more than one of the factors of production? Does the principle of diminishing marginal product still hold true?

The Long Run

The ***long run*** is a period during which the amounts of all inputs can be changed. None of the factors of production are fixed in the long run. The long run, like the short run, is not based on the calendar. Lights Unlimited might be able to expand its retail store and get additional space, equipment, and employees in place in two or three months, changing all of its inputs. For some firms it would take much longer. A power company, for example, might need ten years or more to increase plant capacity.

long run
a period during which the amounts of all inputs can be changed

Scale of Production

The ***scale of production*** is the overall level of use of all factors of production. When all inputs are increased, the scale of production increases. If all inputs are increased, the principle of diminishing marginal product is no longer valid. For example, if Lights Unlimited kept enlarging its store, more employees could be hired without the problem of crowding described earlier.

scale of production
the overall level of use of all factors of production

Global Economy

WHO HAS THE MOST QUALIFIED WORKFORCE?

In today's economy, the playing field is global. You compete for jobs not only with others in the United States but with everyone everywhere. A *Business Week* article asked, "Where will workers be best prepared?" Where do you think? Based on quality of public education, levels of secondary schooling, on-the-job training, computer literacy, and worker motivation, *Business Week* reported the following ranking of national workforces:

1. Singapore
2. Denmark
3. Germany
4. Japan
5. Norway
6. United States
7. Austria
8. Sweden
9. Netherlands
10. Finland

Being able to compete in the global marketplace is crucial to maintaining a healthy domestic economy. Many businesses are increasingly flexible in terms of where they locate and it is likely that many will gravitate to those economies that have the most productive workforces.

Tell students to imagine the following scenario: A business is currently producing and selling two new software programs per year. The business currently employs twenty-five workers. If it were to add a twenty-sixth worker to increase sales, the business would keep measuring production in terms of the short run. Ask students to suggest changes that would ultimately affect other factors of production, which would create a long-run scenario. (For example, also expanding its research facility.) As a student volunteer jots down responses on the chalkboard or an overhead transparency, have class members suggest other factors of production that might cause changes that would create a long-run scenario.

Allow students to independently read the *Global Economy* feature. Then, as a class, discuss what an international company would need to do if it wanted to expand. Ask students to think of the same situation for a statewide business. Explain that companies must use labor in the production process, so they try to locate where labor costs are low. Elicit from students that it would not make sense for a computer-chip company to move into an area where most people are trained in automobile manufacturing, for instance. Ask students to develop a list of the types of industries that would benefit by locating in their community, based on the skills of the community's workforce.

Global Economy

Ask students to discuss why it is important for a country to have a qualified workforce. Encourage them to explain how our country will be affected if the workforces in other countries are more productive than ours. Ask students to imagine that they are decision makers in Washington, D.C., who are trying to make the U.S. economy more productive. Have students develop a plan or set of ideas at the national level that will lead the United States to develop a leading global workforce. Then, share their suggestions with the class for discussion.

Returns to Scale

returns to scale the relationship between changes in the scale of production and the corresponding change in the amount of output

Returns to scale is a term used to describe what happens when the scale of production changes. ***Returns to scale*** is the relationship between changes in the scale of production and the corresponding change in the amount of output. Returns to scale may be increasing, decreasing, or constant.

Many products, such as cars, steel, and home appliances, are produced more efficiently on a large scale. Production is characterized by *increasing returns to scale* when the level of output increases more rapidly than the rate of increase in the use of inputs. For example, if the use of all inputs is doubled and output more than doubles, there are increasing returns to scale.

In some forms of production, doubling all inputs results in exactly twice as much output. That is, output increases at the same rate as all inputs are increased. Using 20 percent more inputs would cause 20 percent more output to be produced. When this is true, there are *constant returns to scale*.

In other situations, output may increase less rapidly than the rate at which input usage increases. This situation involves *decreasing returns to scale*. For example, if the use of all inputs were increased by 50 percent but output increased by only 30 percent, there would be decreasing returns to scale.

Assess

1. They gain income in return for the use of the factors of production. **7-3**
2. Marginal product is the change in total product due to a change in a variable input. **7-4**
3. Short run has at least one fixed factor of production while, in the long run, all factors of production can be changed. **7-4**
4. Only the short run has a limit on the use of some factor of production. **7-4**
5. *Returns to scale* is a term used to describe what happens to output when the scale of production changes over the long run. **7-5**
6. The marginal product of labor decreases as more groomers are added; the marginal product for the fifth groomer is negative because, as more groomers are added, the amount each adds to total output decreases. **7-4**
7. No, hiring another groomer will decrease total product. **7-4**
8. Gerry should change other factors of production such as store size, equipment, and hours of operation. **7-5**

Close

Divide students into four groups. Assign each group one of the four factors of production. Ask each group to describe the role and importance of this factor in opening a plant and tree nursery. Circulate among the groups, correcting any misconceptions. Then, have each group share its findings with the class.

Checkpoint

Content Check

1. What is the motivation for people to use their land, labor, capital, and entrepreneurship to produce goods and services?
2. What is the relationship between total product and marginal product?
3. How is the short run different from the long run in economic terms?
4. Why is the principle of diminishing marginal product only valid in the short run?
5. Explain the relationship between the scale of production and returns to scale in the long run.

What Do You Think Now?

Reread *What Do You Think?* in the Section Two Focus. Then answer the following questions:

6. What happens to the marginal product of labor for Shaggy Dog as groomers are added? Why?
7. Will hiring another worker solve Gerry's problem? Why or why not?
8. What do you think Gerry should do?

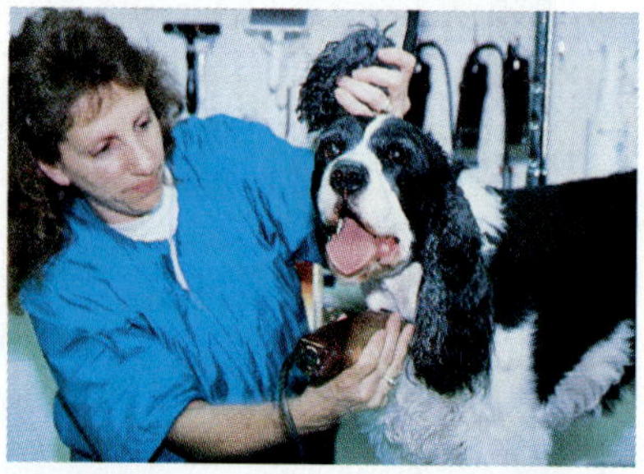

Reteach

Explain to students that factors of production are necessary in order to run a business. If there are people working, there is labor. If there are machines, there is capital. Ask students to identify three businesses that they are familiar with and then determine the factors of production for each. **7-3**

Enrich

Ask each student to develop a song, poem, or rap that talks about a short-run to long-run scenario including factors of production. You may wish to record students' presentations on audiocassette. As a class, discuss the meanings behind the messages. **7-3**

Section Three
Production Creates Costs

What Do You Think?

Billy Joe quit his job at Wal-Mart, where he made $5 an hour. He quit so that he could work full time painting portraits of children. Billy Joe gets $20 for each portrait. The paint, canvas, and brushes cost him about $12 per painting, and it usually takes him two hours to complete a portrait. Billy Joe is looking forward to the extra money he is going to make. Do you think Billy Joe made a good decision?

What's Ahead?

People who are involved in economic activity in both the private and the public sectors are usually concerned with controlling costs. Therefore, it is important to understand what determines costs. In this section, you will see that it is the process of producing a good or service that results in costs.

Terms to Know

explicit costs

opportunity costs

COSTS REPRESENT PAYMENTS TO FACTORS OF PRODUCTION

When businesspeople are asked about the problems they face, their answers almost always include dealing with rising costs. Government officials also talk about rising costs in the public sector of the economy.

Costs are incurred through the production process. The costs that a company incurs represent payments to factors of production or to the supplier of some intermediate good, such as the steel used in making a car. Payments to the factors of production of land, labor, capital, and entrepreneurship are called *rent, wages, interest,* and *profit,* respectively. The four factors of production and their payments are shown in Figure 7-9.

Focus

Write the following question on the chalkboard or an overhead transparency: **What are the costs associated with making a cheeseburger at a fast-food restaurant?** As students enter the classroom, have them jot down on the chalkboard or transparency all the costs they think are involved in this scenario.

Have students review the costs they identified. Elicit from the class that there are a lot of other costs of producing a cheeseburger besides the ingredients. These costs include wages, rent, and profit.

Teach

Analyzing Graphics

Caption Answer
Wages

Write the terms **explicit costs** and **opportunity costs** on the chalkboard or an overhead transparency. Explain that **explicit costs** are payments made to others as part of the cost of running a business. Explain that **opportunity costs** are the value of any alternatives that individuals give up when they make a choice. Provide students with a variety of examples to support the definition of each term. Examples of **opportunity costs** could be the earnings given up by going to college instead of getting a job right out of high school. Another example might be the interest earnings lost by using one's own money to start a business instead of keeping that money in a bank.

Define **marginal product** for students. Explain the relationship between increasing inputs and **diminishing marginal product** in the short run. Then, relate the **short run** to the **long run** by providing example scenarios that involve changes in different factors of production.

Figure 7-9

Payments for the Four Factors of Production

Payments for the factors of production result in costs. ***Which of these payments describes the salary that your economics teacher gets from the school system?***

Payment		Factor of Production
Rent	in exchange for	Land
Wages	in exchange for	Labor
Interest	in exchange for	Capital
Profit	in exchange for	Entrepreneurship

Dollars that are spent for intermediate goods, such as the steel in a car, are eventually used for these same factors of production. Thus, all costs are related to the factors of production at some stage in the production process.

Explicit Costs

Some costs are easy to see and account for. For example, Suzanne and Ben Kanoza have always wanted to own a business. Now that they are both about 40 years old, they have decided to start a business that customizes personal computers for home use. After looking into this type of business, they believe that they can get one started for $110,000. They will use $50,000 of their own money from savings accounts and stock and borrow $60,000 from the bank. The Kanozas figure their new business, Unitech, will have the monthly costs shown in Figure 7-10.

The costs in Figure 7-10 are the explicit costs of running Unitech every month. ***Explicit costs*** are payments made to others as a cost of running a business.

explicit costs
payments made to others as a cost of running a business

Opportunity Costs

When the Kanozas show their cost estimates to the loan officer at the bank, they are surprised by the response they get. The loan officer tells the Kanozas that they have left out some very important costs: salaries to themselves and lost earnings on their $50,000 in savings and stock. These are the opportunity costs of starting and running Unitech.

Item	Monthly Cost
Rent	**$ 1,200.00**
Loan payment	**1,500.00**
Wages to technician	**2,000.00**
Electricity	**500.00**
Telephone	**100.00**
Advertising	**160.00**
Total monthly costs	**$5,460.00**

Figure 7-10

Monthly Cost Estimates for Unitech

The Kanozas can count on these monthly costs to run Unitech. ***What other costs might they have?***

Economic Dilemma

THE PRICE OF GREEN

Some businesses are actively considering alternate methods of production that are more environmentally friendly. This effort is sometimes referred to as *Green Marketing* because of the reduced environmental damage that can result. If you go to a local card shop and look at various greeting cards, you will see on the backs of some that they are printed on recycled paper (in whole or in part). At a bookstore, you also may find books that claim in the opening pages to be printed on recycled paper. The use of recycled paper may reduce the cutting of trees and thus help maintain more forested land. However, it also may be more costly.

It is possible in some parts of the country to produce electricity in an environmentally friendly manner using wind power. However, doing so may result in production costs that are higher per kilowatt hour than the costs of more conventional methods. This possibility raises some economic questions. Would people be willing to pay an extra $0.10 for a greeting card that was printed on recycled paper? Would you? Would people be willing to pay the higher price for electricity if it meant having cleaner air? Would you? Should the choice of whether to use wind power to produce electricity be left to the power companies or should it be made by the regulatory agencies that have oversight responsibility in this industry?

Economic Dilemma

Green Marketing is a major concern in many large industries, such as computer and automobile manufacturing. Ask students to think of items that are designed to reduce environmental damage, such as computer monitors that "power down" after a few minutes to save electricity. In small groups, have students brainstorm how a product or production method could be changed to become more environmentally friendly. Have students in each group vote on whether they would agree to a cost increase of 5 percent for a product if it were environmentally friendly. Have each group share its opinion with the others.

Apply

Analyzing *Graphics*

Caption Answer
Other explicit costs include taxes, health insurance, and equipment rental; opportunity costs include lost wages and lost earnings on investments.

As a class, ask students to think of a local business and its factors of production. Have students discuss the types of payments involved in the four factors of production. Explain that these payments are rent, wages, interest, and profit. Ask students to list the various people or places that receive these payments. On the chalkboard or an overhead transparency, create a two-column chart with the headings **Payments** and **To Whom.** Add students' responses to the chart.
Guided Practice

As a whole class, discuss the particular costs (interest on loans, utility bills, advertising costs, and so on) associated with the businesses from the previous *Apply* activity. On the chalkboard or an overhead transparency, list these costs and classify each as an explicit cost or an opportunity cost.

On the chalkboard or overhead transparency, create the following graphic organizer:

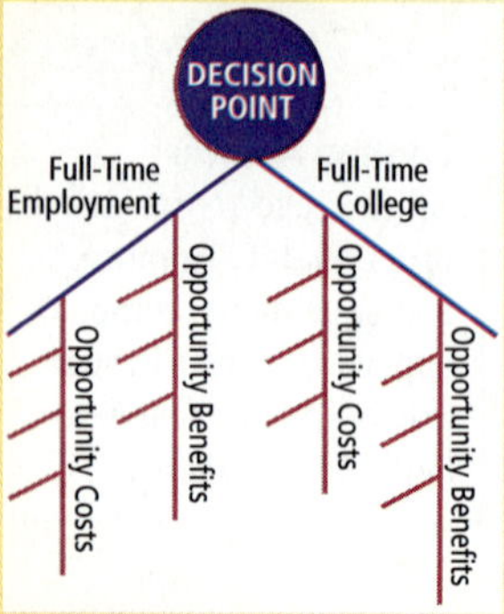

As a class, discuss the pros and cons of attending college versus working at a full-time job after high school. To get students started, elicit reasons students might or might not attend college and discuss how this decision could affect them economically in both the short and long runs. Have each student complete the graphic organizer and then share it with the class. Ask students to predict how the opportunity benefits and costs they listed might change after four years. **Independent Practice**

Economic Spotlight

A FAMILY WHO WORKS TOGETHER, STAYS TOGETHER

Through six decades, Goya Foods has managed to keep its business all in the family. Goya was originally founded as Unanue & Sons in a Manhattan warehouse in 1936. Goya is now the second largest Hispanic-owned company in the United States. The eight Unanues who run Goya, including the president, Joseph Unanue, strongly believe in preserving the family ownership of the business. The company was founded by husband and wife Prudencio Unanue and Carolina Casal because they missed the foods of their native lands of Spain and Puerto Rico.

Goya quickly became known for producing everything from rice and beans to octopus in hot sauce (an Hispanic delicacy), traditional foods that Hispanics in this country sorely missed. Over the years, Goya's business has expanded its product line into broader markets to include such items as frozen foods, desserts, and breads. Today, Goya is taking expansion one step further. The company is introducing Hispanic foods to non-Hispanic communities through coupons and recipes in newspapers and magazine ads and by running television spots.

But this expansion hasn't always been easy. As Goya has built a broader customer base, it has encountered language problems—even within the Hispanic community. For example, beans may be called *frijoles* by Cubans or *habichuelas* by Puerto Ricans. Hispanics have different names for fruits, vegetables, and other products, which poses a labeling problem. Consumers who call a product by a different name might not recognize the product they are looking for, so its identity must be made very clear.

When entering new markets, the Unanue family strategy has been to move more like a tortoise than a hare—approaching one new market at a time. By using this market-to-market strategy, Goya has been able to capture 80 percent of the Hispanic food business in the northeastern United States and 75 percent in Florida. It appears that Goya is one family-owned company that won't be stopped.

Economic Spotlight

Allow students time to read the *Economic Spotlight* feature. Then, on the chalkboard, have students create a class list of some of the payments Goya Foods might make for its factors of production. Ask student volunteers to classify each payment according to the specific factor of production to which it applies. (For example, the cost of translating each product label into Spanish is a labor cost.) Then, tell each student to write a brief description of how he or she thinks Goya Foods' factors of production and related payments might have changed from 1936 to today. Have students share their descriptions with the class and discuss how factors of production might change in any business.

The Kanozas make a total of $5,000 each month at their present jobs. This is income that they would give up by leaving their current jobs, and so it is a cost of the new business. In addition, if the Kanozas didn't use their $50,000 to start the business, it would still be invested and earning about $375 per month. This $375 per month is also an opportunity cost that should be included as part of the cost of Unitech. Adding the lost salaries and earnings on savings to the explicit costs in Figure 7-10 bring the total monthly costs for Unitech to $10,835 ($5,460 + $5,000 + $375).

You can see the importance of the Kanozas considering both explicit costs and opportunity costs in their decision to open Unitech. If projected sales were enough to cover both explicit costs and opportunity costs ($10,835), Unitech would appear to be a worthwhile business. If projected sales were less than $10,835 per month, the Kanozas would have to reconsider their decision. If the Kanozas thought they would get a lot of psychic income from owning their business, they might still do so even if they earned less money.

COSTS AND DIMINISHING MARGINAL PRODUCT

You have seen that in the short run, production is subject to the principle of diminishing marginal product. That is, as added units of labor (or other variable inputs) are used, the marginal product decreases. Each new worker adds less to total output than does the previous one.

This means that in the short run, each added dollar's worth of input adds fewer units to output. So, the added cost per unit of output goes up. Firms that want to increase production without increasing all inputs will find that the additional cost per unit of output becomes greater. Remember the relationship between price and the quantity supplied? The law of supply states that as price goes up, so does quantity supplied. You can see now that this relationship is based on the principle of diminishing marginal product. As the cost per unit of output becomes greater, firms must get a higher price. So, the supply curve is determined by the level of cost. Thus, the supply curve is positively sloped because, in the short run, production is subject to the principle of diminishing marginal product.

COSTS AND THE SCALE OF PRODUCTION

As businesses enter the long run and change the scale of production, the cost of producing each unit is likely to change. Over the long run, costs per unit of output may fall, rise, or stay the same. What happens depends on whether the type of production has increasing, decreasing, or constant returns to scale (see Figure 7-11).

Increasing Returns to Scale	Decreasing Returns to Scale	Constant Returns to Scale
Production Cost per Unit Decreases	Production Cost per Unit Increases	Production Cost per Unit Remains Constant

Figure 7-11

Relationship Between Returns to Scale and Cost of Production

The cost of production per unit of output depends on the type of returns to scale experienced by the production process. ***What type of returns to scale do you think a manufacturer would like to have?***

Economics & Your Community

Opportunity costs for starting a new business can be very high. Small-business owners might have left behind a regular salary in order to try their success at running a business. Invite a small-business owner or a representative of the Small Business Administration (SBA) to visit your class. Have students prepare questions about opportunity costs and benefits ahead of time to ask the speaker. Conclude by having each student write a brief essay on whether he or she would be interested in opening a small business in the future.

Divide the class into groups of three or four students and distribute business sections of a newspaper to each group. Ask each group to identify a product that is currently making the news. Assign the following roles to group members: consumer(s), business owner, and production manager. Ask the consumer(s) to look at the costs of the item from a consumer's perspective. Have the business owner examine the costs from a business perspective. Ask the production manager to discuss how diminishing marginal product might influence costs in the short run and how returns to scale might influence costs in the long run. Have students in each group role-play their viewpoints and rationalizations. Allow 15 to 20 minutes to complete this activity. Conclude by having students summarize the three perspectives role-played in the activity.
Cooperative Learning

Analyzing Graphics

Caption Answer
Increasing returns to scale

Tell students to imagine that they are managers of a local retail business. Ask them to write a report on short-run and long-run adjustments in operations that might be made to improve the business's productivity.

Have students imagine that they are organizing a car wash for a school fund-raiser for which 10 hoses, 15 buckets, and 25 sponges were donated. Given these supplies, have students create a production schedule using the number of workers as the variable input. Ask students to discuss how the concept of costs and diminishing marginal product applies. (Answers may include that workers could get in each other's way and marginal productivity could decrease if more than three or four volunteers washed a car at one time.) Have students vote on what they think would be the optimum number of volunteers to wash cars.

Internet Connection

BROWSING AND BURROWING WITH BOOKMARKS

When you explore the World Wide Web or Gopherspace, it is easy to lose track of where you are. Suppose you follow a series of Web links or gopher menus, and you discover something interesting. How do you figure out where you are and how can you return there easily?

To figure out where you are, you need to understand Uniform Resource Locators (URLs), which indicate the address of a Web page, Gopher site, or any other Internet site. Examples of URLs include **http://alfred.econ.lsa.umich.edu** and **gopher://niord.shsu.edu/11gopher_root%3a%5b_DATA.ECONOMICS%5d**.

The information to the left of the "://" indicates the type of Internet resource. Web pages begin with "http". Gopher sites begin with "gopher". The information to the right of the "://" indicates the Internet address.

If you are using Netscape, finding out your location is easy. The "Location:" box gives the URL of the current document. The address changes as you move through Web space. If you are using Gopher, place your cursor on the item you are interested in and type =.

You can skip burrowing and connect directly to a remote Web page by *opening a URL.* Click on the OPEN icon on the toolbar and enter the URL of the remote Web page. An even better way is to use a bookmark list that stores the addresses of interesting Internet resources. Click on the Bookmarks menu item to view your bookmark list, select an item from the list, or add/delete an item.

To create a bookmark in gopher, select an item and type *a* (add). Gopher will prompt you for a bookmark name. To view your bookmarks, type *v* (view). To delete, select the appropriate bookmark and type *d* (delete).

Internet Application: Find an interesting Web or gopher site somewhere on the Internet. Create a bookmark. E-mail the URL for the site to your teacher.

Economics Application: Use what you have learned about production and supply to answer the following: How have Gopher and WWW affected the productivity of workers whose jobs involve using the Internet? How have they affected the supply of the firms who employ those workers?

Internet Connection

Economics Application: Since Gopher and WWW have made the Internet easier to use, labor productivity has increased. The theory of supply indicates that increased productivity causes an increase in the supply of firms. Intuitively, the same number of now more productive workers should produce more; therefore, supply increases.

If doubling all inputs produced more than twice as much output, then the cost per unit of output would fall. This is the case with increasing returns to scale. If doubling all inputs produced less than twice as much output, then the unit cost of the output would rise. This would represent decreasing returns to scale. In those cases in which there are constant returns to scale, the cost per unit of output would remain constant. Doubling all inputs would exactly double output.

Checkpoint

Content Check

1. Name the payments to land, labor, capital, and entrepreneurship and give an example of each.
2. Why should you consider opportunity costs when making a production decision?
3. In the short run, what happens to the cost of additional production when inputs are added? Why?
4. The rate of output for a product was 1,000 units per month. The company increased all inputs by 20 percent and output increased to 1,500 units per month. Are the returns to scale increasing, decreasing, or constant for this product? What should happen to the production cost per unit?

What Do You Think Now?

Reread *What Do You Think?* in the Section Three Focus. Then answer the following question:

5. What do you think now about Billy Joe's decision to quit his job at Wal-Mart and paint portraits? Consider both explicit costs and opportunity costs in your answer.

Assess

1. Answers may include rent, lease payments for store location; wages, salary for sales staff; interest, payments on small-business loan; profit, lost wages. **7-3**
2. By including *all* costs—not just the most recognizable explicit costs—you get a more accurate cost estimate. **7-3**
3. Cost per unit of additional output increases because of diminishing marginal product. **7-4**
4. The returns to scale are increasing because the 20 percent increase in inputs resulted in a 50 percent increase in output. Production cost per unit should go down due to increasing returns to scale. **7-5**
5. Explicit cost of $12 plus an opportunity cost of $10 equals $22; at a price of $20, Billy Joe is losing money, but if he gets more satisfaction, it might be a good decision. **7-3**

Close

Divide the class into groups of four or five students. Have each group create a graphic organizer that illustrates the four factors of production and their corresponding payments. Photocopy and distribute organizers to each group so all can compare their work. As a class, correct any errors or misconceptions before closing the section.

Reteach

Ask students to create a two-column chart with the headings **Explicit Costs** and **Opportunity Costs.** In the appropriate columns, have students write all the potential costs they anticipate are involved in opening a small desktop-publishing company. **7-3**

Enrich

Tell students to imagine that they are opening a landscaping business after high school graduation and that a family member has decided to quit his or her job to work at the new business. Have students write a paragraph predicting how hiring the family member might affect marginal product in the short run. **7-4, 7-5**

Chapter Close

Your Economic Portfolio

Describe for students the following scenario: For the past three years, Blammo Balloons has produced 300 packages of jumbo balloons per day and sold them for a price of $1.65 per package. Recently, Blammo moved to a larger building and increased its staff from 15 employees to 20. This enabled the company to increase supply by 100 units per day at the same price. It also increased the company's total product and returns to scale. Tell students each to create and properly label a supply curve and a total product curve to illustrate the previous scenario. Also, have them calculate the change in marginal product for Blammo Balloons (100 ÷ 5 = 20). Review students' work and have them make any necessary corrections before filing their curves and calculations in their portfolios.

You may wish to provide the following end-of-chapter materials:

- *Skills & Concepts* worksheet
- *Content Review Workbook*
- Chapter *Assessment*
- Chapter *MicroExam*

Concepts in Brief

1. In a market economy, production decisions are made primarily by individuals acting in their own self-interest. We work in some form of production for the money and psychic income we get in exchange for our work effort.
2. The amount of a good or service that is supplied by a firm or market is related to the price at which the product can be sold. The higher the price, the greater the quantity supplied. This relationship is identified as a *change in the quantity supplied* and can be illustrated in either a supply schedule or a supply curve. The responsiveness of the amount supplied to changes in the product's price can be measured by the price elasticity of supply.
3. If the supply of a good or service at each and every price changes, this is called a *change in supply.* A change in supply is not the result of a change in price. Rather, it is the result of a change in technology or input costs.
4. Individuals own and/or control nearly all the factors of production in a market economy. These factors of production include land, labor, capital, and entrepreneurship. The output that results from production can be measured in units or in dollars. It is better to use units because the dollar measure can be misleading if prices change over time.
5. In the short run, there is at least one factor of production that is fixed in terms of availability. Almost all production is subject to diminishing marginal product in the short run. This means that as the use of a variable input (such as labor) increases, output will increase at a decreasing rate. A point can be reached at which so much of the input is used that output actually declines.
6. In the long run, all factors of production can be varied in terms of the amounts used in production. If all inputs can be increased at the same time, production may become more efficient due to increasing returns to scale. This is true in the production of cars, household appliances, steel, aluminum, and many other products. In some forms of production, there may be constant or even decreasing returns to scale. However, increasing returns to scale is the most common situation.

7. Costs are a natural result of the production process. It is important to consider both explicit costs and the opportunity costs when making economic decisions. Failure to do so will often result in bad decisions with undesirable results. Because of the principle of diminishing marginal product, the cost of production per unit of output increases as the rate of production increases in the short run. In the long run, the production cost per unit of output depends on whether there are increasing, decreasing, or constant returns to scale.

Economic Foundations

1. Market supply of a product is 1,000 units at $8 and 1,200 units at $9. Calculate the price elasticity of supply.
2. Explain the difference between a change in quantity supplied and a change in supply.
3. Who controls the factors of production in a market economy?
4. The total product for a company is 10,565 golf balls. If the company can produce 10,580 golf balls by adding one more worker, what is the marginal product of labor?
5. What distinguishes the short run from the long run in economic terms?
6. Explain the relationship between costs and level of production in the short run.
7. Explain the relationship between costs and level of production in the long run.
8. What payments are made to the four basic factors of production?
9. Differentiate between the three kinds of returns to scale.

Economic Foundations

1. Percentage change in price is 12.5 percent; percentage change in quantity supplied is 20 percent; price elasticity is 20.0 ÷ 12.5, or 1.6. (p. 156)
2. A change in quantity supplied is the quantity that will be supplied if price changes. It is indicated by movement along a supply curve. A change in supply means that a different quantity will be supplied at all prices. It is indicated by a shift in the entire curve. (pp. 156–157)
3. Individuals (p. 160)
4. 15 golf balls (10,580 − 10,565 = 15; 15 ÷ 1 = 15) (p. 162)
5. In the short run, the amount of at least one input is fixed and the amount of at least one other input can change; in the long run, the amounts of all inputs can be changed. (pp. 162, 165)
6. Cost per unit of output goes up at a faster rate than production. (pp. 162–163)
7. With increasing returns to scale, costs decrease as production increases; with constant returns to scale, costs and production increase at the same rate; with decreasing returns to scale, costs increase at a greater rate than production. (pp. 165–166)
8. (1) Land: rent; (2) labor: wages; (3) capital: interest; (4) entrepreneurship: profit (p. 168)
9. (1) Increasing: level of output increases more rapidly than the rate of increase in the use of inputs; (2) constant: output increases at the same rate as all inputs are increased; (3) decreasing: output goes up less rapidly than the rate at which input usage goes up (p. 171)

Your Economic Vocabulary

Build your economic vocabulary by matching the following terms with their definitions.

average product
capital
change in supply
change in the quantity supplied
diminishing marginal product
entrepreneurship
explicit costs
factor of production
labor
land
law of supply
long run
marginal product
price elasticity of supply
returns to scale
scale of production
short run
supply
supply curve
supply schedule
total product

1. a table that shows the quantities of a good or service that would be supplied by a firm at different prices
2. a graphic representation of the quantities that would be supplied at each price
3. the human factor of production
4. the quantities of a product or service that a firm is willing and able to make available for sale at different prices
5. a change in the number of units made available for sale due to a *price change*
6. measures the responsiveness of the quantity supplied to changes in the product's price
7. the managerial ability and risk taking that contribute so much to a productive economy
8. a change in the number of units supplied at every price
9. anything used to produce a good or service
10. previously produced goods used to produce other goods
11. a broad measure representing all the basic natural resources that contribute to production
12. the amount that total product increases or decreases as a result of adding one additional unit of an input
13. all the units of a product produced in a given period of time
14. any period during which the usable amount of at least one input is fixed while the usable amount of at least one other input can change
15. states that the quantity of goods supplied will be greater at a higher price than it will at a lower price
16. the principle that as more of one input is added to a fixed amount of other inputs, the marginal product decreases
17. a period during which the amounts of all inputs can be changed
18. the overall level of use of all factors of production
19. the relationship between changes in the scale of production and the corresponding change in the amount of output

Your Economic Vocabulary

1. supply schedule
2. supply curve
3. labor
4. supply
5. change in the quantity supplied
6. price elasticity of supply
7. entrepreneurship
8. change in supply
9. factor of production
10. capital
11. land
12. marginal product
13. total product
14. short run
15. law of supply
16. diminishing marginal product
17. long run
18. scale of production
19. returns to scale
20. explicit costs
21. average product

Thinking Critically About Economics

1. Answers may include that we work for the rewards that we get, usually money in the form of a wage or salary. Answers may include that some people may place a high value on nonmonetary benefits, such as pleasant working conditions, prestige, and fringe benefits.
2. Because it usually costs more to produce additional units in the short run. Diminishing marginal productivity causes the marginal cost to rise as more is produced; firms must then charge higher prices to cover the production costs.

(Continued)

Thinking Critically About Economics (Continued)

3. Mostly, the supply of camcorders has risen due to technological advances in their production. Other examples may include personal computers, CD-ROM equipment, and cellular phones.
4. As the cost of gasoline and diesel fuel (both tractor fuels) rose, costs of wheat production would rise, resulting in less incentive to produce wheat at a constant price. More fuel-efficient tractors and technological advances that increase crop yields per acre could offset this effect.

20. payments made to others as a cost of running a business

21. the number of units of output produced per unit of input

Thinking Critically About Economics

1. Why do people work if it is not a pleasurable activity? Why would someone choose a lower paying job over a higher paying one?
2. Why are supply curves generally positively sloped? What relevance do production and cost concepts have in this regard?
3. Camcorder sales have been increasing. What factors do you think have contributed to the increase in supply and/or quantity supplied of this product? Can you think of some other products for which supply has increased recently?
4. Why might an increase in gasoline and diesel fuel costs cause a decrease in the supply of wheat in the United States? What technological changes might offset this effect?
5. Explain how the principle of diminishing marginal product relates to studying for a test.
6. Why do increasing returns to scale result in a lower cost per unit of output?
7. Suppose you decide to start a housecleaning business with some friends next summer. List the types of costs you would expect in this new business. Which of the costs would be explicit costs and which would be opportunity costs?

Economic Enrichment

You and a friend are designing a newsletter for your school's Spanish club using graphics and word processing programs on the computer in the school library. In the process, you come up with the idea to provide customized newsletters to businesses in your area. Each business could send the newsletter to its employees and customers.

Make a table of the factors of production that you would need in order to start producing these newsletters. Classify each factor as labor, capital, land, or entrepreneurship. In a short paragraph, explain whether you would expect to see diminishing marginal product from the factors you classify as labor and why.

Thinking Critically About Economics (Continued)

5. As you spend additional time studying for a test, the marginal product (your additional knowledge and improved test score) decreases. Each additional study hour adds to grade improvement but it adds less and less. If you study so long that you don't get enough sleep, the marginal product may be negative—you could could be so tired that you would perform poorly and end up with a lower grade.
6. Increasing returns to scale means that if all inputs are simultaneously increased by a given proportion, output will go up by a greater proportion; since costs are directly linked to inputs, costs would go up less rapidly than output; therefore, the cost per unit of output would fall.
7. Answers may include (1) explicit costs: gasoline for transportation, cleaning materials, advertising, work clothes, and equipment; (2) opportunity costs: lost wages from other employment and the pleasure that could have been experienced by using work time for leisure activity.

Economic Enrichment

Students' factors of production will vary but may include compensation for the hours they spend working on the newsletter (labor), profits (entrepreneurship), computer and software (capital), access to the library after school (land), paper on which to print the newsletters and floppy disks on which to copy them (capital), a car or other transportation for deliveries (capital). If the partners have to hire additional laborers to produce more newsletters, the amount of profit for each person will decrease.

Math and Economics

In Figure 7-6, you saw the following sales data for Lumin Company:

Year	Unit Sales	Dollar Sales
1	121,292	$6,082,662.00
2	128,570	6,360,358.00
3	124,998	6,492,834.00
4	121,747	6,576,924.00
5	126,253	6,956,750.00
6	124,727	7,078,885.00

Sketch a graph showing the dollar sales for Lumin. The vertical axis should indicate dollars and the horizontal axis should indicate years. Then sketch a second graph that shows unit sales for Lumin. Place unit sales on the vertical axis and years along the horizontal axis. Compare these two graphs and provide a written explanation for the differences you see.

Writing About Economics

Inez LaRoosa, the owner of Mama Mía's Pizzeria, is trying to determine how many cooks are needed in the main kitchen. The main kitchen prepares the sauce, dough, pasta, and specialty items for three pizzerias. LaRoosa was doing just fine until she opened the third pizzeria. Now she can't seem to produce enough food. She hired two more cooks, but matters only got worse.

You have been hired as a consultant to Mama Mía's Pizzeria. LaRoosa says she knows how to make a good Italian dinner, but she doesn't understand much about economics. Write a three-part proposal to LaRoosa in which you explain (1) how you plan to analyze this problem (use plenty of creativity here), (2) what data you will need for your analysis, and (3) how supply and production at Mama Mía's are linked. Cover the following areas in your explanation of how supply and production are linked: total product, marginal product, diminishing marginal product in the short run, and the relationship between returns to scale and production costs in the long run.

Math and Economics

Students' graphs should appear as follows:

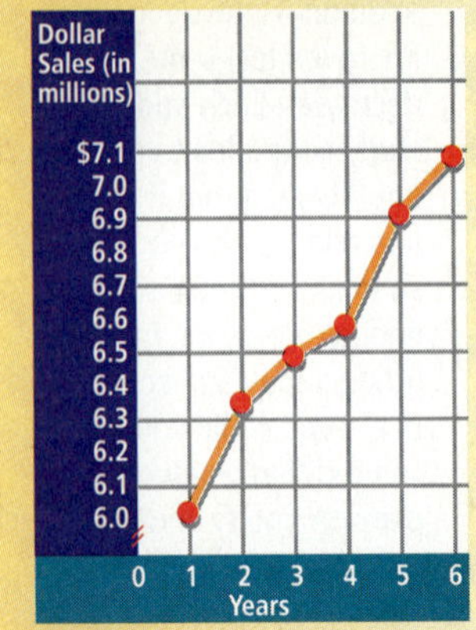

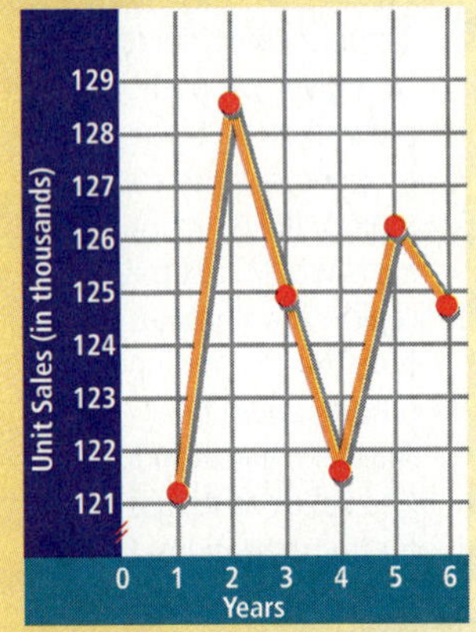

Students should explain that the consistent increase on the dollar-sales graph might give the company a false feeling of security; the unit-sales graph indicates some sharp decreases in the number of lamps sold over the six-year period.

Writing About Economics

Students' proposals will vary but should include an explanation of how opening the third pizzeria and hiring two additional cooks relates to the concepts of total product, marginal product, and diminishing marginal product in the short run; proposals also should address plans for increasing returns to scale and decreasing production costs in the long run.

Social Goals of the U.S. Economy

Economic Freedom on the Internet

Bob and Arminda Alexander ran a coffee store on Maui. Their shop was located on Front Street in Lahaina, a prime tourist spot. By all accounts, things were going well. Then Bob discovered the Internet.

"After exploring the Internet for three days, I thought, 'We could put the shop online,' " recalls Bob. For $1,000 in design and setup fees and $200 a month to a firm to manage their home page, the Alexanders did just that. The online business, Hawaii's Best Espresso Company (**http://hoohana.aloha.net/~bec/**), broke even in less than one month.

This is one example of a successful business enterprise being started on the Internet by two individuals. However, running a business over the Internet brings up several issues. How does the business get paid for its goods and services? If the customer decides to pay by credit card, how is the customer's credit card number kept secure? What are other forms of payment over the Internet?

To help resolve some of these payment and security issues, David Chaum founded DigiCash. The purpose of DigiCash is to provide a safe, secure, private means of conducting business transactions on the Internet. An online payment transaction generally involves three parties. The customer pays, the merchant receives the payment, and a bank does the accounting, making sure that money from the customer ends up in the merchant's account.

In the case of DigiCash's E-cash, the customer buys E-cash coins from the bank for his or her digital wallet. When the customer places an order over the Internet, the merchant's computer sends a payment request to the customer's computer. The E-cash software pops up, the customer approves the payment, and the software sends E-cash coins in the proper amount to the merchant. The merchant then connects with the bank payment server and sends the E-cash coins to the bank. The bank verifies the transaction and then transfers the money to the merchant.

Solutions such as DigiCash's E-cash have made it easier and more practical for people to start up businesses on the Internet. No longer is it necessary for merchants to worry about whether they will get paid for their goods and services. Nor do customers have to worry about sending their credit card numbers over the Internet. Everyone wins, because anything that makes it easier to start a business encourages a greater degree of competition, which should give consumers better prices and/or service.

SOURCE: Furger, Roberta, "Gold Rush on the Digital Frontier," in *PC World* (October 1995): 260.

After students have read the feature article on this page, have them create a chart showing the pros and cons of shopping on the Internet from the perspectives of consumers and sellers. (Answers will vary but may include that the pros are more choices and competitive prices for the consumer, convenient shopping from home, and the ability of businesses to increase their scope of consumers; possible cons are no personal interaction between consumer and seller, risk of loss or damage of product in the mail, and increased competition for retailers and catalog distributors.) Discuss with students which businesses are well suited for the Internet and which ones are not. (Many businesses such as clothing retailers, novelty retailers, and computer retailers are well suited; personal service industries such as beauty salons, doctors, and child-care centers are not well suited.) Ask students to share any experiences they have had browsing or shopping on the Internet. Ask students to think of their own entrepreneurial ideas that could be successful over the Internet, such as homework tutoring or providing up-to-the-minute sports scores. Ask students to search the Internet for businesses that would be competitive with theirs and to investigate set-up and management costs and how these costs would be paid. Have students share their ideas and information with the class.

Chapter 8 Demand, Supply, and Prices

Chapter Theme

Demand and supply are the key factors involved in the working of a market economy. When the market is in equilibrium, the quantity of goods supplied equals the quantity demanded. Chapter 8 explores the role of price and analyzes how changes in demand and supply affect market equilibrium, why government may block the functioning of the market system, and the results of these actions.

Section	Special Features
Market Equilibrium	Economic Spotlight Internet Connection
The Market out of Balance	Economics & Your Community Economic Talk Eye on Market News Multicultural Highlights
Governments Impact Market Equilibrium	Perspectives: Thinking Like a Producer Econ & You Media Link Economic Dilemma Global Economy

Video Activity

Chapter 8, Beef Prices

Search Chapter 8, Play to 9

Review with the class the causes of a market surplus. Ask students to imagine that they are beef producers dealing with a surplus of beef in the marketplace. As a class, brainstorm different marketing strategies to counteract the current decrease in demand.

	Print Resources	Media Resources	Assessment
	Effective Teaching Model Lesson Plans *Skills & Concepts* worksheet *Problem Solving* worksheet *Casebook* *Economic Measurement Workbook* *Content Review Workbook* *Spanish Resources*	VHS CD-ROM Videodisc *Arctic Express* *Interactive* ECONOMICS Template software	*Your Economic Portfolio* Chapter *Assessment* Chapter *MicroExam*

Special Learners	Print Resources	Media Resources	Assessment
Visual Activity Kinesthetic Activity	*Teacher's Connection to the Internet* *Life Skills* worksheet	Overhead and *Transparencies 8-1* to *8-5* Computer	*Checkpoint* Section 1 Quiz
ESL	*Reteach* worksheet *Enrich* worksheet	Overhead and *Transparencies 8-6* to *8-11* Computer VCR Camcorder	*Checkpoint* Section 2 Quiz
Cooperative Learning Activity Auditory Activity		Overhead and *Transparencies 8-12* to *8-13* Computer	*Checkpoint* Section 3 Quiz

Careers Activity

Each summer, as outdoor temperatures rise, so does consumer demand for air-conditioning. Air-conditioning technicians design, install, repair, and maintain systems that control indoor temperatures. When temperatures go up, they are able to charge the consumer more for the services that they supply.

Aspiring technicians must have a high school diploma and should complete two years of technical training, intensive in algebra, trigonometry, physics, English, and technical writing. Income for a trained air-conditioning technician ranges from $20,000 to $40,000 per year.

Tell students to imagine that they are considering careers as air-conditioning technicians. Have them list the ten states in which they would be likely to find the most air-conditioning work and the ten in which they would find the least. Have them explain in writing how geographic location might affect the price of their services.

CHAPTER 8

Teaching Materials

Program Resources

- Student text
- *Effective Teaching Model Lesson Plans*
- *Overhead Transparencies 8-1 to 8-12*
- *Life Skills* worksheet
- *Problem Solving* worksheet
- *Reteach* worksheet
- *Enrich* worksheet
- *Skills & Concepts* worksheet
- *Casebook*
- *Economic Measurement Workbook*
- *Content Review Workbook*
- *Spanish Resources*
- Video package
- *Teacher's Connection to the Internet*
- *Arctic Express*
- *Interactive ECONOMICS*
- Template software

Assessment

- Section Quizzes
- Chapter *Assessment*
- Chapter *MicroExam*

Overview

Section One
Market Equilibrium

Section Two
The Market out of Balance

Section Three
Governments Impact Market Equilibrium

Teacher to Teacher

To illustrate the concepts of shortages and surpluses, bring to class one item of value to students (for example, a homework pass) and ask who would like to have it. As students' hands go up, explain that you have only one item, so only one student can have it. Write on the chalkboard students' suggestions for determining who will get the item. Elicit that you could offer it to the student willing to pay the highest price. Relate this concept to real-life examples of rising prices and shortages. Ask students how they think the price of the item might be affected if you had a surplus. (Price would probably decrease.) Summarize that, in the real world, there must be some way to determine who gets the available resources.

Harlan Day
Purdue University
W. Lafayette, IN

Demand, Supply, and Prices

Learning Objectives

8-1
Explain the equilibrium between demand and supply.

8-2
Graph equilibrium price and equilibrium quantity.

8-3
Demonstrate how price acts as a rationing device.

8-4
Analyze the effects of a shortage or a surplus and how they are eliminated.

8-5
Determine the effects of a change in demand on the market equilibrium.

8-6
Determine the effects of a change in supply on the market equilibrium.

8-7
Show how price floors and price ceilings are used to block the market system.

Outside Resources

- Blank overhead transparencies
- Graph paper
- Posterboard
- Index cards
- Colored pencils or markers
- Butcher paper
- Markers or paints
- Newspapers and news magazines
- Camcorder and VCR
- Tracing paper
- Computer
- Online information service or Internet access
- Ping-Pong ball or small, rubber ball

Vocabulary

equilibrium price, p. 187
equilibrium quantity, p. 187
shortage, p. 191
surplus, p. 192
price floor, p. 201
price ceiling, p. 203

Focus

Write the word **equilibrium** on the chalkboard or an overhead transparency. Have students brainstorm and then list on a sheet of paper all the words that they associate with equilibrium.

As a whole-class activity, list words students associate with **equilibrium.** Lead students to a definition of equilibrium as the condition of two forces exactly balancing one another. Then, ask students which two forces control equilibrium in a market economy. (Demand and supply)

Teach

Emphasize that the function of a market is to bring consumers and producers together and that the interaction of demand and supply is an essential part of a market system. Review the concepts of demand and supply.

Explain that in a market economy the forces of demand and supply, if allowed to operate freely, will create a natural equilibrium. Equilibrium is illustrated on a graph as the point where the supply and demand curves intersect. Compare the concepts of **equilibrium price** and **equilibrium quantity.**

Section One

Market Equilibrium

What Do You Think?

When the price of hiking boots was $70, producers made 1.8 million pairs. At that price, people in the United States would want to buy 1.2 million pairs of hiking boots. Jocelyn Aders watched as the price of the hiking boots she wanted went down from $70.00 to $67.50 to $65.00. She decided to wait until it dropped to $55.00 before she bought, since that price would be within her budget.

Terms to Know

equilibrium price

equilibrium quantity

What's Ahead?

Individual producers and consumers direct the workings of a market economy. Each participant in the market economy acts in his or her own best interests in giving direction to the economy. In this section, you will review some important concepts about supply and demand. You will learn how the equilibrium price and quantity are determined in the marketplace.

THE MARKET SYSTEM

In a market system, people acting in their own self-interests make the decisions that guide the economy. Every time you make a purchase, you guide the direction of the economy. If you buy a new wool sweater, you signal to producers that people want wool sweaters. You do not buy a wool sweater with the idea of increasing employment in woolen mills or adding to the profits of mill owners. You buy a wool sweater because you know you will like wearing it or giving it as a gift. Your decision to buy the sweater is based on your own self-interest. No one makes you buy it.

Meanwhile, producers of wool sweaters respond to consumers' signals by employing more factors of production to make more sweaters. Producers don't have to make more sweaters. No government agency tells them to do so. They make more because they expect to make money. The producers

make more sweaters because it is in their own self-interest to do so.

A system of markets, such as the market for wool sweaters, is the heart of our economic system. We depend on free markets to communicate information between consumers and producers. Markets provide the mechanism for exchange, as illustrated in Figure 8-1. Consumers exchange money for goods and services from producers. Producers then exchange that money for factors of production used in making their products. The owners of these factors use that money in their own roles as consumers. So, the exchange process starts over again. At each stage, the exchange is made more efficient because of the existence of the market system.

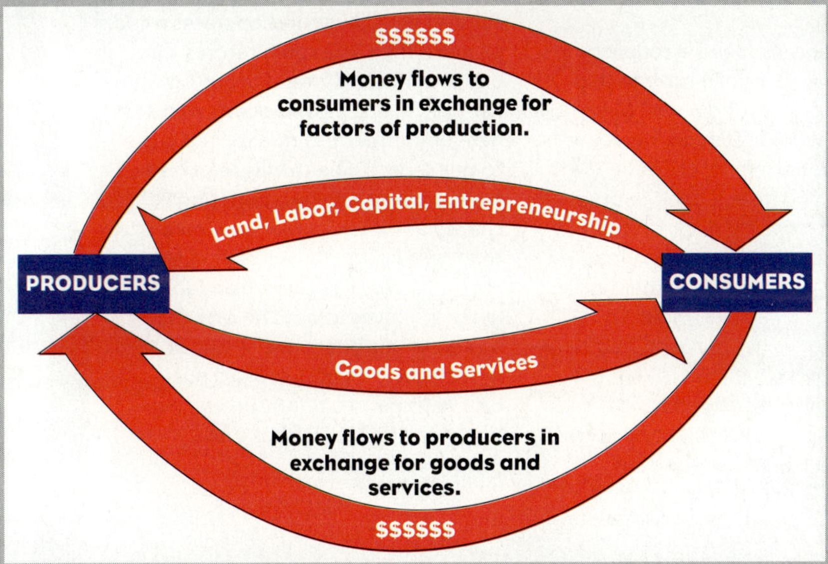

Figure 8-1

Markets Facilitate Exchanges

Money flows between consumers and producers in a circular fashion. Consumers pay money to producers in exchange for goods and services. Producers make payments to land, labor, capital, and entrepreneurship as they produce goods and services. ***What else is exchanged in a market system, such as the one illustrated here?***

Apply

Display *Overhead Transparency 8-1* and ask a student volunteer to summarize the information on the flowchart. Then, ask students to suggest scenarios in which one of the exchanged elements has been altered or eliminated. As each scenario is described, encourage students to explain the consequences of changing even one element in this crucial balance. To get students started, tell them that one example of this type of change is the producer laying off workers to avoid bankruptcy. This reduces the money flow to consumers, so labor flow to the producer is reduced, the producer must reduce amount of goods and services going to consumers, and finally the money flow from consumers to the producer is reduced. As students describe their scenarios, have them show on *Figure 8-1* the progression of change in the flow between producers and consumers.

Guided Practice

Analyzing Graphics

Caption Answer
Information is exchanged.

Tell students that when we make a purchase, we are actually voting for the production of a good or service. Work with students to make a list of goods and services that are no longer produced. (Answers may include services: the Pony Express or home delivery of ice; goods: whale-oil lamps or reel-to-reel tape recorders.) Then, make another list of goods and services that have more recently come into existence, such as laser surgery and hand-held videocassette cameras. Ask students what they think brought an end to each of the goods that are no longer produced. What prompted the production of the new goods? What incentives does the market price provide to consumers and producers?

Have students work in groups of four or five to create a market exchange flowchart using the information from the section entitled *The Market System,* found in the first section of this chapter. You may wish to refer students to *Figure 8-1* in their textbook as an example. Make sure students include the following in their flowcharts: consumer decides to purchase → consumer exchanges money for product → producer exchanges that money for factors of production → producer decides to produce → producer (including owners and employees) exchanges money as a consumer → consumer decides to purchase.

Independent Practice

Economic Spotlight

WHERE DID THE NINE-CENT COOKIE GO?

You probably don't remember the nine-cent cookie: a cold, small cookie handed to you over the counter in a paper bag. In fact, you probably don't even remember the 25-cent cookie! In the late 1970s, Debbi Fields introduced the 25-cent cookie, which was much larger than the old "nine center" and was served on a napkin while it was still warm from the oven.

Today, Americans spend a couple million dollars a year on chocolate chip cookies. Nobody knew how well Mrs. Fields cookies would catch on, however. Not even Fields herself. In 1977, she borrowed $50,000 from a bank to open her first cookie store. By noon on the first day of business, she began to fear that her first day would also be her last. Not a single cookie had been sold. To make matters worse, her husband had bet her that she wouldn't have $50 in the cash register at the end of the day. So, Fields decided to take matters into her own hands. She called a friend to watch the store. Then, she took her cookies out to the street in search of customers. Fields gave away all of her unsold cookies so she could bake more fresh ones. It was love at first bite! The people who sampled her cookies came back looking to buy more. By the end of the first day, she had exactly $50 in the till! Within a week, her store was profitable.

The demand for Mrs. Fields Cookies was so great, she opened more stores. That meant borrowing more money, which was difficult because most bankers believed that the cookie business wouldn't last. Today, Fields owns and operates a chain of more than 700 cookie stores throughout the United States, Europe, and the Far East. Fields moved slowly and kept her commitment to quality and customer service. She continues to sell freshly baked cookies, donating to charity any cookies that are more than two hours old. According to Fields, success has come from doing what she loves to do. She says that she never set out to make lots of money, just the best cookies possible. With her resulting success, you might say Debbi Fields is one "smart cookie."

Economic Spotlight

After students have read about Debbi Fields, discuss as a class the problems involved in keeping up with demand. Brainstorm a list of these problems from the viewpoint of both the producer and the consumer, who is affected by the producer's actions. Then, on the chalkboard or an overhead transparency, organize the list into a chart of these problems. (Producer problems include financing, quality control, and hiring; consumer problems include dissatisfaction if demand is not met and inferior future products if producer lets quality slip.)

The function of a market is to bring consumers and producers together. The interaction of demand and supply is an essential part of a market system. Because demand and supply are so important, we will briefly review these concepts. Then we will look at how demand and supply interact in a market system.

A Review of Demand

Demand is defined as the quantities of a product that consumers are willing and able to buy at various prices. The law of demand is that consumers will buy a greater quantity at a lower price than at a higher price. The market demand for a product is the sum of all individual consumers' demands. So, the market demand represents the total amount that all consumers are willing and able to buy at each price.

The market demand can be shown by either a table or a graph. Figure 8-2 illustrates a hypothetical demand schedule and demand curve for wheat. Note that wheat follows the law of demand. The quantity demanded becomes less as the price goes up. Looking at the demand curve, you quickly see the inverse relationship between price and quantity. At high prices such as $4.40 per bushel, the amount demanded is fairly low (1,600 million bushels). At lower prices, the amount demanded goes up.

A Review of Supply

Supply is the quantities of a product firms are willing and able to make available for sale at various prices. How much a firm supplies at any price depends on the firm's cost of production. Because of diminishing marginal product, the cost per unit of output rises as more is produced in the short run. The price a firm gets for a product must cover production costs. So, we can expect that firms will increase the amount supplied if price goes up.

Price per Bushel	Millions of Bushels Demanded
$2.80	2,400
3.00	2,300
3.20	2,200
3.40	2,100
3.60	2,000
3.80	1,900
4.00	1,800
4.20	1,700
4.40	1,600

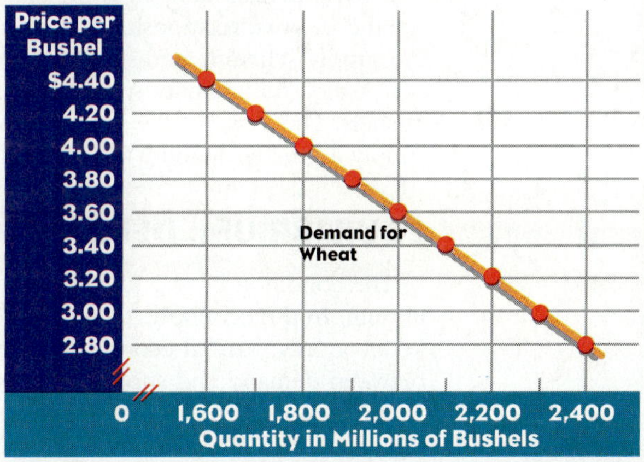

Figure 8-2

Hypothetical Demand Schedule and Demand Curve for Wheat

Each of the nine price and quantity combinations given in the demand schedule are represented by dots on the demand curve. Connecting these points allows you to estimate quantity demanded at prices not listed in the demand schedule. ***How many bushels of wheat would be demanded at a price of $3.70?***

Display *Overhead Transparency 8-2* to review the basics of demand with students. Guide students to use the graph to understand what a demand curve illustrates (the quantities consumers will buy at various prices) and what the law of demand states (inverse relationship between price and quantity demanded).

Analyzing *Graphics*

Caption Answer
1,950 bushels of wheat would be demanded.

Display *Overhead Transparency 8-3* to review the basics of supply with students. Then, have students analyze the graph and explain what a supply curve illustrates. (The quantities producers will produce at certain prices) Have students describe the law of supply. (A positive, or direct, relationship between price and quantity produced)

Analyzing Graphics

Caption Answer
2,050 bushels of wheat would be supplied.

Review and compare demand/supply schedules and demand/supply curves. (Schedules show specific prices and quantities and curves show all prices and quantities within a specific range.) Display *Overhead Transparency 8-4.* Have students explain how they might use the provided information to estimate various inbetween prices not shown on the schedule.

Price per Bushel	Millions of Bushels Supplied
$2.80	1,600
3.00	1,700
3.20	1,800
3.40	1,900
3.60	2,000
3.80	2,100
4.00	2,200
4.20	2,300
4.40	2,400

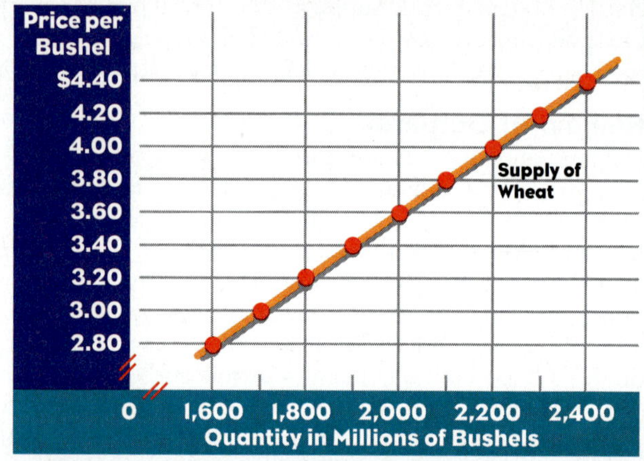

Hypothetical Supply Schedule and Supply Curve for Wheat

Each of the nine price and quantity combinations given in the supply schedule are represented by dots on the supply curve. Connecting these points allows you to estimate quantity supplied at prices not listed in the supply schedule. ***How many bushels of wheat would be supplied at a price of $3.70?***

If each producer produces more at a higher price than at a lower price, the same will be true for all firms combined. Adding together the quantities supplied by all firms at each price gives the market supply of the product.

A hypothetical market supply of wheat is illustrated in Figure 8-3. You can see the positive relationship between price and the quantity supplied in both the supply schedule and supply curve. As price goes up from $2.80 to $4.40 per bushel, the quantity supplied goes up from 1,600 to 2,400 million bushels. The slope of the supply curve is positive because, in total, all firms supply a greater quantity the higher the price.

EQUILIBRIUM: DEMAND AND SUPPLY IN BALANCE

The condition of two forces exactly balancing one another is called equilibrium. In the economy, those two forces are demand and supply. In a market economy, natural economic forces lead to an equilibrium, or balance, between demand and supply. If the quantity demanded equals the quantity supplied, the market is in equilibrium.

Finding Equilibrium

In Figure 8-4, the demand and supply schedules we have been working with are shown in a single table. You can see in the table that at prices higher than $3.60, the quantity supplied is greater than the quantity demanded. At every price less than $3.60, the quantity demanded is greater than the quantity supplied. Only at a price of $3.60 is there equilibrium in the market, with the quantity supplied equal to the quantity demanded. The price at

Price	Quantity Demanded	Quantity Supplied
$2.80	2,400	1,600
3.00	2,300	1,700
3.20	2,200	1,800
3.40	2,100	1,900
3.60	2,000	2,000
3.80	1,900	2,100
4.00	1,800	2,200
4.20	1,700	2,300
4.40	1,600	2,400

Figure 8-4

Hypothetical Demand and Supply Schedules for Wheat

Putting the supply and demand schedules together in one table allows you to see the price at which quantity supplied equals quantity demanded. ***At a price of $3, what is the relationship between supply and demand?***

which the quantity demanded equals the quantity supplied is called the ***equilibrium price*** (or market price). In this case, then, the equilibrium price is $3.60.

At the $3.60 price, the quantity demanded is 2,000 units, as is the quantity supplied. Thus, 2,000 units represent the equilibrium quantity. The ***equilibrium quantity*** is the quantity that is both demanded and supplied at the equilibrium price.

equilibrium price
the price at which the quantity demanded equals the quantity supplied

equilibrium quantity
the quantity that is both demanded and supplied at the equilibrium price

Graphing Equilibrium

Figure 8-5 shows the supply and demand curves for wheat on the same graph. You will see these curves several times throughout the rest of this chapter.

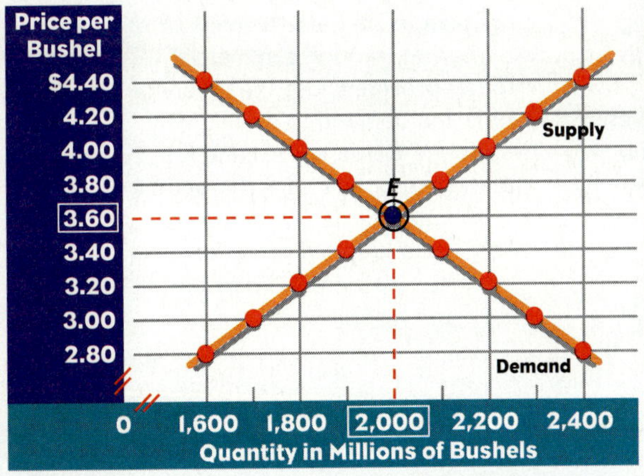

Figure 8-5

Balance Between Demand and Supply

Equilibrium occurs at the point where the supply and demand curves intersect. ***Would there be equilibrium at a price of $4.20?***

Analyzing *Graphics*

Caption Answer
2,300 bushels are demanded and 1,700 bushels are supplied.

To help students better understand the elements of *Figure 8-5,* have them re-create each part of the equilibrium graph. First, distribute a sheet of graph paper to each student. Then, display to the class *Overhead Transparency 8-2,* the demand curve for wheat. Have students re-create the demand curve on their graph paper. Next, lay *Overhead Transparency 8-3,* the supply curve for wheat, on top of *Overhead Transparency 8-2* so that the two graphs overlap. Have students use a different color of ink to add this supply curve to their original demand curve. After both curves are complete, have students mark the intersection of the two curves and label this point **E,** for equilibrium. Next, have students draw a dotted line from **E** to the vertical axis and label $3.60 as the **equilibrium price.** Finally, ask them to draw a dotted line from **E** down to the horizontal axis and label 2,000 as the **equilibrium quantity.** Note: Collect these graphs or have students save them for use in the second section of this chapter.

Analyzing *Graphics*

Caption Answer
No, the quantity supplied (2,300) would be greater than the quantity demanded (1,700).

Have students conduct a survey of their friends and family members about some need that they have for products that do not yet exist today (for example, a machine into which you could simply dictate the answers to your homework that would write them in a correctly spelled form). Tell students to find out how much the respondents would be willing to pay for the good they describe. Ask students to answer the following questions: **Is the price high enough to encourage someone to produce the goods? When do you think the goods might be produced and why? What role will market price play in the decision about when these goods will be produced?**

Have students construct a hypothetical demand curve for one of the goods described in the previous activity. Ask students who would be willing to produce the good and at what price. Ask students to make a hypothetical supply curve for the good. Ask students what the market equilibrium price for the good might be if it were produced.

Internet Connection

POWER SEARCHES USING GOPHER AND THE WEB BROWSERS

As you have learned, the Internet is a great research tool. The Internet offers a tremendous amount of information from libraries, schools, government agencies, and businesses. Two good locations to start any research project are the Global Electronic Library at **gopher://marvel.loc.gov/11/global** and the WWW Virtual Library at **http://www.w3.org/hypertext/DataSources/bySubject/Overview.html**.

To find the information you need, you could browse through Gopher menus or Web pages, but a more efficient way is to use one of the electronic search methods available on the Internet. There are a variety of such methods, but we will focus on two: Veronica for Gopher and WebCrawler for the World Wide Web.

Most Gopher servers have menu items labeled *Veronica Searches* or something similar. You select appropriate keywords to search for and follow directions. Veronica searches through the menu titles in Gopher space to find titles that contain the specified keywords. The results come in the form of a Gopher menu. You then select from the menu to access them.

The easy way to access WebCrawler using Netscape is to click on the directory button *Net Search,* which is located under the *Location* box. If you use a different browser and you don't appear to have direct access to WebCrawler, you can open the URL at **http://webcrawler.com/WebCrawler/**.

WebCrawler asks you to choose keywords; it returns a list of Web pages with the specified keywords that ranks the items on a scale of 1 to 1,000. Clicking on any item in the list connects you to that Web page.

Internet Application: Pick a topic on some aspect of economics that interests you. Try both a Veronica search (even via browser) and a WebCrawler search. Do they give you the same results? Which do you prefer?

Economics Application: Now that the government is no longer subsidizing the Internet, more and more people are getting access to the Internet through commercial Internet providers. Use the theory of supply and demand to explain why, despite the increased demand for Internet access, the price charged by commercial Internet providers has fallen. Use a graph, if possible.

Internet Connection

Internet Application: Narrow the search topics down to something relevant to your class. If you don't have direct Gopher access, you can undertake a Veronica search by using a Web browser to access a Gopher site. Veronica searches and WebCrawler searches will generate somewhat different results.

Explanation for the Economics Application is in the *Teacher's Connection to the Internet.*

What does market equilibrium look like on a graph? In Figure 8-5, the equilibrium price and quantity are shown in boxes. From this graph, you can see that equilibrium occurs at the point where the demand curve crosses the supply curve. That is, the quantity demanded and the quantity supplied are equal where the two lines cross. This is an important point that you will see again and again as you study economics.

The equilibrium point, or the intersection of the demand and supply curves, is labeled *E* (for equilibrium) in Figure 8-5. Only at this point does the quantity demanded equal the quantity supplied. At any price above \$3.60, the quantity supplied is greater than the quantity demanded. At any price below \$3.60, the quantity demanded is greater than the quantity supplied.

This relationship between the quantity supplied and the quantity demanded is true in all markets. Any market is in equilibrium, or balance, when the quantity demanded equals the quantity supplied. In a graph, this is the point where the demand curve crosses the supply curve. To find the equilibrium price and equilibrium quantity for a market, you first find the point where demand crosses supply. Then read over to the price axis to find the equilibrium price. The equilibrium quantity is found from the quantity axis directly below where the two curves cross.

Checkpoint

Content Check

1. How does your purchase of a bicycle helmet guide the market?
2. If there is equilibrium in the market for oats to feed horses, what do you know about the quantity supplied and the quantity demanded?
3. Graph the supply and demand curves to represent a market equilibrium for corn.

What Do You Think Now?

Reread *What Do You Think?* in the Section One Focus. Then answer the following questions:

4. What determines how far the price of hiking boots will drop?
5. Do you think the price of hiking boots will ever get to \$55 so that Jocelyn can buy a pair?

Assess

1. You signal to producers to make bicycle helmets. **8-1**
2. They are equal. **8-1**
3. Students' curves should identify the equilibrium price and quantity at the point where the upward-sloping supply curve crosses the downward-sloping demand curve. **8-1, 8-2**
4. The interaction between the quantity supplied and the quantity demanded in the market **8-3**
5. Answers should reflect an understanding of the possibility of changes in both supply and demand as well as in price. **8-1, 8-3**

Close

As a class, use *Figure 8-4* as a guide to create a hypothetical demand and supply schedule for a product of students' choice (such as quantities of a type of car, computer, or soft drink). Then, on graph paper or on the computer, create a combined demand and supply curve from that information.

Reteach

Pair students who understand graphing with those who are demonstrating difficulty. Have one student help the other draw on graph paper a horizontal axis, labeled **Quantity,** and a vertical axis, labeled **Price.** Have students keep this "base graph" in their notebooks for quick reference. **8-2**

Enrich

Have students each choose from *Chapter 6* or *Chapter 7* of their textbook a demand schedule and a supply schedule for a given product. Have them each create a combined demand and supply schedule for their chosen product and then create on graph paper or the computer a combined supply and demand curve. Finally, have them find and label the **equilibrium price** and **equilibrium quantity. 8-2**

Focus

In small groups, have students brainstorm a list of products that are in demand but hard to find and a list of products that are so plentiful they rarely seem to be sold out.

As a whole class, discuss why certain items are harder to find than others. Have students give examples of products that used to be easier to purchase than they are now. Discuss students' thoughts about why this change has occurred.

Teach

Relate the discussion from *Focus* to the definitions of **surplus** and **shortage** by explaining that, with hard-to-find, in-demand products, there may be a shortage. When too many products are readily available, there may be a surplus. Explain that the market is not at equilibrium when there is either a shortage or a surplus.

Point out that price helps consumers decide how much to buy and producers how much to produce, so it serves as a rationing device. Review with students the four reasons for an overall change in demand and relate this concept to changes in quantity demanded and price.

FOCUS

Section Two

The Market out of Balance

What Do You Think?

Alonzo Borland, a Kansas wheat farmer, is talking on the phone to his sister Grace in New Jersey. "It's been a great year. We got the plowing done on schedule, we had perfect rainfall and sunshine, and the harvest is better than we expected. In fact, all around the country, total wheat production is way up. I just hope I can make some money this year." Grace is not sure why Alonzo is worried after such a great year.

Terms to Know

shortage

surplus

What's Ahead?

The market is in equilibrium when the quantity supplied equals the quantity demanded. What happens when the market is not in equilibrium? In this section, you will see what happens to the market when there is either a shortage or a surplus in the market. You will also see what happens to equilibrium when either demand or supply change.

PRICE AS A RATIONING DEVICE

You know that price is important in determining both the quantity demanded and the quantity supplied. Consumers look at prices as they decide how to spend their money. Producers look at prices as they decide what goods or services to produce. So, price acts as a signal for both consumers and producers. In this way, prices help to distribute both finished goods and raw materials among competing uses. You will see that when there is a shortage of something, price tends to rise. When there is a surplus, price tends to fall. In the following sections, you will examine how price changes help to eliminate either a shortage or a surplus.

A Shortage in the Market

What does it mean to say there is a shortage of some product? What does it mean when a newscaster announces that there is likely to be a shortage of heating oil next winter? When cold weather hits the orange groves of Florida, people in New York experience a shortage of orange juice in the grocery stores. What does that mean?

What Is a Shortage? A shortage exists when people are willing to buy more than producers have for sale at a particular price. A ***shortage*** is the condition in which the quantity demanded is greater than the quantity supplied at a certain price. A shortage of orange juice means that consumers want to buy more at the present price than is available for sale. That is, there is a shortage when the quantity demanded at a certain price is greater than the quantity supplied.

shortage
the condition in which the quantity demanded is greater than the quantity supplied at a certain price

What Does a Shortage Look Like on a Graph? Figure 8-6 takes another look at the wheat market. You can use Figure 8-6 to understand a shortage. At a price of $3.20, the quantity supplied is 1,800 units. This can be found by following the dashed line from the price of $3.20 to the supply curve at the point marked *A*. Then from *A*, follow the dashed line down to the quantity axis at 1,800 units. You can verify that 1,800 units would be supplied at a price of $3.20 by checking the supply schedule in Figure 8-4.

But, what about the quantity demanded at that price? From the demand curve, you can see that 2,200 units are demanded at a price of $3.20. You can find this quantity by extending the dashed line from the $3.20 price over to the demand curve at *B*. Then from *B*, follow the line down to the quantity axis at 2,200 units. Looking back to the demand schedule in Figure 8-4, you also can see that 2,200 units are demanded at a price of $3.20.

At a price of $3.20, there is a shortage of wheat. Consumers would want to purchase 2,200 units, but suppliers are willing to supply only 1,800 units. The quantity demanded is greater than the quantity supplied at that price. Not everyone who wants to buy wheat at that price is able to do so. There is a shortage of 400 units. This is the distance between *A* and *B*.

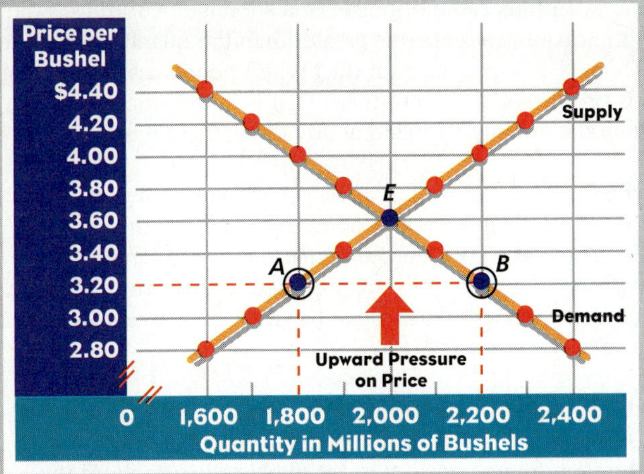

Figure 8-6

Shortage in the Wheat Market

A shortage results when the quantity demanded is greater than the quantity supplied at a certain price. The distance between *A* and *B* (400 units) is a measure of the amount of the shortage. ***What do you think happens to price when there is a shortage of a product in the marketplace?***

Apply

Display *Overhead Transparency 8-6*. Explain that a **shortage** occurs when the quantity demanded is greater than the quantity supplied at a certain price. Explain that Point **A** on the supply curve stands for the quantity supplied at a given price, and Point **B** on the demand curve stands for the quantity demanded at the same price. The difference between these two points (as observed on the horizontal axis) is the amount of the shortage. Point out the shortage (400 units) shown in *Figure 8-6*. Ask students how they think this shortage could be eliminated. (Elicit from students that the upward pressure on price will lead the supplier to produce the equilibrium quantity, thus eliminating the shortage.) Have each student describe in writing this upward movement along both curves toward the equilibrium price and quantity. Tell students to store their descriptions in a safe place so they can use them again in the *Analyzing Graphics* activity for *Figure 8-7*.

Guided Practice

Analyzing Graphics

Caption Answer
There is upward pressure on price; price goes up.

Economics & Your Community

Have students visit local stores to note possible shortages and surpluses of various products. In class, have students work in small groups to brainstorm a list of common characteristics of the surplus products (easy to find, lower than normal price, no additional status involved in ownership, and so on) and a separate list of common characteristics of the products in short supply (hard to find, higher than normal price, some additional status involved in ownership, and so on). Hand out posterboard to the groups and have each group create a poster illustrating these common characteristics and then summarize its findings for the class. Correct any misconceptions.

Some students may have difficulty understanding the math concept of shortages and may have trouble reading *Figure 8-6.* Refer these students to the demand and supply schedule shown in *Figure 8-4* on p. 187 of their textbook. First, ask students to key the figures from the schedule into a spreadsheet on the computer. Then, to illustrate the shortages in the schedule, tell students to create a fourth column and label it **Shortage.** Have them create a formula in this column to calculate the difference between each number in the **Quantity Demanded** column (column **B**) and its corresponding number in the **Quantity Supplied** column (column **C**)—for example, **=(B3 - C3).** Point out that a negative result indicates a shortage because the amount demanded is higher than the amount supplied.

How Is a Shortage Eliminated? Some people are willing to pay more than $3.20 per bushel for their wheat. You can see this is true by looking at the demand curve. For example, enough consumers are willing to pay $4.20 per bushel for 1,700 units to be sold at that price. So, there are consumers who stand ready to buy wheat at prices above $3.20. Some of them are likely to pay more than $3.20, rather than do without the wheat.

Suppliers are likely to know when the quantity demanded is greater than the quantity supplied and that some people are willing to pay a higher price. The suppliers in such a situation will probably raise their prices. Thus, a shortage causes upward pressure on the price. This is shown by the arrow pointing up in Figure 8-6. This upward pressure is due to natural economic forces on both the demand and supply sides of the marketplace.

As price rises, the amount demanded becomes less. Some consumers may drop out of the market while others will cut back on their use of the product. At the same time, producers will increase the amount they supply as price rises. As the amount demanded decreases and the amount supplied increases, the shortage is reduced.

As long as the quantity demanded is greater than the quantity supplied, this process continues. There is upward pressure on price. This, in turn, decreases the amount demanded and increases the amount supplied. Only when there is no shortage is there no longer upward pressure on price.

A Surplus in the Market

At times, U.S. car manufacturers have produced more cars than people have been willing to buy at existing prices. When weather and other conditions cooperate, the agricultural sector may produce more wheat or corn than consumers wish to purchase. You probably can guess that these conditions represent a surplus. What does that mean in the market?

surplus
the condition in which the quantity supplied is greater than the quantity demanded at a certain price

What Is a Surplus? A surplus is the opposite of a shortage. A ***surplus*** is the condition in which the quantity supplied is greater than the quantity demanded at a certain price. There is a surplus of a product when people are not willing to buy as much as is produced at a given price. That is, if the amount demanded is less than the amount supplied at any price, there is a surplus.

What Does a Surplus Look Like on a Graph? A surplus is illustrated in Figure 8-7. At a price of $4.20, the amount demanded is 1,700 units. This is determined from the point labeled *C* on the demand curve. As indicated by Point *D* on the supply curve, 2,300 units are supplied at that price. There is a surplus of 600 units. This surplus is shown as the distance between *C* and *D* in Figure 8-7.

How Is a Surplus Eliminated? Suppliers have more of the product than they can sell at this high price. They are likely to reduce price to try to increase sales. At the same time, consumers are likely to know about the

EconomicTalk

Distribute index cards and have each student write on a card a scenario that describes a **shortage** or a **surplus** of a product. Then, have students pass their cards to the students seated behind them. (Students in the last row should pass their cards to students in the front row.) Have each student write on the back of the card whether he or she thinks the scenario describes a surplus or a shortage. Continue to pass and read the cards until they reach the original writers. Tally the number of correct answers and have students with the top five scores share their scenarios with the class. Discuss the elements in each scenario that made it easy to identify a shortage or surplus.

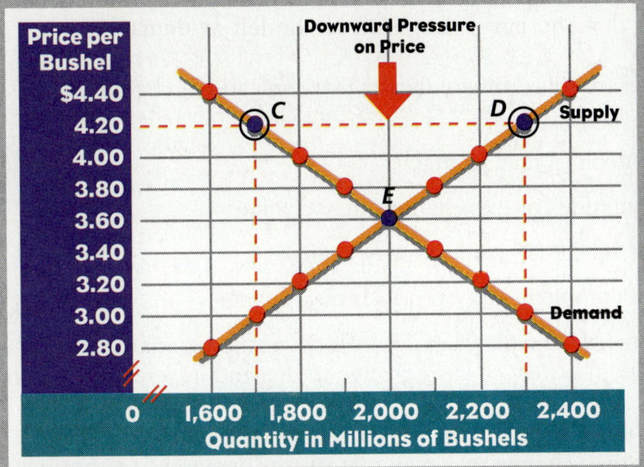

Figure 8-7

Surplus in the Wheat Market

A surplus results when the quantity supplied is greater than the quantity demanded. The distance between *C* and *D* (600 units) is a measure of the amount of the surplus. ***What would you expect to happen to price when the quantity supplied is more than the quantity demanded?***

surplus. They may recognize that they have greater bargaining power and may offer to buy the product, but only at a reduced price. Thus, when there is a surplus, there is downward pressure on price. This is shown by the arrow pointing down in Figure 8-7.

When car companies produce too many cars, they frequently offer rebates to improve sales. A rebate is a lowering of price. If you get back a $500 check from the company after buying a car, that is like having the price reduced by $500. In fact, the rebate often can be deducted from the price at the time of purchase.

Forces on both the demand and supply sides of the market react with downward pressure on price when there is a surplus. As price comes down, the amount demanded increases. This helps reduce the surplus. Also, as price falls, the amount supplied decreases as firms reduce production. This also acts to reduce the surplus.

As long as the quantity demanded is less than the quantity supplied, price continues to fall. As price falls, the amount demanded increases and the amount supplied decreases. When there is no longer a surplus, the downward pressure on price is eliminated.

CHANGES IN DEMAND

You have seen that, in a market economy, natural economic forces lead to a balance between demand and supply. But, in Chapter 6, you learned that demand may change. The demand curve may not stay in

Analyzing *Graphics*

Caption Answer
There would be downward pressure on price; price would go down.

Display *Overhead Transparency 8-7.* Explain that a surplus occurs when the quantity supplied is greater than the quantity demanded. Ask students how to calculate the amount of a surplus. (By figuring the difference between the quantity demanded at a given price and the quantity supplied at that price) Point out that Point **C** on the demand curve stands for the quantity demanded at a given price, and Point **D** on the supply curve stands for the quantity supplied at that price. Point out the surplus (600 units) shown in *Figure 8-7.* Ask students how they think this surplus could be eliminated. (Lead students to understand that the downward pressure on price will lead the supplier to produce the equilibrium quantity, thus eliminating the surplus.) Have each student take out his or her description of how a shortage is eliminated (from the *Analyzing Graphics* activity for *Figure 8-6*). Tell students to add to that description an explanation of the downward movement along both curves toward the equilibrium quantity to eliminate the surplus. Students may wish to use their completed explanations as a handy reference tool.

EyeOnMarket*News*

Bring to class newspapers and news magazines. Ask each student to scan the papers and magazines to find information about shortages or surpluses and their causes and effects. Then, have each student write a short news story about one of the articles, speculating about the cause and possible future effects of the shortage or surplus. Have a volunteer cameraperson videotape each news story, creating a "shortage and surplus" news segment. As a class, view the news segments and discuss each shortage and surplus.

Have students take out the graphs they created for *Figure 8-5* in the first section. Ask them to transfer onto this graph the lines from *Figure 8-6* that show what happens when the quantity demanded is greater than the quantity supplied. Have students use colored pencils or markers to fill in this area with one shade or color. Then, instruct students to transfer onto their graphs the lines from *Figure 8-7* that show what happens when the quantity supplied is greater than the quantity demanded and fill in this area with a second shading or color. Finally, have students make a key, labeling each color or shade appropriately as a surplus or shortage.

Independent Practice

Divide the class into small groups of three or four students. Hand out butcher paper and markers or paints to each group. Tell each group to independently draw a flowchart that shows the possible cycle from shortage to surplus back to shortage. (Quantity demanded exceeds quantity supplied → price goes up → producer produces more and quantity demanded goes down → quantity demanded and quantity supplied reach equilibrium → if producers keep producing more → quantity supplied exceeds quantity demanded → price goes down → quantity supplied goes down while quantity demanded goes up → start over.) Have groups exchange papers and correct any errors. Then, display the flowcharts in the classroom as a reference for students during the study of this chapter.

the same place. It may shift to the right as demand for the product increases. Or, the demand curve may shift to the left as demand for the product falls.

To review, there are four primary factors that can cause a change in demand:

1. Consumers' incomes may change.
2. Consumers' attitudes or expectations may change.
3. The prices of substitute products may change.
4. The prices of complementary products may change.

Other factors, such as consumer expectations, weather conditions, and population changes, also may cause a change in demand in certain situations.

As incomes rise, the demand for most products also goes up. But, if income falls, demand falls as well. Consumers' attitudes may change in a way that causes demand to either rise or fall. Advertising is aimed at increasing demand by changing our attitudes about products. But, the advertising that makes us view Pepsi more favorably also may cause the demand for Coke to fall.

If the price of a substitute product goes up, demand for the other product increases. For example, if the price of Pepsi goes up, the demand for Coke rises. This also works in the other direction. If the price of Pepsi comes down, the demand for Coke falls. Changes in the prices of complementary products also affect demand. As the price of gas goes up, the demand for car tires goes down. Gas and tires are complementary because the use of one increases the use of the other. This works in reverse, too. If the price of gas falls, people drive more and the demand for tires goes up.

What Happens to Equilibrium If Demand Increases?

When the demand for a product goes up, the equilibrium price and quantity are affected. An *increase in demand* means that consumers are willing to buy more at each price than they would have before the rise in demand. If the supply does not change, price will surely rise. The original quantity supplied no longer satisfies demand at the original price. There is a shortage at the original price. As you have seen, price is pushed up when there is a shortage. But, remember that if price goes up, the quantity supplied goes up also as producers respond to the higher price.

Figure 8-8 will help you see exactly what happens. The supply curve and original demand curve shown in Figure 8-8 are the same as the supply and demand curves used earlier in this chapter. They cross at Point *E* at a price of $3.60 and a quantity of 2,000 units. This is the original equilibrium.

Suppose that demand goes up and consumers now are willing to buy 100 more units of wheat at each price. This is shown by the new, higher demand curve. With this higher demand, consumers want to buy 2,100 units rather than 2,000 units at a price of $3.60 (Point *E*). There will be a shortage of 100 units if the amount supplied does not change. This shortage is represented by the distance between Points *E* and *F*.

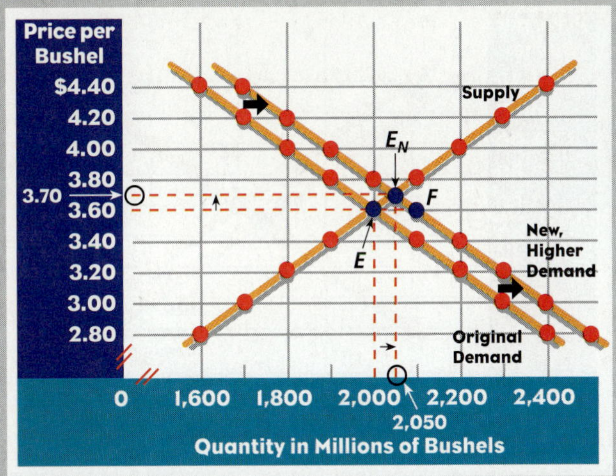

Figure 8-8

Effects of an Increase in Demand

When demand shifts to the right, the equilibrium price and quantity both go up. ***What might cause an increase in the demand for wheat?***

This is not the new equilibrium, however. Remember that when there is a shortage, there is upward pressure on price. As price rises, the quantity supplied goes up as well. A new equilibrium price is reached when the new, higher demand curve crosses the supply curve. This is at Point E_N in the middle of Figure 8-8. The new equilibrium price is $3.70. This is found by following the dashed line to the left from the point where the new, higher demand curve crosses the supply curve.

At a price of $3.70, consumers want to purchase 2,050 units. This is the quantity directly below the intersection of the new, higher demand and supply curves. This quantity demanded is exactly the same as the amount that would be supplied at a price of $3.70.

So, there are two important changes when there is an increase in demand. If demand goes up and the supply curve remains the same, the following occurs:

1. Prices rise.
2. Quantity exchanged rises.

What Happens to Equilibrium If Demand Decreases?

When the demand for a product falls, consumers are willing to buy fewer units at each price. This affects both equilibrium price and equilibrium quantity. With a lower level of demand, there is a surplus if the supply does not change. A surplus puts downward pressure on price. As price falls, the quantity supplied by producers also falls. This process goes on until the quantity supplied and the quantity demanded are once more in balance.

You can use Figure 8-9 on page 196 to see how this happens. The original equilibrium is at a price of $3.60 and a quantity of 2,000 (Point *E*). Demand and supply are in balance. But suppose that demand falls to the level given by the new, lower demand curve. The first effect is a surplus of 100 units at the $3.60 price. Consumers now are willing to buy only

Analyzing *Graphics*

Caption Answer
Answers may include an increase in consumers' incomes, more favorable consumer attitudes, an increase in prices of substitutes, or a decrease in prices of complementary products.

Allow a student to lead the class in a review and discussion of the four factors that can cause a change in overall demand. (Changing consumer incomes, changing consumer attitudes, changing prices of substitute products, and changing prices of complementary products) Support or clarify students' responses.

Display *Overhead Transparency 8-8.* Ask student volunteers to elicit from their classmates in which direction the demand curve moves when demand increases and supply stays the same. (To the right) Have students analyze the graph to determine the two changes that occur when the demand curve shifts to the right and supply stays the same. (Price increases and quantity increases.)

Multicultural *Highlights*

High prices don't seem to affect demand at Neiman Marcus stores. European American Stanley Marcus learned to create demand in his stores by selling fantasy, wishes, dreams, and hopes—and by providing a luxurious shopping experience. The concept of Christmas gift wrapping was pioneered by Neiman Marcus stores as was the first weekly retail-fashion show in the United States.

Today, Neiman Marcus is one of the last holdouts in luxury shopping. Brainstorm with students how the demand for products at Neiman Marcus stores differs from demand in other areas of the marketplace.

Analyzing *Graphics*

Caption Answer
Answers may include a decrease in consumers' incomes, less favorable consumer attitudes, a decrease in prices of substitutes, or an increase in prices of complementary products.

Display *Overhead Transparency 8-9.* Ask students in which direction the demand curve moves when demand decreases and supply stays the same. (To the left) Have students analyze the graph to determine the two changes that occur in the market when the demand curve shifts to the left and supply stays the same. (Price decreases and quantity decreases.)

Ask the class to suggest two reasons supply might change. (Technological changes and changes in input prices)

Figure 8-9

Effects of a Decrease in Demand

When demand shifts to the left, the equilibrium price and quantity both go down. ***What might cause the demand for wheat to decline?***

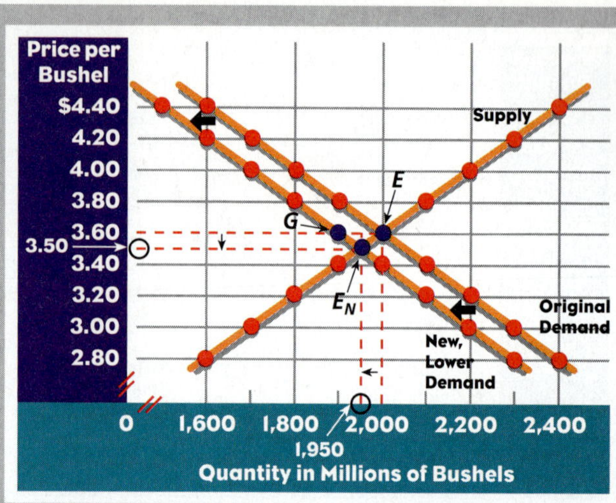

1,900 units, while producers still are supplying 2,000 units. This surplus is shown as the distance between Points *E* and *G* in Figure 8-9.

This surplus results in downward pressure on price. As the price falls, producers cut back on the amount supplied. Price goes on falling, and the amount supplied falls until a new equilibrium is reached. This is at the point where the new, lower demand crosses the supply curve. In Figure 8-9, this is Point E_N.

The price at this new equilibrium is $3.50, and the quantity is 1,950 units. The 1,950 units satisfy consumers at a price of $3.50. Also, suppliers only want to supply 1,950 units at a price of $3.50. The market is once more in balance.

Thus, if demand falls while the supply curve stays the same, the following occurs:

1. Prices fall.
2. Quantity exchanged falls.

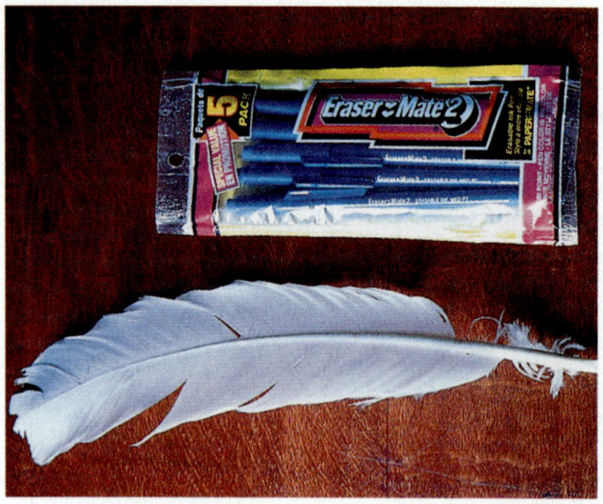

CHANGES IN SUPPLY

A shift of the supply curve also can upset the balance between demand and supply. Remember that the two main causes of a change in supply are a technological change and a change of input prices. If input prices go up, the firm's costs go up. Therefore, the quantity the firm supplies at each price is less. Higher costs result in a decrease in supply. This shifts the supply curve to the left.

Technological changes usually result in a greater supply. Using a more advanced technology increases productivity. As productivity increases, the cost per unit of output goes down. Supply increases as shown by shifting the supply curve to the right.

What Happens to Equilibrium If Supply Increases?

An *increase in supply* means that producers are willing to supply more at each price. If there is an increase in the supply of wheat, the supply curve shifts from the original supply to the new, greater supply, as shown in Figure 8-10. This shift shows that firms supply 100 more units at each price. For example, at the original equilibrium price of $3.60, firms now supply 2,100 units rather than 2,000 units.

At the $3.60 price, there now is a surplus. Producers still supply 2,100 units, but consumers only want to buy 2,000 units. This surplus of 100 units is shown as the distance from *E* to *F*. The existence of the surplus means that there is downward pressure on price.

As the price begins to fall, the amount demanded goes up. This follows from the law of demand. Consumers are willing and able to purchase more at lower prices than at higher prices. As the amount demanded goes up, the surplus is reduced.

At the same time, producers are cutting back on the amount supplied, due to the fall in price. This further helps to lower the amount of the surplus. After all changes, the price has fallen just enough that the quantity demanded and quantity supplied are balanced again.

In the example shown in Figure 8-10, the new equilibrium price is $3.50. At this price, consumers want to buy 2,050 units, as shown by their demand curve. Given the new greater supply, we see that producers want to supply 2,050 units at a price of $3.50. Thus, the quantity demanded and the quantity supplied are once more in balance at Point E_N.

If supply increases while the demand curve remains the same, the following results can be expected:

1. Prices fall.
2. Quantity exchanged rises.

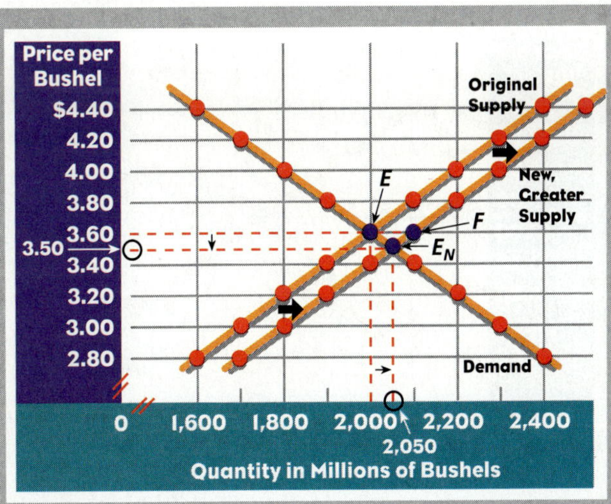

Figure 8-10

Effects of an Increase in Supply

When supply shifts to the right, price falls and the quantity exchanged rises. ***Why might the supply of wheat increase?***

Display *Overhead Transparency 8-10.* Have students tell you in which direction the supply curve moves when supply increases and demand stays the same. (To the right) Then, ask students to analyze the graph to determine the two changes that occur in the market when the supply curve shifts to the right and demand stays the same. (Price decreases and quantity increases.)

Non-native speakers of English may find it easier to conceptualize the information presented in graphs or flowcharts than to explain what is taking place. Assist students by paraphrasing the information in *Figure 8-10* and reinforcing the concepts by using synonyms to expand meaning (decreases: goes down, lowers; increases: goes up, rises; shifts: moves; and quantity: number, amount). Have native speakers of Spanish use the program glossary in *Spanish Resources* to review the definitions of unfamiliar terms. Ask them to make a check mark next to each term as they look up its meaning.

ESL

Analyzing *Graphics*

Caption Answer
Answers may include improvements in technology, better than average weather conditions, or a decrease in the cost of inputs.

Display *Overhead Transparency 8-11.* Ask a student volunteer to show in which direction the supply curve moves when supply decreases and demand stays the same. (To the left) Have the class study the graph to determine the two changes that occur in the market when the supply curve shifts to the left and demand stays the same. Call on individuals to respond and then have class members agree or disagree with the analyses. (Price increases and quantity decreases.)

What Happens to Equilibrium If Supply Decreases?

Supply shifts to the left when the cost of production goes up. This often is caused by a rise in the costs of inputs to the firm. Higher costs for labor, fertilizer, fuel, and machines might combine to cause a reduction in the supply of wheat. This is shown in Figure 8-11 as the shift from the original supply to the new, lower supply. The first effect of this drop in supply is a 100-unit shortage of wheat. At the original equilibrium price of $3.60, consumers want to buy 2,000 units. But now with the reduced supply, producers only want to supply 1,900 units. This 100-unit shortage is shown as the distance from *E* to *G*.

We know that when there is a shortage there is upward pressure on price. As the price rises, consumers reduce the quantity they demand in keeping with the law of demand. This helps to reduce the shortage. As price goes up, producers expand production along the new, lower supply curve. This process goes on until the market is in balance again.

Figure 8-11

Effects of a Decrease in Supply

When supply shifts to the left, prices rise and the quantity exchanged falls. ***What might cause the supply of wheat to fall?***

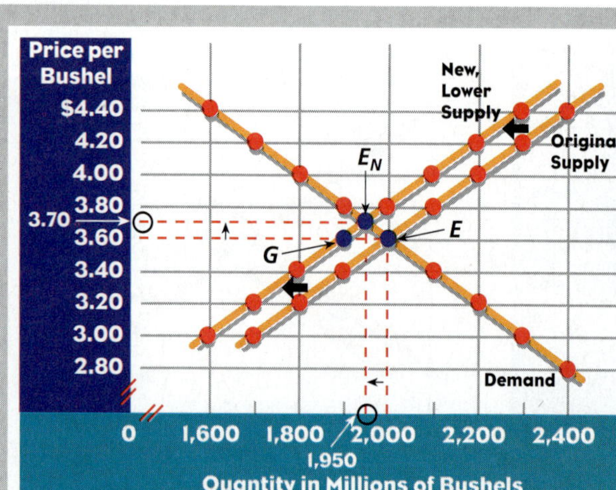

Analyzing *Graphics*

Caption Answer

Answers may include bad weather or an increase in the cost of inputs.

In the case we have shown, the new equilibrium is where the demand curve crosses the new lower supply curve at Point E_N. The price at this level is $3.70. At this new equilibrium price, consumers want to buy 1,950 units. Producers want to supply this same amount at that price. So, at a price of $3.70, the market is in balance. The quantity demanded and the quantity supplied are both 1,950 units.

If demand stays the same and supply decreases, we can expect the following results:

1. Prices go up.
2. Quantity exchanged is less.

Checkpoint

Content Check

1. Prepare a graph of a shortage and describe how the market will work to eliminate the shortage.
2. Prepare a graph of a surplus and describe how the market will work to eliminate the surplus.
3. Complete the following chart by identifying the effects each change in demand and supply will have on equilibrium price and quantity:

	If Only Demand		If Only Supply	
	Increases	Decreases	Increases	Decreases
Price Will:				
Quantity Exchanged Will:				

What Do You Think Now?

Reread *What Do You Think?* in the Section Two Focus. Then answer the following questions:

4. Why is Alonzo worried about making money after such a good harvest? Think about the effect of an increase in supply on the price farmers get for the wheat. Is it possible that a good crop year could mean lower incomes for farmers?

Assess

1. See *Figure 8-6;* upward pressure on price will eliminate the shortage. **8-4**
2. See *Figure 8-7;* downward pressure on price will eliminate the surplus. **8-4**
3. Demand increases: price and quantity increase; demand decreases: price and quantity decrease; supply increases: price decreases, quantity increases; supply decreases: price increases, quantity decreases. **8-5, 8-6**
4. If supply increases, price will decrease, and Alonzo won't make as much money per unit sold, but quantity exchanged will increase, which might make up for the lower price. Answers should reflect an understanding that farmers' incomes will depend on the price elasticity of demand. **8-6**

Close

Distribute one sheet of graph paper and four sheets of tracing paper to each student. To help students understand how demand and supply curves shift, have them plot the information from *Figure 8-5* from their textbook on their graph paper. Using this graph as a base, and assuming that price stays the same, have students use one piece of tracing paper for each of the following shifts in the supply or demand curve: increase in demand (to the right), decrease in demand (to the left), increase in supply (to the right), and decrease in supply (to the left). Have students label their new curves and keep their graphs as a reference to demand and supply curves.

Reteach

Have students illustrate the charts they completed in question 3 of *Checkpoint* by adding arrows to show increases and decreases. For example, in the box listing what happens if demand increases, the answer is *price increases,* so an up arrow (↑) should be placed in that box. Review responses with the group. **8-5, 8-6**

Enrich

Have students use the charts they completed in question 3 of *Checkpoint* as a guide to write equations for each concept. For example, "If supply stays the same but demand increases, price will increase" could be written as follows: **demand ↑ → price ↑**. Have students share their work. **8-5, 8-6**

Focus

As students enter the classroom, tell them that you are going to hold a class auction (either hypothetical or real) of a product or service of your choice that is currently in demand by students. Have them jot down on scrap paper the highest and the lowest price they would be willing to pay for that product or service.

Hold the auction. (You may need to explain that an auction is a public sale where items are sold to the highest bidder.) After the product has been "sold," discuss with students how an auction clearly illustrates the natural forces of supply and demand in action. Then, as a whole class, brainstorm reasons students think the natural forces of supply and demand might need to be controlled sometimes by an outside force such as the government.

FOCUS

Section Three

Governments Impact Market Equilibrium

What Do You Think?

Every so often, political debate in Washington, D.C., turns to the question of whether the mandatory minimum wage should be increased. Some of your representatives and senators suggest raising the minimum wage to help young people earn more money to help with their educational expenses. Would you support an attempt to increase the minimum wage knowing that Congress wants to do so in part to help you earn more at your after-school job?

Terms to Know

price floor

price ceiling

What's Ahead?

Sometimes political forces cause politicians to want to alter the results of the market system in terms of the prices that result. In this section, you will learn how the government may try to hold prices down with a price ceiling. You also will see how the government may try to raise some prices by using a price floor.

THE GOVERNMENT MAY BLOCK THE MARKET SYSTEM

There are times when the government may act to block the market system, thus preventing a balance between the quantity demanded and the quantity supplied. Elected officials may give in to special interest groups who believe the market price is either too high or too low. The following are just a few examples of how the government may prevent a balance between the quantity demanded and the quantity supplied. There are many other examples in our economy:

- The government may allow only a certain amount of imported steel to enter the economy. This cuts down on supply and, as you have seen, results in a higher steel price.
- The government may buy grain products. This increases the demand and results in a higher price.

- The government may set rent controls to keep apartment rents below the market level.
- The government may set a minimum wage to keep wages higher than they would be otherwise.

Programs that block the market often can be evaluated using demand and supply concepts. Looking at two types of government actions will illustrate how such programs can be analyzed. First, you will see how a price floor may be used to keep prices higher than the market system would allow. Then, you will see how a price ceiling can keep price down.

A Price Floor

A ***price floor*** is a minimum price set by government that is *above* the market equilibrium price. In our example, if there is no interference with the wheat market, an equilibrium price of $3.60 results. But, what if wheat farmers convince the government that $3.60 is too low a price? The farmers and government might agree that $4.00 per bushel is a better price (at least for some wheat growers). If the government decided that no wheat will be sold below that price, the $4.00 becomes a price floor. A price floor is illustrated in Figure 8-12.

price floor
a minimum price set by government that is *above* the market equilibrium price

Why do we use the term price floor? If you were on the second floor of a building and dropped your pencil, where would it stop? On the floor. The floor would keep your pencil from falling farther. Similarly, a price floor keeps price from falling below a certain level. To be effective, a price floor must be above the equilibrium price. If a price floor were lower than equilibrium price, it would not be useful. Such a price floor would already be below the natural market price.

If the government said that there would be a price floor of $4 per bushel of wheat, how would the amount supplied compare to the amount demanded? From Figure 8-12, you see that the amount supplied would be 2,200 units.

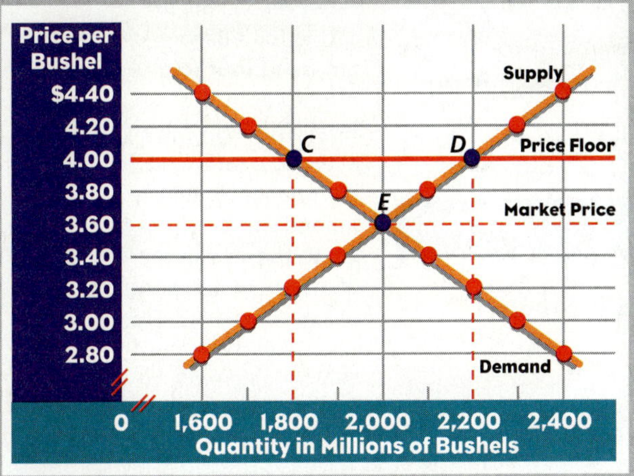

Figure 8-12

A Price Floor Is Set Above Equilibrium

A price floor at $4.00 prevents the market from balancing the quantity demanded and the quantity supplied at $3.60. A surplus results, consumers pay a higher price, and they buy less. ***As a producer how would you feel about this price floor?***

Teach

Ask students to summarize in one sentence what they experienced in the *Focus* auction concerning the natural forces of supply and demand and the reasons for controlling these forces. Relate these reasons to those listed in the textbook for why government may block the market system. Make sure students understand the definitions and uses of **price floor** and **price ceiling.** Point out that, to be effective, price floors must be set *above* the equilibrium price and price ceilings *below* the equilibrium price.

Apply

Distribute graph paper to students. Have each student copy the graph in *Figure 8-12,* illustrating a price floor. Then, instruct them to shade the area above the market price with a pencil and label this area **Surplus Product.** Have them use colored pencils or markers to shade or color the area above the market price and between the demand and supply curves to show how surplus product increases as price rises. Tell students to save this graph to use with *Figure 8-13.*
Guided Practice

Analyzing Graphics

Caption Answer
Answers may include that producers probably would like a price floor because it keeps price up, but the surplus would create long-term problems.

Perspectives

Thinking Like a Producer Tell pairs of students to imagine that they are U.S. wheat farmers and to brainstorm a list of the ways a government floor on the price of wheat could benefit them. Then, have them list how a price floor could hurt consumers. After the lists have been made, have students create a chart that summarizes their information. As a class, discuss students' responses for different costs and benefits and then summarize them in a master chart on the chalkboard or an overhead transparency.

Draw the following graphic organizer on the chalkboard or an overhead transparency to help students understand the difference between price floors and price ceilings:

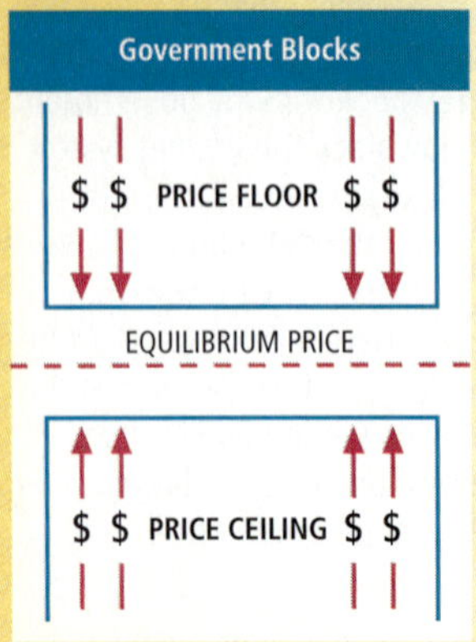

This illustration may be of particular help to students who are having difficulty grasping the idea of a price floor being above the equilibrium price and a price ceiling being below the equilibrium price.

Econ & You

RATIONING CONCERT TICKETS

How much would you pay for a ticket to see a concert by your favorite band? Ticket prices for concerts vary depending on the performer and the number of seats available for each show. The primary determinant of ticket prices is the interaction between supply and demand. In many cases, the supply of tickets is limited by the capacity of the facility in which the concert is to be held. Thus, the supply can be represented as a vertical line at the number of seats available. In the following graph, this supply curve is labeled *Capacity Quantity.*

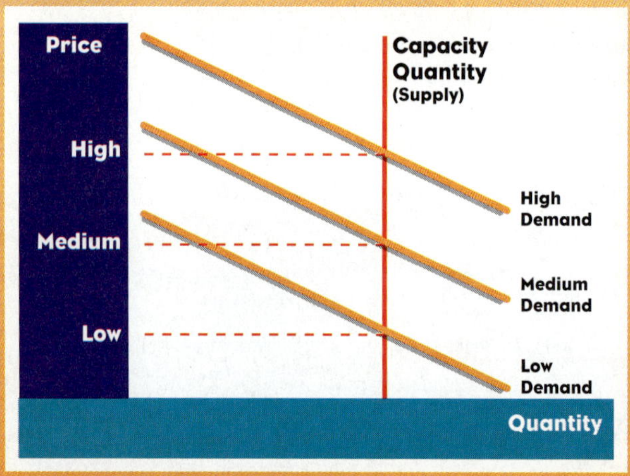

The Supply and Demand of Concert Tickets

The demand depends on the popularity of performers. For some performers in some areas, the demand is relatively low. This would be true for a band that is just starting and is not widely recognized. For some, the demand might be very high and for others there might be a mid-level demand. These possibilities are represented by the three demand curves in the graph. When demand is low and supply is at capacity quantity, you can see that price is low. At the medium demand, you see that price is somewhat higher. Finally, when demand is high the price is high as well.

Suppose a very popular singer is going to appear in your area and tickets are priced at $300. Will you go? It depends on your willingness and ability to pay that high a price. This price will block some people from even thinking about attending such a concert. However, tickets to shows for a Barbra Streisand tour sold out at about this level. The high price acted as a rationing device to allocate the limited supply of tickets to those with the ability and willingness to pay that much. Do you think this is fair? Why or why not?

Econ & You

Have students work in small groups to create a hypothetical "Capacity Supply and Demand Graph" similar to the one shown in *Econ & You*. Each group's graph should apply to a favorite singer or band performing at a local facility. After all groups have created their graphs, have volunteers present them to the class. Discuss whether students agree with the capacity quantity and the level of demand shown in each graph. Point out that, although the capacity of each facility actually sets the supply, promoters choose the facility carefully to try to match the demand.

But, the amount demanded at $4 is 1,800 units. The quantity supplied would be greater than the quantity demanded by 400 units. This 400-unit surplus is shown as the distance from *C* to *D* in Figure 8-12.

In a free market, you know that when there is a surplus, price is pushed down. The amount demanded increases, and the amount supplied decreases. This continues until price falls enough so that the quantity demanded and the quantity supplied are balanced. But, with a price floor, such a free market adjustment is blocked. The market is kept from working.

We are left with an unbalanced market situation. The quantity supplied is greater than the quantity demanded at the government's set price. Producers produce more than consumers buy. What happens to the extra production? The government must either buy up the surplus or keep producers from producing so much. To cut down on production, firms must be kept from producing more than the government wants them to by some type of penalty. When the government buys the surplus, it is really we who buy it since our tax dollars are used for the purchase. Taxpayers often pay to store the surplus as well.

Look at the result of the price floor for consumers. At the free market equilibrium, price is $3.60, and consumers purchase 2,000 units. With the price floor at $4.00, consumers purchase less (1,800 units) but pay a higher price ($4.00).

A Price Ceiling

A ***price ceiling*** is a maximum price set by government that is *below* the market equilibrium price. A price ceiling is the opposite of a price floor. It keeps the price from going above some upper limit. If you threw your pencil up in the air as hard as you could, it would hit the ceiling. The pencil would not go any higher because the ceiling would limit how high it could go. A price ceiling keeps price down to the level the government thinks is right. To be effective, a price ceiling must be below the equilibrium price. If it were above the equilibrium price, the natural market price would already be below the ceiling.

price ceiling
a maximum price set by government that is *below* the market equilibrium price

Suppose the government thought that wheat producers were making too much money at the expense of consumers. The government might set a ceiling price of $3.20 per bushel. This is shown by the horizontal line at $3.20 in Figure 8-13.

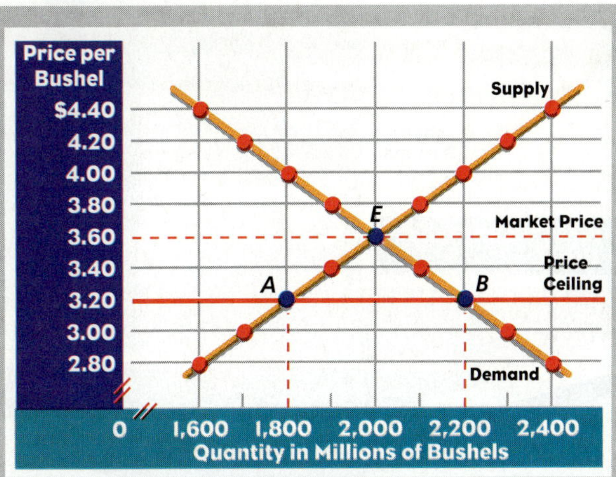

Figure 8-13

A Price Ceiling Is Set Below Equilibrium

A price ceiling at $3.20 blocks the market from working and balancing the quantity demanded and the quantity supplied at a price of $3.60. A shortage results. Consumers pay less but cannot purchase as much as they want at that lower price. ***As a consumer how would you feel about this price ceiling?***

Tell students to add to the graphs they created for *Figure 8-12* the price ceiling shown in *Figure 8-13*. Then, ask them to shade the area below the market price with a pencil and label it **Product Shortage.** Have students use colored pencils or markers to shade the area below the market price and between the demand and supply curves to show how product shortage increases as price decreases. Finally, have students compare the shading on these new graphs with the shading on the graphs they completed in the *Independent Practice* in the second section of this chapter. Have them brainstorm how the shaded or colored areas on both graphs relate to one another and ask them to share their thoughts with the class. (Price floors create surpluses; price ceilings create shortages.) Correct any misconceptions.

Independent Practice

Analyzing *Graphics*

Caption Answer
Answers may include that consumers probably would like a price ceiling because it keeps price down, but shortages could create problems.

MediaLink

Have students use an online information service or direct Internet access to contact an economics forum, bulletin board, RoundTable, or access system (such as the congressional online service *THOMAS,* named after Thomas Jefferson—electronic address: **http://thomas.loc.gov**). Have students search for legislation or other issues dealing with price ceilings, price floors, surpluses, or shortages. Discuss with students how easy access to this previously guarded information empowers U.S. citizens by giving *everyone,* not just high-powered lobbyists, the power to be a government watchdog.

To illustrate to students the concepts of price floor and price ceiling, bounce a Ping-Pong ball or small, rubber ball on the floor. Ask students what stopped the ball and sent it bouncing back up. (The floor) Tell students that, like a ball, falling prices are stopped by a price floor, which keeps them from falling below a minimum level. Next, bounce the ball off the ceiling. Ask students what stopped the ball from bouncing higher. (The ceiling) Discuss with the class that a price ceiling stops prices from going above a maximum level.

Economic Dilemma

THE MINIMUM WAGE PRICE FLOOR

The minimum wage was first instituted in the United States in 1938 when it was $0.25 per hour. Since that time, it has been increased from time to time and always with considerable public debate. At the start of 1995, about 2.5 million Americans were earning the minimum wage. Would raising the minimum wage help the poor of the country? That is the issue of much of the political debate.

The minimum wage is an example of a price floor, where the wage is the price paid for labor services. The effects of a minimum wage can be seen with the help of the following supply and demand diagram.

Market equilibrium is shown at the intersection of the Labor Supply and Labor Demand curves. Market Wage is the equilibrium price, and *L*2 is the equilibrium amount of labor. Raising the minimum wage clearly reduces the amount of labor hired (employment). The decrease is shown as the drop from *L*2 to *L*1 in the diagram. David Neumark of Michigan State University has found evidence that there may be a 1 to 2 percent drop in employment for every 10 percent increase in the minimum wage. The job losses hit the hardest among the already poor—low-skilled workers, teenagers, and welfare mothers. These are all groups that supporters of minimum wages talk about wanting to support. Yet, economics would suggest that raising the minimum wage may have an effect that is the opposite of what is intended. The debate goes on.

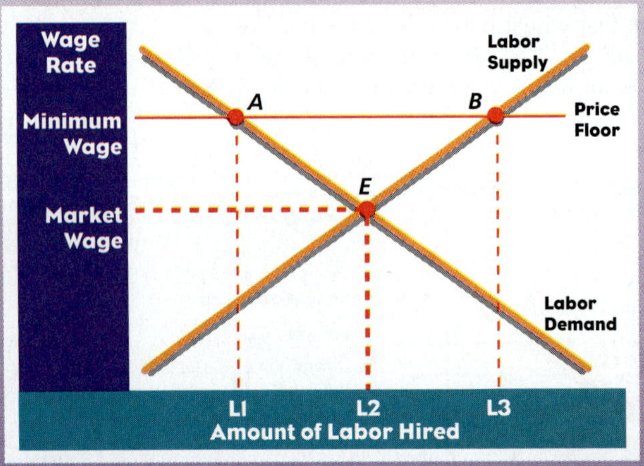

Minimum Wage

Economic Dilemma

Divide the class into two groups: students who agree with having a government-set minimum wage and those who disagree. Ask students to think about how they might be affected by a minimum wage now, as employees, and possibly in the future, as business owners. Allow the groups time to research the topic outside of class and then have the groups debate whether there should be a minimum wage. Be sure to allow time for every student to state his or her case.

At a price of \$3.20, consumers want to buy 2,200 units. Producers, on the other hand, are willing to supply only 1,800 units. A 400-unit shortage results. This is shown as the distance from *A* to *B* in Figure 8-13. You have seen that a shortage normally results in upward pressure on price. In a free market, price rises. The amount supplied increases, and the amount demanded decreases. When the price rises to \$3.60, there is no shortage. The quantity demanded and the quantity supplied balance at that price.

But, this cannot happen if there is a price ceiling. If the \$3.20 price is enforced, the quantity supplied is less than the quantity demanded. The government would have to find a different way to allocate the 1,800 units among consumers who want to buy 2,200 units at that price. Ration coupons are sometimes used in cases like this. However, a large system of people

Global Economy

WHAT'S A DOLLAR WORTH?

The U.S. economy is only one part of the global economy, but it is a very important and influential part. Evidence of this is seen in the market for U.S. dollars. Fluctuations in the value of the U.S. dollar make headlines in newspapers around the world. This is because the dollar is the dominant world currency. What determines the value of the dollar in the worldwide money market?

The value of the dollar compared to other currencies is determined by supply and demand conditions in the global economy. An increase in the demand for dollars raises the value of the dollar, while decreases in demand lower its value.

A weak dollar is a dollar with a low exchange value. Because the U.S. dollar is used around the world, its value affects not only the U.S. economy but the economies of other countries. After one period in which the value of the dollar had fallen, *The Wall Street Journal* reported that, "The Dow Jones Industrial Average dropped 3.7% and Japan's Nikkei stock index fell 3.4%. Stocks fell 4.8% in Britain, 2.2% in Germany and 1.5% in France. Global bond markets also sustained losses, pushing up long term interest rates in the U.S. and abroad." ("The Unloved Buck." *The Wall Street Journal* (June 27, 1994): A1, A8.)

Such events can have widespread effects. Here are three examples:

- An increase in interest rates can slow economic growth in all the major economies of the world.
- A lower value for the dollar increases the cost of items that we import which can cause inflationary pressure in the U.S. economy.
- A weaker dollar may have a positive effect on our balance of payments and unemployment rate because it shifts consumer demand more to goods produced in the United States and away from goods that we import from abroad.

Global Economy

Divide the class into three groups. Assign each group one of the three examples listed in *Global Economy* concerning how the U.S. economy affects the global economy. If necessary, allow each group time to research its assigned global effect and illustrate the concept by creating a flowchart or a political cartoon.

Have students work in groups of three or four for a portion of one class period to develop a visual representation of price floor, price ceiling, and equilibrium. (Tell students to select an example other than the bouncing ball from the previous activity.) In each group, one student should be responsible for illustrating price floor, another for price ceiling, and another for equilibrium price. (If there is a fourth student in a group, he or she should demonstrate the group's concepts to the rest of the class.) Have each group select a spokesperson, rehearse the group's description, and present its three concepts to the class. **Cooperative Learning** usually is needed to issue and keep track of the use of the coupons. This can be very costly. It is sometimes possible for the government to produce enough of the product to make up for the shortage. However, this also costs taxpayers money. Finally, the government can set the price ceiling and let the consumers and producers deal with the shortage problem. In this case, many illegal nonmarket transactions are likely to take place. Those consumers who can afford to pay more will offer secret payments to suppliers to get the product.

Checkpoint

Content Check

1. Using Figure 8-12 as a guide, draw a graph of a price floor at $4.20. Identify the quantity supplied, the quantity demanded, and the amount of surplus. Explain the effects on consumers of a price floor of $4.20.
2. Using Figure 8-13 as a guide, draw a graph of a price ceiling at $3. Identify the quantity supplied, the quantity demanded, and the amount of surplus. Explain the effects of a price ceiling of $3 on consumers.

What Do You Think Now?

Reread *What Do You Think?* in the Section Three Focus. Then answer the following questions:

3. Is the minimum wage an example of a price floor or a price ceiling?
4. Consider the effect of the minimum wage on wages and employment. Would you support an attempt to increase the minimum wage knowing that Congress wants to do so in part to help you earn more at your after-school job?

Assess

1. Students' curves should identify the quantity supplied as 2,300; quantity demanded: 1,700; and amount of surplus: 600. Explanations should include that, if free market adjustment is blocked, consumers will purchase less at a higher price because no downward pressure on price is allowed. **8-7**
2. Students' curves should identify the quantity supplied as 1,700; quantity demanded: 2,300; and amount of shortage: 600. Explanations should include that, if free market adjustment is blocked, there will be a continued shortage because upward pressure on price is not allowed. **8-7**
3. Price floor **8-7**
4. Students should consider that a price floor will result in fewer people being hired. **8-7**

Close

Divide the class into small groups of four or five students. Have each group write a scenario that involves the use of a price ceiling or a price floor. Tell students not to state whether their scenarios describe a price ceiling or price floor. Then, have a volunteer from each group read its scenario to the class. Have the class brainstorm which concept the scenario describes and then discuss whether the scenario made its point effectively.

Reteach

Have partners work together writing a brief scenario of price floors and price ceilings on the front of each of five index cards. Have students identify each as a price floor or price ceiling on the back and exchange cards with another set of partners. Students should then identify the scenarios and verify their responses on the backs of the cards. **8-7**

Enrich

Have student pairs brainstorm a list of possible consequences of either a long-term shortage caused by a price ceiling or a long-term surplus caused by a price floor. Then, have each student choose one consequence and write a short essay explaining the problem and how to solve it. **8-7**

Concepts in Brief

1. In a free market economy, individuals make the decisions that guide the direction of the economy. Demand and supply are the key factors involved in the working of a market economy. When the market is in balance, the quantity supplied equals the quantity demanded. This balance is called *equilibrium*. The price at which this balance is reached is called the *equilibrium price*. In a graph, the equilibrium is determined where the demand curve crosses the supply curve.

2. Price acts as a rationing mechanism in a market economy. If there is a surplus because the quantity supplied is greater than the quantity demanded, there will be natural downward pressure on price. This pressure decreases the quantity supplied and increases the quantity demanded. The eventual result is the elimination of the surplus.

3. This rationing role of price also acts to eliminate a shortage. A shortage exists when the quantity demanded is greater than the quantity supplied. When this is true, natural economic forces put upward pressure on price. This pressure decreases the quantity demanded and increases the quantity supplied. The shortage is eventually eliminated.

4. Changes in demand affect market equilibrium. If demand increases while supply stays the same, price rises as does the quantity bought and sold. If demand decreases while supply stays the same, price falls, as does the quantity bought and sold.

5. Changes in supply affect market equilibrium. If supply increases while demand stays the same, price falls, but the quantity bought and sold increases. If supply decreases while demand stays the same, price rises and the quantity bought and sold decreases.

6. For various reasons, the government may block the functioning of the market system with a price floor or a price ceiling. A price floor is set above the equilibrium price and keeps price from reaching equilibrium. A surplus results from a price floor. This causes other problems for government to handle.

7. A price ceiling is the opposite of a price floor. A price ceiling is set below the market price to keep price from rising. This results in a shortage of the product. Illegal nonmarket transactions are likely to result, and the government must find some nonprice mechanism for allocating the limited product.

Chapter Close

Your Economic Portfolio

As a class, ask students whether they believe that market forces should always control prices naturally, that the government should regulate prices, or that a mixture of both should be allowed. Have each student write three paragraphs defending his or her choice. In the first paragraph, have students explain their choices. In the second, have them defend their choices. And, in the third, have them describe historic examples of how their ways of controlling the economy were implemented effectively. Review students' work and correct any misconceptions before filing their paragraphs in their portfolios.

You may wish to provide the following end-of-chapter materials:

- *Skills & Concepts* worksheet
- *Content Review Workbook*
- Chapter *Assessment*
- Chapter *MicroExam*

Economic Foundations

1. When a market is in equilibrium, what is the relationship between the quantities supplied and demanded?
2. What happens to price and the quantities supplied and demanded when there is a shortage?
3. What happens to price and the quantities supplied and demanded when there is a surplus?
4. If demand increases, what is the effect on equilibrium price and quantity?
5. If demand decreases, what is the effect on equilibrium price and quantity?
6. If supply increases, what is the effect on equilibrium price and quantity?
7. If supply decreases, what is the effect on equilibrium price and quantity?
8. When government sets a price floor, what is the effect on the market? on consumers? on taxpayers?
9. When government sets a price ceiling, what is the effect on the market? on consumers? on taxpayers?

Your Economic Vocabulary

Build your economic vocabulary by matching the following terms with their definitions.

equilibrium price
equilibrium quantity
price ceiling
price floor
shortage
surplus

1. a maximum price set by government that is *below* the market equilibrium price
2. the price at which the quantity demanded equals the quantity supplied
3. the condition in which the quantity demanded is greater than the quantity supplied at a certain price
4. a minimum price set by government that is *above* the market equilibrium price
5. the condition in which the quantity supplied is greater than the quantity demanded at a certain price
6. the quantity that is both demanded and supplied at the equilibrium price

Economic Foundations

1. When a market is in equilibrium, the quantity supplied equals the quantity demanded. (pp. 186-187)
2. When a shortage occurs, the quantity demanded is greater than the quantity supplied and there is upward pressure on price. (p. 191)
3. When a surplus occurs, the quantity supplied is greater than the quantity demanded and there is downward pressure on price. (p. 193)
4. If demand increases, equilibrium price and quantity both rise. (pp. 194-195)
5. If demand decreases, equilibrium price and quantity both fall. (pp. 195-196)
6. If supply increases, the equilibrium price falls and the equilibrium quantity rises. (p. 197)
7. If supply decreases, equilibrium price rises and the equilibrium quantity falls. (p. 198)
8. When government sets a price floor, a surplus results in the market, consumers buy less because of higher prices, and taxpayers often pay the price of buying and storing the surplus. (p. 201)
9. When government sets a price ceiling, a shortage results in the market, consumers pay less but cannot buy all they want, and taxpayers pay the price for whatever action government takes to deal with the shortage. (p. 203)

Your Economic Vocabulary

1. **price ceiling**
2. **equilibrium price**
3. **shortage**
4. **price floor**
5. **surplus**
6. **equilibrium quantity**

Thinking Critically About Economics

1. An arrangement of economic units in which exchanges take place freely between units with a minimum of governmental control. The free interplay of the forces of demand and supply determines the prices of goods and services in such a market system.
2. A market reaches equilibrium when demand and supply are in balance. There is then no tendency for a change in that market. Consumers can buy all they want and producers can sell all they produce.

(Continued)

Thinking Critically About Economics

1. What is meant by the concept of a market system? What roles do demand and supply play in such a system?
2. "When the quantity demanded and the quantity supplied are in balance, the market is in equilibrium." Explain what this statement means.
3. Suppose that there is a news report of a shortage of gasoline. What does this mean? If the market system were left alone, how would this shortage be eliminated?
4. If growing conditions were ideal in the next crop season, a surplus of wheat might be produced. What does the phrase *surplus of wheat* mean in this context? How would a market system reduce or eliminate this surplus?
5. Some years ago, there was a "cranberry scare" in the United States. In the fall of the year, there were widespread stories that cranberries had been contaminated by a cancer-causing chemical. This affected consumers' attitudes and reduced the demand for cranberries. Use your knowledge of supply and demand to analyze this situation. What probably happened to price? What probably happened to the quantity sold that holiday season? Use a graph to help explain your answer. (You may assume that supply did not change.)
6. The wage rate is the price that is paid per labor hour for the use of a person's labor skills. A minimum wage enacted by government is then a type of price floor. Explain how the minimum wage affects the labor market. Begin by drawing a graph of the demand and supply of labor. Assume that demand will have a negative slope and supply will have a positive slope.
7. Rent controls are often suggested as a method for keeping housing costs down. Explain how this type of price ceiling affects the rental housing market.
8. Pick some product or service that you buy on a regular basis and explain how the concepts of demand and supply relate to that product. Can you identify any changes in demand and/or supply that have influenced the price and the quantity people consume?

3. A report of a shortage of gasoline would suggest that the quantity of gasoline demanded is greater than the quantity being supplied. If the market system were left alone, prices would rise until these two quantities became equal.
4. The phrase *surplus of wheat* means that more wheat is produced than people are willing to buy. In a market system, such a surplus would lead to price cuts, as producers tried to reduce inventories. As prices fell, consumers would increase the quantity demanded. This process would continue until the quantity demanded and the quantity supplied became equal.
5. Consumers' preferences for cranberries were reduced, resulting in a downward shift of

(Continued)

Thinking Critically About Economics (Continued)

demand. This probably resulted in both a lower price and fewer cranberries being bought and sold.

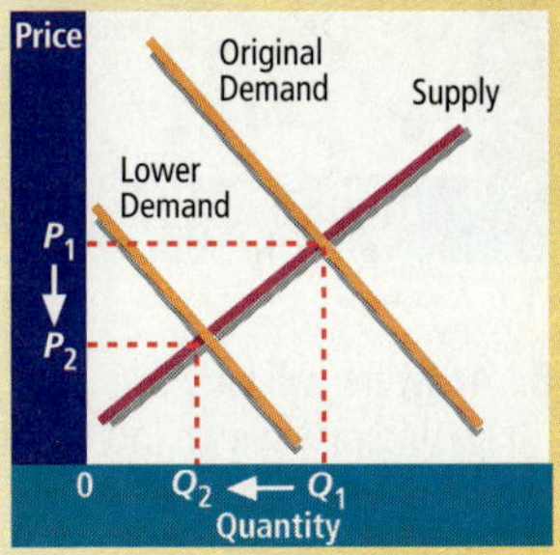

6. The minimum wage is an artificial level below which wages may not legally fall. In the graph that follows, without minimum wage laws, the wage would be at W_1, and L_1 hours of labor would be hired. With higher minimum wages, only L_M hours of labor would be hired. Thus, although some workers would be paid more, fewer hours of labor would be hired than without the minimum wage.

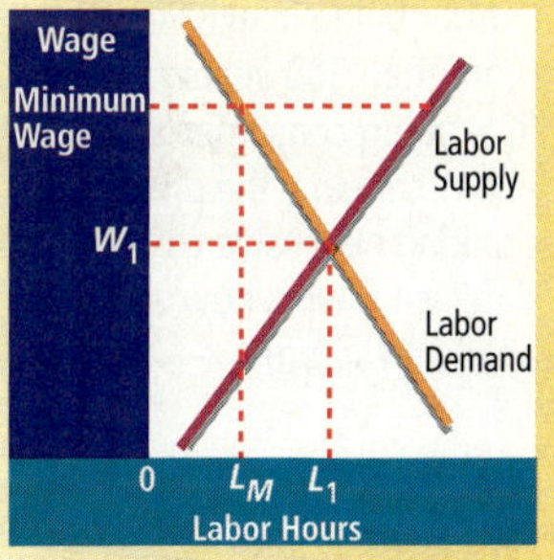

7. In the graph that follows on p. 210, without controls, rent would settle at R_1, with H_1 units of housing made available and rented. With rent controls, the rent would be held below the market level at R_C, where H_D units would be demanded; however, only H_S units would be made available. A shortage would result.

(Continued)

Economic Enrichment

Coffee houses may seem new to some people because of the boom in this business over the last decade. However, coffee houses probably first appeared in the seventeenth century. There is evidence of coffee houses in Italy at that time, and the first U.S. coffee house was the London Coffee House in Boston which opened in 1689. Today, there are more than 4,500 coffee houses and the number is growing rapidly with expectations there will be close to 10,000 by the year 2000. What do you think might be some of the supply and demand changes that are affecting this market?

Math and Economics

Grace Hopkins works at a local grocery store after school and on weekends. She currently works 20 hours a week and earns minimum wage. She is excited because she has heard that Congress plans to pass an increase of $0.50 per hour in the minimum wage. If Grace continues to work 20 hours a week, how much will her earnings go up? (Do not consider taxes in your calculations.) Suppose that due to the higher wage, the store reduces the number of work hours for each employee by 15 percent. What would be the net effect on Grace's earnings considering the lost hours and the higher wage?

Writing About Economics

General Motors, Ford, Chrysler, and Honda are among the car companies that have offered special finance rates and/or rebates on selected vehicles in recent years. Look for three current print advertisements for special financing rates or rebates on cars. Cut these out or make photocopies. Prepare a booklet that includes the advertisements, an explanation of why the car makers would make these offers, and an explanation of how you think the makers decide on the cars that will receive such incentives. Prepare a cover for your booklet that is illustrated and includes a title that reflects the content.

Thinking Critically About Economics (Continued)

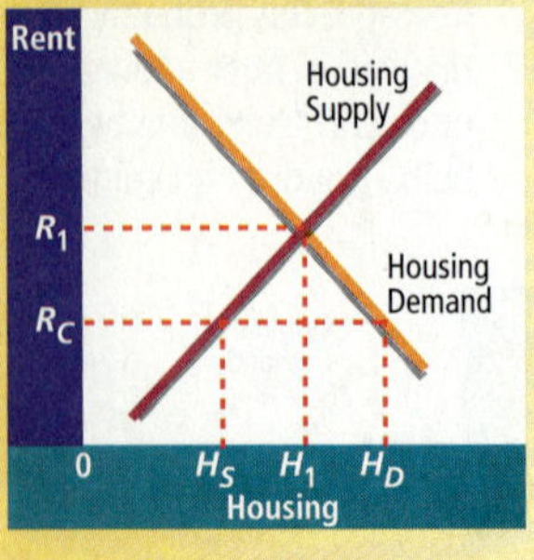

8. Answers will vary but should provide an interesting basis for a class discussion about changes in supply and demand in the marketplace.

Economic Enrichment

Answers will vary, but students should analyze projections for the future of the coffee market and describe in detail what they think will happen to the supply of coffee if the demand more than doubles in the course of a few years. As a class, you may wish to discuss why the coffee market now is expanding so rapidly after being in existence for more than 300 years. (Changing consumer attitudes about caffeine, the prestige of drinking expensive coffees, different flavors now available, and so on)

Math and Economics

Answers may vary according to the current U.S. minimum wage. Using an example wage of $4.75 per hour, students' answers should be as follows: Grace's earnings would increase by $10 (20 x $4.75 = $95.00, 20 x $5.25 = $105.00, $105 - $95 = $10). If the minimum wage were to increase and the store decreased Grace's hours by 15 percent, Grace would lose

(Continued)

Math and Economics (Continued)

$15.75 in potential earnings; what's worse, Grace would make $5.75 less per week than she made at her old, lower wage (20 x 0.15 = 3, 3 x $5.25 = $15.75, $105.00 - $15.75 = $89.25, $95.00 - $89.25 = $5.75).

Writing About Economics

Students' booklets will vary but should include an explanation that the car makers would offer special finance rates and rebates on some cars for a number of reasons, including the following: to improve lagging sales of specific models, to decrease a large inventory before they have to pay taxes on it, and to entice buyers to try a particular make or model of a car for the first time. Students also should explain that car makers are unlikely to make these types of deals on cars that are already selling well at a higher price.

Price Determination—The Equilibrium of Demand and Supply

Analyzing Primary Source Documents

Alfred Marshall (1842–1924) was a highly influential teacher of economics at both Oxford and Cambridge universities in England. He received acclaim with the publication of *Principles of Economics* in 1890. Prior to the publication of this book, some economists believed that price was determined by the cost of producing goods. These economists focused on the supply side of markets. Other economists thought that price was dependent on the usefulness of the goods. This approach focused only on demand. Marshall argued that price was determined by both cost (supply) and utility (demand).

In explaining this relationship between cost of production and utility (or supply and demand), Marshall compared the situation to a pair of scissors. In *Principles of Economics,* he wrote,

> We might as reasonably dispute whether it is the upper or the under blade of a pair of scissors that cuts a piece of paper, as whether value is governed by utility or cost of production. It is true that when one blade is held still, and the cutting is effected by moving the other, we may say with careless brevity that the cutting is done by the second; but the statement is not strictly accurate and is to be excused only so long as it claims to be merely a popular and not a strictly scientific account of what happens.

The accompanying figure illustrates the analogy Marshall was using. Supply can be thought of as one blade of a scissors and demand as the other blade. You need both blades of a scissors to effectively cut a piece of paper. Likewise, you need both supply and demand to determine prices in a market economy. In Marshall's time, this theory suggested a new way of looking at price. Today, the relationship between supply and demand as described by Marshall is at the core of many important economic concepts.

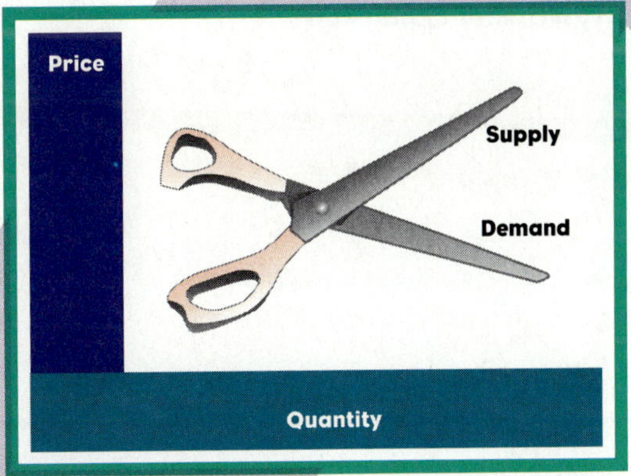

SOURCE: Marshall, Alfred, *Principles of Economics,* 8th ed. (New York: Macmillan, 1920), 348.

After students have read the feature article on this page, use a pair of scissors to demonstrate how one blade cannot work alone to cut. Challenge student volunteers to try to cut a sheet of paper without using both blades of the scissors. As a class, brainstorm other analogies that show how supply and demand work together. (Answers may include pen and ink and CPU and computer monitor.) Then, divide students into pairs and have them brainstorm tangible analogies for other economic concepts in Part 2. Tell students to think of ideas that will help them and their classmates understand and remember the concepts more clearly. Encourage students to think of creative and humorous comparisons that are easy to retain. Then, have each pair demonstrate its analogy to the class and explain its relevance to a particular concept in economics. (Students could use margarine to illustrate the concept of marginal product, a rubber band to show elasticity, or oil and vinegar to show a relationship similar to that between price ceiling and price floor.) You may wish to photograph each demonstration for a bulletin board or videotape each demonstration to show to other economics classes. Have students vote for the most effective demonstration if more than one pair demonstrates an analogy for the same economic concept.

Chapter 9
Business Firms in the Economy

Chapter Theme

The three main forms of business organization are discussed in this chapter. Topics include size, number of firms, sales, forms of financing, and mergers. Nonprofits, multinationals, and franchises are introduced.

Section	Special Features
Proprietorships, Partnerships, and Corporations	Economics & Your Community Economic Spotlight Perspectives: Thinking Like a Lawyer
U.S. Businesses: A Closer Look	Multicultural Highlights Media Link Economic Dilemma
Business Growth and Expansion	Global Economy Econ & You Eye on Market News Economic Talk Internet Connection

Video Activity

Chapter 9, Indies vs. Giants

Search Chapter 9, Play to 10

Elicit from students the possible long-range effects of giant corporations that continually outcompete small businesses in the marketplace. Discuss who will suffer or gain the most from this trend and why. Ask students what they think small businesses could do to compete more successfully with these giants.

	Print Resources	Media Resources	Assessment
	Effective Teaching Model Lesson Plans *Skills & Concepts* worksheet *Problem Solving* worksheet *Casebook* *Economic Measurement Workbook* *Content Review Workbook* *Spanish Resources*	VHS CD-ROM Videodisc *Arctic Express* *Interactive* ECONOMICS Template software	*Your Economic Portfolio* Chapter *Assessment* Chapter *MicroExam*

Special Learners	Print Resources	Media Resources	Assessment
Kinesthetic Activity Auditory Activity	*Reteach* worksheet	Overhead Computer Camcorder	*Checkpoint* Section 1 Quiz
Dysphasia	*Enrich* worksheet	Overhead and *Transparencies 9-1* to *9-4* *Computer*	*Checkpoint* Section 2 Quiz
Visual Activity Cooperative Learning Activity	*Teacher's Connection to the Internet* *Life Skills* worksheet	Overhead Computer VCR Camcorder Audio	*Checkpoint* Section 3 Quiz

Careers Activity

Businesses of all types often find that the best way to keep their finances in order is through the services of a budget analyst. Budget analysts are responsible for continually evaluating a business's procedures and expenditures and providing financial advice on how to operate within a set budget.

Future budget analysts should develop good math skills and obtain a bachelor's degree in accounting. A master's degree and CPA certification are even more advantageous. Beginning budget analysts can earn from $25,000 to $35,000 per year. With more experience, they may earn $90,000 or more annually.

Have students imagine that they are budget analysts working for a small furniture company known for its hand-designed, fine wood chairs. Have students explain in writing why or why not the company should start using a less expensive wood blend and cutting out its chair frames by machine to save costs.

CHAPTER 9

Teaching Materials

Program Resources

- Student text
- *Effective Teaching Model Lesson Plans*
- *Overhead Transparencies 9-1* to *9-4*
- *Life Skills* worksheet
- *Problem Solving* worksheet
- *Reteach* worksheet
- *Enrich* worksheet
- *Skills & Concepts* worksheet
- *Casebook*
- *Economic Measurement Workbook*
- *Content Review Workbook*
- *Spanish Resources*
- Video package
- *Teacher's Connection to the Internet*
- *Arctic Express*
- *Interactive* ECONOMICS
- Template software

Assessment

- Section Quizzes
- Chapter *Assessment*
- Chapter *MicroExam*

Overview

Section One
Proprietorships, Partnerships, and Corporations

Section Two
U.S. Businesses: A Closer Look

Section Three
Business Growth and Expansion

Teacher to Teacher

Before class, clip from newspapers or magazines advertisements for several different businesses. (Be sure all three types of business organization are represented.) Distribute one clipping to each student and discuss as a class the similarities and differences among these businesses. Students probably will point out that some businesses are large and some are small. Build upon this idea, pointing out that most very large companies are corporations and many small businesses are proprietorships or partnerships. Tell students size isn't the only differentiating factor, however. Go on to give a brief overview of the three forms of organization and ask students to volunteer more examples of each.

Laurence H. Jaffe
Rutgers University
New Brunswick, NJ

Business Firms in the Economy

Learning Objectives

9-1
Compare the advantages and disadvantages of proprietorships, partnerships, and corporations.

9-2
Explain why private organizations must pass the test of the market in a market economy.

9-3
Describe the relative importance of the three forms of business organizations in the U.S. economy.

9-4
Distinguish between the major forms of business financing.

9-5
Contrast the three kinds of mergers and how they are viewed by government.

Outside Resources

- Blank overhead transparencies
- Highlighters (two colors)
- Computer
- Integrated software (desktop publishing or graphics, spreadsheets, databases)
- Posterboard and colored markers
- Cardboard or construction paper
- John C. Howell, *Forming Corporations and Partnerships: An Easy, Do-It-Yourself Guide* (Blue Ridge Summit, Penn.: Liberty House, 1986).
- Outside speakers: Small Business Administration employees or volunteers
- Camcorder and VCR
- Index cards
- Local *Yellow Pages*
- Classified advertising sections from local newspapers
- Stock market pages from local newspapers
- Video: *NYSE: A Portrait* (Syosset, N.Y.: New York Stock Exchange, Educational Products).
- Copies of *Business Week* and other business magazines
- Business section from *The Wall Street Journal* or *USA Today*
- Outside speaker: State government official

Vocabulary

proprietorship, p. 215
unlimited liability, p. 216
partnership, p. 217
partnership agreement, p. 217
corporation, p. 218
articles of incorporation, p. 218
charter, p. 219
stock, p. 219
limited liability, p. 219
dividends, p. 221
test of the market, p. 221
multinational business, p. 227
nonprofit organization, p. 227
franchise, p. 228
line of credit, p. 231
bond, p. 232
interest, p. 232
common stock, p. 232
merger, p. 233
horizontal merger, p. 233
vertical merger, p. 233
conglomerate merger, p. 234
conglomerate, p. 234

Focus

Write the headings **Proprietorship, Partnership,** and **Corporation** on the chalkboard. As students enter the classroom, ask them what comes to mind when they see these words. Tell students to jot down descriptive words or phrases under each heading.

Based on the information on the chalkboard, ask students to determine some similarities and differences among these different forms of business. Be sure to correct any of the students' misconceptions. For example, if a student wrote **large number of people** under **Corporation,** explain that it may be true sometimes but not all the time.

Section One
Proprietorships, Partnerships, and Corporations

What Do You Think?

Maria and Maurine Vanuta worked in their uncle's bakery when they were in high school. Now the sisters have started a partnership, MMV Muffins. The Vanutas borrowed money to start the business, using their homes and savings to guarantee a bank loan. At first, business was good, but in the last year competition from a new supermarket has caused a big drop in sales. MMV Muffins is behind on loan payments, owes money for utility bills, owes money to suppliers of baking supplies, and is behind on worker's compensation payments to the government. It looks as if MMV will go out of business. Maria and Maurine are worried that creditors will force them to turn over their personal savings and sell their homes to get the money to pay for MMV's business debts.

What's Ahead?

Knowing the different ways in which businesses can be organized can help you understand how businesses function in the economy. In this section, you will learn about three forms of business organization: proprietorships, partnerships, and corporations.

Terms to Know

- proprietorship
- unlimited liability
- partnership
- partnership agreement
- corporation
- articles of incorporation
- charter
- stock
- limited liability
- dividends
- test of the market

FORMS OF BUSINESS ORGANIZATION

Imagine that you want to open a bicycle repair shop. You will do so only if you think you can provide a service for which customers are willing to pay. You will find out how many people own bicycles in your area of the city and how often they repair them. Once you assure yourself of a demand for repair services, you need to know if you can provide the service needed. You check on the cost of tools and supplies. You find out what space is available for your shop and how much it costs. Don't forget that you have to include the opportunity cost of your time. When you determine that the business can be successful, you are ready to start.

But what form of organization should your business take? Should it be a proprietorship, a partnership, or a corporation? Before you can answer this question, you must understand each form. Each form has certain advantages. If that weren't the case, all three would not exist. Each form also has very important disadvantages of which you should be aware.

Proprietorships

A ***proprietorship*** is a form of business in which there is one owner. If you want to open a bicycle repair shop as a proprietorship, the process is simple. You check to be sure that you satisfy any state or local laws and then you open the shop. Few regulations govern proprietorships. You can borrow the money you need, buy tools and supplies, and hire any necessary labor.

proprietorship
a form of business in which there is one owner

In a proprietorship, the owner and the business are one and the same. The money that the shop makes is your money. But, you also suffer any losses. If business is bad and you can't pay your bills, the bank (and others) can collect from any source of money you have. You feel the pride of ownership and success. But, you also bear the burden of failure.

Advantages of a Proprietorship. Setting up a proprietorship has many advantages. Check this list and compare a proprietorship with other forms of organization:

1. *Easy to start.* There is usually little red tape involved in starting a proprietorship. Almost anyone with a good idea and the willingness to accept some risk can start a business as a proprietorship.
2. *Little government regulation.* Once started, a proprietorship does not face much regulation. Accurate tax records must be kept and there are certain employment guidelines that must be met. But, there are not many regulations in most cases.
3. *Profits stay with owner.* The owner does not have to share money from the business with anyone else. All of the profit stays with the owner.
4. *Pride of ownership.* A proprietor usually has a lot of pride in the business. The owner can see the progress of the business and feel proud to run it.
5. *Complete control.* The owner has complete authority over business decisions. The owner decides which product or service to sell, the hours the firm should be open, and all other aspects of the business. The owner is boss.
6. *Lower taxes.* The taxes for a proprietorship are the same as for personal income. Remember that the business and the owner are the same. In many cases, taxes are lower than if the business were a corporation, particularly if the business has a low profit.

Teach

Write **Proprietorship, Partnership,** and **Corporation** on the chalkboard. Then, define each term for students, noting key points on the chalkboard under the appropriate heading. Below **Proprietorship,** write **one owner;** below **Partnership,** write **two or more owners;** and below **Corporation,** write **organization of people legally bound together by a charter to conduct some type of business.** Ask students to suggest examples of each form of business from your local community and list these responses in the appropriate columns on the chalkboard. Next, discuss the advantages of each of the three forms of business. As you discuss advantages that are common to another form of business, discuss the applicability to the other form as well. For example, both proprietorship and partnership are easy to start, so mention those together. Next, review each of the disadvantages using the same strategy. For example, corporate earnings are double taxed: once as corporate profits and once as stockholder income.

Finally, summarize the forms of business ownership by applying the key concepts or terms students need to know, such as unlimited liability or agreements (for example, partnership agreements and articles of incorporation).

Apply

On the chalkboard or an overhead transparency, copy an outline of the following chart listing only its ten headings.

	Proprietorship	Partnership	Corporation
Start Up	Easy	Easy	Difficult
Gov't. Regulation	Minimal	Minimal	Substantial
Fund-Raising	Difficult	Less Difficult	Easy
Liability	Unlimited	Unlimited	Limited
Profits	Owner	Partners	Owner/ stockholders
Control	Owner	Partners	Prof. Managers
Risk of Loss	Owner	Partners	Owner/ stockholders

Work with students to fill in the information to complete the comparison chart. Then, ask students to discuss whether the advantages of each type of business organization outweigh the disadvantages and to explain the reasons for their responses. **Guided Practice**

Have students write about opening their own businesses. Ask each student to describe in an essay the type of business she or he would like to own. Tell students to explain what tasks would be involved in running the business (such as sales and accounting); what qualities they would look for in potential employees, if they hire any at all; and what business tasks they would enjoy doing. **Independent Practice**

Disadvantages of a Proprietorship. A proprietorship may sound very attractive as a form of business organization. But, there are some important disadvantages that must be considered. Sometimes these disadvantages outweigh the advantages:

unlimited liability the concept that an owner's personal assets can be used to pay bills of the business

1. *Unlimited liability.* **Unlimited liability** is the concept that an owner's personal assets can be used to pay bills of the business. The owner's personal assets, which may include the owner's home, car, or savings account, may be used to pay debts of the business. This means that the owner risks all the money put into the business, plus all other savings or assets.
2. *Limited life of the business.* The business stops when the owner dies or becomes unable to run it any longer. Once more, the business and the owner are one. If the owner dies, the business ceases to exist. The assets can be sold or assigned to someone else who may start the business again. But, then it becomes a new firm with different ownership.
3. *Difficult to raise money.* It is difficult and expensive to raise money for a proprietorship. This is particularly true when the business is just getting started and has no record of success. But, even a successful proprietorship may be seen as risky by lenders. Often the owner of a proprietorship has difficulty borrowing money. When the owner is able to get a loan, it is often at a high rate of interest and is thus expensive for the business.
4. *Risk of loss is not shared.* In a proprietorship, the owner bears the entire risk of loss.

Partnerships

A ***partnership*** is a type of business organization in which there are two or more owners. Each person involved agrees to provide some portion of the work and start-up money and then to share the profits or losses. For example, you alone might not have enough money to open your bicycle repair shop. In this case, you can form a partnership with someone else who can bring more money into the business. Often a partnership is formed by one person who has the skill to run the business and another who has the money to get it started.

partnership
a type of business organization in which there are two or more owners

Taking on partners is often how a proprietorship grows. Each new partner brings something to the business and shares in the good or bad fortune of the firm. New partners may contribute their personal skills, money, or even ideas to the business. Suppose that two of your friends come into your repair shop with a new idea. They have figured a way to change old one-speed bikes into 18-speed mountain bikes at a much lower cost than that of building new mountain bikes. You might offer them partnerships in the firm in exchange for their idea. They will then share in the profits and operations of the firm. They will also share responsibility for the losses. You will no longer have complete control. The three of you together will make decisions about the partnership.

The partners in a partnership must agree on their respective responsibilities and on how the profits or losses from the business will be split between them. These issues are usually specified in a ***partnership agreement*** that becomes a legally binding document. This agreement lasts for the life of the partnership, unless the partners agree to make changes. While it is not necessary to have a lawyer familiar with partnerships write the agreement, it is a good idea.

partnership agreement
a legally binding document that specifies how the responsibilities and profits or losses from a partnership will be split between the partners

Advantages of a Partnership. A business organized as a partnership has many of the same advantages as a proprietorship. The following are the main advantages of organizing a business as a partnership:

1. *Easy to start.* As in a proprietorship, there is usually little red tape involved in starting a partnership. The partners need only agree about how they will share both responsibilities and rewards.
2. *Little government regulation.* Like proprietorships, most partnerships do not face many regulations. But, they must keep good records for tax purposes and meet guidelines related to employment practices.
3. *Not difficult to raise funds.* It is easier to raise funds for the operation of a partnership than for the operation of a proprietorship. All partners' financial assets are considered by a bank or other lender. This makes it possible for the partners to borrow more together than any one of them could alone. Also, each partner may have some money available to put into the business directly.
4. *Combination of skills.* Partnerships are often more efficient than proprietorships. Using the different skills of each partner may increase the efficiency of the firm. One partner may be good at

Have students brainstorm a list of tasks that they regularly perform at school, home, or work. Then, have them indicate by voting whether they prefer to do that task alone or with a partner. Have students look for patterns in their responses and then analyze whether they are better suited to a partnership or a sole proprietorship.

Ask students to create a graphic organizer to compare a proprietorship to a partnership. Have students use a highlighter to show the advantages of a partnership over a proprietorship and a different highlighter to show the disadvantages of a partnership. As a class, have students summarize their organizers orally, comparing their responses. Correct any misconceptions.

Divide the class into groups of three or four students. Tell students to imagine that they are involved in a partnership that will conceptualize and design a movie theater in their city. Ask each student in the group to develop his or her own vision of how the theater will be operated, what the interior will look like, how many employees the business will need, and so on. Then, have students gather into their groups again to discuss their ideas, come to a compromise, and agree upon the details of their business. Students should be encouraged to listen to each other's ideas and work together to draw logical conclusions. Then, have each group use cardboard or construction paper to create a model of its proposed theater. Ask the groups to present their ideas to the class as a whole.

Ask each student to read aloud or summarize his or her essay from the *Independent Practice* activity. Then, pair students whose business ideas are similar and have them discuss forming a partnership. Ask the pairs to answer the following questions: **Who will perform the tasks to run the business? How will our personalities, work ethics, and talents blend together? What are the advantages and disadvantages in a partnership?** As a class, have each "partnership" discuss why its particular relationship would or would not work.

Divide the class into pairs of students. (You may wish to partner with an unpaired student.) Have each student assume the role of a potential business partner. Have each pair draft a partnership agreement, paying attention to the wording and details of the agreement. Direct students to address the following points: the type of business, the duties of each partner, the contributions of each partner to the business, and the distribution of profits and losses between partners.

Have students conduct a panel discussion to answer the following question: **What are the most important points to consider when starting a business and when choosing a business partner?** Ask a volunteer to list students' points on the chalkboard as they are offered. Then, have students use desktop publishing or graphics software or colored markers and posterboard to create a help-wanted advertisement seeking a business partner.

selling and the other better at record keeping. The first, then, should have sales responsibilities and the second should handle accounting and taxes. The owner of a proprietorship is not likely to have as many skills as the two or more people in a partnership.

Disadvantages of a Partnership. There also are disadvantages to forming a partnership. While some resemble the disadvantages of proprietorships, others result from the partnership itself. There are four major disadvantages of a partnership:

1. *Unlimited liability.* The members of the partnership have unlimited liability for the debts of the business. Just as with a proprietorship, the owners' personal assets can be used to pay debts of the firm. Even a partner who has not put any money into the business is subject to unlimited liability.
2. *Profits are shared.* The partners must share the profits according to their original agreement. Even if one of the members of the partnership puts in more work than originally agreed on, the split of profits will follow the original agreement. This also works in reverse. A partner who doesn't work as much as is expected still gets the share of profits specified in the agreement.
3. *Limited life of business.* The business stops when any one of the partners dies or is unable to participate. Thus, a successful business may have to be ended even though other partners may want to continue it. A new partnership often can be formed to continue the business, but sometimes this is not easy. Part of the firm's assets may have to be sold to pay off the deceased partner's share.
4. *Disagreements.* There is always the potential for disagreement among the partners. Unlike a proprietorship in which one owner makes all decisions, partners must reach an agreement. While they all may have the same plan, their choices of how to carry it out may differ. These disagreements can lead to inefficient operations and even to the end of the partnership.

corporation
an organization of people legally bound together by a charter to conduct some type of business

articles of incorporation
a written application to the state requesting permission to form a corporation

Corporations

A ***corporation*** is an organization of people legally bound together by a charter to conduct some type of business. It is a legal entity separate from its owners. The types of business a corporation can participate in are determined by the articles of incorporation. ***Articles of incorporation*** are a written application to the state requesting permission to form a corporation. The articles of incorporation give the name, address, and type of business for the corporation; the names of the initial directors of the firm; and the amount of money being put into the business.

If the articles of incorporation satisfy state and federal laws, a charter will be issued and the corporation becomes a legal entity. A ***charter*** is the legal authorization to organize a business as a corporation. A lawyer familiar with the laws concerning corporations should be hired to write the articles of incorporation.

charter
the legal authorization to organize a business as a corporation

Suppose that your bicycle repair and conversion business continues to grow. You find that if you had the money to buy some new equipment, you could increase production. You may even consider making your own brand of bikes. You might consider forming a corporation. Doing so would allow you to sell stock to raise more money. Shares of ownership in a corporation are called ***stock.*** The sale of stock is one way a corporation can raise money. More will be said about stock later in this chapter.

stock
shares of ownership in a corporation

You could trade your share of the business for some of the stock. Your partners could do the same. And other people could buy some of your company's stock. Then, all the stockholders would elect a board of directors. The board of directors supervises the operation of the business but usually does not take an active part in running it. The board of directors also selects the people who run the company. In your case, you would be the most likely choice for president. Your original partners would be wise choices for other corporate officers such as vice president and treasurer. You would continue to run the business, but now you would be responsible to all the stockholders.

Some of the advantages and disadvantages to forming a corporation are clear from the previous discussion. After reading the following information about the advantages and disadvantages of corporations, you will be able to compare corporations with the other kinds of business organization.

Advantages of a Corporation. There are more than 2 million corporations in the United States. You might expect, then, that there are some real advantages to this form of business organization. Here are the most important advantages:

1. *Easy to raise funds.* The corporate form is the most effective for raising money. This is particularly true if large amounts of money are needed to run the business. Corporations have more alternate methods of getting money than either proprietorships or partnerships.
2. *Limited liability.* ***Limited liability*** is the concept that owners of a business are only responsible for its debts up to the amount they invest in the business. This means that the stockholders (owners) only risk the money they paid for their stock. If the corporation goes bankrupt or is sued, the owners' other assets cannot be used to pay the debts of the business.
3. *Unlimited life.* The corporation does not cease to exist if a major stockholder dies. Even if all the owners of stock died, the corporation would continue. For example, USX, formerly U.S. Steel, has outlived Andrew Carnegie, its founder, and J. P. Morgan, its second owner. It almost certainly will exist long after all the present stockholders have died.

limited liability
the concept that owners of a business are only responsible for its debts up to the amount they invest in the business

Bring to class guidelines for drafting articles of incorporation, such as John Howell's *Forming Corporations and Partnerships: A Do-It-Yourself Guide,* or ask a local small business owner to share a copy of his or her documents with the class. In the same groups as in the previous activity, have students use the sample to draft articles of incorporation for their new corporation. Remind students to include the name, address, and type of business; the names of the initial directors of the business; the purpose for which the corporation is organized; the amount of money being invested in the business; and the way stock in the corporation will be issued.

Economics & Your *Community*

Ask students to visit the office of your county clerk and investigate the registration of a type of business of the students' choice. (These records are often computerized and found in the archives. Have students ask for their location.) Have students note how many businesses of this type exist. Students then should write a report about their findings. Encourage students to include in their reports statistics, informal survey responses, and literature that illustrates the demand for their chosen product or service.

Have students assume the roles of members of the board of directors of a major corporation. Tell them to prepare a list of questions for a prospective officer of the corporation regarding his or her background, qualifications, other board appointments, conflicts of interest, and so on.

Ask students to create a partially completed graphic organizer to compare a proprietorship to a corporation. Have them trade papers with a partner and instruct students to complete their partners' organizers and return them. Have the creators evaluate and correct responses and then give the organizers back to their partners.

Ask students to imagine that they own the store or business where they work. (If students currently are not employed, ask them to think of a business where they worked previously or where they would like to work.) Then, ask each student to write how his or her attitude might be different if he or she were an owner rather than an employee. Ask students if they think they might work harder and more efficiently if they were entitled to participate in the profit-sharing plan. Have students discuss how sharing profits can benefit a business and its employees.

Economic Spotlight

ROLE MODEL, ENTREPRENEUR, AND PHILANTHROPIST

It's hard to believe that the first woman to become the world's highest paid entertainer was, at age 13, turned away from a juvenile detention home due to a lack of beds. That entertainer, Oprah Winfrey, has come a long way since then, but she hasn't forgotten her roots. Today, Winfrey is dedicated to giving much of her time and money back to society. From a multimillion-dollar grant to help people get off welfare to a one-million-dollar donation to Morehouse College to a never-ending crusade against child abuse, Winfrey's dedication to helping others is legendary. According to this philanthropist, herself a victim of abuse, "No one makes it alone. Everyone who has achieved success in life was able to do so because something or someone serves as a beacon to light the way."

Winfrey says, "My father turned my life around by insisting I be more than I was and by believing I could be more." Just like her father, she has served as a beacon to others by succeeding against the odds. After enduring an abusive childhood that resulted in an unwanted pregnancy and juvenile detention, the future talk-show queen set her sights on broadcasting. Her first experience was in high school, working after school at WVOL radio. She worked her way through college as a TV reporter. Then, after college, she became a street reporter at WJZ-TV in Baltimore, where she eventually took over the role of coanchor of the evening news. This news experience led Winfrey to her first talk-show opportunity as cohost of WJZ-TV's "People Are Talking." Seven years later, she was offered the job of hosting "AM Chicago Show," a talk show that was at the bottom of the ratings and up against talk-show king Phil Donahue. According to Winfrey, almost everyone except her best friend thought she would fail because "I was black, female, and overweight." In two short months, Winfrey overtook Donahue in the local ratings. The show was expanded from a half-hour to a one-hour format, and the name was changed to "The Oprah Winfrey Show." The rest, as they say, is history.

Winfrey attributes much of her success as a talk-show host to her willingness to share her inner feelings with the audience, talking freely about matters such as her abusive childhood, her weight problem, and her bout with drugs. No doubt Oprah Winfrey's intelligence, ambition, and concern for others have also contributed to her success.

Economic Spotlight

After students have read the *Economic Spotlight* feature, point out to students that Oprah Winfrey's company, Harpo Productions, produces not only her talk show but also other types of entertainment, such as television specials and made-for-TV movies. Ask students whether they think Harpo Productions is a proprietorship, partnership, or corporation and why. (Probably a corporation because the company is large and diversified) As a class, brainstorm the advantages of that form of business organization, given the nature of Winfrey's type of work. (Responses may include that many people are interested in buying Harpo stock, so Winfrey can easily raise money for new projects; there is limited liability for slander, copyright, or other lawsuits; and there is less personal risk to Winfrey in producing an unsuccessful program.)

4. *Specialized management.* Most corporations are big businesses. They can afford to have specialized managers in all parts of the business. They can hire people who are experts in marketing, accounting, and forecasting. Smaller businesses just cannot afford such specialization.

5. *Risks are shared.* In a corporation, the risks of the business are spread among many owners. Each stockholder takes some risk. But, no one person has to accept all the risk.

Disadvantages of a Corporation. Our economy depends heavily on corporations, but there are some disadvantages to this form of business organization:

1. *Difficult to start.* It is easier to start a proprietorship or partnership than a corporation. Government approval must be obtained to form a corporation.

2. *Less direct control.* In large corporations, the owners are usually far from the day-to-day operation of the business. Professional managers actually run the business and are in charge of the firm's operations. This is more common in large corporations than in small ones.

3. *Double taxation.* To some extent, most corporations are subject to double taxation. The corporation's profits are taxed by corporate income taxes. The corporation pays dividends to stockholders out of the firm's after-tax income. ***Dividends*** are that part of a corporation's income paid to its stockholders. The stockholders then pay personal income taxes on the dividends. So, each dollar of a corporation's earnings may get taxed twice.

4. *Limited activities.* Corporations are limited to activities stated in their articles of incorporation. The articles of incorporation state the purpose of the business. Unless these are written carefully and in broad terms, the corporation's activities can be limited. This is not a problem for proprietorships or partnerships.

dividends
that part of a corporation's income paid to its stockholders

BUSINESSES MUST SURVIVE THE TEST OF THE MARKET

In our market economy, we depend a great deal on the private sector to produce goods and services. More than 80 percent of our total production comes from private businesses. These businesses are guided by supply and demand in deciding what to produce and how to produce it.

All firms, large or small, must satisfy the test of the market. The ***test of the market*** is being able to provide goods that satisfy consumers' needs and desires at prices consumers are willing to pay. And, the business must be able to pay all the necessary factors of production in doing so. Small firms are more likely than large firms to fail this market test. Small firms, and new firms especially, have little money to spend on a product that may fail in the

test of the market
being able to provide goods that satisfy consumers' needs and desires at prices consumers are willing to pay

A board member of an office supply manufacturer may also serve on the board of a chain of discount stores that sell office supplies. Ask students if they think it is ethical for a person to serve as the director of several corporations in the same line of business and what legal problems might result. (Answers may include that, ethically, it might be difficult to act impartially; legally, it might be difficult to avoid monopolistic recommendations.)

Ask each student to brainstorm a list of companies that are in the same line of business but that are different legal business entities. For example, a pizza parlor could be a local "Mom and Pop" store on the corner (proprietorship) or it could belong to a franchise such as Pizza Hut or Domino's Pizza (corporation). Ask students if and how the advantages and disadvantages of business ownership are reflected in tests of the market. For example, a small pizza parlor may suffer greatly if prices rise due to an increase in the cost of cheese. A corporation that does higher volume business may have more flexibility in dealing with the increase.

Invite local Small Business Administration (SBA) employees or volunteers to speak to your class about the forms of business organization of their individual organizations. Beforehand, ask each guest to focus the discussion on his or her original form of business organization and whether that form has ever changed. Ask students to come to class prepared with questions about how to form a business. Ask guests to bring copies of different forms required of prospective business owners.

Perspectives

Thinking Like a Lawyer Ask students to consider what issues might concern them if they were lawyers who specialized in business organization. Ask them how they might advise a client on which form of business organization to file if that client were a small-business owner with many personal assets. Have student volunteers role-play a scenario in which a lawyer advises a client on the form of business he or she should set up, given the client's particular assets. Videotape the sessions. After the lawyers have advised the clients, rewind and replay the performances. Allow the rest of the class to critique the lawyers' legal advice.

marketplace. A large firm can afford to try some risky products, because one failure out of many products may not ruin the company.

Each year, thousands of firms fail the test of the market and go out of business. At the same time, other new firms start up. You probably notice start-ups in your community such as clothing stores, restaurants, bakeries, bicycle shops, automotive repair shops, and sporting goods stores. You probably also know of some businesses that have recently closed. The market economy is ever-changing. Some businesses fail, while others succeed. In recent years, there have been about 90,000 business failures each year in the United States.

As long as we rely on the market system and the private sector, these changes will continue. The market system tends to respond fairly to consumers' wishes. It may not always respond perfectly. It may not always respond the way you personally would like. But, it certainly provides goods and services more in line with what consumers want than command-oriented economies do.

Assess

1. A proprietorship is easy to start and is under little government control; a proprietor has complete control and pride of ownership and keeps all profit; a corporation makes it easier to raise funds, the owners have limited liability, and management can be specialized. **9-1**
2. A partnership has unlimited liability, shared profits, a limited life, and a potential for disagreement among owners; a corporation has double taxation, is difficult to start, gives owners little direct control, and has limitations on activities. **9-1**
3. It goes out of business. **9-2**
4. Yes; the Vanutas have unlimited liability because they are in a partnership, so they are required to use their personal assets to pay the firm's debts. **9-1**
5. Answers should reflect that both the creditors and the Vanutas knew about unlimited liability prior to debt. **9-1, 9-2**

Checkpoint

Content Check

1. Compare the advantages of proprietorships to the advantages of corporations.
2. Compare the disadvantages of partnerships to the disadvantages of corporations.
3. What happens to a company if it does not pass the test of the market?

What Do You Think Now?

Reread *What Do You Think?* in the Section One Focus. Then answer the following questions:

4. Can MMV Muffins' creditors force Maria and Maurine Vanuta to turn over their personal savings and sell their homes to pay the debts? Why or why not?
5. Do you think this is fair to the Vanutas? Do you think this is fair to the creditors? Explain.

Close

On the chalkboard, create a three-ringed graphic organizer. Write one of the following headings near each of the circles: **Proprietorship, Partnership,** and **Corporation.** Work with students to fill in the diagram with the characteristics of each business organization.

Reteach

Have students who need reinforcement work together to create a wall chart that highlights the key advantages and disadvantages of the three forms of business organization. Supervise students' work and prompt revisions as necessary. Display the chart during the remainder of this chapter. **9-1**

Enrich

Have students write to your local SBA office requesting literature on starting a proprietorship. Be sure students use proper business-letter writing techniques. Mail the letters and then have students share with the class the information that they receive. **9-1**

F O C U S

Section Two

U.S. Businesses: A Closer Look

What Do You Think?

In the nineteenth century, a young immigrant to the United States was disappointed to find that land was so expensive he couldn't follow his dream of becoming a successful farmer in New Jersey. As he searched for another way to earn a living, he thought there might be a good market for gun powder. He had enough knowledge in chemistry to produce gun powder, so he found a site on the Brandywine River, close to Philadelphia, and started a new business. Now that gun powder is relatively less important in our economy, do you think this company would still be in business today?

What's Ahead?

There are more proprietorships, by far, than partnerships or corporations in the United States. However, sales by corporations represent the vast majority of total sales in the United States. Both large and small companies are redefining the term *multinational business*. In this section, you will learn about the size and number of firms in the United States and be introduced to the topics of nonprofits, multinationals, and franchises.

Terms to Know

multinational business

nonprofit organization

franchise

DISTRIBUTION OF THE THREE FORMS OF BUSINESS

Think about the last time you went shopping. As you walked down the street or through the shopping center, what kinds of stores did you see? Some were probably small proprietorships or partnerships, such as some shoe stores, hardware stores, or bookstores. Many of the larger stores were probably corporations, such as Sears, J. C. Penney, Wal-Mart, or Kmart.

Focus

Display *Overhead Transparency 9-1* as students enter the classroom and, on the chalkboard, write the following question: **Which of these types of business organization do you think has the most sales?** Post a volunteer at the door to hand each student a blank index card as he or she enters the room. Have students answer the question from the chalkboard on the card.

Have the volunteer tally students' responses on the chalkboard in a three-columned chart: **Proprietorships, Partnerships,** and **Corporations.** Compare a tally of students' responses to the most recent statistics *(Figure 9-2):* Sales by corporations are nine times greater than those of partnerships and proprietorships *combined.* Tell students that, in this section, they will learn why this is so.

Analyzing *Graphics*

Caption Answer
Proprietorships are relatively easy to start.

Teach

On the chalkboard or an overhead transparency, display the following chart:

Business Organization	% of Businesses	% of Total Sales
Proprietorship	74	6
Partnership	8	4
Corporation	18	90

Explain that there are more proprietorships than any other form of business, and they represent about 74 percent of all the businesses in the United States. Explain that, although there are many more proprietorships than corporations, corporations make up 90 percent of overall sales. Name several examples of proprietorships from your local community and point out that these businesses tend to be small in size and often do not employ many people. Make it clear that although certain size trends may be apparent, size does not determine the form of business organization. Point out to students a few of the small corporations in your community.

Explain that a **multinational business** is one that sells and produces products in more than one country. A **nonprofit organization** is one that does not have profit as a main reason for operating. A **franchise** is a type of business contract in which a franchisee uses products, names, or other services of a larger, parent company. Provide examples of these kinds of business operations.

Figure 9-1

Percentage of Businesses Organized as Proprietorships, Partnerships, and Corporations

The vast majority of businesses in the United States are organized as proprietorships. ***Why do you think there are so many more proprietorships than partnerships or corporations?***

SOURCE: *Statistical Abstract of the United States: 1994,* 114th ed. Washington, D.C.: U.S. Bureau of the Census, 1994, 539.

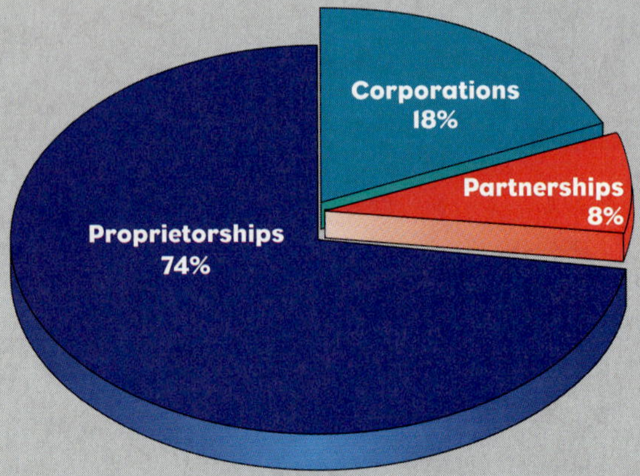

Number of Firms

Our economy often appears to be dominated by very large businesses. Names such as General Motors, Mobil, Pepsi, and Wal-Mart are familiar to everyone. Yet, there exist many more small firms than large ones. Small firms remain unknown outside of a relatively small geographic area. However, they are an important part of our economy. New firms almost always start out small. If successful, they may grow to become large firms with national reputations.

As Figure 9-1 shows, the majority of companies in the United States are proprietorships. In 1994, there were almost 15 million proprietorships compared to more than 3.7 million corporations and roughly 1.6 million partnerships. Proprietorships represent about 74 percent of all companies; corporations, 19 percent; and partnerships, 8 percent. These proportions have been about the same since 1960.

Size of Firms

Many retail stores are fairly small and are proprietorships or partnerships. But, what about the products they sell? Compaq computers, Levi's jeans, Head tennis racquets, Pioneer stereos, and almost all other products come from corporations. In manufacturing, corporations are the dominant form of business organization.

Multicultural *Highlights*

In order to encourage the awareness of cultural diversity in the local business community, ask students to work in small groups to identify different businesses in their community that are owned and operated by people of varying ethnic backgrounds. Have each group share its list with the class. If students point out that a particular ethnic group is not represented in the list, work together as a class to find a business in your local or a neighboring community that is owned by someone from that ethnic group. Have the groups work together to create a comprehensive graph illustrating the economic diversity of their business community.

If you look at sales, rather than the number of firms, proprietorships and partnerships appear much less important. Corporations clearly produce a greater dollar value of sales than the other two combined. The sales of corporations are measured in trillions of dollars. Such numbers are too high to be meaningful to most of us. Perhaps it would mean more to note that the sales of corporations amount to more than $43,000 for each person in the United States. Figure 9-2 uses a pie chart to show the percentage distributions of the dollar value of sales for corporations, partnerships, and proprietorships.

In the pie chart in Figure 9-1, the number of proprietorships is far larger than the other two types of organizations. But, the pie chart in Figure 9-2 tells a different story. There you see that corporations account for most of the sales. You can see that the proprietorships are fairly small businesses, and the real giants of business are the corporations.

To see how big corporations are, look at Figure 9-3 on page 226. It lists the 20 largest corporations with headquarters in the United States. The dollar value of sales for these firms is huge. In total, these 20 firms had sales of more than $1 trillion. For just these 20 corporations, sales represent more than $4,000 per person in the United States. These firms employed a total of 4,456,400 people. That represents more than 3 percent of the total labor force. The employment of just those 20 firms is about the same as the entire population of the Detroit metropolitan area.

In 1994, the largest U.S. corporation, as measured by sales, was General Motors. GM had sales of $138,222,000,000. That represented about $540 per person in the United States. Comparing the sizes of corporations with the

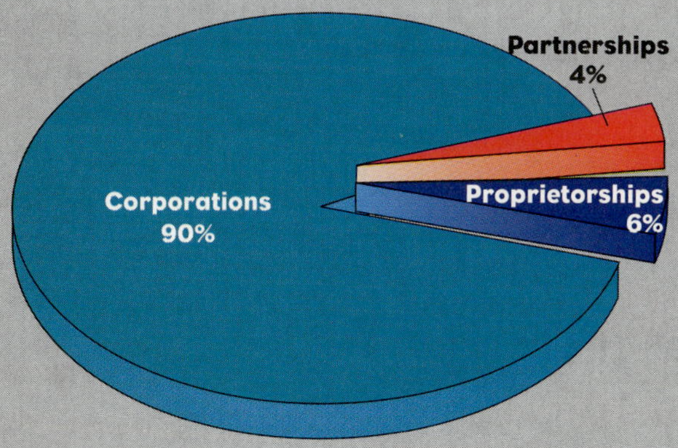

Figure 9-2

Percentage of Sales for Businesses Organized as Proprietorships, Partnerships, and Corporations

Sales by corporations are nine times greater than those of partnerships and proprietorships combined. ***Why do you think corporations have such a large share of all sales?***

SOURCE: *Statistical Abstract of the United States: 1994*, 114th ed. Washington, D.C.: U.S. Bureau of the Census, 1994, 539.

Apply

Ask students to randomly survey 10 to 20 local businesses to find out if each business is a proprietorship, partnership, or corporation. Help students use the information that they gather to create a local-area business pie chart similar to *Figure 9-1* in their textbook. Then, tell students to summarize in one paragraph how their local percentages compared to the percentages for the entire country. Have students store their lists of businesses in a safe place to use again in an upcoming activity. **Guided Practice**

Display *Overhead Transparencies 9-1* and *9-2*. Tell students to compare the two charts and then write a two-paragraph essay. In the first paragraph, have students explain the reasons behind the percentage variances in the two charts (most large businesses are corporations, corporations dominate the manufacturing industry, and corporations start out with more capital and resources so they can produce more). In the second paragraph, have students respond to the following statement: **Since proprietorships and partnerships bring in only 10 percent of all sales, they are unnecessary in the marketplace.** Discuss students' individual responses as a class. **Independent Practice**

Analyzing *Graphics*

Caption Answer
Most really large businesses are corporations.

MediaLink

Ask each student to think of a business he or she might like to start. Then, have students look in the Yellow Pages to find information on companies that already exist in those fields. Tell students to create individual databases that include the business name, address, phone number, and form of organization of five to ten different companies in their chosen fields of business. (Tell students to contact these companies by letter, phone, or e-mail to find out whether the companies are proprietorships, partnerships, or corporations.) Have each student share the business that he or she is interested in and the forms of organization of the surveyed businesses. Help students identify from their research some of the steps they might need to take in order to set up their own businesses.

Ask students to use computer software with charting capabilities to analyze and expand upon the information in *Figure 9-3* in their textbook. Ask them to divide each company's sales figure by its employment figure to calculate the company's dollar sales per employee. Ask students, individually or in small groups, to create bar graphs to visually compare the companies' dollar sales per employee.

Analyzing *Graphics*

Caption Answer
General Motors

Students with dysphasia (language disorders) may express difficulty in predicting, confirming, and integrating concepts. Support language development by asking strategy questions that emphasize meaning and structure as cues to the answers. Use confirming questions such as "Does the bar chart look right to you?" to validate students' responses and emphasize revision for meaning.

Dysphasia

Company	Sales	Employment	Corporate Headquarters
General Motors	$138,220,000,000	710,800	Detroit, MI
Ford Motor	$108,521,000,000	322,200	Dearborn, MI
Exxon Corp.	$97,825,000,000	93,000	Irving, TX
Wal-Mart Stores	$67,435,000,000	472,500	Bentonville, AR
AT&T	$67,156,000,000	310,700	New York, NY
IBM	$62,716,000,000	278,900	Armonk, NY
General Electric Co.	$60,562,000,000	226,500	Fairfield, CT
Mobil Corp.	$56,576,000,000	62,800	Fairfax, VA
Sears, Roebuck	$50,838,000,000	382,500	Chicago, IL
Philip Morris Co.	$50,621,000,000	167,000	New York, NY
Chrysler	$43,600,000,000	115,900	Highland Park, MI
Kmart	$34,557,000,000	320,000	Troy, MI
Texaco	$33,245,000,000	33,700	White Plains, NY
duPont de Nemours	$32,621,000,000	119,500	Wilmington, DE
Citicorp	$32,196,000,000	81,300	New York, NY
Chevron	$32,123,000,000	48,400	San Francisco, CA
Proctor & Gamble	$30,067,000,000	104,800	Cincinnati, OH
Boeing	$25,438,000,000	161,700	Seattle, WA
Amoco Corp.	$25,336,000,000	46,700	Chicago, IL
PepsiCo, Inc.	$25,021,000,000	397,500	Purchase, NY

Figure 9-3

Sales and Employment for 20 Largest U.S. Corporations

These U.S. corporations are enormous, both in dollar sales and in the number of people they employ. ***Which of these companies is the largest employer?***

SOURCE: *Forbes* 153, no. 9 (April 25, 1994): 199, 202, 215–17.

sizes of selected countries also helps you to understand how large some corporations are. For example, in Figure 9-4 you can see that sales of some U.S. companies are greater than the total production of Portugal, Colombia, and Morocco, as well as some other countries not listed.

MULTINATIONAL BUSINESSES

The world of business today is the entire world. Many large and small companies based in the United States sell and produce products in markets around the globe. Not long ago, when people thought of international business, they thought of selling to consumers in other countries. That concept

Country or Corporation	Total Production (Countries) or Sales (Corporations)*
Japan	$3,386,000,000,000
United Kingdom	$1,002,000,000,000
France	$1,191,000,000,000
Austria	$288,000,000,000
General Motors	$138,220,000,000
Ford Motor	$108,521,000,000
Exxon Corp.	$97,825,000,000
Portugal	$65,000,000,000
IBM	$62,716,000,000
Sears, Roebuck	$50,838,000,000
Colombia	$40,000,000,000
Kmart	$34,557,000,000
Morocco	$27,000,000,000

*** Data are 1993 sales for corporations and 1991 GNP for countries**

Figure 9-4

Economic Sizes of Selected Countries and U.S. Corporations

You can see that by these measures, Exxon Corp. is bigger than Portugal. ***Find out how they compare in terms of employees versus population.***

SOURCES: For corporations: *Forbes* 153, no. 9 (April 25, 1994): 199, 202. For countries: *Statistical Abstract of the United States: 1994*, 114th ed. Washington, D.C.: U.S. Bureau of the Census, 1994, 862.

has become broader and the terms *multinational business* or *global business* are more common than *international business.* A ***multinational*** (or global) ***business*** is one that sells and produces products in multiple countries.

multinational business
a firm that sells and produces products in multiple countries

While many U.S. companies, such as Coca-Cola, General Motors, KFC, and Whirlpool are multinational, there are many non-U.S. multinationals as well. The automotive market is a good example. Companies such as Toyota and Honda sell and produce cars outside of Japan. In fact, most of the cars they sell in this country are now produced in the United States. Honda even exports cars that are produced in the United States to other countries.

Whirlpool is an excellent example of a multinational company. It produces in Europe, South America, and Asia, in addition to the United States. Whirlpool has taken products developed in Europe and adapted them for other markets around the globe. For example, Whirlpool took a type of microwave oven manufactured in Sweden that can cook crispy products and introduced it to other markets in Asia and the United States. Whirlpool's corporate attitude is that there are "no foreigners." There is one large global market with varying product needs.

NONPROFIT ORGANIZATIONS

So far, you have been reading about organizations that are driven largely by the profit motive. But, there is another type of organization, called a ***nonprofit organization,*** that does not have profit as its objective. Examples

nonprofit organization
an organization that does not have profit as its objective

Ask students to classify each company shown in *Figure 9-3* into categories of similar businesses. Then, have them compare the companies in each category based on the dollar sales per employee. Explain to students that this type of information could help companies predict the amount of dollar sales they should generate per employee in their market.

Analyzing Graphics

Caption Answer
Exxon has about 93,000 employees (see *Figure 9-3*), while Portugal has a population of more than 10,000,000.

Ask students to go to the local library to research how many proprietorships, partnerships, and corporations existed in the United States in 1960, 1970, 1980, and 1990. Point out that the percentage of each type of business has remained relatively stable, but there has been overall growth in each category. Ask students to plot the increases of each of the three types of business formations, using spreadsheet software with charting capabilities, if possible.

include the American Red Cross, most museums, most educational institutions, and religious institutions. There are well over 20,000 nonprofit organizations in the United States.

FRANCHISES

franchise
a contract between a parent company (franchisor) and some other business or individual (franchisee) that details the terms under which the franchisee does business with products, names, or other services of the franchisor

A ***franchise*** is a contract between a parent company (franchisor) and some other business or individual (franchisee) that details the terms under which the franchisee does business with products, names, or other services of the franchisor. There are essentially three types of franchise operations.

The first is a retail franchise granted by a manufacturer. Automotive dealerships are good examples of this type of franchise. The second type is a wholesale franchise granted by a manufacturer. For example, Coca-Cola grants franchises to bottlers who buy Coca-Cola syrup, add other ingredients, and then bottle and sell the product to retailers.

Economic Dilemma

GOING OUT OF BUSINESS—AGAIN?

You may have seen advertisements for going-out-of-business sales. Or, you may have walked past a retail store that had a big sign in the window that said, "GOING OUT OF BUSINESS," with other wording to lead a shopper to believe that great savings could be had by making a purchase at that store. But, does this mean the store is really closing?

In some cities, you can walk by certain stores and see such signs that are yellowed with age. Some stores have been going out of business for years and years, but they open up shop every day. Could it be that some stores use "going out of business" as a ploy to attract customers into the store and to give them a sense, perhaps false, that prices are greatly reduced? In one midwestern town, two jewelry stores put up "going out of business" signs at about the same time. One store closed up about six weeks after announcing that it was quitting business. It really was. The other store is still operating—and apparently has "gone out of business" several times before.

Should such behavior be allowed? Is it ethical for a business to mislead customers in this manner? Should customers be on guard against such practices? If they are fooled, is it their own fault for not shopping around to be sure they get the best price?

Ask students to think of a nonprofit organization in their community or state. Then, tell each student to write an essay on what might be the company's motives for operation and what are some of the internal and external benefits involved in running that nonprofit organization. Ask student volunteers to create a bulletin board entitled **Money Isn't Everything.** Display students' work and encourage students to read each other's essays.

Have students take out their lists of businesses from the *Guided Practice* on p. 225. Beside the name of each business and its form of organization, have students list whether the company is classified as nonprofit, multinational, a franchise, or none of these. If students do not know the classification of a business, encourage them to call the store's manager or owner or research the information in the library. Your local chamber of commerce or business organization also may have this information on record.

Economic Dilemma

Tell students to imagine that they are the owners of a clothing store and they want to sell some of last season's clothing to make room for new merchandise. Divide the class into two groups. Have one group discuss how to use a false "going out of business" strategy to boost sales and the other group discuss how to use other sales techniques. Then, bring the whole class together and have the two groups debate their different approaches. Elicit from students that, although some sales techniques may be quite effective, they also may be unethical. Discuss the possible long-term effects of unethical business practices.

The third type of franchise is probably the one with which you are most familiar. These are service-sponsored retail franchises. Local business people are granted the right to provide specific service sector products. McDonald's fast-food restaurants are perhaps one of the most visible examples of service-sponsored retail franchises. Others would include H&R Block tax preparation offices, gasoline stations, car rental agencies, and many motel chains. About 40 percent of all franchises are restaurants or gasoline stations.

Checkpoint

Content Check

1. What type of business organization is represented by the largest number of firms in the United States? Why?
2. What type of business organization is responsible for the largest volume of dollar sales in the United States? Why?
3. In what types of business are franchises most common?

What Do You Think Now?

Reread *What Do You Think?* in the Section Two Focus. Then answer the following questions:

4. The business started by the farmer turned gun powder maker eventually became duPont de Nemours, a corporation featured in Figure 9-3. Do you think the owners of most proprietorships have the goal of growing their businesses into giant corporations someday? Why or why not?

Assess

1. Proprietorships; ease of start up **9-3**
2. Corporations; size of business and amount of funding needed to sustain a large volume of sales are more available in the corporate form of organization **9-3**
3. Restaurants and gasoline stations **9-3**
4. Answers should reflect an understanding of profit and growth as business goals and the advantages of the corporate form of ownership for very large firms. **9-1, 9-3**

Close

Ask students to complete the following graphic organizer by identifying nine businesses from their community (if possible) or from a larger community. To conclude the section, have volunteers define the six headings.

	Multi-national	Non-profit	Fran-chise
Proprietor-ship			
Partnership			
Corporation			

Reteach

Ask students to write the names of five to ten businesses on separate index cards. Have students exchange cards and write on the backs whether the businesses are multinational, nonprofit, franchises, or none of these. Have students collect their original cards and verify the answers. **9-2**

Enrich

Ask students to look in the classified advertising section of a local newspaper for franchise opportunities. Encourage a small-group discussion of the advantages and disadvantages of being a franchisee and the advantages of owning a similar but non-franchise operation. **9-2, 9-3**

Focus

As students enter the classroom, ask them to jot down on the chalkboard ways that people acquire financing (through credit cards, loans, borrowing, and so on).

As a class, review students' responses from the previous activity. Introduce the terms **line of credit, interest,** and **merger** to relate students' responses to how businesses acquire needed funds. Point out that businesses look to these and other forms of financing to support or grow their operations.

Teach

Explain to students that financing a business expansion requires money. A **line of credit** is an arrangement whereby a business can obtain cash very quickly. That is, the amount of the loan is approved when the money is needed—ideally, without delay. Also, explain that there are other ways of obtaining capital. These include various kinds of stocks, bonds, and mergers.

Explain that a **bond** is a certificate that states the amount of money a corporation has borrowed from a bond holder and lists the repayment terms. Explain that there are different types of **common stock** and that common stock provides partial ownership in the company.

Section Three

Business Growth and Expansion

What Do You Think?

Remember the problems facing Maria and Maurine Vanuta's business, MMV Muffins? The business is behind on loan payments, owes money for utility bills, owes money to suppliers of baking supplies, and is behind on worker's compensation payments. The Vanutas are afraid they will have to go out of business if they can't make the payments. But, the sisters are optimistic that they can compete with the large grocery on a quality basis in the long run—if they just can hold on for awhile. MMV Muffins needs to obtain additional money to get over this difficult period. But how?

Terms to Know

- line of credit
- bond
- interest
- common stock
- merger
- horizontal merger
- vertical merger
- conglomerate merger
- conglomerate

What's Ahead?

All types of business firms find at times that they need to have access to more money than they have on hand. Sometimes they may need money to get the business going. Sometimes they may need it to help run the business when sales revenue is low. And, sometimes they may need it to help the company merge with another company. In this section, you will learn about ways a business can obtain money. You will also learn about different types of mergers.

FINANCING A BUSINESS

Every business needs money to get started and to run day-to-day operations. Start-up money for most proprietorships and partnerships comes from the savings of the people involved and some funds borrowed from banks or friends. Borrowing from a bank usually requires some form of collateral as security to back up the loan. The people starting the company may pledge their homes and/or other assets as security. If business is bad and they are unable to repay the loan, they risk having to sell their property to pay the loan.

Line of Credit

Once the business has been established, money that comes in from sales is often enough to meet the cash needs of running the business. But, this is not always the case. Sometimes businesses need additional cash to help them get through a period of low sales. For this reason, partnerships and proprietorships try to establish a line of credit with a local bank. A ***line of credit*** is an arrangement through which the business can access needed cash quickly. Obtaining a line of credit is similar to getting a loan. The business files an application with the bank for approval to borrow up to some limit, such as $100,000. Once the application is approved, the business can access the money as needed without going through the time-consuming loan application process each time.

line of credit
an arrangement through which a business can quickly access needed cash from a bank

Global Economy

ECONOMIES IN TRANSITION—AND CONFUSION

The term *economies in transition* refers to economies that are trying to make a relatively rapid leap from command economies to free-market economies. An example is Russia. In countries such as Russia, nearly all business activity used to take place in government-owned enterprises. But, as many such economies have moved more to market-based economies, the way in which businesses are organized has become a source of much confusion.

After the country's economic transition began, private businesses in Russia sprang up almost spontaneously as people recognized the opportunity to make money. For example, small stands, many perhaps only 10 feet by 15 feet in size, started to appear as free-standing shops. These businesses sold a variety of items, from Coke products; to candy bars from the United States and western European countries; to knockoffs of brand name radios, CD players, and watches that were imported from Asia and Poland.

A major problem emerged for all kinds of businesses. There was no legal structure in place to guide the conduct of business. There weren't adequate laws relating to contracts, for example. So, a surprising amount of business was settled on a handshake rather than a formal contract. Even when contracts between parties were made, they were difficult to enforce because of a lack of clear contract law. Issues were decided on a case-by-case basis by a vastly overloaded court system that was not designed to handle such matters. Transactions were made based on a handshake because contracts were essentially meaningless and getting a dispute heard in court could take so long that it would not be worth the wait.

On the chalkboard or an overhead transparency, show the following graphic organizer to help students understand the different types of mergers:

Type of Merger	Characteristics
Horizontal	Same Industry Same Level or Stage in Production Process
Vertical	Related Industry Different Stages in Production Process
Conglomerate	Different Businesses

Ask students to think of an example for each type of merger. As students volunteer their examples, reinforce why each is classified the way it is. Create an additional column on the chart in which to list students' examples. For further practice, you may wish to have students search newspapers and business magazines outside of class for additional examples of mergers. Have students bring their articles to class. Then, work together as a class to determine which type of merger each article describes.

Global Economy

Engage students in a discussion of what the United States would be like without government regulation of mergers. For example, companies such as General Motors could grow so powerful that they could keep other automobile producers out of the market. Have students identify a few large companies, such as Sony and IBM, and discuss what might happen in the United States and around the world if they merged. Divide the class into two groups—government regulators and corporate representatives—and have students debate the appropriate balance between a corporation's freedom to profit and the public's right to be protected from a monopoly.

Bond

bond
a certificate stating the amount the corporation has borrowed from the holder and the terms of repayment

Corporations can issue bonds to raise funds. A ***bond*** is a certificate stating the amount the corporation has borrowed from the holder and the terms of repayment. Bonds can be issued for any amount, but bonds of $1,000, $5,000, and $10,000 are very common. If a firm wanted to raise $1 million by selling bonds, it might offer to sell a thousand $1,000 bonds.

interest
the payment for using some else's money

People who buy bonds get a yearly payment in exchange for the corporation's use of their money. A $1,000 bond paying 6 percent would give the lender $60 per year in interest. In financial dealings, ***interest*** is the payment for using someone else's money.

Each bond has a maturity date. That is, each bond has a date when the amount of the bond must be paid back to the buyer. Suppose you bought a $1,000 bond that paid 9 percent and had a 10-year maturity. You would get $90 each year in interest and, at the end of 10 years, you would get your $1,000 back.

Stock

common stock
a type of stock that gives the holder a partial ownership of the corporation

Corporations also can sell stock. There are several types of stock, but the most important is common stock. ***Common stock*** is a type of stock that gives the holder a partial ownership of the corporation. If a corporation issued 10,000 shares of common stock and you bought 1,000 of them, you would own one-tenth of the business. In turn, the corporation would have use of the money you paid for the stock.

Econ & You

IS SERVICE IN YOUR FUTURE?

The greatest growth in jobs in recent decades has been in the service sector. Projections for the future see this trend continuing. In the late 1970s, about 30 percent of all nonfarm jobs were in goods-producing activities. These include such things as mining, construction, and manufacturing. The other 70 percent were in service-producing activities.

By the mid-1990s, the percentage of jobs in goods-producing sectors had fallen to 21 percent, while service-producing jobs had increased to 79 percent of the total. By the year 2005, the mix is expected to be 18 percent goods-producing and 82 percent service-producing jobs. It is likely that your career will find you producing some type of service, not some type of product. But, what are the service sector activities? The largest category is retail trade. Some other service sectors that employ a lot of people are finance, insurance, real estate, advertising, computer-related services, health services, and government employment.

Apply

Bring to class several copies of a newspaper that carries stock market information. Using the chalkboard or a flip chart, show students how to read the stock market page. Have students choose a stock and, for one week, keep a record of its opening and closing prices. Discuss as a class how fluctuating stock prices might affect both stockholders and the company itself.
Guided Practice

Have students imagine that they want to raise $5 million to grow their corporation. To accomplish this, they decide to sell bonds at 7 percent interest with a 12-year maturity date. On the chalkboard or an overhead transparency, copy the following chart, filling in only the three headings at the top of the chart and **$1,000, $5,000,** and **$10,000** in the first column.

Amount of Bond	Annual Interest at 7%	Total Interest Paid With a 12-yr. Maturity Date
$ 1,000	$ 70	$ 840
$ 5,000	$350	$4,200
$10,000	$700	$8,400

Have students copy the chart onto a sheet of paper and perform the calculations to complete their charts. Ask a volunteer to fill in the rest of the chart on the chalkboard or transparency. Allow the rest of the class to verify the volunteer's answers.
Independent Practice

Econ & You

Ask each student to use the statistics found in the *Econ & You* feature in the textbook to create two charts: one for the 1970s and one for the 1990s. (A pie chart is most effective.) Ask students to compare their charts to those of their classmates and discuss why the percentage of jobs in producing goods decreased. (Responses may include that advances in technology eliminated many jobs in manufacturing and that other countries are able to produce goods more cheaply due to lower costs for wages and materials.) Ask students to predict what percentage of workers they think will be providing goods and what percentage will be providing services by the year 2025. Instruct them to create a third chart to reflect these projections.

Owners of common stock are not guaranteed any payment. They may receive dividends if the company is successful, and the market value of the stock may go up. For example, shares that were purchased for $15 may go up to $20, $25, or more. If the company is not successful, the owners of common stock lose money. If a corporation goes out of business, bondholders' interest will be paid and bonds will be repaid before common stockholders receive anything.

MERGERS: ONE WAY BUSINESSES GET BIGGER

In addition to growing by selling more, many firms grow by buying other businesses. A corporation buys another corporation by buying its stock. This could be all of a corporation's stock or just enough to control the company. When two firms combine in this way, they have merged. A ***merger*** is the combining of one company with another company it buys. There are three kinds of mergers: horizontal, vertical, and conglomerate.

merger
the combining of one company with another company it buys

Horizontal Mergers

A ***horizontal merger*** is a merger of two companies in the same industry. An example would be a merger between two large retailing corporations, such as Kmart and Sears. The term *horizontal merger* indicates that the two firms operate at the same level, or stage, in the production process. Sears and Kmart are both at the retail sales level. Other examples of horizontal mergers are the merger of two coal mining companies, or two airlines, or two companies that make bicycles.

horizontal merger
a merger of two companies in the same industry

Horizontal mergers are watched carefully by the Antitrust Division of the Federal Justice Department. If horizontal mergers reduce competition in an industry, they may not be in the public interest. The merging of two small companies would probably cause little harm. There even could be benefits to the public if as a result products could be produced at a lower cost because of the merger. However, if the companies already had a large share of the market, the government would probably block the merger. For example, if General Motors and Ford wanted to merge, the government probably would not allow them to do so. Such a merger would give the new firm too much control over the automobile industry.

Vertical Mergers

A ***vertical merger*** is a merger of two companies that are at different stages in the same production process. For example, a merger between a steel company and a car manufacturer would be a vertical merger. The steel would be an input to making cars. A merger between a department store chain and an appliance manufacturer would be a vertical merger, because the appliances could be sold through the department stores. The appliance manufacturer

vertical merger
a merger of two companies that are at different stages in the same production process

Show the class the 12-minute videotape *NYSE: A Portrait,* available from the New York Stock Exchange. Then, have students create a flowchart that illustrates how the stock exchange functions.

Ask students to imagine that they are government officials who are trying to set ground rules for establishing what are acceptable and what are unacceptable mergers. Divide the class into groups of four or five students and ask each group to come up with an example of an unacceptable merger. Then, as a whole class, discuss and analyze why these mergers might be unacceptable.

Have students work together in small groups to create examples of mergers. Encourage students to use various methods of presentation, such as advertisements and videotaped or audio taped public service announcements. Have each group present its work to the class.

EyeOnMarketNews

Have students analyze a newsworthy merger that was either considered and rejected or actually approved. For example, in 1995, Microsoft considered buying Intuit (makers of the software program Quicken®). However, Microsoft chose not to merge to avoid government scrutiny regarding the company's size. (Articles about this proposed merger can be found in past issues of *Business Week* or other business magazines.) Have students debate whether it was a good move for their chosen companies to either merge or veto the mergers.

and the department store chain operate at different levels, or stages, in the process that moves appliances from the manufacturer to individual buyers.

The Antitrust Division of the Justice Department also keeps a close eye on vertical mergers. If such a merger might reduce competition, the government may block the merger. Suppose there were many firms that made steel but only a few that mined iron ore. Now suppose that one of the steel producers merged with one or more of the ore companies. The steel company could then restrict the flow of ore to the other steel companies. This could reduce competition in steel production. Therefore, the government might not permit this merger.

Conglomerate Mergers

conglomerate merger
a merger of two companies that are in different businesses

A ***conglomerate merger*** is a merger of two companies that are in different businesses. One example of a conglomerate merger was the purchase of Montgomery Ward (a large retail sales firm) by Mobil (an oil firm). The two businesses have little in common. Some people were alarmed by this conglomerate merger because they thought Mobil should use its money to expand oil production. But, remember that horizontal and vertical mergers are often discouraged by the government. Had Mobil tried to use its money to expand in the energy field, the merger may well have been blocked.

conglomerate
a firm made up of many divisions and/or subsidiaries that may not have much in common in their lines of business

This type of merger results in the formation of large conglomerates. A ***conglomerate*** is a firm made up of many divisions and/or subsidiaries that may not have much in common in their lines of business. What they have in common is that they are owned by one firm. An example of a conglomerate that almost everyone knows is PepsiCo. PepsiCo owns divisions and subsidiaries such as Pepsi-Cola North America, Frito-Lay, KFC, Pizza Hut Worldwide, and Taco Bell Worldwide.

The government less actively opposes conglomerate mergers because it is not certain that they reduce competition. For example, Frito-Lay would not be in competition with Pepsi-Cola or other parts of PepsiCo. KFC, Pizza Hut, and Taco Bell are all in the same fast-food sector of the economy. However, each of these has a small enough market share that their joint ownership probably does little to reduce competition.

Ask students to look through the business section of a national newspaper such as *The Wall Street Journal* or *USA Today* for companies that have merged or are in the process of merging. Have students identify the companies and the types of mergers that occurred. If the mergers were horizontal or vertical, ask students to discuss how the mergers could affect competition.

Divide the class into pairs of students. Distribute to each pair the business section of a national newspaper such as *The Wall Street Journal* or *USA Today*. Ask one student in each pair to identify a company that would be a good candidate for a merger. Have the student's partner decide what type of company might be a good target and explain why. Also, ask the first student to name the type of merger that would occur. Have students switch roles and analyze another potential merger.

Invite to class a member of your local chamber of commerce or a member of your state government who monitors business activity (speakers might include someone from the office of the Secretary of State or the Comptroller of Public Accounts). Ask the speaker to discuss what is done to attract business to your state and what concerns the government has when a merger is proposed. Also, ask the individual to discuss what your state can do to help small businesses prosper. Ask the speaker to discuss the state's goals for bringing new business to your area.

Economic*Talk*

Divide the class into groups of three or four students. Have one student in each group begin telling a story using at least one of the vocabulary terms in the chapter. After 10 to 15 seconds, have a timekeeper signal (by ringing a bell or by saying, "Stop") that the next student in each group is to continue, being sure to use at least one vocabulary term in his or her story segment. Remind students that the purpose of this activity is to use the vocabulary terms in a logical context. Videotape or audio tape the groups' stories and play them back for the whole class to help students review the vocabulary terms.

Internet Connection

COMMERCIAL USE OF THE INTERNET

The Internet was originally the domain of government and educational institutions, but it hasn't taken long for businesses to become involved. Firms have begun to use the Internet for commercial purposes: to provide product and company information, customer service, and even direct sales. More than 25,000 firms have Internet addresses.

For marketing purposes, firms ranging from Microsoft to Volvo have created company Web pages. Several of the top 20 U.S. corporations, listed in Figure 9-3 of this chapter, have them.

AT&T	**http://www.att.com**
IBM	**http://www.ibm.com**
General Electric	**http://www.ge.com**
Citicorp	**http://www.tti.com**

There are now more than 700 electronic shopping sites selling a wide range of items including CDs, books, and software. Virtually anything sold by mail order can be obtained from cyberspace. Two electronic shopping sites are CyberMalls at **http://www.cybermalls.com/index.htm** and Hello Direct at **http://www.hello-direct.com/hd/**.

Many newpapers and magazines are being published in online versions. Most of these are available from the online services but many have sites on the Web. Two Web versions of newspapers are the *Raleigh News & Observer* at **http://merlin.nando.net** and the *San Francisco Examiner* at **http://cyber.sfgate.com/examiner/**.

Internet Application: One way to find companies with Gopher sites or Web pages is to search with Veronica or WebCrawler for the company name. The Web also has at least one list of commercial Web sites at **http://www.directory.net/dir/directory.html**.

Find a Web page or Gopher site of some interesting business. E-mail a description of the site, including its URL, to your teacher.

Economics Application: Most people begin to use the Internet through school or a job. After graduation or job change, many users lose their access. To satisfy demand for continued access, a growing number of commercial Internet providers have sprung up. These providers are not the same as the online services that we covered in Chapter 4. These small firms give the same type of Internet access as was provided through schools and employers but without the user-friendliness of the online services. Do you think commercial Internet providers are more likely to be proprietorships, partnerships, or corporations? What about commercial online services?

Internet Connection

Internet Application: It's worth browsing through the Web directory of firms to get a sense of the wide range of firms on the "net." The examples of business Internet sites given in this lesson are all Web pages. Many businesses, however, have sites on Gopher. One example is the Bell Atlantic Gopher whose URL is **gopher://ba.com:70/1.** If your students have access to Gopher but not a Web browser, they still ought to be able to do this exercise.

Explanation for the Economics Application is in the *Teacher's Connection to the Internet.*

Divide the class into groups of three or four students. Ask each group to think of three companies that might be good candidates for a vertical merger. Remind students that vertical mergers are between companies involved in different stages of a production process. Have three students in each group represent the three companies involved in the merger and work together to iron out the details of which steps each company will be responsible for in the production of an item or service. If there is a fourth student, have him or her use graphics software or posterboard and colored markers to create a flowchart illustrating a vertical merger in process. (If there is no fourth student in the group, assign this task to another group member.) Allow groups ten minutes to complete their assignments and then have all the groups present their production processes to the class. As a conclusion, engage the whole class in a discussion of whether the businesses actually are good candidates for a vertical merger and, if so, of the advantages and possible disadvantages of the merger in the long run.
Cooperative Learning

Ask students to go the library to research current data on a conglomerate such as PepsiCo. Have them identify all the companies that their conglomerates own. Ask each student to present a two-minute summary to the class concerning the different companies that his or her conglomerate holds. Help students analyze the logic behind the inclusion of each company in their chosen conglomerates.

Why do you think one company would want to buy another company that is in an unrelated type of business? One reason is that most companies try to increase the value of their assets for the owners (stockholders). If it appears that they can make a larger return on their investment in a different industry, it may make sense to do so. A company has to be careful, however. Just because managers have the expertise to manage a large car company, for example, doesn't mean they will be equally successful managing a food processing company.

Another reason for merging with a company in an unrelated business is to stabilize stockholder returns. By having assets in a number of different industries, the company is less likely to be hurt when there is a downturn in one part of the economy.

Assess

1. Common stock **9-4**
2. Vertical merger **9-5**
3. Conglomerate merger **9-5**
4. No; it would be a horizontal merger. **9-5**
5. The Vanutas can consider incorporating or adding a partner to provide additional means of raising money. **9-4**

Close

Divide the class into three groups: one that just conducted a vertical merger, a second that just conducted a horizontal merger, and a third that just became a conglomerate. Ask group members to role-play a board of directors responsible for explaining to stockholders the type of merger, what that means, what the advantages are, and how the stockholders and company likely will be affected. Allow 10 to 15 minutes for the role-playing activity. Then, have a spokesperson from each group summarize the group's conclusions for the other groups. Correct any misconceptions about mergers before closing the chapter.

Checkpoint

Content Check

1. Which would give you some ownership of a corporation: buying a corporate bond or shares of the corporation's common stock?
2. How would you classify the merger of a personal computer manufacturer with a discount electronics retail chain?
3. If a clothing company, such as Levi Strauss, were to merge with a beverage company, such as PepsiCo, what type of merger would it be?
4. If the Zeos computer company merged will Dell computers, would it be a conglomerate merger? Explain.

What Do You Think Now?

Reread *What Do You Think?* in the Section Three Focus. Then answer the following question:

5. What can the Vanutas do to obtain additional money to get over this difficult period for MMV Muffins?

Reteach

Ask students to think of ways a company can grow. Have them suggest specific examples, such as bond sales or stock offerings. As students come up with each example, help them briefly summarize how their responses achieve the desired effect. **9-4, 9-5**

Enrich

Ask students to identify growing companies that have expanded in the past five years. Have students research the companies and their methods of expansion (mergers, bond and stock offerings, and so on) and report what they learned about these specific companies and their expansion methods. **9-4, 9-5**

Concepts in Brief

1. A proprietorship is a form of business owned entirely by one person. There are more proprietorships than any other form of business in the United States. In part, this is because they are easy to start. The major disadvantage of a proprietorship is that the owner faces unlimited liability. This means that the owner's personal assets can be used to pay debts of the firm should the business fail.
2. A partnership is very similar to a proprietorship. In a partnership, two or more people own the business together. They agree to share in the work and in the profits of the business. Each partner's share of the work or profits need not be equal. Partnerships are easy to start. With more than one owner, it is usually easier to raise money for the firm's operations. The major disadvantage of a partnership is that the partners are subject to unlimited liability.
3. A corporation is a form of business that is itself a legal entity. The owners are people who have purchased common stock in the business. In a corporation, these owners are usually separate from the managers who run the daily affairs of the business. A corporation becomes a legal entity when its articles of incorporation have been approved and it receives a charter. The articles of incorporation specify the corporation's purpose, how it is financed, and other details about its formation. Two major advantages of a corporation are limited liability for the owners and the availability of more ways to raise money.
4. All businesses must meet the test of the market if they are to survive. This means they must provide goods or services for which consumers are willing to pay. Therefore, the goods must give consumers satisfaction, and they must be affordable. Firms that are not able to do this will eventually go out of business.
5. While proprietorships represent more than 70 percent of all U.S. firms, they make less than 10 percent of all sales. This means that most proprietorships are fairly small firms. Fewer than 20 percent of the businesses in the United States are corporations, but they account for about 90 percent of all sales. Therefore, most corporations are fairly large firms.
6. The 20 largest firms in the United States have sales of more than $1 trillion a year. This equals more than $4,000 for every man, woman, and child in the country. Those same 20 firms employ more than 4 million people. That is about the same as the population of the Detroit metropolitan area.

Chapter Close

Your Economic Portfolio

Ask each student to imagine being in a preliminary meeting with business advisors to discuss founding the business of her or his dreams. Ask each student to compose a summary report that, if the idea is successful, will become the basis for a detailed business plan for the proposed company. Have each student explain the name and purpose of the company; whether the company will be a proprietorship, partnership, or corporation; whether it will be a nonprofit venture, a franchise, or an individual business; what the business purpose is; how business operations will run; what the officers' responsibilities will be; and whether the goods or services will be produced and sold locally, nationally, or multinationally. Students also should include information about the company's founder(s) and prerequisite business experience, how the business will be financed at start up and in the future, and the company's strategy for surviving the test of the market. Finally, have students include their business goals for the next two years, five years, and ten years, including plans for possible expansions, mergers, and so on. Review and discuss the reports with their student authors. Then, have students make any necessary corrections before filing their final drafts in their portfolios.

You may wish to provide the following end-of-chapter materials:

- *Skills & Concepts* worksheet
- *Content Review Workbook*
- Chapter *Assessment*
- Chapter *MicroExam*

7. Multinational businesses view the world as their marketplace. They produce and sell in countries all over the world. Franchising is a means of doing business whereby a franchisee uses products, names, or other services of the franchisor. Some organizations, called nonprofits, do not have profit as their main objective.

8. Money to start or run a business can be obtained from several sources. Proprietorships and partnerships use money mostly from the owner(s) and from bank loans. Corporations also can raise money by issuing bonds or selling stock.

9. Mergers are one way in which firms can grow and expand. A merger takes place when one firm buys all the stock in another firm (or enough to control the company being bought). When one firm buys another that is in the same line of business, it is a horizontal merger. When the two firms are at different stages in one production process, it is a vertical merger. If the firms are in unrelated types of businesses, it is a conglomerate merger.

Economic Foundations

1. What are the three kinds of business organization?
2. What are the advantages and disadvantages of organizing a business as a proprietorship?
3. What are the advantages and disadvantages of organizing a business as a partnership?
4. What are the advantages and disadvantages of organizing a business as a corporation?
5. What is meant by *test of the market*?
6. Compare the sizes of the three kinds of business organizations. Use both the number of businesses in each category and the sales volume of each.
7. How has the definition of *multinational business* changed over the years?
8. What is the relationship between a franchisor and a franchisee?
9. How do the three kinds of business organizations raise money?
10. Why does government watch horizontal mergers closely?
11. Why might government prevent a vertical merger?
12. Why does government usually not oppose conglomerate mergers?

Economic Foundations

1. Proprietorships, partnerships, and corporations (p. 215)
2. Advantages: easy to start, little government regulation, profits stay with owner, pride of ownership, owner has complete control, taxes may be lower than for a corporation; disadvantages: unlimited liability, limited life of the business, difficult to raise money, risk of loss is not shared (pp. 215-216)
3. Advantages: easy to start, little government regulation, not difficult to raise funds, combination of skills; disadvantages: unlimited liability, profits are shared, limited life of business, disagreements (pp. 217-218)
4. Advantages: easy to raise funds, limited liability, unlimited life of the business, specialized management, risks are shared; disadvantages: difficult to start, less direct control, double taxation, limited activities (pp. 219, 221)
5. Firms must provide goods that satisfy consumers' needs and desires at prices consumers are willing to pay; otherwise, the firms will not be able to stay in business. (pp. 221-222)
6. Proprietorships are the most numerous, but account for only 6 percent of total sales of all firms; partnerships are the least numerous and have the least total sales; corporations are about twice as numerous as partnerships but have the largest percentage of all sales—about 90 percent. (p. 225)
7. Answers may include that *international business* meant *selling* products to consumers in other countries; now the

(Continued)

Economic Foundations
(Continued)

broader term *multinational business* indicates *selling and producing* products in *multiple* countries. (pp. 226-227)

8. A franchisor is a parent company; a franchisee is some other business or individual who does business using products, names, or other services of the franchisor. (p. 228)
9. Proprietorships and partnerships: through personal loans and establishing a line of credit with a bank; corporations: through loans, issuing bonds, and selling stocks (pp. 230-233)
10. Because horizontal mergers tend to reduce competition in an industry (p. 233)
11. Because a vertical merger might restrict competition (pp. 233-234)
12. Because conglomerate mergers usually do not reduce competition (p. 234)

Your Economic Vocabulary

Build your economic vocabulary by matching the following terms with their definitions.

1. a firm made up of many divisions and/or subsidiaries that may not have much in common in their lines of business
2. a type of stock that gives the holder a partial ownership of the corporation
3. the concept that an owner's personal assets can be used to pay bills of the business
4. the concept that owners of a business are only responsible for its debts up to the amount they invest in the business
5. a type of business organization in which there are two or more owners
6. a written application to the state requesting permission to form a corporation
7. that part of a corporation's income paid to its stockholders
8. an arrangement through which a business can quickly access needed cash from a bank
9. an organization of people legally bound together by a charter to conduct some type of business
10. a certificate stating the amount the corporation has borrowed from the holder and the terms of repayment
11. the payment for using someone else's money
12. shares of ownership in a corporation
13. the combining of one company with another company it buys
14. a merger of two companies in the same industry
15. a merger of two companies that are at different stages in the same production process
16. a form of business in which there is one owner
17. a merger of two companies that are in different businesses
18. a legally binding document that specifies how the responsibilities and profits or losses from a partnership will be split between the partners
19. being able to provide goods that satisfy consumers' needs and desires at prices consumers are willing to pay

articles of incorporation
bond
charter
common stock
conglomerate
conglomerate merger
corporation
dividends
franchise
horizontal merger
interest
limited liability
line of credit
merger
multinational business
nonprofit organization
partnership
partnership agreement
proprietorship
stock
test of the market
unlimited liability
vertical merger

Your Economic Vocabulary

1. conglomerate
2. common stock
3. unlimited liability
4. limited liability
5. partnership
6. articles of incorporation
7. dividends
8. line of credit
9. corporation
10. bond
11. interest
12. stock
13. merger
14. horizontal merger
15. vertical merger
16. proprietorship
17. conglomerate merger
18. partnership agreement
19. test of the market
20. multinational business
21. charter
22. franchise
23. nonprofit organization

Thinking Critically About Economics

1. Answers will vary but should reflect appropriate research.
2. Answers may include that it is often easier for two or more people to raise the money to start a business. Some disadvantages are problems in distribution of profits and disagreements among partners concerning leadership, job allocation, and ownership.
3. Because corporations have easier access to money markets, and they need large amounts of money to start up and maintain their operations
4. Answers will vary according to the individual firms selected (be sure to check that the necessary resources are available before assigning this question).
5. Yes; if they fail, they go out of business.
6. Answers may include conglomerate merger: a paper producer and a food producer (different companies in unrelated lines of business); vertical merger: a major hardware retailer and a paint company (two companies at different levels in the process of getting paint to consumers); and horizontal merger: two tire manufacturers (two companies at the same level in the same type of business).
7. Here is the rank according to volume of sales: (1) corporations, (2) proprietorships, (3) partnerships. Here is the rank according to number of firms: (1) proprietorships, (2) corporations, (3) partnerships. Answers may include that there are more proprietorships and partnerships because they are easier to (Continued)

20. a firm that sells and produces products in multiple countries

21. the legal authorization to organize a business as a corporation

22. a contract between a parent company (franchisor) and some other business or individual (franchisee) that details the terms under which the franchisee does business with products, names, or other services of the franchisor

23. an organization that does not have profit as its objective

Thinking Critically About Economics

1. List three businesses in your city that you think are proprietorships. Then talk to the owner or manager of one of these to see if you are correct. Ask why the business is operated as a proprietorship and write a paragraph summarizing the owner's answer.
2. Why would some businesses use the partnership form of organization rather than operate as proprietorships? Are there any disadvantages to doing so? If so, what are they?
3. Why do you think most very big businesses are corporations?
4. Choose a corporation that you are familiar with, either because you buy its products or because you know someone who works there. Then go to the library and use *Forbes* magazine's latest list of the Forbes 500 (the Forbes 500 is always in a late spring issue of the magazine) to find out the following information: (a) sales, (b) number of employees, (c) location of home office (city and state), and (d) rank within the 500 by sales volume. Finally, from the *Directory of Corporate Affiliations (Who Owns Whom),* find out either what other companies the firm owns or who owns the firm.
5. Do corporations, partnerships, and proprietorships all have to meet the test of the market? What happens if they fail the test?
6. Think of an example, either actual or hypothetical, of each of the three kinds of mergers. Explain why you classify the examples as you do.
7. Compare the three types of business organizations in terms of the volume of sales each has and how many of each there are in the United States. Why do you think the number of firms and sales are distributed in the way they are?

Thinking Critically About Economics (Continued)

start, but corporations account for more sales because most very big firms are corporations.

8. Selling stock gives part ownership to the stockholder, but selling a bond does not. Answers will vary but may include stock, because it may increase in value if dividend payments are up, or a bond, which will always be worth $10,000 when it matures, even if the company shows poor profits.

8. What is the difference between raising money by issuing bonds versus by selling stock? Which would you rather own: $10,000 worth of General Motors stock or a bond issued by General Motors with a value of $10,000? What do you think is important in making this decision?

Economic Enrichment

You may be one of many people who decide to start your own business rather than work for someone else. More than one-half million new firms are started each year. Both the risks and rewards of opening your own business can be quite high. You might have considerable financial success, but, equally important, you may gain a great deal of personal satisfaction or psychic income.

Pick a type of business you might be interested in starting in your community (for example, a secondhand sporting goods store). Prepare an outline of how you would start up your business. Include the planning steps you would go through, what type of business organization you would use, how you would obtain funding, where you would locate, and, if appropriate, who you would ask to become part of your business.

Math and Economics

In Figure 9-1, you saw that corporations have sales of about $10,914,000,000,000 (written as $10,914 billion). There are about 96,400,000 households in the United States. How many dollars of corporate sales are there per household? If the average household has 2.63 people, is your answer consistent with the information in this book that indicated that corporate sales are about $43,000 per person?

Writing About Economics

Pick a business in a shopping area near where you live. Write a short paragraph describing the business in terms of types of products or services offered, approximate number of employees, hours of operation, and location. Then write a second paragraph that explains what type of business organization you think the business represents and why. Illustrate your paper with a small sketch of the firm and entitle your paper "Organizing for Business."

Economic Enrichment

Students' outlines will vary according to the type of business and the form of business organization they choose; however, all outlines should present a logical plan for setting up the business and should point out appropriate fund-raising methods for the specific forms of business students chose.

Math and Economics

Answers may be presented as $113,215.77 or rounded to $113,216 (10,914,000,000,000 ÷ 96,400,000). The answer should be consistent ($113,216 ÷ 2.63 = $43,047.91, or approximately $43,000 per person).

Writing About Economics

Students' first paragraphs should reflect appropriate research of the chosen businesses. The second paragraphs should describe the forms of business organization in terms of the information given in the textbook. You may wish to photocopy students' illustrated papers, arrange them according to business organization, bind them, and distribute copies to students as concrete examples of each type of business organization.

Chapter 10 Perfect Competition and Monopoly

Chapter Theme

Five characterisitcs define each of the four types of market organizations within the company. In Chapter 10, two types of market organizations—perfect competition and monopoly—are studied in depth. Knowing how businesses within these markets are organized helps students understand the economic issues that face these markets.

Section	Special Features
Market Characteristics	Economic Dilemma Global Economy
Many Firms, Homogeneous Product	Internet Connection Eye on Market News Perspectives: Thinking Like a Producer Econ & You
Single Seller, Unique Product	Media Link Economic Spotlight Economics & Your Community Multicultural Highlights Economic Talk

Video Activity

Chapter 10, AT&T

Search Chapter 10, Play to 11

Divide the class into two groups to debate the advantages and the disadvantages of government subsidies of perfectly competitive businesses. Next, have them debate the merits of government regulation of monopolies.

	Print Resources	Media Resources	Assessment
	Effective Teaching Model Lesson Plans *Skills & Concepts* worksheet *Problem Solving* worksheet *Casebook* *Economic Measurement Workbook* *Content Review Workbook* *Spanish Resources*	VHS CD-ROM Videodisc *Arctic Express* *Interactive ECONOMICS* Template software	*Your Economic Portfolio* Chapter *Assessment* Chapter *MicroExam*

Special Learners	Print Resources	Media Resources	Assessment
Auditory Activity Limited English Proficiency		Computer Overhead and *Transparency 10-1*	*Checkpoint* Section 1 Quiz
	Teacher's Connection to the Internet	Overhead and *Transparency 10-2* Computer Camcorder VCR	*Checkpoint* Section 2 Quiz
Kinesthetic Activity Cooperative Learning Activity Visual Activity	*Life Skills* worksheet *Reteach* worksheet *Enrich* worksheet	Computer Overhead and *Transparencies 10-3* to *10-5* Audio	*Checkpoint* Section 3 Quiz

Careers Activity

The cable company that services your community may be a monopoly, responsible for serving every cable subscriber in its area. Cable television technicians install, inspect, and repair the cables that deliver the company's television signals. They also respond to customers' questions and complaints.

Although a few cable companies hire and train inexperienced technicians, most prefer candidates with two years of technical training in electronics, wiring, broadcasting theory, and physics. Cable technicians are paid $7 to $15 per hour, depending upon the region of the country.

Tell students to imagine that they are cable television technicians whose customers are complaining because the cable company does not provide two popular music video stations in its lineup. Have students write letters detailing what customers can do to change the situation.

Teaching Materials

Program Resources

- Student text
- *Effective Teaching Model Lesson Plans*
- *Overhead Transparencies 10-1* to *10-5*
- *Life Skills* worksheet
- *Problem Solving* worksheet
- *Reteach* worksheet
- *Enrich* worksheet
- *Skills & Concepts* worksheet
- *Casebook*
- *Economic Measurement Workbook*
- *Content Review Workbook*
- *Spanish Resources*
- Video package
- *Teacher's Connection to the Internet*
- *Arctic Express*
- *Interactive* ECONOMICS
- Template software

Assessment

- Section Quizzes
- Chapter *Assessment*
- Chapter *MicroExam*

Overview

Section One
Market Characteristics

Section Two
Many Firms, Homogeneous Product

Section Three
Single Seller, Unique Product

Teacher to Teacher

Bring to class one apple or other item of value for each student. Keep all but one of the items out of students' sight and tell the class that you will sell that item to the highest bidder. (You probably will sell it for more than its normal value.) Ask students why the selling price is so high. (It is the only item of its kind available.) Next, give the money back to the buyer and distribute the remaining items to the class. Inform students that you will buy someone's item for $1 (or any amount of your choosing). When several students offer their items, ask why you should choose to buy from one person and not another. (No reason, since the items are identical) Use this illustration to lead into a class discussion of monopoly and perfect competition.

Laurence H. Jaffe
Rutgers University
New Brunswick, NJ

Perfect Competition and Monopoly

Learning Objectives

10-1
Describe the five characteristics of market organizations.

10-2
Identify the four kinds of market organization.

10-3
Describe the five characteristics of perfectly competitive markets.

10-4
Draw the demand curve and explain the level of output and price for a firm in perfect competition.

10-5
Describe the five characteristics of monopolistic markets.

10-6
Draw the demand curve and explain the level of output and price for a monopoly.

243

Outside Resources

- Blank overhead transparencies
- Posterboard
- Camcorder and VCR
- Graph paper
- Business section of newspapers
- Tracing paper
- Audiocassette recorder
- Computer
- Index cards
- Integrated software (spreadsheets)
- *Monopoly®* game

Vocabulary

market organization, p. 245
price taker, p. 248
price setter, p. 248
perfect competition, p. 250
homogeneous product, p. 251
economic profit, p. 254
monopoly, p. 257
natural monopoly, p. 258
patent, p. 258

FOCUS

Section One
Market Characteristics

What Do You Think?

When you walk into a store to buy a new shirt with your favorite college or sports team logo, the price is clearly marked. The seller has set the price and you can either buy at that price or do without the shirt. It seems that the sellers of products have total control over the price. Is that always true?

Terms to Know

market organization

price taker

price setter

What's Ahead?

There are four types of market organizations: perfect competition, monopolistic competition, oligopoly, and monopoly. These market organizations are defined by five characteristics. In this section, you will learn about these five characteristics and how they are used to identify market organizations. Knowing how businesses are organized in relation to one another is helpful in understanding firms' economic decisions and public policy issues.

HOW MARKETS DIFFER

You have seen that firms can be organized as proprietorships, partnerships, or corporations. These three kinds of business organization refer to ownership and internal control of the business. To understand the workings of a market economy, you also need to know how firms are organized with respect to each other. In this chapter, you will begin your study of the organization of firms within the economy.

Market Organization

Every firm is part of some market. General Motors, Ford, Honda, and Chrysler are four of the firms that make up the seller's side of the automobile market. Wheat farmers from Montana, Iowa, Ohio, and Nebraska are part of the wheat market. Cannondale, Specialized, Huffy, and Peugeot are active in the bicycle market. Kroger, Safeway, and IGA all sell products in the retail

Focus

Before class begins, tear as many scraps of paper as there are students in the class. Then, select five different industries to write on the papers. (Examples of industries include automobile, computer software, computer hardware, television broadcasting, bicycle, retail grocery, retail clothing, and in-line skates.) Write one of the five industries on each of the scrap papers, creating a good balance. Fold the scrap papers and place them in a grab bag or other container. As each student enters the classroom, have him or her choose a scrap of paper from the grab bag. Students should then form five groups according to the industries they selected. Ask each group to brainstorm a list of major firms (national or local) associated with its chosen industry.

Have each group share with the class its chosen industry and its list of related firms. Discuss the similarities and differences among the firms competing within the same industry. Ask a student volunteer from each group to record on paper the names of the students in his or her group along with the industry the group selected. Tell students that they will work together in these groups again to complete the *Independent Practice* later in this section.

grocery market. When the term *market* is used this way, it refers to the industry or activity that represents the firm's most important line of business. ***Market organization*** refers to the way participants in markets are organized and how many participants there are. The word *industry* often means the same as *market*.

Forms of Market Organization

Firms can be placed in one of four major types of market organization: perfect competition, monopolistic competition, oligopoly, and monopoly. You will see that firms behave differently depending on their type of market organization. In later sections of this chapter and then in Chapter 11, you will take an in-depth look at each of the types of market organization and learn about the characteristics that define them.

market organization
the way participants in markets are organized and how many participants there are

Economic Dilemma

SUBSIDIES ON TRIAL

Should the government subsidize the agricultural sector of the economy? And, if so, by how much? These questions have been debated for years, on family farms and in the halls of Congress. The Commodity Credit Corporation, a part of the Department of Agriculture, is involved with various farm subsidy programs. In a recent year, it spent more than $16 billion to subsidize agriculture.

Some in favor of subsidizing agriculture would argue that these expenditures are important to preserve a way of life that has a rich heritage in the United States. They also might argue that it is important to our national interest to have a healthy and stable agricultural sector because of the valuable food products and raw materials that agriculture provides.

Others suggest that this industry should not be subsidized because doing so promotes inefficiency. They argue that it does not make sense to pay people not to produce, which is what some programs do. Others emphasize that we should be more selective in our decisions about what products should be subsidized. For instance, there is probably less debate about $2 million in subsidies for wheat than a $235 million subsidy for tobacco. Of course, if you live in North Carolina, or another tobacco producing state, you may well have reason to favor subsidies that flow to tobacco growers.

Teach

Explain to students that the term *industry*, a particular branch of manufacture and trade, often means the same as *market*. Point out that **market organization** refers to the way in which participants in a market are organized and how many participants there are. Analyze how the five characteristics of market organization compare with the four different types of market organization in order to link the two concepts for students. Emphasize that most industry in the United States falls between monopoly and perfect competition. These market organizations are called monopolistic competition and oligopoly. Monopoly and perfect competition are at the extremes in American society.

Economic Dilemma

Divide the class into three groups and have students work collaboratively to create a bulletin board entitled **To Subsidize or Not to Subsidize?** Have one group research the history of agricultural subsidies; the second group search online databases to find the current types of federal agricultural subsidies; and the third group gather or create relevant graphics, such as tables, charts, maps, and illustrations, to visually represent the agriculture industry in the United States. (Note: Given the differences in the level and type of expertise required to complete each group's assignment, you may wish to group your students according to ability level.)

Apply

Copy the outline of the following graphic organizer on the chalkboard or an overhead transparency, omitting the labels in each section. Explain to students that the inner circle represents the three forms of business organization, the middle circle represents the four types of market organization, and the outer circle represents the five characteristics of market organization. Allow students time to copy the graphic organizer into their notebooks. Then, ask student volunteers to label the sections of each circle on the graphic organizer that you have displayed. Discuss the importance of the characteristics of each circle. Emphasize the relationships among the circles by pointing out the importance of the position of each circle. Then, have students copy the labels onto the organizers in their notebooks.

Guided Practice

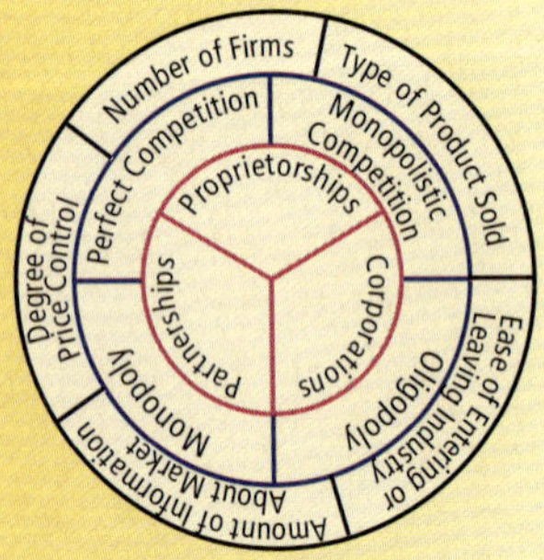

CHARACTERISTICS OF MARKET ORGANIZATION

There are five characteristics that can be used to differentiate between the forms of market organization. You will explore each the following five market characteristics in the next few pages:

1. number of firms;
2. type of product sold;
3. ease of entering or leaving the industry;
4. amount of information about the market; and
5. degree of price control.

Number of Firms

The number of firms that are active in the market differs from industry to industry. Compare the number of firms selling electric power in your hometown with the number of firms selling groceries. In some markets, there are many firms trying to get your business. In others, there may be just a few firms or even just one firm. The number of firms in active competition with

Global Economy

CATTLE FROM CANADA AND MEXICO

Many people think of the United States as a country with sophisticated manufacturing industries and a wide array of services. But, we also have a strong agricultural sector that is a reasonable example of perfect competition. The United States produces about 10 percent of the world's wheat, 20 percent of the world's cotton, 40 percent of the world's corn, and about 50 percent of the world's soybeans.

These products and others are exported primarily to Canada, the European Union (EU), Japan, Mexico, Russia, South Korea, and Taiwan. The United States also exports agricultural products to other countries. For example, cotton, soybeans, and fresh fruit are imported to Indonesia. Total U.S. exports of agricultural products exceed $40 billion per year.

The United States is also a major importer of agricultural products, mainly from Canada, the EU, and Mexico. Our main agricultural imports from Canada are cattle, pork, beef, and canola. Our primary imports from the EU include wine, beer, dairy products, and processed vegetables. From Mexico we import fresh vegetables and fruit, as well as cattle. Agricultural imports from other countries include coffee from Brazil and Columbia. Our total imports of agricultural products are typically between $20 billion and $25 billion per year.

Global Economy

Divide students into groups of five or six and hand out a sheet of posterboard to each group. Have each group apply the five characteristics of market organization to agriculture and classify it into a type of market organization. (Large number of firms + homogeneous products + easy entry and exit + good information flows + no control over prices = perfect competition) Tell five members of each group to each choose one of these characteristics related to agriculture and illustrate it on the posterboard. If there is a sixth group member, have her or him design the layout of the poster and add labels for each illustration. Display each group's poster on the classroom walls or bulletin board under the title **Agriculture: It's Perfect!** or another title of students' choice.

each other influences how each one behaves. This is especially true with respect to how each firm prices its product, what services each firm offers, and how much each produces.

Type of Product Sold

In some markets, the products offered by every firm are very similar. Wheat from one farm is very much like wheat from another farm. Gasoline from Shell is nearly identical to gasoline from Mobil. However, in other markets, the product of one firm may be quite different from that of another firm. A Bic pen is very different from a Cross pen. A Cadillac is very different from a Ford. The extent to which products differ among sellers also influences each seller's behavior.

Ease of Entering or Leaving the Industry

It is relatively easy to enter some industries but very hard to get started in others. If you wanted to open a ice-cream shop, it would not be too difficult. This is not to say it would be easy to operate a successful ice-cream shop. However, it would be relatively easy to get started. You would need just a small amount of space and some fairly inexpensive, low-tech equipment.

The same is true for growing corn, wheat, tomatoes, or most other agricultural products. Although agriculture is becoming a more complex industry and uses more sophisticated capital equipment every year, it is still easier to enter this industry than many others. Businesses that are easy to enter are also usually easy to leave. You can quit and sell your buildings, machines, and land fairly easily and without too much loss of value.

On the other hand, some businesses are very difficult to enter. To successfully enter the automobile industry, for example, you would probably have to spend hundreds of millions of dollars. The amount of technical knowledge and sophisticated equipment necessary would be huge. The same is true for the steel and telephone communications industries. In the phone industry, entry is further restricted by government controls.

Industries—such as metal engraving or newspaper printing—that use a lot of sophisticated equipment also can be difficult to leave. The equipment is usually highly specialized; so it has few, if any, other uses. This makes it hard to sell the equipment without a substantial financial loss. So, once a firm such as this is in business, there is a lot of pressure not to leave.

Amount of Information About the Market

In some industries, firms know a great deal about their markets. They know how much rival firms pay for inputs, how other firms operate, and how much others charge for their products. Wheat farmers, for example, know how much other wheat farmers pay for seed, fertilizer, tractors, and fuel. They also know the selling price for the wheat produced. In fact, television stations in agricultural areas generally report prices for wheat and other products on regular newscasts.

The flow of information among firms is not always this complete. In the production of computers, cars, tents, radios, and most other products, there is not a perfect flow of information

Regroup students into the groups they formed in the *Focus* activity at the beginning of this section. Have each group brainstorm examples of the five characteristics of market organization that are particular to the industry that it selected in *Focus.* Direct each group to prepare a chart listing examples of each characteristic. Then, tell a student from each group to read these examples aloud or list them on the chalkboard. Have the rest of the class work together to guess the type of industry to which these examples of characteristics relate. Then, help the whole class determine the type of market organization for that industry.

Independent Practice

Some students, especially those who experience problems associated with limited English proficiency (LEP), may have difficulty with the concepts of **price taker** and **price setter.** Emphasize to students that the terms are from the point of reference of the firm, not the market. Explain that as a **price taker,** a firm has to *take* the price that is determined by forces totally out of its control. A **price setter,** however, can influence where the price is *set* because it has some control. Have students draw side-by-side cartoons on one sheet of paper. One cartoon should illustrate a price taker and the other should illustrate a price setter. Tell students not to label their cartoons. Then, have them pass each drawing around the classroom, allowing each student to write **price setter** or **price taker** under each cartoon. Review the cartoons as a class. Pair students who correctly labeled the most drawings with students who mislabeled the most to discuss the differences between the two concepts.

Limited English Proficiency

Analyzing *Graphics*

Caption Answer
Great many firms, homogeneous product, complete freedom of entry and exit, perfect information, and no control over price

Display *Overhead Transparency 10-1* and have students copy the matrix into their notebooks. Remind students to keep this matrix handy because they will be using it throughout this chapter and Chapter 11.

among firms. Each firm has some trade secrets it tries to protect. When one firm finds a new and better method of production, it keeps it a secret as long as possible.

One firm might not even know exactly what prices the other firms charge. The list price for a product often does not represent the actual sales price. Sellers may find it difficult to determine what price is actually charged by another seller. For example, a car buyer may look at the same car at different dealers. The sticker price might be identical at each dealer, but the actual price offered might vary quite a bit among the different dealers.

Degree of Price Control

Some firms have a good deal of control over the prices they charge, while others have very little control. The degree of control a firm has over price is determined in part by the other four market characteristics you just read about. You will see this as you study the major forms of market organization in this chapter and in Chapter 11.

price taker
a firm that takes a price determined by forces outside the firm's control

price setter
a firm that has some control over the price at which its product sells

If a firm has no control over price, we say the firm is a price taker. A ***price taker*** is a firm that takes a price determined by forces outside the firm's control. On the other hand, a ***price setter*** is a firm that has some control over the price at which its product sells. There are different degrees to which a firm that is a price setter can determine price. In some situations, the firm may have a great deal of control over price. In other cases, there is only a very small degree of control in the hands of a single firm. You will see examples of these situations as you read the rest of Chapter 10 and Chapter 11.

Market Characteristic	Market Organization			
	Perfect Competition	Monopolistic Competition	Oligopoly	Monopoly
Number of Firms				
Type of Product Sold				
Ease of Entry and Exit				
Amount of Information				
Degree of Price Control				

Figure 10-1

Market Organizations and their Characteristics

This matrix summarizes the five market characteristics that are used to define the four types of market organization. You can draw this matrix on a piece of paper and fill it in as you learn more about the various types of market organization. ***How do you think perfect competition is defined by each of the five market characteristics?***

Identifying Markets by Their Characteristics

The four types of market organization and their five defining characteristics are summarized in the matrix in Figure 10-1. As you move through this chapter and the next, you will learn how each type of market organization is defined by the five characteristics.

The most important defining characteristic of markets is the number of firms selling in the market. In perfect competition, there are a great many firms, while in a monopoly, there is just one firm. Monopolistic competition and oligopoly lie between these two extremes. Most business in the United States takes place in these last two market structures: monopolistic competition and oligopoly. In terms of total sales in the economy, monopoly and perfect competition are not as important. However, it is very important for you to understand perfect competition and monopoly because they are referred to in many public policy debates.

Checkpoint

Content Check

1. What is the difference between market organization and forms of business organization (as described in Chapter 9)?
2. How are the four forms of market organization related to the five characteristics of market organizations?
3. Explain what is meant by the characteristic called *degree of price control.*

What Do You Think Now?

Reread *What Do You Think?* in the Section One Focus. Then answer the following question:

4. Do sellers always have total control over price?

Assess

1. Market organization describes how firms are organized in relation to one another; business organization describes how firms are organized and controlled from within. **10-2**
2. The five characteristics are used to define and differentiate between the four forms of market organization. **10-1, 10-2**
3. It is largely the result of the other four market characteristics, and it varies from price takers (who have no control) to price setters (who have some control). **10-1**
4. No; their control varies, depending upon the number of firms in active competition and the extent to which their products differ. **10-1**

Close

Explain that the most important defining characteristic of market organization is the number of firms. Copy the following continuum on the chalkboard or on an overhead transparency, omitting the label **Perfect Competition.** Have students copy the continuum in their notebooks and write **Perfect Competition** in the appropriate place beneath the continuum. Encourage students to use this continuum as a quick reference and tell them that it will be used again later in this chapter.

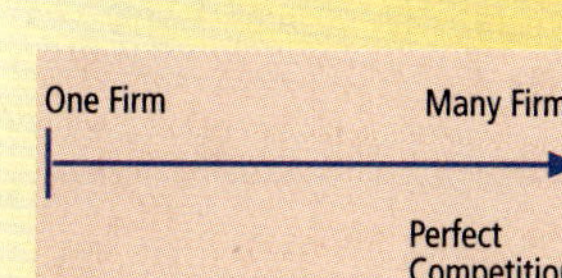

Reteach

If some students are having difficulty assimilating the information about market organization, help them create an outline of the main ideas in the first section of this chapter. First, tell students to list the section title, heads, and subheads in outline form. Then, have them add details in list form under each subhead. **10-1, 10-2**

Enrich

Instruct students to complete the perfect competition portion of the matrix shown in *Figure 10-1,* if they have not done so already. Then, have them add a box beneath the perfect competition column and write one industry that represents the particular type of market organization. **10-1, 10-2**

Focus

Write the following statement on the chalkboard: **Perfect competition is a paradox.** As students enter the classroom, ask them to work in small groups to brainstorm what the paradox of perfect competition is. If students do not know what a *paradox* means (a self-contradictory situation), have them look up the definition in the dictionary or brainstorm the meaning with other students.

When class begins, keep students in the same small groups in order to brainstorm a list of words that they associate with *competition.* Have each group write its list of words on the chalkboard or an overhead transparency. Help students understand the paradox of perfect competition by circling only the listed words that describe perfect competition. Cross out those that do not. Lead students to understand that **perfect competition** is, in many ways, the exact opposite of many people's concept of competition, or rivalry, in everyday life.

FOCUS

Section Two

Many Firms, Homogeneous Product

What Do You Think?

Jacky Barber owns a farm in northern Indiana. Like many of the owners of the almost 2 million farms in the United States, Jacky produces products for which the forces of supply and demand determine price. If the current market price for wheat is $3.50 a bushel, that is what Jacky will get when she sells her crop. The individual farmer has no control over price. Does this sound like a perfectly competitive market to you?

Terms to Know

perfect competition

homogeneous product

economic profit

What's Ahead?

In some ways, perfect competition is held as an ideal form of market organization. Agriculture is an industry that comes close to perfect competition. In this section, you will learn to identify the characteristics of perfectly competitive markets. You also will earn about market forces in a perfectly competitive market and how they affect output and price levels for producers.

PERFECT COMPETITION

perfect competition
a form of market organization in which a great many small firms produce a homogeneous product

Perfect competition is a form of market organization in which a great many small firms produce a homogeneous product. Let's examine perfect competition in terms of the five characteristics of market organization.

Great Many Sellers

In a perfectly competitive market, there are a great many sellers of a product. An industry that comes close to satisfying the characteristics of perfect competition is agriculture. There certainly are many farms in the United States. Although the number varies from year to year, there are about 2.2 million firms involved in agriculture.

Most of these firms are small farms operated as proprietorships. Even big farms are very small in relation to the entire market. For example, there are about 2.4 billion bushels of wheat grown each year in the United States. A farmer with 50,000 acres, with each acre yielding 40 bushels of wheat, would produce 2,000,000 bushels of wheat (50,000 acres × 40 bushels per acre). This is less than one-tenth of 1 percent of total wheat production (2,000,000/2,400,000,000). A 50,000-acre wheat farm certainly is considered to be very large. So, even a very large farm is likely to produce only a very small fraction of total output.

Homogeneous Product

Each firm in a perfectly competitive market produces a product that is just like the output of other firms in that market. A bushel of wheat from one farm is very much like a bushel of wheat from any other farm. A buyer of the wheat, such as General Mills, would not care whether the wheat had been grown on the Myers farm in North Dakota or on the Durkin farm in Montana. General Mills not only wouldn't care, but it also would have almost no way of knowing which farm produced which bushel of wheat.

When the output of one firm so closely resembles that of other firms, we say the product is homogeneous. A ***homogeneous product*** is a good or service that varies little from producer to producer. That is, the products of all producers are exactly the same. There is no way to tell them apart. There are no brands or trademarks. In such a case, buyers do not care from which firm they buy.

homogeneous product
a good or service that varies little from producer to producer

Complete Freedom to Enter or Leave the Industry

In perfect competition, there must be complete freedom for new firms to enter the industry as well as for exiting firms to leave. The entering and exiting also must be fairly easy to do. Each year, some farmers leave farming while others start farming. In recent years, more people have been leaving than entering agriculture, so the number of farms has been declining.

No one forces a person to start or to quit farming. This decision is made by individuals. Farmers do not try to block others from starting in or from leaving the industry. The amount of money necessary to get started in agriculture on a small scale is not great. At least, the amount is not large when compared with the cost of entering many other industries.

Perfect Information About the Market

In perfect competition, information flows freely and completely among participants in the market. *All buyers and sellers have perfect information.* Each seller knows the prices others charge for products as well as the prices paid for inputs. Each producer can have the same information regarding production methods.

Teach

To help students understand the concept of perfect competition, describe its five defining characteristics of market organization. Then, define the price and level of output in perfectly competitive markets. Illustrate the horizontal demand curve in perfectly competitive markets and explain that it is the result of suppliers producing and consumers buying at one set market price. Because production must meet the quantity demanded at the market price, the rate of output is an amount at which economic profit is zero. Explain that this causes the following:

- The price equals the average cost of producing each unit of output.
- The average cost of production is at the lowest possible unit cost.
- The price equals the added cost of producing that unit of output—no more, no less.

Apply

Continue the *Focus* discussion regarding perfect competition as a paradox. Tell students that to identify the characteristics of something, it is useful to understand both what that item is and what it is not. Point out that a more comprehensive way to define perfect competition is through its five characteristics of market organization. Copy the following graphic organizer on the chalkboard or an overhead transparency, labeling only the inner circle.

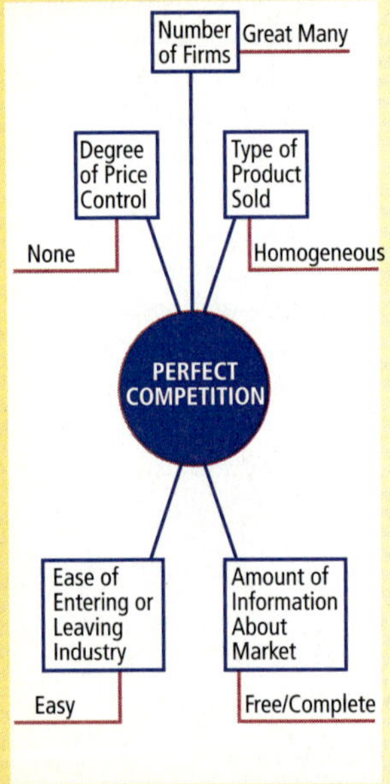

Have student volunteers add to each of the small outer boxes of the graphic organizer one of the five basic characteristics of market organization. As a class, discuss these five characteristics and how they identify perfectly competitive markets. Then, ask student volunteers to write on the lines stemming from the five small boxes the five specific characteristics of perfect competition. Have students copy the graphic organizer into their notebooks and save it to work on in the *Close* activity.

Guided Practice

Internet Connection

Moving Files with FTP

A great deal of information available on the Internet cannot be found in Gopherspace or the WWW. It can only be found in File Transfer Protocol (FTP) archives. Many computers on the Internet have FTP sites containing collections of text files, free software, and other data. Like Gopher sites and Web pages, these sites are open to the public.

FTP is a powerful way for you to transfer files from a remote computer to your local computer. Before Gopher and WWW, the major data archives on the Internet were FTP sites. FTP was the original way to send and receive Internet files. While many items from FTP sites are being made available via Gopher or WWW, there may come a time when you need to obtain a file only available via FTP.

If you access the Internet through a text-based computer, DOS, or UNIX, you can use FTP by typing **ftp ftp.site.name** where ftp.site.name is the Internet address. If your computer uses a graphical interface, Windows, or a Macintosh system, click on *FTP* and enter ftp.site.name. When you get a log-in prompt, type *anonymous*. When you get a password prompt, type in your e-mail address. After a few moments, you should get an "ftp>/" prompt.

FTP sites have one or more public access directories through which you can browse by using DOS commands (dir for a listing of files; cd to change directory.) Once you find a text file you are interested in, you can retrieve it by typing *get file-name* and pressing "Enter." When you are finished browsing and retrieving, you can exit FTP by typing *quit* "Enter."

If you don't have access to FTP, you can still access FTP archives with a Web browser. Use your browser to open a URL with **ftp://ftp.site.name**.

Internet Application: Connect to the FTP site at **ftp.eff.org (ftp://ftp.eff.org).** Browse around to find something interesting. E-mail the document to your teacher and explain why you liked it.

Economics Application: Based on what you learned in Chapter 10 about market organization, would you describe the commercial Internet providers as an example of perfect competition or monopoly? Why?

Internet Connection

Internet Application: This site is maintained by the Electronic Freedom Foundation. There are a number of useful documents including the electronic version of the *Everybody's Guide to the Internet* mentioned in Chapter 1. The site gives detailed instuctions about how to find and obtain this file.

The file is large, over 4 MB, so make sure you have sufficient disk space. This site is accessible via WWW through **http://www.eff.org/pub/.**

Explanation for the Economics Application is in the *Teacher's Connection to the Internet.*

In agriculture, for example, firms have nearly perfect information about the market. There is a wide network of sources that provides information to farmers. Farm cooperatives, university agriculture extension programs, seed and fertilizer companies, equipment dealers, and many government agencies help to spread information throughout the industry.

A great deal of information also is available to farmers through the news media. Radio, television, and newspapers give daily information about prices, sales, and factors expected to influence the market in the future. The daily papers in cities such as Minneapolis, Chicago, Bismarck, Great Falls, and hundreds of others list such information. Newspapers often list prices, price changes from the previous day, and volume for such products as wheat, oats, barley, and soybeans, as well as hogs, cattle and calves, and sheep. For many of these products, information will be given for several subgroups, too. Different types of wheat and different weight classes of cattle, for example, will be included.

No Price Control

You have now seen that in perfect competition there are a great many firms selling products that are perfect substitutes for each other. There is free entry into, or exit from, the industry. And, all firms have complete knowledge about the market. From these characteristics of perfect competition, you should expect that *no one firm has any control over the market price for its output.*

Once more, think about the example of agriculture. Suppose the market price for No. 1 hard winter wheat is $3.50 per bushel. No buyer will pay more and no seller will sell for less. Suppose you went to the grain market with 5,000 bushels and said you wanted $4.00 per bushel. Buyers would likely tell you to move your trucks aside so the next seller could unload. They would not pay more than the $3.50 market price because they could buy as much as they wished at $3.50. Keeping your 5,000 bushels from the market would have no effect since they would be such a small part of total wheat production.

On the other hand, the seller has no reason to offer to sell below the market price. If you were willing to sell the 5,000 bushels of wheat at $3.00, buyers would gladly buy it from you at that price. They would save $0.50 per bushel. But, you would lose $0.50 per bushel, or $2,500. Assuming that you are raising wheat to earn money, it is most unlikely that you would sell it for less than buyers would be willing to pay. This is especially true since you would know exactly what buyers were willing to pay.

PRODUCING IN A PERFECTLY COMPETITIVE MARKET

Producers in a perfectly competitive industry sell at the market price. The sellers take that price as given. They cannot sell anything at a higher price and have no reason to sell at a lower price. For this reason, perfectly

Divide the class into five groups. Assign each group one of the five characteristics of market organization that define perfect competition. Allow groups five to seven minutes to brainstorm a way to role-play the assigned characteristics. When they have finished brainstorming, have a student volunteer write the five defining characteristics on the chalkboard to use as a tally sheet. Then, have each group make its presentation to the class. Have students vote on which characteristic they think the group is portraying. Tally correct responses on the chalkboard and pronounce the group with the most correct votes the winner.

Independent Practice

Have students write a short essay that answers the following question: **Does perfect competition really exist?** (Answers should address the following points: Will producers really want to enter a market in which the price for a product is set? Is it possible for products to be truly homogeneous? Can supplied information really be "perfect"—in other words, reliable, valid, and unbiased? Are there really any products that are perfect substitutes for each other?) Ask volunteers to read their essays aloud and then discuss the different opinions as a class, making sure to correct any misconceptions.

EyeOnMarketNews

In a perfectly competitive market such as agriculture, information flows freely and completely among participants. For example, agricultural market prices are readily available to any interested party via radio, television, and newspapers. Bring to class several daily newspapers from your area and ask students to locate specific information regarding current prices, price changes, and volumes exchanged for several agricultural products (examples might include feed corn, soybeans, and pork bellies). Have students scan the newspaper for information about other markets. Is the information complete? As a class, discuss whether these other markets also can be classified as perfectly competitive and why or why not.

Direct students to use either graph paper or a computer program with charting capabilities to re-create the left-hand side of *Figure 10-2* (showing a market demand and supply curve for wheat). Next, have students label the graph **Perfect Competition** and label the *equilibrium price P_E*. Then, have them shade the area on the graph showing prices at which consumers will not purchase as much wheat as is produced. Next, have them shade differently the area on the graph that shows the prices at which sellers will not produce as much as consumers would like to buy. Have students save this graph as a quick reference and to use with the *Analyzing Graphics* activity for *Figure 10-2*.

Analyzing *Graphics*

Caption Answer
Any change to the determinants of supply or demand, as studied in chapters 6 and 7, could cause the supply and demand curves to shift, which, in turn, would cause the market price to change.

competitive firms are price takers. They must accept a price that is determined by market conditions that are outside of their control and sell whatever amount they wish at that price.

The Demand Curve for the Firm

What determines the price in such cases? Price is determined by the interaction of market demand and market supply, as you saw in Chapter 8. The left-hand side of Figure 10-2 shows a diagram of the market demand and supply for wheat. The equilibrium price of $3.50 per bushel is determined at the point where the demand curve crosses the supply curve.

The demand for the output of any one firm is shown on the right-hand side of Figure 10-2. At the $3.50 market price, buyers are willing to purchase all that each producer wishes to sell. *In perfect competition, the demand for any firm's output is therefore a horizontal line at the market price.* Every seller takes the market price and sells all that is produced at that price.

Output and Price Levels

economic profit total revenue minus total costs

Because of the characteristics of perfect competition, firms will be led to produce an amount of output at which economic profit is zero. ***Economic profit*** is defined as total revenue minus total costs. A perfectly competitive firm will be led by market forces to produce so that total revenue equals total

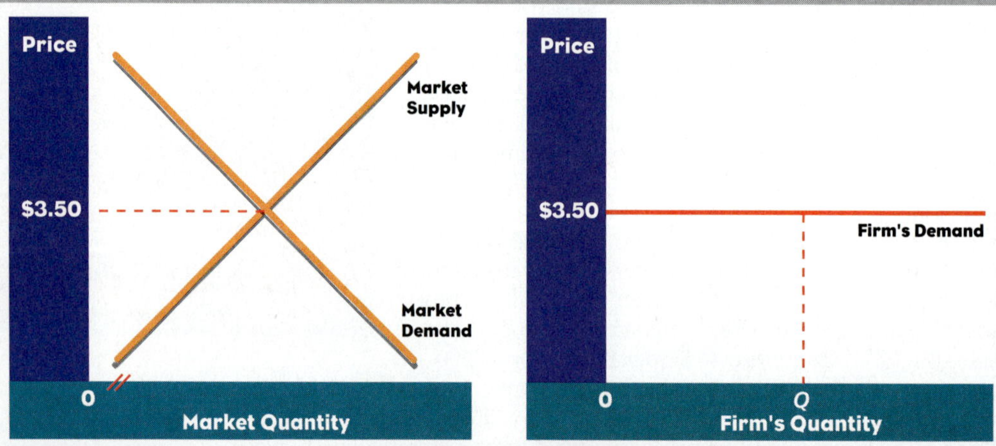

Figure 10-2

Supply and Demand in Perfect Competition

The demand curve for the output of a perfectly competitive firm is a horizontal line at the level of the market price. ***What could cause the market price to change?***

Perspectives

Thinking Like a Producer Have students imagine that they are producers in a perfectly competitive market. Ask them what decisions they can make as producers if they are reacting to a market-determined price and homogeneous products. Have each student describe his or her ideas in a modified version of a marketing plan. The plan should include three main parts: market analysis (the purpose of the business and an analysis of the market), marketing strategy (including goals/expectations; target market; marketing mix; and positioning strategy), and an action plan (what, who, when, how, and how much). As a class, discuss the principles behind producing in a perfectly competitive market.

Econ & You

THE COST OF ENTRY FOR APPLES

The agricultural sector of the economy is often used as an example of a perfectly competitive market. One of the characteristics of a perfectly competitive industry is that entry is relatively easy. Suppose that your family decides that it wants to enter the segment of the agricultural market that grows apples. You may be in for a big surprise. Some library research may tell you that to make a living growing apples you need to have a minimum of 140 acres of producing apple trees. A mature, producing orchard, without living quarters on the property, can easily cost $1,800 an acre or more. That means that for a 140-acre orchard you are likely to have to pay $252,000 for the land and the trees.

At a cost of entry of a quarter of a million dollars, this may not seem an easy industry to enter, especially when this cost covers only one of the factors of production. You would still need to purchase a fair amount of equipment to run the orchard. So, agriculture may not be as easy to enter as one might think.

Have students take out the graphs they shaded in the previous *Apply* activity. Group students into pairs and have them analyze their completed graphs, drawing conclusions about how a firm might form an output and pricing strategy. (Since **economic profit** is zero, price must equal the average cost of producing each unit of output. It also must equal the additional cost of producing that particular unit of output. In addition, the firm must operate with economic efficiency, keeping the average cost of production as low as possible.) Have each student pair present its conclusions to the class. As a class, discuss the practicality and effectiveness of the strategies.

cost. This does not mean that the owner (a farmer, for example) will not make a good living. A farmer's income is a part of the cost of running the business and is included in the firm's total cost. However, there is no excess return to people in that form of production.

If profit were above zero, new firms would enter the industry. This would increase supply—thus, price would fall, and profit would be reduced. If profit were less than zero (negative profit, or a loss), firms would leave the industry. This would decrease supply. Price would rise and profits would rise (losses would become less). These natural economic forces would direct each firm to produce at a level such as *Q* in Figure 10-2. At *Q*, the firm would have a zero economic profit. Remember, though, that each firm would still have enough revenue to pay for all inputs including the owner's salary. But, there would be no excess returns.

This rate of output has several important results. First, price is equal to the average cost of producing each unit of output. This again means that profit must be zero and that there is no excess return to the owners or workers in the industry.

Second, at this level of production, the average cost of production is as low as possible. This is often taken as a measure of economic efficiency. Since perfectly competitive firms produce at the lowest possible unit cost, they are said to be economically efficient.

Econ & You

Ask students whether, given only the following choices, they would rather be farmers or corporate executives. Students should make their decisions by assessing each profession's opportunity costs and benefits, including economic incentives and psychic income. Have each student make a list of the opportunity costs and benefits of each occupation for her or for him. Then, allow students to use a camcorder to record individual television commercials that they create to endorse one of the two careers. Encourage students to use their imagination, humor, props, and the help of other students to produce interesting and informative TV spots. View the commercials as a class and discuss the validity of the "sales pitch" presented in each.

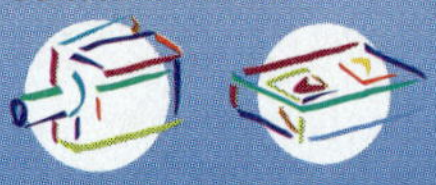

Third, at this level of output, price is just equal to the additional cost of producing that unit of output. If one more unit were produced, the added cost would be greater than the price. But, if one less unit were produced, price would be greater than the added cost. The equality of price and the additional cost of producing one more unit of output is considered a measure of the ideal (optimum) allocation of resources in production. So, in perfect competition, just the right level of resource use is allocated to produce each good.

Assess

1. No single firm has any control over supply or price. **10-3**
2. Answers may include oats, peanuts, and barley. **10-3**
3. Low cost of entry **10-3**
4. The individual farmer's demand curve is a horizontal line at the market equilibrium price. **10-4**
5. Zero economic profit, economic efficiency, and ideal level of output **10-3, 10-4**
6. Many firms produce this homogeneous product. **10-3**
7. Price taker; in agriculture, the producer has no control over price. **10-3, 10-4**

Close

Work together as a class to help students complete the graphic organizers they started in the *Guided Practice* activity at the beginning of this section. Tell students to brainstorm at least ten examples of products that meet each defining characteristic of a perfectly competitive market.

Checkpoint

Content Check

1. What is the effect of having a great number of firms in an industry?
2. Give an example of a homogeneous product (other than wheat).
3. Why is it easy for a producer to enter a perfectly competitive market?
4. Using the following hypothetical industry supply and demand curves for soybeans, draw a demand curve for an individual soybean farmer.

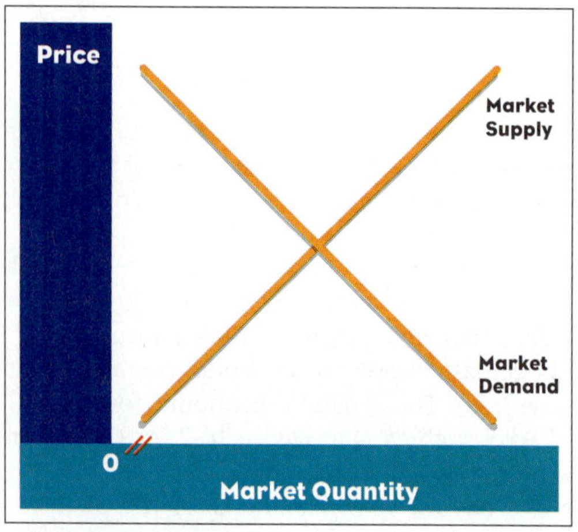

5. Explain three important results of perfectly competitive markets.

What Do You Think Now?

Reread *What Do You Think?* in the Section Two Focus. Then answer the following questions:

6. How does wheat fit the characteristics of a perfectly competitive market?
7. Is Jacky Barber a price taker or a price setter? Why?

Reteach

Pair students who understand the level of output and prices with students who do not. Have each pair create "word equations" to illustrate the concepts covered in the section entitled *Producing in a Perfectly Competitive Market.* For example, students might write, "total revenue - total costs = economic profit." **10-3, 10-4**

Enrich

Direct pairs of students to create two charts, one chart listing the costs and benefits of being a seller and the other of being a buyer in a perfectly competitive market. Have student pairs exchange charts, review the accuracy of the other pair's work, and then review the charts with their creators. **10-3, 10-4**

FOCUS

Section Three
Single Seller, Unique Product

What Do You Think?

Isaiah's water is supplied by the Madeira Water Works. The water meter at his house is read once every three months to determine his water bill. Isaiah's most recent bill was much higher than the previous one for the same amount of water. He thinks it is unfair that Madeira Water Works can just raise the rates and everyone has to pay. After all, it is the only water supplier in Madeira so people don't have a choice. What do you think?

What's Ahead?

There are situations in which buyers have only one seller from whom a product or service can be purchased. This type of situation is called a *monopoly*. In this section, you will learn about the characteristics of monopolies, how they are regulated, and how they are affected by market forces.

Terms to Know

monopoly
natural monopoly
patent

MONOPOLY

A ***monopoly*** is a form of market organization in which there is only one seller of a product. Electricity, water, natural gas, and local telephone service are examples of goods and services that in most communities are provided by monopolies. You can use the five characteristics of market organization to examine monopolies.

monopoly
a form of market organization in which there is only one seller of a product

Single Seller

Monopoly *refers to a situation in which there is a single seller of a good or service.* For most households, there is a single source of electric power. You buy electricity from the local power company, or you don't buy it at all. Just one seller is available to you. True, there are many firms from coast to coast that sell electricity. Montana Power, Ohio Edison, and Consolidated Edison are examples of such firms. But, you cannot shop around for your supplier. In almost any geographic area, there is just one seller of electricity. The same

Focus

Before class, provide one index card for each student. On one card, write **monopoly** and, on three or four additional cards, write **oligopoly.** Write **monopolistic competition** on approximately one-fourth of the remaining cards, and write **perfect competition** on all the rest. As students enter the classroom, hand each person an index card. Group students according to their types of market organization.

After students have formed their groups, have students count off the number of students in each group and write the total for each group on the chalkboard. Remind students that, in the first section, they learned that the most important defining characteristic of market organizations is the number of firms selling in the market. Tell them that each group of students represents a type of market organization. Then, ask which type of market organization each group represents. After students have volunteered their answers, point out that this activity shows that a *monopoly* is a market with one seller, an *oligopoly* is a market with a few sellers, *monopolistic competition* is a market made up of many sellers, and *perfect competition* is a market made up of a great many sellers.

Teach

Continue the discussion from *Focus* about the four types of market organizations. Contrast a monopoly and a perfectly competitive market first by focusing on the number of firms selling in the market and then by contrasting the remaining four characteristics of each. Relate these characteristics to the demand curve for the output of a **monopoly,** which equals the market demand curve for the product. Compare the output and price levels of a **monopoly** to those of a **perfectly competitive market.** Discuss the societal costs and benefits of monopolies.

is usually true of local phone services, natural gas for home heating, and water piped to your home. In each case, there is a single seller.

There are still other cases in which local monopolies may exist. In many smaller cities and towns, there is just one taxi company, one movie theater, one hospital, and one grocery store. As long as the buyer cannot obtain the good or service (or a close substitute) elsewhere, the owners of these lone businesses have local monopolies.

Unique Product

The product of a monopolist is unique. This means that there are no products that are directly comparable. There are no good substitutes. In perfect competition, the product of one firm is a perfect substitute for the product of any other firm. But, in monopoly this is not true. There is no close substitute for electrical power or local telephone access. If you want the kind of satisfaction that comes from consuming such a product, you must buy it from the monopolist who sells it.

Very Difficult to Enter or Leave the Industry

In monopoly, the entry of new firms or the ability of firms to leave is very difficult, if not impossible. There are several reasons for this, and they are at the heart of why monopolies develop in the first place.

First, there usually are very high costs in obtaining machines and other equipment necessary for production. For example, producing electrical power requires a generating plant and a transmission system, plus office and related equipment. These necessary factors of production add up to hundreds of millions of dollars for even a small electric company. This much cost in equipment can prohibit entry into an industry.

A related aspect helps to keep such industries monopolies. Once one firm gets started, it can sell its product at a lower price because costs are spread over a large number of units of output and customers. A new firm entering such an industry starts out with fewer customers and has a higher cost of production per unit of output. The new firm's price has to be higher than the existing firm's price to cover those higher costs.

In many monopolistic industries, the unit costs of production decrease with every additional unit produced. When this is true, it is more efficient (less costly) for one firm to operate than it is for several or many firms to do so. It may be impractical to have more than one firm. For example, having more than one electric power company in a community is not practical and is not in the public interest. A situation such as this in which competition is not practical is called a ***natural monopoly.***

In some industries, competition can be prevented through use of a patent. A ***patent*** is a legal protection for the inventor of a product or process that gives that person or company the sole right to produce the product or use the process for up to 17 years. This protection can keep other firms from entering a new industry.

natural monopoly
a situation in which it is not practical to have competition

patent
a legal protection for the inventor of a product or process that gives that person or company the sole right to produce the product or use the process for up to 17 years

MediaLink

Have students use spreadsheet software to create a table and then use the table to generate a line or bar graph to chart the number of patents issued in the United States in several past years. Write the following statistics on the chalkboard or on an overhead transparency for students to use in their graphs: **Total Number of Patents Granted: 1930: 45,226; 1940: 42,238; 1950: 43,040; 1960: 47,170; 1970: 64,427; 1980: 61,800;** and **1990: 90,366.** Have students draw conclusions about the variances in the number of patents issued and whether it is easier to use a table or a graph to quickly analyze data.

Economic Spotlight

YOUNGEST BILLIONAIRE: KING OF THE SOFTWARE MARKET?

In 1975 at the age of 19, Bill Gates cofounded Microsoft, the first personal computer software company. An over-$10-billion company employing more than 8,000 people, Microsoft towers above other software companies.

Gates scored a perfect 800 on the math section of the Scholastic Aptitude Test (SAT) in high school and enrolled in Harvard University's pre-law program. When Gates and his college friend, Paul Allen, read an article about the first microcomputer, they decided to jointly write a program for it. They adapted the already available mainframe language, BASIC, to this new microcomputer without even having access to the actual hardware. Amazingly, the language worked! The BASIC language that Gates and Allen wrote went on to set the industry standard for more than six years.

Deciding to devote his time to computers, Gates dropped out of Harvard at the end of his sophomore year. Together with Allen, he started a partnership called Microsoft. In 1980, IBM hired Microsoft to design an operating system for its new personal computer. To fill this need, Gates bought the rights to a program named *Q-DOS*. Gates adapted Q-DOS, creating his own MS-DOS (Microsoft Disk Operating System). He then masterminded a deal in which IBM gave up its secret design specifications. This allowed other software makers to create software compatible with the IBM system—and Gates would be paid a licensing fee every time a computer that ran on MS-DOS was sold. Today, Gates receives more than $200 million a year in royalties from this deal.

The contract with IBM made the company vulnerable to antitrust suits. In 1995, the U.S. Department of Justice became convinced that Microsoft's royalty on any machine that is capable of running MS-DOS, whether it uses it or not, violates antitrust law. Considering that eight out of every ten IBM-compatible computers run Microsoft software, many people believe that the company is a monopoly. Microsoft thinks not, contending that it's merely a tough competitor. Is Microsoft doing anything illegal? The judge and jury are still out.

A p p l y

Draw the following graphic organizer of a monopoly on the chalkboard or an overhead transparency. Include the labels for the center circle and the five outer boxes. Ask student volunteers to add one of the characteristics particular to a monopoly on the line extending from each of the outer boxes. Then, ask other student volunteers to describe and give examples of products or services that would meet all five characteristics. Have students copy the completed graphic organizer into their notebooks. **Guided Practice**

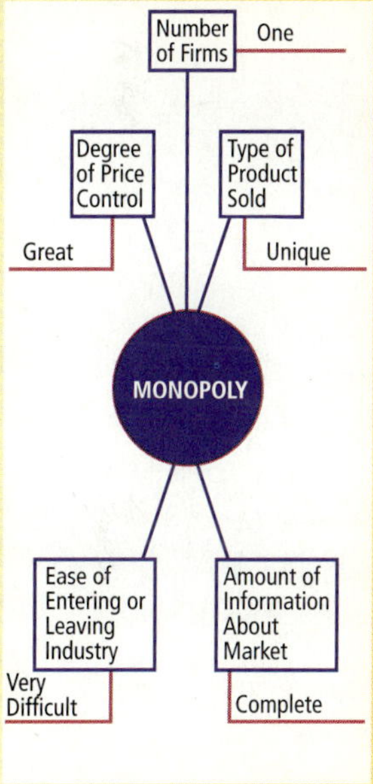

Economic Spotlight

After students have read the *Spotlight* feature about Bill Gates, discuss the following statement made by one of the writers of *People* magazine: "Gates is to software what Edison was to the light bulb." Ask students to individually list similar analogies involving current or past monopolies and, separately, write the rationale behind each analogy. (For example, "The U.S. Postal Service is to mail as gas is to cars. Without the first thing, the second thing goes nowhere.") Have students create matching puzzles from their analogies and rationales and then exchange puzzles with their classmates, match the elements, retrieve their originals, and grade each other's answers.

Explain that there are two main types of monopolies, those created by patents and those that are **natural monopolies.** Elaborate on the concept of **natural monopolies** by explaining that they are most often formed because of a unique raw (natural) resource. Then, point out that some monopolies are maintained by government regulations as franchised monopolies (monopolies protected from competition by a government grant of monopoly privilege using such means as exclusive license, permit, patent, or law). Have students work in small groups to create a chart listing examples of patent monopolies, natural monopolies, and franchised monopolies.

Independent Practice

In some cases, one firm may control access to critical raw material for producing a product. For some years, ALCOA controlled access to bauxite, which is used in the aluminum industry. During that time, ALCOA had a near monopoly in producing aluminum, mostly because it controlled this raw material.

A monopoly may also be maintained by government regulations. Suppose that you could raise enough money to start an electric power company or a telephone company. To start your business, you would have to get approval from one or more regulatory agencies. It is very doubtful that you could get such approval. In most regulated monopoly cases, it is believed that the public interest is best served by having just one firm. If we had two electric companies, there would be twice as many lines running along our highways and through our cities. Each company would have separate electricity generating plants. And, each would have to operate at a smaller rate of output, if the market were shared. This almost certainly would mean higher electricity prices for consumers. So, the government often restricts entry and maintains a monopoly.

Leaving an industry in which a firm has a monopoly may be equally difficult. The equipment is usually highly specialized. Therefore, it may not be possible to sell it except at a very large loss. If the product is considered necessary for consumers, the government may not allow the firm to leave or go out of business. It is hard to imagine an entire city without electricity. Therefore, government would not allow a major electric power company to go out of business.

Complete Information About the Market

The monopolist is the only firm in a market. So, you should expect that *the monopolist knows as much as can be known about the market.* The firm knows how much it pays for inputs, how it produces the product, the selling price, and the number of customers. Local monopolies that are part of a larger industry get a good deal of additional information through trade publications and corporate associations.

A lot of information about regulated monopolies becomes a matter of public record and is available to all other firms. We can say, then, that monopolists generally have very good information about the market in which they sell.

Great Deal of Price Control

In a monopoly, the firm has a great deal of control over price, since the monopolist is the only available seller of the product. With no other firms to supply a substitute product, consumers must either pay the price set by the monopolist or do without the product.

This leads to an important point. The monopolist can set the price but cannot force consumers to buy any particular amount at that price. The firm cannot raise the price and make consumers buy more of the product. Consumers are likely to buy less at a higher price. Even for a product such as electricity, consumers have a choice about how much they buy. Most households could be far more careful about unnecessary use of electricity. Leaving lights on in an empty room and doing laundry in small loads are common wastes of electricity. There are many ways consumers can reduce

Economics & Your Community

Have students take a survey and then draw their own conclusions about whether Microsoft has a monopoly on the software market. Tell each student to survey at least ten students or other computer users about which brands of software the survey respondents use most often and which they prefer. You may wish to direct students to the *Life Skills* worksheet for Chapter 12, which details how to create a survey. After students have conducted their surveys, tally the results and brainstorm with the whole class what conclusions can and cannot be drawn from this informal survey.

the amount of electricity they use. Consumers also can switch, in part at least, to other forms of energy if electricity prices become too high.

Most monopolies are subject to government regulation, so prices are not set just by the firm. Some regulatory agency, such as the Public Service Commission, must approve all prices. Open public hearings usually allow consumers to have some voice in this process along with the company, stockholders, and other interested parties. Therefore, you can see that both consumers and the government have some power to limit the control a monopolist has over price.

PRODUCING AS A MONOPOLY

You now know that monopolists are called *price setters.* This is because they set a price and allow consumers to buy as much as they want at that price. Even when a monopolist is regulated, the firm has considerable input into decisions regarding price.

The Demand Curve for a Monopolist

You also know that a monopolist is the only firm selling the product in a given market. So, it stands to reason that *the demand curve for the output of a monopolist equals the market demand curve for the product.* This is illustrated in Figure 10-3 on page 262. The market demand curve is on the left-hand side, and the monopolist's demand curve is on the right-hand side. These two demand curves are identical.

At the price shown as *P*, the monopolist would sell *Q* units. At that price, the market demand curve also shows that consumers would buy *Q* units. This would be true of any price chosen. The monopolist's demand, then, must be the same as the market demand.

As a warm-up to the following cooperative learning activity, have students brainstorm the kinds of industries included in the board game *Monopoly®*. (Utilities, real estate, transportation) List these industries on the chalkboard. Have students look at a *Monopoly®* game board and add any missing industries to their chalkboard list.

Divide the class into groups of four or five students to create board games similar to *Monopoly®*. Allow each group to choose whether it will create a game based on monopolies or perfect competition. Have each group brainstorm the type of game and the nature of the game it plans to develop. Then, assign one of the following tasks to each group member: create the game board; create the game pieces; create the game board cards; write the rules and directions; and, if there is a fifth group member, create the packaging. You may wish to allot 10 to 15 minutes per class period for several days for students to develop their games and field test their results. When the games are finished, have the groups exchange games and then play and critique them. Discuss whether monopolies or producers in perfect competition are portrayed accurately.

Cooperative Learning

Multicultural *Highlights*

In order to fill the demand for ethnic software titles, software companies such as AfroLink Software of Los Angeles and Afrocentrex of Chicago have formed. Kamal Al-Mansour, president of AfroLink, and Keith Coleman, president of Afrocentrex, are excited about the success of their respective companies. According to Coleman, "There is a real need for ethnically diverse software out there—and not just for African Americans—for all ethnic groups." As a class, have students discuss the following: **Why is there a demand for software with a particular ethnic orientation? What might be the disadvantages if one company had a monopoly over this market?** As a class, brainstorm ideas for new software that would help meet this growing demand.

Analyzing *Graphics*

Caption Answer
Consumers would decrease the quantity demanded.

Display *Overhead Transparency 10-3.* Point out that the market demand curve and the monopolist's demand curve are the same. Relate these two curves to an actual monopolist, such as a utility company or the U.S. Postal Service. Review with students price inelasticity and point out that utilities and the postal service are services that are reasonably price inelastic. However, consumers do have the power to change the quantity demanded. If a firm raises the price of an "essential" service, how can consumers cut down on their demand? Brainstorm with students what they could do to reduce their demand for a service such as electricity. Lead students to understand the importance of conservation and community involvement with governmental regulatory agencies. Have students work together to create public service announcements concerning the conservation of electricity, water, and other monopolistic products and services. Allow students to tape record their PSAs, and then critique the spots as a class.

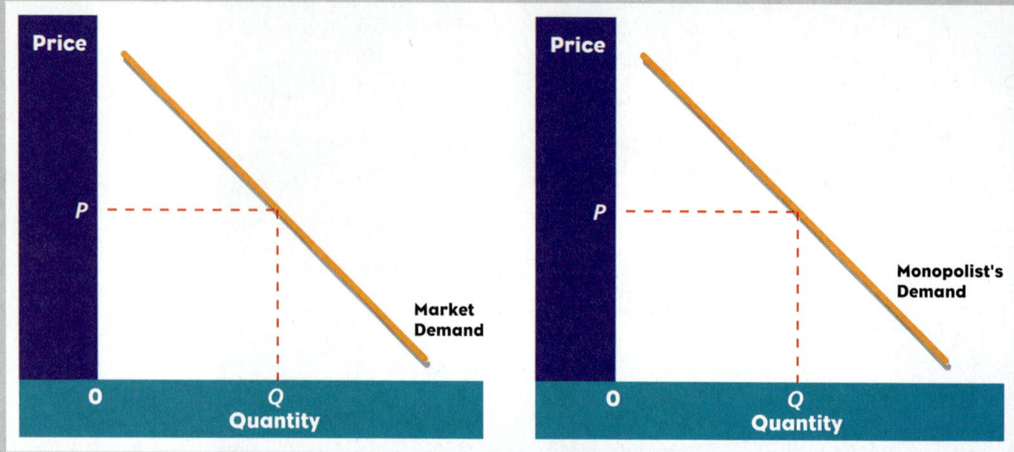

Figure 10-3

Demand in Monopoly

The monopolist's demand curve and the market demand curve are exactly the same. This is because the monopolist is the only firm in the industry. ***What do you think consumers would do if the monopolist raised the price above* P?**

Output and Price Levels

Managers of a monopoly, like those of other firms, will try to produce at a level at which they can make as much money as possible. At low levels of production and sales, the added revenue from increasing sales is normally greater than the added cost of producing the extra output. For example, $20 of added revenue might be obtained by spending $8 in added cost. If so, the firm's profit will increase by $12. As long as the added revenue from new sales is greater than the added cost to produce the output, expansion is favorable.

As a firm expands, the added revenue from sales tends to fall and the added cost from production tends to rise. Firms try to select the level of output with the greatest difference between total revenue from sales and total cost of production. This level of output occurs when added revenue from selling one more unit equals the added cost of producing that unit. Once added revenue and added cost are equal, it is not profitable to expand any more.

So, the monopolist determines the best and most profitable level of output by finding where the added revenue from sales equals the added cost of producing that output. This would be some level such as *Q* in Figure 10-3. The price that corresponds to *Q* along the demand curve becomes the best price to set. This is the price *P*. At *P*, consumers will purchase the *Q* units the monopolist wishes to sell.

Often, a regulatory agency will not permit the monopolist to charge this price. Rather, the agency may force the monopolist to set a price that equals the per-unit cost of production. This will result in a zero economic profit to the monopolist. Even so, production costs will be covered and stockholders will earn dividends since dividends are considered part of the cost of doing business. However, there will not be any excess return to the monopoly. Such a regulated price is illustrated in Figure 10-4 as P_R, which is lower than P. The corresponding quantity produced and sold is Q_R, which is greater than Q.

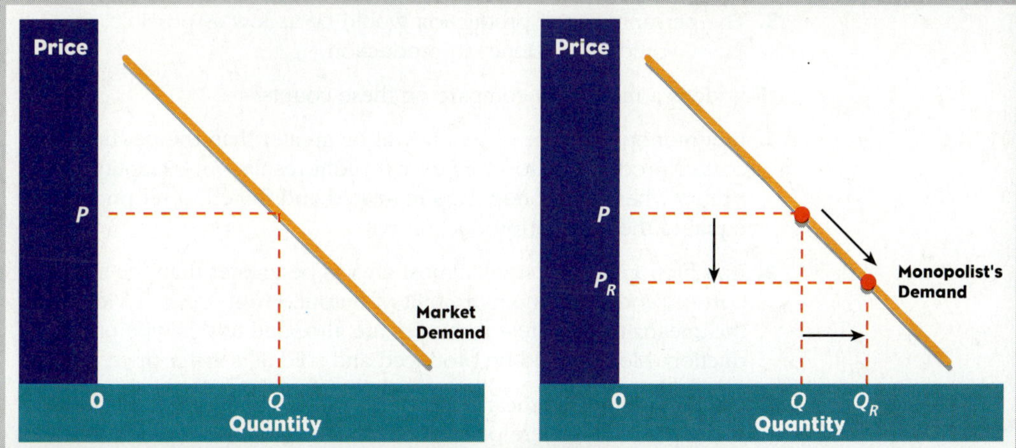

Figure 10-4

Monopolist's Demand with Government Regulation

The market price may not be permitted by a regulatory agency. If the regulatory agency forces price down to P_R, the monopolist will produce and sell Q_R, a larger quantity. ***What do you think would happen to quantity demanded if the regulatory agency approved a rate hike for the monopoly?***

COMPARISON OF MONOPOLY AND PERFECT COMPETITION

If an industry is a constant cost industry (one that can expand or contract without changing the production cost per unit of output), the price charged by a monopolist will be higher than if the industry were perfectly competitive. If the monopolist's price is higher, you should expect that the total quantity purchased by consumers will be less than if the industry were perfectly competitive and price was lower. So, for some monopolies we can expect price to be higher, but the quantity produced to be lower than in perfect competition.

In many monopolistic industries, however, prices are lower than they would be if the same industries were perfectly competitive. This is true when monopolies afford greater economies of scale in production. Electric power is a good example. If there were a great many firms supplying electric power to any area, the cost (and price) of electricity would be much higher.

Help students plot on a graph what would happen if a regulatory agency were to approve a rate hike. Have students use graph paper or computer software with charting capabilities to re-create the right-hand side of *Figure 10-4.* Next, tell students to indicate a point on the demand curve to illustrate a rate increase. Then, have them create a dotted line leading from that point to both the **Price** axis and the **Quantity** axis. Have students label the new price P_I and the new quantity Q_I. Discuss what happened to quantity demanded when the price went up.

Analyzing *Graphics*

Caption Answer
Quantity demanded would go down.

Economic *Talk*

To review the vocabulary for this chapter, play a modified version of the game *Wheel of Fortune.* Divide the class into two teams and provide each team with a bell or other noisemaker. Then, draw 18 blank writing rules side by side on the chalkboard (the number of letters in the three longest vocabulary terms). Have student teams take turns trying to guess the letters in eight of the vocabulary terms for this chapter. (Although there are nine terms, only create eight puzzles since the last term will be obvious.) Tell students to ring the bell when they can solve a puzzle. The team that is the first to guess the correct answer to a puzzle receives one point. However, the team that defines the term also gets a point. After all eight puzzles have been solved and the terms defined, declare the team with the most points the winner.

If students have not already completed the *Life Skills* worksheet for Chapter 10, ask them to complete it now. The worksheet supplies students informations about patents and ties patents to the concept of monopolies. It also contains a sample patent application for students to complete.

In studying perfect competition, you learned that market forces work to assure the following conditions:

1. Price would equal the per-unit cost of production, so there would be no excess profit.
2. Price would equal the added cost of increasing output by one unit, so there would be a desirable allocation of resources in production.
3. The per-unit cost of production would be as low as possible, so there would be efficiency in production.

How does a monopoly compare on these counts?

1. In a monopoly, price generally will be greater than the per-unit cost of production, so some excess profit results. An exception occurs when the monopoly is regulated and forced to set price equal to the per-unit production cost.
2. In a monopoly, price will almost always be greater than the added cost of producing one more unit of output. From society's view, this means that too few resources are allocated to this type of production. More should be produced and sold at a lower price.
3. If there are not significant economies of scale, a monopolist normally produces where per-unit costs are higher than the lowest possible level. When this is true, some economic efficiency is lost. However, if there are economies of scale, per-unit costs will be lower with a monopoly than with perfect competition.

There are other benefits that society gets from monopolies besides the products the firms produce. Many monopolistic firms advertise on radio and television, as well as in newspapers and magazines. The money spent on such advertising helps cover the cost of making radio and television shows available. It also reduces the subscription price for magazines and newspapers. Monopolies are usually big firms that can afford to spend a good deal of money for research and development. All of us stand to benefit from the discoveries of such research. Perfectly competitive firms, on the other hand, are usually small and do virtually no advertising. They also spend almost nothing on research and development.

Figure 10-5 uses part of the matrix first presented in Figure 10-1 to summarize the market characteristics of perfect competition and monopoly. You will be able to complete the matrix after reading Chapter 11 by entering the market characteristics for monopolistic competition and oligopoly.

Market Organization

Market Characteristic	Perfect Competition	Monopolistic Competition	Oligopoly	Monopoly
Number of Firms	great many			one
Type of Product Sold	homogeneous			unique
Ease of Entry and Exit	very easy			very difficult
Amount of Information	complete			complete
Degree of Price Control	none			great deal

Figure 10-5

Market Characteristics of Perfect Competition and Monopoly

This matrix summarizes the five characteristics of perfect competition and monopoly markets. ***For perfect competition and monopoly, name one example that was not used in your textbook.***

Checkpoint

Content Check

1. How does a monopoly compare to a firm in a perfectly competitive market on the five characteristics?
2. Why is it hard to enter and exit a monopolistic market?
3. Explain why a monopolist has complete information about the market.
4. Show how a monopolist's demand curve compares to the market demand curve.
5. Name some benefits society receives from monopolies.

What Do You Think Now?

Reread *What Do You Think?* in the Section Three Focus. Then answer the following questions:

6. Do residents of Madeira have any control over their water bills? Why or why not?
7. Can utility companies charge any price they want? Why or why not?

Reteach

Pair students who understand the differences between perfect competition and monopoly with those who are having difficulty with the concepts. Have each pair brainstorm a list of ten products they use daily and decide whether they purchase these products from a firm that operates in a perfectly competitive or a monopolistic market. **10-3, 10-5**

Enrich

The U.S. Postal Service (USPS) is a franchised monopoly. Have students brainstorm how technology and businesses have taken some of the market away from this monopoly and what effect this has had on the USPS and society. Ask each group to create a cause-and-effect chart to illustrate its findings. **10-5**

Analyzing Graphics

Caption Answer
Perfect competition: lettuce; monopoly: cable TV in some areas

Assess

1. Perfect competition: great many firms, homogeneous product, easy entry and exit, complete information, no price control; monopoly: one firm, unique product, difficult entry and exit, complete information, great deal of price control **10-3, 10-5**
2. It is expensive and a firm may need special licenses, patents, raw materials, and special technology to enter; unique equipment and government restrictions make it difficult to exit. **10-5**
3. The monopolist is the only firm. **10-5**
4. Both curves are the same. **10-6**
5. Research and development, advertising, and lower costs of production. **10-5**
6. Yes, somewhat; they can decrease consumption and they can register complaints with the government to influence the rates. **10-5, 10-6**
7. No; they are regulated by the government. **10-6**

Close

Have students add to the continuum they copied into their notebooks in the *Close* activity for the first section by writing **monopoly** in the appropriate place.

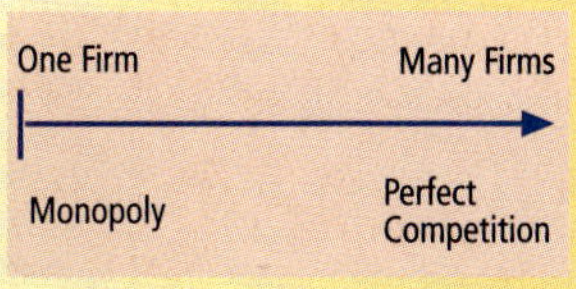

Chapter Close

Your Economic Portfolio

Ask students to imagine that they are in charge of public relations for a new monopoly in a large city. Point out that the company can provide any product or service students choose, but the decisions students make must reflect those of a true monopoly. Tell students to imagine that their company has purchased a full page in the local newspaper to use for an advertisement, announcement, informative article, or other introductory document to let the public know how it will be served by the monopoly and to encourage public good will. Individually, have students write this newspaper ad or article, making sure to include information related to the five defining market characteristics of a monopoly. Encourage students to include graphics, compelling headlines, and subheads to catch and retain the reader's interest. Review students' work and help them make any necessary corrections before filing their ads or articles in their portfolios.

You may wish to provide the following end-of-chapter materials:

- *Skills & Concepts* worksheet
- *Content Review Workbook*
- Chapter *Assessment*
- Chapter *MicroExam*

Concepts in Brief

1. *Market organization* refers to the way in which participants in an industry are organized and how many participants there are. The four types of market organization are perfect competition, monopolistic competition, oligopoly, and monopoly. From the producer's side, market organization is determined by five characteristics: number of firms, type of product sold, ease of entering or leaving the industry, amount of information about the market, and degree of price control.
2. Perfect competition is a form of market organization in which there are a great many firms producing products that are exactly the same. There is a very good flow of information among firms, and it is easy to enter or leave the industry. No one has any control over price.
3. In perfect competition, a firm's demand curve is a horizontal line at the market price. There are three important results of perfectly competitive markets. First, price equals the per-unit cost of production, so there is no excess return to firms in that industry. Second, output is produced at the lowest possible unit cost, so there is economic efficiency. And third, price equals the added cost of producing the last unit of output, so society's resources are allocated well.
4. Monopoly is a form of market organization in which there is just one firm from which a consumer can buy the product. The monopolist has considerable control over price. But, monopolies are usually regulated by the government to prevent misuse of their power.
5. Since there is only one firm in a monopoly, the firm's demand curve is the market demand curve. A monopolist can be expected to produce at a level at which price is greater than the per-unit cost. This means that excess economic returns result. The monopolist is not likely to produce at the lowest possible cost per unit of output. So, production is not as efficient as it could be. Also, since price is above the added cost of producing one more unit of output, the monopolist allocates too few resources to production.
6. In some ways, monopolies can benefit a market society. Due to economies of scale, many products are produced at a lower cost than could be done otherwise. Monopolists also do a good deal of research and development. And, monopolists' support of the media through advertising helps make radio and television shows available and lowers subscription prices for newspapers and magazines.

Economic Foundations

1. List four kinds of market organization.
2. Identify five characteristics that differentiate among forms of market organizations.
3. Describe *perfect competition* by using the five characteristics of market organization.
4. Draw the demand curve for the perfectly competitive firm. How does it compare with the market demand curve?
5. What is the level of output and price for the perfectly competitive firm?
6. Describe *monopoly* by using the five characteristics of market organization.
7. Draw the demand curve for the monopolistic firm. How does it compare with the market demand curve?
8. What is the level of output and price for the monopolistic firm?

Your Economic Vocabulary

Build your economic vocabulary by matching the following terms with their definitions.

1. a good or service that varies little from producer to producer
2. total revenue minus total costs
3. a firm that takes a price determined by forces outside the firm's control
4. a legal protection for the inventor of a product or process that gives that person or company the sole right to produce the product or use the process for up to 17 years
5. a form of market organization in which there is only one seller of a product
6. the way participants in markets are organized and how many participants there are
7. a firm that has some control over the price at which its product sells
8. a form of market organization in which a great many small firms produce a homogeneous product
9. a situation in which it is not practical to have competition

economic profit
homogeneous product
market organization
monopoly
natural monopoly
patent
perfect competition
price setter
price taker

Your Economic Vocabulary

1. **homogeneous product**
2. **economic profit**
3. **price taker**
4. **patent**
5. **monopoly**
6. **market organization**
7. **price setter**
8. **perfect competition**
9. **natural monopoly**

Economic Foundations

1. (1) Monopoly; (2) oligopoly; (3) monopolistic competition; (4) perfect competition (p. 245)
2. (1) Number of firms; (2) type of product sold; (3) ease of entering or leaving industry; (4) amount of information about the market; (5) degree of price control (p. 246)
3. Perfect competition: a large number of firms; firms are selling a homogeneous product; complete freedom to enter or leave the industry; perfect information about the market; no single firm has control over the market price. (pp. 250-251, 253)
4. Students' demand curves for a firm should show a horizontal line at the market equilibrium price. The market equilibrium price is at the intersection of the downward sloping market demand curve and the upward sloping market supply curve. (p. 254)
5. The level of output is the amount at which economic profit is zero, and price is just equal to the average cost of producing each unit of output. (pp. 254-256)
6. Monopoly: only one firm; a unique product; very difficult, if not impossible, to enter or leave the industry; complete information; good deal of control over price. (pp. 257-258, 260)
7. Students' monopolist's demand curves should slope downward to the right. The monopolist's demand curve is identical to the market demand curve. (p. 262)
8. The level of output is at the level with the greatest difference between total revenue from sales and total cost of production, and price is greater than the cost of production, so profit results, unless the price is regulated. (pp. 262-263)

Thinking Critically About Economics

1. Consider the characteristics of a perfectly competitive market. Why do you think governmental policy generally tries to promote competition?
2. What are the good and bad features of a monopoly? Give examples of two goods or services your household buys from firms that have a monopoly. Why do you think those firms have a monopoly?
3. Explain why the demand curve for a perfectly competitive firm is a horizontal line at the market price. Why does the demand curve in the case of a monopoly have a negative slope?

Economic Enrichment

Shelly Egan and her brother Bob have decided to start a business next summer so they can earn money to help with college expenses that fall. They need to choose a business for which entry is easy and inexpensive. It also will be important for them to leave the business easily once college begins. They decide on a house cleaning and lawn care business. They currently have one lawn mower, one electric weed eater, and a small truck. They plan to hire friends as needed to meet the demand if the two of them can't do all the work themselves.

Develop a plan for Bob's and Shelly's business. Include a list of the things Bob and Shelly will need to start and operate their business. Consider the following issues in the plan you develop: How easy will it be to get started? How much money will they need? How will they distribute information to potential customers? Will they have a lot of competition? What will their demand curve look like? Are they more likely to be "price setters" or "price takers"?

Thinking Critically About Economics

1. Answers may include that competition leads to efficient production, a desirable balance between the costs of producing goods and the benefits those goods provide to consumers, and no excess profits.
2. Answers should include that monopolies are good because they can take advantage of economies of scale, they do considerable product research, and they help to subsidize radio, TV, and magazines through advertising expenditures; monopolies are bad to the extent that they may exploit consumers and are often inefficient in production. Answers will vary but may include natural gas, cable TV, electric service, phone service, and water service. Answers may include that these firms fall into the class of natural monopolies.
3. It is horizontal because no single firm in a perfectly competitive industry can control price so they are all price takers, accepting the market price determined by supply and demand. Since the monopoly *is* the industry, the demand curve is negatively sloped; it is identical to the industry, or market, demand curve.

Economic Enrichment

Students' plans will vary, but may include that Bob's and Shelly's business can be classified as perfectly competitive, with complete freedom to enter or leave the marketplace; they probably will not need a great deal of start-up money, but they will need to buy gasoline and oil for the lawn equipment as well as supplies for the cleaning service; advertising could be accomplished with flyers or newspaper ads or through word of mouth; the amount of competition will vary according to the number and quality of competing lawn care and cleaning services in the area; their demand curve will be a horizontal line at the level of the market price; and, because they will have to offer their services at a rate that is competitive with other similar businesses, they will be price takers.

Math and Economics

In a recent year, about 62,600,000 acres of wheat were harvested in the United States. The average yield per acre was 38.3 bushels. What was the total production of wheat in that year? The average price per bushel that year was $3.20 per bushel. How much revenue went to farmers for their wheat production that year?

Writing About Economics

In many areas, cable television companies have a local monopoly. Research the pros and cons of having multiple suppliers of cable in any one geographic area. Then, write a short play that depicts an exchange between owners of a cable television company and government representatives. The play could take place in a courtroom setting, at a city council meeting, or at a congressional committee meeting.

Your script should accurately reflect the following positions: The cable company wants to have a local monopoly and the government wants to promote competition. The dialogue should cover pricing, production costs, benefits to society, and any other areas you think are important to this issue.

Math and Economics

2,397,580,000 bushels ($62,600,000 \times 38.3$); $7,672,256,000 ($2,397,580,000 \times \$3.20$)

Writing About Economics

Students' scripts will vary but should include logical arguments for both parties. The cable company may argue that, due to economies of scale, a regulated monopoly could produce the service for a lower cost and, therefore, provide it at a lower price for consumers; it may also argue that it is better for the environment and society if there is only one set of underground cable lines. The government may argue that competition among cable companies will keep prices low and quality high for consumers; and, in order to compete, companies will be motivated to find better, cheaper, more ecologically sound ways to provide service in the future.

Chapter 11 Monopolistic Competition and Oligopoly

Chapter Theme

In Chapter 11, students learn the characteristics of the two most prevalent forms of market organization in the United States: monopolistic competition and oligopoly. Students will study the market characteristics of firms having these types of organization and how they differ from monopolies and perfectly competitive firms.

Section	Special Features
Many Firms, Differentiated Products	Multicultural Highlights Economic Dilemma Eye on Market News Econ & You
Few Interdependent Firms	Internet Connection Global Economy Perspectives: Thinking Like a Producer Economic Spotlight Economics & Your Community Economic Talk Media Link

Video Activity

Chapter 11, OPEC

Search Chapter 11, Play to 12

On the chalkboard or an overhead transparency, have students brainstorm a list of paper and plastic products that they use every day. Then, ask respondents to describe how they might be affected if one of those industries were to become a cartel similar to OPEC.

	Print Resources	Media Resources	Assessment
	Effective Teaching Model Lesson Plans *Skills & Concepts* worksheet *Problem Solving* worksheet *Casebook* *Economic Measurement Workbook* *Content Review Workbook* *Spanish Resources*	VHS CD-ROM Videodisc *Arctic Express* *Interactive* ECONOMICS Template software	*Your Economic Portfolio* Chapter *Assessment* Chapter *MicroExam*

Special Learners	Print Resources	Media Resources	Assessment
Auditory Activity	*Enrich* worksheet *Life Skills* worksheet	Computer Overhead and *Transparencies 11-1* and *11-2*	*Checkpoint* Section 1 Quiz
Kinesthetic Activity ESL Visual Activity Cooperative Learning Activity	*Teacher's Connection to the Internet* *Reteach* worksheet	Overhead and *Transparencies 11-3* and *11-4* Computer	*Checkpoint* Section 2 Quiz

Careers Activity

One well-known oligopoly is the airline industry. Annually, this industry employs more than 100,000 flight attendants. Flight attendants look after the safety and comfort of passengers. They are trained to handle air emergencies, inform passengers of safety procedures, take care of passengers' questions and special needs, and serve food and beverages during flights.

Flight attendant candidates must be at least 19 to 21 years old and have a high school diploma. A college education and experience working with the public are helpful. Most newly hired attendants complete four to six weeks of intensive training. Flight attendants work an average of 75 to 85 hours per month and may receive free or discounted air fares. Salaries range from $15,000 to $35,000 per year.

In an oligopoly, when one company makes changes, other similar companies are often affected. Have students make a spider map (wheel with spokes) showing some of the possible ways all flight attendants are affected when one airline goes out of business.

CHAPTER 11

Teaching Materials

Program Resources

- Student text
- *Effective Teaching Model Lesson Plans*
- *Overhead Transparencies 11-1 to 11-4*
- *Life Skills* worksheet
- *Problem Solving* worksheet
- *Reteach* worksheet
- *Enrich* worksheet
- *Skills & Concepts* worksheet
- *Casebook*
- *Economic Measurement Workbook*
- *Content Review Workbook*
- *Spanish Resources*
- Video package
- *Teacher's Connection to the Internet*
- *Arctic Express*
- *Interactive ECONOMICS*
- Template software

Assessment

- Section Quizzes
- Chapter *Assessment*
- Chapter *MicroExam*

Overview

Section One
Many Firms, Differentiated Products

Section Two
Few Interdependent Firms

270

Teacher to Teacher

Hand out one new pencil to each of five students. Ask one student to name a selling price for his or her pencil. Then, ask the other four students to name their prices. Advise students to price their items at or just below the original seller's price, leaving little or no money "on the table." Explain that firms in an oligopoly often follow a price leader in order to remain competitive. Next, tell the class that you need to buy a writing implement. Allow students to offer their own pens or pencils at any reasonable price. Explain that, in monopolistic competition, products are basically similar, but they may vary somewhat among individual firms. For example, all writing implements are basically similar, but some are fancier or last longer. So, firms can set their own prices, as long as they remain competitive.

Laurence H. Jaffe
Rutgers University
New Brunswick, NJ

Monopolistic Competition and Oligopoly

Learning Objectives

11-1

Describe monopolistic competition in terms of the five characteristics of market organization.

11-2

Draw the demand curve and explain the level of output and price for the monopolistically competitive firm.

11-3

Describe oligopoly in terms of the five characteristics of market organization.

11-4

Draw the demand curve and explain the level of output and price for the oligopolistic firm.

11-5

Compare the four forms of market organization.

Outside Resources

- *Yellow Pages*
- Three same-subject student textbooks from different publishers
- *MacWorld,* other computer magazines, or mail-order software catalogs
- Copies of *Money* or other financial magazines
- Blank index cards
- Colored pens or markers
- List of businesses associated with the local chamber of commerce
- Posterboard
- Computer
- Integrated software (desktop-publishing, graphics)
- Assortment of current magazines

Vocabulary

monopolistic competition, p. 272
product differentiation, p. 273
oligopoly, p. 281
pure oligopoly, p. 283
differentiated oligopoly, p. 283
collusion, p. 287
cartel, p. 287

Focus

Before class, gather as many phone books containing the *Yellow Pages* as possible. (You may be able to borrow multiple phone books from your school's media center or various department offices.) As students enter the classroom, divide them into as many groups as you have phone books. Hand out a phone book to each group and tell students to choose a product or service that is listed in the *Yellow Pages.* Instruct the groups to look up their chosen products or services in the *Yellow Pages,* count the number of firms listed under the headings, and record the products and the number of firms on a sheet of paper. Allow groups to choose other products or services and repeat the process. Continue this activity as long as time allows.

As a class, continue the previous *Focus* activity by discussing the types of products each group looked up and the number of firms it found under each listing. Discuss what the number of firms may indicate about the type of market organization. Remind students that the most important of the five characteristics of market organization is the number of firms in the market.

FOCUS

Section One
Many Firms, Differentiated Products

What Do You Think?

Weiss, Inc., makes ketchup and distributes it to retail supermarkets. The ketchup is sold as Weiss ketchup in grocery stores throughout the country. The same ketchup is also bottled as the private store brand for the Bates Supermarket chain, which includes 30 stores. So, the same ketchup is sold under two different brands: Weiss and Bates. Do you think these products are the same in the eyes of consumers?

Terms to Know

monopolistic competition

product differentiation

What's Ahead?

Most of the economic activity in the United States takes place in markets that are either monopolistically competitive or oligopolistic. In this section, you will learn about the market characteristics of firms that operate in monopolistic competition. You will see how these firms differ from both monopolies and perfectly competitive firms.

CHARACTERISTICS OF MONOPOLISTIC COMPETITION

monopolistic competition a market organization in which many firms produce goods that are different but similar enough to be substitutes

Monopolistic competition is a market organization in which many firms produce goods that are different but similar enough to be substitutes. You learned in Chapter 10 that five characteristics can be used to classify market organization: number of firms in the market, type of product sold, ease of entering or leaving the industry, amount of information about the market, and degree of price control. In the last chapter, you also learned about perfect competition and monopoly. As the name implies, monopolistic competition has some characteristics of monopoly and some of perfect competition. Overall, it is closer to perfect competition than to monopoly. Now you will learn how monopolistic competition is defined in terms of the characteristics of market organization.

Many Sellers

In monopolistic competition, there are many firms from which a given type of product can be bought. Although there are more firms in an industry classified as perfectly competitive, monopolistic competition does provide many different suppliers from which to choose.

Imagine, for example, that you want a haircut. You have many choices about where to buy that service. If you look in the *Yellow Pages* of your local phone book, you will find many listings under the headings *Barbers* and *Beauty Salons.* Even in fairly small cities, the combined listings can run more than 10 pages. In almost any city, there are many places where you can get a haircut.

Differentiated Product

In monopolistic competition there is product differentiation. **Product differentiation** is the concept that the product of one firm can be distinguished from the products of other firms. There may be actual physical differences between products, or the differences may be superficial. This can be illustrated in the market for breakfast cereals. There are very clear taste and physical differences among corn flakes, raisin bran, and puffed rice, for example. Almost anyone would be able to taste the differences among these cereals. And, anyone with reasonably good eyesight could tell them apart on the store shelf. The containers' colors and brand names make them clearly different.

product differentiation
the concept that the product of one firm can be distinguished from the products of other firms

Product differences may not always be so clear. Consider two different brands of the same kind of breakfast cereal: Post Raisin Bran and Kellogg's Raisin Bran. Many people have a strong preference for one brand over the other. Others claim to have no preference at all. There is not as much physical and chemical difference between these cereals as between raisin bran, corn flakes, and puffed rice. Why, then, do some people form such strong brand preferences? The answer involves psychological reasons. To some people, the ads for Kellogg's Raisin Bran may be more appealing. Other consumers may like the color and design of the Post Raisin Bran box better than the other box. The reason for brand preferences is not as important as the simple fact that preferences do exist and are sometimes very strong.

Teach

Explain that **monopolistic competition** is closer to *perfect competition* than to *monopoly* by pointing out the similarities and differences in their five characteristics of market organization. Point out that **product differentiation** is the main characteristic that separates monopolistic competition from perfect competition. Emphasize that products can be differentiated through physical, superficial, and psychological criteria. Discuss the role advertising plays in this process. Illustrate that, in a monopolistically competitive market, the demand curve has a negative slope and the firm's demand curve is less steep than the market demand curve.

Multicultural *Highlights*

A few years ago, David Filo and Jerry Yang decided the Internet needed its own *Yellow Pages.* Shortly thereafter, *Yahoo* (Yet Another Hierarchical Officious Oracle) was born. *Yahoo* is a catalog of World Wide Web home pages that are organized by subject. Filo and Yang, European-American and Asian-American (respectively) Ph.D. students at Stanford University, began *Yahoo* as a personal list of their favorite Web sites. Now, *Yahoo* boasts more than 200,000 daily users! Elicit from students specific market characteristics of Filo's and Yang's business. Ask what type of market organization it is. If possible, allow students to take a look at *Yahoo* at **http://www.yahoo.com/**.

Apply

List the terms **physical, quality, function, packaging,** and **brand name** on the chalkboard. Brainstorm with the whole class students' favorite brands of items such as cereals, athletic shoes, and cars. As individual students express their preferences, have them clearly identify why they prefer a certain product over a substitute. Have students classify their preferences under one of the five category headings listed on the chalkboard. Keep a running tally of preferences and total each category at the end of the discussion. Point out which category scored the highest, making it the most important to students. Discuss why this preference seems to be so important. Reinforce that, in monopolistic competition, there must be product differentiation and that this is the most important characteristic separating monopolistic competition from perfect competition.
Guided Practice

For products to be considered differentiated, consumers must be able to tell one product from another. The differences may be in physical characteristics, function, quality, or just in the brand, trademark, or package. Consider the example of a haircut. In a sense, one haircut is just like any other haircut. It makes little difference where you go. On the other hand, we know that people develop very strong preferences and loyalties to particular businesses and even to specific hairstylists. This appears to be true for both men and women.

Here are ten representative names from one phone book of places where a person can get a haircut:

1. Bell Hair Designs
2. Campus Barber Shop
3. Mirror's Image
4. Razor's Edge
5. The Squire Barber Salon
6. Creative Hair Designers
7. Luau's Salon of Beauty
8. Star Barber Shop
9. Sande's Hair Shoppe
10. Guy's and Gal's Hair Styling

Knowing only that each place takes both female and male customers, which would you choose? If you ask 100 people this question, probably each of the ten choices will be selected. Firm names alone will create some kind of preference. "Luau's Salon of Beauty" has a different image than "Star Barber Shop." Some of the names may appeal more to women than to men and vice versa. Some will appeal more to young people, while others will appeal more to older consumers.

The important point is that the product (or service in this example) becomes differentiated in our minds as soon as we know the producer's name. This service also may be differentiated by the shop's location, its cleanliness and design, and the quality of the haircuts. The fact that products are differentiated in monopolistic competition is the most important characteristic separating this form of market organization from perfect competition.

Relatively Easy to Enter or Leave the Industry

With respect to the ability of firms to enter or leave the industry, monopolistic competition is much closer to perfect competition than to monopoly. *Entry into and exit from monopolistically competitive industries is relatively easy.* Usually, there are few, if any, regulations imposed by the government. Getting started in business in monopolistic competition requires less money than, say, steel production or the production of electric power.

For example, think about the restaurant industry. Look in the *Yellow Pages* for your area under the heading *Restaurants*. You probably will find many firms listed. They all have at least one thing in common. They are all places where prepared meals can be bought. But, they also may be very different from one another. At some restaurants, the meals may be eaten only in the restaurant; while at others, the meals may be taken out. In some cases, either choice is possible. The types of food available may differ quite a bit: from salads and sandwiches to lobster and prime rib. Many of the restaurants in your area may be fairly new. Perhaps they opened within the past five years. Other restaurants may have gone out of business in the past five years. Businesses in monopolistic competition enter and leave the industry with relative ease and freedom.

Reasonably Complete Information About the Market

Firms in a monopolistically competitive industry have reasonably complete information about conditions that may affect the business. Each firm knows approximately how much other firms pay for labor, raw materials, and other inputs. All firms can find out the prices that the others charge. They all have the same access to existing technology. Through trade associations, government publications, and private sources, all firms can learn a great deal about the demand for the product or service produced.

Think about restaurants again. If you opened a sandwich shop, you would know approximately how much other similar firms paid for bread, meats, cheeses, labor, rent, and other inputs. You could find out what prices they charged for similar products by watching their ads or visiting them. You could get information from government publications about how much money local residents spend at restaurants. And, you could get a more personal feel for demand by observing business at other similar restaurants.

Economic Dilemma

BUSINESS OR BRIBE?

The textbook industry at all levels of education is a pretty competitive business. There are lots of publishers involved and many publishers print more than one title for each subject. This means that the people who decide which books will be purchased (mostly teachers) have a lot of choices. For most subjects, there are several to many quality texts available. That's certainly quite true in the subject area of economics—and we think you got the best of the best.

In today's changing world, texts are increasingly being integrated with technology-based supplements. Examples include CD-ROMs, computer simulations, Internet connections, and videotapes and disks. Unfortunately, some schools do not have the hardware or equipment to fully utilize these supplements. This restricts the level of sales for the supplements and/or the entire text package. In turn, the lower sales make it harder for publishers to justify the very high cost of producing good simulations, CDs, and other quality learning aids.

In the past, some publishers have told schools that if they order the text package the publishers will provide all or part of the necessary equipment. Is this ethical? Is it a bribe? Or, is it a mechanism to get state-of-the-art learning packages into the hands of students? What do you think?

Economic Dilemma

Have students analyze the amount of product differentiation within the textbook industry by comparing same-subject textbooks. Explain that one way firms differentiate themselves from others is by creating a competitive analysis that compares the strengths and weaknesses of their products with those of other similar products. Brainstorm with the whole class categories to use in a textbook comparison. (Number and quality of visuals, depth of coverage of subject matter, number and type of special features, name recognition of authors, and so on) As a group, create a form for the comparison and make several copies. Have students work in small groups to create a competitive analysis for at least three same-subject textbooks from three different publishers.

Explain to students that many firms differentiate their products from others by giving away "freebies" to the customer. As a class, discuss whether it would be a good idea to give away freebies in each of the four types of market organization. Ask students whether they think these items are truly free. If not, who do they think ultimately pays for them? Then, have students brainstorm situations in which giving away freebies might be unethical. When might it be illegal? Ask students if they can think of any situation in which giving away freebies would be unethical but not illegal (or vice versa). Have each student write an essay examining these issues and defending his or her position.

Reinforce the concept of **product differentiation,** which occurs when many firms produce substitute goods in a market. Lead students in a game in which one student names a product, the next student names a substitute product, and a third student describes the differences between them (with help from the previous two students, if necessary). Start the game with the first student in the first row in the classroom and end with the last student in the last row. When everyone has participated, ask students if they observed any trends in their responses. In other words, was one type of difference more common than others? Discuss whether students think the differences among similar products are more important when the products are offered at the same price or when one is less expensive than the other.

Copy the outline of the following graphic organizer onto the chalkboard or an overhead transparency, omitting all labels except **MONOPOLISTIC COMPETITION** in the center circle. Direct students to copy the graphic organizer into their notebooks, filling in each of the five outer boxes with one of the five characteristics of market organization. Then, tell students to fill in one characteristic specific to monopolistic competition on the line radiating from each box. Have students exchange papers and check their answers.

Independent Practice

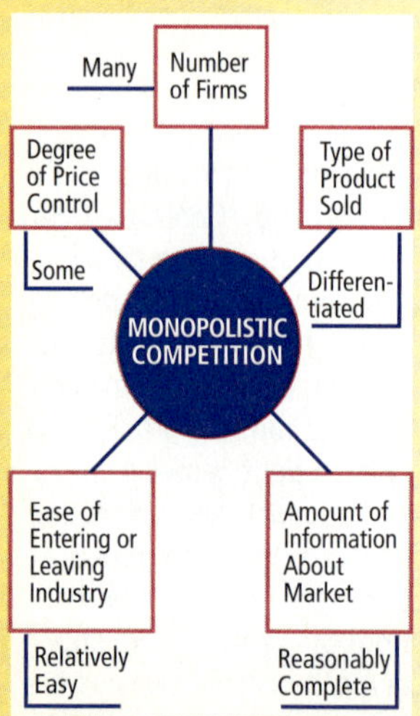

Some Price Control

Firms in monopolistic competition have some control over price but not very much. This is mainly because there are many firms producing products that are good substitutes for each other. If the price of Coke were much higher than the price of Pepsi, few cola drinkers would buy Coke. The degree of price control any firm has depends on how different the consumers think its product is. If buyers view two products as very different, the price difference between them can be greater. For example, economic reasoning would suggest that the price difference between Kellogg's Raisin Bran and Post Raisin Bran would be less than the price difference between Kellogg's Raisin Bran and a box of generic raisin bran cereal. Kellogg's and Post Raisin Bran cereals are generally seen as more alike than Kellogg's and a generic box of the same type of cereal.

The same situation can be observed in the restaurant business. Those that serve similar meals usually have prices that are close. A spaghetti dinner will not differ much in price from one family restaurant to another. A breakfast of two eggs, bacon, hash browns, and juice costs about the same regardless of where you buy it as long as the restaurants are of a similar type. As the type of meal or the type of restaurant becomes more different, price difference also increases. A steak dinner at an elegant restaurant will cost more than the same dinner at a cafeteria-style steak restaurant. But, as long as the products and services are close substitutes, individual firms cannot exert much price control.

PRODUCING IN A MONOPOLISTICALLY COMPETITIVE MARKET

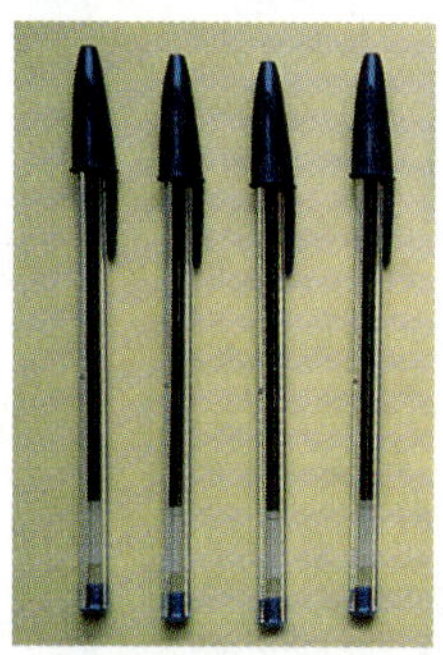

There are many close substitutes in a monopolistically competitive market. Remember, though, that even the closest substitute products are not exactly the same. There is some product differentiation. In fact, if we defined products narrowly, each firm would have a monopoly. You could not produce jeans and sell them under the Levi's name. If you wanted to open a fast-food restaurant, you could not construct a building with golden arches and call it McDonald's. These two firms have a legal monopoly over the use of those names. Bic has a monopoly in the production of Bic pens. There are other pens that are very similar, but they do not carry the Bic name. So, all such firms have some monopoly power. They are the only ones that can make and sell those exact products.

The Demand Curve for a Monopolistically Competitive Firm

As Figure 11-1 shows, the demand curve for a firm in monopolistic competition will have a negative slope. More can be sold at lower prices than at higher prices. The small amount of monopoly power resulting from product differentiation is what gives the firm some slight control over price. This control over price is reflected in the negative slope of the demand curve.

The demand curve for the firm looks flatter than the market demand curve. This is because for the individual firm, the quantity demanded is likely to be fairly responsive to changes in price. If Mobil raised the price

EyeOnMarket*News*

Bring to class issues of *MacWorld,* other computer magazines, or mail-order software catalogs. Divide the class into groups of three or four and allow students to skim the advertisements. Tell each group to make a chart that lists software companies across the top and types of available software along the side. Make sure students include the following types of software: operating system, groupware, network mail, spreadsheet, word processing, database, and presentation. Then, tell them to list in each software category at least one product supplied by each company. As a class, compare charts and discuss which products seem to be the most widely advertised. Does one firm have a true monopoly in computer software?

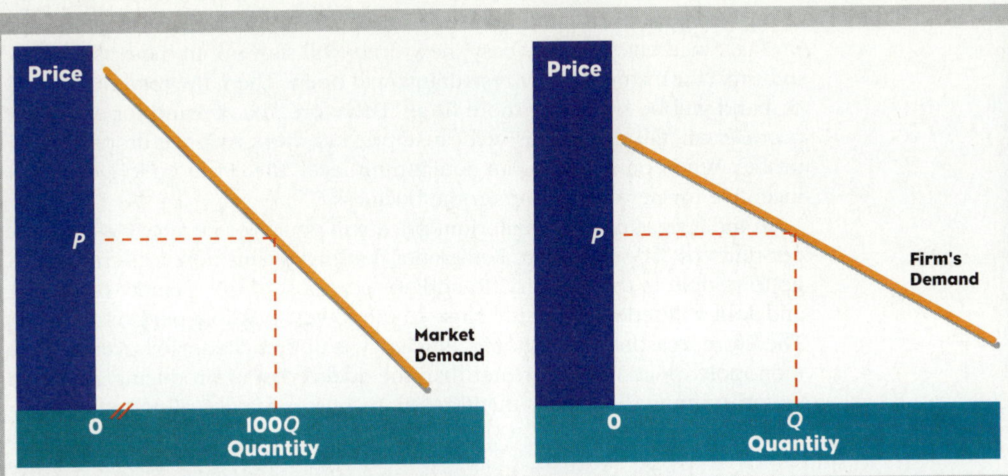

The Demand Curve for Monopolistic Competition

The left-hand diagram shows the demand curve for the market. The demand curve for a monopolistically competitive firm is shown in the right-hand diagram. The firm's demand curve is less steep than the market demand curve because the firm's sales are more sensitive to price changes than is the market in general. ***What do you think would happen to a firm's sales if it lowered price below the current level* P?**

of a gallon of regular gas to \$0.05 above what others are charging, it would lose some sales but not all of its sales. In comparison, wheat farmers asking \$0.05 more than the market price per bushel would lose all their sales. People with a strong brand preference for Mobil gas probably would pay the higher price. But people don't form a brand preference for wheat. What if Mobil raised its price to \$1 more than what other gas stations charge per gallon? Do you think many people would have a strong enough brand preference to continue buying Mobil?

Output and Price Levels

In determining how much to produce and what price to charge, firms in monopolistic competition act much like monopolists. If the sale of an added amount increases revenue more than it increases costs, the firm is well-advised to do so. If the added costs go up more than the added revenue, the firm should not sell more. By making such comparisons, the firm might settle on *Q* in Figure 11-1 as the best amount. And, from the demand curve, you know that *Q* units can be sold at the price *P*. Therefore, *P* is the best price to charge.

Suppose that the firm represented by the demand curve in the right-hand side of Figure 11-1 sells 1 percent of the total industry sales. That is, that firm has 1/100 of the total market. If the average price for the industry is also at *P*, all firms in total will sell 100 times *Q*. This is the amount labeled 100*Q* on the left-hand side of Figure 11-1, which represents the market demand.

Analyzing *Graphics*

Caption Answer
It would sell more, and much of the increase would probably come at the expense of other firms selling a similar product or service.

Display *Overhead Transparency 11-1,* which shows the demand curve for a firm in a monopolistically competitive market. Have students compare this curve to two others that they analyzed in Chapter 10. Display *Overhead Transparencies 10-2* and *10-3.* Point out to students that *Figure 10-2* represents a demand curve for a firm in perfect competition, and *Figure 10-3* is a curve for a monopoly.

Have students work in small groups to create a cause-and-effect chart to illustrate what happens in monopolistic competition when profits are high. Students' completed charts may look like the following: large profits → new firms enter market → total market demand shared by more firms → demand for individual firm's product falls → price drops → profits drop → no new firms enter market.

Have students create posters or other visuals to summarize the similarities and differences in market characteristics of the three forms of market organization they have studied. Tell students that they can refer to the information in *Figure 11-2* but their work should graphically represent their findings. After presenting and explaining their work, discuss as a class the importance of selecting visuals, icons, and examples for presentation graphics that are clear and meaningful to the target audience.

Suppose prices become very high in such an industry and there are large profits. Since entry is fairly easy, new firms will start up. In the restaurant industry, for example, new restaurants will open. Then, the total market demand will be shared by more firms. Therefore, the demand for each firm's product will fall some. This will cause price to drop. As price drops, so will profits. When profits fall to an equilibrium level, there will no longer be incentive for new firms to enter the business.

In the long run, this equilibrium price will equal (or be very close to) the per-unit cost of production. Remember that this means no excess returns go to people in this industry. In addition, the cost of the quantity produced and sold will tend to be fairly close to the lowest possible per-unit cost. Therefore, reasonable economic efficiency is approached. However, as with monopoly, price will be greater than the added cost of producing an added unit of output. This means that too few resources may be allocated to that industry.

Econ & You

CREDIT UP CLOSE

The market for credit cards can be described as monopolistically competitive. There are many companies offering credit cards to consumers and each card has some differentiating feature(s). Many are very nearly identical except for the name of the issuing institution. In a recent year, more than 6,000 issuers of credit cards sent about 2 billion pieces of mail soliciting business. So, there are lots of firms offering cards that are pretty close substitutes for one another.

Which card is best? That depends. Maybe you want one with your photo on the front and would pay more to have such a card. Maybe you want one with no annual fee but a higher interest rate on unpaid balances. There is a big array of choices to pick from and you are not limited to just one credit card. You can have many, but be careful. Credit card debt can rise quickly if you are not careful and soon you may have trouble paying all those monthly bills that seemed far away when you said, "Charge it." Many people have ten or more bank, gas, and store credit cards ,and the average balance for bank cards runs about $1,700. You can see how people can get into debt too far by using credit cards.

You can get a free and informative booklet about credit cards from the Board of Governors of the Federal Reserve System. The booklet title is "Shop: The Card You Pick Can Save You Money." To request one, write to Board of Governors of the Federal Reserve System, Washington, D.C. 20551-0001.

Econ & You

Bring to class copies of *Money* or another financial magazine that lists credit card rates and fees. Have students make a chart listing at least four different credit card companies, their interest rates, and their annual fees. Have each student decide which company is most suitable for his or her needs and write a short summary explaining why. Have students consider such issues as whether they are going to pay in full each month or carry a balance in their account. You may wish to have students complete the *Life Skills* worksheet for Chapter 13 at this time. This worksheet explains how to establish credit and contains a credit card application for students to complete.

COMPARISON OF MONOPOLISTIC COMPETITION WITH MONOPOLY AND PERFECT COMPETITION

A firm in monopolistic competition has some monopoly power due to product differentiation. But, that power is not very strong since there are many substitute products available. While firms have some control over price, they don't have nearly as much control as monopolists. Because there are so many other firms in the same market, firms in monopolistic competition also have some characteristics of perfect competition. In fact, they often have so little control over price that they are fairly close to perfectly competitive firms. Figure 11-2 provides an update to the matrix first presented in Chapter 10 that compares the four forms of market organization.

Market Organization

Market Characteristic	Perfect Competition	Monopolistic Competition	Oligopoly	Monopoly
Number of Firms	great many	many		one
Type of Product Sold	homogeneous	differentiated		unique
Ease of Entry and Exit	very easy	relatively easy		very difficult
Amount of Information	complete	reasonably complete		complete
Degree of Price Control	none	some		great deal

Figure 11-2

Market Characteristics of Perfect Competition, Monopolistic Competition, and Monopoly

This matrix summarizes the five characteristics of perfect competition, monopolistic competition, and monopoly markets. ***Can you predict the market characteristics for oligopoly?***

Divide the class into three groups, one for each of the market organizations studied thus far. Have each group copy the five row headings and one applicable column heading from *Figure 11-2* onto a sheet of paper. Then, ask students to copy their graphic organizer four times. At the top of each page, have each group identify an industry within their market organization. Have each group research local or well-known firms in its chosen industry (by phone, in the library, and so on) and complete its organizers. Have each group present its findings to the class.

Analyzing *Graphics*

Caption Answer
Answers may include few interdependent firms, products that are the same or differentiated, relatively difficult to enter and exit, fair amount of information, and varied degrees of price control.

Assess

1. Perfectly competitive: homogeneous; monopolistically competitive: differentiated **11-1**
2. Perfectly competitive: none; monopolistically competitive: varying degrees **11-1, 11-2**
3. Students' demand curves should be similar to the curve on the right-hand side of *Figure 11-1.* The demand curve is less steep than the market curve. **11-2**
4. Production continues as long as revenues from sales are greater than the added cost of production; the demand curve tells the price at each quantity. **11-1, 11-2**
5. Perfect competition, because they both have many firms and ease of entry and exit **11-1**
6. It depends on the consumer, but probably yes because of product differentiation. **11-1, 11-2**
7. Answers will vary, but prices are probably different. **11-1, 11-2**

Close

Have each student add **monopolistic competition** to the correct location on the continuum that he or she started in Chapter 10. As a class, discuss why **monopolistic competition** appears close to the **perfect competition** end.

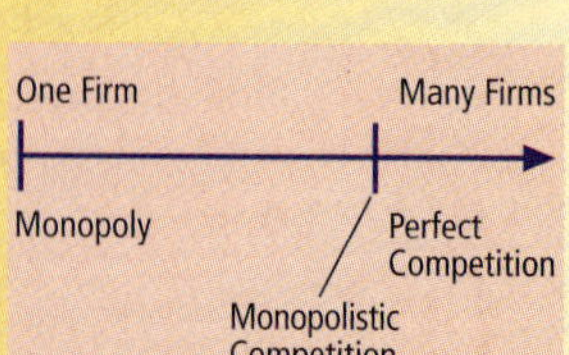

Checkpoint

Content Check

1. Compare the type of products sold in a perfectly competitive market to the type sold in a monopolistically competitive market.
2. Compare the degree of price control in a perfectly competitive market to the degree in a monopolistically competitive market.
3. Draw the demand curve for a monopolistically competitive firm and explain how it relates to the market demand curve.
4. How does a monopolistically competitive firm decide how much to produce and what price to charge?
5. Is monopolistic competition closer to perfect competition or to monopoly? Why?

What Do You Think Now?

Reread *What Do You Think?* in the Section One Focus. Then answer the following questions:

6. Do you think consumers would be willing to pay a higher price for Weiss ketchup? Why or why not?
7. Check prices on a national brand ketchup and a store brand ketchup. Was your original thinking correct?

Reteach

Pair students who understand monopolistic competition with those who are having difficulty. Have each pair draw a five-part illustration to show the five defining characteristics of a monopolistically competitive market organization. You may wish to display students' work on a bulletin board. **11-1, 11-2**

Enrich

Have students research a firm to find out whether it is a proprietorship, partnership, or corporation and whether it operates in perfect competition, monopolistic competition, oligopoly, or monopoly. Have students write a brief background story about the firm that they choose. **11-1**

Section Two
Few Interdependent Firms

FOCUS

What Do You Think?

Reggie and her grandmother were looking at used cars. Reggie needed a car to drive between school and work. They looked at Buicks, Fords, Chryslers, Toyotas, Acuras, Mercuries, Audis, Chevrolets, Nissans, and Volkswagens. There were so many models and styles and colors to choose from they had to keep track of what they liked by making notes. Do you think the auto industry is monopolistically competitive?

What's Ahead?

In some industries, there are relatively few firms or a few dominant firms with many smaller firms selling similar products. These industries are called *oligopolies.* In this section, you will learn about the market characteristics of oligopoly, how firms determine output levels and price, and how oligopolies compare to the other three market organizations.

Terms to Know

oligopoly

pure oligopoly

differentiated oligopoly

collusion

cartel

OLIGOPOLY

Oligopoly is a form of market organization in which there are relatively few firms. There is no absolute number of firms that separates oligopoly from monopolistic competition. In some industries that are oligopolies, there may be quite a few firms.

oligopoly
a form of market organization in which there are relatively few firms

Like monopolistic competition, oligopoly has some characteristics of both perfect competition and monopoly. Overall, the industries that would be classified as oligopolies are closer to monopolies in terms of how the firms behave. Most economic activity in the United States takes place in industries that are classified either as oligopolies or as monopolistically competitive. In the next few pages, you will read about oligopoly in terms of the five characteristics of market organization.

Focus

Before students enter the classroom, write the name of an oligopolistic industry (such as automobiles, steel, package delivery, pharmaceuticals, or petroleum) on the chalkboard or an overhead transparency.

As students enter, divide them into five groups. Have each group brainstorm the names of several firms that represent the industry that you selected. Then, assign one of the five characteristics of market organization to each group. Have the groups define their assigned characteristics according to the chosen industry.

Ask students to stay in the same groups as in the previous activity. On the chalkboard or an overhead transparency, create a chart of the five characteristics of market organization. Discuss with the whole class the five defining characteristics of the industry selected previously. Have a student from each group record examples of his or her group's assigned market characteristic in an appropriate place on the chart. Circle the best examples of the five characteristics and explain to students that these examples represent the chosen industry, which operates in an oligopolistic market.

Internet Connection

GOVERNMENT ANTITRUST POLICY AND THE INTERNET

In Chapter 5, you learned that promoting competition in the private sector is one of the major functions of government. In the real world, most industries are less than perfectly competitive. Promoting competition is a serious concern for government policy makers. Most monopolies in the United States today are regulated monopolies. This means that they are allowed to be the sole suppliers, but they are supervised by some government agency to make sure that they do not restrict supply and charge excessively high prices. In addition, the government is always wary of mergers between businesses in monopolistically competitive or oligopolistic industries. If an agency weren't watching over mergers in these types of industries, there would be increased concentration and monopoly power.

Two government agencies with responsibilities in the area of promoting competition are the Antitrust Division of the Justice Department, which enforces antitrust law, and the Federal Trade Commission, which protects against unfair business practices.

The Antitrust Division has a Web page, **http://gopher.usdoj.gov/atr/atr.html**, which provides policy statements of the agency and descriptions of current cases. This information is also available from the agency's Gopher site, **gopher://gopher.usdoj.gov/1/atr**.

Vanderbilt University has a very interesting Web page on antitrust policy, **http://www.vanderbilt.edu/Owen/froeb/antitrust/antitrust.html**. It includes a collection of business merger case studies, a summary of antitrust/merger law, and a regularly updated link called "In the News," which describes current merger activities.

The Federal Trade Commission has a Web page that provides a description of the agency, news releases, and an explanation of how the FTC begins an investigation, how the investigation proceeds, and the various ways an investigation is concluded, such as consent orders, cease and desist orders, and penalties. The URL is **http://www.ftc.gov**.

Internet Application: Visit the Vanderbilt Antitrust Policy Web page to find an interesting merger case in the news. E-mail the names of the firms involved to your teacher. Are these firms oligopolies or monopolistically competitive?

Economics Application: Based on what you learned in Chapter 11 about market organization, would you describe the commercial on-line services (CompuServe, America Online, Prodigy) as examples of monopolistic competition or oligopoly? Why?

Internet Connection

Remind students to carefully follow the directions to select an appropriate browser to read the Vanderbilt Antitrust Policy Web page. This resource is particularly good for making students aware of current events in this area.

Explanation for the Economics Application is in the *Teacher's Connection to the Internet.*

Be sure to check South-Western's Web and Gopher pages for updates to addresses.

Few Interdependent Sellers

We usually think of an oligopoly as an industry in which there are few firms. But, it is hard to assign an absolute number to the term *few.* The degree to which firms act independently of one another is more important than the exact number of firms. If there are a great many firms, such as in wheat production, we expect each to act on its own. That is, each firm will act independently of the others. But, think about the car industry where a relatively small number of firms dominate the industry. Each firm takes the actions and reactions of the other firms into account when making economic decisions. This interdependence that influences economic behavior is one key element of oligopoly.

Identical or Differentiated Products

In oligopoly, the products produced by different firms can be either nearly identical or differentiated. Consider the case of steel beams used in building bridges. The product is very much the same whether it is produced by Bethlehem Steel, USX (formerly U.S. Steel), or any other steel producer. In this case, the industry is a pure oligopoly. A ***pure oligopoly*** is an oligopoly in which the products are the same for all firms. The aluminum industry is also a pure oligopoly.

pure oligopoly
an oligopoly in which the products are the same for all firms

In other oligopolistic industries, there is considerable product differentiation. As with monopolistic competition, this product differentiation can be actual physical differences or differences perceived by the consumer due to brands, trademarks, packages, or other factors. Consider, for example, the car industry. The products are clearly differentiated. A Jeep is very different from a Cadillac. A Buick is different from a Toyota. Even products that are very similar in a strict physical sense may be viewed as very different by consumers. The Mercury Sable and Ford Taurus are very similar, yet some people would buy one and not the other. Thus, the two cars are considered differentiated. An industry such as this is called a *differentiated oligopoly.* A ***differentiated oligopoly*** is an oligopoly in which the product is differentiated.

differentiated oligopoly
an oligopoly in which the product is differentiated

Teach

Fine-tune the definition of **oligopoly** that students provided in *Focus* by relating the five characteristics you circled on the chart to the ones discussed in the textbook. Explain that, overall, oligopolies are closer to monopolies than to other types of market organizations. Emphasize that the key element of an **oligopoly** is the interdependency of the few firms operating in the industry. Compare **pure oligopoly** to **differentiated oligopoly,** especially in relation to the degree of price control. Define **collusion, cartel,** and *price leader* and explain how each affects price in an oligopolistic market. Illustrate that the demand curve for an individual oligopolist is negatively sloped, but that there is no single type of demand curve applicable to all oligopolies. Explain the kinked demand curve used to describe oligopolies. Discuss the costs and benefits to society of oligopolistic industries.

Apply

Copy the following graphic organizer on the chalkboard or an overhead transparency, labeling only the center and outer boxes. Ask for student volunteers to write the defining characteristics of an **oligopoly** on the single line radiating from each outer box. Discuss these characteristics as a class. Then, have students copy the completed graphic organizer into their notebooks.

Guided Practice

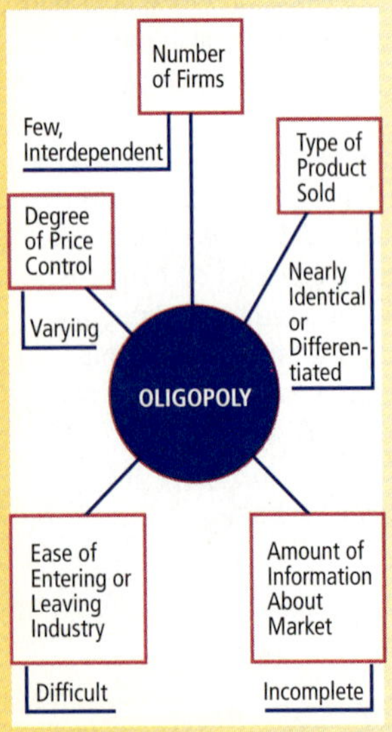

Difficult to Enter or Leave the Industry

It is fairly difficult to enter an industry that is oligopolistic. There are a couple of reasons for this.

First, most oligopolistic industries use very expensive and sophisticated equipment. It would cost a great deal of money to enter the car or steel industries at a scale that would be economically efficient. Hundreds of millions of dollars would be necessary to make even a serious attempt.

Second, because the products have a brand, buyers develop brand preferences that can be quite strong. Some people have always bought the same brand of car. This is true of many other products including televisions, stereo equipment, and other home appliances. The buyer for a large construction firm may prefer one company's steel beams because of the product's past performance. This might happen even though other companies produce very similar steel beams. A new firm would have a hard time overcoming people's existing brand preferences. Therefore, it would be difficult to get those important first-time sales.

Global Economy

MADE IN ________?

There was a time when U.S. companies dominated car sales in this country. There were very few imports and there were no foreign companies producing cars in the United States. This changed quite rapidly during the last half of the twentieth century. Foreign imports came in at lower prices, with models more to the liking of the modern consumer and with better quality ratings. Detroit, the one time auto capital of the world, was stunned and caught by surprise.

As we move toward the third millennium, this industry is in a continued state of change. It has become a truly global market. Japanese and German manufacturers are making cars in the United States. U.S. companies are selling and making cars and trucks in Europe and elsewhere. For example, in the early 1990s, I was personally surprised when the first car I saw upon walking out of the Moscow (Russia) airport was a Chevrolet Astro Van that was pretty similar to the one in my driveway thousands of miles away.

There are many joint ventures between U.S. companies and their foreign competitors. It is now hard to say whether some vehicles are foreign or domestic. Companies sell transmissions, engines, and even body designs to their competitors. Parts may be made anywhere in the world and assembled in the United States. How much of the final product is domestic is hard to determine, and trying to make such a determination probably is becoming less and less important.

Global Economy

As a homework assignment, have students choose 10 to 15 products that they or their families use at home and find out in what country each of the products is made. For each product, have students write on each index card the name of a product and the country in which it was made. Create a bulletin board that is divided into two sections: **Made in the U.S.A.** and **Made Elsewhere.** Have students post their products on the appropriate sides of the bulletin board. Then, discuss the economic impact on U.S. producers of our buying habits.

Leaving oligopolistic industries also can be pretty difficult. Because most of these industries use highly specialized machines, it is often very hard for a firm to exit and sell the equipment without great loss. When a firm does leave, it commonly does so by selling out to another firm. If the firm is in the same line of business, this creates a horizontal merger. An example of this occurred when Chrysler bought American Motors primarily to acquire the Jeep line of vehicles.

Incomplete Information About the Market

In oligopolistic industries, firms have less complete information about the market than in other forms of industry organization. Firms usually know how much other firms pay for labor, but there is much less reliable information for other inputs. One car company may pay more for steel than another car company does. This can be true even though the published list price for the steel is the same for all car companies. Because of their size, some oligopolistic firms can get a price reduction that other firms cannot get. This is true even in the money markets. When two firms go to a major bank, they may find that the interest rate to borrow money is not the same for both of them.

More trade secrets exist in oligopolistic industries than in any other type. Each car company will try to keep new designs, new advertising programs, and even major personnel changes secret as long as possible. Chemical companies such as Dow or Monsanto closely guard new product development, sales, and cost information. However, it is very difficult for these firms to prevent information from leaking out. People change jobs and move from one company to another. The firms are likely to buy things from the same suppliers and sell to the same buyers. So, information that either a supplier or a buyer may obtain can leak out (even accidentally) to other firms in the industry.

Varying Degree of Price Control

Firms in a differentiated oligopoly have a great deal of control over price. These large firms spend a lot of money on advertising to create and maintain consumer brand preferences. The car buyer who has bought a new Buick every three years since 1980 is not likely to change now. Therefore, that buyer is probably not very sensitive to price. And, surely the difference in price between a Buick and a Chevrolet will not be important to a buyer with such a strong brand preference.

Firms in a pure oligopoly have some control over price, but they usually have less control than firms in a differentiated oligopoly. A manufacturer of steel beams cannot price the beams much higher than other manufacturers do. Any firm's steel beams are likely to be satisfactory. In many cases, such products are bought solely on the basis of price. So, even favorable company preferences based on past performance may not give any one firm the ability to charge a higher price without hurting sales.

Review the concepts of a **pure oligopoly** and those of a **differentiated oligopoly.** Focus students on what might happen if a differentiated oligopoly, such as the automobile industry, suddenly became a pure oligopoly. Tell each student to write a newspaper article alerting consumers to this change. Also, have students include their own speculations about the immediate and long-range effects of this change on both the industry and consumers.

Independent Practice

Ask students to come up with clever ways to remember the market characteristics of an oligopoly. Then, independently, have students brainstorm a list of possible oligopolies and add them to a blank overhead transparency (not yet projected). Ask volunteers to share their devices for remembering the characteristics. Then, display the transparency naming possible oligopolies. Based on the characteristics students used to define **oligopoly,** review the list as a class, eliminating the "candidates" for oligopoly that do not meet the definition.

Perspectives

Thinking Like a Producer

Have students think of a new product that they would like to market. (Students may wish to use the product they developed for the patent application in the *Life Skills* worksheet for Chapter 10.) Have them decide which type of market organization would be the most likely in which to market their product and explain why. Then, tell students to imagine that they want to convince an investor to help finance their invention. Have them describe their product, its market organization, and their initial marketing strategy in a properly styled business memo.

Distribute a blank index card to each student. Have each student think of a product and write its name on the front of the card. Then, tell him or her to determine whether that product is within an industry that exists in perfect competition, monopoly, monopolistic competition, or oligopoly. Have students write the types of market organization on the backs of the cards and then pass their cards to you. Read the name of the product written on the front of each card and ask the whole class to vote on its type of market organization. Tally the votes for each suggestion and then work together as a class to determine whether the class, the student, or both are correct. Retain all correct (or corrected) cards to use as flash cards to help students who need further reinforcement.

To help nonnative speakers of English make the transition from economics terms possibly known in their native language to the English-language equivalent, have proficient bilingual students or an ESL teacher write the type of market organization in students' native languages in a second color above the English on the index card. (Use multiple colors for different languages.) Native speakers of Spanish can refer to *Spanish Resources* for support. Have students use these cards as vocabulary acquisition flashcards to help them remember the terms in English.

ESL

Economic Spotlight

THE OVERNIGHT SENSATION

How did a 1965 "C" term paper in Economics 43A at Yale University turn into FedEx, Frederick Smith's "overnight" sensation? Smith was given a "C" on his economics paper because his professor thought that Smith had thrown it together at the last minute. Smith based his paper on the hub-and-spoke concept used today by most major airlines. With this concept, a hub, or central, office in a middle-America location such as Little Rock or Memphis serves as a "feeder" to spoke cities in the far reaches of the country.

Smith didn't let the "C" convince him that his idea wouldn't fly. In April 1973, the former Marine pilot bought 14 small aircraft housed at Memphis International Airport and launched the overnight package delivery industry. Somewhere between 7 and 18 packages were shipped the first night. (No one knows the exact number because tracking wasn't an issue back then.) Overcoming great skepticism and on-going loan problems, Smith quickly grew FedEx into a phenomenal success. His company, then named Federal Express, was the first in U.S. history to report $1 billion in revenues within 10 years of start-up without the benefit of mergers or acquisitions. Today, the company's 5,000 employees ship 1 million to 1.5 million packages a night on more than 400 airplanes and thousands of trucks from 93 airports and several hundred smaller hubs. At the Memphis Superhub, computer monitors outnumber people by five to one, and more than 250 video cameras monitor packages moving over 171 miles of conveyer belts. The Superhub even has its own meteorology department to track the weather in 165 FedEx regions twice a day.

In 1994, the Federal Express Corporation officially changed the company name to FedEx to reflect customers' widely used nickname for the company. In fact, the public has coined a new verb inspired by Federal Express. To "FedEx" is now nationally understood to mean to "ship overnight." The name change was also a response to the needs of the company's fastest growing segment: international business. Non-native English speakers who had difficulty pronouncing "Federal Express" have found the new name much easier to pronounce. In fact, customers in almost 200 countries around the world have learned to "FedEx" with great enthusiasm. As a result, FedEx is able to bill itself as the world's largest express company.

Economic Spotlight

Frederick Smith is a classic example of an entrepreneur who had a great idea. Have students determine whether they have what it takes to be an entrepreneur like Smith by honestly assessing whether they are self-motivated, have a strong bond with their families, work hard at everything they do, are willing to listen to others, and are often in the right place at the right time. Also, ask students if they consider themselves to be managers, venture capitalists, planners, or doers and have them label their risk tolerance as high, moderate, small, or none. (Most entrepreneurs are doers with a moderate risk tolerance.) Then, have students write an essay entitled "Am I An Entrepreneur?," analyzing their entrepreneurial potential.

Collusion and Cartels. Because there are relatively few separate firms in an oligopoly, there is often incentive for them to make joint decisions. This is especially true of pricing decisions. ***Collusion*** is the situation of firms acting together rather than separately. So, if two or more firms make joint decisions, we say there is collusion between the firms. If this collusive behavior becomes formal and well organized, the firms become what is called a *cartel.* A ***cartel*** is a formal organization of firms in the same industry acting together to make decisions.

collusion
the situation of firms acting together rather than separately

cartel
a formal organization of firms in the same industry acting together to make decisions

The objective of having collusion and/or forming a cartel is to give the group of firms the power of a monopoly. All of the firms then can act as one and earn greater profits than if they acted separately. To consumers, this usually means a higher price and a lower level of output for purchase.

The most famous cartel probably is the international cartel known as OPEC (Organization of Petroleum Exporting Countries). This cartel has controlled oil prices and output throughout the world. In the United States, cartels are illegal. This does not mean firms do not practice collusion. However, it is often done secretly and is very hard to prove.

Price Leadership. In some oligopolistic industries, cooperation between firms exists but falls short of being a full cartel. Price leadership, for example, happens when one firm in an industry sets a price and other firms follow. The other firms then sell their product at the price set by the leader rather than set their own prices. It is illegal in the United States for managers of firms to decide collectively on a pricing strategy. Such action is considered collusion and is viewed as an attempt to form a cartel. However, it is not illegal for one firm to react to the price set independently by another firm.

The firm that acts as the price leader may vary from year to year. Often, the largest firm in the industry will be the price leader, but this is not necessarily the case. As long as all the other firms will follow, any firm can act as the leader.

PRODUCING AS AN OLIGOPOLIST

Managers in oligopolistic businesses probably pay more attention to the actions and reactions of other firms than do managers in any other industrial setting. You can see this in the car industry, in the steel industry, in banking, and in other oligopolistic industries. In the car industry, consumers see the result in terms of similar prices, similar designs, and similar timing of the release of new models.

The Demand Curve for an Oligopolist

The demand curve for an oligopolist is negatively sloped. As with monopolistically competitive firms, this is due mainly to the product differentiation that exists between firms. Unlike in the other forms of industry organization, there is not one type of demand curve that is good for all oligopoly cases. Probably the most famous type is a *kinked demand curve* such as the one shown in Figure 11-3 on page 288.

The demand curve is kinked because the responsiveness of the quantity demanded to a price change differs depending on whether the firm raises or

Point out to students that, sometimes, **cartels** or companies in **collusion** may practice *disinformation* to increase their profits. Discuss the ethics of disinformation, which is the deliberate release of false information. Explain that this term originated in political circles when one government would try to confuse another government's intelligence operations by "leaking" false information. Today, this term has been applied to companies' practices of leaking information about their products in order to generate sales, increase stock prices, and increase product prices. Emphasize that, like collusion, disinformation is extremely hard to prove. Ask students if they can name any possible examples of disinformation. (OPEC's declared gas shortage in the 1980s, perpetual going-out-of-business sales, unsubstantiated rumors of future price increases, and so on) As a class, discuss the ethical differences between a government's use of disinformation for defense and other political reasons and a company's use of it for profit.

Bring to class several magazines and newspapers and have students scan them for ads that represent oligopolistic industries. As a class, discuss the concept of price leadership and ask students to suggest examples of price leadership that they have observed in the real world. Ask students if any of the ads they pointed out earlier shows signs of price leadership by one particular firm.

Economics & Your Community

Contact your local chamber of commerce for a list of member businesses. Have small groups of students choose from the list three to four businesses that are of interest to them. Have each group look for telephone listings for these businesses in the local *Yellow Pages.* Remind students that the businesses, if listed, will be classified under the type of industry. Have them identify from the chamber of commerce information, a phone call, or the *Yellow Pages* each company's form of organization (proprietorship, partnership, or corporation) and then speculate about the company's type of market organization. As a whole class, discuss each group's conclusions.

Analyzing *Graphics*

Caption Answer
It is more elastic above the kink; a price increase from *P* decreases quantity more than an equal price decrease will increase quantity.

Display *Overhead Transparency 11-3,* which is one way of showing the market demand and the firm's demand in an oligopolistic market. Point out the kink in the firm's demand curve. To illustrate how this kink is created, have each student create two cause-and-effect charts. Tell students that one chart should show what happens when a firm raises its price and the other should show what happens when a firm lowers its price. (Firm raises price → no other firms follow → firm loses customers to other firms; firm drops price → other firms follow → sales in the market expand → firm's share of the market stays the same but sales increase because total quantity demanded in the market increases.)

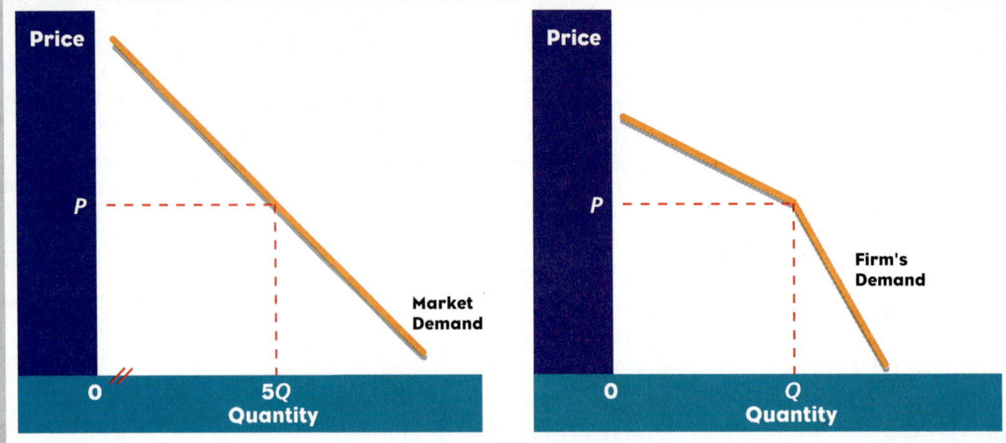

The Demand Curve for an Oligopolist

The demand curve for an oligopolistic firm is shown to the right of the market demand curve. The firm's demand is often drawn as a kinked demand curve. This shows that sales may be more responsive to a price rise than to a drop in the firm's price. ***Would you say that the demand curve for the oligopolist in the right-hand graph is more or less price elastic above the kink than below the kink?***

lowers price. Suppose the current price is at the level marked *P* in Figure 11-3. At *P*, the firm shown in the graph has 20 percent, or one-fifth of the total market. The firm's sales are *Q* units. In the left-hand graph, you can see that sales by all of the firms in the market are five times *Q* (5*Q*).

Suppose the firm lowers price to try to get a greater share of the market. The kinked demand curve shows that other firms will also cut price to prevent this firm from getting part of their sales. Therefore, the firm in the right-hand graph will not have much of an increase in sales by lowering price. So, its demand curve is very steep below the existing price *P*.

Now suppose this firm raises price. Other firms will not necessarily follow. If the others do not increase price, the firm that does will likely experience a large drop in sales. For this reason, the demand curve for the firm is very flat above the existing price *P*.

The kinked demand curve approach to an oligopolist's demand and pricing behavior does not explain all cases of oligopoly. It does, however, help to explain why some oligopoly prices do not change as frequently as prices in other industries. Many other approaches to oligopoly explain demand for the firm when the kinked demand curve is not appropriate.

Output and Price Levels

In deciding the levels of output and price, oligopolistic firms behave very much like firms in other situations discussed earlier. If selling an

Economic*Talk*

Divide the class in half. Then, on the chalkboard or an overhead transparency, write a scrambled version of one of the vocabulary terms for this chapter (for example, **poolliogy** for oligopoly). For an added challenge, combine two of the shorter vocabulary terms for students to unscramble. Award a point to the first group to identify the term and spell it correctly. Award another point to the first team to define the term correctly. Award yet another point to the first team to name a real-life example of the term. Repeat this process until all the vocabulary terms for this chapter have been guessed. Declare the team with the most points the winner.

added unit of output makes revenue go up more than costs go up, it will be profitable to sell that added output. On the other hand, if the added costs go up more than the added revenue, it will be better not to sell more.

In cases in which a cartel is formed or price leadership is followed, these principles may be altered by individual firms. Some firms may produce and sell less while others may produce and sell more. As a result of their decision, some firms may sacrifice profit for the overall good of the industry.

COMPARISON OF OLIGOPOLY WITH OTHER MARKET STRUCTURES

Firms in oligopolistic markets have some amount of monopoly power. Generally they have more monopoly power than do firms in monopolistic competition. This is due largely to the smaller number of substitute products available in oligopolies. There are fewer firms to provide competition.

This monopoly power, along with the relatively difficult entry of new firms, means that high profits may result. There is no guarantee of high profits, of course. In the automotive sector, we sometimes see that even with relatively few firms in a large market it is possible to lose money. In an oligopoly, however, prices will stay high enough to be profitable for most, if not all, firms involved.

In oligopoly, production is likely to occur at a level where the per-unit cost of output is not as low as possible. This means that the product is not produced as efficiently as is technically possible. In this regard, oligopoly is very similar to monopoly. The similarity continues if we compare price to the extra cost of producing an added unit of the product. As in monopoly, price is higher than this added cost, so we can conclude that too few resources are used in producing that product. For society to be best served, more should be produced and it should be sold at a lower price.

Firms in oligopolistic industries do benefit society, however. Pharmaceutical companies, car companies, petroleum companies, chemical companies, and others spend a great deal of money on research and development. Some of that money does not pay off since the research does not always produce usable products. But, much of the spending supports successful research that may benefit the whole society in the long run. In this respect, oligopolies are like monopolies.

Have students work in groups of four or five to role-play a price change in an oligopolistic market. Assign the following roles: a firm making a price change, a firm reacting to a price change, a consumer reacting to a price change, a facilitator describing the price scenario to the group, and, if there is a fifth member, a recorder taking notes of what happens throughout the process. If there are only four group members, the facilitator may also serve as the recorder. Allow the groups three to five minutes to play out at least two or three different scenarios. Have the recorders for all the groups describe to the class what happened in each of their scenarios. Discuss with the whole class whether the players acted as players in an oligopolistic market would. **Cooperative Learning**

MediaLink

Advertising is one means by which companies differentiate their products. Have each student use desktop-publishing software and/or graphics software to create an advertisement for the product he or she marketed in *Perspectives: Thinking Like a Producer* (p. 285) or the invention he or she patented in the *Life Skills* worksheet for Chapter 10. You may wish to bring to class several current magazines to allow students to scan the ads for ideas. Make sure students' ads stress how their product is different from other products.

Explain to students that an *icon* is an easy-to-recognize symbol for something. Show students several examples of icons (such as those for no smoking areas, handicap access, and women's or men's rest rooms). Divide the class into five groups—one for each market characteristic—and distribute a sheet of posterboard and several colored markers to each group. Lead each group to create an icon for its market characteristic. Then, have the groups adapt their icons to accurately represent each type of market organization. (For example, for perfect competition, price control might appear as a dollar sign in a red circle with a line through it.) Tell the groups to make posters of their work. Display all the posters on a wall as a reference for students.

Analyzing Graphics

Caption Answer
Answers may include perfect competition: corn; monopoly: natural gas; monopolistic competition: shoe retailers; and oligopoly: auto industry.

Firms in oligopolistic industries, like those in monopolistic and monopolistically competitive industries, also spend a lot of money for advertising. Many of the television specials and sports broadcasts are paid for by oligopolistic firms through advertising. Magazines with national distributions are full of ads by these companies. These firms also support broadcasts on public radio and television through donations.

Figure 11-4 gives a complete summary of the characteristics of the four forms of market organization. An example of each type of market structure is also included in this chart.

Market Organization

Market Characteristic	Perfect Competition	Monopolistic Competition	Oligopoly	Monopoly
Number of Firms	great many	many	few and interdependent	one
Type of Product Sold	homogeneous	differentiated	differentiated or homogeneous	unique
Ease of Entry and Exit	very easy	relatively easy	difficult	very difficult
Amount of Information	complete	reasonably complete	incomplete	complete
Degree of Price Control	none	some	varying degree—often considerable	great deal
Example	wheat	hair cuts	steel	electric power

Figure 11-4

Market Characteristics of Perfect Competition, Monopolistic Competition, Oligopoly, and Monopoly

This matrix summarizes the five characteristics of all four forms of market organization. ***Name an industry, besides the one given, that belongs in each group.***

Checkpoint

Content Check

1. Use the five characteristics of market structure to describe oligopoly.
2. Explain why the demand curve for an oligopolistic firm may be kinked.
3. How does an oligopolistic firm decide how much to produce and what price to charge?
4. Is oligopoly closer to perfect competition or to monopoly? Why?

What Do You Think Now?

Reread *What Do You Think?* in the Section Two Focus. Then answer the following questions:

5. Describe the auto industry in terms of the five market characteristics.
6. What market organization do you think the auto industry fits into?

Assess

1. Relatively few firms, homogeneous or differentiated products, relatively difficult to enter and exit, fair amount of information, some price control **11-3**
2. The quantity is more responsive to a price increase than a price decrease as is shown on the demand curve by a kink where quantity drops rapidly. **11-4**
3. It continues to produce as long as added revenue from sales is greater than added cost of production. The demand curve identifies price. **11-3, 11-4**
4. Monopoly because of some control over price, difficult entry and exit, fewer firms, and (sometimes) differentiated product **11-3**
5. Few firms, yet they are interdependent; differentiated product; difficult to enter and exit; some information; and some price control **11-3**
6. Oligopoly **11-5**

Close

Have students add to the continuum they copied into their notebooks in the *Close* activity in the first section by writing **oligopoly** in the appropriate place on the continuum. Have class volunteers verbally explain the reasoning behind their choice of location.

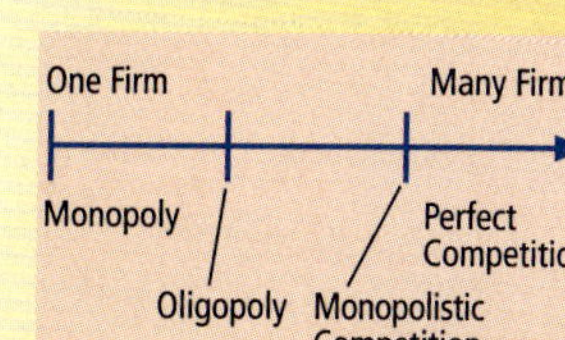

Reteach

Pair students who understand the four types of market organization with those who are having difficulty. Have each pair create four continuums similar to the one they completed in *Close* to show the differences in the number of firms. Tell students that each continuum should represent one of the other four characteristics of market organization. **11-5**

Enrich

Have students write a brief essay to explain the following statement: **An oligopolistic market is a game of sorts—one in which each player must try to guess the opposition's moves, bluffs, countermoves, and counterbluffs as many moves ahead as possible.** Discuss students' conclusions as a class. **11-3, 11-4**

Chapter Close

Your Economic Portfolio

Have students choose one of the four types of market organization and write a two-page newsletter directed to the employees of companies in that category. Point out that students' newsletters might provide news about the advantages of the chosen type of market organization (refer to *Figure 11-4*) or helpful hints (real or imaginary) on how to succeed in the market. Encourage students to use desktop-publishing software to create a newsletter with attractive headlines, related illustrations, and an easy-to-read format. Tell students to spell check before printing. Read students' newsletters and correct any misleading or inaccurate information before filing them in their portfolios.

You may wish to provide the following end-of-chapter materials:

- *Skills & Concepts* worksheet
- *Content Review Workbook*
- Chapter *Assessment*
- Chapter *MicroExam*

Concepts in Brief

1. Monopolistic competition is a form of market organization in which firms create products that, while different in some ways, are good substitutes for one another. Firms have good information about the market, and it is fairly easy to enter or leave the industry.
2. In monopolistic competition, price is usually very close to the unit cost of producing the product, so there is little, if any, excess return. The degree of economic inefficiency is small since output is produced close to the lowest possible cost. There is some misallocation of resources since price is greater than the cost of producing one additional unit.
3. Oligopoly is a form of market organization in which there are just a few firms. In some cases, the output is very much the same no matter which firm it comes from. In other cases, products are very different between firms. It is usually quite difficult to enter or leave an industry that is oligopolistic.
4. In oligopoly, price is likely to be greater than the cost per unit of output, so excess profits result in the industry. At the level of output that is best for the firm, price is greater than the added cost of producing one more unit of the product. So, too few resources are allocated to production. Also, oligopolistic firms are not likely to produce at the lowest unit cost and therefore some economic efficiency can be lost.
5. Firms in oligopolistic industries tend to advertise heavily and thus help support newspapers, magazines, radio, and television. Oligopolists also spend a great deal of money on research and development, which is often of great benefit to society in the long run.

Economic Foundations

1. Describe monopolistic competition using the five characteristics of market organization.
2. Draw the demand curve for the monopolistically competitive firm. How does it compare with the market demand curve?
3. What determines the level of output and price for the monopolistically competitive firm?

Economic Foundations

1. Many firms, all offering a given type of product; product differentiation; relatively easy entry into and exit from the industry; reasonably complete information about the market; and some control over price (pp. 273–276)
2. Students' demand curves should slope downward to the right. It should be similar to the market curve but not as steep. (pp. 276–277)
3. The level of output is where an added quantity increases revenue by the same amount as it increases costs. (pp. 277–278)
4. Few firms, with products either nearly identical or differentiated; fairly difficult entry into or exit from the industry; incomplete information about the industry; great deal of control

(Continued)

4. Describe oligopoly using the five characteristics of market organization.
5. Draw the demand curve for the oligopolistic firm. How does it compare with the market demand curve?
6. What is collusion and how is it used by cartels?
7. What determines the level of output and price for the oligopolistic firm?
8. What is the difference between a pure oligopoly and a differentiated oligopoly?

Your Economic Vocabulary

Build your economic vocabulary by matching the following terms with their definitions.

1. the situation of firms acting together rather than separately
2. a form of market organization in which there are relatively few firms
3. a market organization in which many firms produce goods that are different but similar enough to be substitutes
4. an oligopoly in which the products are the same for all firms
5. the concept that the product of one firm can be distinguished from the products of other firms
6. a formal organization of firms in the same industry acting together to make decisions
7. an oligopoly in which the product is differentiated

cartel
collusion
differentiated oligopoly
monopolistic competition
oligopoly
product differentiation
pure oligopoly

Thinking Critically About Economics

1. Review what is meant by the term *monopolistic competition.* How does this form of market organization resemble a monopoly? How does it resemble perfect competition?
2. From a recent issue of *Time* (or any other weekly news magazine) pick out ads for industries you consider oligopolies. Explain your choices, using the characteristics of oligopoly as a guide.

Economic Foundations
(Continued)

over price in differentiated oligopoly, less control in pure oligopoly (pp. 283–287)

5. There is not one type of demand curve that applies to all oligopoly cases; students' demand curves may be either negatively sloped or kinked. In the case of the kinked demand curve, the curve has a different slope, depending on whether price increases or decreases, unlike the market demand curve. (pp. 287–288)
6. Firms within a cartel are said to be in collusion when they act together to make joint decisions about pricing or other issues. (p. 287)
7. The level of output is at the point where an added quantity increases revenue by the same amount as it increases costs. (p. 289)

(Continued)

Economic Foundations
(Continued)

8. In a pure oligopoly, the products are all about the same; in a differentiated oligopoly, products have different characteristics. (pp. 289–290)

Your Economic Vocabulary

1. **collusion**
2. **oligopoly**
3. **monopolistic competition**
4. **pure oligopoly**
5. **product differentiation**
6. **cartel**
7. **differentiated oligopoly**

Thinking Critically About Economics

1. Monopolistic competition resembles a monopoly in that each firm has some control over price and each is the only firm to produce that exact product (e.g., only one firm can sell Levi's jeans). Monopolistic competition resembles perfect competition in that there are usually many very similar substitutes (e.g., Wrangler, Chic, Lee), and so the degree of price control is modest.
2. Examples may include the auto, steel, airline, and oil refining industries; all of which have relatively few firms, are difficult industries to enter, and have firms that exercise some control over price.

(Continued)

Thinking Critically About Economics (Continued)

3. Students' answers will vary but should include which countries are members of OPEC, how much of the world's oil supply they produce, how much influence OPEC has on the price of oil, and the effects such events as the Persian Gulf War had on OPEC's strength. (The Gulf War temporarily weakened OPEC because many nations began looking for other oil sources just in case OPEC's production faltered due to the war. As a result, OPEC lowered prices. Ultimately, however, OPEC regained any lost ground and raised prices back to former levels.)
4. Perfectly competitive firms are price takers, accepting the price determined by the market forces of supply and demand. In other market structures, firms have some control over price and do not produce perfectly homogeneous products. Since products are not identical, price can be raised (or lowered) with a corresponding decline (or increase) in sales. Thus, the demand curves must be negatively sloped.

3. Using news magazines and reference materials, write a brief history of the OPEC oil cartel. In your report, indicate how key world events, such as the Persian Gulf War, have affected the strength of OPEC throughout its life.
4. Explain why the demand curve for a perfectly competitive firm is a horizontal line at the market price, while demand curves for firms in the other market structures all have negative slopes.

Economic Enrichment

Picture the intersection of two busy streets. On two of the four corner lots there are gas stations. One is a Shell station, a national brand, and the other is Gary's Gas and Go, a local company that is a combination convenience store and gas station. The price of regular unleaded gas at the Shell station is $1.39 per gallon, while at Gary's the comparable price is $1.35. You have probably experienced situations such as this many times. The product itself, unleaded regular gas, is essentially the same at the two stations. In fact, it comes from the same refinery in a nearby city. Why does anyone buy their gas at the Shell station, where ten gallons of gas costs an extra $0.40?

Math and Economics

A firm has determined that a 10 percent price cut would increase sales by 8 percent, whereas a 10 percent price increase would cause sales to drop by 12 percent. Remember from Chapter 6 that price elasticity is calculated as the percentage change in quantity demanded divided by the corresponding percentage change in price. What is the price elasticity for a price cut? What is the price elasticity for a price increase? What do your calculations for these two price elasticities tell you about the likely market structure in which this firm operates?

Economic Enrichment

Answers may include that some consumers may have a credit card that only can be used at the Shell station; some may feel that, due to their traffic habits, the Shell station is more conveniently located; some may not wish to deal with the traffic congestion and long lines created by the local station's convenience store customers; and some may have a loyalty to the Shell brand because they have a preconceived idea that gas from a national chain is superior to gas from a local station.

Writing About Economics

Go to the cereal aisle at a local supermarket and make a list of all the brands of cold cereals that you find. In addition to writing down the brand name (for example, Cheerios), write down the name of the company that markets the product (for example, General Mills).

When you get home, make two separate lists based on what you found. The first list should group the cereals into broad product types (for example, put all raisin brans together). In the second list, put the brands into groups according to the company that markets each cereal (for example, Cheerios would go in the General Mills group). Write a report of your findings. Include the two lists, a description of the market structure of the cold cereal industry, and an explanation for your choice of market structure.

Math and Economics

The price cut has a price elasticity of demand of 0.8 (0.08 ÷ 0.10). The price increase has a price elasticity of demand of 1.2 (0.12 ÷ 0.10). Because sales are more responsive to a price increase than to a price decrease, the demand curve would be kinked. Since an oligopoly is the only form of industry organization with a kinked demand curve, the firm must be operating in an oligopoly.

Writing About Economics

Information on students' lists should be divided according to the given criteria. Students should analyze their data according to the characteristics of market organization and form the following conclusions: (1) There are definite market leaders (including Post, Kellogg's, and General Mills), but smaller brands (such as store brands) are able to enter the market relatively easily and do have a substantial impact on the market. (2) There are many substitutes for each type of cereal, but each firm claims that its product has some unique characteristics.
(3) There appears to be some degree of price control, but not much; therefore, the cold cereal market is probably a monopolistic competition.

Chapter 12 Improving the Market Economy

Chapter Theme

The United States has generally favored a competitive free market economy that depends on a balance between private costs and private benefits to determine the quantity of goods produced and consumed. Sometimes, however, people do not bear the full cost of their actions, resulting in positive or negative externalities. Government generally supports positive externalities and, sometimes, encourages natural monopolies to provide public goods effectively.

Section	Special Features
Markets May Not Always Work Well	Multicultural Highlights Econ & You
The Shifting of Costs	Media Link Economics & Your Community
The Shifting of Benefits	Perspectives: Thinking Like an Education Analyst Economic Dilemma Eye on Market News Global Economy
Sometimes Having a Single Supplier Is Best	Economic Talk Economic Spotlight Internet Connection

Video Activity

Chapter 12, EPA Regulation

Search Chapter 12, Play to 13

As a class, brainstorm the various costs associated with the oil spill caused by the Exxon *Valdez.* Encourage students to be comprehensive in their thinking and to consider both short- and long-range effects. Discuss how these costs were shifted to people who were not directly involved with the production or consumption of Exxon products. Have students volunteer suggestions about actions the EPA could take to prevent future catastrophes such as this.

	Print Resources	Media Resources	Assessment
	Effective Teaching Model Lesson Plans *Skills & Concepts* worksheet *Problem Solving* worksheet *Casebook* *Economic Measurement Workbook* *Content Review Workbook* *Spanish Resources*	VHS CD-ROM Videodisc *Arctic Express* *Interactive ECONOMICS* Template software	*Your Economic Portfolio* Chapter *Assessment* Chapter *MicroExam*

Special Learners	Print Resources	Media Resources	Assessment
	Reteach worksheet	Overhead and *Transparencies 12-1* and *12-2*	*Checkpoint* Section 1 Quiz
Cooperative Learning Activity Auditory Activity Kinesthetic Activity		Overhead and *Transparencies 12-3* to *12-5* Camcorder VCR	*Checkpoint* Section 2 Quiz
Visual Activity	*Enrich* worksheet *Life Skills* worksheet	Overhead and *Transparencies 12-6* and *12-7* Computer	*Checkpoint* Section 3 Quiz
Limited English Proficiency	*Teacher's Connection to the Internet*	Overhead and *Transparency 12-8* Computer	*Checkpoint* Section 4 Quiz

Careers Activity

Environmental engineers find ways to reduce or eliminate the harmful effects of negative externalities such as pollution. They test food, water, soil, and air samples for harmful substances; inspect buildings, machinery, and public transportation for dangers; and implement any corrective measures when standards have been violated.

Environmental engineers must have a bachelor's degree in engineering; a master's degree is helpful. Special licenses also are required to work in public health or safety. Entry-level salaries start at $25,000. But, with a master's degree and experience, yearly income can rise to $100,000.

As a class, list several negative externalities that can be observed in your community or state. Then, divide the class into small groups and assign one externality to each group. Have each group design a way to reduce the negative effects of its externality. Encourage students to prepare diagrams and written explanations of their solutions.

CHAPTER 12

Teaching Materials

Program Resources

- Student text
- *Effective Teaching Model Lesson Plans*
- *Overhead Transparencies 12-1* to *12-8*
- *Life Skills* worksheet
- *Problem Solving* worksheet
- *Reteach* worksheet
- *Enrich* worksheet
- *Skills & Concepts* worksheet
- *Casebook*
- *Economic Measurement Workbook*
- *Content Review Workbook*
- *Spanish Resources*
- Video package
- *Teacher's Connection to the Internet*
- *Arctic Express*
- *Interactive* ECONOMICS
- Template software

Assessment

- Section Quizzes
- Chapter *Assessment*
- Chapter *MicroExam*

Overview

Section One
Markets May Not Always Work Well

Section Two
The Shifting of Costs

Section Three
The Shifting of Benefits

Section Four
Sometimes Having a Single Supplier Is Best

Teacher to Teacher

Explain to students the definitions of positive and negative externalities. Then, point out several examples of each in your community. (Negative externalities may include building an industrial facility near a residential area, and positive externalities may include renovating a dilapidated building near your school.) After students understand these concepts, have them independently think of another example of an externality producer in your city or community. Then, have them write a short essay describing how third parties are affected by these externalities. Allow volunteers to use their own creativity to illustrate their essays. Then, display their work on a bulletin board entitled **Good Neighbor Policy?**

Laurence H. Jaffe
Rutgers University
New Bruswick, NJ

Improving the Market Economy

Learning Objectives

12-1

Explain the relationships between marginal private costs and supply and between marginal private benefits and demand.

12-2

Analyze negative externalities in terms of marginal costs and benefits.

12-3

Describe how the effects of negative externalities on the market system can be controlled.

12-4

Analyze positive externalities in terms of marginal costs and benefits.

12-5

Describe how the effects of positive externalities on the market system can be encouraged.

12-6

Recognize how the government improves the market economy by providing public goods and controlling natural monopolies.

Outside Resources

- Blank overhead transparencies
- Graph paper
- Markers
- Posterboard
- Index cards
- Newspaper and magazine articles about Exxon and the *Valdez* oil spill or other companies that have produced negative externalities
- Camcorder and VCR
- Outside speaker: A representative from the Environmental Protection Agency (EPA)
- Local newspapers
- Local television cable company program guides
- Friedman, Milton, and Rose Friedman, *Free to Choose.* New York: Harcourt Brace Jovanovich, 1980.

Vocabulary

marginal private benefit (MPB), p. 299
marginal private cost (MPC), p. 299
externality, p. 302
negative externality, p. 303
marginal social benefit (MSB), p. 305
marginal social cost (MSC), p. 306
positive externality, p. 310
subsidy, p. 312
exclusion principle, p. 317

Focus

Write **marginal** on the chalkboard. On a sheet of paper, ask students to jot down what comes to mind when they think of the term.

As students share their responses, write them on the chalkboard. Then, ask students to speculate about what the terms **marginal private benefit** and **marginal private cost** mean. Lead students to the definitions that a **marginal private benefit (MPB)** is the added benefit that individuals directly involved in an activity receive from increasing the activity by one unit and that a **marginal private cost (MPC)** is the added cost individuals directly involved in an activity pay to increase the activity by one unit.

Section One
Markets May Not Always Work Well

What Do You Think?

One hot and humid summer evening, Betsy Center sat on the front porch of her family's home outside Little Rock, Arkansas. She was reading a Tom Clancy novel, sipping iced tea, and listening to music that filtered through an open living room window. How might this event have affected other people in the neighborhood?

Terms to Know

marginal private benefit (MPB)

marginal private cost (MPC)

externality

What's Ahead?

In a free market economy, the quantity of a product that is produced and consumed depends on a balance between private costs and private benefits. However, the costs or benefits of people's actions sometimes are greater than what they may seem. This creates what economists refer to as *externalities.* In this section, you will learn about how a market economy reaches a balance between marginal private costs and marginal private benefits but fails when externalities are involved.

THE MARKET CAN BE SUCCESSFUL

When a market is perfectly competitive, the economy benefits in three ways:

1. Economic efficiency results. This means that products are produced at the lowest possible cost per unit.
2. Firms in the industry do not make excessive profits. This is because price equals the cost per unit of producing the product.
3. There is the best possible allocation of resources to production in the industry. For the good of society, neither too much nor too little is produced because price equals the added cost of producing an added unit.

A graph of supply and demand helps explain why just the right amount is produced when markets are competitive. The graph in Figure 12-1 shows

Multicultural *Highlights*

After students read *What Do You Think?,* reinforce the idea that one individual's actions *can* affect society. Relate the example of 28-year-old Hispanic business owner Roy Nieto. Nieto's consulting business, RSN and Associates, matches U.S. companies with potential partners in Latin America—benefiting the individual businesses involved *and* the U.S. and Latin American economies. Yet, Nieto feels that his efforts are hindered by the fact that he has never mastered the Spanish language. To remedy this, he plans to dedicate two years of his life to studying Spanish abroad. As a class, discuss the private costs and benefits of Nieto's decision and the potential effects on society.

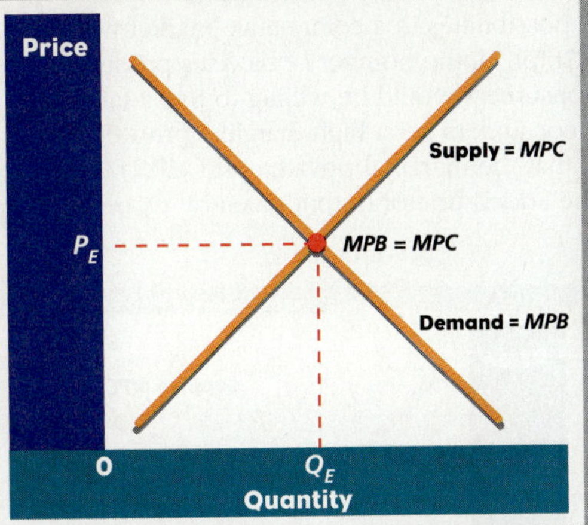

Figure 12-1

Demand and Supply Curves for Bicycles

The demand curve represents the marginal private benefit of consuming one more unit. The supply curve represents the marginal private cost of producing one more unit. The market is in equilibrium when the marginal private benefit equals the marginal private cost at the price P_E. This is where the demand and supply curves cross. ***How many bicycles are demanded and produced when this market is in equilibrium?***

demand and supply curves for bicycles. Here's a quick review of what demand and supply curves show:

Demand: A demand curve shows the quantities that people are willing and able to purchase at various prices.

Supply: A supply curve shows the quantities that producers are willing and able to make available for sale at various prices.

marginal private benefit (MPB) the added benefit that individuals directly involved in an activity get from increasing the activity by one unit

marginal private cost (MPC) the added cost individuals directly involved in an activity pay to increase the activity by one unit

Marginal Private Benefit (MPB)

The demand curve reflects willingness of individuals in the marketplace to buy. Think of it as showing the added benefit received from each unit. This is called *marginal private benefit*. ***Marginal private benefit* (MPB)** is the added benefit that individuals directly involved in an activity get from increasing the activity by one unit. It is *marginal* because it shows the benefit from each added unit. It is *private* because you consider only your own personal satisfaction, or benefit, in deciding whether to buy. You can see that marginal private benefits decrease as more units are consumed. This is due to diminishing marginal utility.

Marginal Private Cost (MPC)

The supply curve shows the firm's cost of producing each added unit. This cost is called the *marginal private cost*. ***Marginal private cost* (MPC)** is the added cost individuals directly involved in an activity pay to increase the activity by one unit. It is *marginal* because it is the cost of producing one more unit. It is *private* because the only costs included are those that the individual producer must pay. Marginal private costs increase as more units are produced because of the effect of diminishing marginal product.

Analyzing Graphics

Caption Answer
Q_E bicycles

Teach

On the chalkboard or an overhead transparency, copy the following chart.

PERFECT COMPETITION	
Economic Benefits	Economic Costs
• Efficiency • No Excessive Profits • Minimal Waste of Resources • Externalities	• Externalities

Explain that, in a perfectly competitive market, the best rate of production occurs when MPB = MPC. Point out that MPB is the same as demand and MPC is the same as supply. Finally, discuss that an **externality** is a cost or benefit received by people who are not directly involved in the production, sale, or use of a good.

Apply

Display *Overhead Transparency 12-1*. Have students copy the figure onto graph paper. Then, ask students to explain to you how the graph would change if *MPB* were greater than *MPC*. (See *Figure 12-2*.) Use a second color to indicate this change on the original graph. Have students do the same with their individual graphs. Finally, work with students to determine what the graph would look like if *MPC* were greater than *MPB*. (See *Figure 12-2*.) Use a third color to show this change on the transparency. Have students use a third color to add this information to their graphs as well. Discuss which relationship between *MPB* and *MPC* is the ideal in a competitive market. (*MPB* equal to *MPC*)

Guided Practice

Analyzing Graphics

Caption Answer
Marginal private costs would be greater than marginal private benefits.

Best Rate of Production

Figure 12-2 illustrates three possibilities in a competitive market with only private costs and benefits. In Graph *A*, the number of bicycles produced is represented by Q_1. At that rate, consumers would be willing to pay a fairly high price for the product. That is, consumers get a high marginal private benefit (MPB_1). But, you can also see that the marginal private cost (MPC_1) to produce that output is lower. Should the added unit of output given by Q_1 be produced?

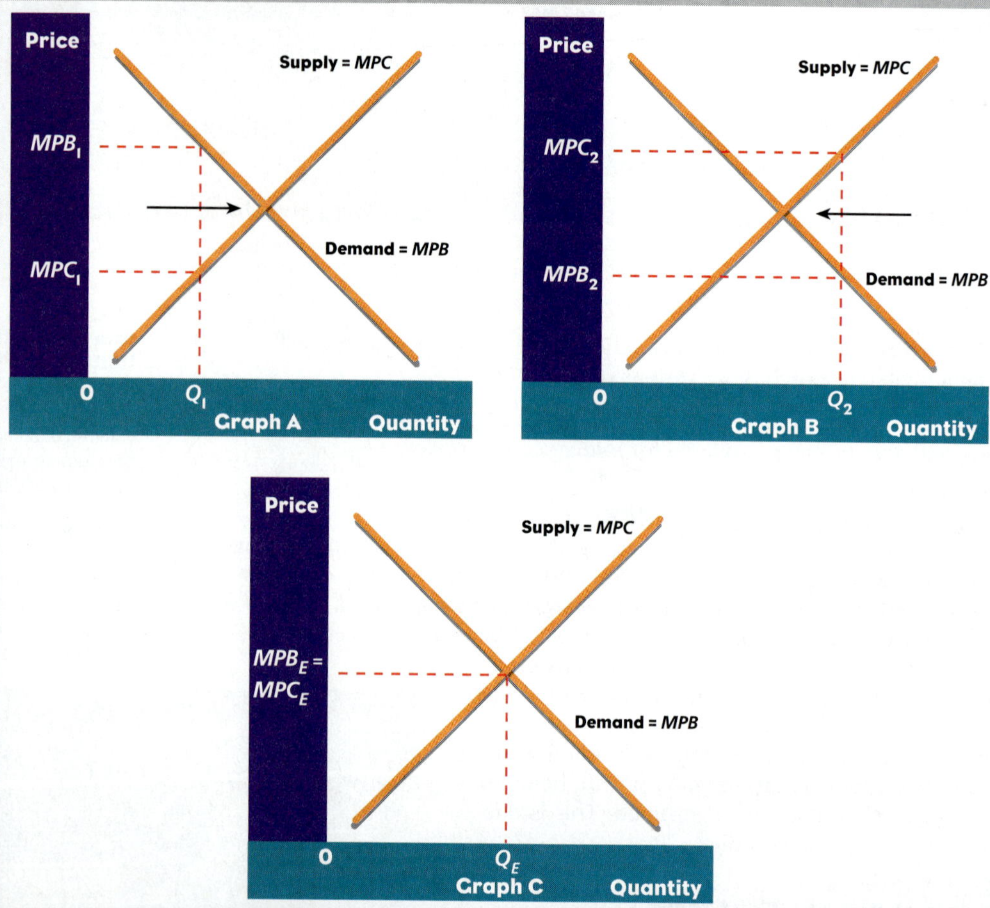

Figure 12-2

The Relationship Between MPB and MPC in a Competitive Market

If marginal private benefits are greater than marginal private costs, as in Graph *A*, output should be increased. If marginal private costs are greater than marginal private benefits, as in Graph *B*, less should be produced. The best rate of production and the best allocation of resources occur when marginal private costs equal marginal private benefits, as in Graph *C*. ***In Graph C, if more than Q_E units were produced, how would the marginal private costs and marginal private benefits compare?***

Econ & You

YOUR EXTERNALITIES ARE SHOWING

It would be rare to find an individual who does not contribute to pollution in some way. Answer the following questions for yourself:

1. Do you ever leave a light on when you are not using it?
2. Do you ever play a radio or similar device loudly enough that it could interfere with someone else?
3. Do you ever drive or catch a ride when you could walk or ride a bike?
4. Do you actively try to conserve on heating and/or air conditioning use?
5. Do you personally recycle paper, bottles, and cans?
6. Have you ever littered?

Identify other similar questions that might be relevant.

The answer is *yes.* The added benefit from consuming the product is greater than the added cost of making it available. So, it is desirable to produce that bicycle.

Now look at Graph *B* in Figure 12-2. The added cost of producing the unit given by Q_2 is MPC_2. This is a high cost. But, the added benefit consumers would get from that unit is just MPB_2. You can see that MPB_2 is much less than MPC_2. So, for Q_2, the added cost would be greater than the added benefit. It would not be desirable to produce that many bicycles.

It is desirable to produce Q_1 but not Q_2. Think again about why this is true. For Q_1, the added benefit is greater than the added cost. But, for Q_2, the added cost is greater than the added benefits. This leads to a general conclusion: *It is only desirable to produce an additional unit if the added benefit that results is greater than or equal to the added cost.*

In Graph *C* of Figure 12-2, Q_E represents the best rate of production. For units to the left of Q_E (less than Q_E), the added benefit is greater than the added cost. Those units would be worth producing. For units to the right of Q_E (greater than Q_E), the added cost is higher than the added benefit. So, it would not be desirable to produce those units. At Q_E, which is the best rate of production, the added costs are exactly equal to the added benefit. That is, at Q_E, MPC = MPB.

When all costs and benefits are private, the economy's scarce resources are allocated in the best possible way when *MPB* = *MPC.* This happens when price equals the added cost of producing the last unit. In perfectly competitive markets, this is a natural result. The market system is successful in providing the best possible allocation of resources.

Ask students to imagine that they are holding a graduation party in one of their classmates' backyards. Tell them that they all are contributing to the cost of having the party catered. Ask students to list in a two-column chart on the chalkboard what they believe are the marginal private benefits for them (party is a good source of entertainment, they will get to eat good food) and their marginal private costs (payments to the caterer for the food, the labor to prepare the food, and the fuel to deliver it). Ask students what the externalities may be (noise pollution from loud voices or music, litter, and so on).

Have each student think of one externality that exists in his or her community. Ask students to write a one-page description of that externality and discuss whom the externality affects. Then, have students exchange papers with their classmates. On the back of the classmate's paper, have the student-partner analyze the problem and write possible solutions to decrease the externality.

Independent Practice

Have students create posters that illustrate the message "Give a Hoot, Don't Pollute." Or, if students wish, have them create their own antipollution slogans. Point out that this type of externality involves more than just litter; excess noise as well as air, water, and soil contaminants are all forms of pollution. Students also may wish to investigate the ideas of "thought pollution" or "visual pollution." If possible, hang their posters in the school halls.

Econ & You

After students have read *Econ & You* in their textbook, ask the class to answer the six questions listed in the special feature with a show of hands to indicate "yes." Have a volunteer graph the results. Then, if the results indicate a high percentage of students contributing to these types of externalities, discuss ways to influence a change in their behaviors. If the results indicate a low percentage, discuss how students are limiting these externalities.

SOMETIMES THE MARKET CAN FAIL

So far in this and previous chapters, it has been assumed that all costs and benefits are private. The benefits all go to the people who buy the product. The costs are all paid for by the producers. When this is true, all the costs and benefits go only to people involved in market transactions. In such cases, we say that all costs and benefits are *internalized*. None of the benefits or costs spill over to people who are not involved in the market transaction.

In some cases, however, this assumption is not correct. It is possible that some of the benefits or costs will go to third parties. Third parties are people not directly involved in the production or purchase of the product. When all the benefits or costs are not internalized, externalities exist. As you recall, an ***externality*** is a cost or benefit passed on to people not directly involved in a transaction. Three terms are used to describe these cases, and any of the three is correct: *spillovers, third-party effects,* or *externalities*. Each of these terms refers to cases in which all the costs of production or the benefits of consumption do not go to the people directly involved in producing or using the product.

externality
a cost or benefit passed on to people not directly involved in a transaction

The market system does not work well when there are spillovers. Resources are not allocated to different types of production in the best possible way. In the following sections, you will look more closely at the effects of such externalities. You will also look at some examples of spillover benefits and costs. In addition, you will consider some ways to correct this failure of the market system to allocate resources in the best possible way.

Checkpoint

Content Check

1. Explain why the demand curve is the same as the marginal private benefits curve.
2. Explain why the supply curve is the same as the marginal private costs curve.
3. What happens to the market system when there are externalities?

What Do You Think Now?

Reread *What Do You Think?* in the Section One Focus. Then answer the following question:

4. Might Betsy's activities have any spillover effect on others?

Assess

1. Both reflect willingness of individuals in the marketplace to buy, and the added benefit received from each unit is private. **12-1**
2. Both curves reflect the firm's private cost of producing each added unit. **12-1**
3. The market system does not work well because resources are not allocated to different types of production in the best possible way. **12-1**
4. Betsy's activities may have no effect on others, but if the music is loud, it could interfere with a neighbor's music, keep someone from sleeping, or annoy someone who wants to have a relaxing evening on the front porch. **12-1**

Close

As a whole-class activity, ask students to share events or personal experiences in which externalities have affected them. Encourage students to discuss how the externality made them feel and what, if anything, was done to change it.

Reteach

On the chalkboard, write the following three equations:
MPB > MPC = output ↑
MPB $<$ MPC = output ↓
MPB = MPC
Have students who are experiencing difficulty with these concepts create graphs or written narratives to explain what each equation means and how it affects the rate of production. Correct any misconceptions. **12-1**

Enrich

Have students create their own equations to symbolically illustrate the different ways in which MPB and MPC can affect the rate of production. Then, have students exchange papers and have each student write a short scenario to illustrate one of their classmate's equations. Pair students to discuss their scenarios. **12-1**

Section Two

The Shifting of Costs

What Do You Think?

The Millikin Paper Company operates in the beautiful foothills of the northern Rocky Mountains. It has been in business at this location for more than 60 years. Recently, EPA (Environmental Protection Agency) officials found that the company has been discharging waste water into the Grey Wolf River, resulting in fish kills and a reduction of recreational activities on the river. Should the government step in and shut down the plant?

What's Ahead?

There are times when individuals, families, social groups, and businesses do not bear the full cost of their activities. This creates various forms of pollution. In this section, you will learn how economists analyze such situations and about how to develop possible solutions.

Terms to Know

negative externality

marginal social benefit (MSB)

marginal social cost (MSC)

Focus

Write the term **negative externality** on the chalkboard. As students enter the classroom, hand each an index card. On the card, have students write three examples of what they think are negative externalities.

Ask student volunteers to read aloud their examples as you have the remaining students circle similar responses on their own index cards. On the chalkboard or an overhead transparency, list students' examples as they are offered. Discuss with students the common characteristics that make all the examples negative externalities. Correct any misconceptions.

NEGATIVE EXTERNALITIES

A ***negative externality*** is the result when *costs* are shifted to people who are not directly involved with the production or consumption of a good. When the costs of externalities shift to third parties, producers and consumers of the good do not pay the full cost to society of providing the good. In other words, the social costs of providing the good are greater than the private costs. The social costs include all costs: the private costs plus the costs that are shifted to third parties in the form of externalities. Therefore, the social costs are higher than the private costs. The difference between the social costs and the private costs is a measure of the cost of the externality.

negative externality the result when *costs* are shifted to people who are not directly involved with the production or consumption of a good

Water Pollution Is a Negative Externality

Suppose the Sulfa Chemical Company builds a new plant on the banks of the Green River. The company uses pure water from the river in the production of chemicals. Waste water containing various chemical impurities is

Teach

Be sure that students understand that a **negative externality** is the result of a cost being shifted to people who are not directly involved with the production or consumption of a good. Explain that negative externalities result when marginal social costs are greater than marginal private costs. Explain that a **marginal social cost** results when the cost affects people not involved in the transaction.

On the chalkboard or an overhead transparency, draw the following graphic organizer to help students understand how marginal social costs relate to marginal private costs.

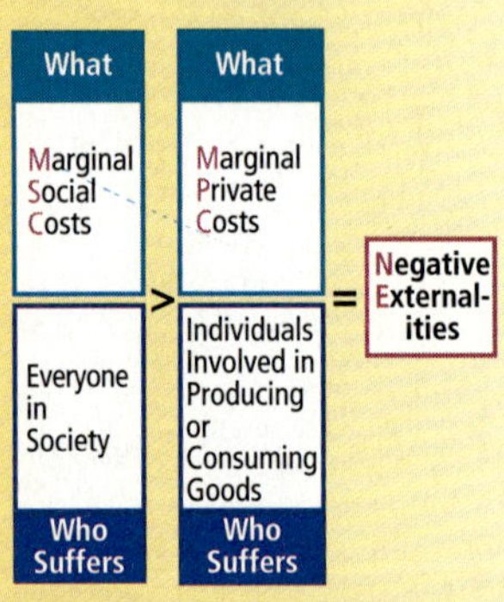

Apply

Lead students to brainstorm a list of companies that are well known for contributing to negative externalities. (For example, Exxon for the *Valdez* oil spill on March 24, 1989, which caused tremendous ecological damage to Prince William Sound, and Union Carbide for its poisonous gas leak in Central India on December 3, 1984, which killed an estimated 1,600 people and injured an additional 50,000). If possible, distribute copies of newspapers and magazine articles on the Exxon *Valdez* oil spill or other examples for students to read. Lead a

(Continued)

dumped back into the river downstream. As a result, fish die. The town of Greenville, which is downstream from Sulfa Chemical, has to add new equipment for water treatment because the Green River is the town's main source of water. People for the next 50 miles downstream find that the Green River is no longer safe for recreation. The river can no longer be used for boating, fishing, swimming, or water skiing.

To whom does the Sulfa Chemical Company shift part of the production costs? Who are the third parties in this case? People who used to enjoy fishing in the river have to go elsewhere. This creates a cost to all of them. Every resident of Greenville has to pay more for water because of the added cost of water treatment. Some people are affected by both these added costs.

Society as a whole bears some of the cost of producing the chemicals. The private costs of making the chemicals, as shown by the company's records, are less than the true total costs. Some of the costs are shifted to third parties. So, the social cost is greater than the private cost. There are costs to society in addition to the costs to the company. If the water returned to the river had been as clean as the water the company took out, there would have been no spillover to other people. The company would have internalized all the costs. The private costs would then have been the total cost to society of making the products. There would be no negative externality, and private costs would be the same as society costs.

Examples of such water pollution are very common. Indeed, it is hard to find a major river or lake that has not been polluted in some way. Almost all major industries have dumped wastes into our water. Producers of steel, coal, cars, chemicals, wood products, paper, and food are only a few. Lake Erie and the Ohio River are highly polluted. But, the problem is not found just in the industrial Northeast and Midwest. The Yellowstone River at some locations is also polluted.

Air Pollution Is a Negative Externality

Another common type of negative externality is air pollution. Industries all too often treat the atmosphere as a free "dump" for waste products. Each year, hundreds of millions of tons of air pollutants are released into the air. Almost everyone shares in creating this problem, including you. One of the biggest sources of air pollution is the exhaust of cars and trucks. Industrial plants, many electric power plants, agricultural burning, and solid waste disposal also contribute to air pollution.

Air pollution causes an increase in health costs for many people. In some cities, air pollution sometimes gets so bad that people are warned to stay indoors and refrain from heavy physical activity. Air pollution also damages vegetation and personal property. For example, people living near a source of air pollution may have to paint their homes more often. In all these cases, as with water pollution, the firms or people involved shift part of the cost of activities to other members of society. Once more, the social cost is greater than the private cost.

Individual Activities Can Result in Negative Externalities

Negative externalities can take less obvious forms. Consider, for example, how one family can affect a neighborhood. They have a horse trailer that sits in the street in front of the house and makes an otherwise very pretty street less attractive. They have a disassembled car in their driveway. Their six-year-old son leaves his bike and other toys in their side yard and in neighbors' yards. Their house needs painting, and the yard is overgrown with weeds. Their two dogs bark throughout the night, keeping even people living several houses away awake. This family allows part of the cost of enjoying their lifestyle to spill over to others in the neighborhood. You can plant a nice hedge to separate your yard from theirs and to give you a more pleasant view. But, this is a cost you have that is due to someone else's activities.

When people in an apartment play their stereo and television loudly, other people who live in the same building are affected. There is a negative externality. Due to the activities of others, some people incur a cost in the form of psychological discomfort, loss of sleep, or even moving to a quieter place.

ANALYSIS OF NEGATIVE EXTERNALITIES

Negative externalities result in the social costs of some activity being greater than the private costs. So far in our analysis, it has been assumed that private costs and social costs are equal, and that no costs are shifted to third parties. Figure 12-2 on page 300 assumes that this is the case and that the competitive market system will yield the best allocation of resources.

(Continued)

discussion on what the social and private costs were and how these costs affected production and society.
Guided Practice

Divide the class into two groups. Have one group represent a company that wants to make a profit at any cost and the other group represent a company that wants to make a profit but is willing to pay the full cost of its negative externalities. Have each side debate how paying for or not paying for negative externalities can help or hurt its company.
Independent Practice

Divide the class into groups of three or four students. Assign the following roles: cameraperson, talent, writer(s). Using a camcorder, have each group create a public-service announcement (PSA) about negative externalities to which we as individuals unknowingly contribute. Encourage students to be creative and humorous while encouraging their audience to be more conscientious, realizing how their actions affect others. Allow 20 to 30 minutes for each group to create and record its PSA. Share all videos with the class and discuss the effectiveness of the proposed solutions to each externality.
Cooperative Learning

MediaLink

Using a camcorder, ask groups of students to record a brief segment exposing or focusing on a negative externality in their neighborhood, school, downtown, or any other easily accessible and safe area in their community. Share the videotapes with the class and discuss how the negative externalities affect members of the community. As a class, choose one or two of the most serious negative externalities presented and compose a class letter detailing the circumstances involved. Mail the letter and a copy of the videotape to the assignments editor of your local television news department as a possible news story.

Analyzing *Graphics*

Caption Answer
Answers could include various forms of air or water pollution, noise pollution, or visual pollution, such as trash discarded along a highway.

As a class, discuss how the advances in and popularity of such technology as cellular phones, beepers, and "boom boxes" have increased negative externalities. (Talking on cellular phones in movie theaters, listening to loud radios in public places, beepers sounding in quiet public places, and so on) Work with students to generate a list of the private benefits and social costs associated with this technology. Ask students to brainstorm ways to decrease these social costs without substantially reducing private benefits.

Have students conduct a poll among at least ten of their friends and family members concerning their willingness to improve the market economy. Tell students to ask respondents if they are willing to sacrifice lower prices on products such as automobiles for such benefits as cleaner air. Also, have them find out if respondents are willing to pay higher taxes to enforce pollution control laws.

Invite a representative from the Environmental Protection Agency (EPA) to speak to students about the kinds of costs that companies impose on society and what companies can do to reduce their existing marginal social costs. Ask the speaker to explain the purpose of the EPA and what measures the agency takes to reduce social costs.

Marginal Social Benefit (MSB)

marginal social benefit (MSB) the added benefit that society gets from increasing an activity by one unit

What is the economic impact of negative externalities? The demand curve in Figure 12-3 shows the diminishing marginal private benefits *(MPB)* from consumption. For now, assume that all the benefits are private. The only benefits to society are internalized to private individuals. So, you can say that society's benefits *are the same as private benefits*. ***Marginal social benefit* (MSB)** is the added benefit that society gets from increasing an activity by one unit. Marginal social benefit is the same idea as marginal private benefit, which was defined earlier in this chapter, except that it applies to society instead of individuals. In Figure 12-3, the demand curve, *MPB,* can be labeled *MSB* as well because all benefits are internalized.

Figure 12-3

Negative Externalities and Marginal Costs

Negative externalities result in marginal social costs *(MSC)* that are greater than marginal private costs *(MPC)*. The market system leads to more production than is desirable. ***Name two situations in which you think the marginal social costs are higher than the marginal private costs.***

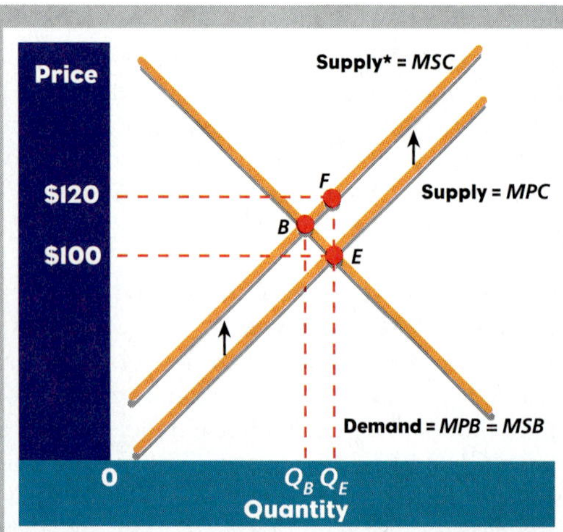

Marginal Social Cost (MSC)

marginal social cost (MSC) the added cost that society pays to increase an activity by one unit

The curve labeled *Supply = MPC* in Figure 12-3 shows the quantities that producers are willing and able to make available for sale, considering only private costs. This is the supply (or marginal private cost) curve that firms use to determine the rate of production. In Figure 12-3, another supply curve is drawn above the firm's own supply. This new supply curve, labeled *Supply* = MSC,* reflects the full cost of producing the good. Since all costs are included in this higher supply curve, it is the marginal social cost *(MSC)* curve. ***Marginal social cost* (MSC)** is the added cost that society pays to increase an activity by one unit. The vertical distance between the two supply curves is the amount of the full cost that is shifted to third parties for each unit produced. This is the distance labeled *FE* in Figure 12-3.

Spillover Costs

Left to competitive market forces, Q_E units would be produced and sold. The last unit produced would cost the firm that produced it $100. But, the full cost of that unit would be $120. The difference, or $20, would be shifted to third parties in the form of pollution costs. In this case, the distance *FE* equals $20 per unit. Suppose 1 million units are produced (Q_E = 1 million). The total pollution cost to society will be $20 million. That is, the cost of this negative externality will be $20 million.

Most people would agree that such a spillover of costs is not in the public interest. Let's compare the full cost of producing Q_E units with the price people are willing to pay for those Q_E units. The full cost is $120 per unit. That is, the marginal private cost *(MPC)* of $100 plus the pollution cost of $20 is the full marginal cost to society *(MSC)* of $120. According to consumer demand, people will be willing to pay only $100 per unit for Q_E units. The cost to society of producing the last unit is greater than the benefit received from the last unit. Therefore, society will be better served if fewer than Q_E units are produced.

Best Rate of Output

How many units should be produced? What is the best rate of output? The best rate is found on the graph where the full marginal cost is just equal to the full marginal benefit. In Figure 12-3, this is where *MSC* crosses *MSB* (which equals *MPB)* at Point *B*. At this point, the marginal social cost of supplying the last unit is exactly the same as the marginal social benefit obtained from that unit. This best rate of output is labeled Q_B on the horizontal axis.

Suppose firms did pay the full cost of making products. If they did, the *MPC* curve would be the same as the *MSC* curve. No costs would be shifted to third parties. The competitive market would naturally lead to the production of the best rate of output, Q_B. Knowing this best rate of output is helpful in deciding what should be done to control negative externalities.

PUBLIC POLICY FOR NEGATIVE EXTERNALITIES

When negative externalities are present, *MSC* is greater than *MPC*. For now, continue to assume that all the benefits are private, or *MSB* = *MPB*. You now know that the best rate of output is found on the graph where marginal social cost is the same as marginal social benefit. That is, the best rate of output, Q_B, is where *MSC* = *MSB*. The question is, "How can you get firms to produce Q_B units?" If you can do this, the best possible allocation of our scarce resources will result.

Making Pollution Illegal

One way for government to control negative externalities is to pass laws making pollution illegal. Of course, there would have to be some penalty for people who broke the law. To avoid this penalty, owners and managers of businesses would have to buy machines to clean the air and water they use before discharging either back into the environment. More labor and other inputs probably would be necessary, too. So, the firms' costs would go up. As costs went up, the prices the firms would have to charge for each unit produced would go up as well. That is, the firms' supply curves would shift upward. If no externalities were left, marginal social cost and marginal private cost would be the same.

Economics & Your *Community*

For the remainder of this chapter, have students look in local newspapers on a daily basis for examples of negative externalities. Tell students to clip these articles and organize them into a booklet. Then, as a class, write a letter to the mayor or other government official summarizing these social costs and suggesting logical ways to remedy them or to prevent similar situations. Remind students to use proper business-letter writing style. Make a copy of the letter and booklet before mailing them so you can refer to them should you receive a response.

Have students conduct a panel discussion to decide who (producers, government, local communities, and so on) should pay the cost of cleaning up pollution caused by industry. Ask students to identify a specific violation and then suggest a win/win agreement between that industry and taxpayers so that spillover costs to the community are reduced.

On the chalkboard or an overhead transparency, copy the outline and the headings of the following graphic organizer.

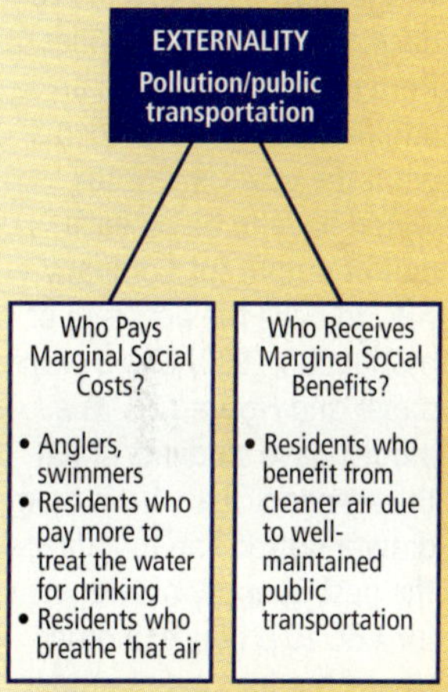

Tell students to imagine that a large automotive service center contracting with your city is located near the lake the city uses for its water supply. The center specializes in servicing, cleaning, and disinfecting city buses, and it dumps many gallons of petroleum and chemical waste in the lake each day. Have each student copy the graphic organizer into his or her notebook and complete it using the information from the scenario. (Some possible responses are given in the graphic organizer.) Have students keep their completed organizers in a safe place so they can refer to them to complete the *Apply* activity on p. 311.

Analyzing Graphics

Caption Answer
The rate of production would be the quantity associated with the point where the original supply curve intersects the demand curve; this quantity would be greater than Q_B.

Give students the following (fictitious) information: Company ABC produces a widget that costs $75 to produce. Negative externalities from air pollution equal an additional $30. Ask students what the government tax would have to be on each unit of output for Company ABC to have the best rate of production. ($30) Using graph paper and *Figure 12-5* as a model, have students graph the scenario. Then, have them draw a dotted line to indicate the best quantity of widgets for ABC to produce in order to pay the full cost of production. Tell students to label this quantity Q_B. Completed graphs should look like this:

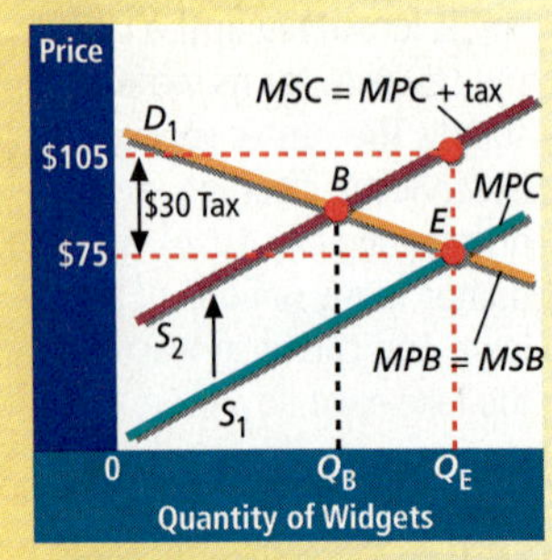

This situation is shown in Figure 12-4. The *Original Supply* curve shows the quantities that firms would produce at each price before the passage of laws against pollution. This curve also represents the marginal private cost of production if firms did contribute to pollution problems. If firms did obey the antipollution laws, the supply curve would shift to the curve labeled *New Supply* due to the added costs of complying. With this new supply curve, firms would charge a higher price for each unit because of the higher production costs. All the costs would be internalized. Marginal private costs *(MPC)* and marginal social costs *(MSC)* would be the same. There would be no negative externalities. Having decided to obey the laws against pollution, firms naturally would be led to produce the best amount of output (Q_B).

Figure 12-4

The Effect of Antipollution Laws

If the government passed a law prohibiting pollution, firms would have to clean up waste products. This would raise production costs so that marginal private costs *(MPC)* would be the same as marginal social costs *(MSC)*. The new supply curve would be above the original supply curve, and the best rate of output, Q_B, would be produced. ***What would be the rate of production if there were no laws prohibiting pollution?***

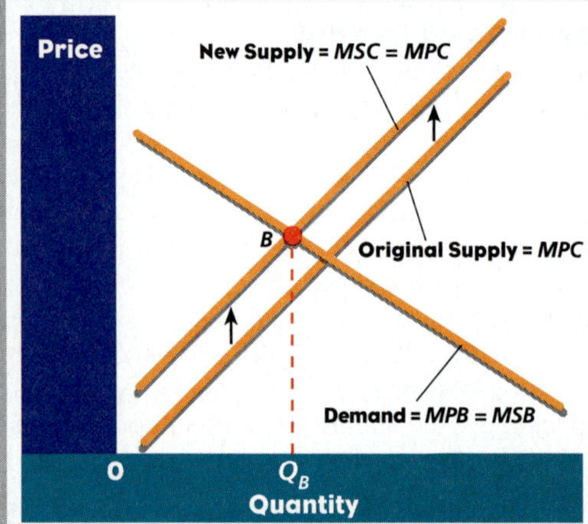

Using a Tax to Curb Pollution

A second common way to deal with the problem of negative spillovers is to use taxes. Any tax that is in some way tied to the rate of output could be used. The tax could be on the output itself or on an input. The tax even could be on the actual pollution. The easiest tax to use, however, is usually a tax on output.

To understand how such a tax would work, look at Figure 12-5. To start, suppose that firms only consider the private costs of production. Also, continue to assume that all of the benefits are internalized—that is, that $MPB = MSB$.

The free, competitive market system would ignore any negative externalities. Production would take place where marginal private costs were equal to marginal private benefits. This is at the point labeled *E* in Figure 12-5. The number of units produced would be Q_E units.

But, suppose there are negative externalities that equal $25 per unit of output. The marginal social costs then would be $25 more than the marginal private costs. This is shown by the distance *FE* in Figure 12-5, as well as by the difference between $85 and $60 on the vertical axis. If firms had to internalize that pollution cost of $25 per unit of output, less would be produced.

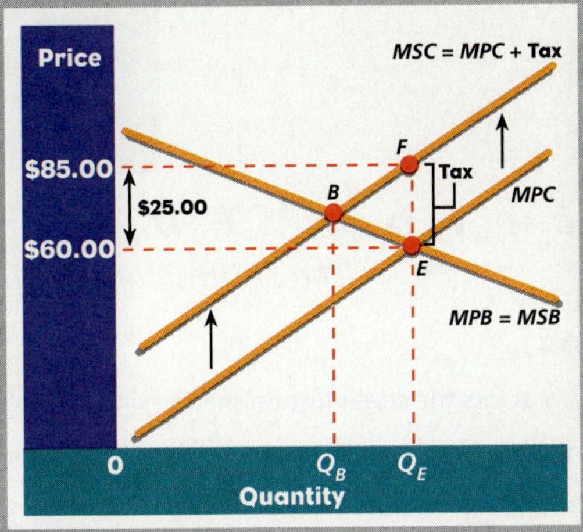

Figure 12-5

The Effect of a Tax on Output

When there are negative externalities, a tax on output can be used to decrease production from Q_E to Q_B units, which is the best rate of production. In this example, the amount of the tax is $25. ***Why is Q_B a better rate of production for society than Q_E?***

The government could put a tax on each unit of output equal to the pollution cost per unit, $25. Firms would have to pay the tax plus the cost of producing each unit. The cost for each additional unit of output would then be equal to *MPC + Tax*. Since the tax equals the pollution cost, the sum *MPC + Tax* would equal *MSC*. Firms would then base output decisions on the *MPC + Tax* curve, which is exactly the same as the *MSC* curve.

The result is that firms would find Q_B to be the best output rate. And, as you have seen before, Q_B is the best amount from the viewpoint of the entire society. That is, at Q_B, the *MSC* curve crosses the *MSB* curve. Marginal social costs are equal to marginal social benefits and resources are allocated in the best possible way.

Checkpoint

Content Check

1. Explain the difference between marginal social cost and marginal private cost.
2. How do laws that make pollution illegal affect a supplier's level of production?
3. How do taxes on output affect a firm's output decision?

What Do You Think Now?

Reread *What Do You Think?* in the Section Two Focus. Then answer the following questions:

4. If a company is polluting the environment, should it be forced to shut down? Why or why not?

Reteach

To help students understand negative externalities, ask them to think of all the negative externalities that a gas station located at a busy intersection might create. **12-2**

Enrich

Ask students to write a brief description of the externalities the following taxes could pay for: highway use tax for vehicles over 55,000 pounds (wear and tear on roads), alcohol and tobacco taxes (health-related costs shifted to the public when patients can't pay), and vaccine manufacturer's tax (fund for families of people injured or killed by vaccines). Discuss the fairness of these types of taxes. **12-3**

Analyzing Graphics

Caption Answer
At Q_B, marginal social costs equal marginal social benefits.

Assess

1. Marginal social cost includes the cost of the externality. Marginal private cost is the cost to the producer only. **12-2**
2. To avoid the penalty for polluting, businesses buy machines to clean the air and water they use, so their costs and the price charged for each unit produced go up. All costs are internalized, so firms produce output at the best rate—with the full marginal cost equal to the full marginal benefit. **12-2**
3. Firms must pay the tax plus the cost of producing each unit; since the tax equals the pollution cost, firms base output decisions on the *MPC + Tax* curve, which is the same as the *MSC* curve. **12-3**
4. Responses will reflect independent thinking, but students may answer no; the best outcome for society is to find the rate of output at which the marginal social costs and the marginal social benefits are equal. **12-3**

Close

Ask students to imagine that they are government representatives who must create one universal law to establish unacceptable criteria for polluters. Have students draft their law and then submit it to the "voters" (schoolmates, friends, or family) for feedback. As a class, revise the law according to these responses.

FOCUS

Section Three

The Shifting of Benefits

What Do You Think?

The Kelinsky family across the street just finished having a professional landscaping firm redo their yard. The new trees and shrubs and flowers make quite a showplace. The Kelinsky's are very happy with the results and their increased enjoyment of their yard. How might others benefit as well?

Terms to Know

positive externality

subsidy

What's Ahead?

There are times when the overall benefits from an activity are greater than the benefits to just those who are directly involved. Economics can help you understand such situations and how governments encourage these positive externalities.

POSITIVE EXTERNALITIES

positive externality the result when *benefits* are shifted to people who are not directly involved with the production or consumption of a good

A ***positive externality*** is the result when *benefits* are shifted to people who are not directly involved with the production or consumption of a good. There are situations when third parties benefit from an economic activity, even though they are not directly involved in it. This means that the social benefits of the activity are higher than the private benefits. It may be hard to believe that you ever get something for nothing, but it is possible. Unfortunately, though, there may be fewer cases of positive externalities than of negative ones.

Mass Transportation Can Create Positive Externalities

People who live in big cities that have mass transportation systems may enjoy a positive spillover from these systems. When people use the mass transit system rather than driving private cars, there is less air pollution. Other people in the city, even those who don't use the mass transportation system, benefit because of the cleaner air. The benefit from the system is greater than just the benefit to direct users. This positive externality results in social benefits that are greater than private benefits.

Individual Activities Can Create Positive Externalities

Consider again the family next door. Suppose they decide to spend some of their time and money fixing up their house and yard. They build a garage big

Focus

Write the term **subsidy** on the chalkboard or an overhead transparency. As students enter the classroom, ask them to jot down on a sheet of paper what they think of when they read this word.

Ask students to volunteer their responses. Explain that the government sometimes gives money to individuals and companies that encourage positive actions or attitudes in society. Then, relate this concept to the Kelinsky family named in the textbook and how their new trees and shrubs make the neighborhood look better. Explain to students that this is an example of a positive externality. Ask students to determine if the Kelinskys should receive a subsidy.

Teach

Explain that a **positive externality** is the result of benefits being shifted to people who are not directly involved with the production or consumption of a good. The government may give companies a **subsidy,** or incentive, to encourage these positive externalities. For example, keeping employees physically fit might be something the government wants to encourage, so companies with physical fitness programs might be entitled to a tax credit. The positive externality would be healthier people, which should result in fewer workdays missed due to illness, which would keep families' earnings up and health-related costs down. This, in turn, would allow the families to spend more money on goods and services in their community.

Perspectives

Thinking Like an Education Analyst Elicit from students that education has many positive externalities, including a reduction in crime, a more globally competitive workforce, a higher standard of living, and a better quality of life. Ask students to imagine that they are education analysts. Ask them to brainstorm a plan to convince their state government to increase state funding for education on the basis of the positive externalities received from improved education.

enough for their trailer and their son's bicycle and other toys. They paint the outside of the house and improve their yard. They get some benefits from doing these things. The property is more enjoyable for their personal use, and the value of their property goes up. But, there is a spillover of benefits to others as well. Your family and other neighbors will get some benefits. You will enjoy the use of your own yard more if there is a more pleasant view next door. If the people next door improve their house and property, the neighborhood is improved and your house becomes more valuable. So, the social benefits of the improvements made by one household are greater than just the private benefits.

Education and Health Care Create Positive Externalities

You will get many private benefits from your education. You are more likely to enjoy a wider variety of activities as you get more education. You will have a better understanding of the world around you, and you probably will earn more money. But, education also provides some external benefits. As more people are educated, the number of crimes tends to decrease. There is a likelihood that welfare payments will decrease. And, the democratic process works better when people are better educated, because they are more able to understand issues. While you get private benefits from your education, the rest of society gets some benefits, too. So, the social benefits are higher than the private benefits.

There also are positive externalities from many types of medical care. When one person is inoculated against an illness, that person clearly gets a private benefit. But, other members of society benefit, too, because there will be less chance of their getting that illness. Again, the social benefits are higher than the private benefits that go just to the person who is inoculated.

Economic Dilemma

HO-HO-HO OR BAH HUMBUG?

Every year in December during the Christmas season, many families decorate the outside of their homes with lights and other displays. It is not uncommon to find one or more homes in a given area that really "go all out." They may hang thousands of lights, display an animated Santa Claus, or play Christmas music over a loud speaker.

Some people so enjoy seeing such displays that they drive for miles to see what displays people have put up. Occasionally, these drives lead to massive traffic jams. People sometimes have trouble getting to their own homes due to the congestion. Some residents complain about the noise, the light, and the damage to their own property caused by the spectators who come to view the displays of a few neighbors.

Should such displays be encouraged or discouraged? Think about both the positive and the negative externalities that are involved. What suggestions do you have for solving this dilemma?

Economic Dilemma

After students have read *Economic Dilemma,* divide the class into two groups. Have the groups debate whether Christmas displays in public buildings should be encouraged or discouraged. Tell students to cite possible positive and negative externalities to support their viewpoints.

Apply

Tell students to take out the graphic organizer that they created for p. 307. Display a copy on the chalkboard or an overhead transparency. Ask students to identify the negative and positive externalities. (*negative: MSC > MPC;* marginal social costs are greater than marginal private costs; *positive: MSB > MPB;* marginal social benefits are greater than marginal private benefits). Add another heading: **What Is the Response of Government?** Work with students to complete the organizer. (Possible responses include passing antipollution laws or paying subsidies to suppliers of public transportation and taxing the output of the firm or providing subsidies to consumers of public transportation.) Be sure students understand how the government balances the economy by offering subsidies to encourage positive externalities.

Guided Practice

Tell students to imagine that one of their state senators is opposed to a national health-care plan. Have students write a formal business letter to their senator, logically supporting their personal opinions on the positive or negative externalities of a national health-care program.

Independent Practice

Analyzing Graphics

Caption Answer
Because the marginal benefits to society are greater than the marginal social costs of producing the amount represented by Q_E

Display *Transparency 12-6* and have one or more student volunteers explain the differences between points ***F*** and ***B*** on the curve labeled **Demand* = *MSB*.** (When the marginal benefits to society are greater than the marginal private benefits, the market system will not allocate enough resources to meet demand for a product. ***F*** represents the quantity that will be produced if only private costs and benefits are considered. ***B*** represents the quantity that should be produced in order for marginal societal benefits to equal marginal private benefits.) Then, ask students what they think could be done to encourage businesses to produce more goods that create positive externalities. (Point out the positive image generated for the company by the product; give tax deductions or tax credits; give government funds, or **subsidies,** to help pay for production.)

Point out to students that, as a nation, we spend money to subsidize the tobacco industry, which employs thousands of people and boosts the economy. Yet this industry creates tobacco products that have been proven to increase our risk for cancer. The government then spends more money on cancer research and on health-related costs for cancer patients who can't afford treatment. We are,

(Continued)

ANALYSIS OF POSITIVE EXTERNALITIES

In this section on positive externalities, assume that the only costs involved are private costs. That is, assume that marginal social costs and marginal private costs are exactly the same *(MSC = MPC)*. When there are positive spillovers, the social benefits are greater than the private benefits. So, the marginal social benefits curve is above the marginal private benefits curve. This is shown in Figure 12-6.

Figure 12-6

Positive Externalities and Marginal Benefits

Positive externalities cause marginal social benefits *(MSB)* to be greater than marginal private benefits *(MPB)*. The market system allocates too few resources to the production of this product. Only Q_E units are produced when the best rate of output is Q_B. ***Why is the Q_E rate of output too small?***

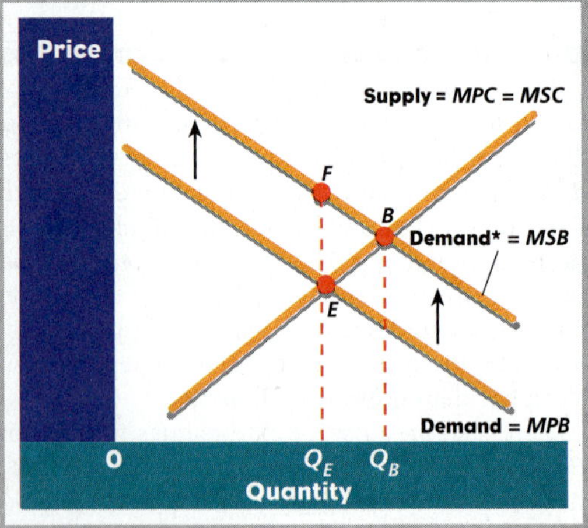

The competitive market economy will fail to take the social benefits into account. Only private benefits will be considered. The result is that firms will produce, and people will buy, the amount shown as Q_E in Figure 12-6. This is where marginal private benefits and costs are equal.

But, from the view of the whole society, Q_E is too little of the good. The marginal benefits to society are greater than the marginal costs of producing the amount represented by Q_E. As you saw in Figure 12-2, this means that more resources should be allocated to this type of production. In Figure 12-6, the amount by which the marginal social benefit is greater than the marginal social cost is the distance *FE*.

The best rate of output can be found only by comparing the marginal social cost with the marginal social benefit. The demand curve labeled *Demand* = MSB* shows the demand that would result if all of society were included, including third parties. Since there are benefits to third parties in cases of positive spillovers, *Demand** is above the demand curve that includes only private benefits.

When you compare the marginal social cost with the marginal social benefit, you see that the best rate of production is Q_B units. This is the rate where *Demand** crosses the supply curve at Point *B*. Society's resources are allocated in the best way when Q_B units are produced.

PUBLIC POLICY FOR POSITIVE EXTERNALITIES

subsidy
a payment made by the government to encourage some activity

Activities that have positive externalities should be encouraged by society. The government can encourage such activities by subsidizing them. A ***subsidy*** is a payment made by the government to encourage some activity. A subsidy

EyeOnMarketNews

Throughout the world, social, economic, and political tensions create positive and negative externalities. Have students create a three-column chart with the headings **News Summary, + Externalities,** and **- Externalities.** Ask students to watch a televised, national, evening newscast and to briefly summarize the top five news stories in the first column of the chart. Then, in class, tell students to identify in the second and third columns of the chart possible positive and negative externalities associated with each news story.

is the opposite of a tax. For example, participants in a market transaction can be given money to get them to make or buy more of the goods that yield positive externalities.

Subsidies are given for a number of activities. Think about the examples used for positive spillovers. Education gets very big subsidies. Education in public schools from kindergarten through high school is nearly free for most people. Even postsecondary education in technical schools, nursing schools, and colleges is subsidized. Tuition fees usually do not cover the full costs of education in such schools. Sometimes the subsidy goes directly to the supplier, such as a public school system. But, it can also go to the consumer through student loan programs, for example. The government also provides large subsidies for medical programs and mass transit. In many geographical areas, government programs have been used to help families or businesses pay for the costs of improving property.

In Figure 12-7 on page 314, you can see how subsidies can work on either the supply side or the demand side. Graph *A* shows a subsidy of *BC* dollars per unit for consumers. With the subsidy, consumers get benefits from consuming the product and from the subsidy. This shifts the demand curve to *Demand**, and the best rate of output (Q_B) results.

Graph *B* of Figure 12-7 shows what would happen if the subsidy were given to suppliers instead. The subsidy to suppliers would lower the cost of production so that the supply curve would shift to *Supply**. *Supply** crosses the original

Global Economy

POLLUTION WITHOUT BORDERS

In 1978, researchers predicted "that the frozen continent would be the world's canary-in-a-coal-mine, showing the early signs that the climate is warming." In 1995, a chunk of ice the size of Rhode Island broke off the Larsen ice shelf on the Antarctic peninsula. A few months later, a large crack, 30 feet wide and 40 miles long, appeared in the ice shelf, another ominous sign to scientists who worry about global warming.

There is concern that as the ice shelves of Antarctica melt, the winds that blow over the ice of Antarctica will be warmer and potentially melt a portion of the continents' ice cover. If only 10 percent of that ice melts, it is predicted that sea levels worldwide could rise by 12 to 30 feet. Think about what this would mean for the thousands of cities around the world in coastal areas.

Perhaps the greatest cause of global warming (if indeed it is taking place—which is not certain) is the accumulation of carbon dioxide and other gases. These gases stem mainly from the burning of coal, gas, and oil. Pollution does not recognize political boundaries between countries. The air pollution caused by traffic in Detroit drifts readily into Canada. The emission of greenhouse gases such as carbon dioxide, methane, and chlorofluorocarbons, may contribute to global warming no matter whether they come from Germany, Japan, the United States, or Brazil.

Global Economy Divide the class into three groups of students for a debate centering on pollution and acid rain. Have one group represent utilities and manufacturing industries, which generate more than 45 percent of all air pollution. Have the second group represent environmentalists who want to force these companies to reduce their output of pollution. Have a third group represent Canadian fishers who believe that pollution generated in the United States is polluting Canadian waters. Have each group develop economic and political arguments to support its viewpoints. Then, have the groups debate their positions in relation to marginal social costs and benefits.

(Continued)

therefore, encouraging both positive and negative externalities at the same time. Have students draw a political cartoon or write a letter to the editor of your school or local newspaper addressing this inconsistency. Encourage students to submit their cartoons and letters for publication.

After students have read *Global Economy,* lead a class discussion about positive externalities that may actually lead to negative externalities over time. For example, the invention and the production of the automobile created many positive externalities, such as the ability to have loved ones, business associates, and so on travel great distances in a short amount of time in order to visit you and the ability to have your friends and family protected by fire-fighting equipment, police protection, and emergency medical services that can be rushed to accident scenes quickly. Yet, automobile exhaust has polluted the atmosphere, and auto accidents have claimed countless victims. As a class, discuss how to prevent future problems caused by current "positive" externalities.

Individually or in small groups, ask students to go to their local library and use an online database, if possible, to research several existing subsidies. Ask students to write a one-page description of some of the U.S. government subsidies that they learned about through their research and to suggest positive externalities that may be created by each subsidy.

demand at Point *A*. So, with the subsidy to suppliers, market forces would make sure Q_B units would be produced. And, as you have seen several times now, Q_B is the best rate of output. At that rate, resources are allocated in the best way.

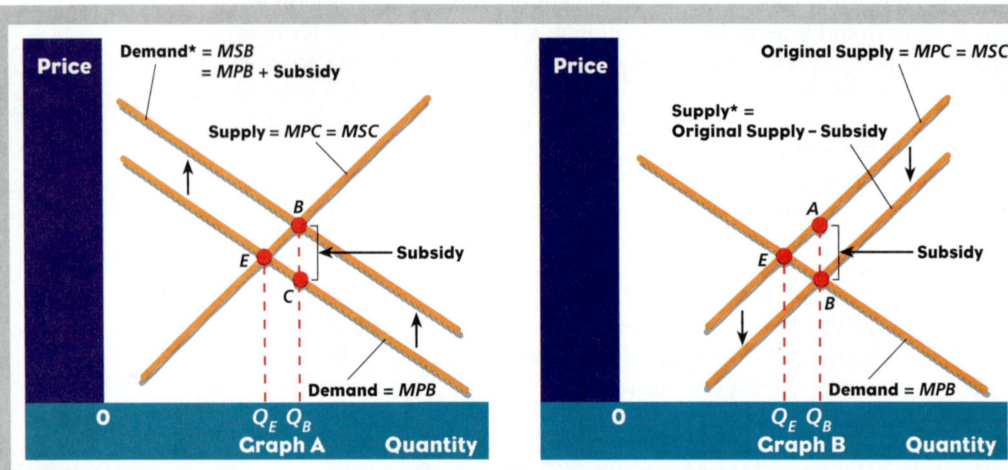

Figure 12-7

A Subsidy Will Affect the Amount Produced and Consumed

A government subsidy to consumers, Graph *A*, or to producers, Graph *B*, can correct the misallocation of resources due to a positive externality. In either case, output would be increased from Q_E units to the best rate of output, Q_B. ***If too great of a subsidy were given in the cases described in these graphs, what would be the result?***

Checkpoint

Content Check

1. Explain the difference between marginal social benefits and marginal private benefits.
2. How do subsidies to suppliers affect a supplier's level of production?
3. How do subsidies to consumers encourage activities that have positive externalities?

What Do You Think Now?

Reread *What Do You Think?* in the Section Three Focus. Then answer the following question:

4. When one family makes its property more attractive, how might others benefit as well?

Analyzing Graphics

Caption Answer
Too much would be produced.

Assess

1. The difference is the added benefit to society of an economic activity; when there are positive externalities, the marginal social benefits of the activity are higher than the marginal private benefits. **12-4**
2. Subsidies decrease the cost of production, so supply increases, the supply curve shifts downward (or to the right), and suppliers allocate resources to produce the best rate of output—which is greater than the amount they would produce without the subsidy. **12-5**
3. With the subsidy, consumers receive the benefit from the product plus the benefit from the subsidy; this increases demand, shifting the demand curve upward (or to the right), and the best rate of output results. **12-5**
4. Others benefit if the "improvements" are to their liking as well. **12-4**

Close

As a class, make a list of five or more externalities that affect students at school. Then, have class members tell whether each externality is negative or positive and list its social and private benefits and costs.

Reteach

To help students understand positive externalities, point out those produced by many nonprofit organizations. One example is Habitat for Humanity (see *Economic Spotlight,* Chapter 17), which builds and refurbishes houses and then sells them at a very low cost to underprivileged families. Have students work together to list the benefits society gains from these efforts. **12-4**

Enrich

Ask groups of students to develop a two-page letter to their local government with suggestions for encouraging positive externalities from community businesses. Suggest that students use a computer program to calculate tangible savings that result from their suggestions. **12-5**

FOCUS

Section Four

Sometimes Having a Single Supplier Is Best

What Do You Think?

For most households there is a single supplier of electric power. This is due, in part, to the high cost of the equipment that is necessary to generate and distribute electricity. Would you, or society in general, be better served by having competition in the supply of electric power?

What's Ahead?

In the United States, we generally have favored a competitive free market economy. Overall, the results have been good. However, there are times when a single supplier and no competition may be better. In this section, you will learn about two such situations: the provision of public goods and the case of natural monopolies.

Term to Know

exclusion principle

PUBLIC GOODS

The market system does not always give good signals about how much should be produced. Either too much or too little may be produced if the market is left alone. A special class of goods that if left alone the market would fail to provide at all, even though society wants them, are public goods.

Everyone Benefits from Public Goods

You will recall that public goods and services are used by the whole society. To expand on this definition a little, public goods are goods that cannot be sold one unit at a time to individuals. Once the good is available for one person to consume, it is available for everyone to consume. An example of a public good is national defense. Everyone gets some benefit from national defense. Some people get more and some get less, but the same amount of benefit is available for everyone.

Economic*Talk*

On the chalkboard, write the following pairs of terms:

1. **externality/third-party effect**
2. **externality/spillover**
3. **MSC/MSB**
4. **tax/subsidy**

Ask students to determine whether the economic relationship between each pair of terms is equal or opposite. (1. equal, 2. equal, 3. opposite, 4. opposite) Then, have student volunteers explain the relationship between the terms in each pair.

Focus

Contact your local cable television company and request copies of its basic cable and premium station offerings. Distribute the booklets to students to review in small groups. Ask this question: **What available channels are not offered by this company in your area?**

Have volunteers suggest names of channels not offered by your supplier. Ask students to consider why they are not provided. Then, based on this example, have the class brainstorm the meaning of **exclusion principle.**

Teach

Explain to the class that the **exclusion principle** is the principle that a person can keep others from benefiting from his or her private property. Point out that the **exclusion principle** only applies to private goods and services—*not* to public goods and services. Tell students that, sometimes, goods or services can be supplied best by a single supplier. Because it makes no sense to have several companies compete for the provision of these goods or services, a natural monopoly occurs, which can be regulated by the government. For example, natural gas or another public utility may be more effectively supplied by one company because it is inefficient for two or more companies to have the same type of utility lines and highly specialized equipment.

Apply

Ask students to suggest a list of public goods and private goods. As a class, brainstorm who pays for and uses each good. Ask students if they think individuals can be excluded from using a good that is paid for with tax dollars. Point out that this does occur, and have students suggest examples. (Examples may include someone under 12 not being admitted without an adult to a museum or public swimming pool, campers not being allowed to camp in certain areas of a national park, or community football teams unable to practice on their school fields due to legal liability.) Then, explain to students that these situations are not really exceptions to the exclusion principle. No single individual is able to exclude others from using these public goods. Rather, they are excluded by a system of rules and regulations. Also, one person's consumption of the public good does not exclude another person from using that same good.
Guided Practice

Economic Spotlight

SHE RUNS THE USA (NETWORK)

Could hearing one guest speaker change your life forever? It did for Kay Koplovitz. When Koplovitz heard science-fiction writer Arthur C. Clarke, author of *2001*, speak on the future impact of satellite technology on communications, she immediately changed her major to communications and wrote her master's thesis on satellites and global communications.

After graduate school, Koplovitz worked her way up the ladder in the communications industry, first working for satellite companies, then running her own communications management firm, and then joining forces with UA-Columbia. There she launched the first advertiser-supported basic cable network in the United States: MSG Sports (Madison Square Garden Sports), which later became the USA Network.

Koplovitz has many other "firsts" to her credit too. She was the *first* to negotiate national cable rights for major league sports, the *first* to begin 24-hour cable programming, and the *first* to sign licensing agreements for the right to rebroadcast more than 100 different program titles. In fact, the USA Network has become quite famous for its rebroadcasts of such shows as "Miami Vice" and "Murder, She Wrote."

Since the network's beginning, Koplovitz has served as president and CEO. She is a true pioneer in the cable industry, blazing a communications trail for other cable networks to follow. But, is this trail heading in the wrong direction? The U.S. Congress thinks so. It has stepped in to try to control the cable industry so that a single company cannot dominate it. Striving to stimulate competition in the cable marketplace, Congress has passed several laws to regulate the industry. One such law worries Koplovitz because it allows broadcasters to charge cable operators for their signals. This, in turn, encourages cable operators to charge viewers extra for access to specific cable channels.

USA Network is included in most basic cable services and does not cost customers extra. Koplovitz wants to keep it that way. She feels so strongly about the issue, she has even imposed penalties on cable operators that have tried to move the USA Network out of their basic cable service. As the years go on, she will definitely have a fight on her hands in her efforts to keep USA "free." But, if anyone has a proven ability to come out on top, it's Kay Koplovitz.

Economic Spotlight

After students have read *Economic Spotlight,* discuss as a class the exclusion principle in relation to the cable industry. Ask students who they think is being excluded—cable subscribers, nonsubscribers, or cable networks? (All are, in some form; subscribers are excluded from enjoying more cable networks on their basic service, nonsubscribers are excluded from viewing *any* cable broadcasts, and some cable companies are excluded from exposure to the vast audience of basic cable subscribers.) Who is doing the excluding? (Cable operators) Should cable service operate as a natural monopoly? Why? (Answers may include "no" because a natural monoploy would limit consumers' options. Or, "yes" because it would lower the delivery price.)

No One Can Be Excluded from Using Public Goods

If we tried to sell national defense through the market system, we would fail. Why should you or I voluntarily pay for something we know we can get for free once others pay for it? Of course, everyone would reason this way. So, if left to the market, we would have no national defense. This doesn't mean that we don't get any benefit from it. It just means that people will not express their demand for defense through the market system. Therefore, national defense must be provided through the public sector. Our demand for this service is expressed through the political system rather than through the market system.

A lighthouse is another example of a public good. Once the lighthouse is built along a rocky coastline, all boaters can benefit from it without any direct payment. The owner of a small sailboat and the captain of a huge oil tanker both benefit from the warning light. Neither of them can be kept from benefiting from the light.

The ***exclusion principle*** is the principle that one person can keep others from benefiting from a private good. If you buy a new tennis racquet, you can exclude others from using it. This is true of all private goods. But, one person cannot exclude others from benefiting from public goods. If you hike through Glacier National Park, you cannot prevent others from also doing so. If you get some benefit from national defense, you do not exclude others from benefiting, too. Since our demand for public goods cannot be expressed well through the market system, the public sector provides them and they are paid for by taxes.

exclusion principle
the principle that one person can keep others from benefiting from a private good

NATURAL MONOPOLIES

If one firm can produce enough to satisfy the market more cheaply than if there are more than one, that firm is a natural monopoly. You have learned that natural monopolies exist in industries in which competition is not practical. Because competition does not exist in these markets, prices are not controlled by the laws of supply and demand. Thus, the market system fails to function in the control of prices, output, and profits.

Natural monopolies usually occur in industries in which average cost falls as output increases through the range of potential sales. To see why this is so, look at Figure 12-8 on page 319. The average cost curve shows that average cost decreases as output increases. If a monopolist produced so as not to make excess profits, production would be Q units. The average cost would be relatively low, as shown on the vertical axis. But, if two firms tried to share the market equally, the average cost per unit would go up. Each firm would produce $\frac{1}{2}Q$, and as shown in Figure 12-8, the average cost would be higher. Neither firm could capture enough of the demand to produce at the lowest possible average cost. This would mean that the price to consumers would have to be higher as well.

The two firms would likely have price-cutting wars until one of them were forced out of business. The firm that survived would then have a low average cost and almost surely would reduce output and increase price.

Have students make a list of the public utilities (natural monopolies) in your area. Divide the class into as many teams as there are public utilities. Write the following questions on the chalkboard or an overhead transparency and tell the teams to prepare to answer them orally: **Is the utility truly a natural monopoly? Why or why not? What agency regulates the utility? How? Do you think the utility provides service at the lowest possible cost? Why or why not?**

Independent Practice

Language Experience Activities (LEAs) use the student's own language abilities and personal responses to record an experience. Summarize class findings from the previous activity and ensure that limited-English-proficient students understand public utilities and monopolies by asking for oral examples of each. Write students' ideas in standard English on the chalkboard. Have students read and copy the ideas into their notebooks for additional reinforcement.

Limited English Proficiency

Tell students that, in 1980, economist Milton Friedman and his wife Rose Friedman wrote a book entitled *Free to Choose,* which also was made into a TV series. In the series, the authors advocated opening the entire world to free trade and competition. Have students go to the library and read excerpts from the book. Based on what they read, have them write an essay about whether they favor or oppose a system of only free competition.

Internet Connection

REACHING OUT ACROSS THE INTERNET WITH TELNET

In this chapter, we want to explore the services available from telnet sites. Telnet is the command used to get one computer to connect to another computer on the Internet. Telnet also allows computer systems to make a variety of services available to the public without requiring users to have accounts on those systems. These services include online library catalogs; Gopher, Web, and other information servers; electronic books; databases; and a wide range of other resources. Your teacher may give you some specific examples of telnet services to try.

If you access telnet through a text-based interface (DOS or UNIX), type **telnet remote_computer**, where remote_computer is the Internet address of the telnet site. If you use a graphical interface (WINDOWS or MAC), click on *telnet* and enter the Internet address of the remote_computer.

Telnet is not as user-friendly as Gopher or WWW. Different telnet services use different commands, but for public access telnet sites, the important commands are usually explained when you log in. Write these down! Ordinarily this information will include how to end the telnet session. If it doesn't, you can always type *ctrl-]* and then *quit.*

You might not have access to telnet, but you may be able to reach telnet sites with a Web browser. Use your browser to open a URL with **telnet://remote_computer**. Not all browsers are configured for telnet. If you're not sure, try opening a telnet URL.

Internet Application: The federal government maintains a gateway to federal information systems on the internet. This is called FedWorld and has the URL **telnet://fedworld.gov**. Telnet to FedWorld and set up an account in your name. Explore the FedWorld site and find something relevant to this chapter (regulation, for example). E-mail a description of what you find to your teacher.

If you have access to the Web but not telnet, you can still access FedWorld. What do you think the Internet address is?

Economics Application: Market failure is a major reason for government regulation. The chapter indicates that market failure is caused by externalities such as pollution. In the United States, the principal regulatory body for pollution control is the Environmental Protection Agency (epa.gov). Use Gopher or Web to access the EPA Internet site and identify a major current issue for the agency. E-mail a description to your teacher.

Internet Connection

Economics Application: The EPA Web page is **http://www.epa.gov**. The EPA Gopher site is **gopher://gopher.epa.gov**. Current EPA issues can be found by examining the press releases or speeches available on the EPA Web page.

Explanation for the Internet Application is in the *Teacher's Connection to the Internet.*

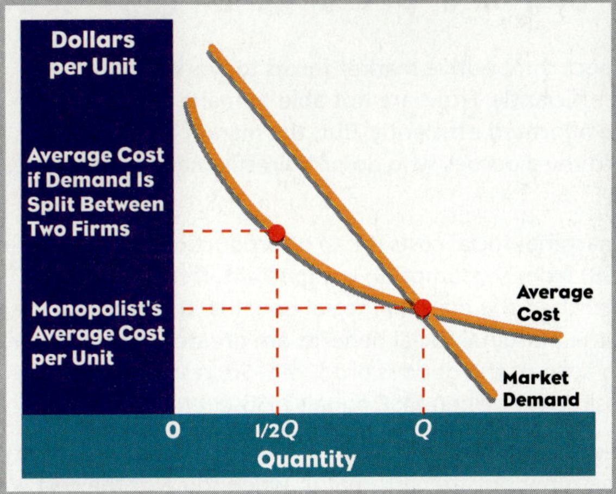

Figure 12-8

Average Cost for a Natural Monopoly

A natural monopoly may result when average cost falls over the entire range of possible production. A monopolist could produce *Q* units at a lower cost per unit than could two firms splitting the market. ***If there were three firms sharing equally the market described by this graph, would the average cost be higher or lower than if there were two firms, each with one-half of the market?***

The natural monopolist then would make excessive profits. To prevent such profits, the government usually regulates natural monopolies so that price just equals average cost and *Q* units are produced.

Examples of natural monopolies include electric power, natural gas, and local telephone services (although new technologies may be changing this). As you know, these services are commonly called *public utilities*. They are not necessarily owned by the public sector, however. Public utilities, just like other *corporations*, are usually owned by stockholders. But, they are closely regulated by public sector officials.

Checkpoint

Content Check

1. What is a public good?
2. How does the exclusion principle relate to a good such as a CD player you may own?
3. What determines whether a natural monopoly is likely to exist in an industry?

What Do You Think Now?

Reread *What Do You Think?* in the Section Four Focus. Then answer the following question:

4. Would society be better served by having several electric power companies serve each market?

Reteach

Divide the class into four groups. Tell each group that it represents a company that wants to supply water to your town. However, one of the four companies already supplies all your town's water. Ask the groups to discuss how they will compete and what will happen if they compete to supply water. **12-6**

Enrich

Ask each student to imagine that the personal-computer hardware and software industries in the United States have become natural monopolies. As a small group, have students discuss the pros and cons of this market organization from the perspectives of consumers and both industries. **12-6**

Analyzing Graphics

Caption Answer
The average cost (cost per unit) would be higher with three firms than with two firms.

Assess

1. A public good is available for everyone to consume. Public goods cannot be sold one unit at a time to individuals, and one person cannot exclude others from benefiting from them. **12-6**
2. You may exclude others from using the CD player because it is a private good. **12-6**
3. If competition is not practical because one firm can produce enough to satisfy the market more cheaply than can several firms in competition, that industry is a natural monopoly. **12-6**
4. Society would *not* be better served. Natural monopolies usually occur in industries in which average cost falls as output increases through the range of potential sales. If more than one firm tried to share the electric-power market, the average cost per unit would go up and the price to consumers would go up as well. **12-6**

Close

Divide the class into groups of three or four students. Ask each group to think of a government-regulated natural monopoly and then outline a plan that details how that business could successfully become a competitive enterprise. Ask students to list the obstacles that could occur in this process. Then, have the groups share their lists and plans with the class for feedback and revision.

Chapter Close

Your Economic Portfolio

Tell each student to choose a private business that, in his or her opinion, produces many more positive externalities than negative externalities. (For example, a professional baseball franchise) Have students create a chart that has two columns: one labeled **+ Externalities** and one labeled **- Externalities.** Tell them to name the chart **Competition** and then to list all of the externalities in the appropriate columns. Next, ask students to imagine that the business they chose suddenly became a government-regulated monopoly. Direct them to create a second, similar chart, name it **Monopoly,** and list in it the externalities that would be produced by the business as a monopoly. Ask students to explain whether these externalities are different and, if so, how. Have students write an explanation of how the business owner and consumers would be affected by this change from competition to monopoly. Remind students to include information about the exclusion principle and private costs and benefits versus social costs and benefits. Review students' charts and correct any misconceptions before filing them in the students' portfolios.

You may wish to provide the following end-of-chapter materials:

- *Skills & Concepts* worksheet
- *Content Review Workbook*
- Chapter *Assessment*
- Chapter *MicroExam*

Concepts in Brief

1. Normally, we can expect competitive market forces to work fairly well. Goods are produced efficiently. Firms are not able to make excessive profits. And resources are allocated efficiently. But, the market can fail when benefits or costs go to third parties who do not directly make or consume a product.
2. The relation of the marginal social costs (MSC) of production to the marginal social benefits (MSB) from consumption is important. If the marginal social costs are greater than the marginal social benefits, too much of the good is produced. If the marginal social benefits are greater than the marginal social costs, too little of the good is produced. So, resources are allocated in the best possible way when MSC equals MSB.
3. Negative externalities result when the marginal social cost of some activity is greater than the marginal private cost; that is, when some of the cost is shifted to third parties. Pollution is a negative externality. *Negative spillovers* or *negative third-party effects* are other terms used for negative externalities.
4. Negative externalities can be reduced or eliminated by laws that prohibit pollution. They also can be reduced or eliminated by the use of a tax on the input or output of a firm causing pollution. The tax per unit of output should equal the difference between the marginal private cost and the marginal social cost.
5. Positive externalities result when the marginal social benefit from an activity is greater than the marginal private benefit; that is, when some of the benefit from the activity is shifted to third parties. *Positive spillovers* or *positive third-party effects* are other terms used to describe positive externalities.
6. Activities involving positive externalities should be encouraged. This can be done through the use of government subsidies on either the supply side or the demand side. On the supply side, a subsidy reduces the firm's costs and encourages more production. On the demand side, a subsidy increases the benefits consumers receive and causes demand to increase. The subsidy per unit should be equal to the difference between the marginal social benefit and the marginal private benefit.
7. Some goods have such big positive spillovers that they are provided entirely or nearly so by the government. When such a good cannot be provided by the private sector, it is called a *public good.* National defense is an example of a public good.

Economic Foundations

1. Output will increase. (pp. 300–301)
2. Output will decrease. (pp. 300–301)
3. The best level of production and allocation results when marginal private costs equal marginal private benefits. (pp. 300–301)
4. When there are negative externalities, marginal social costs are higher than marginal private costs. (p. 303)
5. The level of output would be too high (p. 306). Passing laws against the externality or levying a tax against it discourages the activity with the negative externality, leading to the best rate of output. (pp. 307–309)
6. When there are positive externalities, marginal social benefits are greater than marginal private benefits. (p. 310)

(Continued)

8. The exclusion principle is useful in distinguishing between public and private goods. If one person can exclude others from enjoying the benefits of some good, the good is considered a private good. But, if one person cannot exclude another, such as from the benefits of national defense, the good is a public good.

9. A natural monopoly can result when the average cost of producing a product decreases over the entire range of potential sales. If more than one firm tried to operate in such a market, a price war would be likely. All but one firm would be forced out of business, and the remaining monopoly could then charge a high price and make big profits. The government usually regulates such natural monopolies closely. Public utilities, such as electric companies, are examples of natural monopolies.

Economic Foundations

1. In a competitive market with no externalities, if marginal private benefits are greater than marginal private costs, what is the rate of output?
2. In a competitive market with no externalities, if marginal private costs are greater than marginal private benefits, what is the rate of output?
3. In a competitive market with no externalities, what relationship between marginal private costs and marginal private benefits results in the best rate of production and allocation of resources?
4. What is the relationship between marginal private costs and marginal social costs when there are negative externalities?
5. What level of output would an unregulated industry produce when there are negative externalities? What could be done to cause the best rate of output to be produced?
6. What is the relationship between marginal private benefits and marginal social benefits when there are positive externalities?
7. What level of output would an unregulated industry produce when there are positive externalities? What could be done to cause the best rate of output?
8. How does the exclusion principle apply to public goods?
9. Under what circumstances is a natural monopoly likely to occur? What would happen if two firms instead tried to share such a market equally?

Economic Foundations
(Continued)

7. The level of output would be too low (p. 312). The best level of output can be caused by using subsidies to encourage the activity with the positive externality. (p. 312)
8. The exclusion principle means that, unlike with private goods, one person cannot prevent another person from benefiting from a public good. (p. 317)
9. A natural monopoly is caused by natural market forces when competition is inefficient and it is better for only one company to provide a good or service (p. 317). The cost of production would be higher for both firms, so prices would go up for consumers (p. 317).

Your Economic Vocabulary

(see page 322)

1. **externality**
2. **negative externality**
3. **marginal social cost (MSC)**
4. **subsidy**
5. **marginal social benefit (MSB)**
6. **positive externality**
7. **marginal private cost (MPC)**
8. **exclusion principle**
9. **marginal private benefit (MPB)**

Thinking Critically About Economics

(see page 322)

1. Negative externalities and their solutions may include 1) clutter: student cleanup teams; 2) traffic congestion: locate schools in uncrowded places or widen streets; and 3) property damage: increase patrols or establish a property repair fund.
2. Because one person cannot exclude another from the benefits of police protection, it is a public good. Answers may include that, through a market system, people might not pay for police protection because they would assume that others would pay and that they could benefit for free. If everyone assumed this, no one would pay and there would be no police protection.
3. Externalities and their solutions may include a) air pollution from exhaust: improve emissions devices on vehicles; b) thermal pollution from nuclear generators: levy a tax tied to water temperature to force

(Continued)

Thinking Critically About Economics (Continued)

firms to cool water more before discharging it; c) noise pollution: make stadiums absorb more sound; and d) water pollution: tax firms according to the volume of waste materials discharged and use the revenue to clean up water sources.

4. Students' graphs should appear similar to the following:

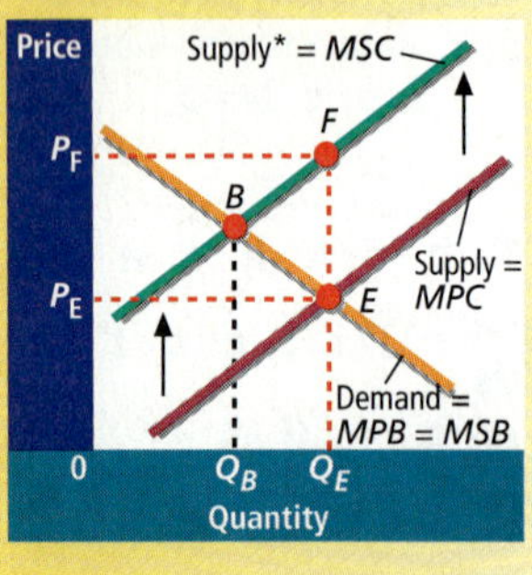

5. For a, c, d, and f, one person's consumption does not significantly limit another's, and one person cannot keep another from consuming the good or service. In the other two cases, b and e, one person can keep another person from consuming the good (e.g., I can prevent you from eating my banana split or from driving my car).

Your Economic Vocabulary

Build your economic vocabulary by matching the following terms with their definitions.

exclusion principle
externality
marginal private benefit (MPB)
marginal private cost (MPC)
marginal social benefit (MSB)
marginal social cost (MSC)
negative externality
positive externality
subsidy

1. a cost or benefit passed on to people not directly involved in a transaction
2. the result when *costs* are shifted to people who are not directly involved with the production or consumption of a good
3. the added cost that society pays to increase an activity by one unit
4. a payment made by the government to encourage some activity
5. the added benefit that society gets from increasing an activity by one unit
6. the result when *benefits* are shifted to people who are not directly involved with the production or consumption of a good
7. the added cost individuals directly involved in an activity pay to increase the activity by one unit
8. the principle that one person can keep others from benefiting from a private good
9. the added benefit that individuals directly involved in an activity get from increasing the activity by one unit

Thinking Critically About Economics

1. It is generally recognized that many positive externalities result from education. But, there may be some negative externalities, too. Examine your own school carefully to see if you can find any negative spillovers. For example, consider the noise that spills over to people who live near the school. Suggest a way of correcting each of the negative externalities you find.
2. Why is police protection considered a public good? Explain what would happen if communities tried to offer police services as a private good through the market system.
3. Identify negative externalities for each of the following activities. Then suggest ways of correcting each of the negative externalities you identify.
   a. driving a car
   b. producing electric power
   c. a professional football game
   d. car production

Economic Enrichment

Answers may include anyone who drinks the water, people who no longer are able to use the river for recreation, fishers who may harvest fewer or no fish, and consumers who no longer can eat the river's seafood products due to contamination. The dollar amount could be measured in terms of the dollars needed to prevent future damage or to correct the damage that has been done. Corrective measures might include posting a government agent on site to uphold regulations and to teach the company how to properly dispose of waste; if negative externalities continue, the company should be fined and forced to pay for the damages.

4. Use a graph of marginal private costs, marginal social costs, and marginal private benefits to explain the concept of negative externalities. You can assume there are no positive externalities.

5. How does the exclusion principle relate to the following?

   a. a city park **c.** a highway **e.** a car

   b. a banana split **d.** national defense **f.** a school

Economic Enrichment

The Toy-Co Manufacturing Company is located along the Pheasant River. In the production of children's toys, Toy-Co dumps several waste products into the river. Who are some third parties likely to be affected by Toy-Co's use of the river? How might you measure the dollar amount of the negative externalities created? What corrective measures would you suggest?

Math and Economics

In 1960, there were about 2.6 pounds of solid waste generated per person each day in the United States. By 1970, that figure was 3.3 pounds per day; by 1980, it was 3.6 pounds per day; and by 1990, it was up to 4.3 pounds per day for every person in the country.

Using the resources available at your library, find out the amount of solid wastes produced by the average person last year and the U.S. population estimates for 1960, 1970, 1980, 1990, and last year. Then, prepare a table that summarizes the following:

a. pounds of solid wastes produced by the average person in the United States in 1960, 1970, 1980, 1990, and last year

b. population of the United States in 1960, 1970, 1980, 1990, and last year

c. total pounds of solid wastes produced by individuals in the United States in 1960, 1970, 1980, 1990, and last year

Based on your table, prepare bar charts that compare the average solid waste production for each year and the total solid waste production for each year.

Writing About Economics

Identify an area around your school, perhaps one-mile square. Conduct a visual survey of the area and make a list of the positive or negative externalities you see. Write a poem about one or more of the externalities. In your poem, explain the source of the externality and who either benefits from or bears part of the cost of the activity as a third party. Include in your poem possible ways to encourage or reduce the externalities.

Writing About Economics

Students' individual poems should include information about various externalities observed around the school; for example, if there is a fire station near the school, students may point out that a positive externality to students and teachers is having fire protection near the campus, and a negative externality to neighborhood residents is the noise caused by the alarms and sirens. The positive externality could be encouraged by observing safety rules and volunteering to help out around the fire station. Negative externalities could be discouraged by asking the firefighters to avoid sounding alarms and sirens more than is absolutely necessary.

Math and Economics

Year	Pounds of Waste Per Person Per Day	Pounds of Waste Per Person Per Year
1960	2.60	949.00
1970	3.30	1,204.50
1980	3.60	1,314.00
1990	4.30	1,569.50
Last Year		

Year	U.S. Population	Total Pounds of Waste in United States Per Year
1960	180,671,000	171,456,779,000
1970	205,052,000	246,985,134,000
1980	227,726,000	299,231,964,000
1990	249,900,000	392,218,050,000
Last Year		

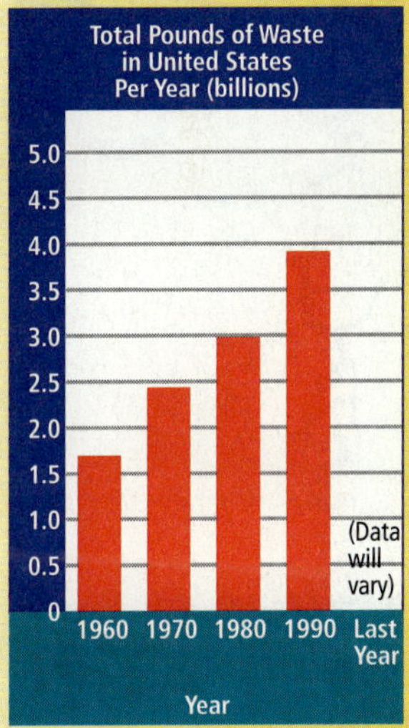

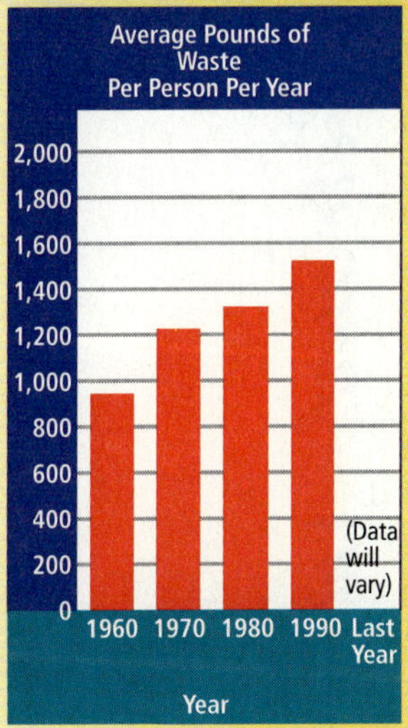

Chapter 13

The Labor Market and Determining Personal Income

Chapter Theme

In this chapter, students study the impact of supply and demand on determining how much labor is hired and at what wage rate and study the forces that may cause wages to be higher or lower than the equilibrium rate. Income (labor and interest), the minimum wage, and labor unions are analyzed.

Section	Special Features
The Labor Market	Econ & You Economics & Your Community Media Link
Other Factors Affecting the Labor Market	Perspectives: Thinking Like a Business Consultant Economic Dilemma Economic Spotlight Multicultural Highlights
Interest: A Source of Income and an Expense	Internet Connection Global Economy Economic Talk Eye on Market News

Video Activity

Chapter 13, Auto Strike

Search Chapter 13, Play to 14

Divide the class into two groups to debate the pros and cons of unionized labor in today's society. After the debate, have the class brainstorm how the labor market might appear today if unions had never been created.

	Print Resources	Media Resources	Assessment
	Effective Teaching Model Lesson Plans *Skills & Concepts* worksheet *Problem Solving* worksheet *Casebook* *Economic Measurement Workbook* *Content Review Workbook* *Spanish Resources*	VHS CD-ROM Videodisc *Arctic Express* *Interactive ECONOMICS* Template software	*Your Economic Portfolio* Chapter *Assessment* Chapter *MicroExam*

Special Learners	Print Resources	Media Resources	Assessment
ESL Visual Activity		Overhead and *Transparencies 13-1 to 13-4* Computer Camcorder VCR Audio	*Checkpoint* Section 1 Quiz
Kinesthetic Activity Auditory Activity Cooperative Learning Activity		Overhead and *Transparency 13-5* Computer Audio	*Checkpoint* Section 2 Quiz
	Teacher's Connection to the Internet *Enrich* worksheet *Reteach* worksheet *Life Skills* worksheet	Overhead Computer Audio Camcorder VCR	*Checkpoint* Section 3 Quiz

Careers Activity

Do you have a credit card? If so, your credit card application probably was handled by a data entry clerk. Data entry clerks enter personal, business, and financial information into computer systems. This information is used to produce billing invoices, sales reports, and mailing lists.

Data entry clerks must have a high school diploma or its equivalent and should be able to scan and type documents quickly and accurately. English, computer literacy, typing, and business courses help prepare students for careers in data entry. Earnings range from $15,000 to $20,000 per year.

Divide the class into customers of four or five imaginary credit card companies. Give each student a debt amount and each credit card company a daily interest rate. Have each person take a turn as a data entry clerk, entering the name, address, phone number, and debt amount for one of the credit customers (group members). Have students work together to chart the amount each group member owes the company for interest for one day.

CHAPTER 13

Teaching Materials

Program Resources

- Student text
- *Effective Teaching Model Lesson Plans*
- *Overhead Transparencies 13-1* to *13-5*
- *Life Skills* worksheet
- *Problem Solving* worksheet
- *Reteach* worksheet
- *Enrich* worksheet
- *Skills & Concepts* worksheet
- *Casebook*
- *Economic Measurement Workbook*
- *Content Review Workbook*
- *Spanish Resources*
- Video package
- *Teacher's Connection to the Internet*
- *Arctic Express*
- *Interactive ECONOMICS*
- Template software

Assessment

- Section Quizzes
- Chapter *Assessment*
- Chapter *MicroExam*

Overview

Section One
The Labor Market

Section Two
Other Factors Affecting the Labor Market

Section Three
Interest: A Source of Income and an Expense

Teacher to Teacher

Ask students what hourly wage they think they would earn working at a fast-food job in your community. Elicit that they probably would earn the minimum wage. Next, ask students if they think the government should raise the minimum wage by $0.10. What about by $0.50? $1? $5? Ask students why they think the minimum wage rate is not $10 or $15 per hour. Why is it not $100? Discuss as a class an employer's potential cost if he or she had to pay *every* employee at least $10 or $15 per hour. Ask students how they think the employer would be able to afford this. Lead students to understand that one way would be to lay off current employees and/or hire fewer new employees. As a class, conclude that raising the minimum wage can ultimately hurt unskilled laborers.

Harlan Day
Purdue University
W. Lafayette, IN

The Labor Market and Determining Personal Income

Learning Objectives

13-1
Demonstrate how the forces of supply and demand work in the labor market.

13-2
Describe how monopsony and minimum wage laws affect the labor market.

13-3
Present the history of labor unions.

13-4
Explain how interest can be viewed in different ways.

13-5
Compare the various types of interest rates and their impact on the cost of borrowing.

Outside Resources

- Blank overhead transparencies
- Magazines and newspapers
- Art supplies
- World almanac
- Balance scale
- Four weights (one light, two medium, and one heavy)
- Camcorder and VCR
- Audiocassette recorder
- Computer
- Integrated software (spreadsheets, charting)
- Recordings of labor movement songs such as Pete Seeger, *American Industrial Ballads* (Folkways 40058); Woody Guthrie, *Struggle* (Folkways 40025); and Pete Seeger, Jane Sapp, and Si Kahn, *Carry It On: Songs of America's Working People* (Flying Fish 104). A source book is *Carry It On: The Story of America's Working People in Song and Picture* by Pete Seeger and Bob Reiser (Sing Out Corp., Bethlehem, PA, n.d., ISBN: 0-9626704-6-4).
- Pocket calculators
- Outside speaker: Loan officer from a community financial institution
- Several issues of *The Wall Street Journal*
- Crossword-puzzle software
- Several pocket-sized interest tables
- Integrated software (word processing, desktop publishing)

Vocabulary

demand for labor, p. 327
wage rate, p. 327
derived demand, p. 327
supply of labor, p. 329
equilibrium wage, p. 333
monopsony, p. 334
minimum wage law, p. 335
labor union, p. 337
collective bargaining, p. 339
injunction, p. 339
closed shop, p. 340
union shop, p. 340
interest, p. 341
inflation, p. 345
prime rate, p. 345
corporate bond rate, p. 346
federal funds rate, p. 346
discount rate, p. 346

Focus

Write the following on the chalkboard: **What are the characteristics of a good job?** As students enter the classroom, ask them to list on a sheet of paper factors they think contribute most to the quality of a job. (Answers may include high wages, pleasant working conditions, good benefits, flexibility, convenient hours or location, easy or interesting duties, exciting environment, fun co-workers, and opportunities for advancement.)

Have students share their responses and discuss how their answers influence the types of jobs they will seek. Then, ask the class to identify the three items that they think are the most important contributors to job satisfaction.

Teach

Explain to students the terms **demand for labor, wage rate, derived demand, supply of labor,** and **equilibrium wage.** Then, ask students to imagine that only five copies of a new, extremely popular CD are available at only one music store in town and that hundreds of people want to buy the CD. Assuming the store can sell the new CD for any price it wishes, ask students what is likely to happen to the price of the CD. (It will go up.) Ask what would happen if the situation were reversed and the store had unlimited copies of the CD but only five customers wished to purchase it. (The store would either drop the price or let the CD sit on the shelves indefinitely.)

Section One
The Labor Market

What Do You Think?

Bill and Sheri Lati own a messenger service in a large city. They hire people to ride bikes throughout the city to deliver small parcels to various offices. Most of the deliveries involve the medical, legal, and financial sectors of the economy, so confidentiality and reliability are important to the success of the business. The work demands good physical fitness and a thorough knowledge of the city. Lately, the Latis have been having trouble hiring enough messengers to meet the delivery demands of their customers. What might cause this difficulty and how might Bill and Sheri hire more people?

Terms to Know

- demand for labor
- wage rate
- derived demand
- supply of labor
- equilibrium wage

What's Ahead?

Labor is one of the four factors of production in the economy. Each company has some demand for labor to use in the production of the products or services it sells. There is also a supply of labor. Each of us has an equal amount of time to use (24 hours a day). We must decide how much of that time to use for work and how much to use for other activities. In this section, you will see how the forces of demand and supply determine how much labor is hired and at what wage rate labor is paid.

THE DEMAND FOR LABOR

Just as there is a market for cars or stereos, so is there a labor market. People are not bought and sold, but their time and skills are. Suppose a restaurant hires you to wait on customers. The manager doesn't buy you but does buy (pay for) some of your time and ability to take and process orders correctly. So it is with all jobs. A school buys someone's time and ability to act as a teacher. A steel mill buys an engineer's time and ability to watch over a production process.

Determining the Demand for Labor

The ***demand for labor*** is the amount of labor that firms would want to hire at various wage rates. The ***wage rate*** is the price paid for each unit of labor. The amount of labor demanded depends on the demand for the good or service produced. One hundred years ago, when people used horses instead of cars for transportation, blacksmiths were in high demand. As cars came into use, fewer services of blacksmiths were needed. Thus, the demand for blacksmiths declined. But, at the same time, the need for skilled workers in the automobile factories rose. Due to the higher demand for cars, there was a higher demand for workers to make those cars.

The demand for labor is called *derived demand*. ***Derived demand*** is a demand for an input that is dependent on the demand for the product that the input helps to produce. Demand for the company's product clearly determines the company's demand for labor. If consumers do not want to buy the product, the company will not need to hire any labor. The firm needs labor to produce what it wants to sell.

The level of productivity of the workers themselves also helps determine the demand for labor. *Labor productivity* is measured by the amount of output produced per hour of labor input. Productive labor will be more in demand than unproductive labor. Keep this important point in mind. Anything you can do that will increase your productivity will help you in the labor market. Education and training programs are two means of increasing your productivity.

Wage Rate and Quantity of Labor Demanded

An inverse relationship exists between the quantity of labor a business will hire and the wage rate it must pay. If the wage rate is high, businesses will hire less labor. Perhaps you can already guess why this is true. First, at a high wage, it is cheaper to use methods of production that employ less labor. More equipment, more machines, and even robots may be used. Second, as the wage level goes up, the cost of production goes up and the product's price is likely to rise. As the product's price goes up, fewer units will be demanded. This means there will be less demand for labor to produce the product. The inverse relationship between the wage rate and the quantity of labor demanded is illustrated in Figure 13-1 on page 328.

demand for labor
the amount of labor that firms would want to hire at various wage rates

wage rate
the price paid for each unit of labor

derived demand
demand for an input that is dependent on the demand for the product that the input helps to produce

Next, ask students to name the situation that exists when the supply of the CD matches customers' demand for it. (Balance, or equilibrium) Explain that, just as with product markets, labor markets can be in equilibrium. They also can be unbalanced, with the labor supply higher or lower than the labor demand.

Ask students what is likely to happen to wages if the supply of labor (the number of people who want a job) were greater than the demand for labor (the number of available jobs). (Wages would fall.) Ask students what they think would happen if available jobs outnumbered job seekers. (Wages would rise, and employers might offer other benefits to attract workers.)

Apply

Using the chalkboard or an overhead transparency, work with students to list types of jobs that they think will need more workers in the years to come. (Examples may include accountants; recreation, health-care, and social workers; and real-estate managers.) Ask students what types of skills these jobs require. (Math skills; computer skills; reading, writing, and other communication skills; and a familiarity with modern technology) In a second list, have students brainstorm jobs that have become rare or have disappeared (blacksmiths, sailors on wind-powered vessels, shepherds, and so on) and the skills those jobs required (brute strength, knowledge of obsolete technology, familiarity with the care of grazing animals). Be sure students understand how these examples reflect our changing times and the changing demand for labor, which is a **derived demand.**

Guided Practice

Analyzing *Graphics*

Caption Answer
An increase in the quantity of labor demanded

Point out that the demand for labor has changed radically over the years and will continue to change in the future. Remind students that the demand for labor is called a **derived demand** because it depends on the demand for the product or service that the labor produces. Ask students to name a particular product or service. Then, have others take turns naming types of jobs that would experience a change in the derived demand for labor if the demand for this product or service changed. (For example, for a lawn-care service, answers might include lawn-care workers, lawn-mower manufacturers, uniform makers, and fertilizer producers.)

Figure 13-1

Demand Curve for Labor

The demand curve for labor slopes down to the right. A greater quantity of labor will be demanded at a lower wage than at a higher wage. If the demand for labor increases, the demand curve shifts to the right to L_{D1}. If the demand for labor decreases, the demand curve shifts to the left to L_{D2}. ***Does the movement from Point A to Point B represent an increase in the quantity of labor demanded or an increase in the demand for labor?***

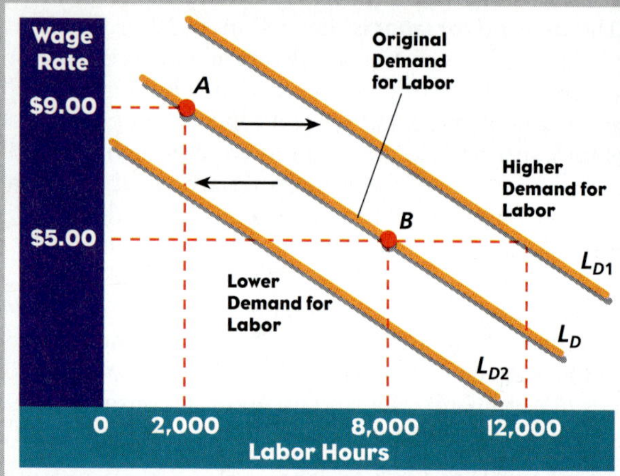

Think of the demand for labor in Figure 13-1 as the total demand for labor each day in a local labor market. Two thousand labor hours is the same as 250 people working an eight-hour day. The wage rate of $9 means $9 per hour of labor hired. At this high wage, only 2,000 hours of labor would be hired in that market each day. But, if the wage rate fell to $5 an hour, 8,000 hours of labor would be demanded. Such a change is called a *change in the quantity of labor demanded.* A change in the quantity of labor demanded can only be caused by a change in the wage rate. Such a change is a movement *along* a labor demand curve.

Change in the Demand for Labor

The entire demand for labor may also change. There are two factors that may cause the demand for labor to change: (1) the demand for the output and (2) the productivity of labor.

An increase in the demand for labor is shown by a shift of the labor demand curve to the right. This is shown as the move from the original demand for labor curve, L_D, to the higher demand for labor curve, L_{D1}. A rise in the demand for labor means that more labor will be hired at *each* wage rate. In Figure 13-1, after the increase in demand for labor, 12,000 labor hours will be demanded at a wage of $5 an hour. This is 4,000 labor hours more than what was demanded at $5 per hour with the original demand for labor.

A decrease in the demand for labor will have opposite causes. Demand for output might fall and/or the productivity of labor might decrease. If the demand for labor goes down, its demand curve will shift to the left to L_{D2}.

Before you read the next section about the supply of labor, think about what kind of work you want to do. What will determine the demand for labor in that line of work? Do you wish to work in an occupation where demand for the product or service will be high? Do you have, or can you develop, the necessary skills to be productive in the kind of work you want to do? Thinking about these questions can help you make better career decisions. Your answers may influence how you participate in the labor market.

THE SUPPLY OF LABOR

How many hours would you work next Saturday if an employer offered to pay you $0.50 an hour? Probably not very many. Why? You probably feel that your time would be better spent doing other things. You may be able to work for someone else at a higher wage. Or, your relaxation and recreation may be worth more to you than $0.50 an hour.

What do you think would happen if the same offer were made to the entire class? Would anyone work for $0.50 an hour? What if the wage offer were slowly raised to $1, then to $2, $3, $4, $5, and so on up to $10 an hour? At some wage, you would surely offer to work some hours. At $10 an hour, perhaps everyone in your class would be willing to work a full eight-hour day. You might even be willing to work ten hours, twelve hours, or more. The ***supply of labor*** is the amount of labor that would be available at each wage rate.

supply of labor
the amount of labor that would be available at each wage rate

Determining the Supply of Labor

What else would determine your willingness to work? Perhaps the hours would be important. What if workers were needed from 3 a.m. to 7 a.m.? Fewer people probably would be interested than if the hours were from

Econ & You

HOMEWORK MAY NOT BE SCHOOL WORK

The 1990s have been a decade of "reengineering," "downsizing," "right-sizing" or whatever else people have called workforce reductions in the corporate world. But, at the same time workforces were reduced, the unemployment rate did not suffer; in fact, it improved. Where did the displaced workers go? Many found new work at home. There has been an increase in the number of people who work at home, either for corporations or for themselves. Nearly 10 percent of U.S. workers are self-employed, many at home.

For example, one woman in New Jersey worked for a company that later moved to another geographic area. She chose not to move with the company. Instead, she started her own business, an editorial production company, in a house in her hometown. Using the Internet, she works with various people from Arizona to Florida to Michigan.

Many college students now can do much of their college work from their residences. Not long ago, they had to spend a lot of time on campus to perform the same tasks. Now, students can access the school library (or other libraries anywhere in the world) electronically. Today's students have the ability to complete a great deal of "library" work without ever physically entering the library. They may even conference with an instructor from the comfort of their own room via e-mail or another computer interface.

Econ & You

Ask students to interview someone who works out of the home about the advantages and disadvantages of this type of work arrangement. Have students list the responses in a two-column chart under the headings **Pros** and **Cons.** In class, discuss students' findings and ask whether they think more people will work from their homes in the future. If so, what types of products are likely to experience an increase in derived demand? (Home office furniture, home computers, fax machines, and so on) How might this increase, in turn, affect the derived demand for other types of labor? (Increased demand for labor to produce all these products and less demand for labor to produce others) How might this affect students? (Job opportunities)

Have students use magazine and newspaper articles, advertisements, photos, original artwork, and other visuals to create a bulletin board or collage depicting changing labor demand. The display should highlight obsolete or declining occupations and skills as well as current jobs in which demand for labor is increasing.

Independent Practice

Tell students that *labor productivity* is the amount of output produced per hour of labor. On the chalkboard or an overhead transparency, ask students to name some words that come from the same root as *productivity* (*produce, producer, product, productive*) and to develop definitions of each. Ask if a product produced by a company must be an object. (No) Then, ask students to give examples of products that are not objects (telephone service, radio broadcasts, and advice)

ESL

In pairs, have students interview each other about their job plans after graduation. Ask them to discuss the probable demand for and supply of labor in their chosen fields and list the skills they will need to develop in order to be productive in those fields.

Have each student summarize his or her plan of action in a short essay. Then, ask volunteers to share their plans with the class. Allow the class to offer additional suggestions for preparing for a particular job market.

Analyzing Graphics

Caption Answer
An increase in the supply of labor

Draw the following two-column chart on the chalkboard or an overhead transparency and have students copy it onto a sheet of paper. Have them list in the first column the forces or events that can cause an increase in the supply of labor. (Improved working conditions, better benefits, and fewer restrictions such as age, race, and gender bias) Have them list in the second column the forces or events that can cause the supply of labor to decrease. (Unpleasant or dangerous working conditions, long training programs, job discrimination)

LABOR SUPPLY	
Increase	Decrease

10 a.m. until 2 p.m. Wouldn't the type of work also be important? What if people were needed to demonstrate the use of swimming pools? More people would want this job than the job of digging post holes three feet deep in rocky ground. In addition to considering the wage, the hours, and the type of work, people consider other factors. You might consider the possibilities for job advancement, the work effort required, and the physical environment in which the work is to be done.

Wage Rate and Quantity of Labor Supplied

Even with all these nonwage aspects of a job, you can still expect that more labor hours will be offered at higher wages than at lower wages. The supply curve for labor increases from left to right. It has a positive slope. For example, in the original supply of labor curve in Figure 13-2, at a wage of $2 an hour only 2,000 hours of labor are offered. As the wage rate goes up, so does the number of labor hours people are willing to work. You can see in Figure 13-2 that when the wage in this labor market reaches $10 an hour, 12,000 labor hours are offered. This change is called a *change in the quantity of labor supplied* and is caused only by a change in the wage rate. This type of change is represented by movement *along* a particular labor supply curve.

Figure 13-2

Supply Curve for Labor

The supply curve for labor slopes up to the right. A greater quantity of labor will be supplied at a higher wage than at a lower wage. An increase in the supply of labor can be shown as a shift from the original supply curve to curve L_{S1}. When the labor supply declines, the supply curve shifts to the left to L_{S2}. ***Does the movement from Point A to Point B represent an increase in the quantity of labor supplied or an increase in the supply of labor?***

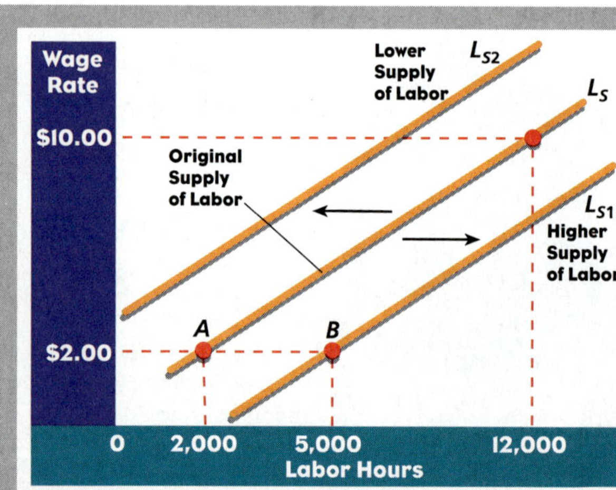

Change in the Supply of Labor

The entire supply of labor may rise or fall over time. A rise in the labor supply will shift the supply of labor curve to the right. More hours would be available at *each* wage. An example is curve L_{S1} in Figure 13-2. After the increase in the labor supply, at the $2 wage 5,000 hours rather than 2,000 hours will be offered. Anything that makes work more enjoyable (or less objectionable) can cause an increase in the supply of labor. Better and safer working conditions or more opportunities for job advancement are examples.

There also are forces that can cause the supply of labor to fall (or to increase less rapidly). Unpleasant labor conditions, artificial labor supply restrictions, or unnecessarily long training or apprenticeship programs can all cut down on supply. Discrimination by race, gender, age, or other characteristic

Economics & Your Community

Today, more and more U.S. companies are offering day care to employees, either at the work site or by arrangement with existing day-care facilities. Working in small groups, have students research the availability of day care for children of employees by contacting the personnel offices of five or more workplaces in the community. Then, ask students to compile their information into a report and present it to the class. Discuss how the availability of day care affects both the number of people who will apply for jobs and the number of laborers companies will need to hire.

also limits supply (even though such discrimination is illegal, it still exists). A decline in the supply of labor is shown by the curve L_{S2} in Figure 13-2. You can see that a shift of the labor supply curve to the left shows a decrease in supply. Less labor is offered at *each* wage.

Women Increase the Supply of Labor

The increasing number of women in the labor force has caused a dramatic rise in the U.S. labor supply. The percentage of women in the labor force over the past several decades has steadily risen. In 1960, 37.7 percent of all women over 16 years of age were in the labor force. By 1980, 51.5 percent of adult women were in the labor force. In 1990, 57.5 percent of women over 16 were in the labor force. By 1995, the labor force participation rate of women had risen to about 59.1 percent.

During the same period, the percentage of men over 16 years of age who were in the labor force dropped from 83.3 percent to 74.8 percent. This decrease is less than the rise for women. So, on balance, a greater percentage of the population is active in the labor force.

These changes in the labor force can be seen in Figure 13-3. The heights of the bars in this figure indicate the percentages of men and women currently

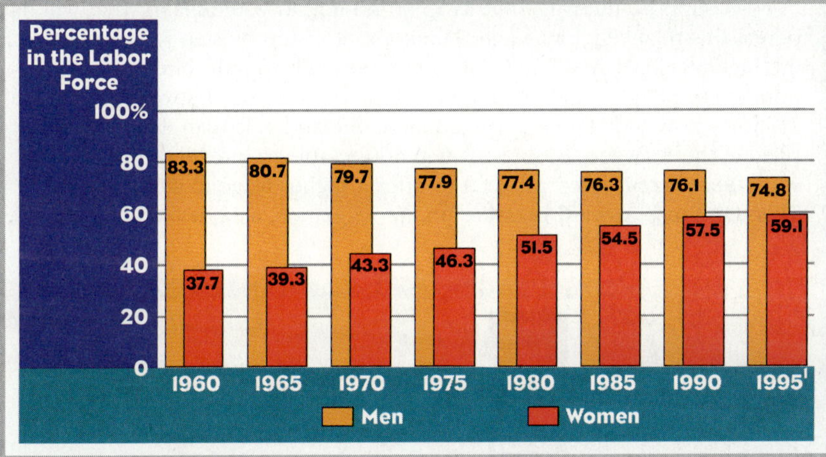

Figure 13-3

Labor Force Participation Rates for Men and Women

The percentage of women who were in the labor force rose from 37.7 percent in 1960 to 59.1 percent in 1995. During the same period, the percentage of men who were in the labor force fell from 83.3 percent to 74.8 percent. ***Do you think that the downward trend in the labor force participation rate for men and the opposite trend for women will continue?***

SOURCE: *Economic Report of the President 1995* (Washington, D.C.: U.S. Government Printing Office, 1995), 317.

[1]The 1995 values are the author's estimates based on data through the end of 1994.

Have students research in a world almanac which four occupations have the *highest* percentage of female workers (secretaries, nurses, nurses' aides, textile sewing machine operators) and which four have the *lowest* (mechanics, guards and police, stock handlers, and mail carriers). Ask students to speculate about why this is so. (Tradition and convention, discrimination, need for physical strength, and so on)

Analyzing *Graphics*

Caption Answer
Answers are likely to focus on the possibility that the two rates may be equal someday.

Media*Link*

Divide the class into four groups. Using a camcorder or audiocassette recorder, have students present a brief multimedia performance on the participation of minorities and women in the labor force. Encourage students to use music, art, literature, dance, drama, and other forms of expression in their performances. For example, presentations could focus on changes in the types of work available to various minority groups and women, rates of participation, or challenges to the group's participation over the years. Show all presentations to the class. Then, discuss with the class important ideas that arise from the presentations.

To help students understand the concept of the market equilibrium wage, arrange a visual demonstration with a balance scale and four different-sized weights. Place the lightest weight on one side and tell students that it represents the number of labor hours offered in a market. Then, place a heavier weight on the other side to represent the number of labor hours demanded by employers. Ask students to describe in economic terms what is happening. (Quantity demanded is greater than quantity supplied.) Ask what companies in this market must do to the wage rate to bring the quantity of labor supplied into balance with the quantity of labor demanded. (Raise it.) Next, demonstrate the effect of raising wages by placing the heaviest weight on the demand side and ask students what happened to the wage rate. (The companies raised it too much and the quantity of labor supplied is now greater than the quantity demanded.) Ask how companies in this market will know when they have set their wages at the market equilibrium. (The quantity of labor supplied and demanded will be equal.) Demonstrate this concept by placing equal weights on either side of the scale. Ask students which point in *Figure 13-4* corresponds to the balanced scale (Point *E*).

Analyzing *Graphics*

Caption Answer
The quantity of labor supplied will be greater than the quantity of labor demanded, and there will be downward pressure on the wage rate.

active in the labor force. You can see that the height of the bars for women has been rising. For men, the height of the bars has been falling.

BALANCING LABOR DEMAND AND SUPPLY

You have learned that product markets are in balance, or equilibrium, when the quantity demanded and quantity supplied are equal. The same is true in the labor market. When the quantity of labor demanded equals the quantity of labor supplied, the labor market is in balance. That is, the labor market is in equilibrium where the demand curve crosses the supply curve.

Remember that the demand curve for labor slopes downward to the right. Companies will demand more labor hours at a lower wage than at a higher wage. For supply, the relationship is reversed. The supply curve for labor slopes upward from left to right. More labor will be offered at a higher wage than at a lower wage.

Look at Figure 13-4. Suppose that the wage rate is $8 an hour. You see that the distance between the points marked *A* and *B* shows the excess of the quantity of labor supplied over the quantity demanded. In other words, the amount of labor demanded is less than the amount of labor supplied. When this happens, there is downward pressure on the wage rate, as indicated by the large arrow pointing down. As the wage rate falls, the quantity of labor demanded goes up (movement to the right *along* the demand curve). At the same time, the quantity of labor supplied falls (movement to the left *along* the supply curve).

Now suppose the wage rate is $3 an hour. Can you explain what will happen at this relatively low wage? Think about it step by step just as you did for the high $8 wage. At $3 an hour, companies will want to hire more labor hours than people will be willing to offer. The distance between points *C* and *D* shows how much greater the quantity demanded is than the quantity supplied at the $3 wage. Businesses will not be able to hire all the labor they want. Some companies will start to offer a higher wage to attract workers. This will cause upward pressure on the wage rate, as indicated by the large

Figure 13-4

Market Equilibrium for Labor

The market equilibrium wage is found where the supply of labor curve crosses the demand for labor curve at Point *E*. The equilibrium wage is $6, and the amount of labor employed is 7,000 labor hours. At a wage above equilibrium ($8), the quantity of labor supplied is greater than the quantity of labor demanded. There is downward pressure on the wage rate. At a wage below equilibrium ($3), the quantity of labor demanded is greater than the quantity supplied. Thus, there is upward pressure on the wage rate. ***What will happen in the labor market if the wage rate is $7?***

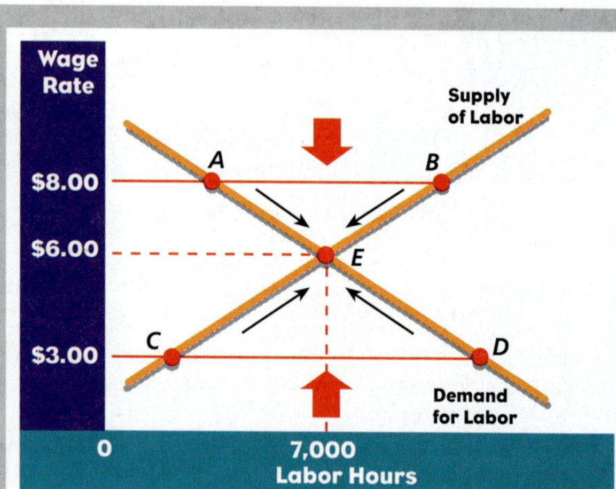

arrow pointing up. As wage goes up, more hours of labor will be offered (movement to the right *along* the supply curve). At the same time, less labor will be demanded (movement to the left *along* the demand curve).

At the high wage, there is downward pressure on the wage rate. At the low wage, there is upward pressure on the wage rate. You should expect that, somewhere in between these two wage rates, there is a balance between the quantity demanded and the quantity supplied. Look at the wage rate of $6 an hour. At that wage, the amount of labor demanded is 7,000 hours. And, at the $6 wage, the amount of labor supplied is also 7,000 hours. Demand and supply are in balance. The labor market is in equilibrium at the wage where the amount of labor demanded is equal to the amount of labor supplied. So, the labor market equilibrium is found where the supply and demand curves cross. This is Point *E* in Figure 13-4. The ***equilibrium wage*** is the wage rate at which the quantity of labor demanded equals the quantity of labor supplied.

equilibrium wage the wage rate at which the quantity of labor demanded equals the quantity of labor supplied

Checkpoint

Content Check

1. Why do you think there has been a rise in the demand for workers with good computer skills?
2. A city official in New Orleans commented in the mid-1990s that it is impossible to hire good police officers for what was the current wage. What could the city have done to attract more people to this job market?
3. Draw fictitious labor demand and labor supply curves to illustrate a labor market. Label your graph carefully and indicate the equilibrium wage as well as the amount of labor that would be employed.

What Do You Think Now?

Reread *What Do You Think?* in the Section One Focus. Then answer the following questions:

4. Do you think that if Bill and Sheri increase the wage rate they offer for new employees it will help their problem? Explain.
5. What else, besides increasing wages, could Sheri and Bill do to find more messengers?

Reteach

Ask students to create a diagram that visually explains the relationship of the quantity of labor demanded to the quantity of labor supplied at the market equilibrium wage. Tell students not to label the parts of their diagrams. Then, have each student exchange diagrams with a partner and add the appropriate labels. (Diagrams should reflect the balance between the quantity demanded and supplied.) **13-1**

Enrich

Ask students to write an essay using the five *Terms to Know* in this section and comparing the following economic situations: a society in which the quantity of labor supplied has always been greater than the quantity demanded and one in which the quantity of labor demanded has always exceeded the quantity supplied. **13-1**

Assess

1. Because there has been an increase in the demand for products and services that use computer technology in the production process **13-1**
2. Increase the rate of pay and offer more and better benefits, such as more day care, better health insurance, improved retirement programs, and more flexible work schedules **13-1**
3. Students' graphs should resemble the one in *Figure 13-4* (p. 332). **13-1**
4. By increasing the wage, they should be able to stimulate an increase in the quantity of labor supplied by the local labor pool. **13-1**
5. They could provide company bikes, longer lunch periods, paid vacations, and the ability to share shifts with other messengers. Talking with current employees about their needs would provide ideas for other options. **13-1**

Close

Divide the class into three teams. Allow 20 minutes for each team to develop eight to ten *Jeopardy*-style questions about the labor market. Have teams take turns asking the other two teams one of their questions. Continue this process until 15 different questions have been answered. Discuss the class's answers and declare the team with the most correct answers the winner.

Focus

Before students arrive, write **$4.25** on the chalkboard. As students enter the classroom, ask them to prepare a brief estimate of their total expenses for a week, including food, clothing, transportation, entertainment, and other expenses. Then, have students estimate how many hours they would have to work each week at the wage of $4.25 per hour to meet their expenses.

Have volunteers share their calculations with the class. If appropriate, ask students who currently have jobs to describe their own budgets and work schedules. Discuss whether it is difficult to make ends meet while working for minimum wage, how a family might increase its income, and whether a lower minimum wage for trainees is fair.

Section Two
Other Factors Affecting the Labor Market

What Do You Think?

Students at Northview High School recently participated in a letter writing campaign to members of Congress concerning the minimum wage. They urged the members of Congress who represent them to push for an increase of $2 an hour in the minimum wage because they feel that student workers in their community do not earn enough. Do you agree with the students at Northview?

Terms to Know

- monopsony
- minimum wage law
- labor union
- collective bargaining
- injunction
- closed shop
- union shop

What's Ahead?

Under certain conditions, wages may stay above or below the equilibrium that would be established by a free and competitive labor market. We have been assuming that the labor market functions in a free and competitive way. But, this may not always be true. A variety of noncompetitive forces may cause wages to be higher or lower than this equilibrium. In this section, you will learn about three such forces.

MONOPSONY IN THE LABOR MARKET

One noncompetitive force in the labor market occurs when a given labor market is dominated by one employer. That single employer may have enough influence over the market to keep wages low, since laborers either work for that employer or not at all. This influence is sometimes called a *monopsonistic influence*. A ***monopsony*** is a market in which there is only one buyer. (It is similar to the word *monopoly* which means one seller.) If there is only one buyer of labor (one employer) in a labor market, that employer can influence wage rates considerably.

monopsony
a market in which there is only one buyer

This often happens in university towns where the community is small relative to the size of the university. When this is true, an abundant supply of people want sales, clerical, and other such jobs. Students, spouses of students and faculty, and other people from the town compete for jobs. Most jobs in such an area are with the university. A university may employ as much as 50 or 60 percent of the labor force of a town.

As a result of the abundant labor supply in university-dominated towns, nonprofessional jobs with universities tend to be low paying. In large cities where a university represents a small part of the total population, wages for university workers are likely to be more competitive.

MINIMUM WAGE LAWS

The second noncompetitive force that can affect the wage rate is a minimum wage law. A ***minimum wage law*** is a law that sets the lowest wage that can be paid for certain kinds of work. The Fair Labor Standards Act of 1938 marked the beginning of a national minimum wage in the United States. Some states had their own minimum wage laws even before 1938. In 1950, the minimum wage was just $0.75 an hour. In 1956, it was increased to $1.00 an hour. By the late 1960s, the minimum wage was $1.60 an hour. Starting in 1974, there were increases nearly every year that resulted in a minimum wage of $4.25 an hour beginning April 1, 1991. There is considerable debate about increasing the minimum wage above this level.

minimum wage law
a law that sets the lowest wage that can be paid for certain kinds of work

The Reasoning Behind Minimum Wage Laws

Why would Congress want to set a minimum wage? One reason usually given is that a minimum wage helps provide low-income families with more money to spend. The reasoning Congress seems to use is as follows. If the market wage is $4 an hour and a person works 40 hours per week, the income earned will be $160 (40 hours × $4/hour). But, if the government forces employers to pay $4.25 an hour, the income earned will be $170 (40 hours × $4.25/hour).

At this point in your study of economics, perhaps you already can see a problem with the reasoning that a higher minimum wage means more money to spend. You now know that the demand curve for labor slopes down to the right. This means that if the wage increases, the amount of labor that companies will demand decreases. Fewer labor hours will be employed at a higher wage than at a lower wage. So, when Congress forces the minimum wage up, you should expect that some low-wage workers will be laid off and some may end

Teach

Explain to students that you are going to examine three forces that can cause wages in a market to be higher or lower than the equilibrium wage that a totally free market would set for labor. On the chalkboard or an overhead transparency, draw a three-section chart and fill in these headings: **Monopsony, Minimum Wage Laws,** and **Labor Unions.** Then, fill in the columns with the following information:

MONOPSONY

- Single employer with strong influence over wages
- Common in university towns
- Wages often below market equilibrium

MINIMUM WAGE LAWS

- Set by government
- $4.25 in 1995
- Raise wages above market equilibrium
- Designed to ensure minimum income to poor families

LABOR UNIONS

- Developed to offer more control to workers over working conditions
- Feature collective bargaining
- Rights protected and restricted by laws
- Membership increasing only slightly, if at all

Discuss with students whether they think a totally free labor market could exist today in our country. (Most will say no, since so many artificial forces, such as minimum wages and labor unions, are common in our society.) Ask students if they can imagine a society in which a totally free labor market might exist. (Answers may include a frontier society such as in the early days of this country or in a less-developed country in which employers hold all the power and labor unions are not allowed.)

Apply

Write the words **monopoly** and **monopsony** on the chalkboard or an overhead transparency. Underline the prefix *mono-* and ask students for its meaning. (One) Then, with the help of students, fill in characteristics and an example of each term in the appropriate column. (Characteristics of a **monopoly** include a single seller of a good or service; a lack of competition that often leads to higher prices, lower quality, and lack of consumer choice; and the temptation for government to intervene and break up the monopoly; electric utility companies are an example. Characteristics of a **monopsony** include a single employer or buyer of labor, and a lack of competition for labor that can lead to downward pressure on wages and a lack of choices of where people can work; a coal company town of the 1920s and 1930s is an example.) Point out the similarities of these two economic conditions.
Guided Practice

Analyzing *Graphics*

Caption Answer
Some students will argue that it will be the distance between L_E and L_D, since that many labor hours will be cut. Others might argue that it will be the distance between L_S and L_D, since that is the difference between the quantity of labor supplied at W_M and the quantity of labor demanded at that wage.

up working fewer hours. Those who keep their jobs with no cut in their work hours will earn more. But, some workers will earn less or even nothing at all.

Analyzing the Effect of Minimum Wage Laws

To analyze this problem, draw a graph on a piece of paper. Label the vertical axis *wage rate* and the horizontal axis *labor hours*. Draw a downward sloping line for the demand for labor and an upward sloping line for the supply of labor. Make a small circle where these two lines cross and label it *E*. This is the equilibrium point where the labor demand and supply are in balance. Draw a line from Point *E* to the vertical axis. This shows the equilibrium wage, or the market wage. Drawing a line down from *E* to the horizontal axis shows the amount of labor hired at that wage.

Now draw a horizontal line across the graph above the equilibrium wage (that is, above where demand crosses supply). This line represents the government's minimum wage. How much labor will firms want to hire at this wage? You can tell from your demand curve. It is less than the number hired at the equilibrium wage, isn't it? Thus, fewer labor hours would be employed with the minimum wage than without it.

Compare your graph with the one in Figure 13-5. The size and exact shape of the curves may differ, but your graph should look very much like Figure 13-5.

Figure 13-5

Minimum Wage and Supply and Demand for Labor

The minimum wage (W_M) is set by government above the market equilibrium wage (W_E). At the minimum wage, fewer units of labor will be employed, but those who still have jobs get a higher wage per hour. ***If the government mandates a minimum wage at W_M, how much unemployment will result?***

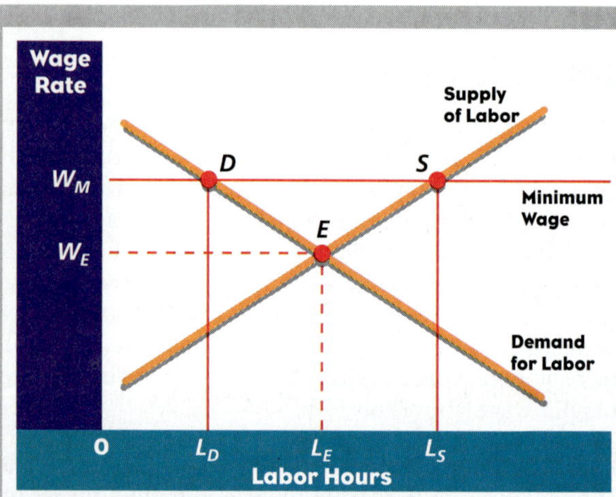

In Figure 13-5 you see that at the minimum wage (W_M) the quantity of labor demanded will be at Point *D*. This is L_D labor hours on the horizontal axis. But, at that wage, the quantity of labor supplied will be at Point *S*, or L_S labor hours on the horizontal axis. The quantity of labor supplied will be greater than the quantity demanded, so there will be unemployment. Some people who have jobs at the market wage (W_E) are pushed out of those jobs.

What groups of people will be hurt the most? Those who are not skilled, that is, the less productive workers. Young people make up a large part of this group. They have yet to learn productive and marketable skills. This is why unemployment is particularly high among teenagers. And, the minimum wage makes this problem worse than it would be otherwise.

Perspectives

Thinking Like a Business Consultant Tell students to imagine that they are business consultants working for a plastics factory whose workers have just voted to join a union. The factory president wants the consultants to prepare an annotated list of potential positives and negatives of this unionization. What would the consultants include on their lists? (Negatives: probable higher salary and benefit costs; more paperwork to conform to union regulations; possible increase in paid holidays; positives: benefits from greater worker motivation and participation in running the factory; less combative relationship between management and workers)

LABOR UNIONS

Labor unions represent a third noncompetitive force that can affect the wage rate. The labor movement came about because workers wanted more control over working conditions and other job-related matters. Many workers felt that the market system gave too much power to management and not enough to labor. Employees had only their own labor with which to bargain. Laborers had to work for whatever management would pay or quit. Each employee acting alone had very little bargaining power. If management decided fewer workers were needed, some were fired. Workers had the choice of either accepting the working conditions and hours set by management or not working at all. Often, the choices were not good ones for the workers. Because they had to support themselves and their families, they were forced to work despite the conditions or wages.

Workers Band Together

How did workers try to solve their problem? They started to band together in groups called *labor unions.* A ***labor union*** is an organization of workers formed to give workers greater bargaining power in their dealings with management. The first labor union was a group of tailors in Philadelphia. They called themselves the Noble and Holy Order of the Knights of Labor.

labor union
an organization of workers formed to give workers greater bargaining power in their dealings with management

Economic Dilemma

FAIR PAY OR FOUL?

It is generally accepted that there should not be pay discrimination according to factors, such as gender or race, that do not directly relate to the ability to perform a specific job. Thus, a male teacher and a female teacher with similar experience and training should earn the same amount for the same work. A male nurse should earn the same as a female nurse with a comparable background.

Yet it is well documented that, on average, women earn less than men. Some people have argued that the differential is caused by women being employed predominately in lower paying occupations. But, how can we arrive at a fair compensation mechanism when the jobs are different?

The concept of "comparable worth" has been suggested as a solution to this problem. This approach says that the pay for various jobs should be based on the skills required for a job, the level of responsibility that the job entails, and the amount of effort required to perform the job. While it is difficult to quantify these three aspects of a job, doing so is seen as a step in the right direction. A number of states now have comparable worth laws, most notably the state of Washington, where much of the original impetus for this approach began.

Fairness is a hard goal to achieve because our definitions of what is fair often differ. As we try to reach for fairness in compensation of employees, the stumbling block will be the difficulty in identifying and comparing required job skills, responsibility, and effort.

Economic Dilemma

After students have read *Economic Dilemma,* discuss as a class the concept of comparable worth. Have students work in groups of three or four to develop a method for determining comparable hourly salaries for a nurse, a police officer, and a popular musician. As a class, discuss the groups' different methods of calculating comparable worth.

African-American leader Jesse Jackson has said in defense of the minimum wage that it is "the poor person's labor union." Ask students to discuss how this statement might be true. (Answers may include that a minimum wage helps ensure that the lowest paid workers, often those who are not represented by unions, can still earn enough to afford basic necessities.)

Ask small groups of students to research in a world almanac the increases in the federal minimum hourly wage since 1950 and to create a line graph to show each increase and the year it occurred. Have students create a second line graph to show the percentage of the average national wage that the minimum wage has represented every five years since 1950. Then, have students describe the general trend in the ratio of the minimum wage to the average wage. (It dropped from 54 percent in 1950 to 38 percent in 1991.)

Independent Practice

Point out that teenagers are often hurt the most by minimum wage laws because they have yet to develop productive and marketable skills and, therefore, may not yet be as valuable to employers as more experienced workers are. Have students conduct surveys of their classmates to determine how many of them would like to have part-time jobs but have been unable to find work. Have students tabulate the results of their survey, estimate the "unemployment rate" among classmates, and discuss as a class the reasons unemployment may be higher or lower than expected.

Have students prepare bulletin boards or other displays on influential figures of the labor movement. Leaders might include Mary Harris (Mother) Jones, Cesar Chávez, Samuel Gompers, Eugene Debs, Elizabeth Flynn Rodgers, Richard Davis, Walter Reuther, and George Meany.

Divide the class into four groups. Ask each group to research, learn, and perform a selection of songs from the labor movement of the early 1900s. Have students provide historical background about the specific songs and composers (if known) and about the role music and singing played in the labor movement. For suggested sources, see *Outside Resources* at the beginning of this chapter.

Obtain one or more of the recordings of labor-movement songs listed in *Outside Resources* and play selections for students in class. Discuss how music and song may have aided workers in forming unions. (Raised morale, communicated valuable information)

Economic Spotlight

THE ENDORSEMENT GAME SLAM DUNKS OR SLIPUPS?

It bounced up, then down, and then back up again. No, it's not a basketball. It's Michael Jordan's marketability as a high-powered endorser. When Jordan decided to hang up his basketball shoes and go looking for new challenges, he sent Nike Corporation stock prices on a roller-coaster ride that would last for a year and a half. Nike, which had signed Jordan to a lucrative, multiyear athletic-shoe endorsement, watched its stock drop from $80 to $42 a share when the superstar decided he had shot his last free-throw.

On October 6, 1993, Jordan retired the Chicago Bull's number 23 jersey that had seen him through three consecutive NBA championships. His decision also threatened to send Nike's highly profitable "Air Jordan" marketing campaign into retirement. Stating that he was no longer challenged by basketball (and that he wished to shelter his family from the media circus surrounding the tragic murder of his father), Jordan said good-bye to basketball.

But, only a few months into his "retirement," Jordan sent Nike stocks on the rebound when he announced that he would try his hand at major league baseball. Jordan's career decision came just before the onset of the longest major league baseball strike in history. Refusing to cross the picket line, Jordan returned to basketball, rejoining the Chicago Bulls in 1995. Jordan's double-dribble from basketball to baseball and back again to basketball had sent advertisers and their stockholders into a frenzy.

Much of the wild speculation subsided with Jordan's return to basketball. Today, the hoopster is among the world's highest paid advertising endorsers, influencing $300 million to $400 million in annual sales at his peak and making $31 million a year from commercials and other endorsement deals. But, why is Michael Jordan such a moneymaker for advertisers? Could it be because of his charm and quiet confidence? Could it be because he takes seriously his status as a role model for youth everywhere? The truth is it's Michael Jordan the person that is so appealing to consumers.

The superstar refuses to let fame go to his head. "My mother is my root, my foundation," says Jordan. "She planted the seed that I base my life on, and that is the belief that the ability to achieve starts in your mind." Apparently, Michael Jordan has made up his mind to be a winner —on and off the court.

Economic Spotlight

Ask students to look again at the third paragraph of *Economic Spotlight.* Tell students that, in 1994, the major league baseball season came to an abrupt halt in the United States when unionized major league baseball players declared a strike in response to team owners' plans to place caps, or limits, on players' salaries. The players' union and the team owners eventually reached an agreement, but only after cancellation of the major league season and, consequently, the 1994 World Series. Divide the class into two teams and have them debate whether the players' strike was justified in light of the enormous salaries they already make. Tell students to support their arguments with information about unions from this chapter.

In 1869, the union was founded in secret. But, the union gradually came into the open, and by 1886, it had nearly 1 million members. Also in 1886, Samuel Gompers founded the American Federation of Labor (AFL). The AFL was formed as a voluntary association of craft unions such as carpenters' and bricklayers' unions. Even though the Knights of Labor died out by 1917, the AFL has survived to this day. In 1955, the AFL merged with the Congress of Industrial Organizations (CIO). The CIO had been formed 20 years earlier during the Great Depression under the leadership of John L. Lewis. The CIO was made up of industrial unions such as the steelworkers' and the rubber workers' unions.

The formation of unions helped to balance out the bargaining power between labor and management. While management didn't need any one worker, it did need workers as a group. While a single worker had little power, workers as a group did have economic power. When workers belonged to a union, individual workers no longer negotiated working conditions with management. Benefits such as wages, hours, vacation time, and insurance coverage were determined through collective bargaining. ***Collective bargaining*** is the process of having the union negotiate with management to determine the terms of employment for all workers rather than having each worker negotiate separately. If management did not listen to workers' demands, workers could threaten a strike—the ultimate union weapon.

collective bargaining
the process of having the union negotiate with management to determine the terms of employment for all workers rather than having each worker negotiate separately

Management Responds

Management, of course, did not like the formation of unions. It struck back by asking the courts to say that unions were conspiracies and should be outlawed. The courts, however, ruled that unions were not illegal. Employers then turned to other weapons of their own, such as injunctions, yellow-dog contracts, and the use of antitrust laws.

An ***injunction*** is a court order to stop someone from doing something (or to make someone *do* something). If unions acted in ways management did not like, management would try to have an injunction issued against the union. And, management usually succeeded. The penalties for violating an injunction included fines and jail sentences. Management also forced workers to sign agreements before they were hired. A *yellow-dog contract* was a contract workers had to sign before they were hired saying that they would not join a union. Anyone who wouldn't sign did not get hired.

injunction
a court order to stop someone from doing something (or to make someone *do* something)

Finally, management used the Sherman Antitrust Act to stop unions. The Sherman Antitrust Act was passed partially to make combinations that were in restraint of trade illegal. The law was aimed at big corporate businesses. But, much of its early use was against unions that used strikes to fight management. Management claimed that the unions' strike activities were in restraint of trade because the strikes limited the flow of goods across state lines.

Legislation Is Passed

By the early 1930s, public opinion began to favor labor unions. Public opinion was against business, because many people blamed business for the Depression. As a result, the Norris-LaGuardia Act was passed in 1932. The act held that labor activity was not in violation of antitrust laws and that yellow-dog contracts were illegal. The act also greatly limited business use of injunctions

Multicultural *Highlights*

César Chávez, a Mexican-American migrant worker born in Yuma, Arizona, in 1927, led the campaign to organize agricultural workers in the 1960s and 1970s. Chávez used the nonviolent tactics of Mohandas Gandhi and Martin Luther King Jr. to win recognition for his United Farm Workers of America (UFWA), the first successful farm workers' union in U.S. history. As a class, have students discuss whether they think certain types of occupations are more or less suitable for union organization and why.

On the computer or by hand, ask students to create bar graphs showing membership in U.S. labor unions and the percentage of the labor force that was unionized using these figures:

Year	Union Membership (millions)	Percentage of Workforce
1930	3,401	11.6
1940	8,717	26.9
1950	14,267	31.5
1960	17,049	31.4
1970	19,381	27.3
1980	19,843	21.9
1990	16,740	16.1

Ask students to discuss the general trend in union membership and reasons for the trend. (Decline in numbers of workers in traditionally unionized heavy industry occupations; rise in anti-union sentiment and activity; foreign competition keeps wages low)

Have students research the following labor legislation: Sherman Antitrust, Norris La Guardia, National Labor Relations, and Taft-Hartley.

Divide the class into groups of five or six students. Have the groups conduct a mock negotiation between management and labor over a contract to build a 20-story office building. Have two or three students represent the management team and two or three others represent the union. Have the remaining student play the role of mediator, conducting the negotiation and recording the different positions. Have the two sides negotiate such issues as salary, benefits, paid holidays, sick leave policy, and any other relevant concerns. Allow 10 minutes for each side to prepare and 20 minutes for the negotiations. Then, have the groups report to the class on their negotiations and bargaining strategies.

Cooperative Learning

against unions. This opened the door for the development of labor unions. The stress between labor and management, however, increased. Armed conflicts between labor and the people hired by management to keep unions in check were common.

Partly as a result of such conflicts, the National Labor Relations Act, also called the Wagner Act, was passed in 1935. One of the most important pieces of labor legislation, this bill defined management practices that were unfair to labor. Management could no longer interfere with or restrain union activities. It could not discriminate against workers who wanted to join unions and could not act against workers who filed charges against business. Employers had to recognize and bargain with unions that were properly formed. The law also established the National Labor Relations Board that set up procedures for conducting union elections.

As a result of the National Labor Relations Act, union activity grew. There were restraints on management but almost none on unions. But, after World War II, unions began a flurry of strike activity and public opinion started to turn against unions. In 1947, the Taft-Hartley Act was passed. This act specified which union actions were unfair labor practices. For example, the closed shop was made illegal. A ***closed shop*** is a business that agrees to hire only those workers who are members of a union. A union shop was and is still legal, however. A ***union shop*** is a business that requires workers to join a union shortly after taking a job. The Taft-Hartley Act also set up emergency procedures to allow government to interfere with union activity if labor problems threatened national security.

closed shop
a business that agrees to hire only those workers who are members of a union

union shop
a business that requires workers to join a union shortly after taking a job

Today, there is a better balance between the power of unions and the power of management. People still join unions, and union growth is greatest in white-collar jobs such as teaching. Overall, however, the percentage of all nonagricultural workers who belong to unions has declined.

Checkpoint

Content Check

1. Under what conditions might there be a monopsony in the labor market?
2. Why do labor unions exist?
3. How does collective bargaining work?

What Do You Think Now?

Reread *What Do You Think?* in the Section Two Focus. Then answer the following questions:

4. Who ends up being hurt the most by a minimum wage?
5. Who ends up benefiting from a minimum wage?

Assess

1. When there is one large employer that dominates a labor market **13-2**
2. They developed and continue to exist in order to give workers a more equal footing with employers when determining wages, benefits, and working conditions. **13-3**
3. A union bargains collectively for all its members so that each worker doesn't need to bargain individually with the employer. **13-3**
4. Workers with the fewest skills are generally hurt the most by an increase in the minimum wage because they are the most likely to be laid off or not hired to begin with. **13-2**
5. Workers who are not laid off or do not have their work hours reduced benefit most from an increase in the minimum wage. **13-2**

Close

Ask students to list the three forces discussed in this section that influence the labor market. (Monopsony in the labor market, minimum wage, and labor unions) Have them choose the one they feel has had the greatest effect on their own community's or familys' economic situations and then write several paragraphs describing and analyzing the effect. Post the essays on a bulletin board for students to read before or after class.

Reteach

In order to clarify how establishing a minimum wage can lead to loss of jobs for some workers, ask students to imagine that they manage a fast-food restaurant and that the minimum wage is being increased by $0.50 per hour. Ask them to describe the kind of worker they would lay off first to curtail expenses. **13-2**

Enrich

Have students respond creatively to the history of labor unions by composing a labor protest song or a lyric from management's point of view, writing a story or poem about the concerns of workers and management, or creating a visual that embodies the history or values of those involved in management-labor relations. **13-3**

Section Three

Interest: A Source of Income and an Expense

What Do You Think?

Many of you may have elderly grandparents who have savings from which they get interest payments. For some people, this interest is an important source of income. The higher the interest rate, the higher the income of people with interest income. Do you think high interest rates are a good thing?

What's Ahead?

The income that individuals get depends on the quality and quantity of the factors of production over which they have control. We can work for wages to earn income. In fact, most of the income earned in the United States is labor income. We also may own stocks in corporations. This allows us to share in the profits earned by those firms. We may own land or the right to natural resources which gives us rental income. We also can get interest income from lending money to people who invest it in productive machinery or from investing the money ourselves. Interest income is the second most important source of income in the United States. In this section, you will learn about different ways of looking at interest and its role in the economy.

Terms to Know

interest

inflation

prime rate

corporate bond rate

federal funds rate

discount rate

INTEREST INCOME

Interest is the price paid for the use of money. The concept of interest dates back at least to biblical times when all payments for the use of money were considered evil. Money was thought of as useless and nonproductive. The collection of money for the use of money was called *usury,* and it was considered sinful and illegal. Not until the development of modern business did people accept interest as a justifiable charge for the use of money. Modern businesses often must borrow large sums of

interest
the price paid for the use of money

Focus

Before students arrive, write on the chalkboard **"Neither a borrower nor a lender be"** (from William Shakespeare's *Hamlet*). As students enter the classroom, ask them to jot down on a sheet of paper what they think about this well-known piece of advice.

As a class, discuss whether students believe this is good or bad advice. Elicit from students what dangers the advice hints at, how a borrower or lender can minimize these dangers, and under what conditions it might be acceptable to borrow or lend.

Teach

Explain to students that, in spite of the dangers of borrowing and lending implied by the statement from *Hamlet*, borrowing and lending money is extremely common in today's world. In fact, some forms of business would be impossible without it. Explain to students that **interest** is the price paid for the use of money, and discuss the two situations in which interest is commonly paid. (Borrowers pay interest to use money when they want to buy something; lenders earn interest on savings accounts and investments when they let other people or organizations use their money.)

Tell students how measures of **interest** charged and paid are usually expressed (as a percentage rate) and whether this percentage is always the same. (The rate varies widely, based on several elements.) Explain the differences among the four particular interest rates and how **inflation** influences interest rates.

Apply

Ask students if interest has always been an important part of business economics and what it was known as in the past. (No, it once was thought of as evil. It was called *usury.*) Discuss with students why they think interest was regarded in this manner. (Early economies were based on "real" property, such as land, gold, and farm animals, and many other forms of wealth were neither understood nor accepted. People rich in money may have been considered exploiters.)

Ask for examples of how business ventures were affected once interest was accepted as a justifiable charge for the use of money. (Entrepreneurs could borrow money to improve and expand their businesses; merchants could borrow money to outfit a ship, buy cargo, sell it at a profit, and then repay the loan.) Ask students how we use the term *usury* today. (*Usury* now describes interest rates that are higher than what is allowed by law.) **Guided Practice**

money to buy the productive equipment they need. The money firms borrow has productive use because it buys productive equipment. So, a charge for its use is fair and reasonable. Today, the term *usury* is used only to refer to the act of charging interest rates above the maximum rates allowed by law.

Two Views of Interest

There are two ways of looking at the concept of interest. One is to think of interest as the price that is paid for the use of money or credit. For example, if you borrow money to buy a car, you must pay interest on the amount you borrow. Another way of looking at interest is as the rate of return that a productive piece of machinery earns. Machines, buildings, and computers are examples of capital equipment that can be productive. Capital contributes to production just as labor does. And, the payment to capital is interest, just as the payment to labor is a wage.

Interest as the Price for Borrowing. Suppose you borrow $1,000 today and agree to repay that $1,000 plus $50 one year from today. You might do this because you prefer current consumption to consumption at a later time. You are willing to pay the extra $50 for the right to use someone else's money for the year. The $50 is the interest you pay. That $50 is the cost of borrowing the $1,000. But, interest is almost never stated in terms of the number of dollars paid. Instead, interest is stated as a percentage, or a rate of interest. The rate is the amount of interest paid per year divided by the amount that is borrowed. In this example, the interest rate is 5 percent ($50/$1,000 = 0.05 = 5%).

Banks, savings and loan associations, and credit unions all pay interest when people save, and they charge interest when people borrow. In either case, the interest paid or charged is stated as a percentage. Interest paid on savings is always less than the interest charged on new loans. For example, a bank may pay 7 percent on your savings but charge you 10 percent on a loan. The 7 percent paid on your savings means that each year you get an added $7 for each $100 in your savings account. The 10 percent loan rate means that for every $100 borrowed for a year you are charged $10 in interest.

Interest as a Return to Capital. Now let's look at interest as a return to capital. Suppose a business buys a $20,000 machine to use in producing some product. To simplify this example, we will assume that the machine is useful for only one year. To find the earnings related to the machine, you subtract all other payments, such as wages, from the revenue obtained by selling the product. If the revenue from sales is $100,000 and all other costs amount to $97,000, the earnings due to the machine are $3,000. The rate of return on the machine, then, is $3,000 divided by $20,000 which is 0.15 or 15 percent. This is the interest earned by that piece of capital equipment. If the company can borrow the money to buy the machine for less than 15 percent, it will find it profitable to do so. But, if the market rate of interest is higher than 15 percent, the company should not invest in the machine.

Internet Connection

INCOME AND EMPLOYMENT FACTS ON THE INTERNET

For most people, the major source of income is their labor. Their income depends on how much they work and the wages they get paid.

The quantity of labor supplied can be measured by the size of the labor force, number of people employed, or number of labor hours worked. Data on the labor force are available from the Statistical Abstract, **http://www.census.gov/ftp/pub/statab/USAbrief/part2.txt**. Data about total nonfarm employment and average weekly work hours are available from the Bureau of Labor Statistics (BLS) database at two addresses: **gopher://hopi.bls.gov/00hopiftp.dev/special.requests/ee/b1nsa.dat** and **gopher://hopi.bls.gov/00hopiftp.dev/special.requests/ee/b2nsa.dat**.

The wage rate depends on a variety of factors including education and training, which affect productivity, field of expertise, and the effects of unions. The BLS database **gopher://hopi.bls.gov/00hopiftp.dev/special.requests/ee/b3he.dat**, gives current statistics on the average hourly earnings in the economy and in each industry.

The AFL-CIO maintains a homepage at **http://www.aflcio.org** that includes a description and history of the AFL-CIO, policy statements, press releases, current news stories related to labor issues ("News On Line"), and links to other union Web sites.

Data about average weekly earnings in the economy and in each industry are available from the BLS database **gopher://hopi.bls.gov/00hopiftp.dev/special.requests/ee/b3we.dat**. The Census Bureau provides information about annual per capita income and annual household income at **http://www.census.gov/org/hhes/income/highlights/p2cap.html** and **http://www.census.gov/org/hhes/income/highlights/h3med.html**.

Internet Application: The Internet has improved the workings of the labor market by making it easier for job seekers and employers to communicate. There are lists of job vacancies on the Internet, and job seekers are submitting applications via e-mail. The Gopher site at Vanderbilt University, **gopher://vuinfo.vanderbilt.edu:70/11/employment**, maintains a list of job opportunities. Fedworld publicizes federal employment opportunities at **telnet://fedworld.gov** or **ftp://fwux.fedworld.gov/pub/jobs/jobs.htm**. E-mail your teacher a description of the sorts of jobs that are currently advertised on the Internet.

Economics Application: *Telecommuting* is the term for people who no longer work in an office but stay in touch by telephone, fax, and modem. Explain how the Internet contributed to the increase in telecommuting in the 1990s.

Ask students to name the two ways the textbook gives for looking at the concept of interest. (The price paid for the use of money or credit; the rate of return that a productive piece of machinery earns) Review the two examples given in the textbook. Then, have students complete the following problems either on paper or with a calculator:

- You plan to borrow \$1,500 for one year and agree to pay \$105 in interest. What is the interest rate you will be charged? (\$105 ÷ \$1,500 = 0.07 = 7 percent)
- You want to borrow \$3,000 for one year at an interest rate of 8 percent. How much total interest will you pay? (\$3,000 × .08 = \$240)
- You deposit \$350 in a savings account. One year later, your account holds \$364. What interest rate have you earned on your savings? (\$364 − \$350 = \$14 ÷ \$350 = 0.04 = 4 percent)
- Your frozen yogurt company buys a new mixing machine for \$50,000. Revenues from sales in the first year after the purchase of the machine are \$325,000. All costs including the cost of the new machine amount to \$318,000 that year. You pay 9 percent interest on the money you used to buy the machine. Assuming the machine is useful for only one year, was buying it a good idea? What was the return on your investment (ROI)? (Yes, your earnings due to the new machine were \$7,000, for an ROI of 14 percent [\$7,000 ÷ \$50,000 = 0.14 = 14 percent].)

Internet Connection

Internet Application: The Vanderbilt Gopher site contains the online version of Job Openings for Economists, which advertises academic vacancies as well as nonacademic positions for economists. The Gopher site contains extensive listings under Worldwide Job Listings via Internet Sources. This Gopher site can be accessed via Gopher or Web browser. For Gopher access, type **gopher vuinfo.vanderbilt.edu** and select "Employment Opportunities."

Economics Application: E-mail and Ftp can be used to communicate. Through Telnet, connect to your company's computer system to access information and do your work while staying at home. Gopher, Web browser, and WAIS can be used to search for information relevant to your job tasks.

Ask students which is always higher: the interest a bank or savings and loan pays on savings, or the interest it charges on loans. (Interest it charges on loans) Ask students what they think this difference in rates represents. (The difference, minus costs associated with operating a bank, represents the profit a bank earns.)

On the chalkboard or an overhead transparency, copy the following graphic organizer.

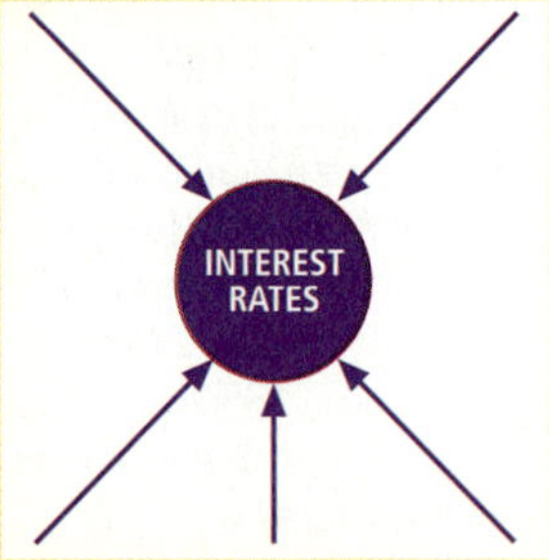

Have students copy the organizer into their notebooks and fill in the branches with the five elements that influence an interest rate. (Time period involved, risk, rate of inflation, costs of making a loan, and tax treatment of interest) Then, have pairs of students discuss the way each element influences interest rates in particular markets.

Independent Practice

Arrange for a loan officer to address the class. Ask the loan officer to prepare a brief talk on the impact of inflation and varying interest rates on the local economy and how the lending institution determines the rates it will charge for various loans and to different borrowers. Encourage the speaker to bring charts, graphs, sample forms, or any other visuals that will help clarify the concepts. Before the speaker arrives, have each student prepare three questions.

Factors That Influence the Interest Rate

On television and radio, as well as in newspapers and magazines, we see and hear many articles and reports about the rate of interest. Actually, there are many different interest rates in the economy. You may have heard of the prime rate, the corporate bond rate, or the federal funds rate. Every lending market has its own interest rate. The rate in each market depends upon many factors. Among these are the time period involved, the risk, the rate of inflation, the costs of making the loan, and the tax treatment of interest.

In general, the shorter the time period of the loan, the lower the interest rate. Lenders prefer a shorter time period because there is less chance of changes that would affect the profitability of the loan. Loans that extend over long periods of time reduce the lender's ability to change and to adjust to changing economic events.

Global Economy

NAFTA DRIVES DEMAND FOR LABOR

The long-term consequences of the North American Free Trade Agreement (NAFTA) may not be known fully until well into the twenty-first century. But, it appears that this agreement, passed in the mid-1990s, is having the beneficial effects that were widely anticipated. There have been ups and downs, especially in the case of Mexico's emerging economy. But, overall, the positive outcomes have dominated.

In Canada, increased employment has resulted as Canadian exports have risen. In addition, the demand for labor in Canada has been bolstered by big expansion in the automotive sector. For example, Ford spent about $2.2 billion to expand production of minivans, trucks, and engines in Ontario. Chrysler also expanded production in Canada. In 1994, Chrysler produced in Canadian facilities a record 695,000 vehicles, mostly minivans and LH models.

Similar events have unfolded in the Mexican economy. In the first eight months of NAFTA, U.S. and Canadian firms invested $2.4 billion in Mexico. Ford spent $60 million to revamp its Cuautitlán plant near Mexico City to produce small cars and trucks for global sales. Ford's export of cars from Mexico to the United States and its export of vehicles from the United States to Mexico were up dramatically in the first year of NAFTA. The president of Ford's Mexico operations commented, "We've created jobs here and in the U.S."

Other positive results have been evident for the United States. Food and beverage producers, manufacturers of consumer goods, and agricultural businesses have benefited. For example, Proctor & Gamble experienced a 75 percent increase in exports to Mexico in the first six months of NAFTA, and the exports to Mexico of Archer-Daniels-Midland tripled in NAFTA's first year.

Global Economy

Free-trade agreements such as NAFTA allow the free movement of goods and services across national borders without the imposition of protective tariffs or quotas. Have students compile a list of free trade's possible positive and negative effects on the U.S. labor market. On the chalkboard or an overhead transparency, compose a class list from students' suggestions. As students volunteer items from their own lists, discuss whether each is a short-term effect that may eventually be overcome or a long-term effect.

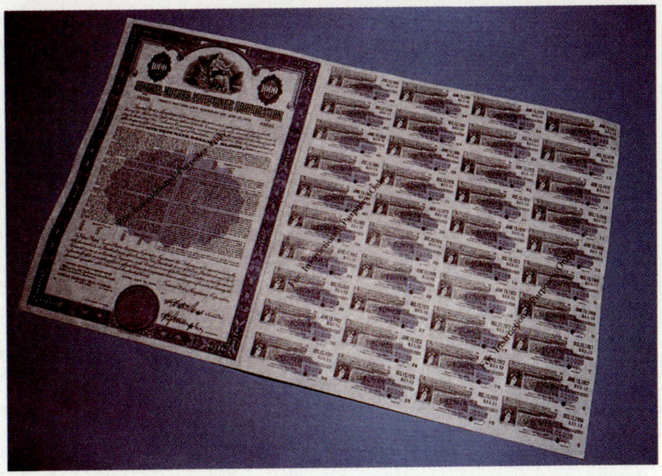

Risk is another factor that influences interest rates. For example, suppose you have the choice of lending your money to IBM or to the Wickey Wackey Widget Corporation. Because IBM is a large, well-established firm, it is more likely that it will repay your money in full and on time. You might then lend money to IBM at a relatively low interest rate. But, you will charge the Wickey Wackey Widget Corporation more since you can't be as sure of repayment in full and on time. There is a general rule in lending money: The higher the risk, the higher the interest.

The rate of inflation also influences interest rates. We will discuss inflation in more detail later, but for now we will define it in broad terms. ***Inflation*** is a rise in the average level of prices. You can see quickly why inflation influences interest rates. Suppose the average level of prices increases 10 percent a year. Next year it will take $110 to buy what $100 buys today. If you are loaned $100 today at 5 percent interest, you will owe $105 a year from now. But, that $105 a year from now won't even be enough to buy what the $100 buys today. It will take $110 to do so. So, the lender will not earn any real interest and, in fact, will lose buying power. It follows, then, that lenders will not want to lend money unless the interest rate is greater than the inflation rate. This means that in times of high inflation, we should expect high interest rates.

inflation
a rise in the average level of prices

The costs a lender has in making a loan will also influence the interest rate. There are costs involved in checking the borrower's credit and in administering the loan.

Finally, the ways in which tax laws treat different forms of interest can influence the interest rate. If a lender can get tax benefits by loaning money in some market, that market's interest rate is likely to be lower. Most of the time, a lender must pay taxes on interest that is collected. For example, if you lend IBM money by buying its bonds, you pay taxes on that interest income. But, if you lend money to the city of Tulsa by buying a bond the city issues, the interest income is tax free. So, you might be willing to lend money to Tulsa at a lower interest rate than you would to IBM. People will be more likely to lend money if the interest income is not taxed.

As you study macroeconomics in Part Three, you will see some ways that national economic policy can influence interest rates. You also will see how interest rates influence investment, productivity, and economic growth.

Particular Interest Rates

What do people in the news media mean when they refer to rising or falling interest rates? Usually, they are referring to the prime rate. The ***prime rate*** is the interest rate that banks charge their best corporate customers. Companies such as General Motors, IBM, and AT&T may be

prime rate
the interest rate that banks charge their best corporate customers

Assign each student one of the four interest rates described in the textbook (prime rate, corporate bond rate, federal funds rate, and discount rate). As a homework assignment, have students look through *The Wall Street Journal* for news and information about their specific types of interest rates. After students have completed their research, have volunteers report to the class any information they found.

Have students work in pairs to role-play the following situation: One student is a loan officer at a bank and is trying to determine the creditworthiness of a second student, who is playing the role of a potential borrower. Ask the first student to write and ask questions that he or she feels will help determine whether the applicant is a good risk. The second student is to provide information to verify his or her ability to repay a loan. Allow 5 minutes for each student to write questions and to determine appropriate ways to prove creditworthiness. Allow another 10 minutes for the role-playing activity. After the activity, have students discuss the kinds of questions "loan officers" asked as well as the types of evidence "applicants" thought were appropriate to reveal.

Obtain copies of an interest table for determining loan principal and interest payments for various amounts at different terms. (Real-estate agents often supply these.) Review how the table is used and then ask students to determine monthly payments for the following loans:

- $15,000 for 15 years at 6 3/4 percent ($132.75)
- $40,000 for 30 years at 9 1/2 percent ($336.40)

(Note: Answers may vary slightly depending on the algorithm used and on whether students rounded off figures.)

Write the following loan terms on the chalkboard:

A. $60,000 for 30 years at 8 3/4 percent

B. $60,000 for 15 years at 8 percent

Ask students which of these loans would result in a lower monthly payment. (Loan A's monthly payment of $472.20 is $101.40 less than B's payment of $573.60. Again, answers may vary slightly.) Then, ask which would result in a greater *total* payment over the life of the loan. (Loan A would require 360 payments totaling $169,992, while loan B would require 180 payments totaling $103,248, a difference of $66,742.) Ask students why a borrower might choose loan A over loan B in spite of the large difference in total payments. (The lower monthly payments might be more affordable for some people.)

charged the prime rate. The risk involved in lending money to those firms is very small. Therefore, the prime rate is usually lower than most other interest rates. It also is often used as a standard indicator of changes in interest rates in general.

Another interest rate that is commonly talked about is the corporate bond rate. As the name implies, the ***corporate bond rate*** is the interest rate paid on corporate bonds. A corporate bond is a certificate issued by a corporation promising to pay bondholders a specific amount of money by a specific date.

A third interest rate that is often reported in the news is the federal funds rate. The ***federal funds rate*** is the interest rate that banks pay to borrow from each other on a short-term basis. The time may be as short as overnight. Such loans have little risk and last for a very short time. Therefore, the federal funds rate usually stays low, even lower than the prime rate.

Another rate we hear about often is the discount rate. The ***discount rate*** is the interest rate that banks must pay to borrow from the Federal Reserve System. (The Federal Reserve System and the discount rate will be discussed more fully later in this text.) The discount rate is lower than the prime rate and the other rates mentioned, but it is not available to private individuals and businesses except banks.

corporate bond rate
the interest rate paid on corporate bonds

federal funds rate
the interest rate that banks pay to borrow from each other on a short-term basis

discount rate
the interest rate that banks must pay to borrow from the Federal Reserve System

Economic*Talk*

Have students use at least 10 of the 18 words in *Your Economic Vocabulary* at the end of this chapter to create a crossword puzzle. Tell students that their clues can be definitions, fill-in-the-blank statements, and so on, but all clues should be based on the reading of this chapter. If your school owns crossword-puzzle software, consider allowing students to use the computer to construct their puzzles. Have each student exchange puzzles with a partner and, after completing the work, return it to the partner for correction.

CONSUMER CREDIT AND INTEREST RATES

The rates charged for consumer credit are usually higher than other rates. There are three reasons for these higher rates:

1. Consumer loans have higher risk.
2. Consumer loans are costly to set up.
3. Consumer loans often run over a relatively long period of time.

Most consumer loans involve much more risk than do loans to corporations that qualify for the prime rate. The costs of checking credit and handling loan accounts are also higher for individuals. This is particularly true in comparison to the dollar amount of a loan. There may be high costs in trying to collect the balance due if the person fails to keep up with the payments. Also, many consumer loans are made for three or more years. It is not uncommon for people to have car loans that run four or even five years.

Consumer credit comes from credit unions, life insurance companies, commercial banks, savings and loan associations, finance companies, charge accounts, and credit cards. The interest charged by these lenders varies, so you should shop around when looking to borrow money. It will always cost you money to borrow money. But, by shopping around, you often can save. Let's look at two common examples of how it pays to shop for interest rates: buying a car and buying a house.

Buying a Car

Suppose that you have saved enough money for a down payment on a car, but you need to borrow $5,000 to make the purchase. You investigate two loan sources. A credit union will lend you the money at a 9 percent interest rate. A local finance company will lend you the same amount at a 12 percent interest rate. (A difference of 3 percent or more on a car loan is not uncommon.) Both loans are for four years. Your monthly payments and total payments for the $5,000 loan would be as follows:

	Monthly Payment	Total Payment
Finance Company (12% Interest)	$ 131.67	$6,320.16
Credit Union (9% Interest)	124.43	5,972.64
Difference in Payment	$ 7.24	$ 347.52

As you can see, there is a $347.52 savings over the four years at the lower interest rate. But, if you don't shop around, you might not borrow at the lowest rate.

Buying a House

At some point, you may want to buy a house, and finding the lowest interest rate will be important. Assume that you want to borrow $90,000 to buy a house. A home loan may be for as long as 30 years, so we will use that time period. You go to a bank and to a savings and loan to see about borrowing the money. The bank will lend you the money at 10.5 percent,

Draw the following graphic organizer on the chalkboard or an overhead transparency and ask students to copy it into their notebooks. Then, have them fill in the circles with the monetary effects of changes in interest rates. Remind the class that the answers are based on the information in this section.

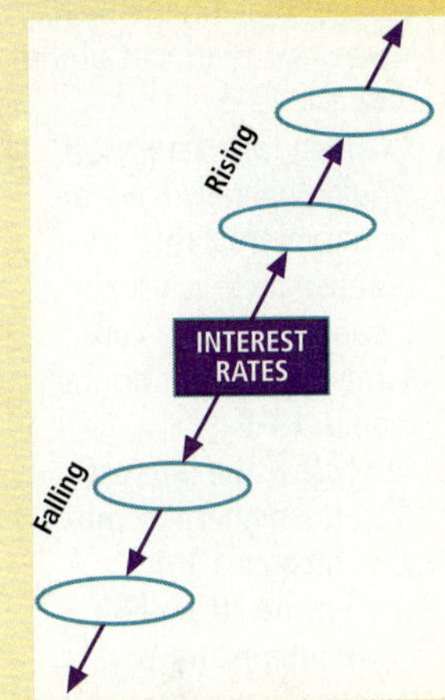

(Answers in the **Rising** circles might be that people living on interest income get more money, and that people might save more if they can earn higher interest on savings and investments. However, people who must borrow money are forced to pay more interest. Answers in the **Falling** circles might be that purchases bought on credit become cheaper, and businesses can expand more cheaply. However, investments that earn interest experience much slower growth.)

EyeOnMarketNews

Some of the tax-reform plans currently being examined by Congress call for eliminating the important and popular income tax deduction for interest paid on home mortgage loans. Using the school or community library, online computer information services, or information from local bankers, real-estate agents, or elected representatives, have students compile a list of advantages and disadvantages of eliminating the mortgage interest deduction. Ask students to share the results of their research with the class. Then, survey class members to determine where they stand on the issue.

and the savings and loan will lend you the money at 10 percent. This does not seem like much of a difference. But is it? Your payments on the $90,000 are summarized as follows:

	Monthly Payment	Total Payment
Bank (10.5% Interest)	$ 823.27	$296,377.20
Savings and Loan (10% Interest)	789.81	284,331.60
Difference in Payment	$ 33.46	$ 12,045.60

A one-half of 1 percent difference in the interest rate means a difference in total payments of $12,045.60 over the 30-year loan. It may surprise you to see that even at the lower rate, you will have to pay $284,331.60 for the $90,000 home loan. The interest payments will total $194,331.60, which is more than twice the amount you will borrow. Interest can add up to a large amount of money. So, it is as important to shop around when you borrow money as it is when you make purchases.

Checkpoint

Content Check

1. Why do you think people are willing to pay a price (interest) to borrow money?
2. Name three factors that may influence the rate of interest charged for a loan.
3. Would you expect the rate of interest for a family's car loan to be higher or lower than the rate paid by General Motors on a loan to expand a factory? Why?

What Do You Think Now?

Reread *What Do You Think?* in the Section Three Focus. Then answer the following questions:

4. How would the rate of interest affect the income of a retired couple who rely on their savings as a primary source of income?
5. As a potential borrower would you like to see lower interest rates? Why or why not?

Assess

1. Because people prefer current consumption to consumption at a later date, they are willing to pay interest in order to be able to buy goods and services now rather than later. **13-4**
2. Answers may include the time period involved, the risk to the lender, the current rate of inflation, the costs of making the loan, or the tax treatment of the interest. **13-5**
3. The loan for a family car would generally have the higher interest rate because there is usually greater risk that a consumer loan might not be repaid. **13-5**
4. The higher the interest rate, the higher the couple's income **13-4**
5. Yes; borrowers prefer lower interest rates because lower rates reduce the cost of repaying their loans. **13-4**

Close

Working in groups, have students create and produce either a videotaped or audiotaped public service announcement (PSA) or a print ad or poster giving information on how to be a responsible and informed borrower. The PSA, ad, or poster should be based on information found in this section. Encourage students to use music, visuals (including computer-generated graphics), humor, and any other communication techniques that will help them get their message across. Arrange to display the projects or have students view all projects in class. You also might want to investigate showing the projects in a community setting such as a social center, bank, savings and loan, or YMCA/YWCA.

Reteach

List the five factors that influence interest rates. (Time period involved, risk, rate of inflation, costs of making a loan, and tax treatment of interest) Have students work in pairs to draft short explanations of how each factor influences interest rates. **13-5**

Enrich

Have students examine a list of current mortgage interest rates from a recent local newspaper to determine interest paid at each rate offered, given a $100,000 loan for 30 years. Ask students to determine whose responsibility it is to know—and offer—the best rates: the real estate agent's, the lending institution's, or the lender's. **13-4**

Concepts in Brief

1. Labor is bought and sold in a market, very much as goods and services are bought and sold. People are not bought or sold, but their labor, skills, and time are.
2. The demand for labor can be represented by a negatively sloped labor demand curve. This means that firms will hire more units of labor at a lower wage than they will at a higher wage.
3. The supply of labor can be represented by a positively sloped labor supply curve. This means that more units of labor will be made available for work at a higher wage than will at a lower wage.
4. When the quantity of labor demanded equals the quantity of labor supplied, the labor market is in balance. This is called an *equilibrium* in the labor market. If the wage is above the market equilibrium, more labor will be supplied than will be demanded. If the wage is below the market equilibrium, the quantity of labor demanded will be greater than the quantity supplied. In either case, economic forces will push the wage toward the equilibrium.
5. The government may set a minimum wage to prevent firms from paying a wage that is considered too low. Congress periodically votes to increase the minimum wage. This puts some people out of work and reduces the hours that others work. This is particularly hard on teenagers and people with less-developed labor skills. If minimum wage earners are not laid off or do not have their hours cut back, they do earn more after increases in the minimum wage than they did before the increase.
6. Labor unions developed because management seemed to have too much control over labor. Since the late 1800s, much conflict has occurred between business managers and unions. Laws favoring both sides have been passed by Congress. Power between unions and management appears better balanced now than 100 years ago.
7. People's incomes depend on the quantity and quality of the factors of production that they control. We all have our own labor to use in whatever form of production we wish. Some people own land and capital, while others have none of these resources within their control.

Chapter Close

Your Economic Portfolio

Tell students to imagine that they have been hired by their state's (un)employment commission to prepare a brochure to explain the concept of the minimum wage to new workers entering the workforce. Ask students to include whatever information they consider important about the minimum wage, including why this country has such laws, how they are intended to help workers, and who determines the minimum wage. Encourage students to use word-processing or desktop-publishing software to make their brochures appealing and easy to read. Suggest that they use eye-catching headlines and subheads, illustrations, bulleted lists, short paragraphs, and other graphic elements that will make the information easy to grasp. Review students' brochures and help them make any necessary corrections. Then, file the finished brochures in students' portfolios.

You may wish to provide the following end-of-chapter materials:

- *Skills & Concepts* worksheet
- *Content Review Workbook*
- Chapter *Assessment*
- Chapter *MicroExam*

8. Interest is the payment made for the use of someone else's money. You get interest when you put money into savings for someone else to use until you want it. You pay interest when you borrow money to buy things before you have enough of your own money to do so. When borrowing money, you should always shop around for the lowest interest rate.

9. Another way of looking at interest is as a return on productive machines and other forms of capital equipment. Just as labor and land are productive, so is capital. The return on capital is called *interest* and is usually stated as a percentage.

Economic Foundations

1. What factors determine the demand for labor?
2. What factors may cause the demand for labor to increase?
3. What has been a major cause of the increase in the supply of labor in the last 35 years?
4. Name three forces that can prevent labor market equilibrium.
5. Which groups do minimum wage laws help and hurt?
6. Why did labor unions develop?
7. Describe the effect on labor of four laws mentioned in this chapter.
8. Why do some people think of interest mainly in terms of income while others think of it mainly as a cost?
9. What factors influence the interest rate charged on a particular loan?
10. List three reasons interest rates on consumer loans are higher than other rates.

Economic Foundations

1. The demand for the good or service produced and the productivity of labor (p. 327)
2. It may increase if the demand for output increases or if the productivity of labor increases. (p. 328)
3. The increasing number of women in the labor force (p. 331)
4. Labor markets dominated by one employer (monopsony), minimum wage laws, and labor unions (pp. 334–335, 337)
5. Minimum wage laws hurt those who are laid off because an employer will not pay a minimum wage that is higher than the wage the laid-off workers were making; they also hurt unskilled workers, especially young people. Minimum wage laws help those who get their salaries raised to the minimum wage without losing their jobs or having their work hours reduced. (pp. 335–336)
6. Because workers wanted more control over working conditions and other job-related matters (pp. 337, 339)
7. The Sherman Antitrust Act was used against unions that used strikes to fight management on the basis that strikes restrained trade. The Norris LaGuardia Act stated that labor activity was not in violation of antitrust laws and that yellow-dog contracts were illegal. The National Labor Relations Act defined management practices considered unfair to labor. The Taft-Hartley Act specified which union activities were considered unfair and set up emergency

(Continued)

Your Economic Vocabulary

Build your economic vocabulary by matching the following terms with their definitions.

1. a rise in the average level of prices
2. the interest rate paid on corporate bonds
3. an organization of workers formed to give workers greater bargaining power in their dealings with management
4. a market in which there is only one buyer
5. the amount of labor that would be available at each wage rate
6. the price paid for each unit of labor
7. the amount of labor that firms would want to hire at various wage rates
8. demand for an input that is dependent on the demand for the product that the input helps to produce
9. the wage rate at which the quantity of labor demanded equals the quantity of labor supplied
10. a law that sets the lowest wage that can be paid for certain kinds of work
11. a business that agrees to hire only those workers who are members of a union
12. the interest rate that banks pay to borrow from each other on a short-term basis
13. the interest rate that banks must pay to borrow from the Federal Reserve System
14. the price paid for the use of money
15. a court order to stop someone from doing something (or to make someone *do* something)
16. the interest rate that banks charge their best corporate customers
17. a business that requires workers to join a union shortly after taking a job
18. the process of having the union negotiate with management to determine the terms of employment for all workers rather than having each worker negotiate separately

closed shop
collective bargaining
corporate bond rate
demand for labor
derived demand
discount rate
equilibrium wage
federal funds rate
inflation
injunction
interest
labor union
minimum wage law
monopsony
prime rate
supply of labor
union shop
wage rate

Economic Foundations
(Continued)

procedures for the government to use to interfere with union activity when national security was threatened by that activity. (pp. 339–340)

8. People who are earning interest on savings and investments see it as income; people who are paying interest on borrowed money see it as a cost. (p. 342)
9. The time period involved, the risk, the rate of inflation, the costs of making the loan, the tax treatment of the interest (p. 344)
10. The risk is higher, they are costly to set up, and they often run over a long period of time. (p. 347)

Your Economic Vocabulary

1. **inflation**
2. **corporate bond rate**
3. **labor union**
4. **monopsony**
5. **supply of labor**
6. **wage rate**
7. **demand for labor**
8. **derived demand**
9. **equilibrium wage**
10. **minimum wage law**
11. **closed shop**
12. **federal funds rate**
13. **discount rate**
14. **interest**
15. **injunction**
16. **prime rate**
17. **union shop**
18. **collective bargaining**

Thinking Critically About Economics

1. What is a *minimum wage*? In what types of jobs are people paid the minimum wage? Why do you think this is so?
2. Describe how the market system would determine an equilibrium wage rate and the level of employment. Use a supply and demand graph for labor to help with your explanation.
3. What determines the demand for bank tellers? Why is the demand for bank tellers called a *derived demand*?
4. Suppose you are in business and you buy a new machine for $40,000. After paying all other expenses, $7,000 is left that can be attributed to the productivity of the machine, which only has a one-year useful life. What is the rate of interest earned by this machine? If you had to pay 20 percent to borrow the money to buy such a machine, would you do so? Would you borrow the money at 10 percent?
5. Teachers' salaries have not been increasing as fast as the pay in many other types of work. Explain why you think this might be true. Use a graph of the supply and demand for teachers' labor to help answer this question. (Hint: Think about how the supply and demand curves may be shifting over time.)

Economic Enrichment

Why is it important for consumers to shop around when they need to borrow money? Where might people go if they want to borrow money to buy a car? Call two different banks, credit unions, or savings and loans and ask what their current interest rates are on a 48-month new car loan. Then, ask what the monthly payments would be for a $10,000 loan. Finally, compare the total payments over the life of the loan. Why might the rates, and resulting payments, be different at each loan source?

Thinking Critically About Economics

1. A minimum wage is a rate of pay set by the government as the lowest hourly payment for labor services. Generally, those with the least work experience and fewest productive and marketable skills, young workers, and workers in jobs that require few, if any, skills are paid the minimum wage. Answers may include that employers feel they can find less expensive ways to accomplish the low-skill tasks performed by those workers.
2. The equilibrium wage rate and level of employment are at the level where quantity of labor supplied is equal to quantity of labor demanded, as illustrated by this graph:

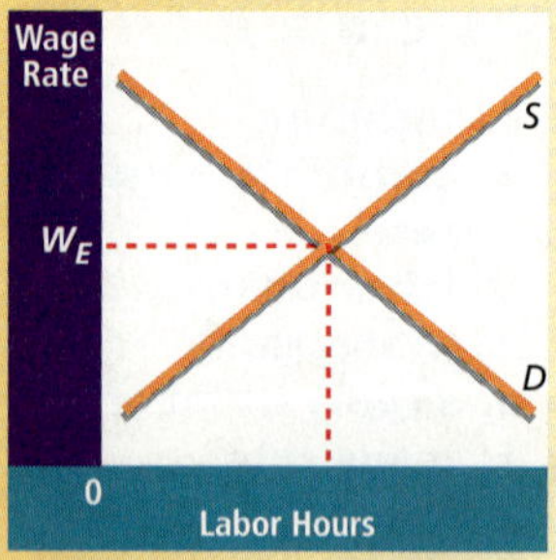

3. The demand for banking services that require a teller creates the demand for tellers. Consumers have a demand for banking services and banks want to fill those needs; therefore, the banks have a derived demand for tellers—demand for tellers arises from the bank's desire to satisfy customers' needs.
4. 17 1/2 percent ($7,000 ÷ $40,000 = 0.175 = 17.5); no, because you would be paying $8,000 (0.20 × $40,000) to earn $7,000;

(Continued)

Thinking Critically About Economics (Continued)

yes, because you would be paying $4,000 (0.10 × $40,000) to earn $7,000—a profit of $3,000;

5. At some initial time, the supply and demand curves for teachers could be represented by S_1 and D_1, with the salary level as S_1; as demand grows with population growth, the demand curve shifts to D_1; at the same time, we have been educating more teachers, so the supply of teachers has also gone up to S_2. The result has been very modest increases in teachers' salaries, as illustrated in this graph:

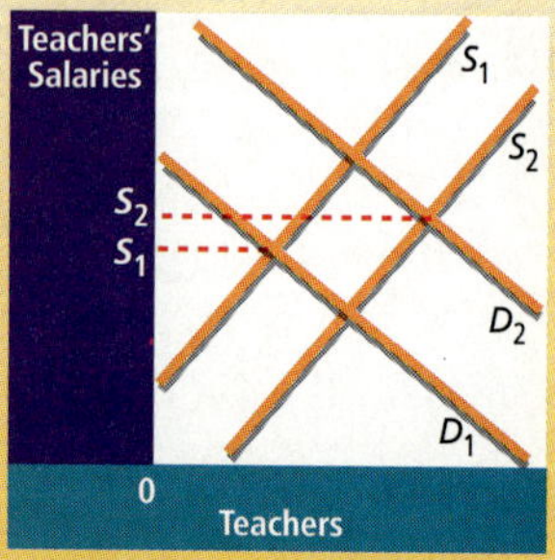

Math and Economics

In the following labor market graph, the wage rates shown are in dollars per labor hour. Use the graph to answer the following questions:

1. How much total income would be earned by labor at each wage rate?
2. If the current wage is $4.00, would you favor having a minimum wage of $4.50? What about $5.00?

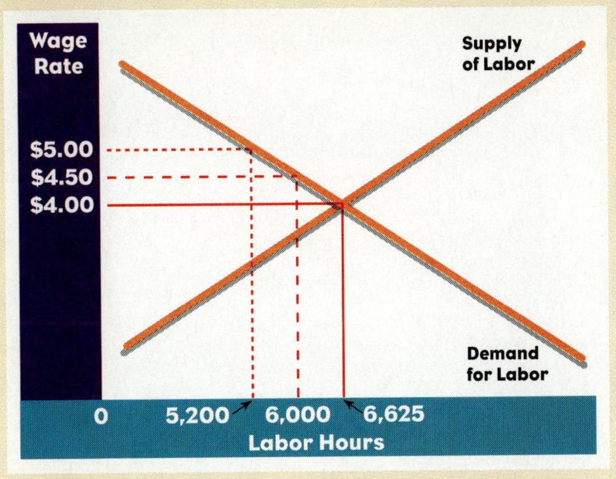

Writing About Economics

Interview an employed adult, other than a parent or guardian of yours, about his or her job. Find out what the adult likes and doesn't like about the job. Get information about the training, education, and/or skills that are needed for that type of work. Ask about the hours, the benefits, and the working conditions. Take careful notes (you might ask if you can audio tape or videotape the interview) and then write an essay about this type of job to share with the rest of your class.

Economic Enrichment

Consumers should shop around when they want to borrow money because interest rates almost always vary. People are most likely to get a car loan from a bank, savings and loan, credit union, or from the auto manufacturers themselves, who often maintain finance divisions that offer special interest rates from time to time. Students' rates, monthly payments, and total payments will vary. Rates and resulting payments vary because of different risks in lending to the types of customers each institution serves and different costs of administering the loan.

Math and Economics

1. At $5.00 and 5,200 hours: $26,000; at $4.50 and 6,000 hours: $27,000; at $4.00 and 6,625 hours: $26,500.
2. Answers may include yes, because earnings would increase by $0.50 per hour for people who are able to keep their jobs, or no, because it would increase the risk of people losing their jobs. More students may answer no to an increase to $5 because the larger increase in the minimum wage will mean a larger decrease in labor demand—which means they may be more likely to lose their jobs.

Writing About Economics

Students' essays should reflect an understanding of various aspects of the job being analyzed. Essays should be carefully written with concern for the rules of grammar, usage, and mechanics.

APPENDIX A

Economic Measurement Concepts

Economists use several types of measurement tools to get data into a manageable form. You already may have learned some of these concepts in your mathematics classes. The focus of this appendix will be on how the following measurement concepts are used in economics: tables and graphs; averages and distributions; ratios and percentages; rates and absolute numbers; index numbers; and real and nominal values.

TABLES AND GRAPHS

Newspapers and magazines present economic information in the form of tables and graphs. Just pick up any newspaper or such popular publications as *The Wall Street Journal, Readers Digest, USA Today, Time, Newsweek,* and *U.S. News & World Report.* You will find examples in nearly every issue. Tables or graphs organize and display economic information in a clear and manageable form.

Tables Summarize Data

Assume you want to gather data on the distribution of income in a high school economics class. You could have all class members write on a piece of paper the income they earn each week, collect this data, and look at it piece by piece. However, the individual pieces of data would not, by themselves, tell you much about how income is distributed in your class.

If you were to look at this data in table form, your results would be much more meaningful. A *table* is a simplified way of showing numbers. Figure A-1 on page 682 is a table that summarizes weekly income for the economics class at Summit High School.

You could analyze this data by setting up some income categories. For example, you might arrange the incomes into the groups shown in Figure A-2 on page 682.

Graphs Show Relationships

From the information given in Figure A-2, you can create a bar graph. A *bar graph* uses the lengths of bars to represent the general relationship between variables. In the table in Figure A-2, the variables are *number of students* and *income categories.* To prepare a bar graph, label the vertical axis *number of students* and the horizontal axis *income categories.*

681

Student No.	Income	Student No.	Income	Student No.	Income	Student No.	Income
1	$15	6	$27	11	$39	16	$57
2	15	7	33	12	45	17	63
3	15	8	33	13	48	18	63
4	21	9	36	14	51	19	69
5	27	10	39	15	51	20	75

Figure A-1

Income Data for Economics Students at Summit High School

This table summarizes student income for a class of 20 students.

Figure A-2

Categories of Income Data for Economics Students

These income categories further summarize the income data for economics students.

Category Number	Income Category	Number of Students in Category
1	$15–$27	6
2	$28–$40	5
3	$41–$53	4
4	$54–$66	3
5	$67–$79	2

The bar graph in Figure A-3 gives you several pieces of information at a glance. First, you can see that more students have incomes in the $15 to $27 range than any other income category. Second, you can see that the fewest number of students have incomes in the $67 to $79 group. Finally, you can see that the general relationship between income and the number of students who receive it is an inverse relationship. That means that, as income goes up, the number of students receiving incomes in that category goes down. And, as income goes down, the number of students receiving income in that category goes up.

A *line graph* is a diagram in which the relationship between variables is represented by a line. The bar graph in Figure A-3 can be converted into a rough approximation of a line graph by plotting a point in the center of the top of each bar and connecting the dots. This is shown in Figure A-4.

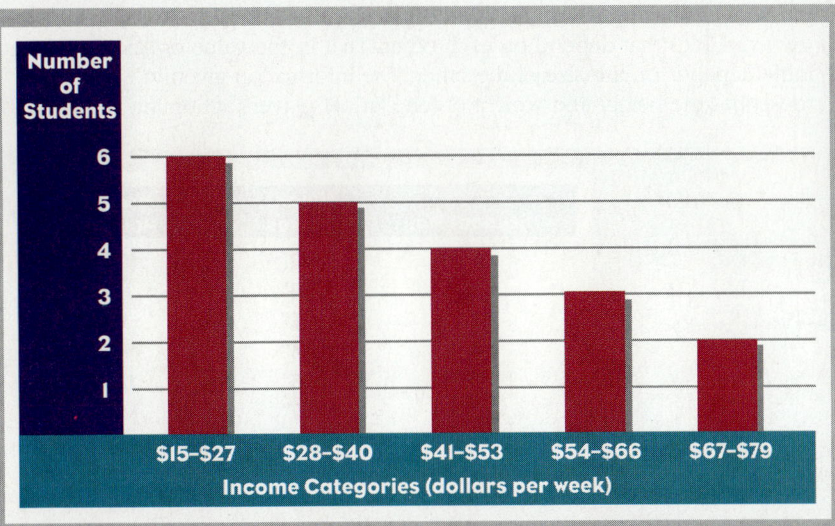

Figure A-3

Bar Graph of Income Data for Economics Students

This bar graph is a visual representation of the data summarized in Figure A-2.

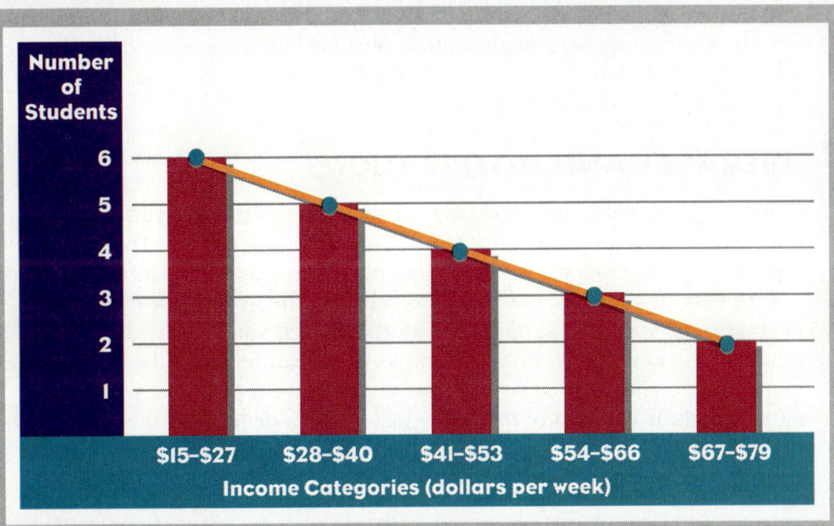

Figure A-4

Line Graph of Income Data for Economics Students

This line graph highlights the relationship between number of students and student income.

Now let's examine another type of graphical relationship. We will look at two variables that depend on each other. That is, the value or size of one variable depends on the size of the other. The information given in Figure A-5 describes the height and weight of ten clarinet players at Summit High School.

Figure A-5

Height and Weight Data for Clarinet Players at Summit High School

This table summarizes height and weight data for ten students.

Student No.	Height Inches	Weight Pounds
1	60"	105
2	61"	110
3	62"	117
4	64"	121
5	66"	128
6	67"	140
7	70"	152
8	72"	180
9	73"	192
10	75"	265
Totals	**670"**	**1,510 lbs.**

To graph these height and weight data points, the vertical axis of your graph should show weight and the horizontal axis should show height. Then, plot the points for the data and it will look like the graph in Figure A-6. From this graph, you can *see* a mathematical relationship. In general, the taller a person is, the heavier he or she is. While this is not always true, it does tell us the general relationship or rule.

AVERAGES AND DISTRIBUTIONS

It can be helpful to describe data points in more general terms. A *distribution* is a list of observations ordered from lowest to highest. In Figure A-5, the heights and weights for Summit clarinet players are presented as a distribution.

One way of summarizing data is to calculate the average or mean. The *average* or *mean* is the sum of the values for each variable divided by the number of observations. In our example, the mean height is the sum of the individual heights divided by the total number of students measured. The mean weight is the sum of the individual weights divided by the total number of students. The mean height and weight for clarinet players at Summit are calculated as follows:

$$\text{Mean height} = \frac{\text{Total height}}{\text{Number of students}} = \frac{670''}{10} = 67''$$

$$\text{Mean weight} = \frac{\text{Total weight}}{\text{Number of students}} = \frac{1{,}510 \text{ lbs.}}{10} = 151 \text{ lbs.}$$

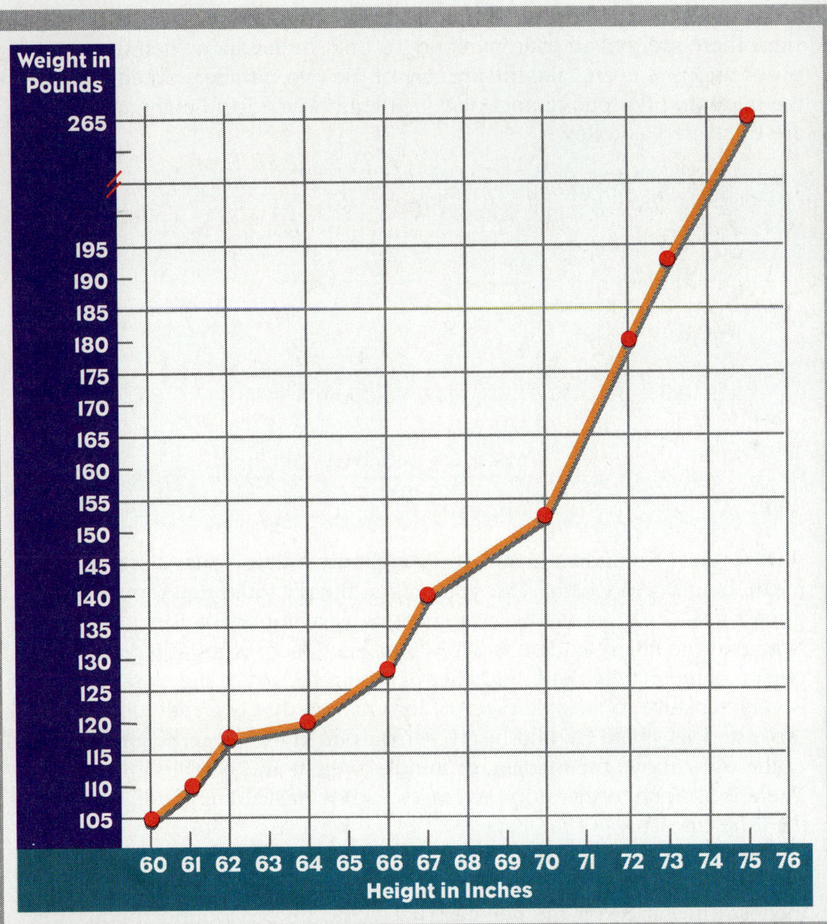

Figure A-6

Line Graph of Height and Weight for Clarinet Players

This line graph is a visual representation of the data in Figure A-5.

The mean height, then, is 67 inches (5'7") and the mean weight is 151 pounds. These average measurements would be one way of describing all ten students at one time. However, it is important to notice that no clarinet player actually is 5'7" tall and weighs 151 pounds.

The median and the range are two other important measures of data. The *median* is the middle number in a distribution. One-half of all the numbers fall above the median, and one-half fall below. When there are an odd number of observations in the list, the median is simply the middle number when the numbers are listed from low to high. Consider the following five numbers:

M
13 16 20 28 35

As indicated by the M, the median is 20, the middle number.

How do you determine the median height and weight for clarinet players, since there are ten, an even number? To find the median when the number of observations is even, take the average of the two numbers on either side of the midpoint. For our clarinet players, then, the median height and weight are calculated as follows:

Height: 60 61 62 64 66 Midpoint 67 70 72 73 75

$$\text{Median height: } \frac{66'' + 67''}{2} = \frac{133''}{2} = 66.5''$$

Weight: 105 110 117 121 128 Midpoint 140 152 180 192 265

$$\text{Median weight: } \frac{128 \text{ lbs.} + 140 \text{ lbs.}}{2} = \frac{268 \text{ lbs.}}{2} = 134 \text{ lbs.}$$

Note that the median height and weight are a little below the average, or mean, height and weight. Can you look at the data and figure out why this is true? If you can, you will know something very important about averages. Note that the tallest student is 6'3" (75 inches) and weighs 265 pounds. This person is much taller and much heavier than the rest of the class. The mean is very sensitive to a single piece of information that is greatly different from the rest. This single tall and heavy person pulled the mean height and weight of the class above the median, or middle, weight and height of the class. There is a moral to this story: Averages can be misleading if you don't look at the other measures of the data.

The *range* is the largest number in a set of data minus the smallest number. The range of height would be 75 inches minus 60 inches, or 15 inches. The range on the weight data would be 265 pounds minus 105 pounds, or a range of 160 pounds. There is quite a wide range on both height and weight here. If the ranges were lower, what do you think would happen to the difference between the mean value and the median value? They would probably be closer to each other since there would not be individual pieces of data that were so much higher or lower than the rest.

When thinking about the concepts of mean, median, and range, it is important to understand how they are applied to economics. For example, you might see in the newspapers or on television that the median family income in the United States is approximately $35,000. Ask yourself why they chose to report the median income and not the mean income. The answer is simple. The range of family incomes in our economy is relatively large (from several thousand to millions of dollars per year). If the mean were reported, it might not give an accurate picture of what the "average" family earns. Since we have a large middle class in America, the median of $35,000 tells us that one-half of the families earns more and one-half earns less. The median gives us a more descriptive picture of family income in our economy.

RATIOS AND PERCENTAGES

A *ratio* shows the relationship of one numerical value to another numerical value. Ratios are often expressed in a form such as 5:1, which is pronounced, "5 to 1." A ratio is calculated by expressing two numbers as a fraction and then reducing the fraction to its lowest terms.

For example, consumers can do only two things with their after-tax incomes: They can spend (consume) or save them. In other words, consumers use their incomes for consumption and savings. Suppose that a family earns $30,000 after taxes and consumes (spends) $24,000. Savings, then, are $6,000. The proportion between these two activities is very important. In our example, the family spends four times as much as is saves:

$$\frac{\textbf{Consumption}}{\textbf{Savings}} = \frac{\$24{,}000}{\$6{,}000} = \frac{4}{1}$$

Our calculation reveals a consumption to savings ratio of 4:1. Another way of stating this proportion is that, on the average, for every $1 the family saves, it spends (consumes) $4. This concept of ratios can be extended to include income. What is the ratio of spending to after-tax income for this family? The answer is $24,000/$30,000 or 24:30 or 4:5. On the average, for every $5 earned, this family spends $4 and saves $1.

A *percentage* is a ratio that has been converted into a base of 100 equal parts. To get a percentage from a ratio, divide the numerator of a ratio by its denominator and multiply the result by 100. For example, what percentage of its income does this average American family consume? Divide consumption ($24,000) by income ($30,000) and multiply the result by 100. This average family consumes 80 percent of its income:

$$\frac{\$24{,}000}{\$30{,}000} = 0.80$$

$$0.80 \times 100 = 80\%$$

Percentages also can show how much a number has changed. For example, suppose you were making $5.00 per hour and then you received a raise to $5.50. The percentage change in your wage rate could be figured by finding the difference between your old wage and new wage, dividing by your old wage, and then converting the result to a percentage:

$$\frac{\$5.50 - \$5.00}{\$5.00} = \frac{\$0.50}{\$5.00} = 0.10$$

$$0.10 \times 100 = 10\%$$

Your new wage, then, would be 10 percent greater than your old wage.

RATES AND ABSOLUTE NUMBERS

Economic reports in the news media can be confusing because so many numbers are used. One of the most frequent mix-ups concerns percentage rates and absolute numbers. For example, you might hear that inflation is up 3 percent, or the money supply is growing at an annual rate of 5 percent, or the economy grew at 7 percent last year. The basic difference between rates and absolute numbers is that *rates* tell you how fast *absolute* numbers are changing. If you drive your car 200 miles at a speed of 50 miles per hour, then 50 miles per hour is the rate at which you are traveling. Two hundred miles is an absolute number that tells the distance you traveled.

The classic economic example of rate versus absolute numbers involves the rate of inflation. The rate of inflation tells us how fast prices are rising. When the headline in a newspaper reads, "Inflation increases to 15 percent," it means that prices are going up at a rate of 15 percent per year. If, in the next week, the same newspaper has a headline reading, "Inflation falls to 10 percent," it does not mean that absolute prices are falling. What it does mean is that absolute prices are rising at a slower rate (i.e., going up more slowly) than before.

To understand how relationships between rates and absolutes appear on a graph, look at the various graphs in Figure A-7 and read over the descriptions of what is happening under each graph. In each graph, the economic variable is some absolute number. Two examples of such absolute numbers would be Gross Domestic Product and sales of a company. The slope of the lines in the graphs tells you something about the rate of change in those absolute numbers.

INDEX NUMBERS

Index numbers are used by economists to show relative changes in factors such as consumer prices and gross domestic product. Index numbers set a base period and measure the changes from the base period to the present. The base period is usually considered to have an index value of 100 (or 100 percent). The other numbers, such as prices in the current year, are then expressed as a percentage of the prices in the base period. For example, for a typical market basket of goods in the 1982–1984 base period, the price index is set at 100. The remaining years' price indexes then show the percentage by which prices have increased over the base period. Figure A-8 on page 690 shows the price index of the same market basket of goods for the years 1980, 1985, 1990, and 1995.

Since the 1985 price index of 107.6 is greater than 100, it shows that 1985 prices were higher than prices in the base period. As you can see, the average level of prices rose steadily from 1980 to 1995. Index numbers are a quick and relatively accurate way to measure increases or decreases in any variable relative to a base period.

NOMINAL AND REAL VALUES

Dollar measurements in economics can be expressed in either nominal or real terms. For example, if you get paid a salary of $300 per week, your nominal income is $300 per week or $15,600 per year. If you receive the same

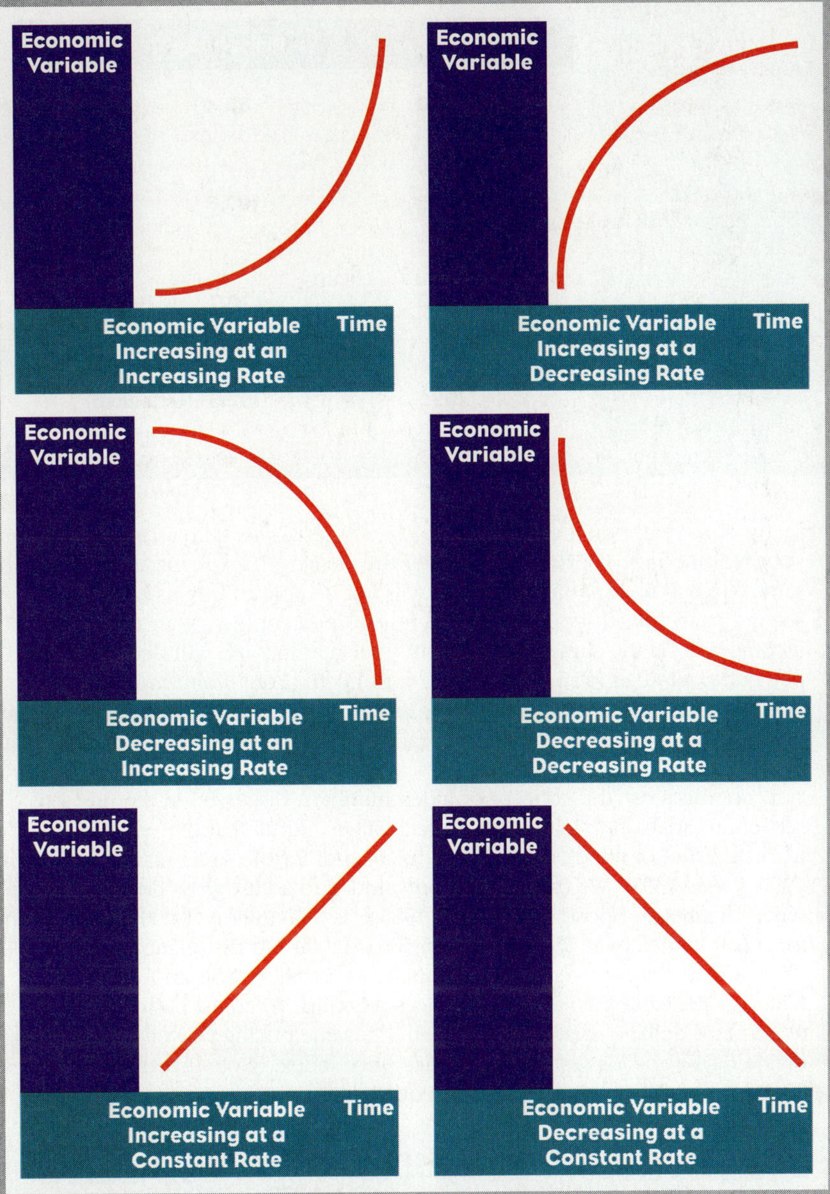

Figure A-7

Absolute Numbers and Their Rates of Change

These graphs are visual representations of a variety of different rates, both increasing and decreasing.

Figure A-8

Price Indexes for Selected Years

The price indexes in this table show the percentages by which prices have increased over the years shown.

SOURCE: *Economic Report of the President: 1995* (Washington, D.C.: U.S. Government Printing Office, 1995), 341.

Year	Price Index
1980	82.4
1985	107.6
1990	130.7
1995	152.5 (estimated)

salary next year, you'll earn another $15,600. But, let's take a closer look at your real income. If prices go up over the year by 10 percent and you get the same $15,600 nominal income, you will not be able to buy as much in the second year. In fact, your salary will buy 10 percent less. Your nominal income will be the same, $15,600, but your real income will decline by 10 percent to $14,040 ($15,600 – $1,560 = $14,040). Your *nominal income* is your income measured in dollars for this year. Your *real income* is the buying power of your nominal income. A real value in economics is a nominal value adjusted for changes in prices.

Economists use the concept of index numbers, discussed in the previous section, to adjust nominal values to real values. Recall that the price index for a market basket of goods in 1985 was 107.6, and, for the same market basket in 1990, it was 130.7. We can use this price index to adjust gross domestic product (GDP) figures. Suppose that GDP in 1985 was $4.0 trillion ($4,000,000,000) and that GDP in 1990 was $5.5 trillion ($5,500,000,000). At first glance, it might look as if GDP increased over the five years by $1.5 trillion. You know, however, that over the same period of time prices went up. To adjust both values of GDP to constant dollars—that is, dollars with the same buying power—you need to divide GDP for each year by that year's price index. (Note that the price index is divided by 100 when used in this equation.)

$$\text{1985 Real GDP} = \frac{\text{1985 Nominal GDP}}{\text{1985 Price Index}} = \frac{\$4{,}000{,}000{,}000}{1.076} = \$3{,}717{,}472{,}118$$

$$\text{1990 Real GDP} = \frac{\text{1990 Nominal GDP}}{\text{1990 Price Index}} = \frac{\$5{,}500{,}000{,}000}{1.307} = \$4{,}208{,}110{,}175$$

As the calculations show, real GDP did not go up $1.5 trillion. After adjusting for inflation, it "only" went up by about $491 million ($4,208,110,175 – $3,717,472,118 = $490,638,057).

APPENDIX B

United States Political Map

World Political Map

691

UNITED STATES
CANADA
Olympia
WASHINGTON
Columbia
River
Salem
OREGON
IDAHO
Boise
Snake River
MONTANA
Helena
NORTH DAKOTA
Bismarck
Red River
SOUTH DAKOTA
Pierre
Minnesota
Missouri
River
WYOMING
Cheyenne
NEBRASKA
Lincoln
Great Salt Lake
Carson City
NEVADA
Sacramento
CALIFORNIA
Salt Lake City
UTAH
Denver
COLORADO
Topeka
KANSAS
Arkansas
River
PACIFIC OCEAN
Colorado
ARIZONA
Phoenix
Santa Fe
NEW MEXICO
OKLAHOMA
Oklahoma City
Red River
TEXAS
Austin
Brazos River
Rio Grande
MEXICO
RUSSIA
ARCTIC OCEAN
ALASKA
Yukon River
CANADA
Juneau
PACIFIC OCEAN
Honolulu
HAWAII
PACIFIC OCEAN

POLITICAL

Projection: Transverse Mercator
MAINE
Augusta
VERMONT
Montpelier
NEW HAMPSHIRE
Concord
Boston
MASSACHUSETTS
Providence
RHODE ISLAND
CONNECTICUT
Hartford
Albany
NEW YORK
L. Ontario
Lake Superior
Lake Huron
Lake Michigan
Lake Erie
MINNESOTA
St. Paul
WISCONSIN
Madison
MICHIGAN
Lansing
IOWA
Des Moines
ILLINOIS
Springfield
INDIANA
Indianapolis
OHIO
Columbus
PENNSYLVANIA
Harrisburg
Trenton
NEW JERSEY
Dover
DELAWARE
Annapolis
Washington, D.C.
MARYLAND
WEST VIRGINIA
Charleston
Richmond
VIRGINIA
Ohio River
Frankfort
KENTUCKY
Jefferson City
MISSOURI
Raleigh
NORTH CAROLINA
Nashville
TENNESSEE
ARKANSAS
Little Rock
Mississippi River
MISSISSIPPI
Jackson
ALABAMA
Montgomery
Atlanta
GEORGIA
SOUTH CAROLINA
Columbia
Tallahassee
LOUISIANA
Baton Rouge
FLORIDA
Lake Okeechobee
ATLANTIC OCEAN
Gulf of Mexico
N
TROPIC OF CANCER

WORLD

Countries of EUROPE Inset

1. Albania	8. Croatia	15. Greece	22. Macedonia	29. Slovakia
2. Andorra	9. Czech. Rep.	16. Hungary	23. Moldova	30. Slovenia
3. Austria	10. Denmark	17. Italy	24. Netherlands	31. Sweden
4. Belarus	11. Estonia	18. Latvia	25. Norway	32. Switzerland
5. Belgium	12. Finland	19. Liechtenstein	26. Poland	33. Ukraine
6. Bosnia	13. France	20. Lithuania	27. Romania	34. Yugoslavia
7. Bulgaria	14. Germany	21. Luxembourg	28. San Marino	(35.) Russia

POLITICAL

Projection: Robinson

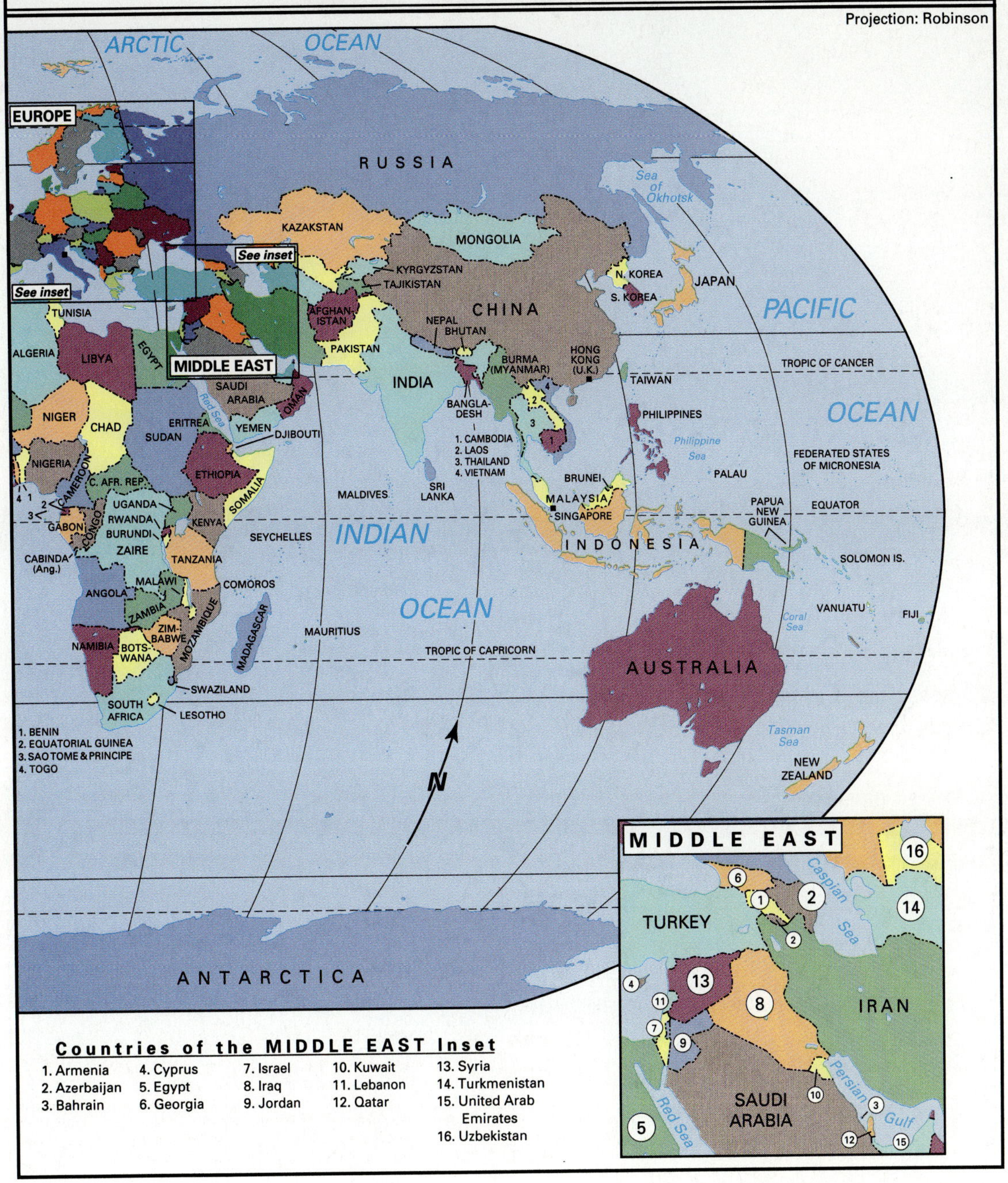

APPENDIX C

Careers in Your Future

Choosing a career is one of the most important decisions you will ever face. Preparing for the career of your choice through education and training is only part of successful career planning. You must also look at what tomorrow's job opportunities will be. In this appendix, you will read about projected trends in population and the composition of the labor force, the link between education and job opportunities, and growth in the service sector. Then, you will see some helpful job search hints. Finally, a variety of career choices are described to give you a broad overview of the types of jobs awaiting you.

The following additional career planning information is provided in the *Life Skills* worksheets, available from your teacher:

Chapter	Career Planning Topic
12	College application
15	Scholarship application
16	Job application
22	Résumé template

POPULATION TRENDS

Employment opportunities are affected in several ways by population trends. Changes in the size and composition of the population between now and 2005 will influence the demand for goods and services, which will affect the demand for jobs. For example, the percentage of the population who is aged 85 and over will grow about four times as fast as the total population, increasing the demand for health services. This may mean an increase in jobs in health services.

The U.S. civilian noninstitutional population, aged 16 and over, is expected to increase to about 219 million by 2005, growing more slowly than it has in the recent past. However, even slower population growth still will increase the demand for goods and services, as well as the demand for workers in many occupations and industries.

The age distribution will shift into the twenty-first century toward relatively fewer teenagers and a growing proportion of middle-aged and older people. The decline in the proportion of teenagers reflects the lower birth rates that prevailed during the 1980s; the impending large increase in the middle-aged population reflects the aging of the "baby boom" generation born between 1946 and 1964; and the very rapid growth in the number of old people is attributable to high birth rates prior to the 1930s and improvements in medical technology that have allowed most Americans to live longer.

697

Minorities and immigrants will constitute a larger share of the U.S. population in 2005 than they do today. Substantial increases in the number of Hispanics, Asians, and African Americans are anticipated.

Population growth varies greatly among geographic regions, affecting the demand for goods and services and, in turn, the number of workers required by various occupations and industries. Projections by the Bureau of the Census indicate that the West and South will continue to be the fastest growing regions, increasing 24 percent and 16 percent, respectively, by 2005. The Midwest population is expected to grow by 7 percent, while the number of people in the Northeast is projected to increase by only 3 percent.

COMPOSITION OF THE LABOR FORCE

Population is the single most important factor governing the size and composition of the labor force. The civilian labor force is expected to reach 151 million by 2005. America's workers will be an increasingly diverse group as we move toward 2005. White non-Hispanic men will make up a slightly smaller proportion of the labor force, and women and minority group members will comprise a larger share.

The changing age structure of the population will directly affect tomorrow's labor force. Compared to the pool of young workers, that of experienced workers will increase. In 1992, the median age of the labor force was 37.2 years; by 2005, it will be 40.5 years. Young people are expected to comprise roughly the same percentage of the labor force in 2005 as they did in 1992. The scenario should be somewhat different for prime-age workers (25 to 54 years of age). The baby boom generation will continue to add members to the labor force, but their share of the labor force peaked in 1985. The proportion of workers in the 25–34 age range will decline dramatically, from 28 percent to 21 percent in 2005. The growing proportion of workers between the ages of 45 and 54 is equally striking. These workers should account for 24 percent of the labor force by the year 2005.

EDUCATION AND JOB OPPORTUNITIES

In recent years, the level of educational attainment of the labor force has risen dramatically. In 1996, at least 27 percent of all workers aged 25 and over had bachelor's degrees or higher, while only 12 percent did not possess high school diplomas. The trend toward higher educational attainment is expected to continue. Projected rates of employment growth are faster for occupations requiring higher levels of education or training than for those requiring less.

Three out of the four fastest growing occupational groups will be executive, administrative, and managerial; professional specialty; and technical and related support. These occupations, which generally require the highest levels of education and skill, will make up an increasing proportion of new jobs. Office and factory automation, changes in consumer demand, and movement of production facilities to other countries are expected to cause employment to stagnate or decline in many occupations that require little formal education. Opportunities for those who do not finish high school will be increasingly limited.

Those who do not complete high school and are employed are more likely to have low-paying jobs with little advancement potential, while workers in occupations requiring higher levels of education will have higher incomes. In addition, many of the occupations projected to grow most rapidly are among those with higher earnings.

GROWTH IN THE SERVICE SECTOR

The long-term shift from goods-producing to service-producing employment is expected to continue. Service-producing industries, including transportation, communications, and utilities; retail and wholesale trade; services; government; and finance, insurance, and real estate are expected to account for approximately 24.5 million of the 26.4 million new jobs available between now and 2005. Expansion of service-sector employment is linked to a number of factors, including changes in consumer tastes and preferences, legal and regulatory changes, advances in science and technology, and changes in the way businesses are organized and managed.

Continued expansion of the service-producing sector conjures up an image of a workforce dominated by cashiers, retail sales workers, and waiters. Although service-sector growth will generate millions of these jobs, it also will create jobs for financial managers, engineers, nurses, electrical and electronics technicians, and many other managerial, professional, and technical workers. As indicated earlier, the fastest growing occupations will be those that require the most formal education and training.

JOB SEARCH TIPS

It takes some people a long time to find the job they want. Don't be discouraged if you have to pursue many leads. Friends, neighbors, teachers, and counselors may know of available jobs in your area of interest. Read the want ads. Consult state employment service offices and private or nonprofit employment agencies, or contact employers directly.

Once you get an interview, keep the following recommendations in mind:

- Be prepared.
- Learn about the organization and review your qualifications for the job.
- Practice the interview with a friend or relative.
- Before you leave for the interview, gather your social security number, driver's license, a résumé (if required), and the names of three references (get permission from the references first).
- On the day of the interview, dress appropriately, arrive before the scheduled time of your interview, and do not chew gum or smoke.
- During the actual interview, answer the questions concisely, use good manners, and be enthusiastic. This is your chance to impress on the interviewer that you will be a good employee who is a benefit to the company.
- Always thank the interviewer and follow up with a letter.

DESCRIPTION OF JOBS

Occupation	Nature of Work	Education and Training	Job Growth Outlook	Earnings at Entry Level
Accountant	Prepare, analyze, and verify financial reports and taxes and monitor information systems that furnish this information.	Bachelor's degree; CPA recommended	Faster than the average	$28,000
Actor	Entertain and communicate through interpretation of dramatic roles.	Formal dramatic training or acting experience	Much faster than the average	Earnings vary greatly
Automotive mechanic	Repair and service automobiles.	High school education and formal training program	As fast as the average	$11,960
Bank Teller	Handle a wide range of banking transactions.	High school education	Declining	Federal minimum wage
Chef	Prepare food.	No formal requirement	Faster than the average	Earnings vary greatly
Computer Analyst	Conduct research, design computers, and discover and use principles of applying computers.	Bachelor's degree	Much faster than the average	$22,700
Economist	Conduct research, monitor economic trends, and develop forecasts. Study the ways a society uses scarce resources to produce goods and services.	Bachelor's degree	As fast as the average	$25,200

Occupation	Nature of Work	Education and Training	Job Growth Outlook	Earnings at Entry Level
Electrician	Install and maintain electrical systems.	4- or 5-year apprenticeship program	As fast as the average	$13,520
Engineer	Apply the theories and principles of science and mathematics to the solution of technical problems.	Bachelor's degree	As fast as the average	$34,000
Home Health Aide	Help elderly, disabled, and ill people live in their own homes instead of in a health facility.	Federal competency exam	Much faster than the average	Earnings vary greatly
Lawyer	Counsel clients as to their legal rights and obligations and represent parties in criminal and civil trials.	Law school and state bar examination	Faster than the average	$36,600
Occupational Therapist	Help individuals with disabling conditions to develop or maintain daily living and work skills.	Bachelor's degree	Much faster than the average	$30,470
Paralegal	Assist lawyers in preparing cases, investigating facts, conducting research, and preparing written reports.	Formal paralegal training programs, associate's degree, or bachelor's degree	Much faster than the average	$23,400

Occupation	Nature of Work	Education and Training	Job Growth Outlook	Earnings at Entry Level
Physician	Examine patients, obtain medical histories, and interpret diagnostic tests.	Medical school, residency, and licensing exam	Faster than the average	$28,618 (first-year resident)
Police officer	Prevent and investigate crimes.	High school education and written and physical exams	More slowly than the average	$18,400
Radiologic Technologist	Use radiation, ultrasound, and magnetic resonance scans to produce images of the interior of the body.	Certificate, associate degree, or bachelor's degree	Much faster than the average	$22,250
Reporter	Gather information and prepare stories about local, national, and international events.	Bachelor's degree	As fast as the average	$22,000
Retail Sales Worker	Assist customers in the selection and purchase of retail items.	No formal training required	As fast as the average	Federal minimum wage
Secretary	Perform and coordinate office activities.	High school education with office skills	More slowly than the average	$16,400
Teacher	Educate children in specific subject areas and teach abstract concepts, problem solving, and critical thought processes.	Bachelor's degree and state certification	Faster than the average	$24,000

Occupation	Nature of Work	Education and Training	Job Growth Outlook	Earnings at Entry Level
Travel Agent	Assist clients with personal and business travel plans.	Vocational training program or associate's degree	Much faster than the average	$12,428
Truck driver	Transport goods by truck.	Commercial driver's license	As fast as the average	$18,000
Veterinarian	Care for pets, livestock, and sporting and laboratory animals. Advise owners on care and breeding.	Doctor of Veterinary Medicine degree and state board exam	Faster than the average	$27,858
Visual Artist	Use a variety of methods and materials to communicate ideas visually.	No formal training required but demonstrated ability and appropriate training as shown in a portfolio	As fast as the average	$21,000

SOURCE: *Occupational Outlook Handbook 1994–1995 Edition* (Washington, D.C.: U.S. Government Printing Office, 1994).

APPENDIX D

Consumer Economic Issues

Consumers face many economic decisions in our complex world. This appendix will examine the importance of managing your money, using credit wisely, investing, managing consumer risk, and your role as a consumer in the marketplace.

MONEY MANAGEMENT

Money management is a plan for controlling and spending income. Money management requires personal application of the decision-making process first introduced in chapters 1 and 2. Money management involves scarcity and opportunity costs as you decide what tradeoffs will be made when you spend your limited income.

Budgeting

A *budget* is an estimate of expected income, expenses, and savings. It is a tool to help you reach your financial goals. Following a budget is a key to good money management. By using a budget, you can make good money decisions and spend your limited financial resources in ways that truly satisfy you.

The first step in preparing a budget is setting goals and priorities. Few people can afford to waste income. Setting consumer goals is a way to decide how to use limited income for the best results.

The second step in preparing a budget is estimating your income for a specific time period. You should estimate the amount of all income that you are sure you will receive, including wages, interest on a savings account or certificate of deposit, stock dividends, and gifts.

After you have estimated your income, the next step is estimating expenses. When your estimate of income is equal to your estimate of expenses, you have a balanced budget, but estimating expenses can be a very difficult step. It helps to separate regular expenses from those that can change from month to month.

Regular expenses such as rent or mortgage payments, telephone bill, loan payments, and insurance are called *fixed expenses.* Some people put a regular savings amount into this category. Although savings is not really an expense, if you save regularly, this fixed amount can be included in this category. Saving this way is a good idea.

705

Expenses that are likely to change from month to month are called *variable expenses*. These include items such as food, clothing, transportation, health care, and entertainment. Even these variable expenses can be estimated to an approximate amount.

Remember, a budget is a plan for estimating income and spending. Adjustments may be made within the budget. One purpose of a budget is to make sure that spending does not exceed income. The more realistic your budget is, the better you will be able to follow it. Self-discipline is also required to follow it and make it work for you.

Savings Accounts

A savings account gives you the opportunity to earn interest on money that you have deposited in it. A savings account can help you establish the habit of saving. Having your own savings account makes it easier for you to cash checks that you may receive. Different financial institutions offer different kinds of savings accounts. You should compare interest rates, bank location, bank business hours, automatic teller access, and the initial deposit amount required before choosing the financial institution for your savings account.

When opening a savings account, you will fill out a signature card. This card serves as the basic record for the account. It lists your name and address and the amount of the initial deposit. You then will be given a passbook in which all of your deposits and withdrawals should be noted.

Checking Accounts

Most financial transactions in the country involve checks. A *check* is a written order for payment. The dollar value of transactions handled by check is far greater than that of transactions involving cash. Checks provide a record of a transaction and are safer than using cash. Different financial institutions offer different types of checking accounts. It is important to find out what types are offered when you are choosing among different financial institutions.

To open a checking account, you will fill out a signature card and make an initial deposit. You then will be given a supply of checks and a *check register*, which is a booklet for record keeping. (Some checking accounts use check stubs or carbon copies of the checks for record keeping rather than check registers.)

Writing checks involves two procedures. The first is filling out the check register or check stub, if appropriate. It is very important to fill out the check register or stub first because you might forget to do it later. If this happened, you could easily lose track of how much money you had in the account. This might cause you to bounce a check, or write a check for money you did not have in the account, which is called *being overdrawn*. This can be both embarrassing and expensive, since most banks charge a fee for bounced checks or overdrawn accounts.

The second procedure in writing checks involves filling out the check itself. Be sure to use permanent ink. Never use a pencil or erasable ink, so that no one else can change the amount of your check in an effort to take money from you. To actually write the check, you should do the following:

1. write the date on the date line;
2. write in the name of the payee (the person or company being paid);
3. write in the amount of the check in numbers next to the dollar sign;
4. write in the amount of the check in words next to the word *dollars;*
5. write in the purpose of the check on the memo line; and
6. sign your name exactly as you signed it on the signature card.

When making a deposit to your checking account, either through an automatic teller machine, by direct deposit from your paycheck, or with the help of a teller at the financial institution itself, make sure you note the deposit in your check register or on your check stub. This will allow you to keep accurate checking account records.

The financial institution will send you a periodic report of the activity in your checking account. The report is usually made monthly and is called a *statement.* Some financial institutions also return your cancelled, or used, checks. The statement lists checks paid, interest payments, deposits, and any service charges made. The statement also includes the balance in your account the day the statement was prepared. This statement will not necessarily agree with your check register or stubs. There may be checks you have written that are still outstanding, some of your deposits may not have been received before the statement was prepared, or an error may have been made—by you or the financial institution. That is why it is very important to *reconcile* your statement, which means to try to make the statement agree with your records. A reconciliation form will be printed on the reverse side of the statement you receive. If you complete the reconciliation form and your statement and records still do not match, report the problem right away. The financial institution will compare your account records with its records and help you find the difference.

CONSUMER CREDIT

Credit is not a form of income. Credit is a borrower's promise to pay at some future time. When you use credit, you are actually borrowing against your future income. A seller or lender trusts you to pay later for goods or services you receive now. Whether the amount borrowed is large or small, the use of credit is an important part of a consumer's life. To use credit wisely, you must be aware of its advantages and disadvantages.

Advantages of Credit

To buy a major consumer good, such as a car, it would take years to save enough money to pay for the good outright. During the time when you were saving, you would not have the benefit of using the good. If you did not really need a car and had other options for transportation, it might be good to save the money. However, if you really needed a car, using credit to buy it would be an advantage. You could use the car when you needed it and pay for it in the future. For example, if you needed the car for a job, using credit would allow you to take the job where you could earn the income needed to buy the car. Another advantage of credit is that it allows you to carry less cash, which is both a convenience and a safety measure. Credit is also convenient when ordering over the telephone or by mail.

Disadvantages of Credit

For most arguments in favor of using credit, there are equally strong reasons for not using it. People tend to buy more when they use credit. They also tend to buy higher priced merchandise. Even though the bills for credit purchases must be paid eventually, some consumers buy on credit as if there is no tomorrow. Some consumers lose control of their spending when they use credit. Another disadvantage of credit is that it costs money. Credit is a financial service that you pay for in interest. This interest can add a great deal to the cost of an item if you carry a balance on your credit cards or loan.

INVESTMENTS

Millions of people set aside a portion of the money they do not spend for food, clothing, shelter and other needed items. Some people put this money into savings accounts, others put the money to work by investing it.

Many consumers invest their money by buying securities. Securities include stocks and bonds. People who buy securities hope that, over a period of time, the value of their investments will grow. They hope the money will earn more interest or dividends than it would in a savings account.

Many consumers choose not to buy securities because investing can be risky. The risk is that money may be lost—investments are not insured as are savings accounts. Securities can and do decline in price sometimes. The more you learn about the kinds of investments available, the better your decisions will be.

Stocks and Bonds

Corporations obtain the money they need to start and continue their operations by selling stocks and bonds. Buying corporate stocks and bonds is a common investment activity.

Stocks represent ownership in a company. When you buy common stock, you become a shareholder and part owner in the company that issues the stock. A *share* of stock is one of the equal parts into which the ownership of a company is divided. If things go well for the company, the price of the stock might increase, increasing the value of your stock investment. There is no limit to how much any stock can increase in price. This is one of the main reasons people buy common stock. *Dividend* is money earned as profits by the company and divided among the shareholders. If the company does well, dividends paid out will be high. So, stocks earn money for stockholders through dividends and through their increasing value. Over a long period of time, stocks have done better than other forms of investments, but this does not mean that every stock will do well. Therefore, it is necessary to know as much as possible about a company before investing in its stock.

A *bond* is a certificate representing a loan of money to a corporation or government. The organization that issues the bond agrees to pay back the money, with interest, within a certain time period. When you buy a bond, you lend an organization money, you receive interest, and you are repaid the money when the time period is up.

How to Invest

You can invest money individually or through a financial group. Either way, the more information you have about different investments, the better your decisions will be. Before investing in a company's stock or bonds, read a company's annual report. The *annual report* describes a company's type of business, sales and earnings, and financial condition. You also should read the financial sections of newspapers, where you will find articles and stock market reports that will increase your understanding. Special magazines and newspapers provide detailed information about stocks and bonds. *The Wall Street Journal, Money, Fortune,* and *Barrons* are all useful sources of investment information. The wise investor will follow the stock market averages to find out how the stock market is doing on a daily basis. The Dow Jones Industrial Average is probably the most widely watched stock market average. Other popular stock market averages are issued by the New York Stock Exchange, Standard and Poor's, and the Nikkei Index (from Japan).

In addition to being informed, you should follow three major investment principles:

1. set investment goals,
2. diversify your investments, and
3. review and revise your investments periodically.

Other Investments

You have a wide range of investment opportunities. Some people choose to invest in real estate, works of art, stamp or coin collections, rare books, antique cars, and thoroughbred horses. Some people invest in certificates of deposit (CDs), which are investments in which the investor agrees to leave money on deposit in a financial institution for a definite period, such as six months or several years. The interest paid is generally higher than that paid for regular savings accounts.

MANAGING CONSUMER RISK

A risk is the possibility of loss. As individuals and as consumers, we face many risks in life. All risks have an element of uncertainty. You do not know for sure that they will happen. You do not know if you will become ill, lose a wallet, or wreck your car. If you knew in advance, you would avoid the loss. It is impossible to completely remove all risks. But you can take steps to reduce them.

Insurance

Insurance is a system by which risks of loss are spread among a number of people. Many people who face similar risks, such as car owners, pay a relatively small amount of money, called a *premium,* to an insurance company. The insurance company, in turn, issues a policy to the consumer, who is the policyholder. The insurance company agrees to pay a certain amount of money if the policyholder suffers losses that are covered by the policy. Insurance policies can cover many different risks, such as automobile accidents, fire, and theft.

Types of Risk

One major category of risk that consumers face is property loss. Consumers are very concerned about the risk of damage to or theft of their property. People whose homes are damaged by fire often lose the use of their homes while they are being repaired or rebuilt. A driver who has been in an accident may lose the use of the car while it is being repaired. These risks of loss of the *use* of property, as well as the loss of property itself, can be covered by insurance.

A second major category of risk that consumers face is the risk of liability loss. To be liable means to be responsible. Most cases of liability are related to car accidents, but many cases involve accidents around the home. An injured person might sue the home owner and the home owner may have to pay an amount decided by the court. People who have been found liable for injuries to someone else are often not prepared to pay the large amount ordered by a court. If a person does not have enough cash to pay, the court can take away his or her home, car, and other property. Many liability lawsuits involve physical injury. Others involve damage to property. Liability insurance is the most important way to protect against risk of liability.

The risk of loss of income is the third major category of consumer risk. The sudden loss of income resulting from the death or disablement of a wage earner can cause financial hardship. Life insurance is intended to protect against the risk of loss of income due to unexpected, early death. Disability insurance is intended to protect against the loss of income due to serious injury or illness.

Finally, consumers face the risk of unexpected major expenses. The most common unexpected major expense consumers face is for health services. Hospital, medical, and dental costs are very high. Most consumers cannot afford to pay them on their own. Many employers provide insurance to protect employees against the risk of major medical expenses. Consumers can buy individual policies if they are not covered through work.

CONSUMERS IN THE MARKETPLACE

The relationship between buyer and sellers used to be described by the phrase *caveat emptor,* which means "let the buyer beware." As the marketplace changed, the relationship between buyers and sellers changed. By the beginning of the 1960s, the relationship could be described by the phrase *caveat venditor,* which means "let the seller beware."

Consumer Rights and Responsibilities

In 1962, President Kennedy proclaimed the Consumer Bill of Rights, which outlines the basic rights of all consumers. Along with these rights, consumers have certain responsibilities to themselves, the economy, society, and the environment. These rights and responsibilities include the following:

Consumer Rights	Consumer Responsibilities
The right to safety	The responsibility to use products safely
The right to be informed	The responsibility to use information
The right to choose	The responsibility to choose efficiently
The right to be heard	The responsibility to express satisfaction or dissatisfaction
The right to redress or remedy	The responsibility to seek a remedy to consumer problems
The right to consumer education	The responsibility to be an educated consumer

Consumer Legislation

The heart of consumer progress in the United States has been the passage and enforcement of laws that benefit consumers. The following is a sampling of consumer laws passed to protect consumers and provide for controls over producers and sellers:

Law	Major Provisions
Pure Food and Drug Act	Guards against unhealthy and adulterated food and drugs
Meat Inspection Act	Requires inspection of red meat products and establishes sanitation guidelines for meat and poultry processing
Federal Trade Commission Act	Established the Federal Trade Commission and declares unfair methods of competition to be illegal
Kefauver-Harris Amendment	Requires that all drugs be tested for safety and effectiveness before being sold to the public
Fair Packaging and Labeling Act	Requires manufacturers to provide specific information on packages
Consumer Credit Protection Act	Requires lenders to make full disclosure of actual annual interest rates and other costs of credit
Equal Credit Opportunity Act	Prohibits discrimination on the basis of age, gender, race, and religion when approving credit

Law	Major Provisions
Fair Debt Collection Practices Act	Prohibits unfair debt collection tactics
Clean Air Act	Requires the reduction of acid rain and pollution from auto emissions and from coal-burning utilities
Child Care Act	Gives tax credits to working parents and gives grants to states to increase the availability of child-care centers

Getting Help for Consumer Problems

If you are dissatisfied with a product or service, it is your responsibility to express your complaint to the merchant. But, what if the merchant will not resolve the problem? In that case, it is your right to report the problem to the appropriate regulatory commission or another consumer group. Working with a commission or an established consumer group is a very effective way to resolve consumer complaints.

Approximately 22 federal government agencies perform regulatory functions and have established programs designed to assist the consumer in dealing with problems and to involve consumers in the government decision-making process. Most government agencies do not handle individual problems. However, if the problem involves the violation of the law, the agency will be interested. Following is a list of some of the federal agencies that protect consumers through enforcement of federal legislation:

- Federal Information Centers
- Department of Agriculture
- Consumer Product Safety Commission
- Federal Trade Commission
- Food and Drug Administration
- Office of Consumer Affairs

In some communities, businesses collectively provide consumer assistance through such organizations as the Better Business Bureau. If there is a bureau in your community, you can ask about the reputation of a company before you do business with it. You also can report to the Better Business Bureau any problems you have with a certain business. Information about your complaint may then be made available to other consumers.

Some important consumer organizations are available to advance the interests of consumers in the marketplace. The National Consumers League, Consumer Federation of America, American Council on Consumer Interests, Consumers' Research, and Consumers Union are all consumer groups organized to push for changes when they feel the quality of life is being threatened.

SOURCE: Adapted from Joseph Bonnice and Rosella Bannister, *Consumers Make Economic Decisions,* (Cincinnati, Ohio: South-Western Publishing Co., 1990), and D. Hayden Green, *Consumers in the Economy,* (Cincinnati, Ohio: South-Western Publishing Co., 1993).

APPENDIX E

Understanding the Economic Numbers

ECONOMIC INFORMATION IS ALL AROUND YOU

An informed citizen should have a reasonable understanding of the economic data that are reported in both the business and popular media. Many people watch one of the morning or evening network news shows, listen to a radio news program, and/or read a daily newspaper on a somewhat regular basis. From such exposure to the world in which we live, almost anyone probably can name at least a few economic measures that he or she has heard or seen reported. As a student of economics, you probably can name more of them than most people. If you read *The Wall Street Journal, Time, Newsweek,* or *Business Week,* you might be able to name dozens of important measures of the economy. The ones you name might be different from those named by a classmate because each of you is likely to focus on one that for one reason or another is of particular interest.

In this discussion, some of the economic measures many economists and businesspeople think are important are described, and some information about their publication schedule is provided. Determining which measures to include was difficult because there are so many measures. As you read through the following paragraphs, you almost certainly will recognize most of the measures as being reported regularly in the mass media.

It is impossible to provide *current* economic data in a printed textbook that will be used in a classroom for several years. The data quickly will become outdated. For this reason, throughout this appendix there are references to online sources of economic information. If you have access to the Internet, you can use these addresses to find the most current data available. For example, the *Economic Report of the President,* which can be accessed online at **gopher://umslvma.umsl.edu:70/11/library/govdocs.erps**, contains much of the economic data you might need. Many economic indicators are updated by the Fed at **http://great-lakes.net:2200/0/partners/ChicagoFed/econind**.

However, it is the nature of the Internet that addresses change and a Web site that is here today might be gone tomorrow. If that should happen, simply contact the Web site for South-Western ECONOMICS at **http://www.thomson.com/swpco/internet/hb29da1.html** for current information on address changes in this text.

713

GROSS DOMESTIC PRODUCT

Gross domestic product (GDP) is the most broad-based measure of economic activity within the country. You can read about GDP in detail in Chapter 14, Measuring Aggregate Economic Activity. GDP is reported by the Department of Commerce on a quarterly basis. The quarterly report of GDP often makes it into the popular news media and is always reported in *The Wall Street Journal,* usually during the third week in January, April, July, and October. You can obtain current GDP figures online from the Census Bureau at **http://www.census.gov/ftp/pub/statab/indicator/gdp.txt** or at **http://www.census.gov/ftp/pub/statab/USAbrief/part2.txt**.

LABOR MARKET REPORTS

The Bureau of Labor Statistics releases data on employment and the unemployment rate on a monthly basis. The employment data are based on a survey of employer payroll records, while the unemployment rate data are based on a broader survey of households. This series is watched closely by businesspeople because of the relation to potential consumer demand. Demand for durable goods and luxury items is particularly sensitive to the unemployment rate.

Employment data are usually reported in the national news media and appear regularly in *The Wall Street Journal,* usually on Monday of the second week of the month. You also can get current employment figures online from the Bureau of Labor Statistics at **http://www.bls.gov/** or from the Census Bureau's *Statistics in Brief* at **http://www.census.gov/ftp/pub/statab/USAbrief/part2.txt**. To examine local and regional unemployment rates, access the Economic Bulletin Board at the University of Michigan at **gopher://una.hh.lib.umich.edu/00/ebb/employment/laus-5.bls**.

PERSONAL INCOME

Personal income includes the income of households from employment (including self-employment), investments, and transfer payments (such as social security). *Disposable personal income* is personal income minus various taxes. These values are important measures of purchasing power.

Data on the level of personal income are provided by the Department of Commerce on a monthly basis. These data are common fare on the evening network news and are always published in *The Wall Street Journal,* usually during the third or fourth week of each month. You can access the Department of Commerce online at **http://www.doc.gov/**. Income information is also available online from the Census Bureau's *Statistics in Brief* at **http://www.census.gov/ftp/pub/statab/USAbrief/part2.txt**.

NEW HOUSING STARTS

New home construction is often viewed as a precursor of things to come because so many other economic activities are tied to housing starts. For example, when a housing start is recorded, construction workers will soon be on the job, new materials (such as lumber, glass, cement, roofing supplies, and heating equipment) will be purchased, and new appliances for kitchens, baths, and laundries will be needed. Private housing starts are counted in the month during which excavation for the foundation begins, while public housing starts are counted when the contract is awarded.

During the third week of each month, the Bureau of the Census publishes data on housing starts for the previous month. This series is published in *The Wall Street Journal* about three weeks into the month following the month for which the data are reported. The Bureau of the Census can be accessed online at **http://www.census.gov/**.

RETAIL SALES

Retail sales are considered to be an indicator of the demand-side strength of the economy. The Bureau of the Census collects monthly data on retail sales using a voluntary survey of retail establishments.

The results are reported in a monthly release of the Department of Commerce titled "Retail Sales." These results are then frequently reported in the popular press, especially around the Christmas holiday shopping season, and they are routinely published in *The Wall Street Journal* during the second week of the month. The data are in nominal terms and are seasonally adjusted. Typically, the reporting focuses on which retail segments were particularly strong or weak in the previous month and offers some explanation of possible reasons. You can reach the Bureau of the Census and get current retail sales data at **http://www.census.gov/**.

CONSUMER ATTITUDES

There are several measures of consumer attitudes, of which the two most commonly cited are probably the Consumer Confidence Index and the Consumer Sentiment Index. The Consumer Confidence Index (CCI) is a monthly series developed by the Consumer Research Center of the Conference Board. The Conference Board publishes the index in two publications: the *Consumer Confidence Survey* and its *Statistical Bulletin*. The Consumer Sentiment Index (CSI) comes from the Survey Research Center at the University of Michigan and is published monthly in its *Survey of Consumer Attitudes*.

The CCI and CSI are both reported in *The Wall Street Journal* from time to time but not on a regular basis. You also may recall them being reported in the popular news media. Both are considered indicators of the future level of consumer spending. You can get information about the CCI online at **http://www.mlinet.com/bci/catBCI.html**. Information about the CSI is available online at **http://www.mlinet.com/bci/pages/u0m058.html**.

PRICE LEVELS

The two most commonly reported measures of prices in the economy are probably the consumer price index (CPI) and the producer price index (PPI). Both are considered measures of inflation, with the PPI being used as an indicator of what might be in store at the consumer level in the future. The CPI and the PPI are based on extensive surveys of consumers and producers, respectively, by the U.S. Department of Labor.

Each month, you can expect to see the CPI and PPI reported in *The Wall Street Journal.* You can find current data on CPI and PPI online at **http://www.census.gov/ftp/pub/statab/indicator/prices.txt** or **gopher://una.hh.lib.umich.edu/00/ebb/indicators/ei.prn**.

THE MONEY SUPPLY

The Federal Reserve is the agency that controls the money supply, and so it is natural to expect that it would be the provider of money supply data. M1 is the most basic measure of the money supply. It is defined to include currency and checking accounts. M2 is a broader measure (including M1 as well as savings deposits, CDs, and money market funds) and is usually considered the best overall measure of the money supply. The money supply data are closely watched by people in business because of the potential impact of the money supply on purchasing power, interest rates, real GDP, and inflation.

Each Thursday, the Fed releases data on the money supply. You might find it interesting to know that it waits to release data until after the New York financial markets have closed to circumvent knee-jerk reactions to the news. *The Wall Street Journal* reports money supply data in a section titled "Closely Watched Reports." The gopher site at **gopher://gopher.great-lakes.net:2200/00/partners/ChicagoFed/finance** provides current information on the money supply.

INTEREST RATES

Notice that the heading for this subsection uses the plural *rates,* not *rate.* This is because there are many interest rates, each of which is important for specific reasons. It may be hard to get universal agreement on which two or three interest rates are the most important, but the prime rate, the federal funds rate, and the discount rate would be high on the list for many business professionals.

The *prime rate* is the rate that large commercial banks charge their best corporate customers. This rate is often viewed as an indicator of the supply and demand conditions in capital markets. The *federal funds rate* is the rate that banks charge one another for very short-term loans (such as overnight) that are used to cover reserve requirements. This rate is also seen as an indicator of the state of money markets. The *discount rate* is the rate that the Federal Reserve charges banks to borrow from the Fed and is one of the instruments of monetary policy. Changes in the discount rate are therefore policy based rather than based on supply and demand conditions as are the prime and federal funds rates. Changes in the discount rate represent what the Fed's intention is with respect to monetary policy and thus may be indicative of an expansionary or restrictive policy.

These, and other interest rates such as mortgage rates, foreign prime rates, and CD rates, are reported daily in *The Wall Street Journal.* Up-to-date information on the federal funds rate, prime rate, and discount rate can be found at **http://great-lakes.net:2200/partners/ChicagoFed/finance/rates_cw.prn**.

INDUSTRIAL PRODUCTION INDEX

This index is released monthly by the Federal Reserve Board. The industrial production index includes agriculture, construction, transportation, communication, trade, finance, service, and government. It is sometimes seen as a gauge of general business fluctuations.

While it is published in *The Federal Reserve Bulletin,* it also is available in a timely manner in the more widely accessible *Wall Street Journal*. For current Industrial Production Index information, travel to **http://great-lakes.net:2200/0/partners/ChicagoFed/econind/indpro_c.prn**.

INDEX OF LEADING ECONOMIC INDICATORS

The index of leading economic indicators is developed by the Bureau of Economic Analysis of the U.S. Department of Commerce. This index is generally accepted as a reasonably good predictor of the future state of economic events, especially unemployment and industrial production. The eleven items that make up the index follow:

1. average weekly hours worked for manufacturing production workers;
2. average initial claims for unemployment insurance;
3. manufacturers' new orders for consumer goods and materials (constant dollars);
4. vendor performance—percentage of companies receiving slower deliveries;
5. contracts and orders for new plant and equipment (constant dollars);
6. index of new private housing units authorized by local building permits;
7. change in manufacturers' unfilled durable goods orders (constant dollars);
8. change in sensitive materials prices;
9. index of stock prices, 500 common stocks;
10. Index of consumer expectations; and
11. money supply (M2 in constant dollars).

The Bureau of Economic Analysis has a Web site at **http://www.bea.doc.gov/beahome.html**, where you can access the Index of Leading Economic Indicators. The index is also published every month in *The Wall Street Journal*.

EXCHANGE RATES

Published exchange rates reflect current trade in currencies between major banks and between banks and their corporate customers. The number of different exchange rates published is large and gives testimony to the truly global nature of today's business world. *The Wall Street Journal* publishes exchange rate data on a daily basis based on what is referred to as an "interbank market." Exchange rate data also are available from the Fed at **http://great-lakes.net:2200/0/partners/ChicagoFed/finance** and at **gopher://una.hh.lib.umich.edu/00/ebb/monetary/noonfx.frb**.

OTHER INTERNET SOURCES OF ECONOMIC DATA

There are many interesting economic sites on the Internet that you might want to visit. Here is a list of some favorites:

Census Bureau

- **http://www.census.gov/ftp/pub/foreign-trade/www/top10.html**
- **http://www.census.gov/ftp/pub/statab/indicator/**
- **http://www.census.gov/ftp/pub/population/www/**

CIA World Factbook

- **http://www.odci.gov/cia/publications/95fact/index.html**

World Bank

- **http://www.worldbank.org/**

GLOSSARY

A

ability-to-pay principle of taxation
the concept that those who can best afford to pay taxes should pay most of the taxes

absolute advantage
exists in the production of a good when one country can produce a good more efficiently than another country

aggregate demand
the total demand of all people for all goods and services produced in an economy

aggregate supply
the total supply of all goods and services in an economy

allocation
the process of choosing which needs will be satisfied and how much of our resources we will use to satisfy them

alternative
a possible course of action

articles of incorporation
a written application to the state requesting permission to form a corporation

asset demand for money
the demand for money in order to hold wealth in the form of money

average product
the number of units of output produced per unit of input

B

balance of payments
the total flow of money into a country minus the total flow of money out of a country

balance of trade
the level of merchandise exports minus the level of merchandise imports

barriers to economic development
economic, social, and political characteristics that prevent an economy from developing

barter
a direct trade of goods or services

benefit principle of taxation
the concept that those who benefit from the spending of tax dollars should pay the taxes to provide the benefits

Board of Governors
a group that supervises the Federal Reserve System

bond
a certificate stating the amount the corporation has borrowed from the holder and the terms of repayment

budget constraint
the mix of goods that can be purchased with a limited amount of income

budget deficit
the amount by which federal government spending exceeds revenues each year

C

capital
goods that are produced and can be used as inputs for further production

cartel
a formal organization of firms in the same industry acting together to make decisions

change in supply
a change in the number of units supplied at every price

change in the quantity supplied
change in the number of units made available for sale due to a *price change*

charter
the legal authorization to organize a business as a corporation

check
a written order to pay money from amounts deposited

civilian labor force
the total number of people in the working age group (16 years and over) who are either employed or actively seeking work

closed shop
a business that agrees to hire only those who are members of a union

collective bargaining
the process of having the union negotiate with management to determine the terms of employment for all workers rather than having each worker negotiate separately

collusion
the situation of firms acting together rather than separately

commercial bank
a type of financial institution that was originally formed to serve businesses but now provides a large number of financial services to both business customers and individuals

common stock
a type of stock that gives the holder a partial ownership of the corporation

comparative advantage
the principle that a country benefits from specializing in the production at which it is relatively most efficient

competition
the rivalry between two or more parties to gain benefits from a third party

complementary products
products that are used together

conglomerate
a firm made up of many divisions and/or subsidiaries that may not have much in common in their lines of business

conglomerate merger
a merger of two companies that are in different businesses

constant dollar GDP
the value of gross domestic product after taking out the effect of price changes

consumer goods
items that are made for final consumption

Consumer Price Index (CPI)
a number used to calculate changes in the average level of prices for a number of items typically bought by urban families

contract
a legally binding agreement between two or more competent persons

corporate bond rate
the interest rate paid on corporate bonds

corporate income tax
a tax on the earnings of corporations

corporation
an organization of people legally bound together by a charter to conduct some type of business

cost-push inflation
a rise in the general level of prices that is caused by increased costs of making and selling goods

creditors
people who have loaned money to others

credit union
a financial intermediary formed around something that its members have in common

criteria
the characteristics of a group of alternatives that will be judged to make a choice

crowding out
the effect on private businesses when increased government borrowing raises interest rates and reduces private borrowing

currency
coins and paper money

cyclical unemployment
unemployment resulting from too low a level of aggregate demand

D

debtors
people who have borrowed money from someone else

decision matrix
a table comparing possible decisions

deflation
a decline in the average level of prices

demand
the quantities of a good that consumers are willing and able to purchase at various prices during a given period of time

demand curve
a graphic illustration of the relationship between *price* and the *quantity demanded* at each price

demand deposit
money that must be paid upon demand by the holder of a check

demand for labor
the amount of labor that firms would want to hire at various wage rates

demand-pull inflation
a rise in the general level of prices caused by too high a level of aggregate demand in relation to aggregate supply

demand schedule
a listing of the quantities that would be purchased at various prices

deposit expansion multiplier
the number that expresses the relationship between a change in bank reserves and the change in the money supply

depression
a severe and prolonged decline in the level of economic activity

derived demand
demand for an input that is dependent on the demand for the product that the input helps to produce

determinants of demand
the factors that determine how much will be purchased at any given price

differentiated oligopoly
an oligopoly in which the product is differentiated

diminishing marginal product
the principle that as more of one input is added to a fixed amount of other inputs, the marginal product decreases

diminishing marginal utility
the principle that as additional units of a product are consumed during a given time period, the additional satisfaction decreases

direct tax
a tax paid by the person against whom the tax is levied

discount rate
the interest rate that banks must pay to borrow from the Federal Reserve System

disposable income
the income that is left after deducting tax payments

distribution effect
the way the benefit or inconvenience of a social issue is spread among the members of the society

dividends
that part of a corporation's income paid to its stockholders

dual economy
an economy in which a modern market economy exists side by side with a primitive subsistence economy

E

economic growth
the change in the level of economic activity from one year to another

economic incentive
the increase in personal satisfaction that may result from some economic activity

economic profit
total revenue minus total costs

economics
the social science that deals with how society allocates its scarce resources among its unlimited wants and needs

economic system
the combination of social and individual decision making a society uses to answer the three economic questions

economies of scale
the concept that some economic activities become more efficient when done on a large scale

efficiency
achieving the maximum benefit from a given amount and combination of resources

Employment Act of 1946
states that the federal government should take responsibility for full employment, price stability, and economic growth

entrepreneurs
individuals who take the risk of producing a product for a profit

entrepreneurship
the managerial ability and risk taking that contribute so much to a productive economy

equilibrium price
the price at which the quantity demanded equals the quantity supplied

equilibrium quantity
the quantity that is both demanded and supplied at the equilibrium price

equilibrium wage
the wage rate at which the quantity of labor demanded equals the quantity of labor supplied

equity
dealing fairly and equally with all concerned

estate and gift taxes
taxes levied on the wealth (money and property) passed from one person to another either at death or as a gift

European Community (EC)
a group of European countries that have joined together and agreed on ways to improve trade among themselves

excess reserves
the difference between actual reserves and required reserves

exchange
giving one thing in return for some other thing

exchange rate
the rate at which one kind of money can be traded for another

excise tax
a sales tax levied only on a specific item

exclusion principle
the principle that one person can keep others from benefiting from a private good

expansionary fiscal policies
causing the economy to run more rapidly primarily by increasing aggregate demand

explicit costs
payments made to others as a cost of running a business

exports
goods and services that one country sells to another country

external debt
the part of the national debt that is owed to people or governments outside the United States

externality
a cost or benefit passed on to people not directly involved in a transaction

F

factor of production
anything used to produce a good or service

Federal Advisory Council
a group that consists of 12 members who meet four times each year with the Board of Governors to discuss the economic situation and policies of the Board

Federal Deposit Insurance Corporation (FDIC)
the agency that insures deposits of individuals and businesses for up to $100,000 in the event of bank failure

federal funds rate
the interest rate that banks pay to borrow from each other on a short-term basis

Federal Open Market Committee (FOMC)
a group that acts on the most important part of monetary policy: the buying and selling of U.S. government securities by the Federal Reserve Banks

Federal Reserve System (the Fed)
the central banking system in the United States

financial intermediary
an organization that helps the flow of money from people with money to save to people who need to borrow money

fiscal policy
the changing of federal government spending and taxes in order to control the level of economic activity

fixed income
an income that is set and does not change from year to year

flexible exchange rate
a system in which the laws of supply and demand are allowed to set the prices, or exchange rates, of each kind of money

foreign aid
the money that more advanced countries provide to help LDCs in their economic development

fractional reserve banking system
a system that requires banks to keep some fraction of their deposits in the form of reserves

franchise
a contract between a parent company (franchisor) and some other business or individual (franchisee) that details the terms under which the franchisee does business with products, names, or other services of the franchisor

freedom of choice
the individual power to choose and receive both the costs and the benefits of a choice

free rider
a person who benefits from a public good without sharing its cost

frictional unemployment
unemployment of people who are temporarily between jobs

full employment
employment of about 95 percent of the labor force

functional distribution of income
the way in which income is divided by economic functions

G

General Agreement on Tariffs and Trade (GATT)
an agreement that gave broad international support to improving trade among countries

gold standard
a system in which each nation sets the value of its money in terms of a certain amount of gold

gross domestic product (GDP)
the total dollar value of all final goods and services produced by resources located in the United States (regardless of who owns them) during one year's time

H

homogeneous product
a good or service that varies little from producer to producer

horizontal merger
a merger of two companies in the same industry

human resources
the people who work or may be able to work

i

imports
goods and services that one country buys from another country

income effect
the effect that increasing or decreasing prices has on the buying power of income

indirect tax
a tax that can be shifted, at least in part, to a party other than the one on whom the tax is levied

individual choice
decisions made by people acting separately

infant mortality rate
the number of deaths of children under one year of age per 1,000 live births

inferior goods
goods for which demand goes down as income goes up

inflation
a rise in the average level of prices

inflationary bias in fiscal policy
the natural tendency for Congress to favor expansionary policies over restrictive policies

injunction
a court order to stop someone from doing something (or to make someone *do* something)

inside time lag
the time it takes to decide on a policy

interest
the price paid for the use of money

International Monetary Fund (IMF)
a bank established to promote economic cooperation by maintaining an orderly system of world trade and exchange rates

investment
an increase in the amount of productive capital in an economy

invisible hand
the incentive for individuals to choose in the best interest of society by pursuing their own self-interests

J

job discrimination
the refusal to hire certain people because of their gender, race, or other characteristics that have nothing to do with their ability to do a job

L

labor
the human factor of production

labor union
an organization of workers formed to give workers greater bargaining power in their dealings with management

land
a broad measure representing all the basic natural resources that contribute to production

law of demand
the quantity demanded of a good will be greater at lower prices than will be the quantity demanded at higher prices

law of supply
states that the quantity of goods supplied will be greater at a higher price than it will at a lower price

less-developed country (LDC)
a poor country with a relatively low level of education and a largely rural population

life expectancy
the average age the people in a country reach

limited liability
the concept that owners of a business are only responsible for its debts up to the amount they invest in the business

limited resources
the condition of there not being enough resources to fulfill all wants and needs

line of credit
an arrangement through which a business can quickly access needed cash from a bank

lobbying
the act of communicating with government representatives to influence their votes on a specific issue

long run
a period during which the amounts of all inputs can be changed

loose monetary policy
a policy of the Federal Reserve that causes the money supply to increase

Lorenz curve
a graphic method of showing the amount of income inequality that exists in society at any point in time

M

macroeconomic equilibrium
what results when the sum of savings and taxes equals the sum of investment and government spending

macroeconomics
that part of economics that examines the behavior of the whole economy

marginal private benefit (MPB)
the added benefit that individuals directly involved in an activity get from increasing the activity by one unit

marginal private cost (MPC)
the added cost individuals directly involved in an activity pay to increase the activity by one unit

marginal product
the amount that total product increases or decreases as a result of adding one additional unit of input

marginal social benefit (MSB)
the added benefit that society gets from increasing an activity by one unit

marginal social cost (MSC)
the added cost that society pays to increase an activity by one unit

marginal utility
the amount of satisfaction a person gets from *one* additional unit of a product

market
exchange activities between buyers and sellers of goods and services

market economy
an economy in which the economic questions are decided mostly by individuals in the marketplace

market organization
the way participants in markets are organized and how many participants there are

member banks
those banks that belong to the Federal Reserve System

merger
the combining of one company with another company it buys

microeconomics
the branch of economics that examines the choices of individuals concerning one product, one firm, or one industry

minimum wage law
a law that sets the lowest wage that can be paid for certain kinds of work

model
a simplified form of reality that shows the relationship between different factors

monetary policy
the changing of the quantity of money in the economy in order to reduce unemployment, keep prices stable, and promote economic growth

monopolistic competition
a market organization in which many firms produce goods that are different but similar enough to be substitutes

monopoly
a form of market organization in which there is only one seller of a product

monopsony
a market in which there is only one buyer

multinational business
a firm that sells and produces products in multiple countries

multiplier effect
the concept that any change in fiscal policy affects total demand and total income by an amount larger than the original amount of the change in spending or taxing

mutual savings banks
banks that were first formed for the same reasons as savings and loan associations and that promote thrift in their members

N

national debt
the amount of money that the federal government owes

natural monopoly
a situation in which it is not practical to have competition

natural resources
the total raw materials supplied by nature

negative externality
the result when *costs* are shifted to people who are not directly involved with the production or consumption of a good

nonprofit organization
an organization that does not have profit as its objective

normal goods
goods for which demand goes up as income goes up

North American Free Trade Agreement (NAFTA)
trade agreement established between the United States, Canada, and Mexico to promote economic growth and prosperity for all three economies by eliminating barriers to free trade

O

objectivity
ruling out aspects of a problem that seem important only because of your strong emotions about them

oligopoly
a form of market organization in which there are relatively few firms

open market operations
the buying and selling of U.S. government securities by the Federal Reserve

opportunity benefit
what is gained by making a particular choice

opportunity cost
the value of any alternative that you must give up when you make a choice

outside time lag
the time it takes for the effects of a policy change to be completely felt in the economy

P

partnership
a type of business organization in which there are two or more owners

partnership agreement
a legally binding document that specifies how the responsibilities and profits or losses from a partnership will be split between the partners

patent
a legal protection for the inventor of a product or process that gives that person or company the sole right to produce the product or use the process for up to 17 years

per capita income
the average income per person

perfect competition
a form of market organization in which a great many small firms produce a homogeneous product

personal distribution of income
how income is shared among people in our society

personal income tax
a tax on the income of individuals

population explosion
rapid growth in the number of people living in a country

positive externality
the result when *benefits* are shifted to people who are not directly involved with the production or consumption of a good

poverty
the condition in which people do not have enough income to provide for their basic needs, such as food, clothing, and shelter

price ceiling
a maximum price set by government that is *below* the market equilibrium price

price elasticity of demand
measures the relative responsiveness of the change in quantity demanded as a result of a change in the product's price

price elasticity of supply
measures the responsiveness of the quantity supplied to changes in the product's price

price floor
a minimum price set by government that is *above* the market equilibrium price

price index
a number that compares prices in one year with some earlier base year

price setter
a firm that has some control over the price at which its product sells

price taker
a firm that takes a price determined by forces outside the firm's control

prime rate
the interest rate that banks charge their best corporate customers

private enterprise
a system in which individuals take the risk of producing goods or services to make a profit

private goods
goods that are privately owned and used to benefit only their owners

private sector
the part of an economy that is owned by individuals and operated for their personal benefit

product differentiation
the concept that the product of one firm can be distinguished from the products of other firms

production possibilities curve
a graphic illustration of the combinations of output an economy can produce if all of its resources are utilized and utilized efficiently, given the state of technology

progressive tax
a tax that takes a larger percentage of higher incomes and a smaller percentage of lower incomes

property rights
the rules that government has established to define who owns what property and how owners may use their property

property tax
a tax levied on real estate, such as a home, land, and buildings

proportional tax
a tax that takes the same percentage of income from all taxpayers

proprietorship
a form of business in which there is one owner

protectionism
the idea that we should limit international trade to protect our own self-interest

psychic income
the nonmonetary reward we get from taking some action

public goods
goods and services available to the whole society

public goods rationale
the argument that some public goods can be produced more efficiently by the government

public institutions
publicly owned organizations established by government to serve the wants and needs of a whole society

public sector
the part of an economy that is owned by the whole society and operated for its benefit

pure oligopoly
an oligopoly in which the products are the same for all firms

Q

quota
a limit on the amount of imports or exports

R

rate of growth
the percentage change in the level of economic activity from one year to the next

real GDP
the value of gross domestic product after taking out the effect of price changes

real GDP per person
the real value of the total output of goods and services divided by the number of people in the economy

recession
the condition in which unemployment is high and GDP falls for two or more consecutive quarters

regressive tax
a tax that takes a larger percentage of lower incomes and a smaller percentage of higher incomes

research and development
the activities undertaken to find new and more efficient methods of production

reserve ratio
the fraction of deposits that the Federal Reserve determines banks must keep on reserve

reserve requirement
the dollar amount banks must keep on reserve

restrictive fiscal policies
causing the economy to run more slowly primarily by reducing aggregate demand

returns to scale
the relationship between changes in the scale of production and the corresponding change in the amount of output

S

sales tax
a tax on goods that are bought

savings and loan association
a financial intermediary that mainly provides a place for people to save money and then lends that money to people to buy houses or other items

scale of production
the overall level of use of all factors of production

scarcity
the condition that occurs because people's wants and needs are unlimited, while the resources needed to produce goods and services to meet these wants and needs are limited

seasonal unemployment
unemployment of people who are out of work because of factors that vary with the time of year

share draft account
an account with a credit union from which withdrawals easily can be made through a draft (a draft is a type of check)

shortage
the condition in which the quantity demanded is greater than the quantity supplied at a certain price

short run
any period during which the usable amount of at least one input is fixed while the usable amount of at least one other input can change

social benefits
the benefits received by a society from a social choice

social choice
decision making by government in the interest of society

social costs
the costs to a society of a social choice

social economy
an economy in which the major economic questions are determined by a government representing the interests of the entire society

social goals
the goals of an entire society

Social Security tax
a tax that provides disability and retirement benefits for most working people

special interest group
an organization of people who are bound together by a common concern

speculation
when someone buys a large amount of a good and hopes to resell it at a much higher price

stock
shares of ownership in a corporation

structural unemployment
unemployment resulting from skills that do not match what employers require or from being geographically separated from job opportunities

subsidy
a payment made by the government to encourage some activity

substitute products
products whose uses are similar enough that one can replace the other

substitution effect
the change in the mix of goods purchased as a result of increasing or decreasing relative prices

supply
the quantities of a product or service that a firm is willing and able to make available for sale at different prices

supply curve
a graphic representation of the quantities that would be supplied at each price

supply of labor
the amount of labor that would be available at each wage rate

supply schedule
a table that shows the quantities of a good or service that would be supplied by a firm at different prices

surplus
the condition in which the quantity supplied is greater than the quantity demanded at a certain price

T

tariff
a tax on imports

tax
a charge imposed by the government on people or property for public purposes

technology
the body of knowledge that is used for the production of goods and services

test of the market
being able to provide goods that satisfy consumers' needs and desires at prices consumers are willing to pay

theory
a simplified description of reality

tight monetary policy
a policy of the Federal Reserve that causes the money supply to decrease

total product
all the units of a product produced in a given period of time

total revenue
the total amount of money a company receives from sales of a product

trade deficit
the result when a country imports more than it exports

trade surplus
the result when a country exports more than it imports

transaction demand for money
the demand for money to make exchanges

utility
the satisfaction one receives from the consumption, use, or ownership of a good or service

U

unemployment
the condition of those who are willing and able to work and are actively seeking work but who do not currently work

unemployment rate
the percentage of the civilian labor force that is considered unemployed

union shop
a business that requires workers to join a union shortly after taking a job

unlimited liability
the concept that an owner's personal assets can be used to pay bills of the business

unlimited wants and needs
the human characteristic of never having all wants and needs satisfied

util
the unit of measurement for utility

V

vertical merger
a merger of two companies that are at different stages in the same production process

W

wage and price controls
government controls on the levels of wages and prices

wage rate
the price paid for each unit of labor

work ethic
the belief that people should work hard and pull their own weight in economic life

World Bank
an organization established in 1944 to help finance reconstruction after World War II

INDEX

D

E

F

G

H

K

L

M

N

O

P

Q

R

S

T

ACKNOWLEDGMENTS

Chapter 1

p. 5: Jeff Greenberg, Photographer; **p. 7:** Jeff Greenberg, Photographer; **p. 9:** Jeff Greenberg, Photographer; **p. 11:** Jeff Greenberg, Photographer; **p. 15:** Jeff Greenberg, Photographer; **p. 21:** Jeff Greenberg, Photographer.

Chapter 2

p. 30: Photograph by Paul Couvrette, Ottawa, Canada; **p. 32:** Jeff Greenberg, Photographer; **p. 33:** The Bettmann Archive; **p. 38: top:** Jeff Greenberg, Photographer; **p. 38: bottom:** Jeff Greenberg, Photographer; **p. 39:** Jeff Greenberg, Photographer; **p. 43:** Jeff Greenberg, Photographer.

Chapter 3

p. 53: Jeff Greenberg, Photographer; **p. 55:** The Bettmann Archive; **p. 58:** Jeff Greenberg, Photographer; **p. 61:** Jeff Greenberg, Photographer; **p. 62:** Jeff Greenberg, Photographer; **p. 65:** Jeff Greenberg, Photographer; **p. 67:** Jeff Greenberg, Photographer.

Chapter 4

p. 77: Jeff Greenberg, Photographer; **p. 79:** Jeff Greenberg, Photographer; **p. 80:** USDA Photo by Doug Wilson; **p. 83:** Jeff Greenberg, Photographer; **p. 85:** Jeff Greenberg, Photographer; **p. 89:** Jeff Greenberg, Photographer; **p. 90:** Scott Willis ©1989 San Jose Mercury News.

Chapter 5

p. 105: Alan Brown/Photonics; **p. 106:** Jeff Greenberg, Photographer; **p. 109:** Oil Spill Public Information Center; **p. 110:** Jeff Greenberg, Photographer; **p. 112:** Photograph by William P. McElligott, Ottawa, Canada; **p. 115:** Photo courtesy of the American League of Lobbyists.

Chapter 6

p. 124: Photograph by Les Amis du Jardin Botanique de Montreal, Montreal, Canada; **p. 125:** Jeff Greenberg, Photographer; **p. 129:** Jeff Greenberg, Photographer; **p. 130:** Jeff Greenberg, Photographer; **p. 133:** Photograph by Paul Couvrette, Ottawa, Canada; **p. 135:** Jeff Greenberg, Photographer; **p. 139:** Jeff Greenberg, Photographer; **p. 141:** Jeff Greenberg, Photographer; **p. 142:** Jeff Greenberg, Photographer.

Chapter 7

p. 154: Jeff Greenberg, Photographer; **p. 160:** Florida Citrus Growers; **p. 163:** Jeff Greenberg, Photographer; **p. 164:** Jeff Greenberg, Photographer; **p. 166:** Jeff Greenberg, Photographer; **p. 168:** Jeff Greenberg, Photographer.

Chapter 8

p. 190: Photograph by Harold Davis, New York, NY; **p. 191:** Jeff Greenberg, Photographer; **p. 192:** Jeff Greenberg, Photographer; **p. 193:** USDA Photo by Doug Wilson; **p. 196:** Jeff Greenberg, Photographer; **p. 198:** Jeff Greenberg, Photographer; **p. 206:** Alan Brown/Photonics.

Chapter 9

p. 216: Jeff Greenberg, Photographer; **p. 218:** Jeff Greenberg, Photographer; **p. 222:** Jeff Greenberg, Photographer; **p. 224:** Erik Von Fischer/Photonics; **p. 225:** Jeff Greenberg, Photographer; **p. 230:** Photograph by Robert Lear, Toronto, Canada; **p. 233:** NYSE; **p. 234: top:** Jeff Greenberg, Photographer; **p. 234: bottom:** Photo courtesy of Pizza Hut, Inc.

Chapter 10

p. 245: Jeff Greenberg, Photographer; **p. 247:** © Jose Carrillo, Ventura, CA; **p. 253:** Jeff Greenberg, Photographer; **p. 261:** Jeff Greenberg, Photographer; **p. 264:** Jeff Greenberg, Photographer.

Chapter 11

p. 273: top: Jeff Greenberg, Photographer; **p. 273: bottom:** Jeff Greenberg, Photographer; **p. 276:** Jeff Greenberg, Photographer; **p. 281:** Photograph by Malak, Ottawa, Canada; **p. 283:** Jeff Greenberg, Photographer; **p. 285:** Jeff Greenberg, Photographer; **p. 289:** Hoffmann-La Roche, Nutley, N.J.

Chapter 12

p. 304: USDA; **p. 305:** Jeff Greenberg, Photographer; **p. 307:** Jeff Greenberg, Photographer; **p. 310:** Jeff Greenberg, Photographer; **p. 317:** Photograph by Al Greening, San Francisco, CA.

Global Economy: p. 313: Adapted from Sharon Begley et al., "Ice Cubes for Penguins," in *Business Week* (April 3, 1995): 56.

Chapter 13

p. 327: Jeff Greenberg, Photographer; **p. 333:** Courtesy of Apple Computer, Inc.; **p. 335:** Jeff Greenberg, Photographer; **p. 339:** Jeff Greenberg, Photographer; **p. 341:** Photograph by Helen Cohen Rimmer, Pincourt, Quebec, Canada.

Chapter 14

p. 359: left: Photograph by Larry White, New York, NY; **p. 377:** Alan Brown/Photonics; **p. 379: left:** Photograph by Larry White, New York, NY; **p. 379: center:** Architect of the Capitol; **p. 383:** Jeff Greenberg, Photographer.

Chapter 15

p. 393: Jeff Greenberg, Photographer; **p. 399:** Photograph by Christine Dameyer and Anne Xu; **p. 405:** Photograph by Harold Davis, New York, NY; **p. 406:** National Archives Trust; **p. 408:** Jeff Greenberg, Photographer; **p. 409:** Jeff Greenberg, Photographer.

Chapter 16

p. 422: Jeff Greenberg, Photographer; **p. 425:** Jeff Greenberg, Photographer; **p. 428:** Jeff Greenberg, Photographer; **p. 429:** Jeff Greenberg, Photographer; **p. 433:** Courtesy of Apple Computer, Inc.; **p. 435:** Photograph by William P. McElligott, Ottawa, Canada; **p. 437:** Jeff Greenberg, Photographer.

Chapter 17

p. 457: Photograph by Christine Dameyer and Anne Xu; **p. 458:** The Bettmann Archive.

Chapter 18

p. 470: Photograph by William P. McElligott, Ottawa, Canada; **p. 482:** Jeff Greenberg, Photographer; **p. 485:** Photograph by Lee Paris, Belmont, MA; **p. 486:** Jeff Greenberg, Photographer; **p. 487:** Photograph by Jack Parsons (Los Gatos, CA), Alan D. Harkrader Jr. (Peoria, IL) and other photographers; **p. 490:** Jeff Greenberg, Photographer.

Econ & You: p. 483: Based on John Wenninger and David Laster, "The Electronic Purse," *Current Issues,* Federal Reserve Bank of New York (April 1995).

Global Economy: p. 488: Based on Lena H. Sun, "A Cultural Bank and Trust," in *The Washington Post National Weekly Edition* (February 27–March 5, 1995): 9.

747

Chapter 19

p. 504: Bureau of Engraving and Printing; **p. 516:** Jeff Greenberg, Photographer; **p. 517:** Photograph by Robert Lear, Toronto, Canada; **p. 519:** Jeff Greenberg, Photographer.

Chapter 20

p. 536: Photograph by NASA; **p. 540:** Jeff Greenberg, Photographer; **p. 542:** Jeff Greenberg, Photographer.

Chapter 21

p. 569: The Bettmann Archive; **p. 576:** Jeff Greenberg, Photographer; **p. 580:** Photograph by Al Greening, San Francisco, CA; **p. 582:** The Bettmann Archive; **p. 583:** The Bettmann Archive.

Chapter 22

p. 594: Photograph by Lee Paris, Belmont, MA; **p. 597:** Photograph by Lee Paris, Belmont, MA; **p. 598:** Photograph by Lee Paris, Belmont, MA; **p. 606:** Photograph by Esther Mugar and David Ryan, San Francisco, CA; **p. 607:** Jeff Greenberg, Photographer; **p. 613:** Photograph by Jack K. Blonk, Laval, Quebec, Canada.

Chapter 23

p. 626: Photograph by Esther Mugar, San Francisco, CA; **p. 627:** Photograph by William P. McElligott, Ottawa, Canada; **p. 634:** Photograph by Gordon Barbery and Esther Mugar, San Francisco, CA; **p. 640:** Photograph by William P. McElligott, Ottawa, Canada; **p. 644:** Jeff Greenberg, Photographer; **p. 645:** Photographs by Lee Paris, Belmont, MA.

Econ & You: p. 631: Shawn Tully, "Teens: The Most Global Market of All," in *Fortune* (May 16, 1994): 90–97. Cyndee Miller, "Teens Seen as the First Truly Global Consumers," in *Marketing News* (March 27, 1995): 9.

Global Economy: p. 641: Dom Del Prete, "Latin America Is a Marketer's Dream Come True," in *Marketing News* (October 10, 1994): 7–8.

Chapter 24

p. 656: Jeff Greenberg, Photographer; **p. 662: top:** Photograph by France Pepper, Montreal, Canada; **p. 662: bottom:** © TSM/Sally Wiener Grotta; **p. 666: bottom:** Photograph by Robert Chadwick, Montreal, Canada; **p. 671:** ICRC/Red Cross.